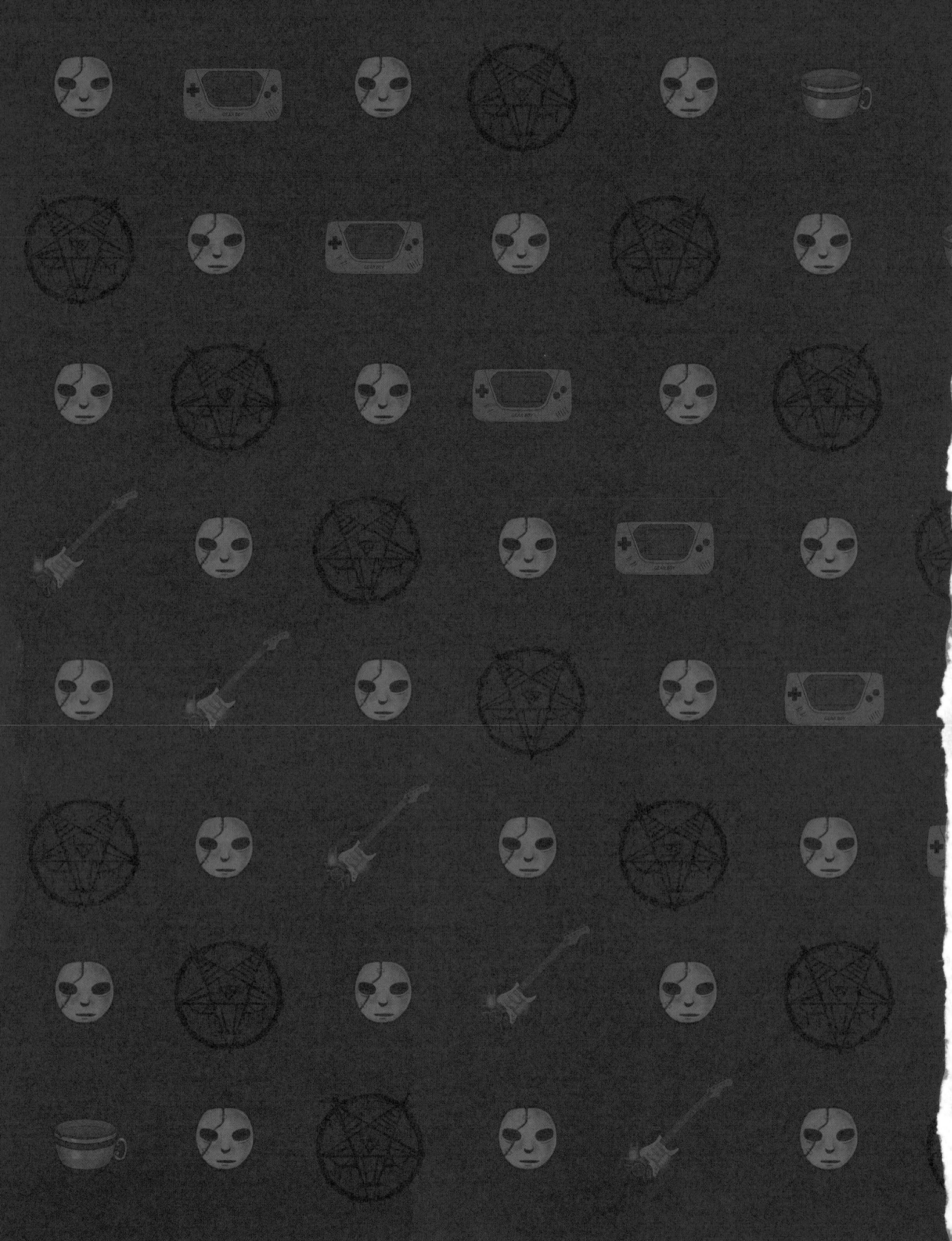

Sally Face
ART, LORE, AND MORE

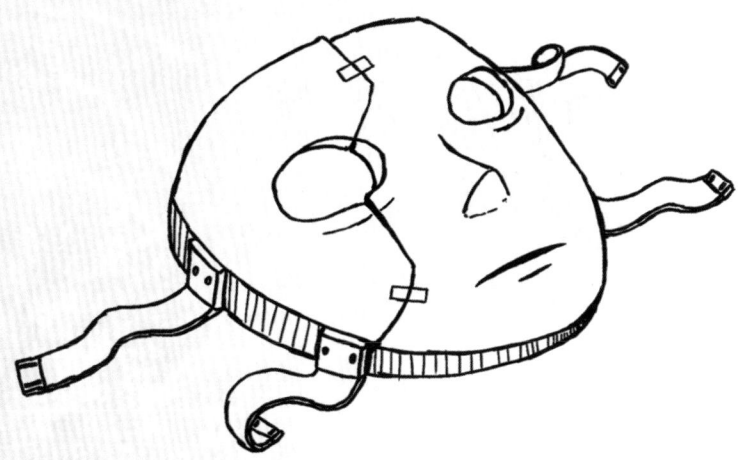

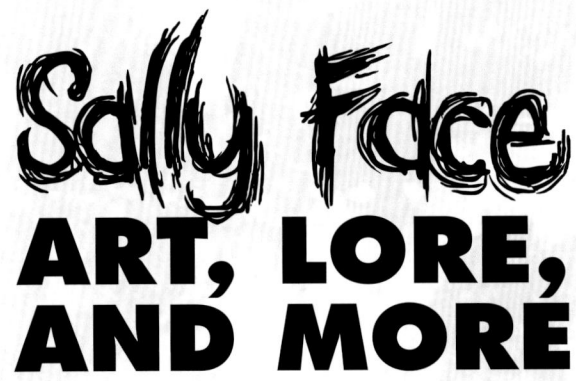

Sally Face
ART, LORE, AND MORE

ISBN: 9781803369792
Published by
Titan Books
A division of Titan Publishing Group Ltd
144 Southwark St
London
SE1 0UP
www.titanbooks.com

First edition: September 2024
4 6 8 10 9 7 5

EU RP (for authorities only)
eucomply OÜ Pärnu mnt 139b-14 11317
Tallinn, Estonia
hello@eucompliancepartner.com
+3375690241

Did you enjoy this book? We love to hear from our readers.
Please e-mail us at: readerfeedback@titanemail.com
or write to Reader Feedback at the above address.

To receive advance information, news, competitions,
and exclusive offers online, please sign up for the
Titan newsletter on our website: www.titanbooks.com

A CIP catalogue record for this title is available from the British Library.

Printed and bound in China.

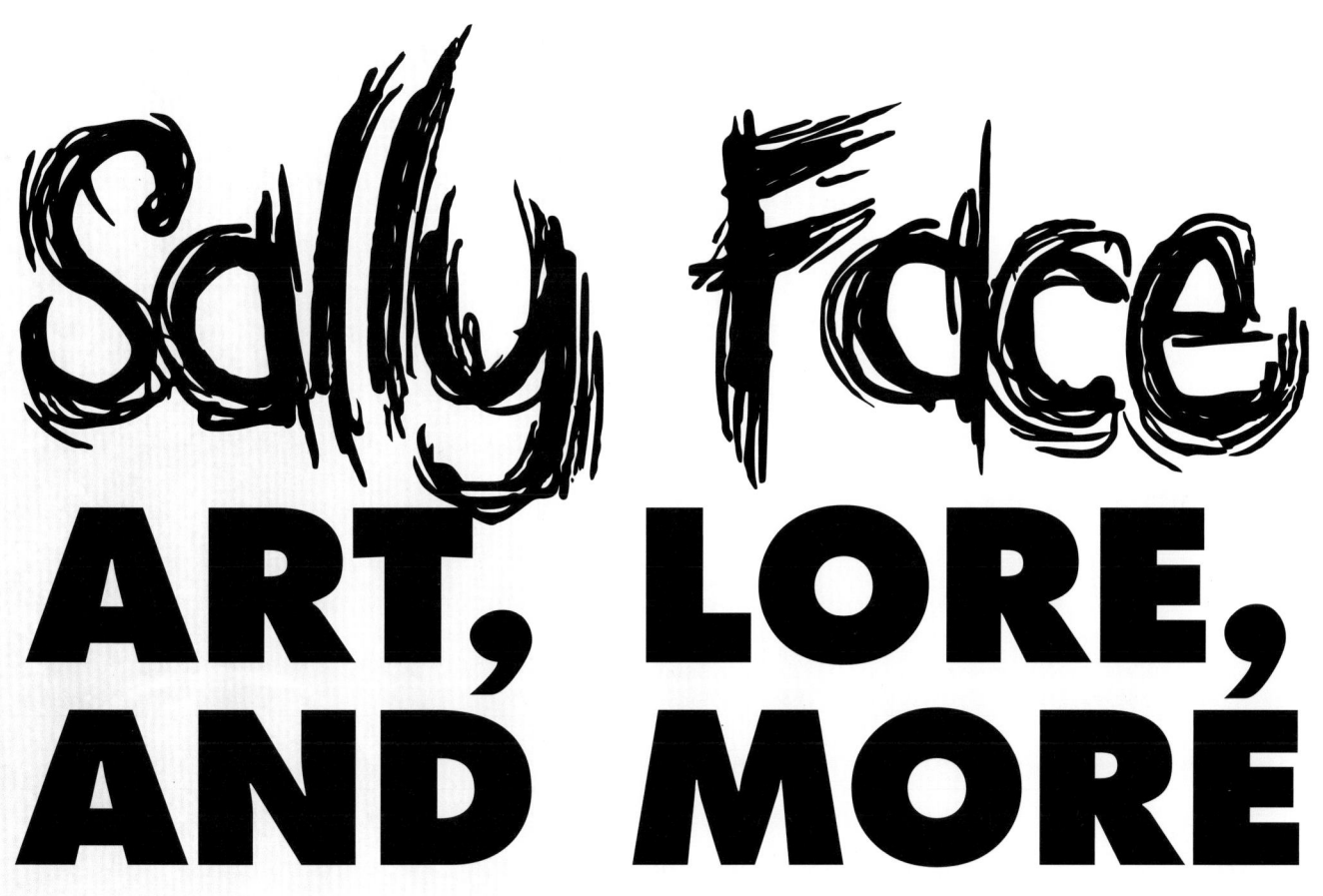

Sally Face
ART, LORE, AND MORE

Steve Gabry

TITAN BOOKS

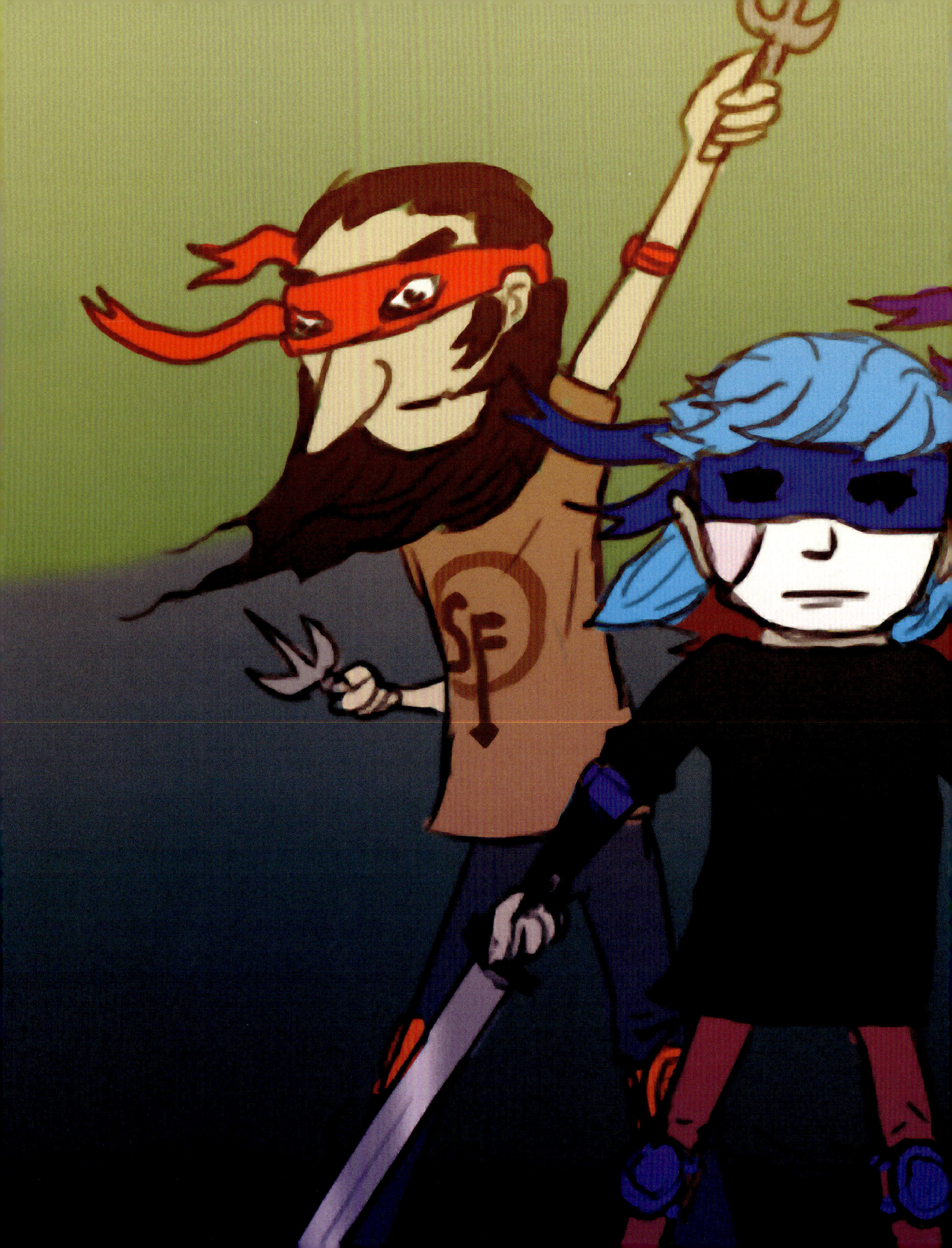

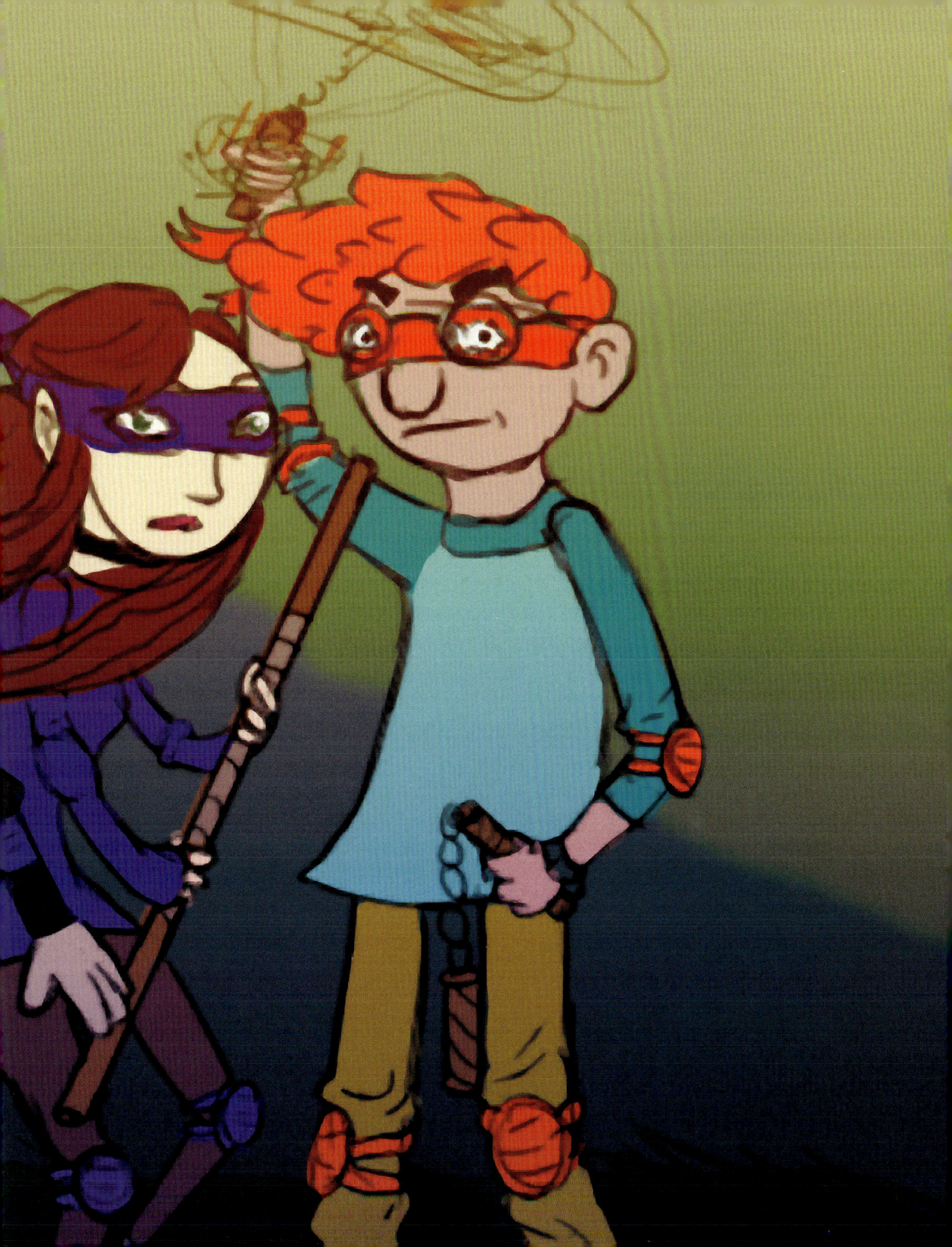

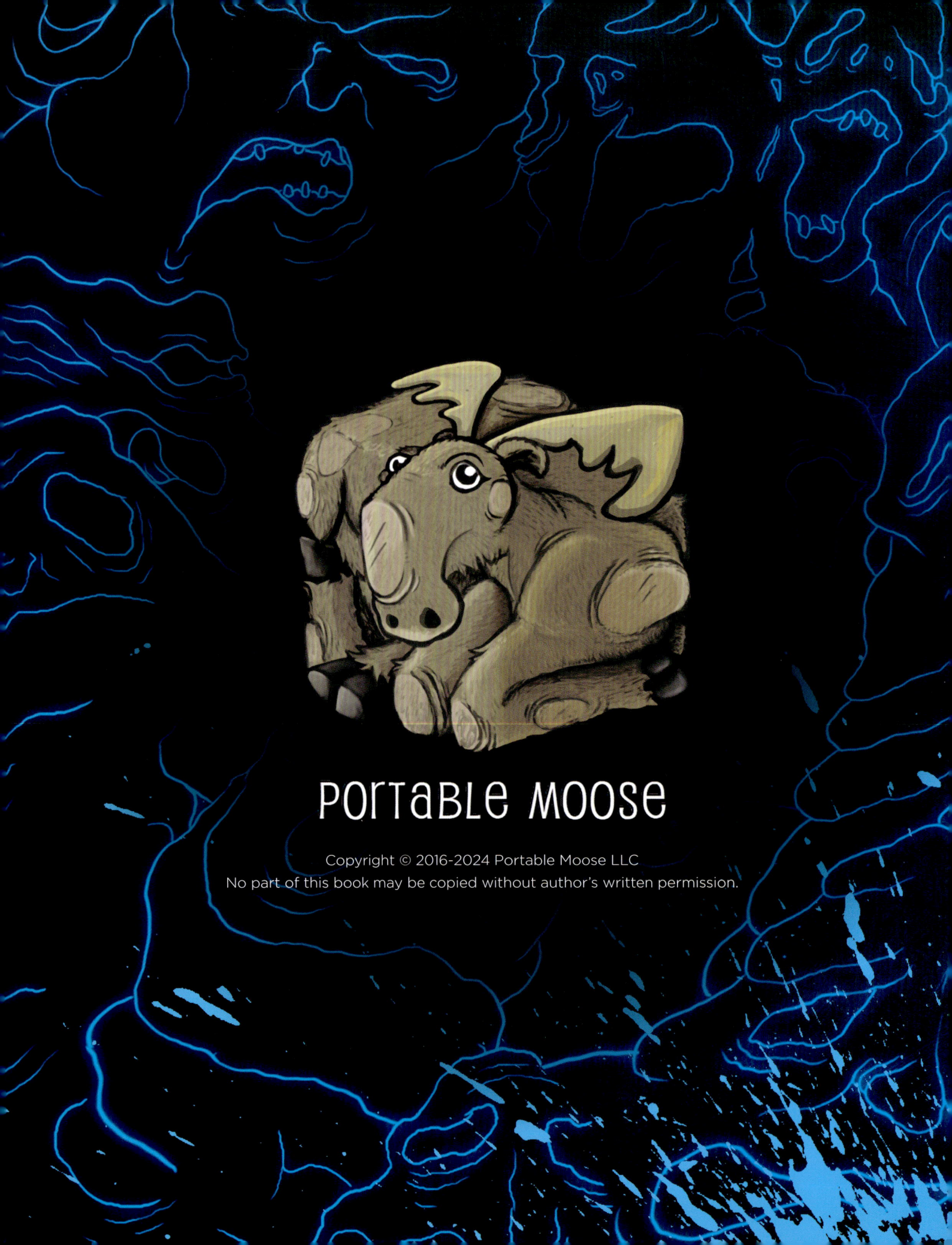

Portable Moose

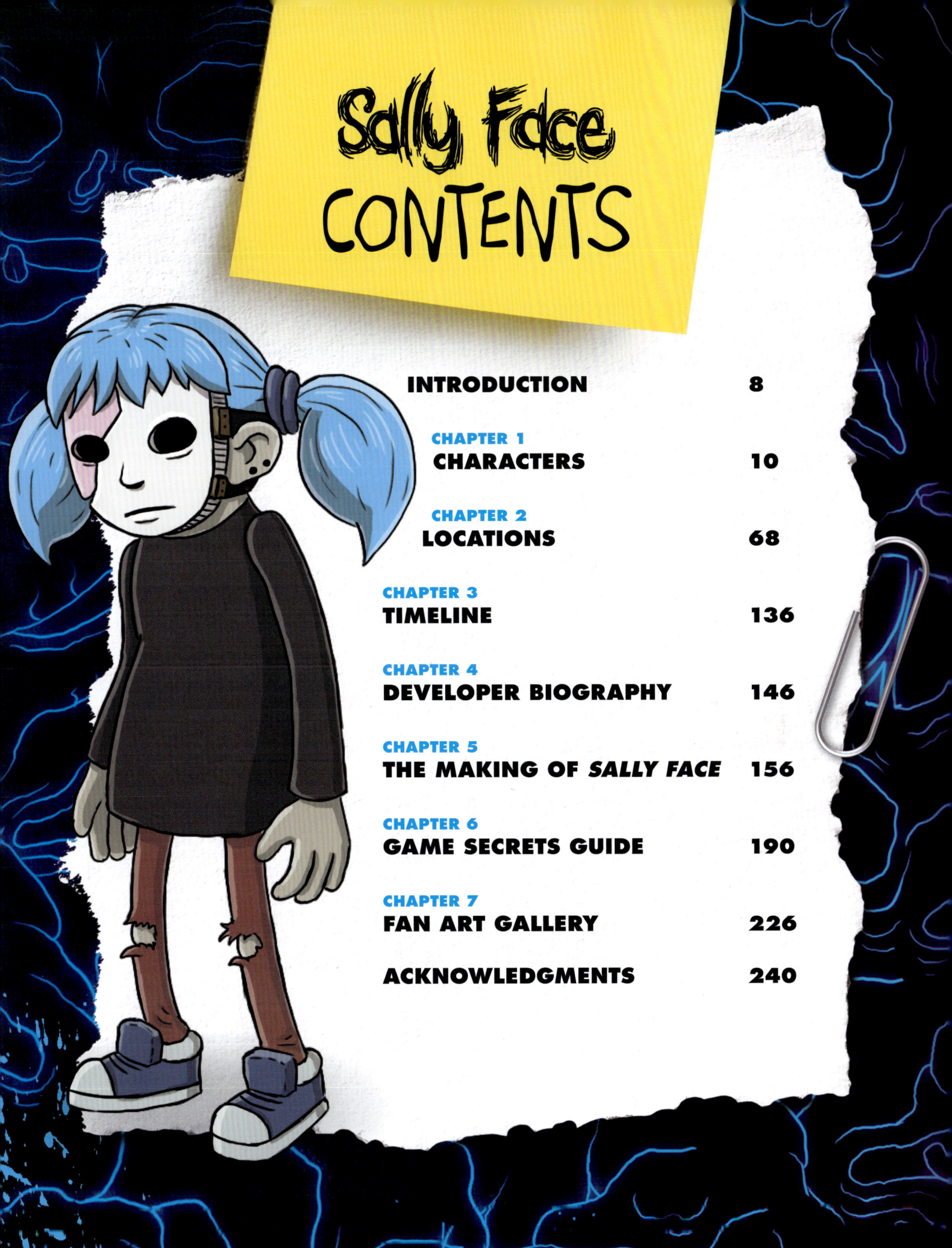

Sally Face
CONTENTS

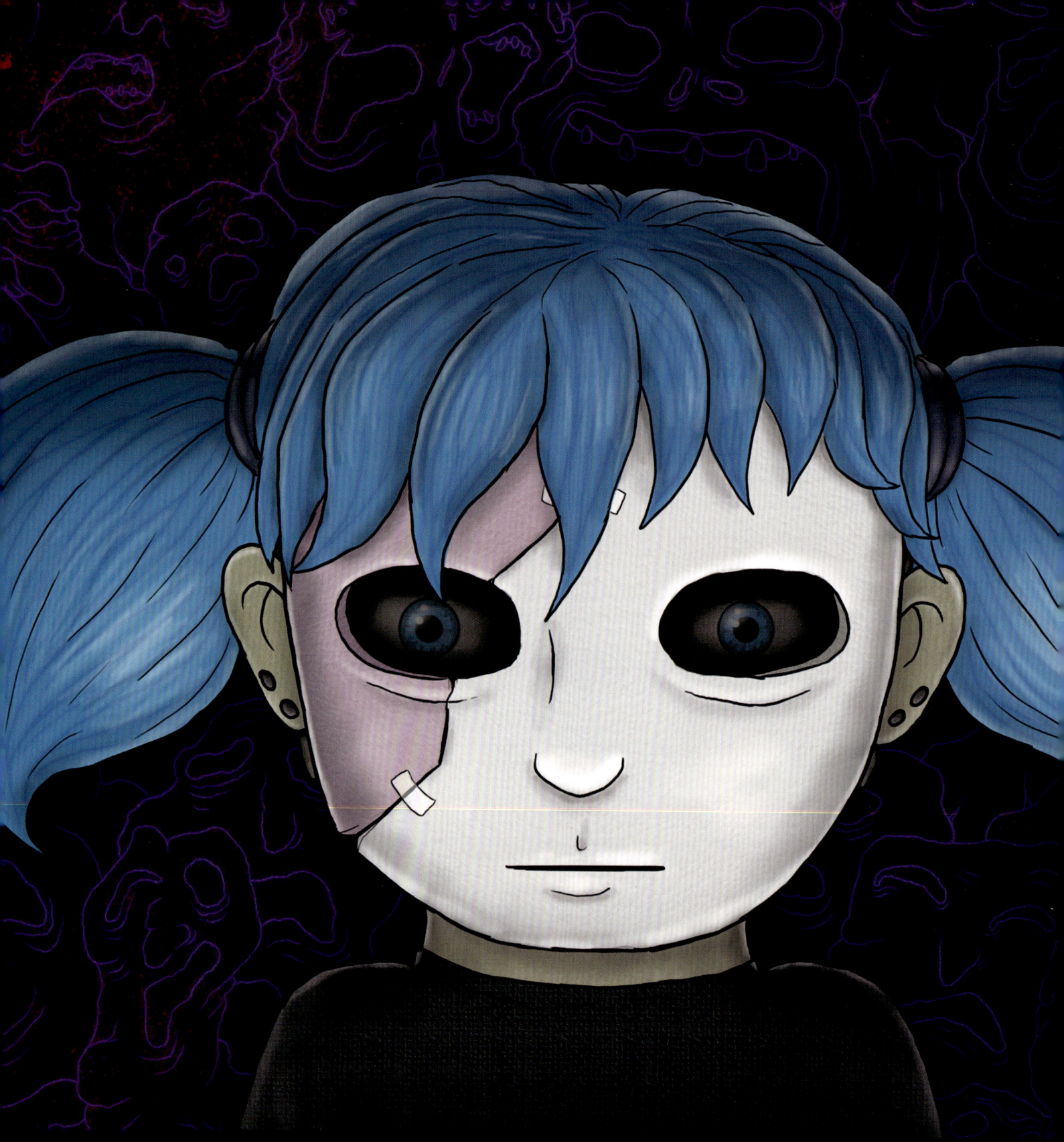

INTRODUCTION

A dark mystery is unfolding...

MY NAME IS STEVE GABRY, and I'm the creator of *Sally Face* and the author of this book! I'm an independent game developer from Pittsburgh, Pennsylvania. Ever since I was a kid, I have drawn monsters and other creepy things. So much so that my mom would often ask, "Why don't you draw something nice?" But I never felt right drawing "something nice". I've always had a strong fascination with the unknown, the paranormal, the oddities, and darker sides to life that influenced the entertainment I consumed. Nowadays, people frequently ask me how I come up with creepy content and the truth is that my mind is always in dark places.

The journey in creating *Sally Face* has been a deeply personal one and it's connected me to many wonderful people around the world. When I first began working on the game, I never imagined it would become as big as it has gotten. The amount of passion I see from the fans on a daily basis is incredible: the fan art, the cosplay, the tattoos, the touching letters—it's amazing to witness and to be a part of. *Sally Face* has become something much bigger than the dark little cartoon game I set out to create; it's become an important part of so many other lives and that means the world to me.

Thank you for all the love and support. I wouldn't have gotten this far without you.

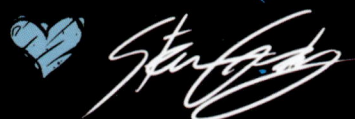

CHAPTER 1

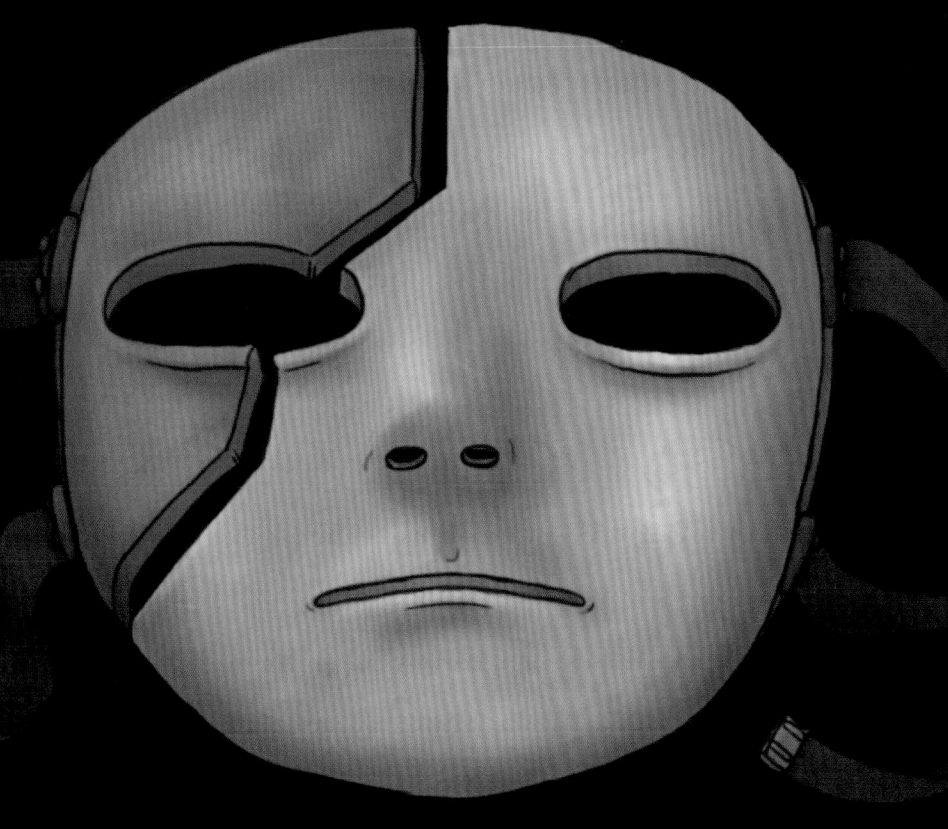

Sally Face

CHARACTERS

SAL "SALLY FACE" FISHER

"Whatever it is, I'll do it. Whatever it takes to save them."

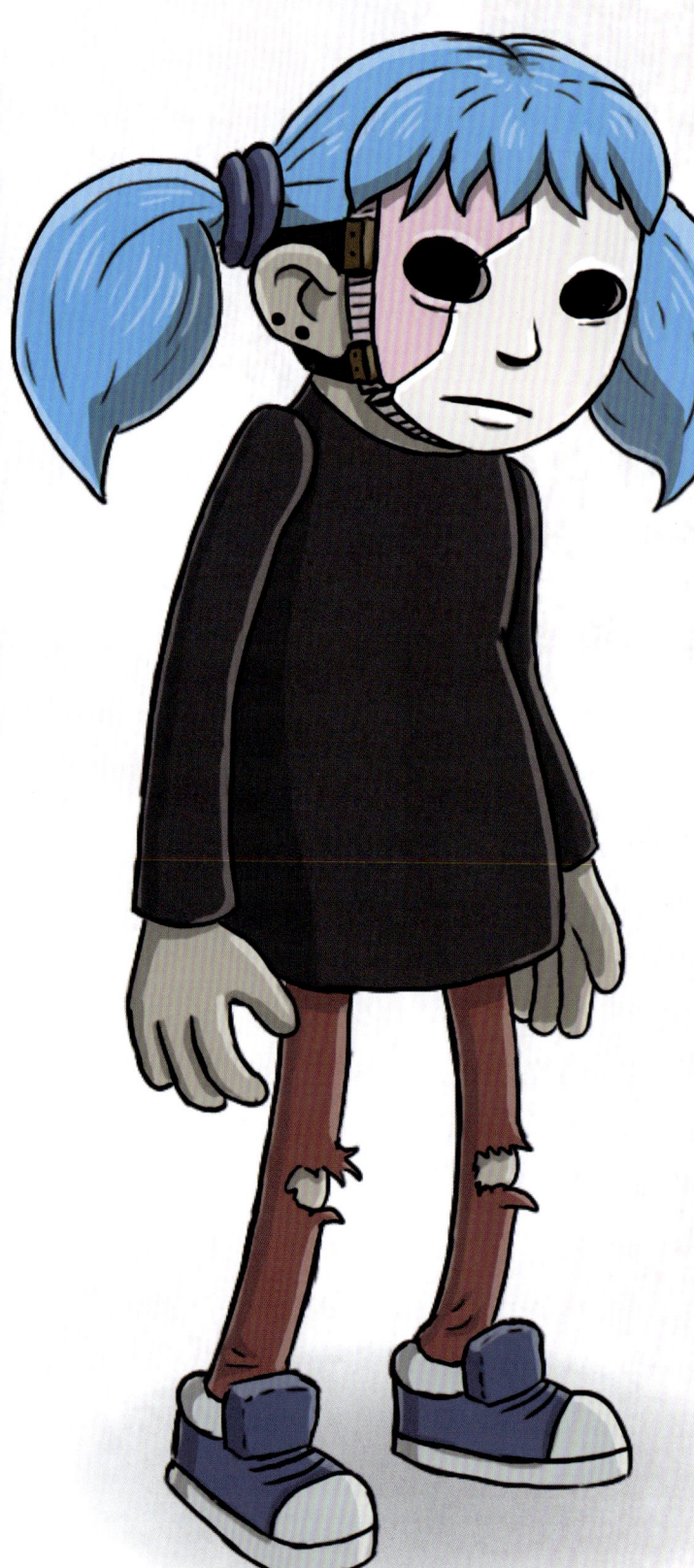

SAL SURVIVED A HORRIFIC ACCIDENT as a young boy that killed his mother and left his face disfigured. Because of this, he now wears a prosthetic face. Since the accident, Sal suffers from PTSD, depression, and frequent night terrors.

Despite his past, Sal remains outgoing and has a very positive and kind personality. He looks for the best in people and isn't quick to judge. He puts his loved ones first and would do anything to make them happy, even if it means making great sacrifices.

Sal is very short and loves video games, movies, and rocking out on his guitar. He was picked on quite a lot by school bullies. They called him "Sally Face" to mock his feminine mask and hairstyle. Sal took the nickname and kept it as his own; this way the bullies couldn't use it against him.

CHARACTER INFORMATION

NICKNAME: Sally Face
BIRTH: December 13th, 1976
DEATH: Electric chair, 2004
HAIR: Blue
EYES: Blue
FATHER: Henry Fisher
MOTHER: Diane Fisher

TEEN HEIGHT: 5'2"
ADULT HEIGHT: 5'6"

FAVORITE FOOD: Pizza
DREAM JOB: Undecided
FAVORITE MUSIC: Rock

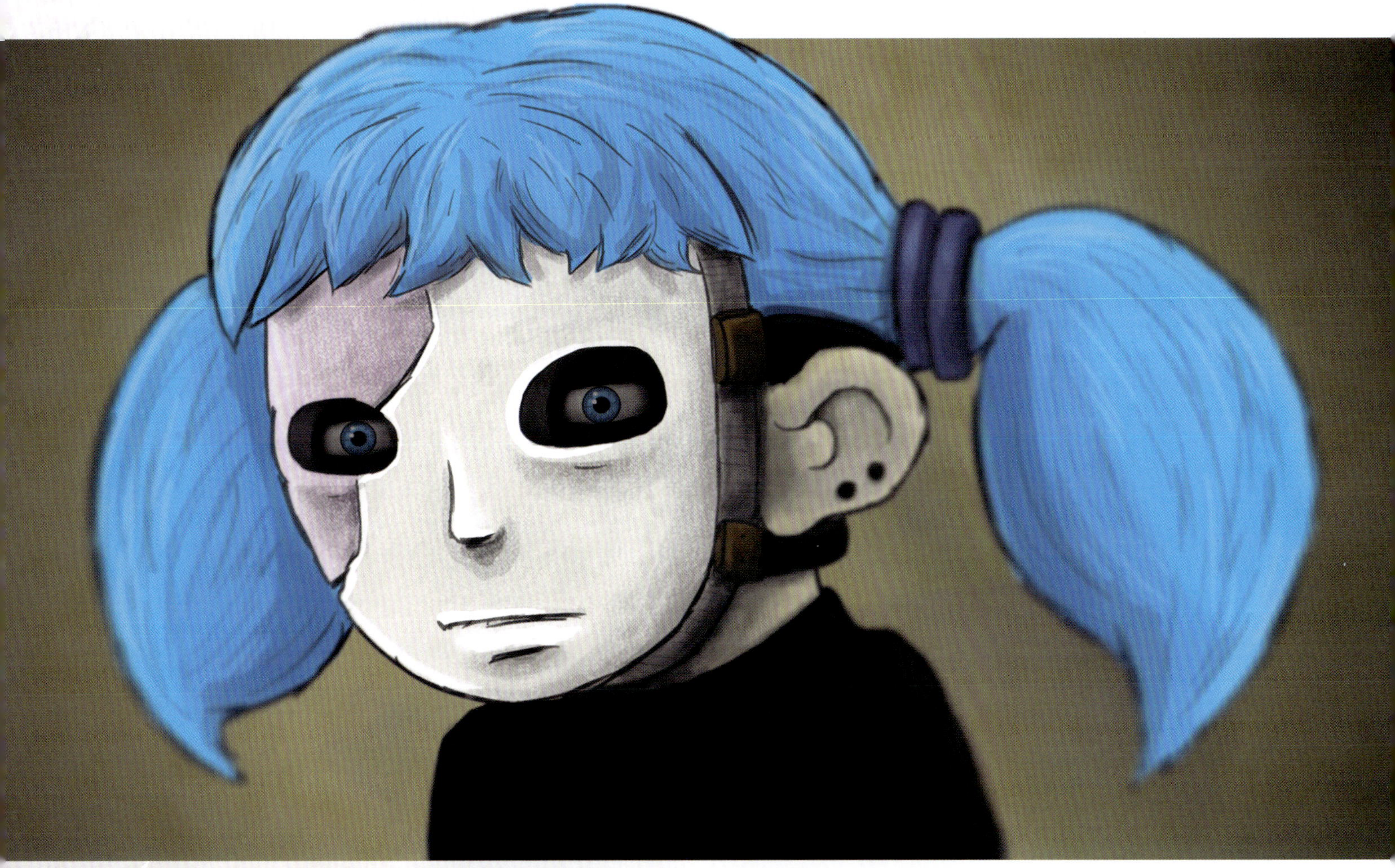

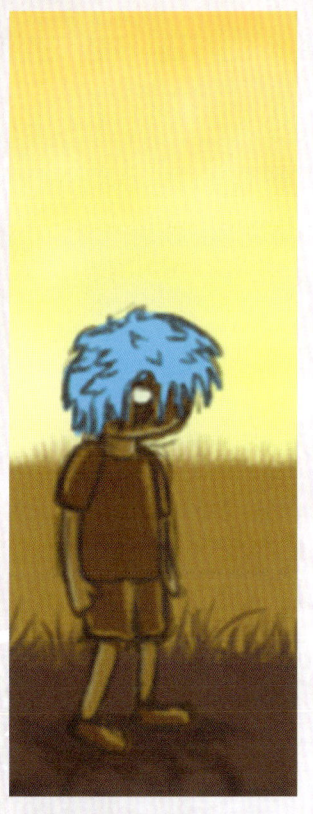
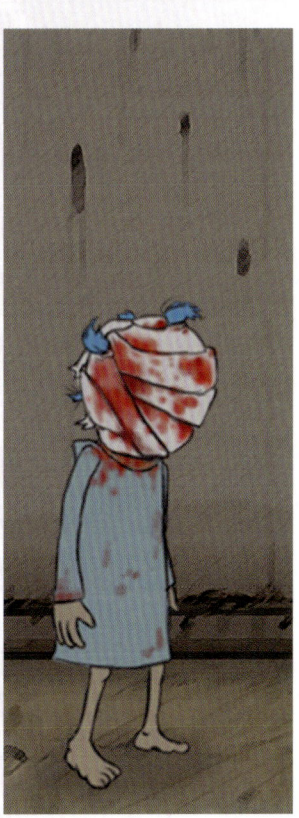
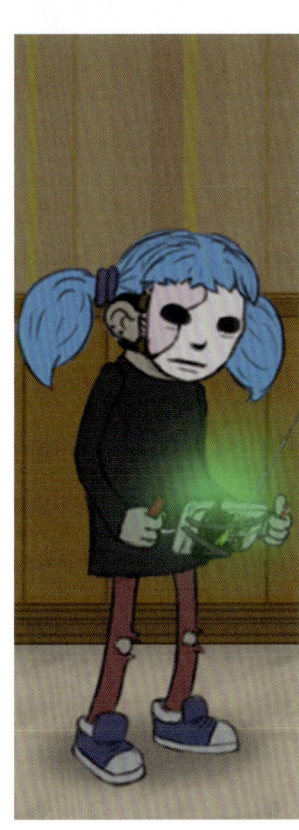
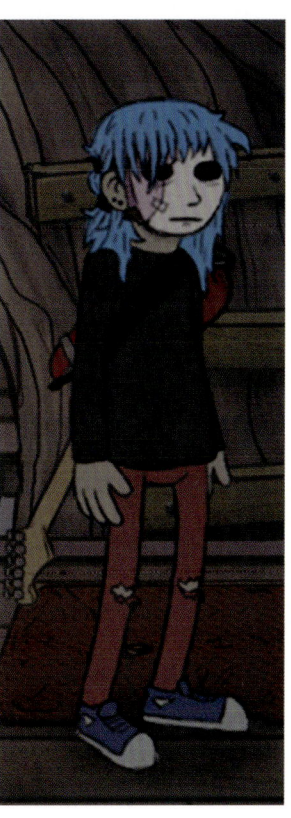

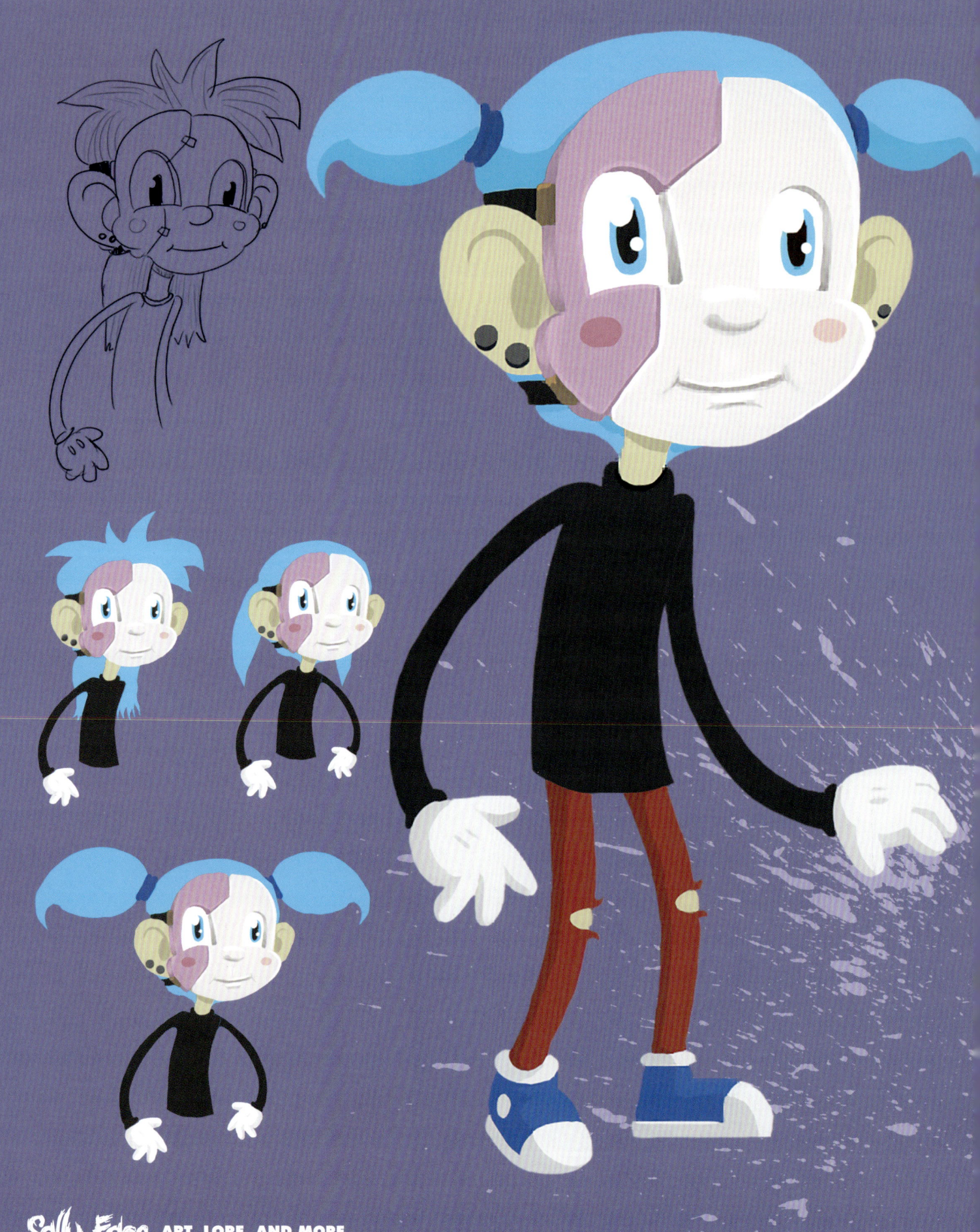

Sally Face ART, LORE, AND MORE

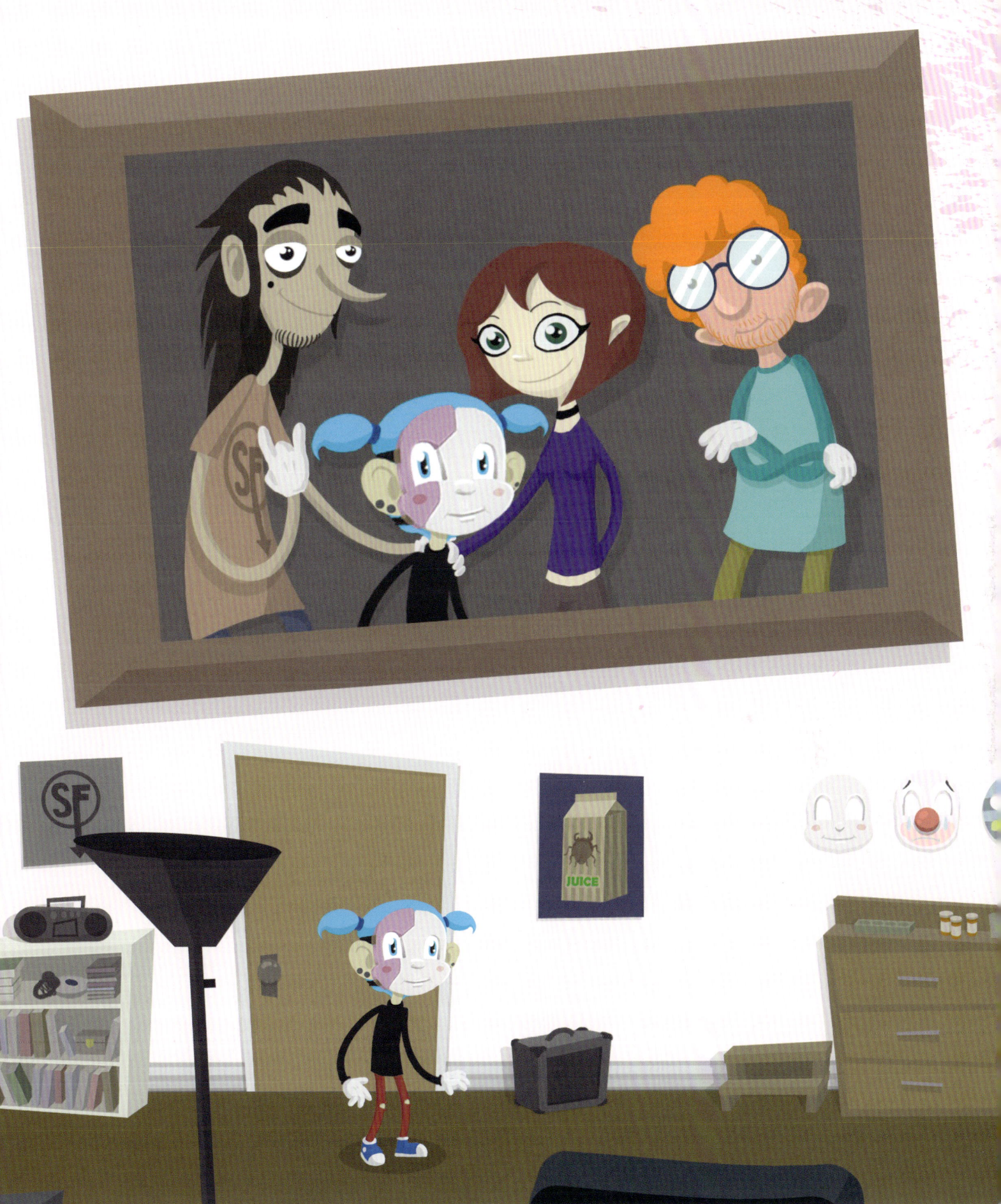

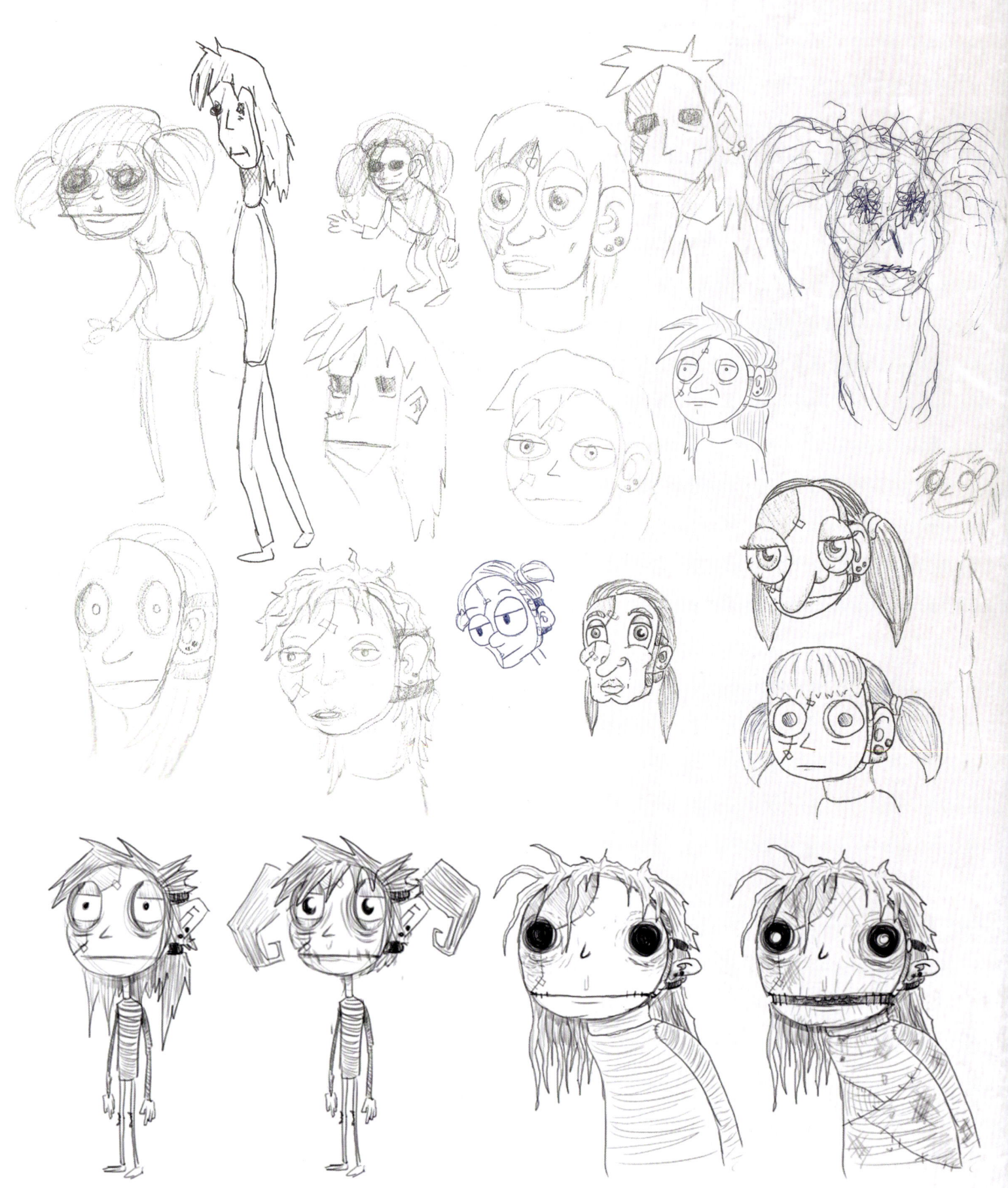

Sally Face ART, LORE, AND MORE

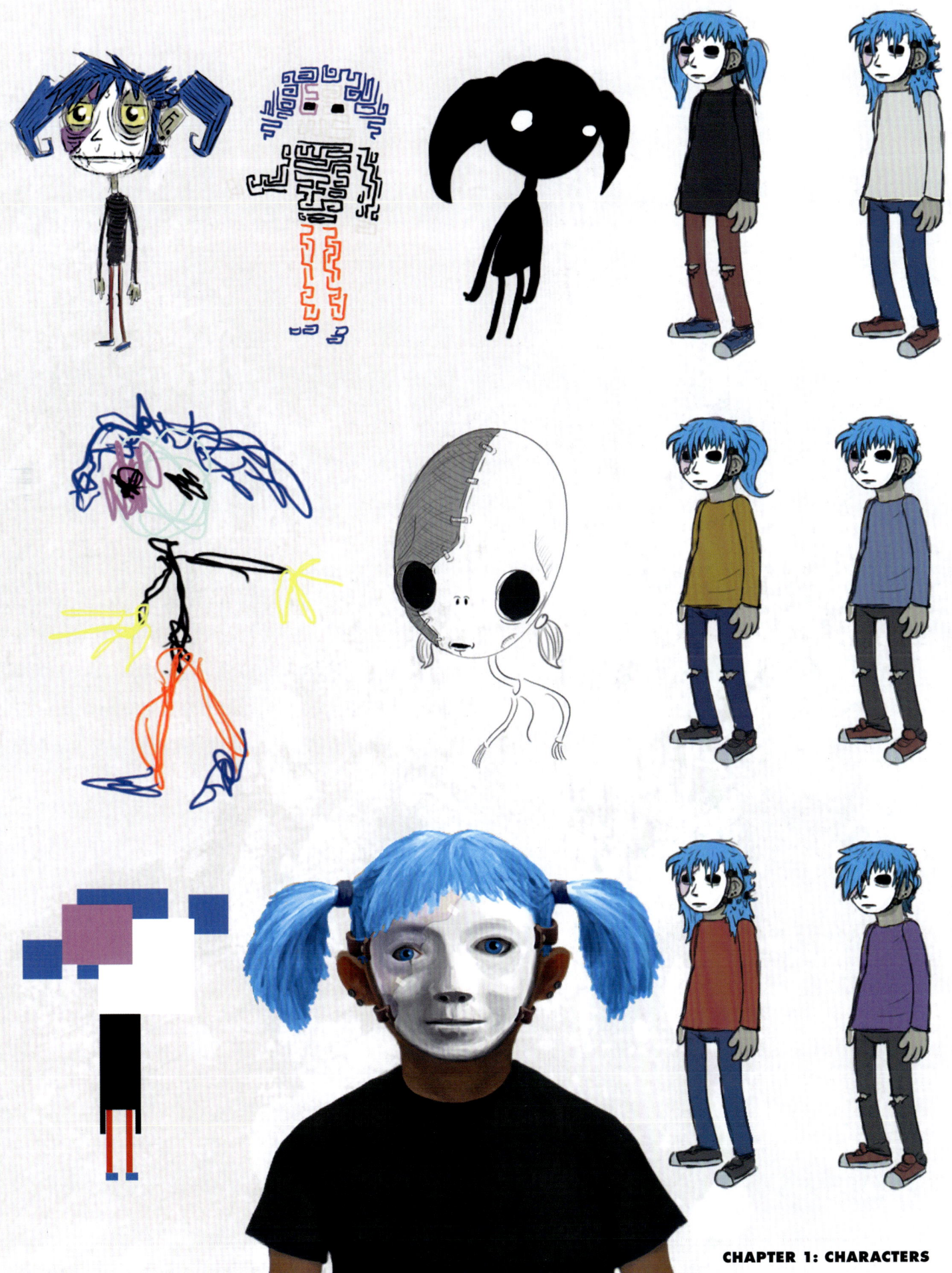

GEAR BOY

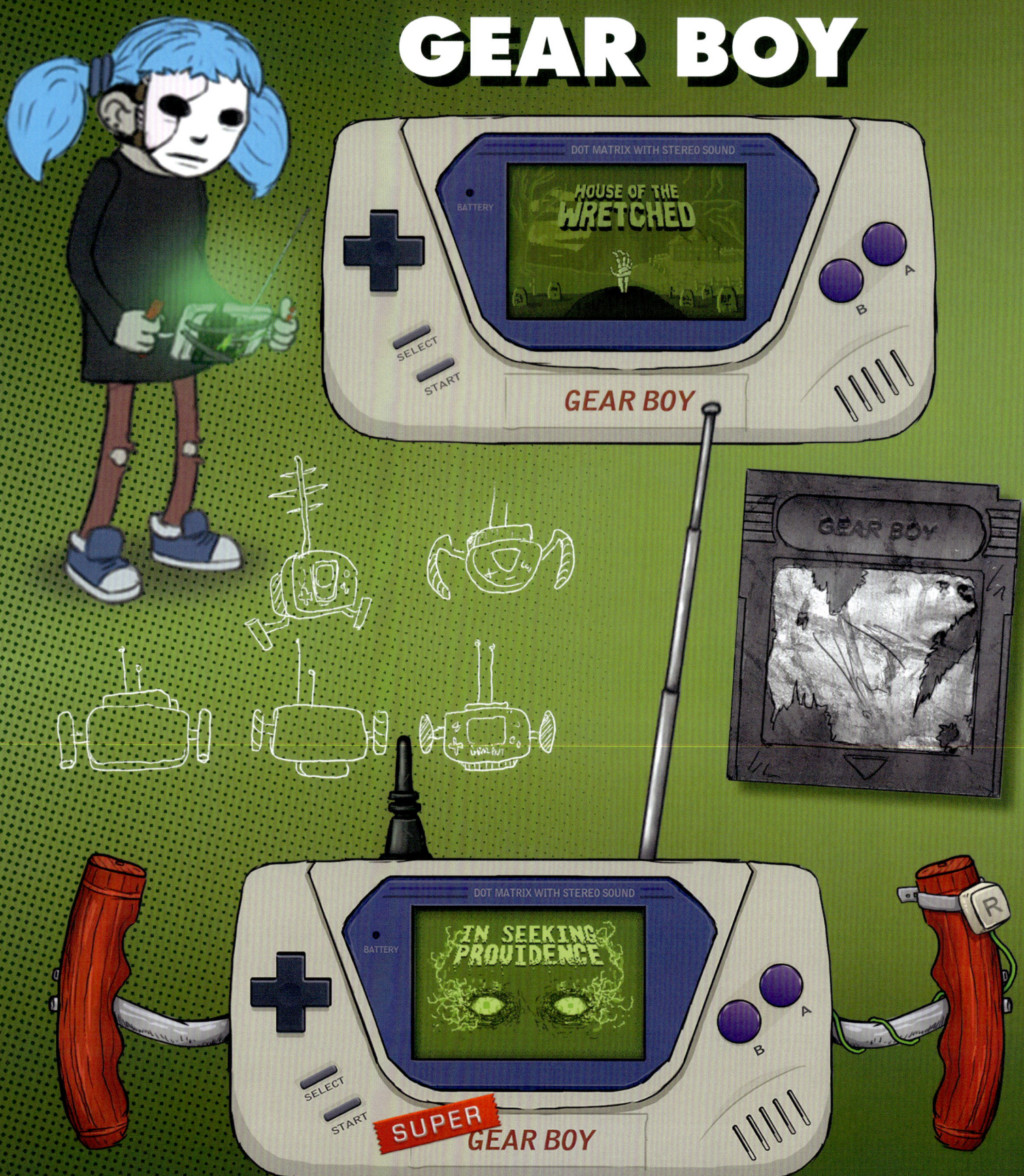

Sally Face ART, LORE, AND MORE

NECRO GUITAR

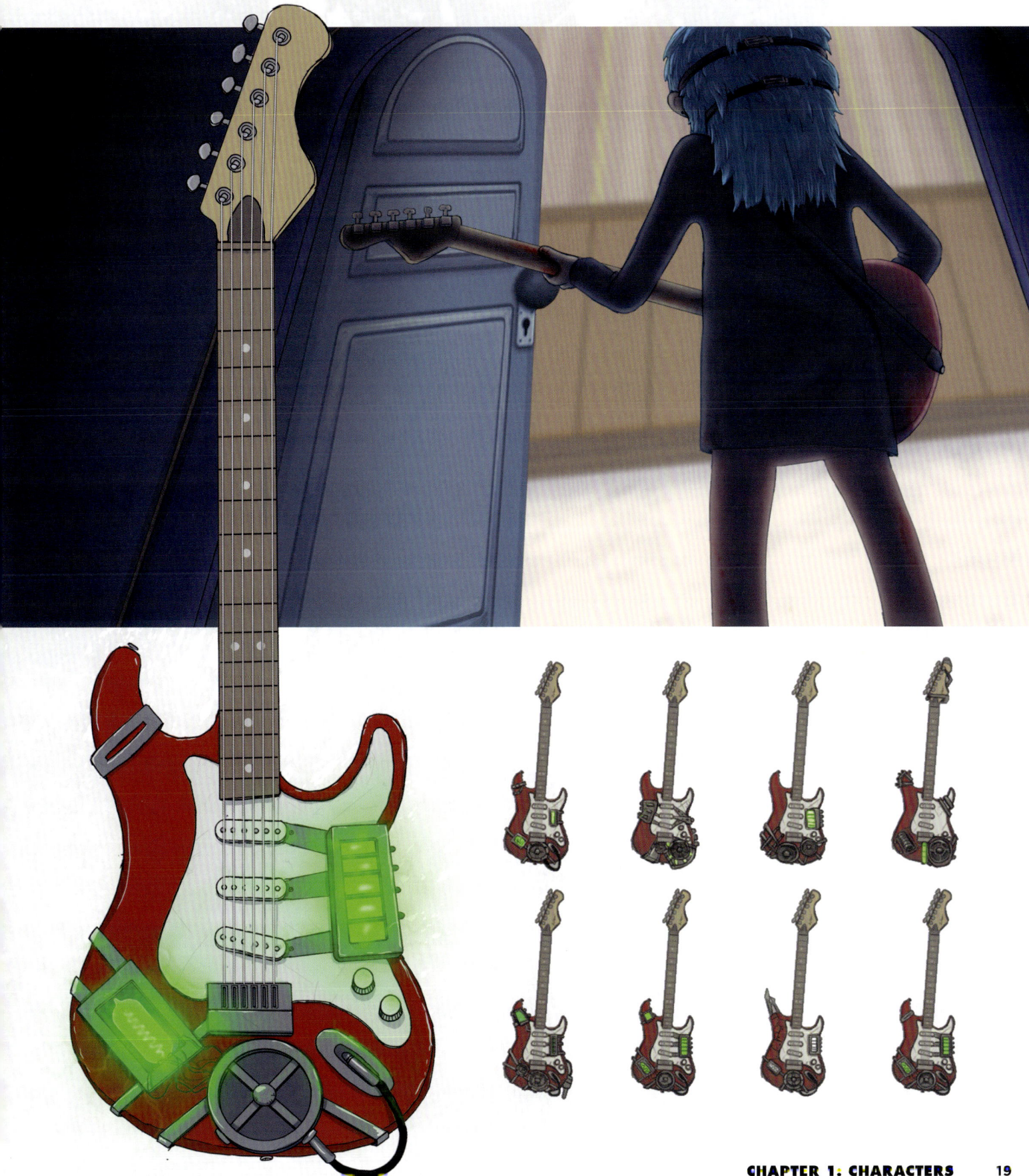

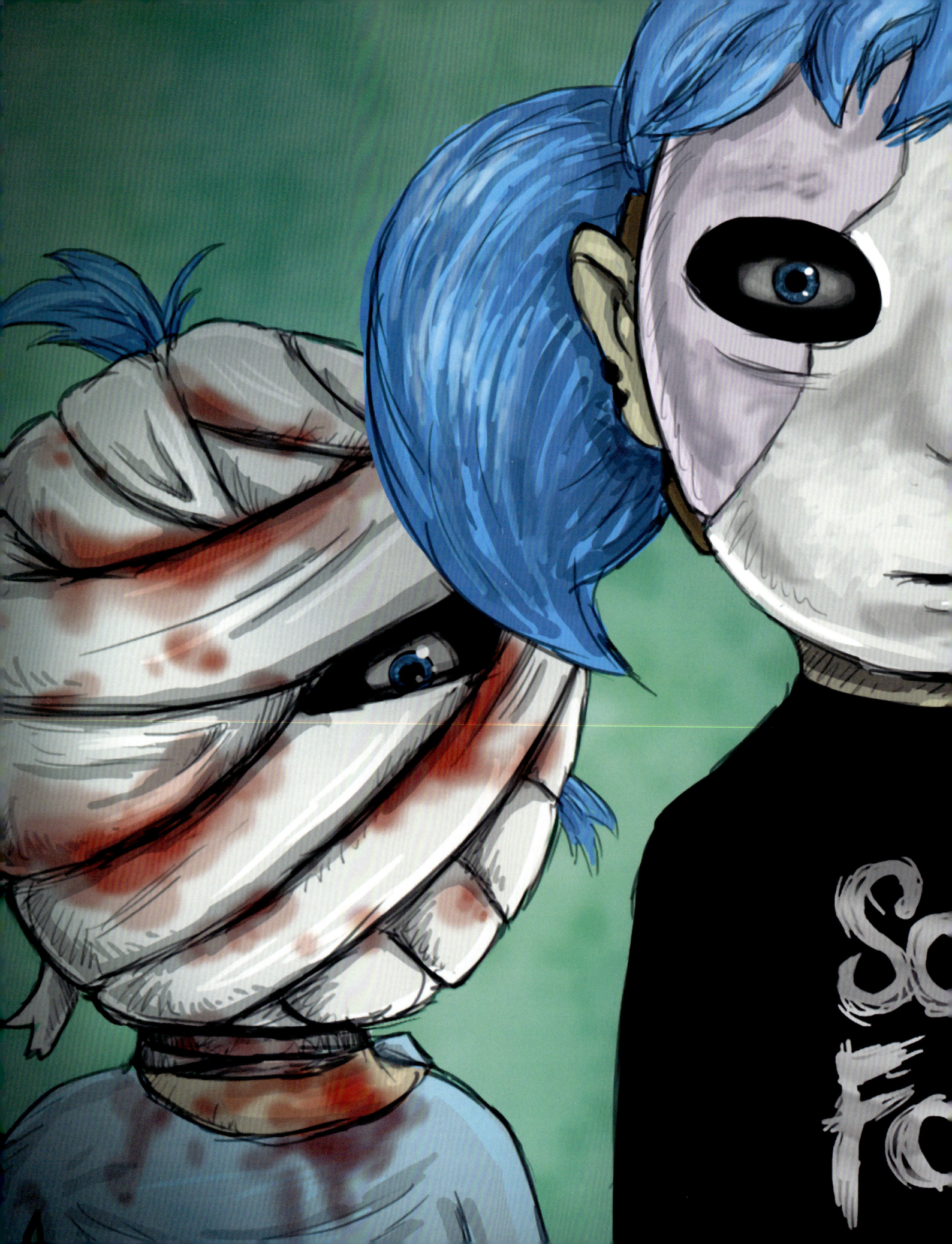

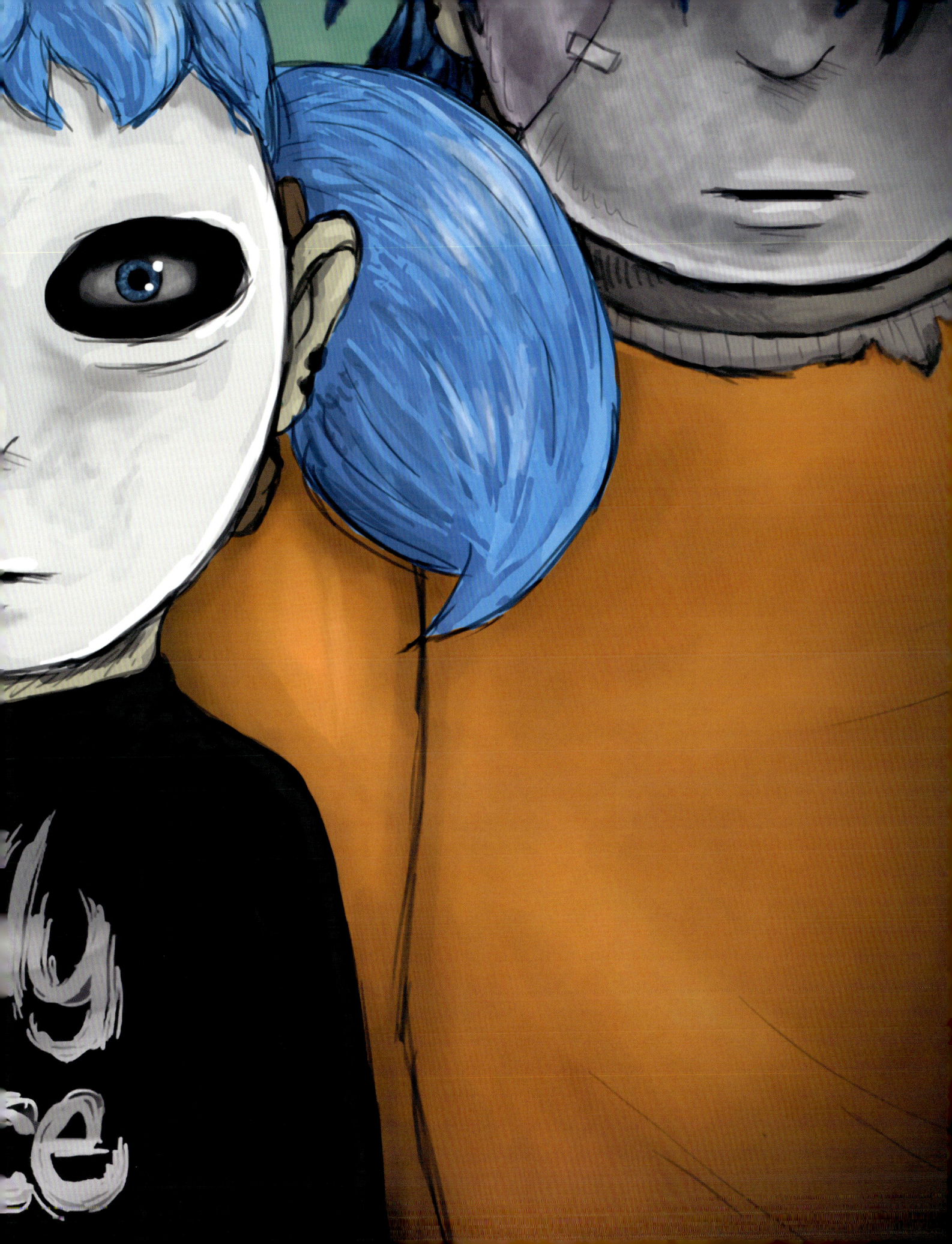

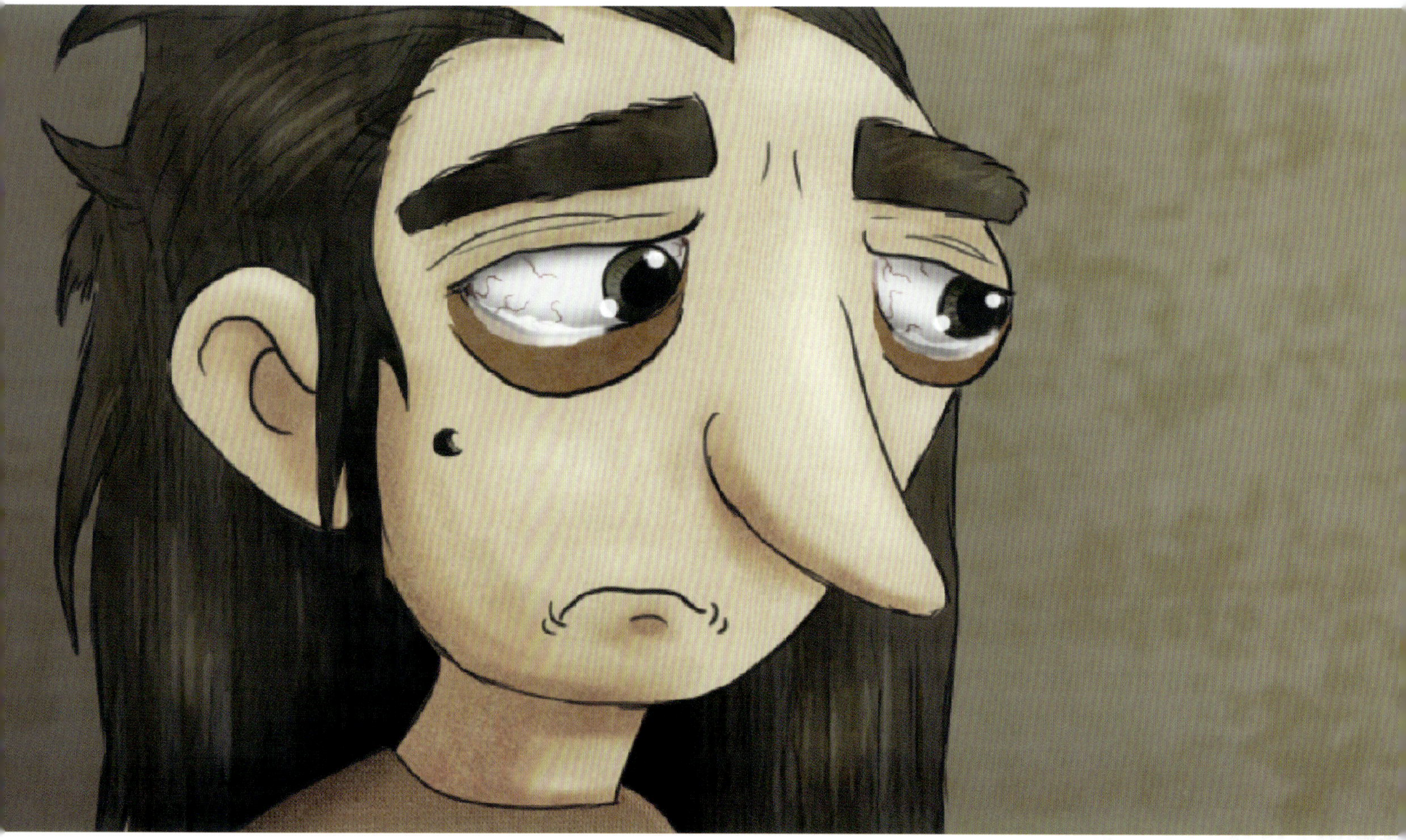

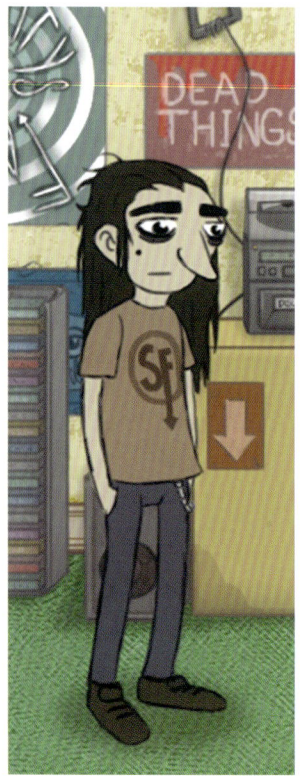

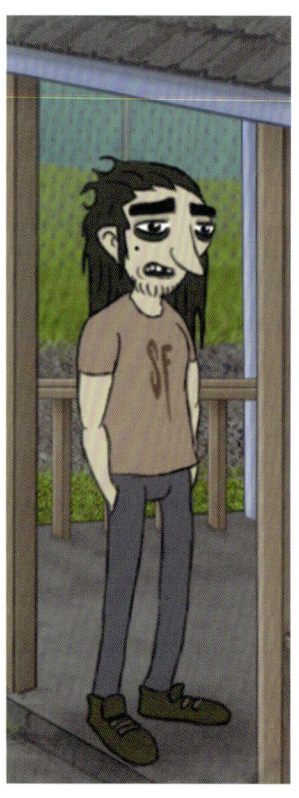

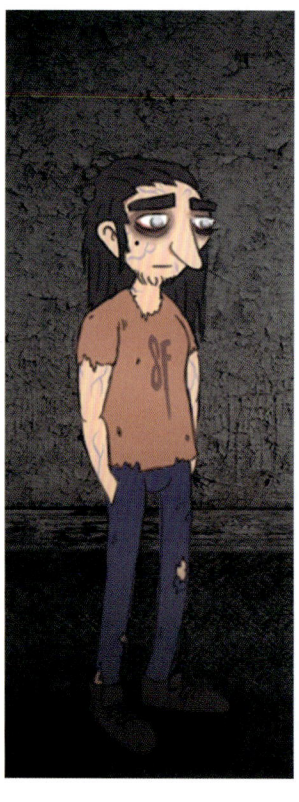

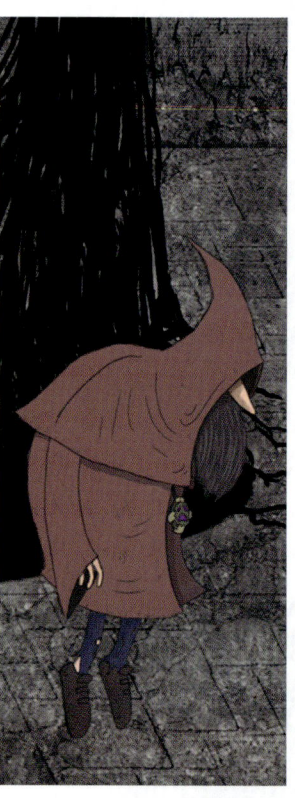

LARRY JOHNSON

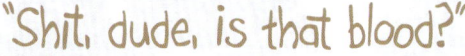

"Shit, dude, is that blood?"

LARRY IS SAL'S BEST FRIEND and local metalhead. He has a laid back, stoner vibe and is known to throw around corny jokes and cheesy puns. When he was a child, his father disappeared without a trace. Larry convinced himself that the disappearance was somehow his fault and that he was "cursed". Since then, he's carried a sadness inside but has buried it deep down and rarely shows it.

Being the tallest in the gang of friends, Larry towers over Sal. He loves painting, listening to music, and playing video games. Larry is also a big fan of horror movies and comic books. His big mouth and anti-authoritarian nature can sometimes get him into trouble, but he is overall a good person—despite how he views himself.

Larry's friends are like family to him and he's very protective of them. If anyone threatens them, Larry takes it personally and can quickly become aggressive. There's a lot of pent up rage under his calm demeanor, though he typically has a lid on it.

CHARACTER INFORMATION

BIRTH: August 16th, 1975
DEATH: Suicide, 1999
HAIR: Brown
EYES: Brown
MOTHER: Lisa Garcia
FATHER: Jim Johnson

TEEN HEIGHT: 5'8"
ADULT HEIGHT: 6'1"

FAVORITE FOOD: Pizza
DREAM JOB: Retired
FAVORITE MUSIC: Metal

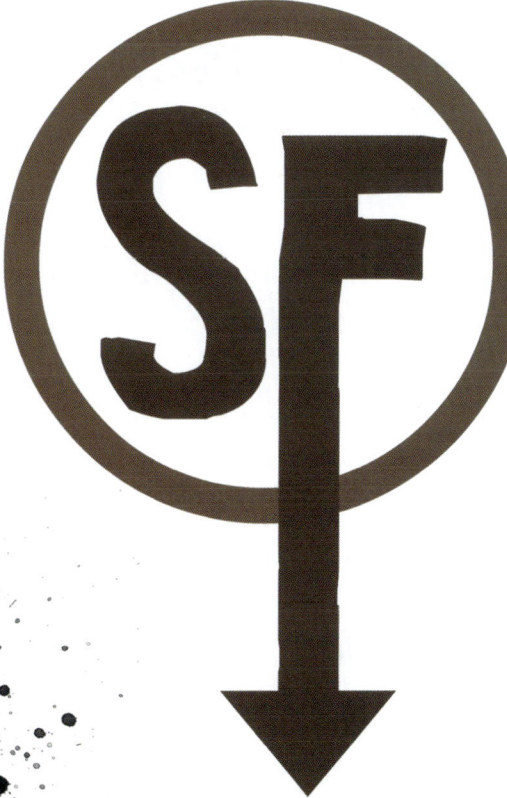

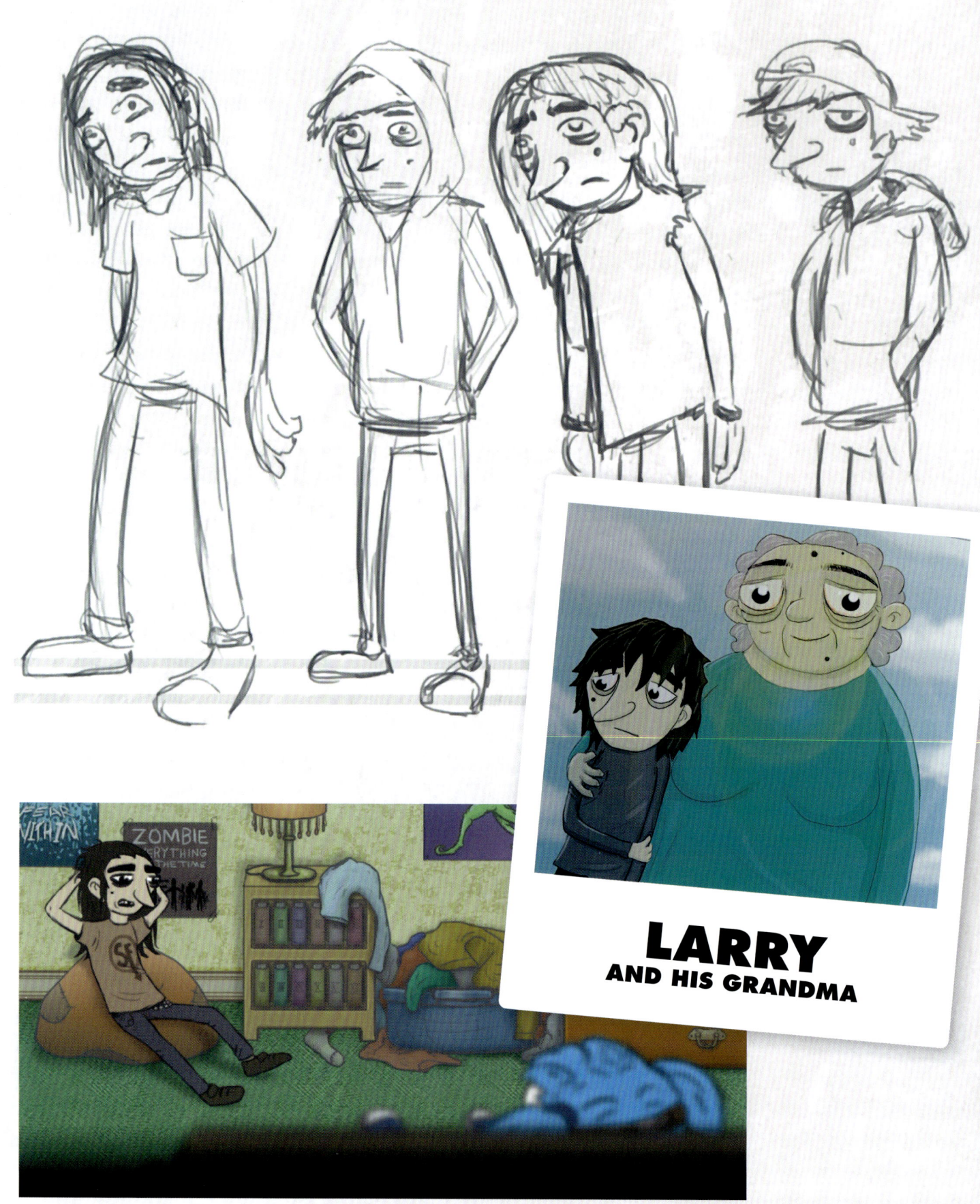

LARRY
AND HIS GRANDMA

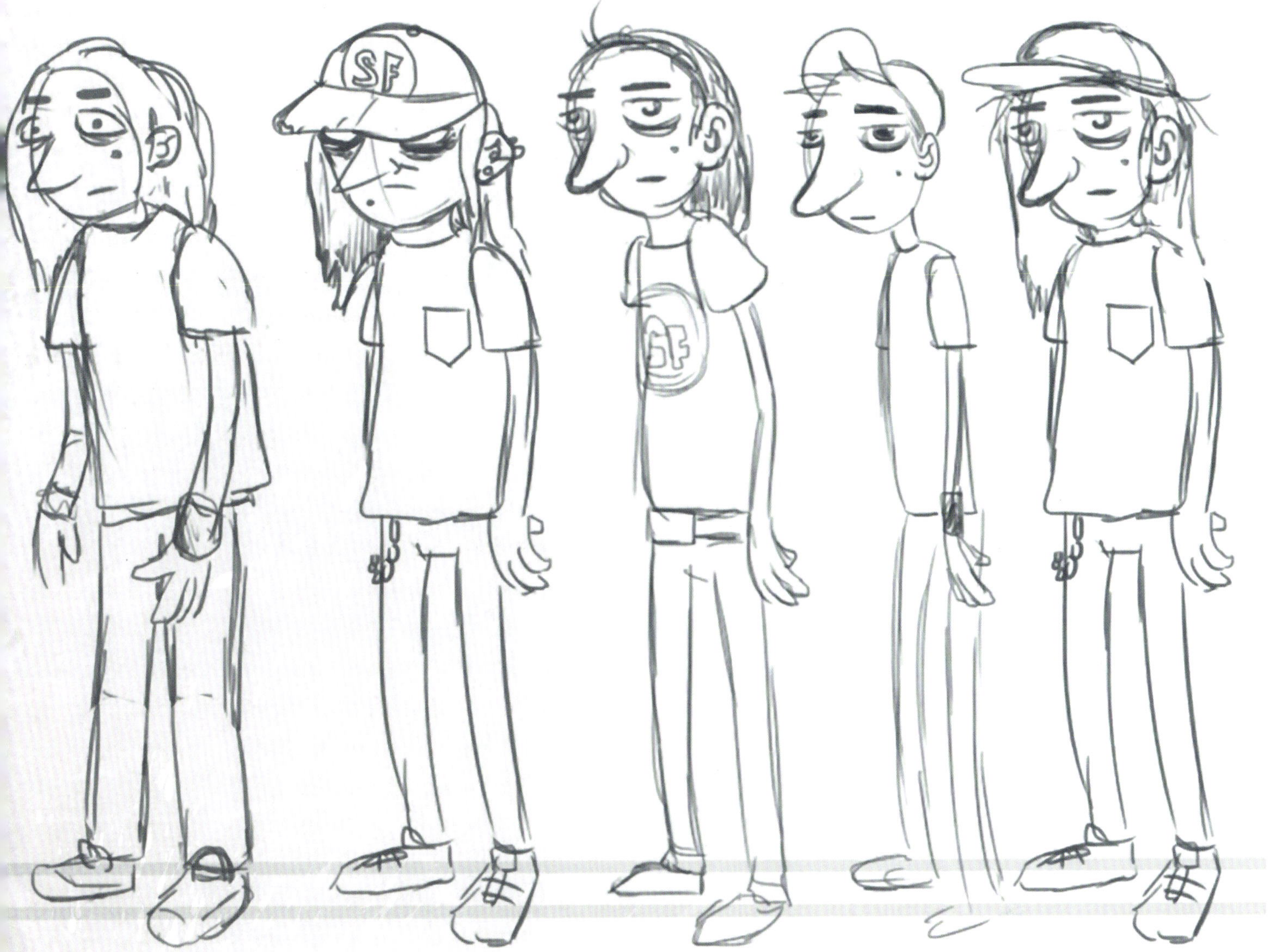

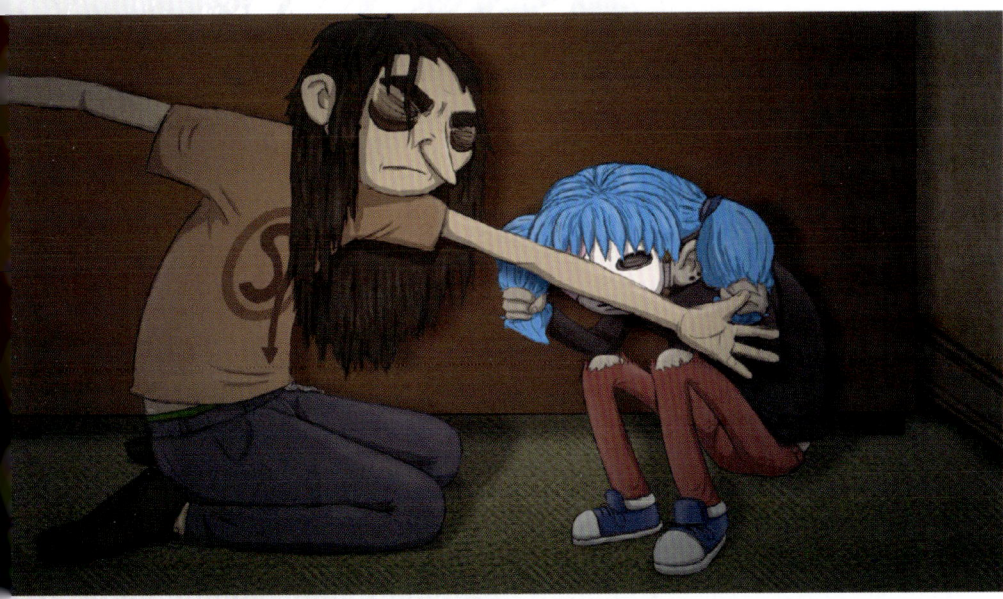

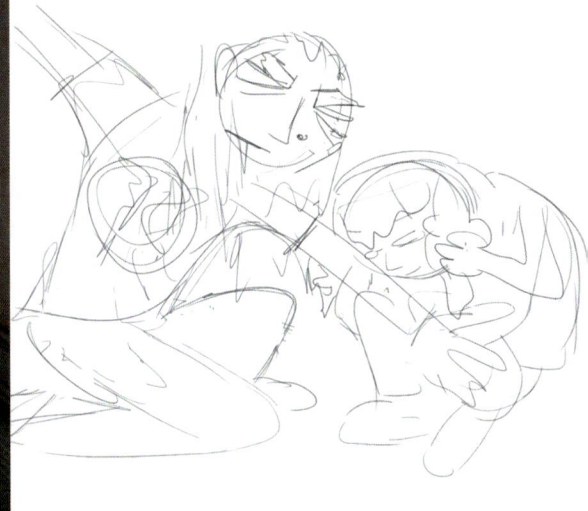

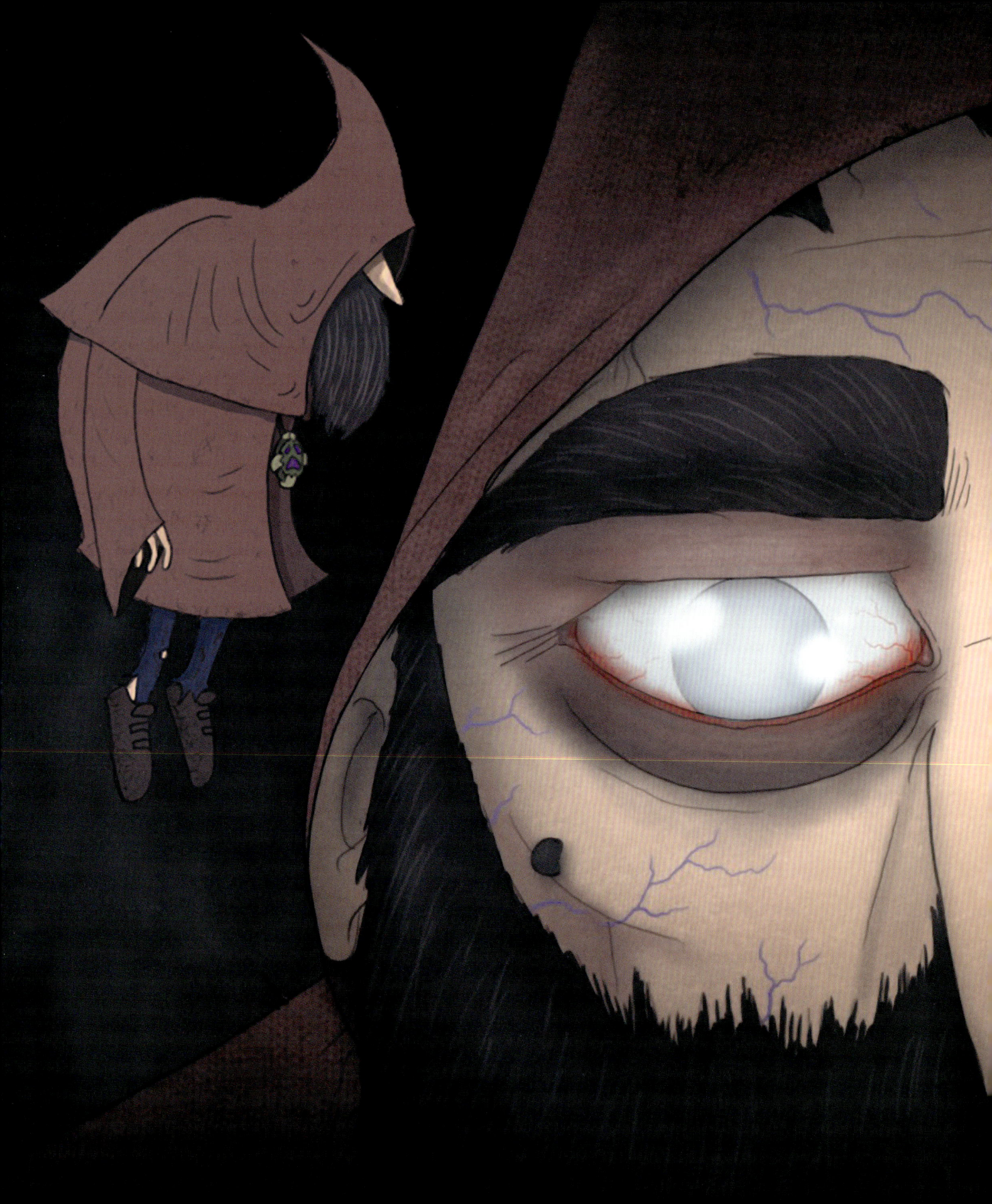

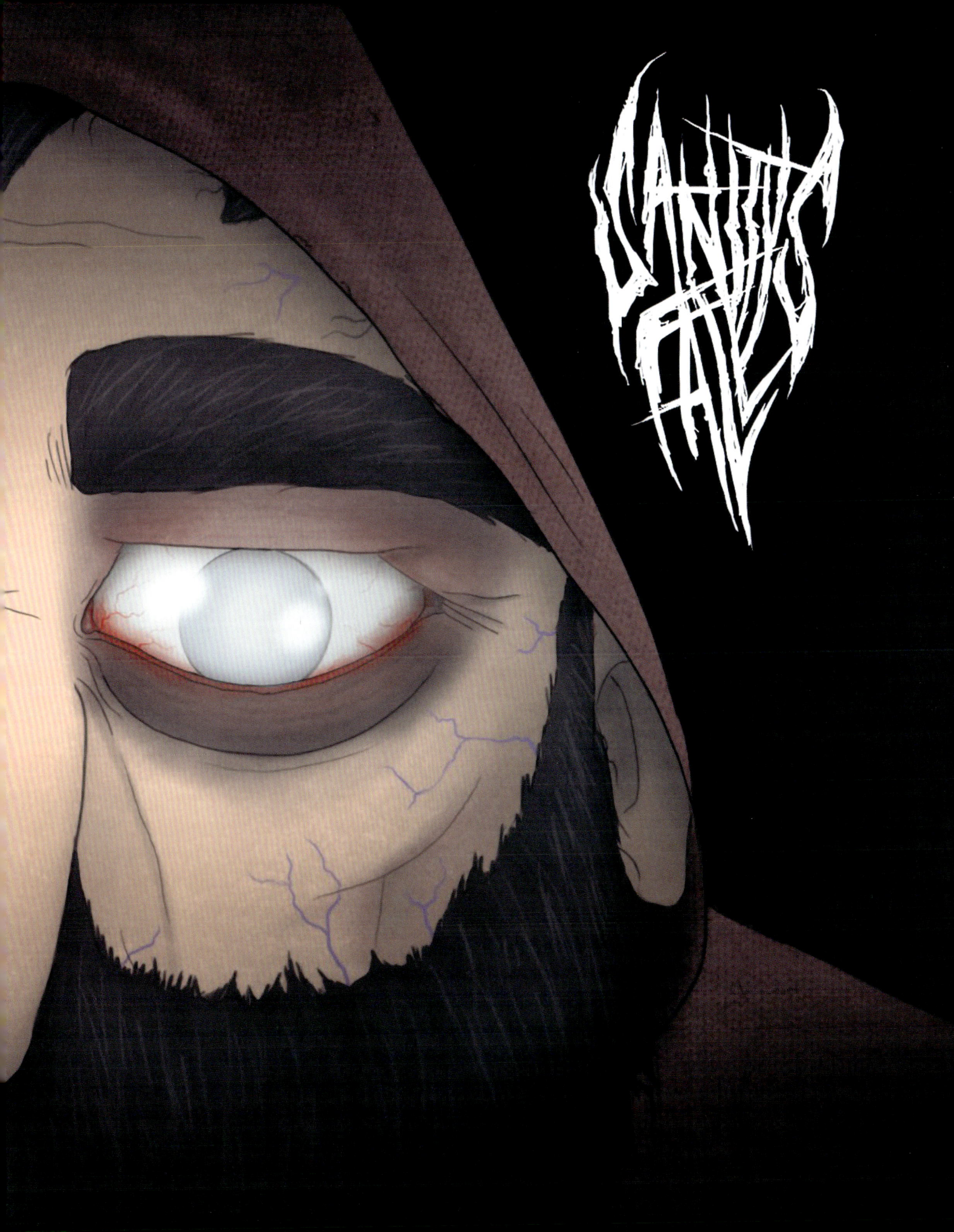

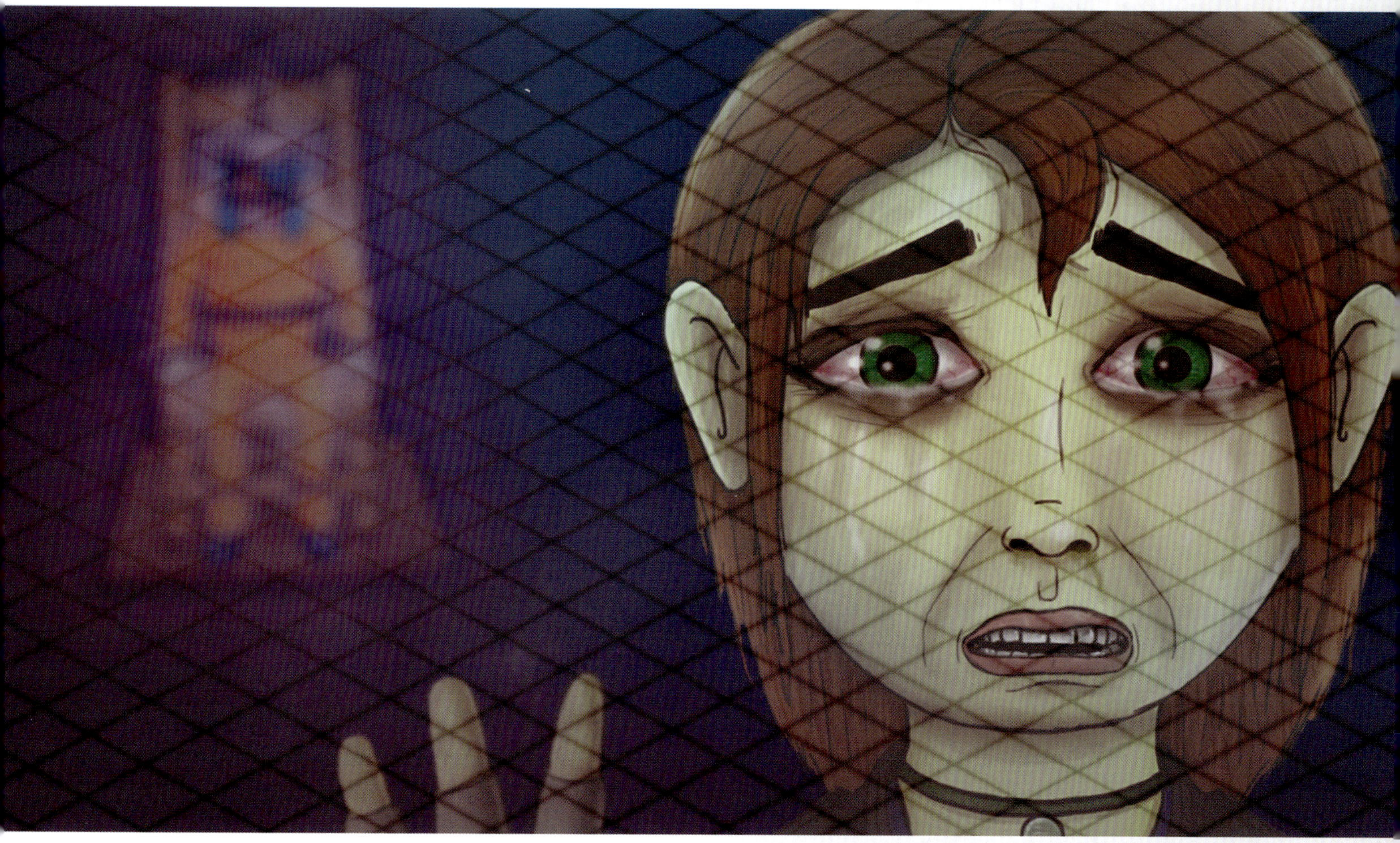

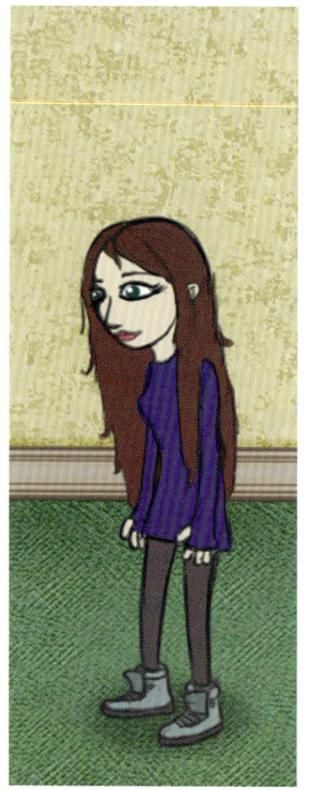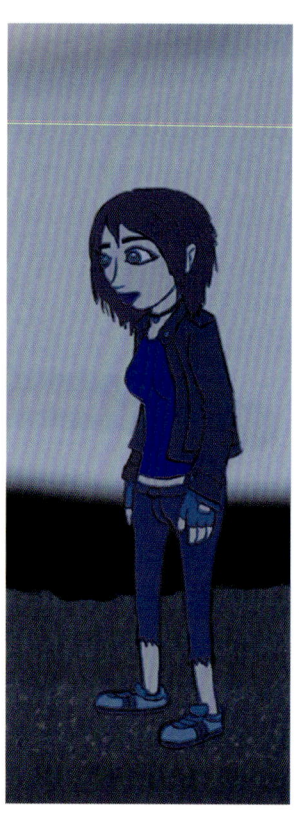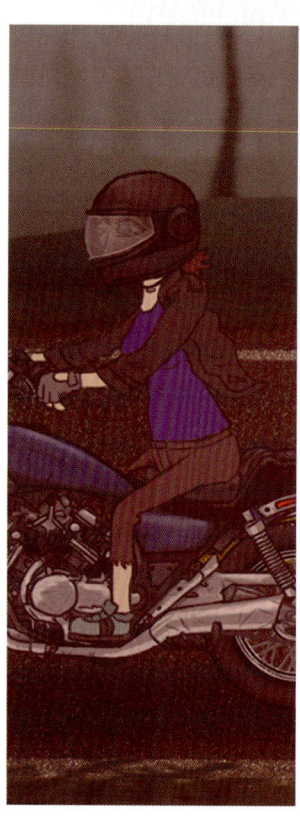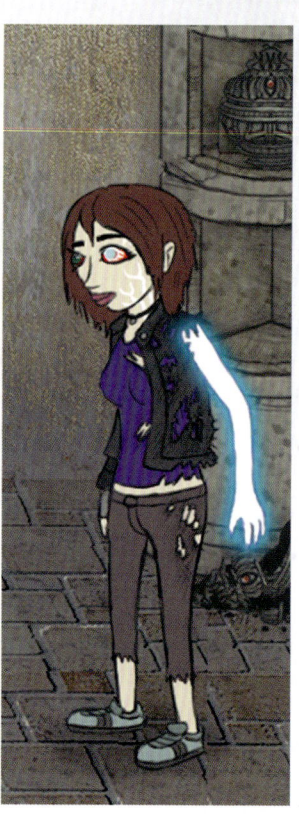

ASHLEY "ASH" CAMPBELL

"I just want you to be happy."

ASHLEY IS A SWEET and caring artist who is always there for emotional support. She is cheerful, especially when she's with her friends. Ash is also the group skeptic and doesn't believe in the supernatural, even as they discover unexplainable things. She never seems to be around when the boys speak with ghosts, so she hasn't witnessed them firsthand. Even so, she remains supportive of their investigations and helps out when she can. Ash will sometimes make fun of the spooky stuff, but is never mean about it.

When everything falls apart, Ash steps in to pick up the pieces. The once naive young girl grows into a strong-willed woman, who's ready to sacrifice everything to save her friends. Ashley has made many mistakes throughout her journey and becomes desperate to set things right.

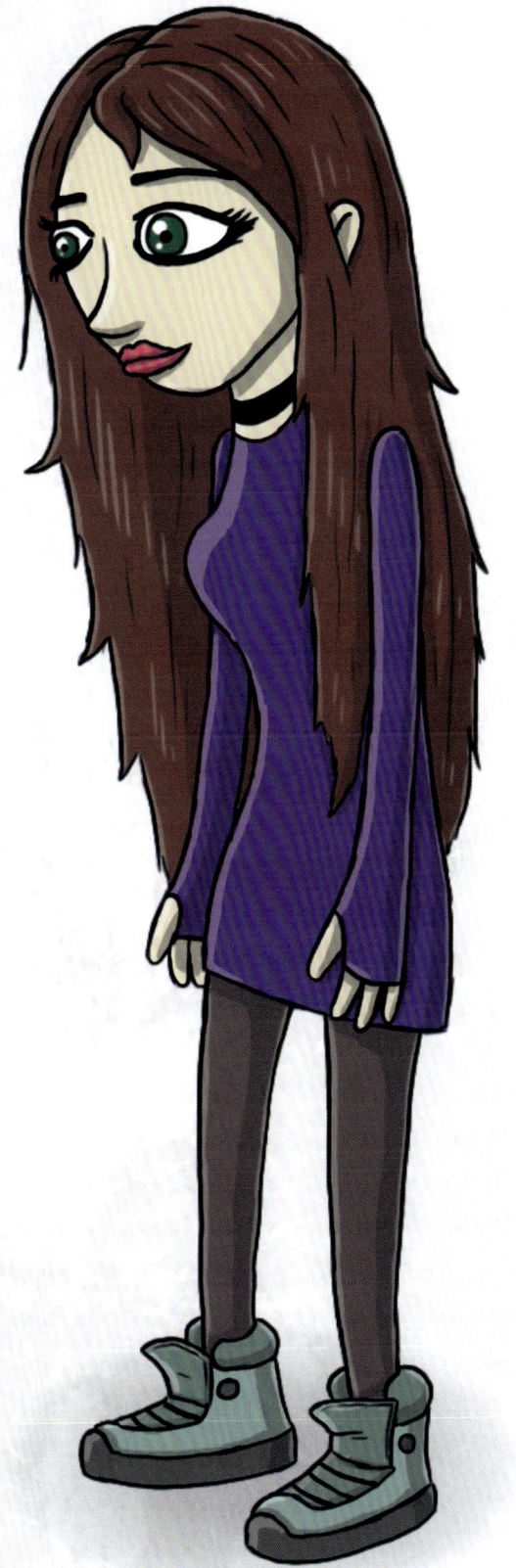

CHARACTER INFORMATION

NICKNAME: Ash
BIRTH: November 30th, 1976
HAIR: Red
EYES: Green
MOTHER: Stephanie Campbell
FATHER: Adam Campbell
BROTHER: Benjamin Campbell

TEEN HEIGHT: 5'5"
ADULT HEIGHT: 5'8"

FAVORITE FOOD: Pasta
DREAM JOB: Art Teacher
FAVORITE MUSIC: Classic Rock

ASHLEY (EMPOWERED)
"MEMORIES AND DREAMS"

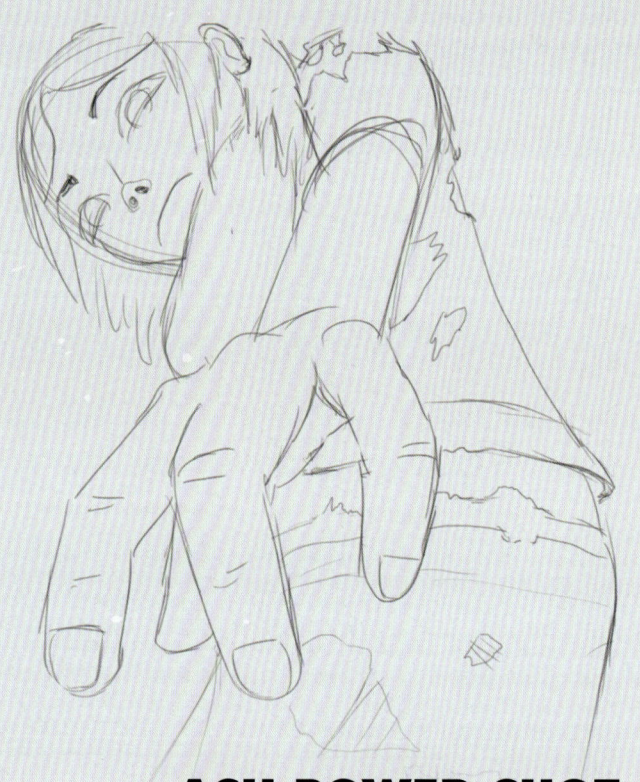

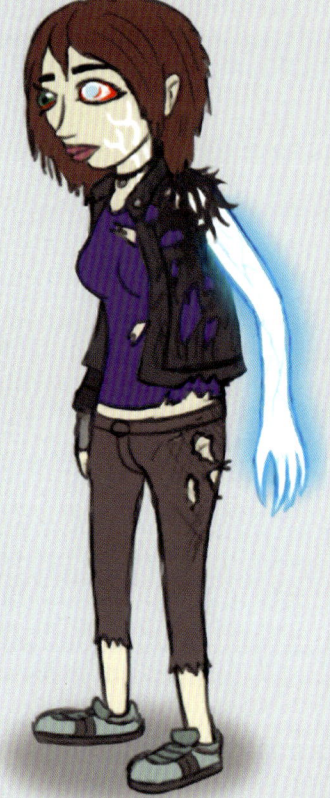

ASH POWER SHOT

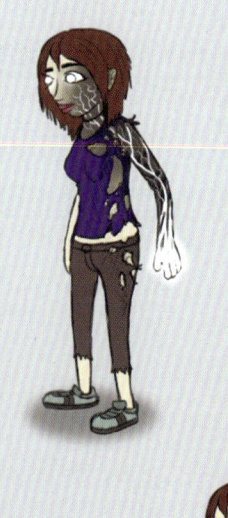 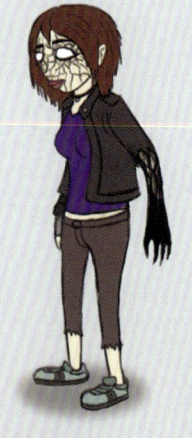 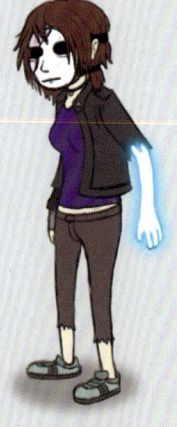 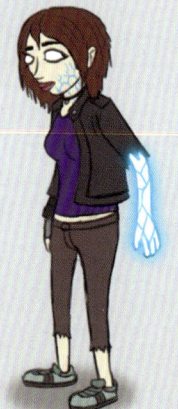 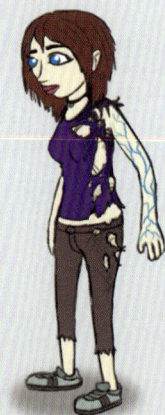 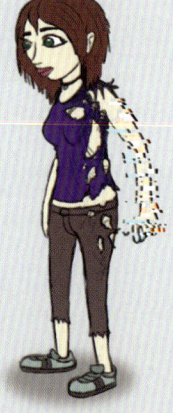 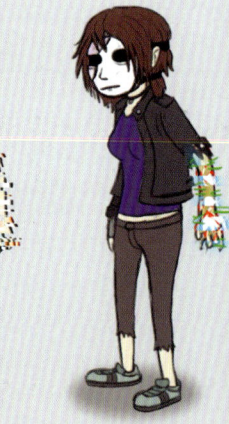

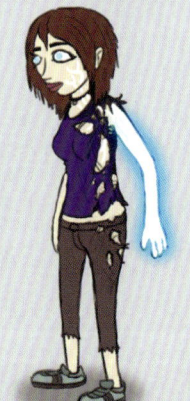 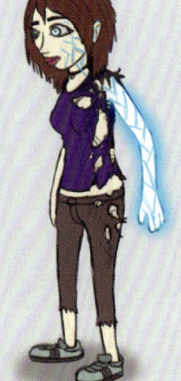 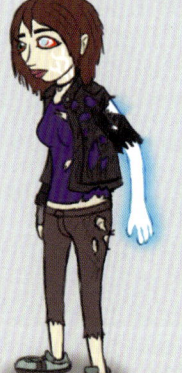 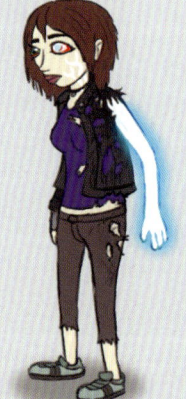

30 **Sally Face** ART, LORE, AND MORE

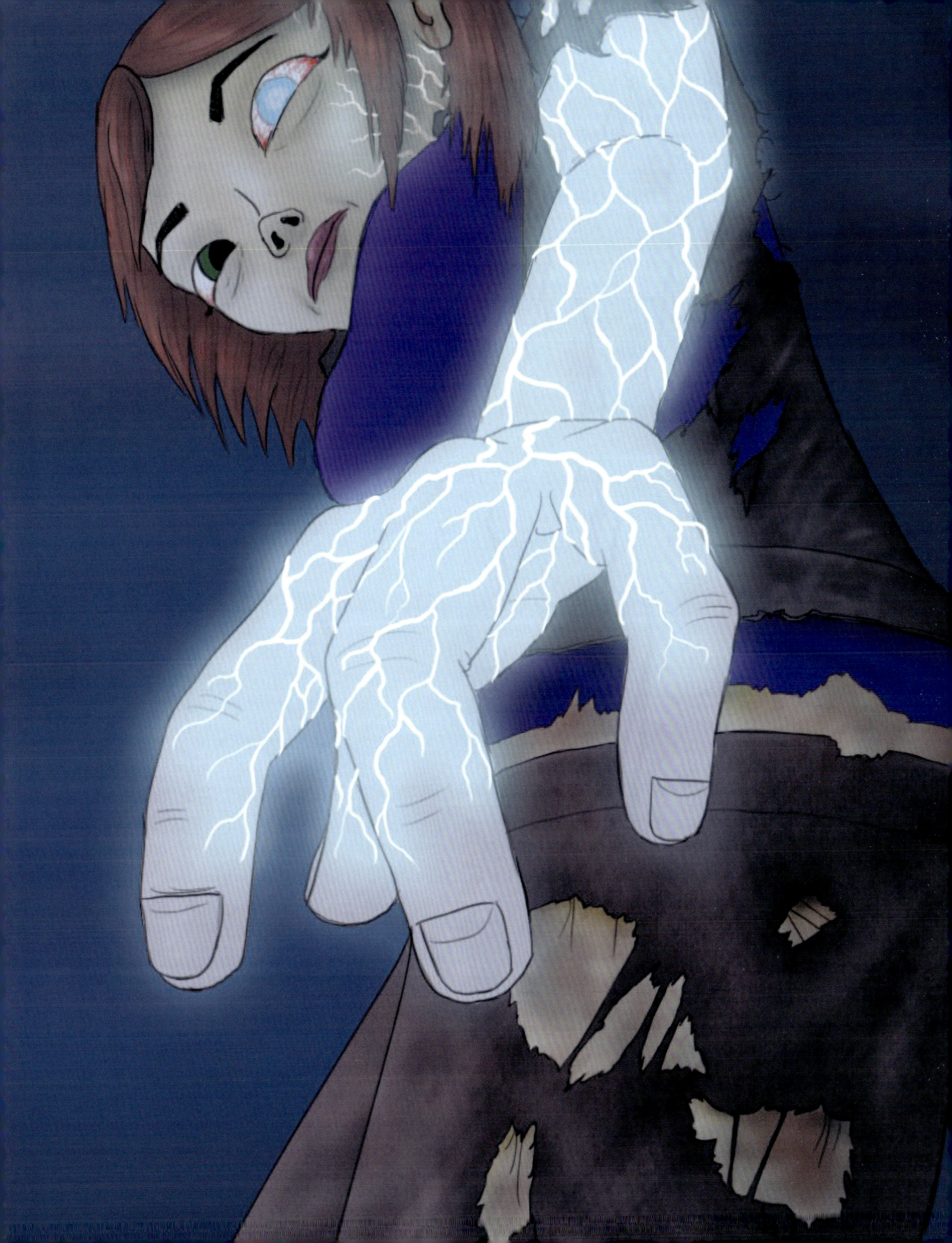

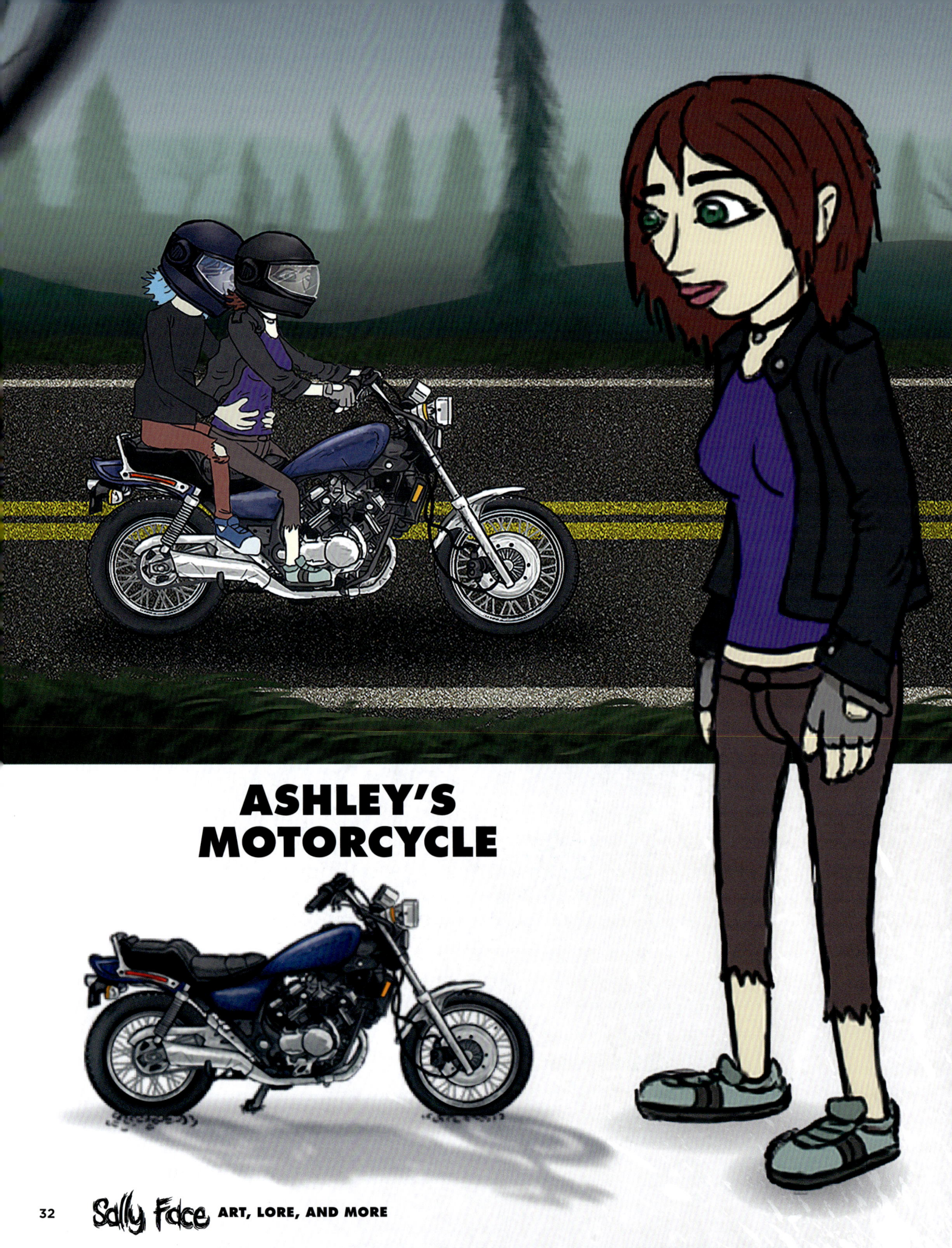

ASHLEY'S MOTORCYCLE

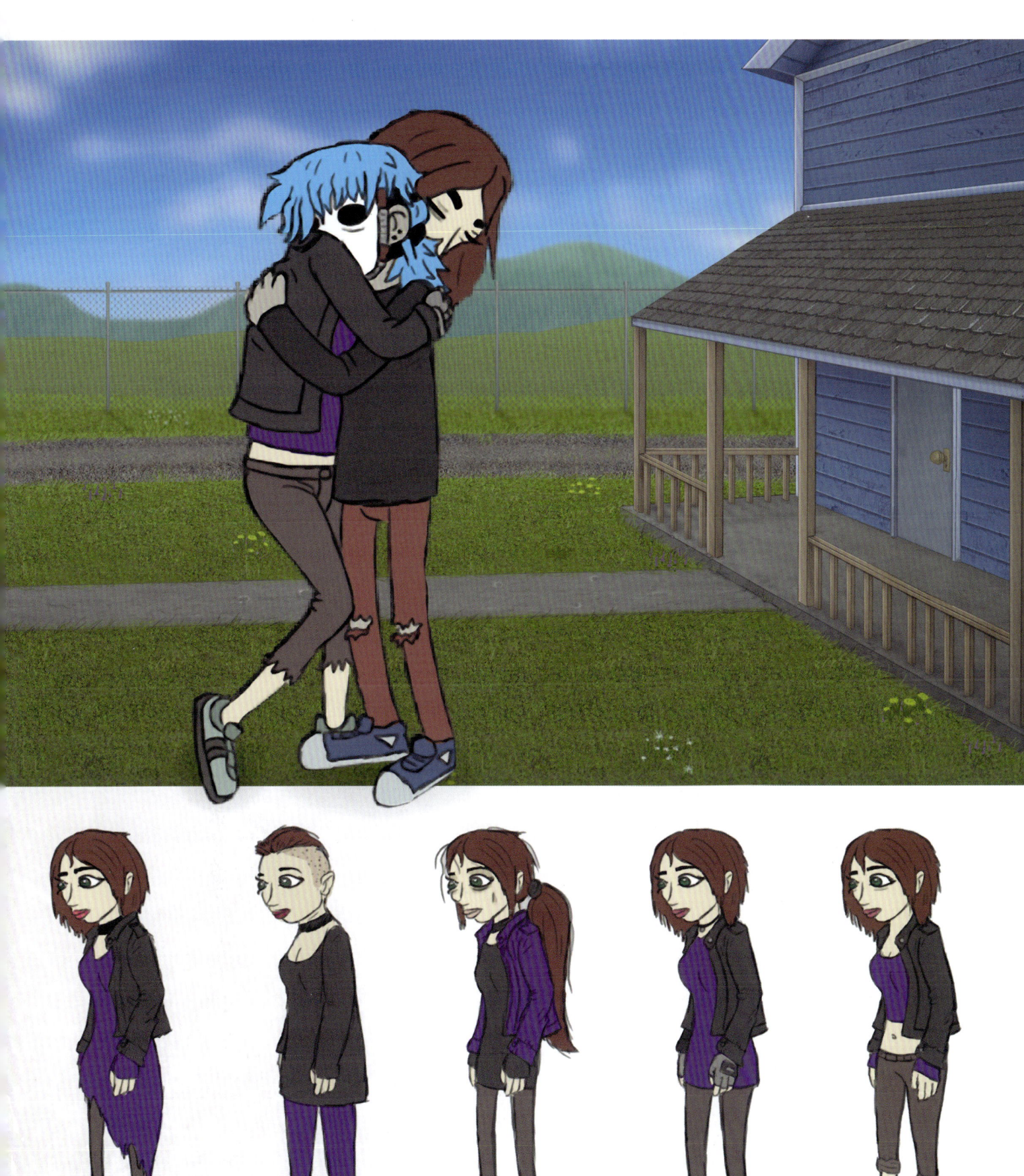

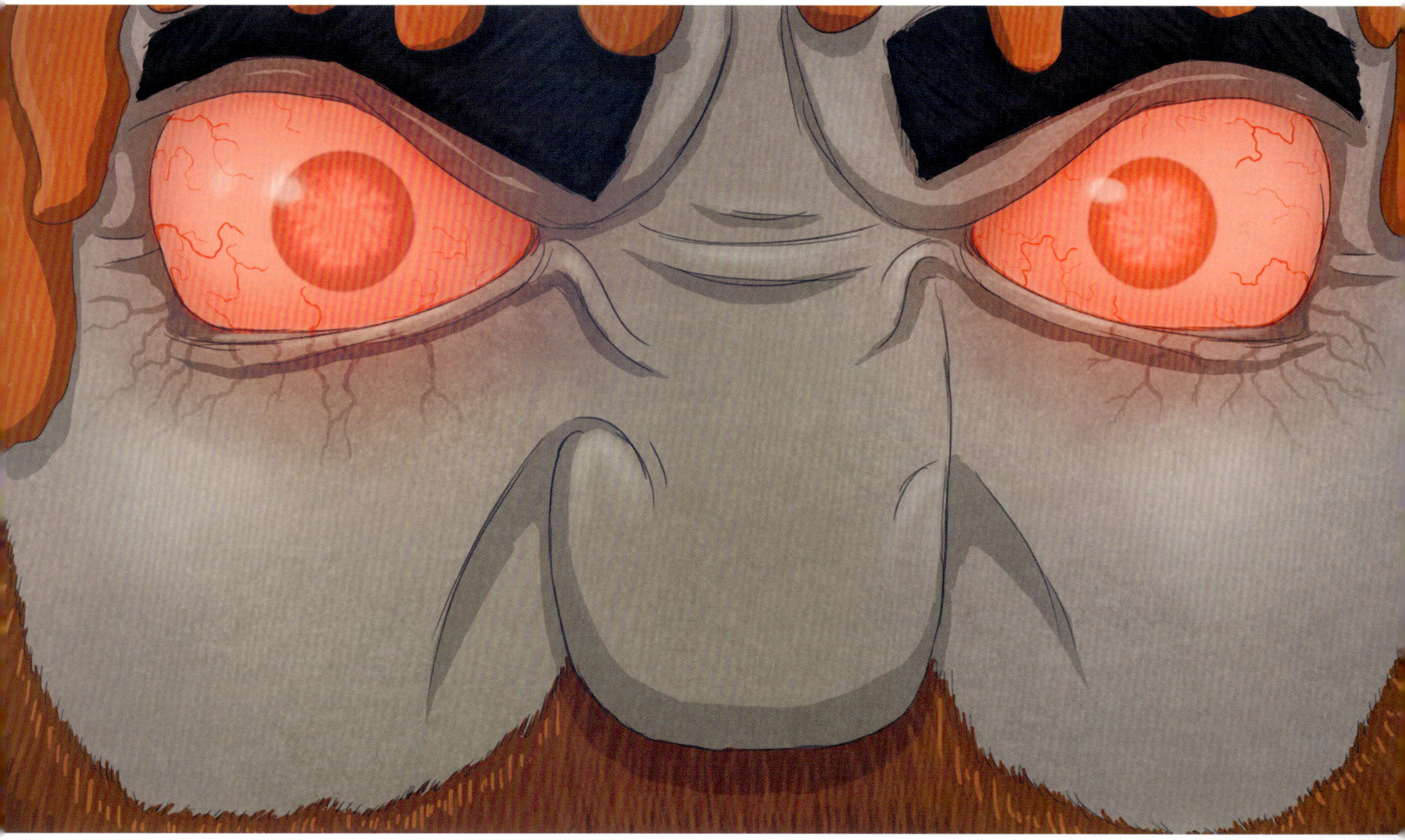

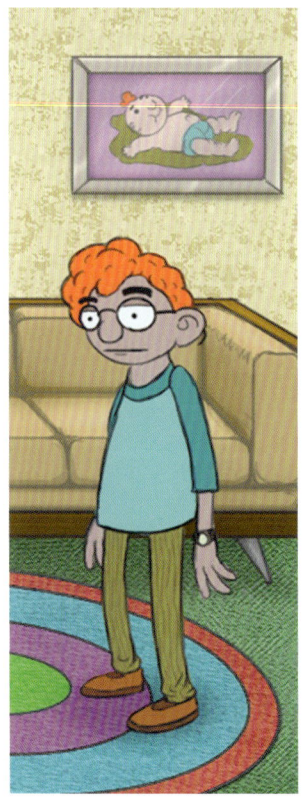
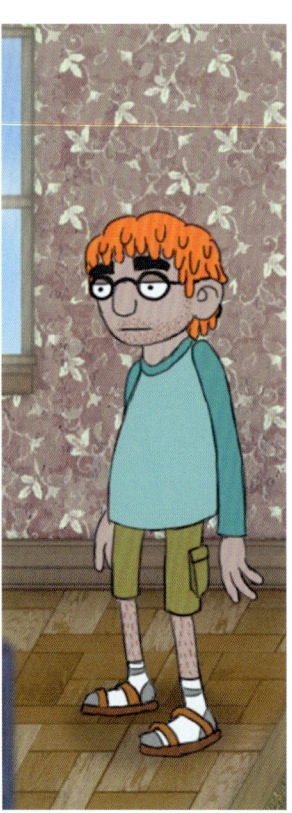
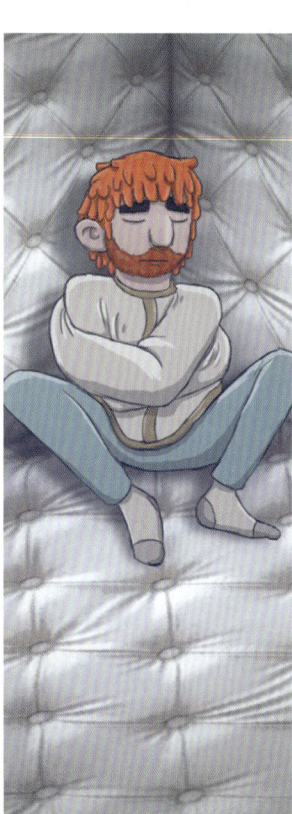
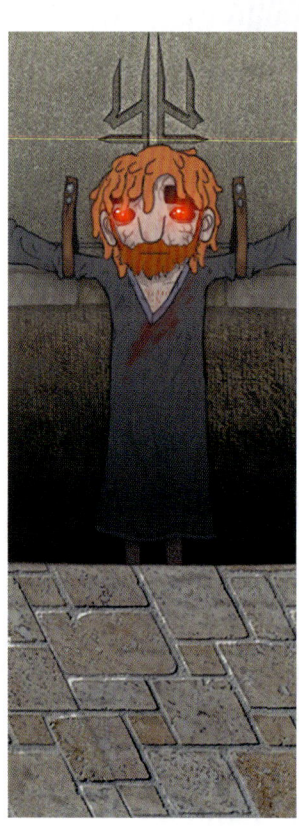

Sally Face ART, LORE, AND MORE

TODD MORRISON

"I've upgraded your Gear Boy to detect supernatural hotspots within close proximity."

TODD IS THE SMART ONE. He's always tinkering with new inventions and is fascinated by the unknowns in life. Todd has a very straightforward and monotone personality. He's a bit unkempt with his physical appearance, especially in his later years. When Sal asks him to help research the paranormal, he jumps onboard right away. Above all else, he loves his boyfriend, Neil, and is happiest when they are together.

With an almost unhealthy thirst for knowledge, Todd always has his nose in a book or his eyes on a computer screen. The lack of social connection has left him a bit awkward and with a pretty blunt way of interacting with others. This also makes him hard to read at times. Because of this, it took Todd a while to really click with his new friends, but now he wouldn't trade that friendship for anything.

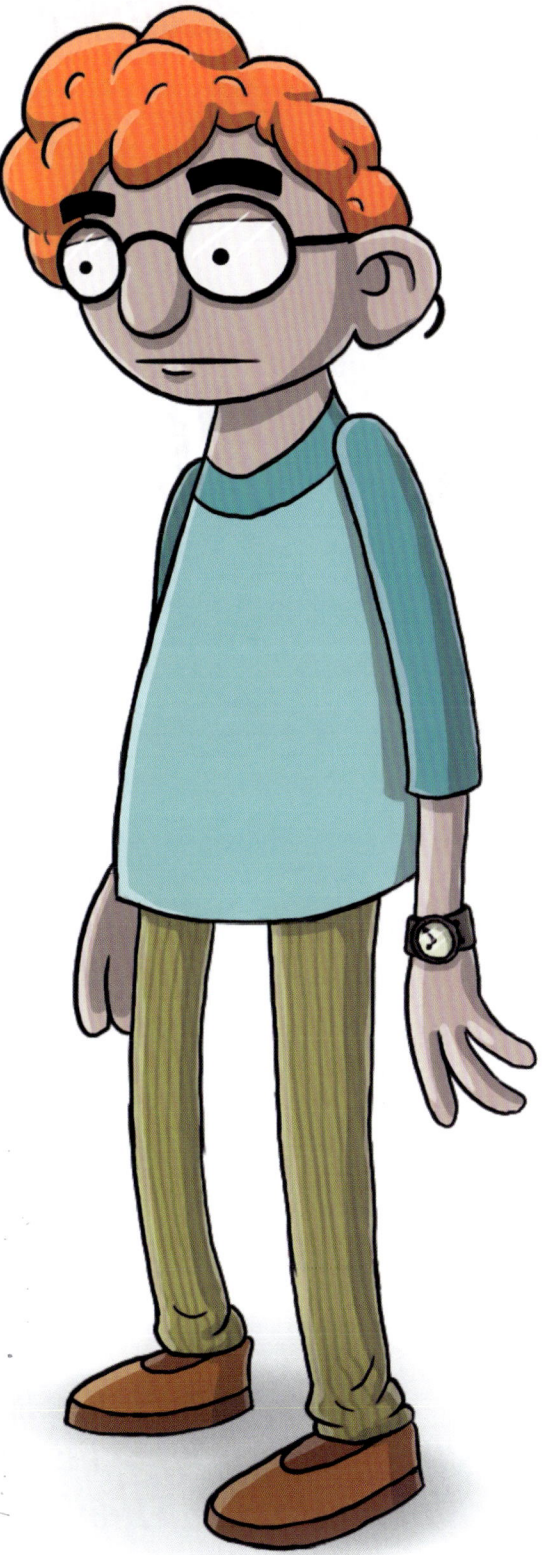

CHARACTER INFORMATION

BIRTH: July 7th, 1977
HAIR: Orange
EYES: Brown
MOTHER: Janis Morrison
FATHER: Ray Morrison

TEEN HEIGHT: 5'7"
ADULT HEIGHT: 5'11"

FAVORITE FOOD: Blueberries
DREAM JOB:
Paranormal Researcher
FAVORITE MUSIC:
Electronic and Rap

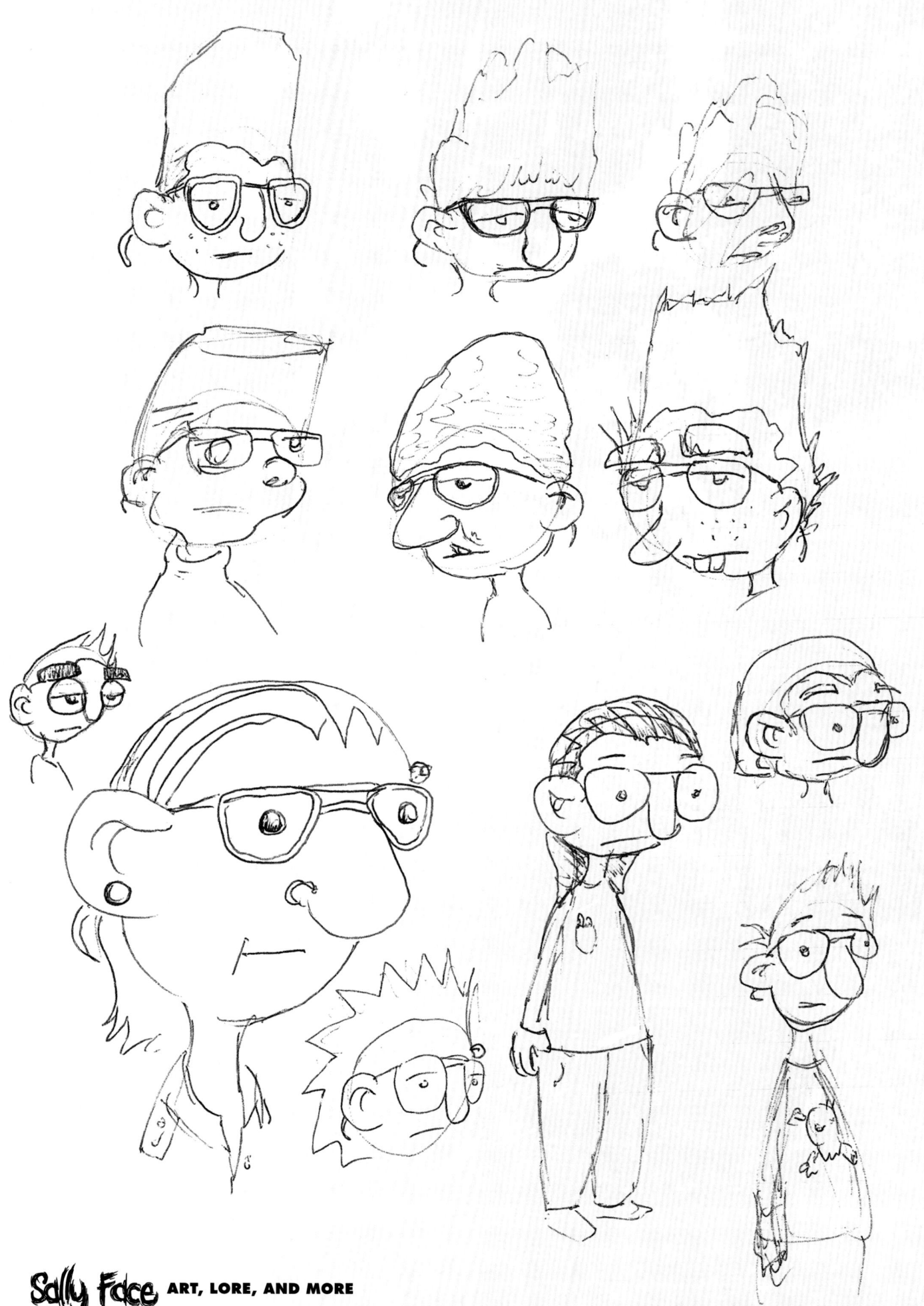

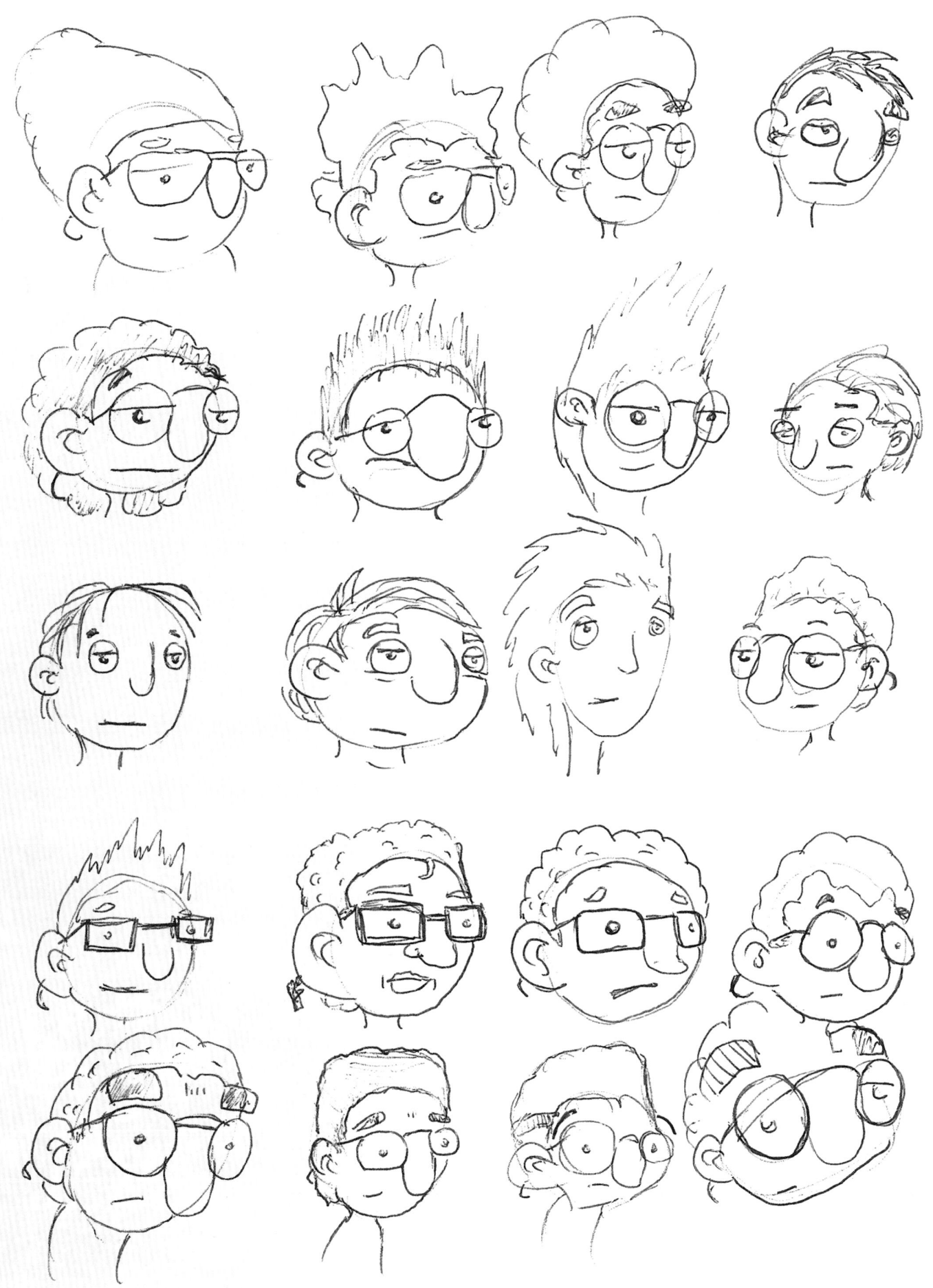

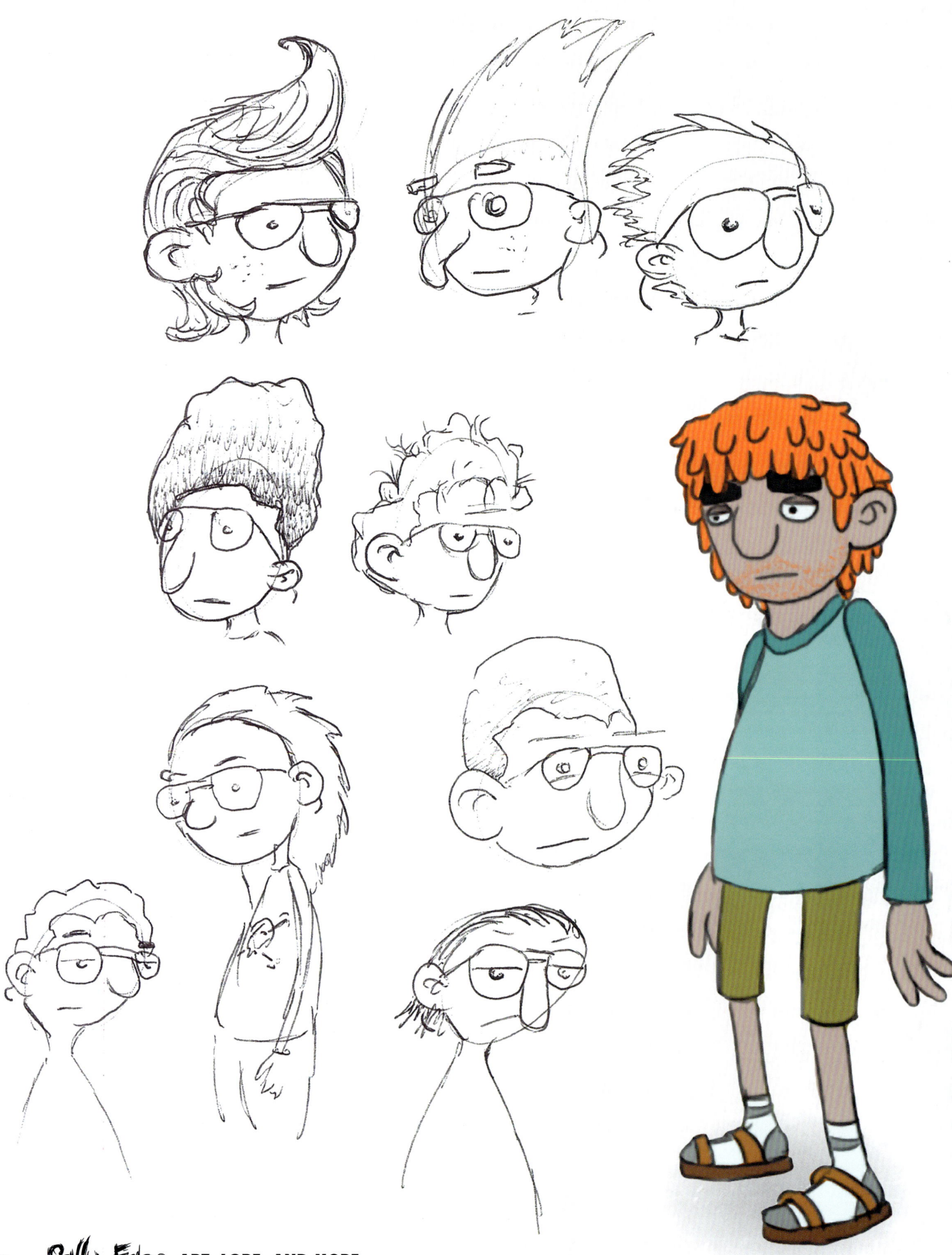

Sally Face ART, LORE, AND MORE

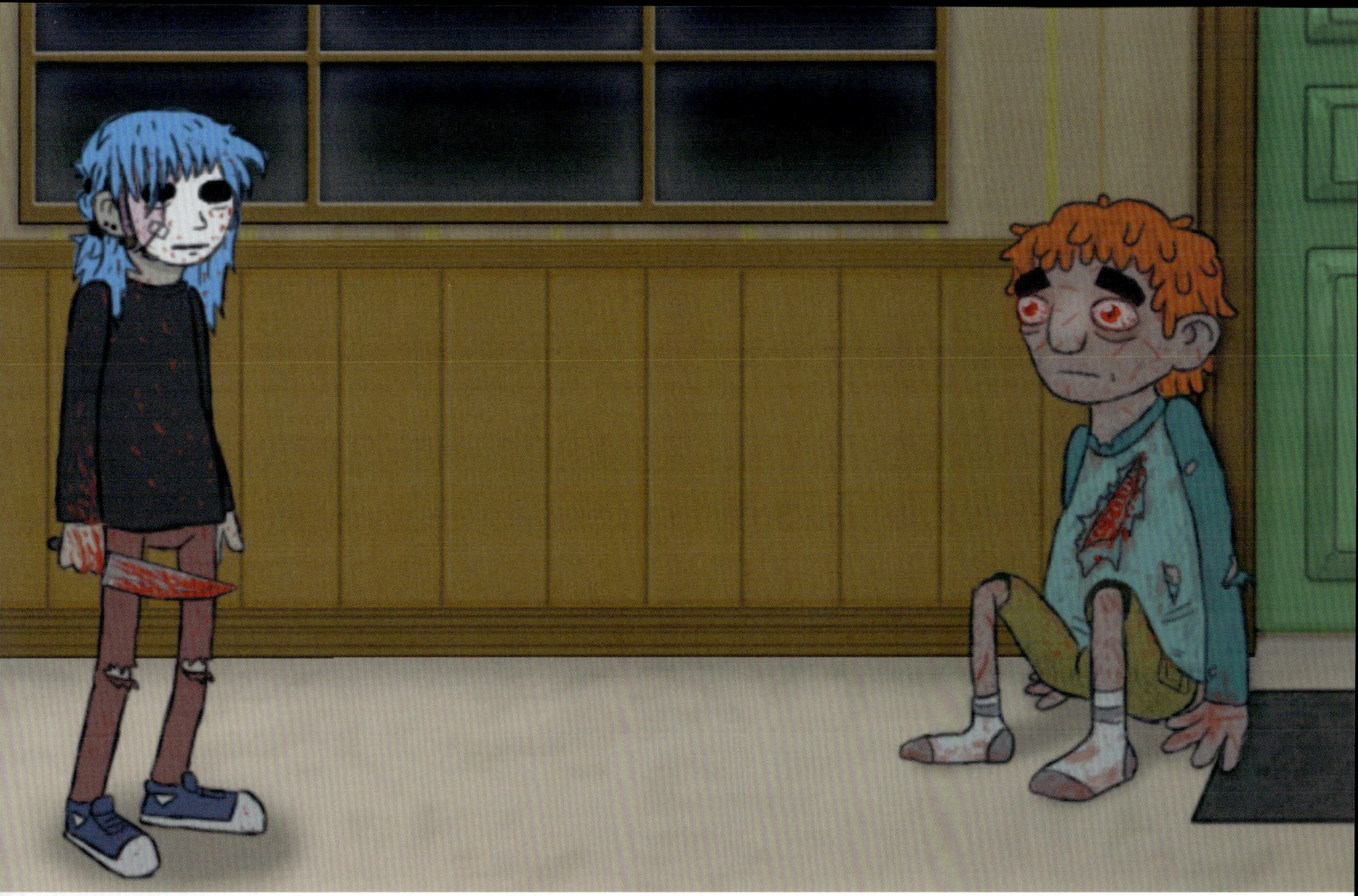

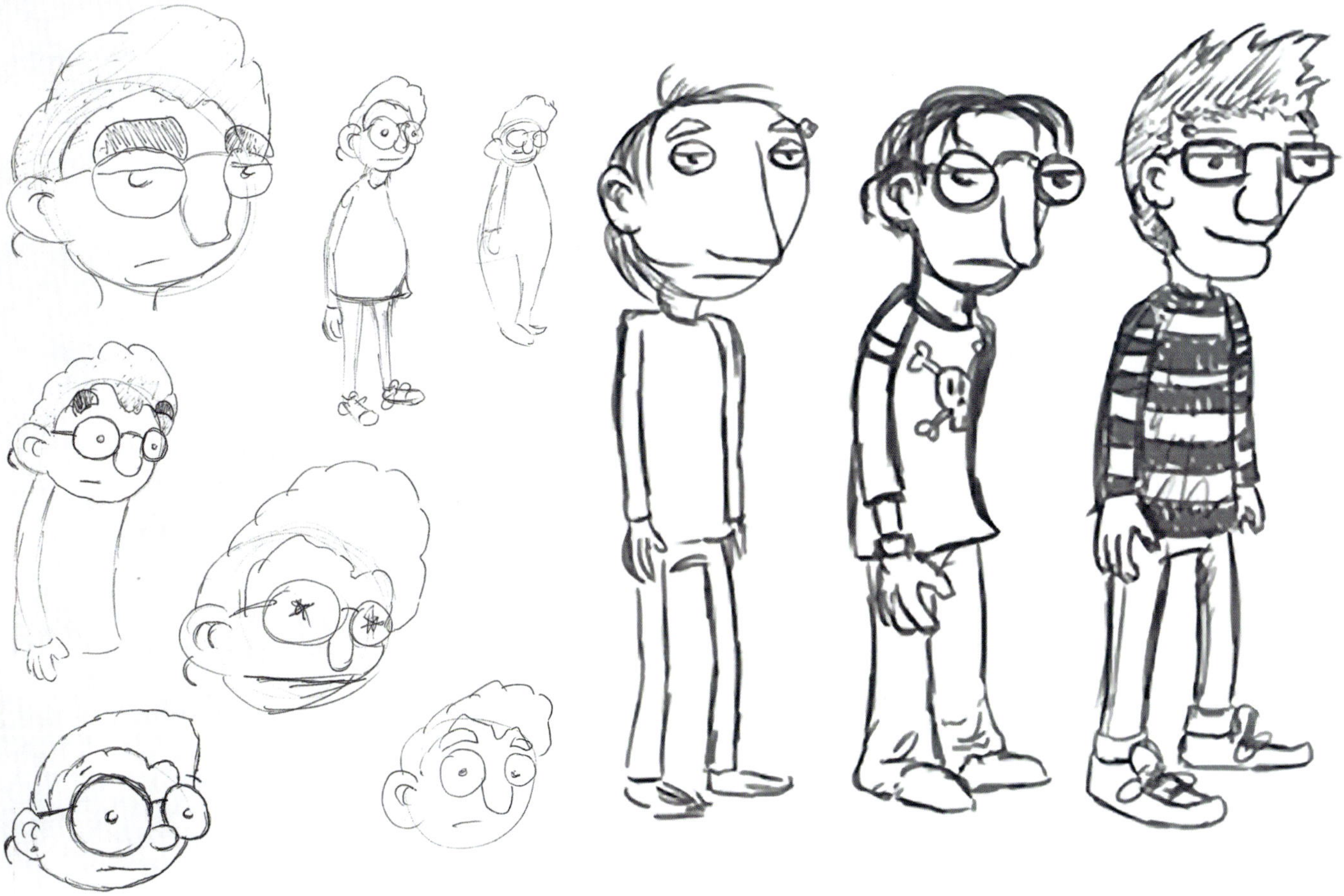

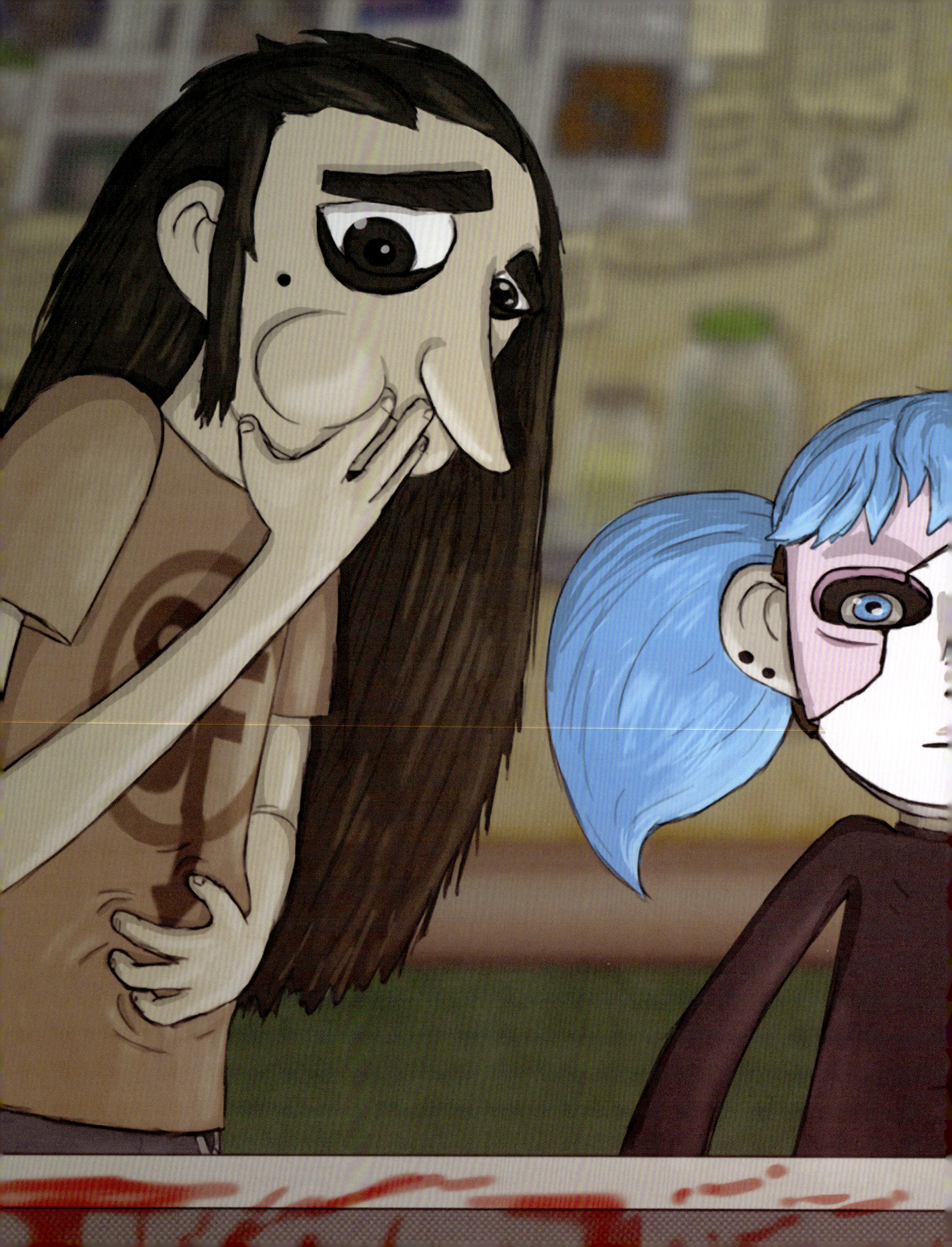

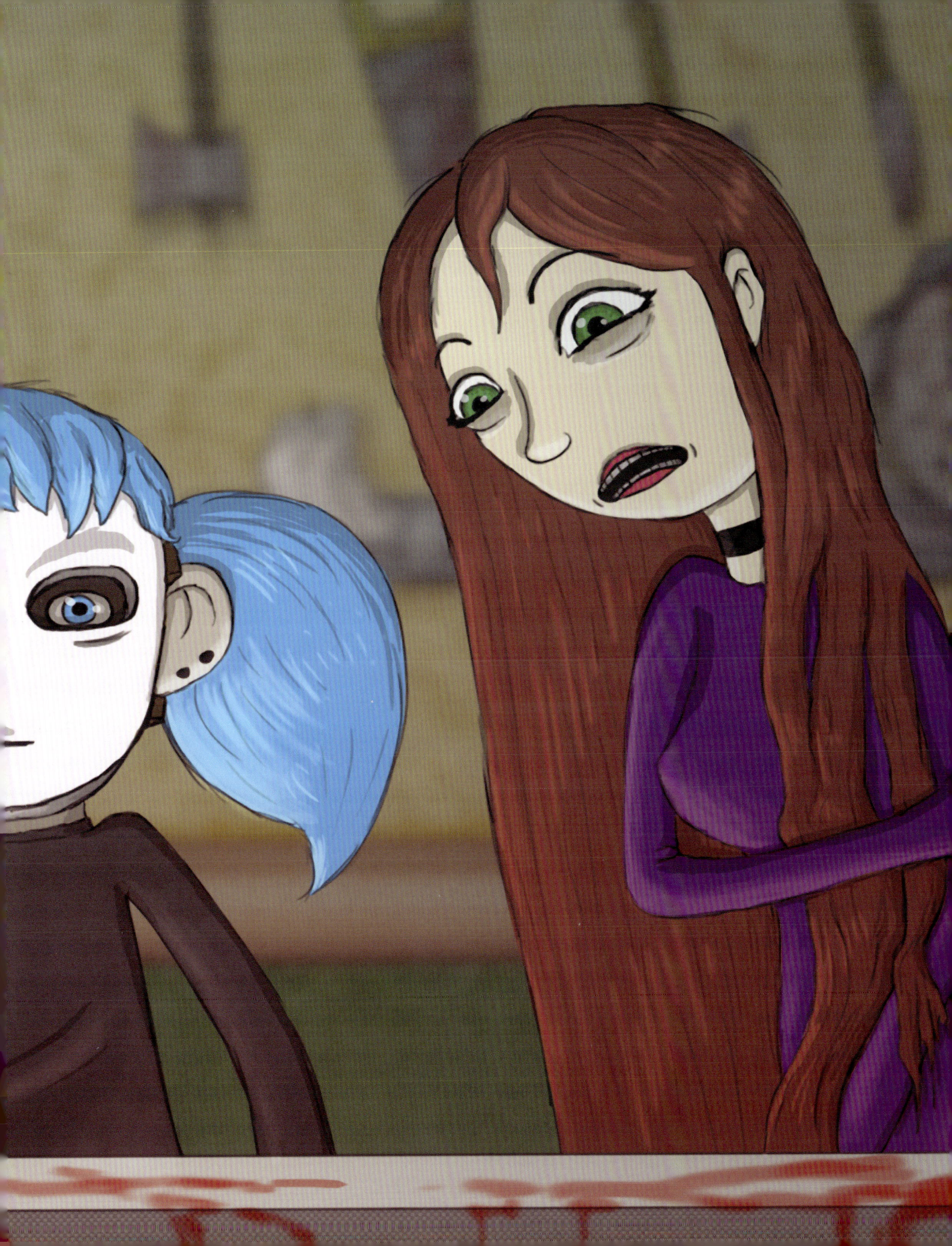

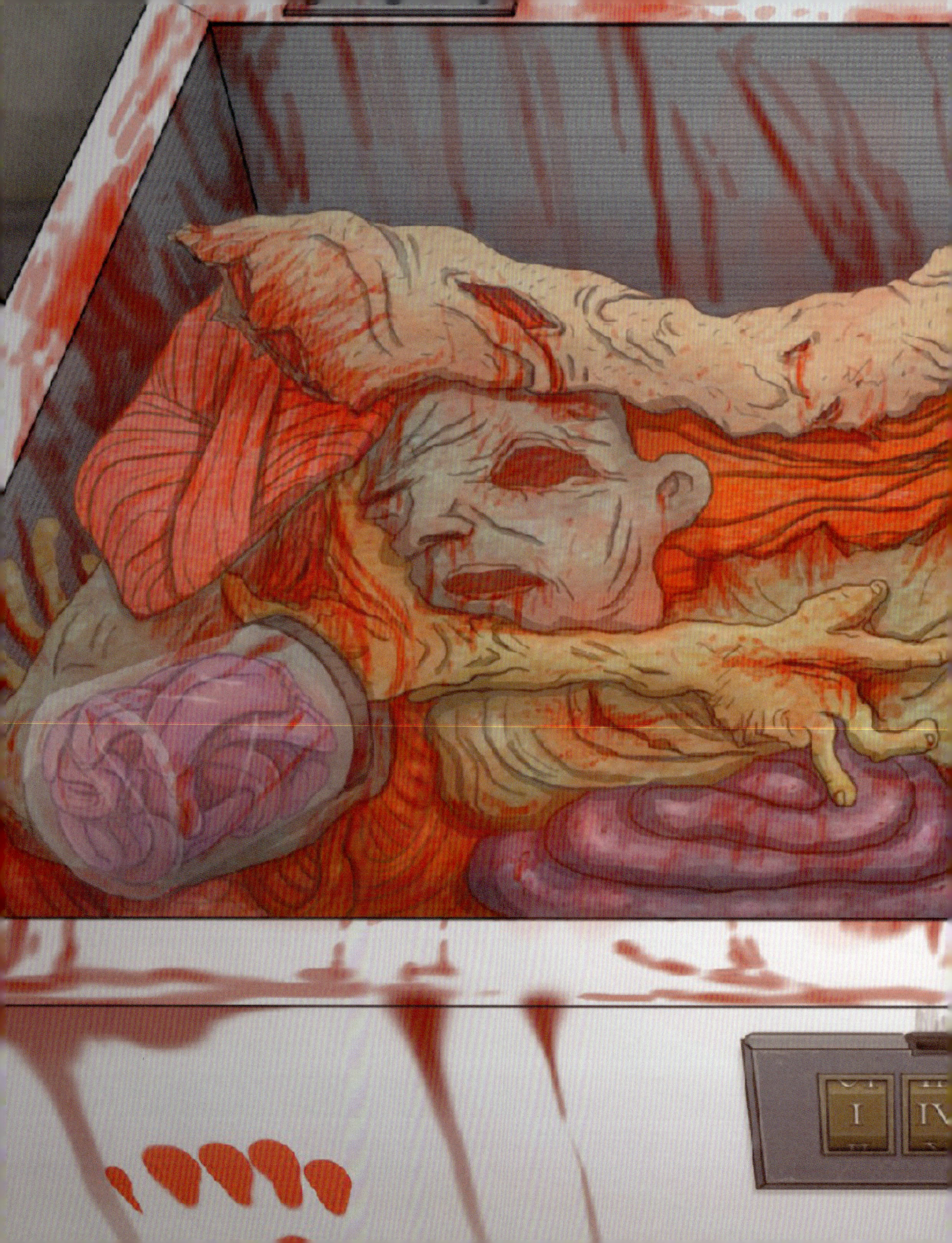

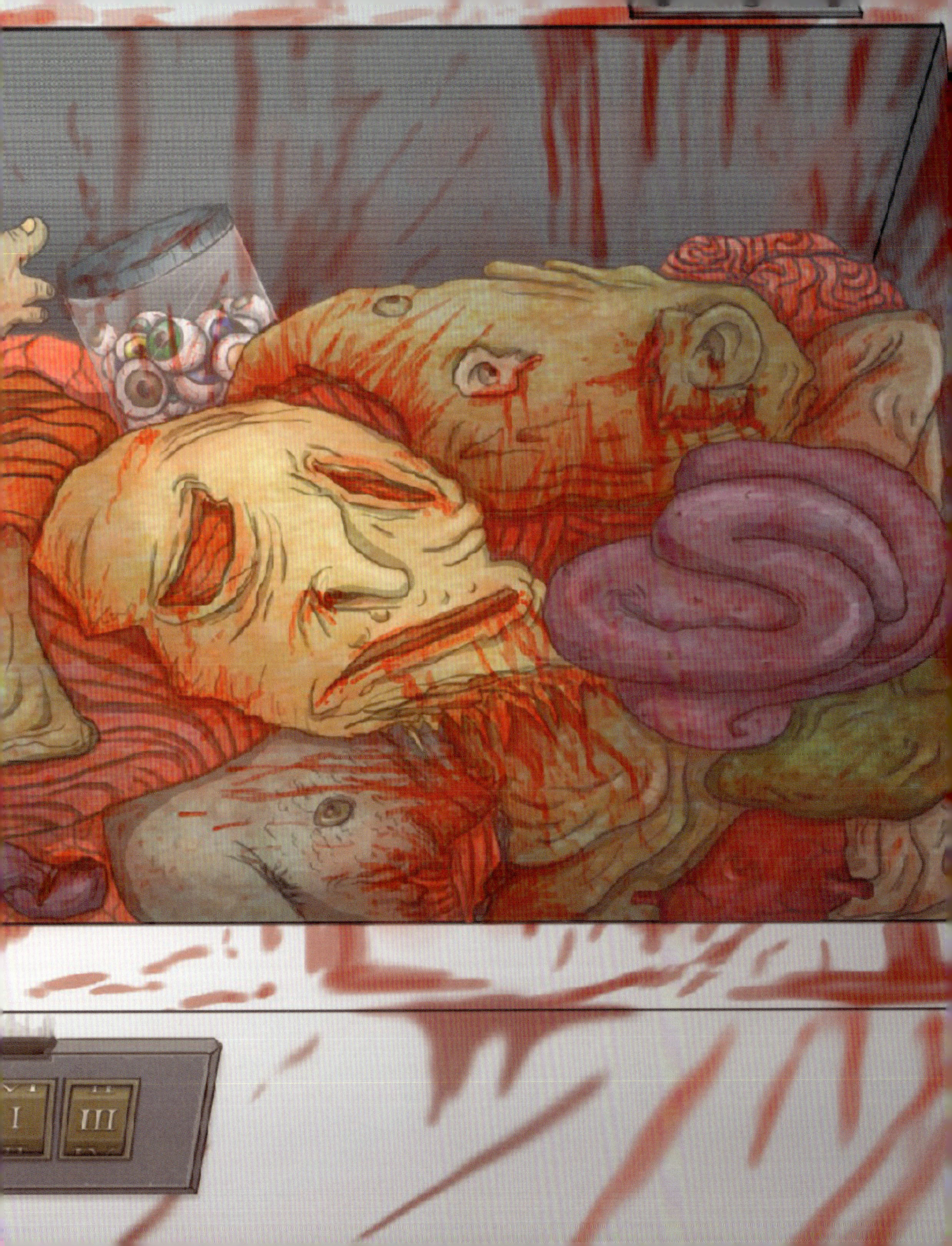

HENRY FISHER

Henry struggled hard after losing his wife, Diane. He fell into alcoholism and a deep depression. During this time, he neglected his son, Sal, at a time when Sal needed him the most. After a few years, Henry began to level out and cut back on the alcohol. Witnessing the negative impact he was having on Sal was the major reason for Henry taking the first step towards recovery.

DIANE FISHER

One day while waitressing, Diane met the love of her life, Henry Fisher. It wasn't long until they were married and soon she became pregnant. Diane loved Sal more than anything and couldn't be happier with her baby boy.

CHARACTER INFORMATION

BIRTH: 1947
DEATH: 1999
HAIR: Blue
EYES: Blue
HEIGHT: 6'3"
SON: Sal Fisher
FIRST WIFE: Diane Fisher
SECOND WIFE: Lisa Johnson

CHARACTER INFORMATION

BIRTH: 1948
DEATH: 1984
MAIDEN NAME: Hatherson
HAIR: Blond
EYES: Yellow
HEIGHT: 5'4"
SON: Sal Fisher
HUSBAND: Henry Fisher

Sally Face ART, LORE, AND MORE

LISA JOHNSON

Lisa is the caretaker of the Addison Apartments. She's very affectionate and hardworking. When a strange man showed up looking for help, she was the first to lend a hand. Jim and Lisa eventually fell in love, married, and had a child.

CHARACTER INFORMATION

BIRTH: 1956
DEATH: 1999
MAIDEN NAME: Garcia
HAIR: Brown
EYES: Hazel
HEIGHT: 5'10"
SON: Larry Johnson
FIRST HUSBAND:
Jim Johnson
SECOND HUSBAND:
Henry Fisher

JIM JOHNSON

A man from another world. Jim came to Earth in an attempt to escape the world-eating Plague of Shadows. When he began to make a life for himself, destiny intervened again. Jim was caught up in a local cult, with hopes to keep his family safe.

CHARACTER INFORMATION

IDENTIFIER: Zarinthkampt 42-79
AGE: Unknown
HAIR: Red
EYES: Yellow
HEIGHT: Unknown
SIBLINGS: Evelyn
SON: Larry Johnson
EX-WIFE: Lisa Garcia

TERRENCE ADDISON

Terrence is the owner of the Addison Apartments, which he inherited from his father. He appears to be a kind yet overly timid man who never leaves his room. He speaks to his tenants through a mail slot and loves making tea.

ALYSON ROSENBERG

Rose is a little old lady that tends to monologue a great deal about death and the unknown. Turns out, she's from a long line of witches and was once connected to the Devourers of God. She tried to stop them at one point, but failed.

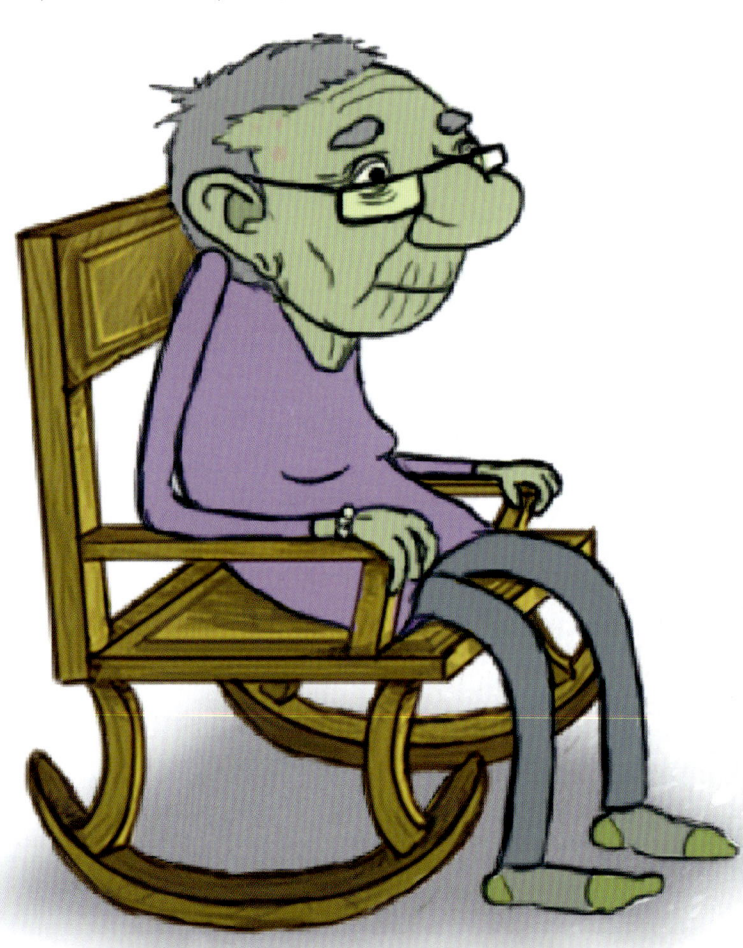

CHARACTER
INFORMATION

BIRTH: 1905
DEATH: 1999
HAIR: Brown
EYES: Black
HEIGHT: Unknown
FATHER: Fredrick Addison
MOTHER: Henrietta Addison

CHARACTER
INFORMATION

NICKNAME: Rose
AGE: Unknown
HAIR: Gray
EYES: Purple
HEIGHT: 5'5"
RELATIVES: Unknown

Sally Face ART, LORE, AND MORE

KENNETH PHELPS

Preacher at Phelps Ministry in Nockfell. Archbishop of the Devourers of God. Lurking in the dark, half-man, half-shadow. Kenneth was the orchestrator behind many of the cult's horrible acts, yet not much is known about him.

TRAVIS PHELPS

Travis has deep anger issues brought on by an unusual and abusive upbringing. It wasn't until later that it was revealed to him that his father wasn't just a preacher. Travis's father was an Archbishop of the Devourers of God.

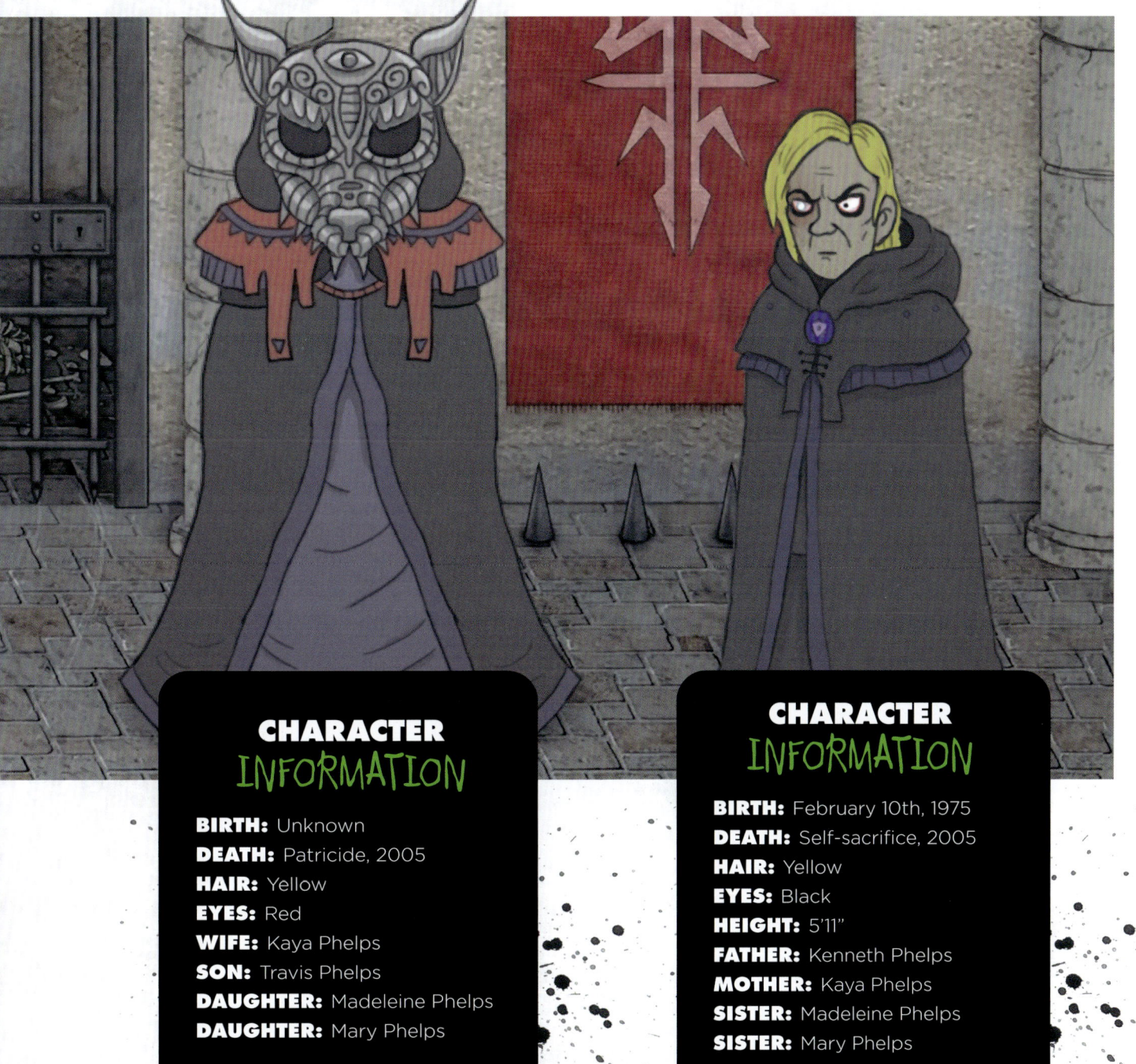

CHARACTER INFORMATION

BIRTH: Unknown
DEATH: Patricide, 2005
HAIR: Yellow
EYES: Red
WIFE: Kaya Phelps
SON: Travis Phelps
DAUGHTER: Madeleine Phelps
DAUGHTER: Mary Phelps

CHARACTER INFORMATION

BIRTH: February 10th, 1975
DEATH: Self-sacrifice, 2005
HAIR: Yellow
EYES: Black
HEIGHT: 5'11"
FATHER: Kenneth Phelps
MOTHER: Kaya Phelps
SISTER: Madeleine Phelps
SISTER: Mary Phelps

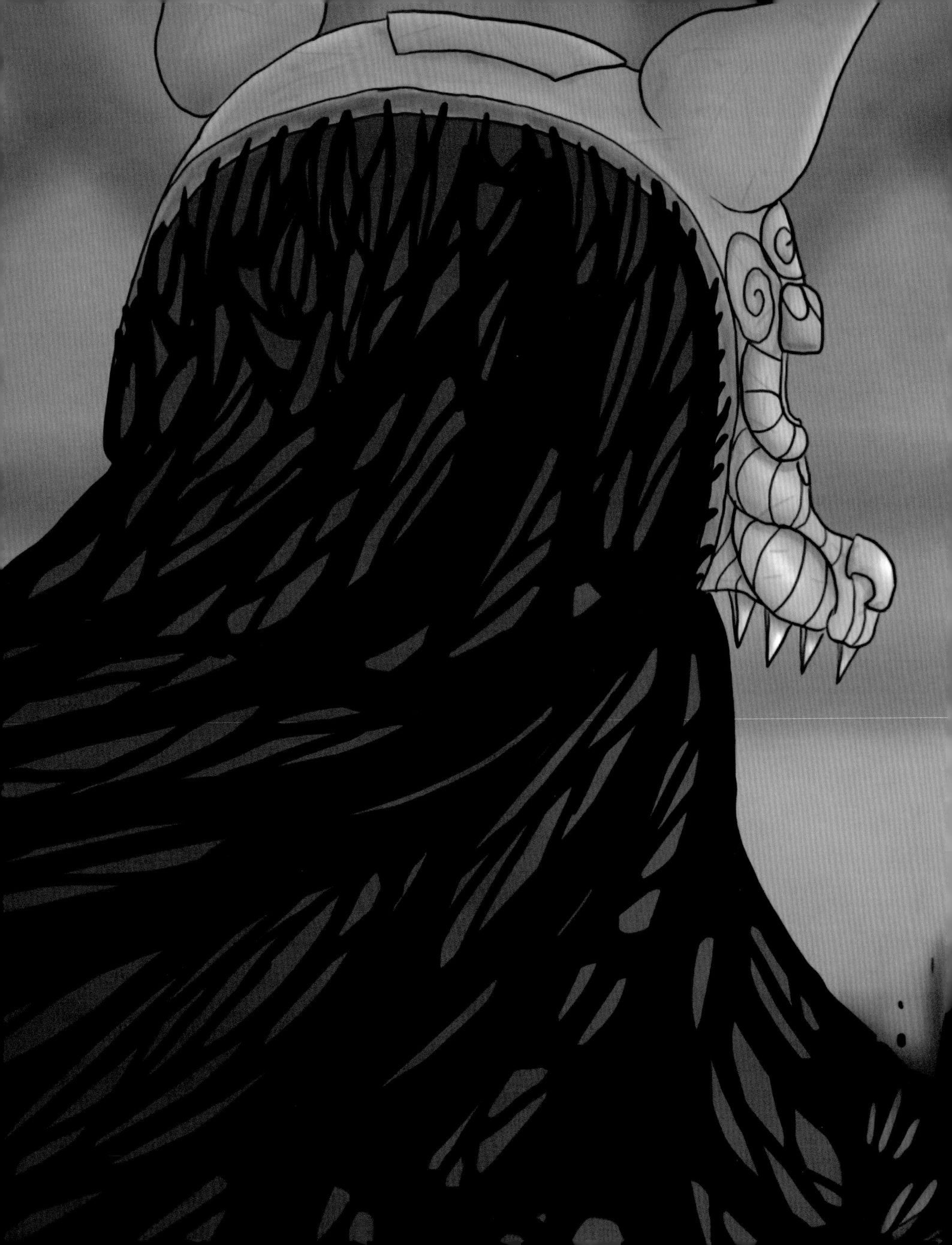

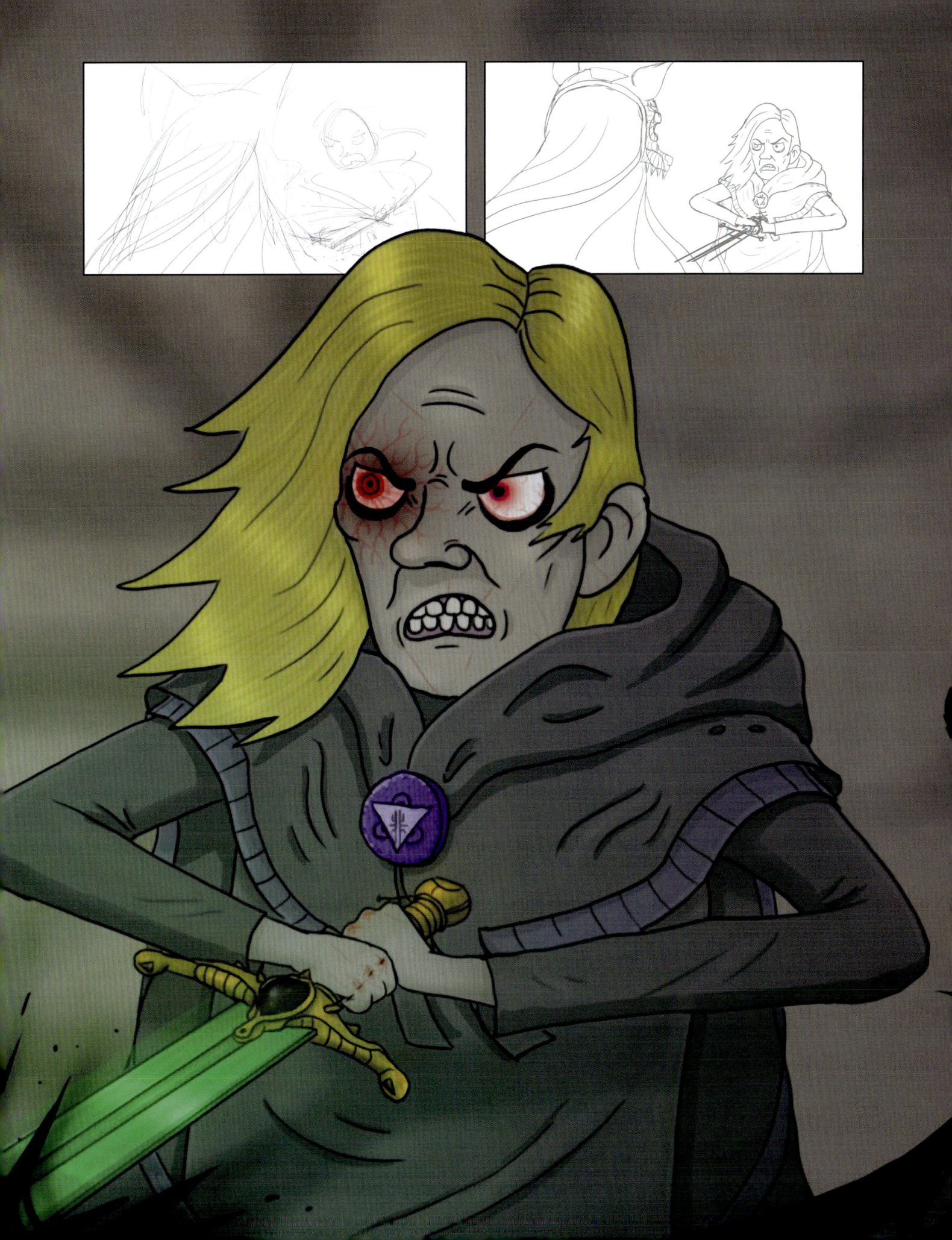

MAPLE COHEN

When they were kids, Maple had a big crush on Larry. Since she wasn't close to the gang, she was often on the sidelines with Chug. The two of them grew close over the high school years and eventually married.

CHARACTER
INFORMATION

BIRTH: 1976
DEATH: 2005
MAIDEN NAME: O'Dea
HAIR: Silver
EYES: Gray
HEIGHT: 5'6"
HUSBAND: Chug Cohen
DAUGHTER: Soda Cohen

CHUG COHEN

Chug is a bit slow, easily frightened, and loves video games and snacks. He likes to hang out with Sal and the gang when they aren't hunting ghosts or doing anything too scary. Chug is a big softy and loves his family with all his heart.

CHARACTER
INFORMATION

BIRTH: 1976
DEATH: 1999
HAIR: Green
EYES: Black
HEIGHT: 5'4"
MOTHER: Katey Cohen
FATHER: Ed Cohen
WIFE: Maple Cohen
DAUGHTER: Soda Cohen

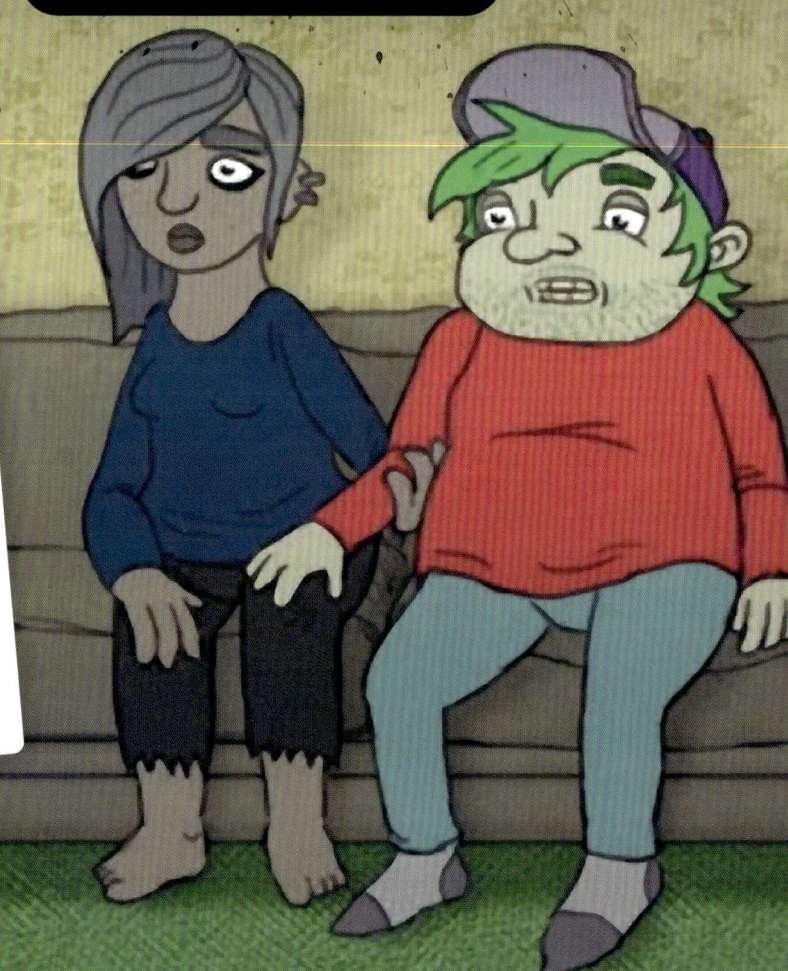

SODA COHEN

Soda Cohen is the daughter of Chug and Maple. She's very fond of Larry and Sal, and calls them her "uncles".

Sally Face ART, LORE, AND MORE

ROBERT SILVA

Rob is a rich entrepreneur who lives next to Sal. Despite his wealth, Rob likes to keep things simple and doesn't live in extravagance. He's a laid back jokester that doesn't seem to take much of anything too seriously.

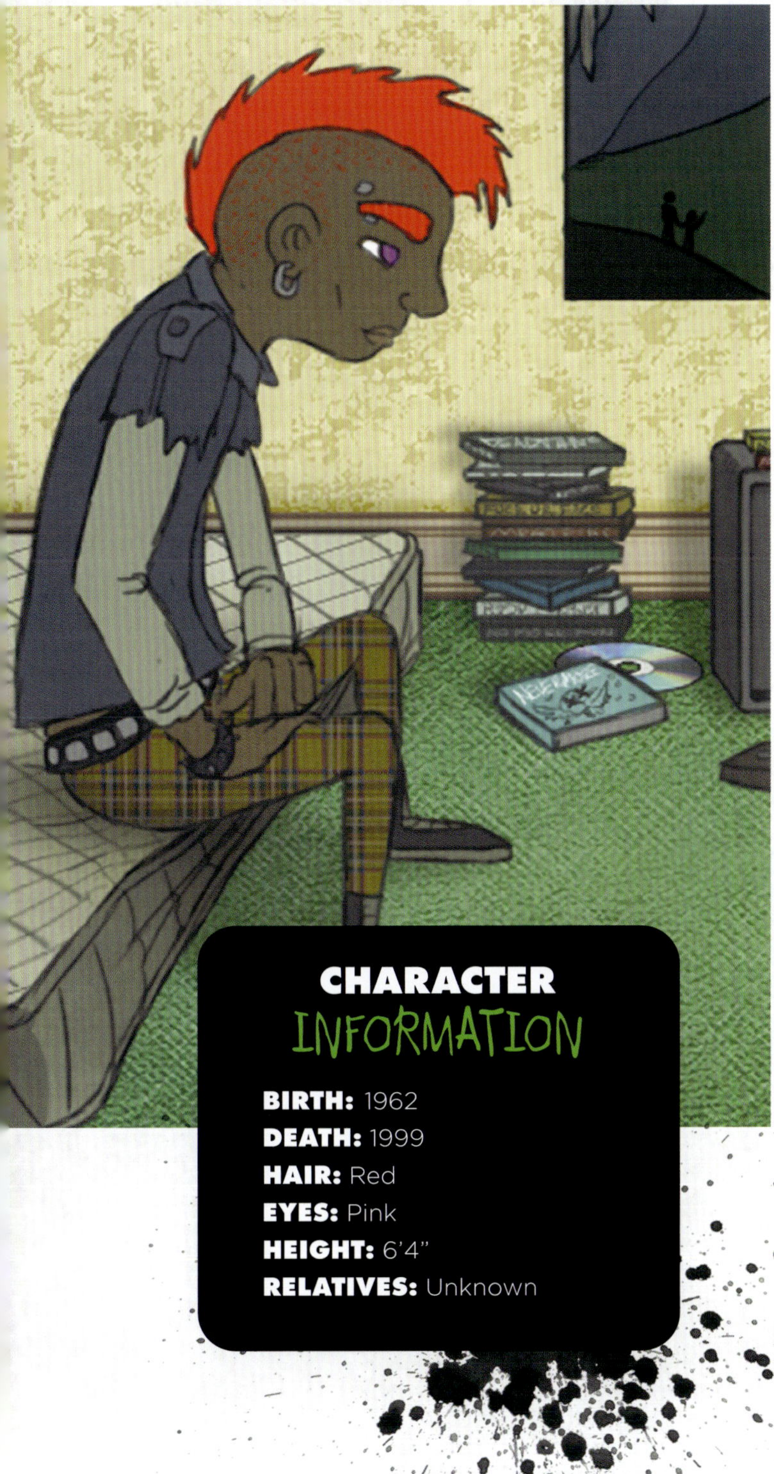

NEIL DOUGLAS

A southern boy who moved up north and still retains that southern hospitality. He met Todd at the library and the two of them hit it off right away. Neil was studying to become a registered nurse before everything fell apart.

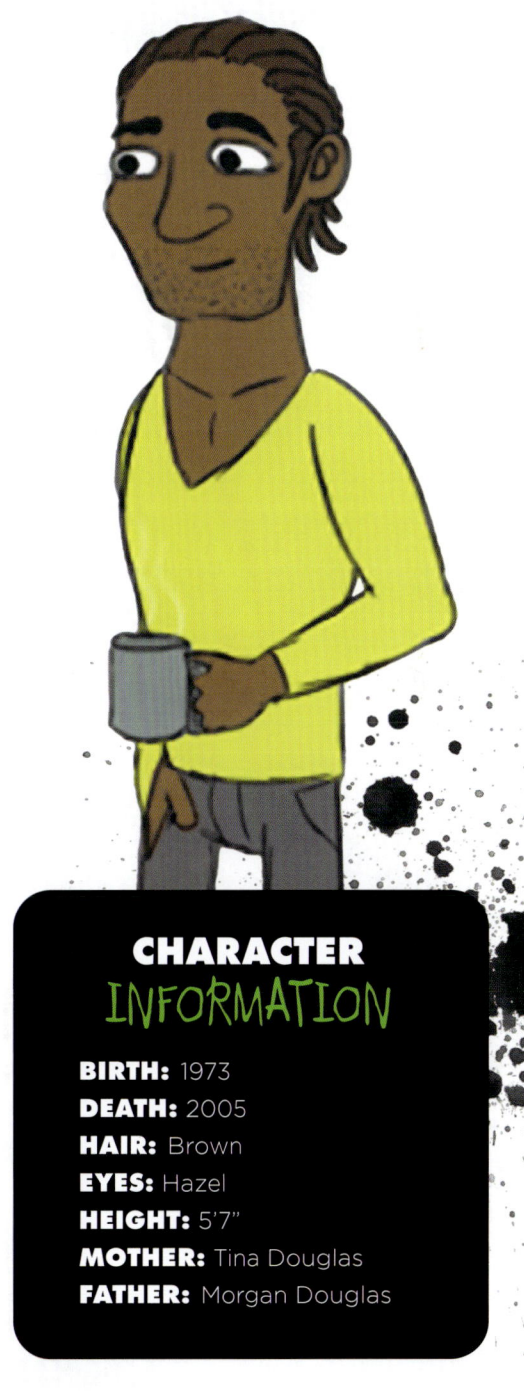

CHARACTER INFORMATION

BIRTH: 1962
DEATH: 1999
HAIR: Red
EYES: Pink
HEIGHT: 6'4"
RELATIVES: Unknown

CHARACTER INFORMATION

BIRTH: 1973
DEATH: 2005
HAIR: Brown
EYES: Hazel
HEIGHT: 5'7"
MOTHER: Tina Douglas
FATHER: Morgan Douglas

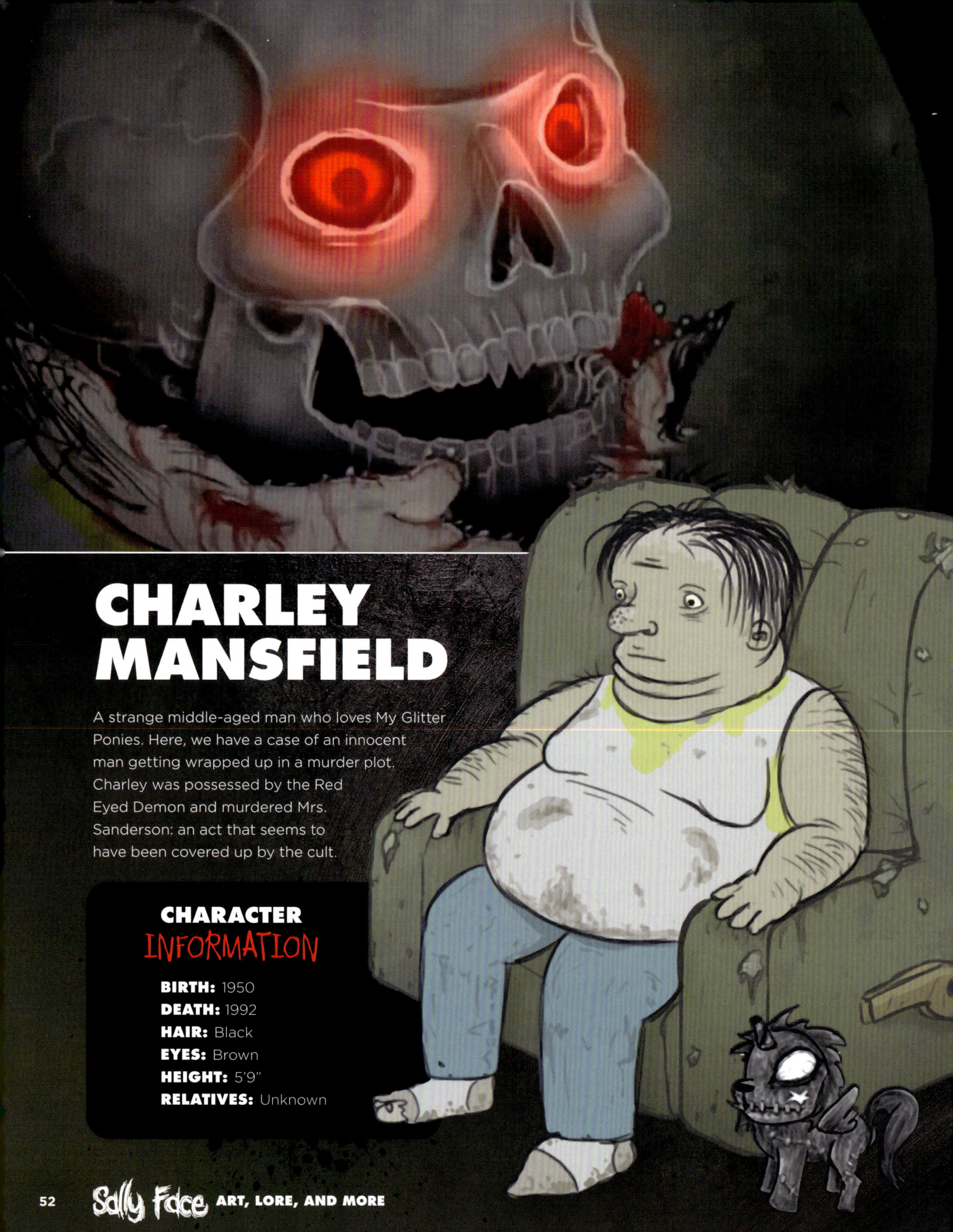

CHARLEY MANSFIELD

A strange middle-aged man who loves My Glitter Ponies. Here, we have a case of an innocent man getting wrapped up in a murder plot. Charley was possessed by the Red Eyed Demon and murdered Mrs. Sanderson: an act that seems to have been covered up by the cult.

CHARACTER INFORMATION

BIRTH: 1950
DEATH: 1992
HAIR: Black
EYES: Brown
HEIGHT: 5'9"
RELATIVES: Unknown

CASSANDRA SANDERSON

Mrs. Sanderson was murdered on the night before Sal and his father moved into the apartments. She had found out that her husband was involved with a cult. In an attempt to gather more information, Sanderson stole a book from the cult. This would turn out to be a fatal mistake.

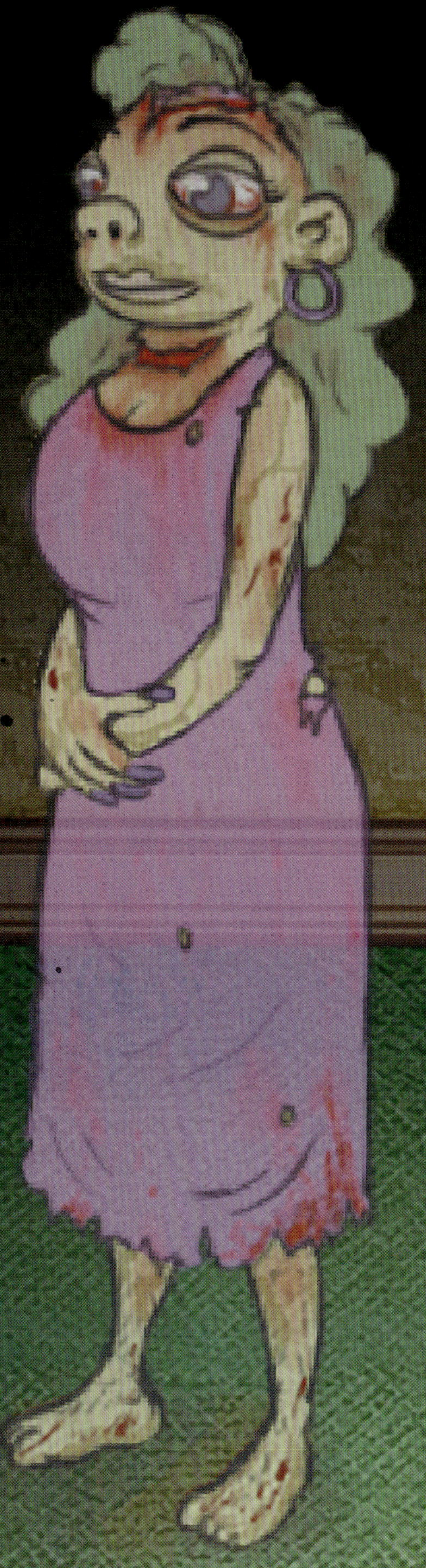

CHARACTER
INFORMATION

BIRTH: 1951
DEATH: 1992
NICKNAME: Sandy
HAIR: Green
EYES: Purple
HEIGHT: 5'8"
HUSBAND: Herman Sanderson

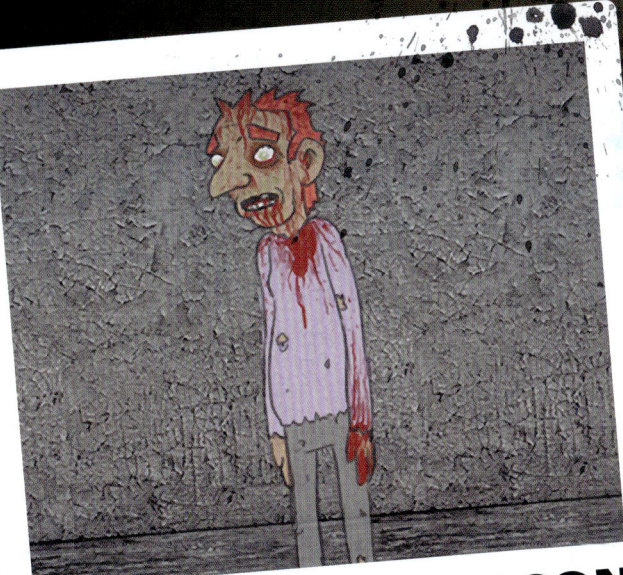

HERMAN SANDERSON

Herman Sanderson was husband to Cassandra and member of the Council of the Devourers of God. After his wife was killed, Herman slowly unraveled and eventually took his own life.

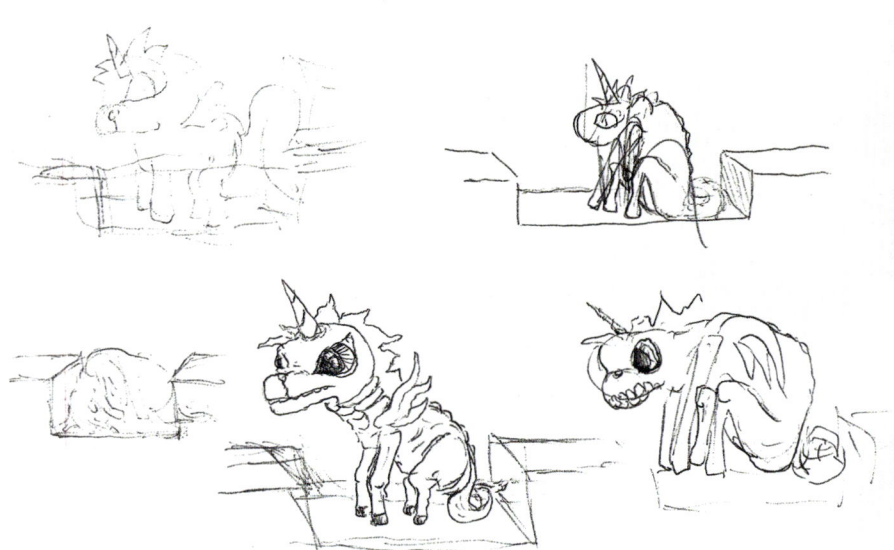

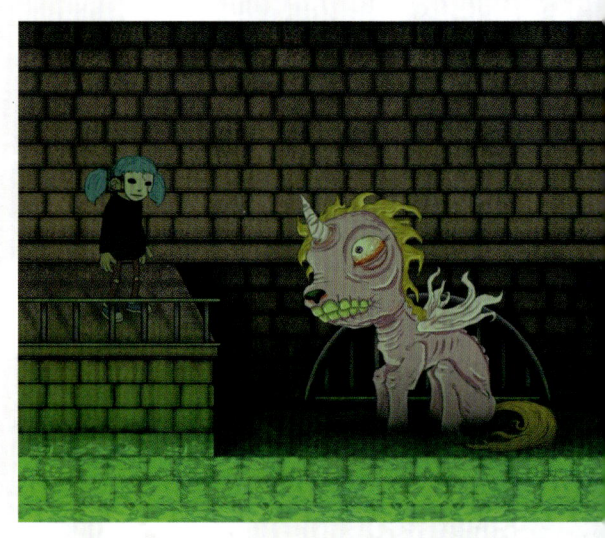

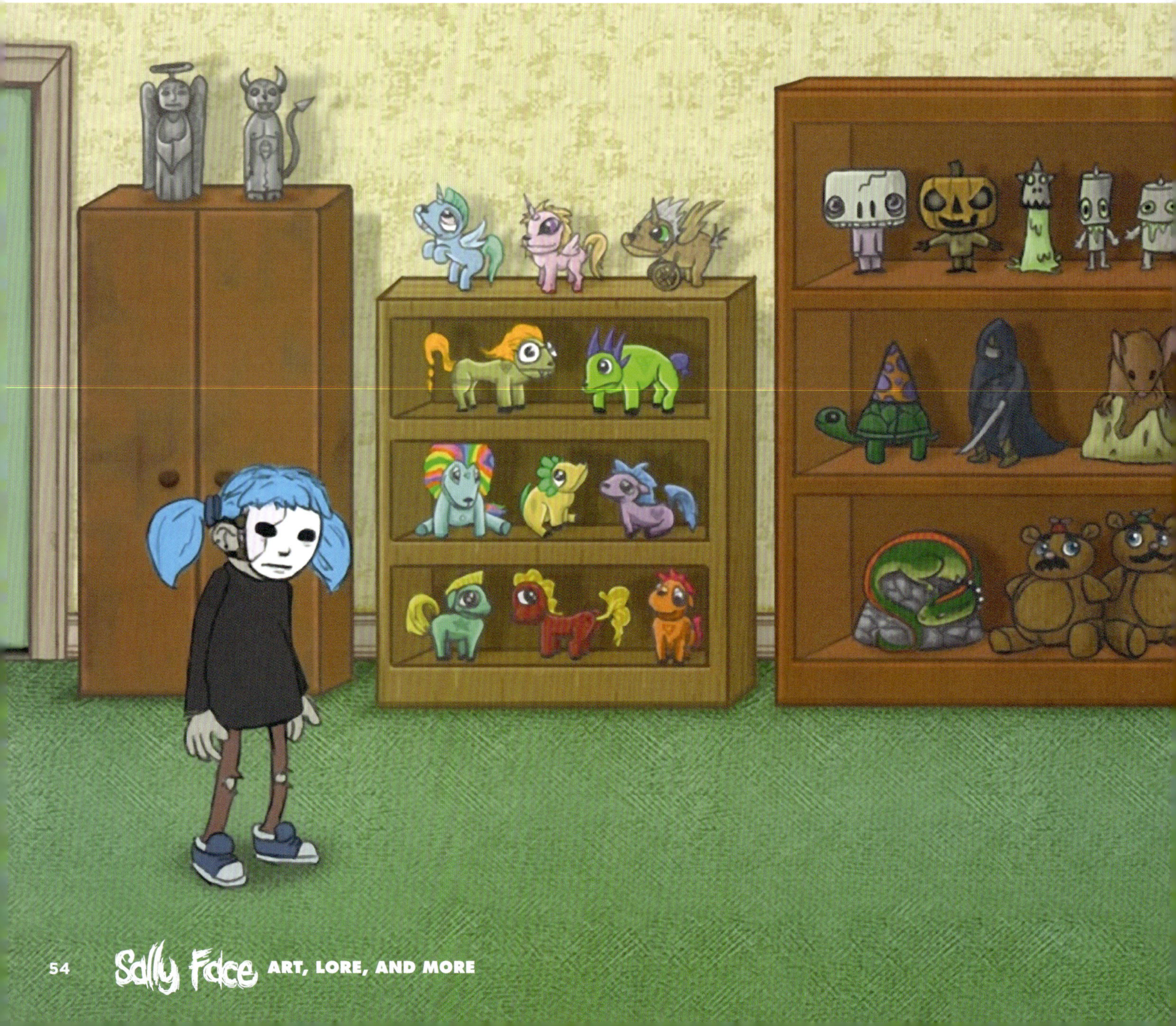

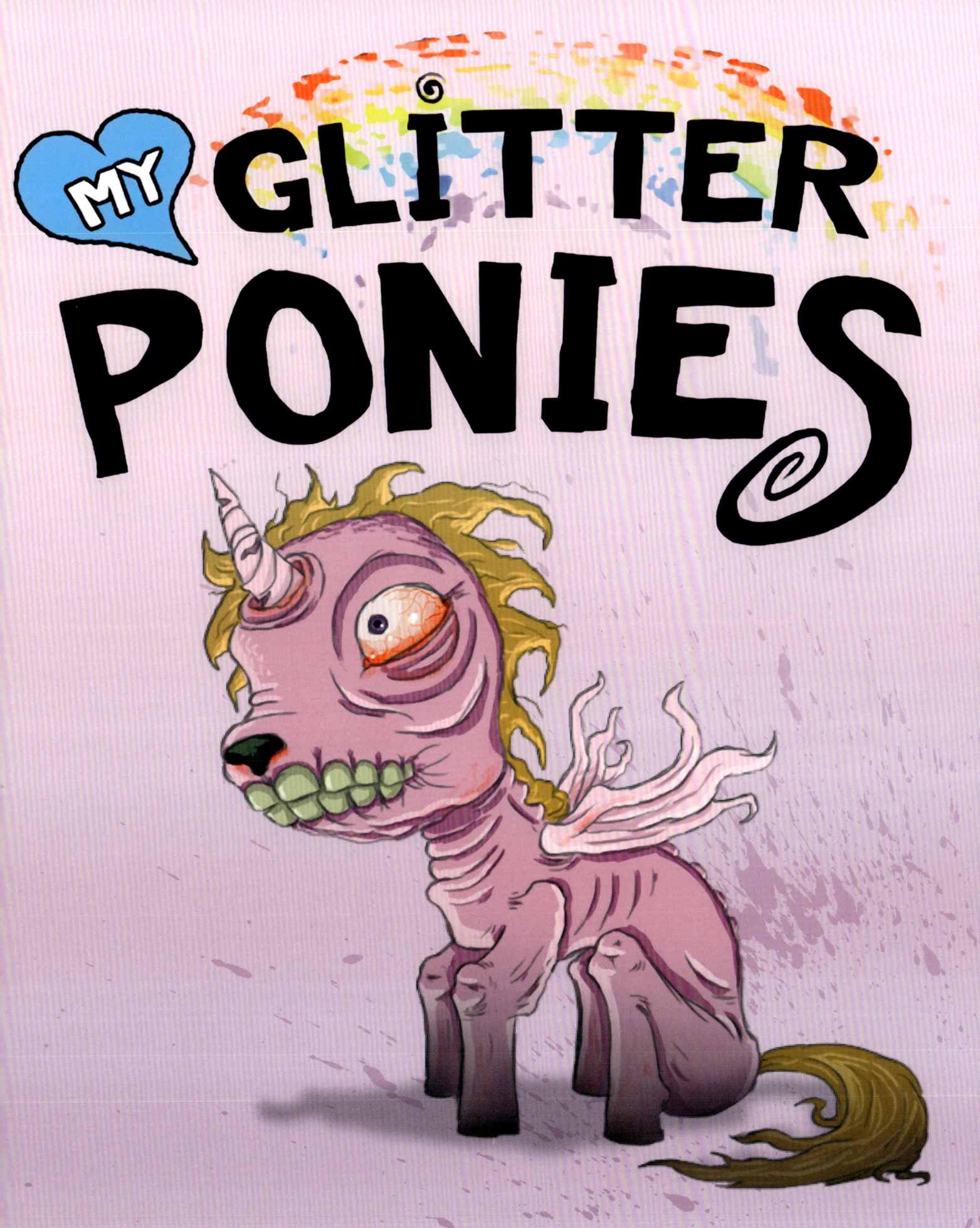

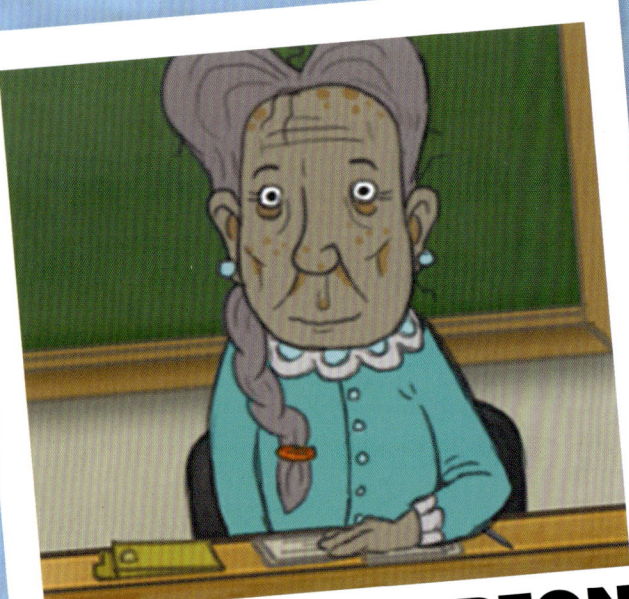

MRS. PACKERTON

The math teacher at Nockfell High School. What's a bit weird is that apparently she also makes bologna for the school lunches... and it smells a bit off...

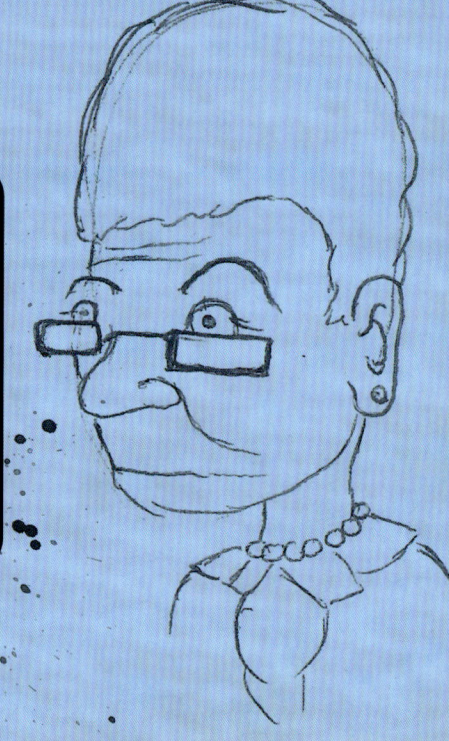

CHARACTER INFORMATION

BIRTH: Unknown
DEATH: Car accident, 1994
HAIR: Gray
EYES: Black
HEIGHT: 5'8"
HUSBAND: Mr. Packerton

Mrs. Packerton's *Signature* BOLOGNA

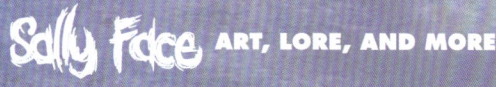

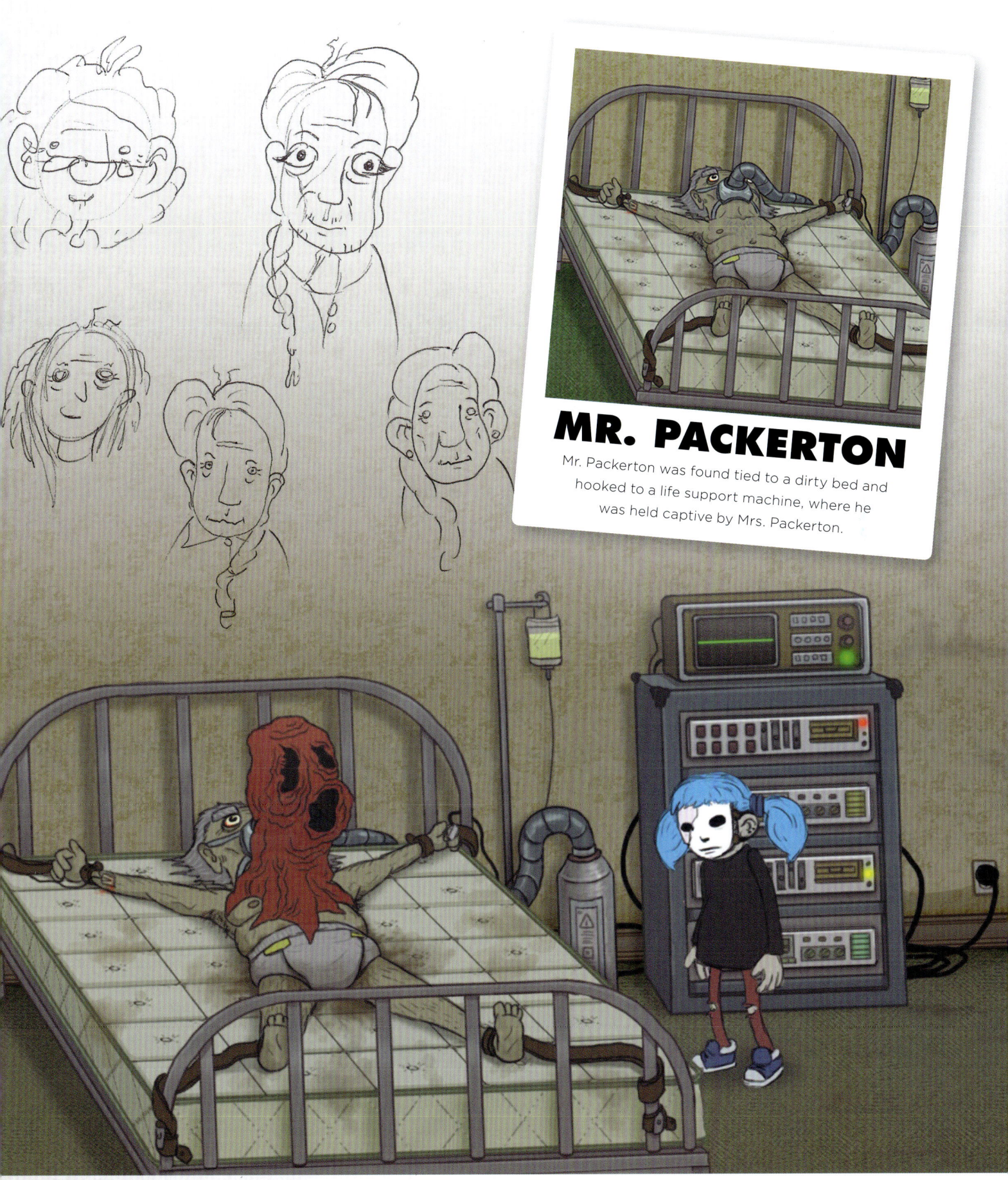

MR. PACKERTON

Mr. Packerton was found tied to a dirty bed and hooked to a life support machine, where he was held captive by Mrs. Packerton.

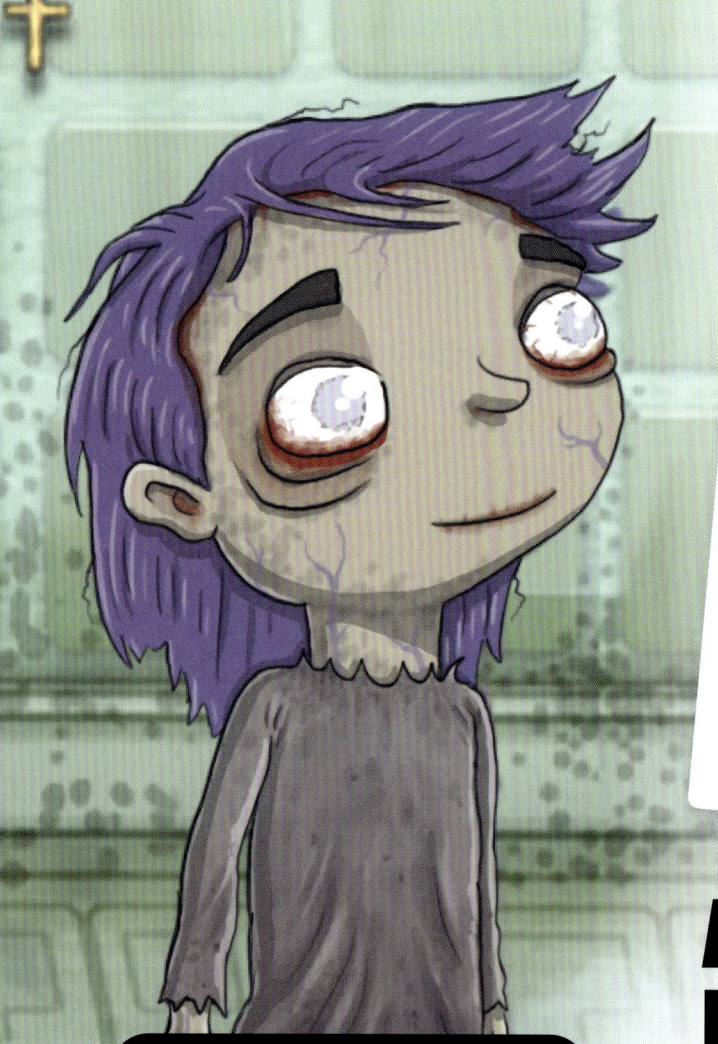

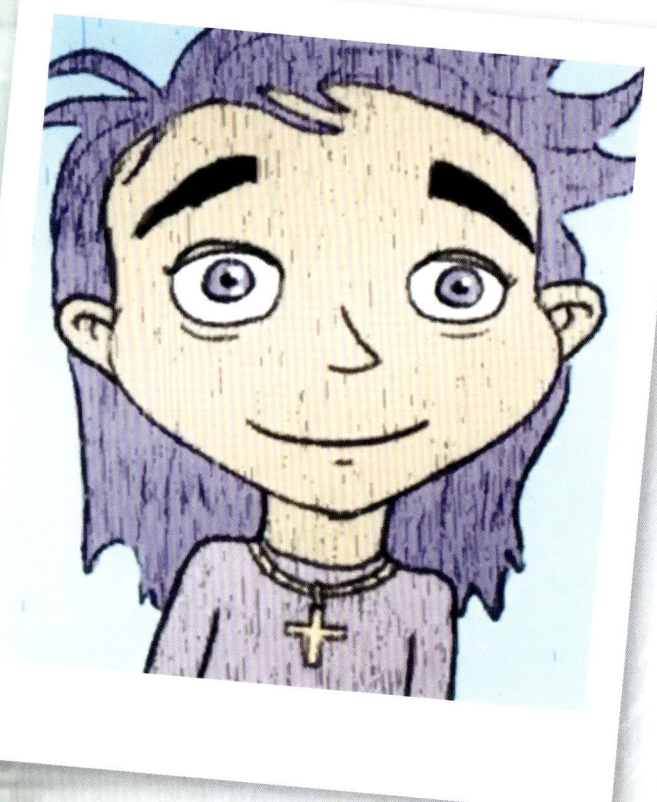

MEGAN HOLMES

Megan is the ghost of a young child who haunts the fifth floor of the apartments. She's typically very playful but can become very sad at times. She was murdered by her father but doesn't have a clear memory of the event.

CHARACTER
INFORMATION

BIRTH: 1980

DEATH: 1987

HAIR: Purple

EYES: Purple

HEIGHT: 4'

FATHER: Luke Holmes

MOTHER: Stacy Holmes

SISTER: Stephanie Holmes

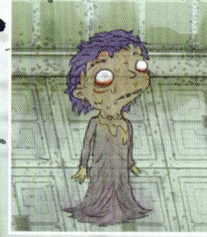
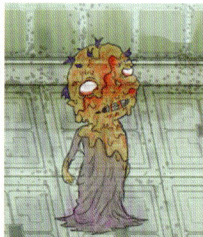
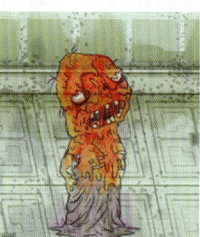
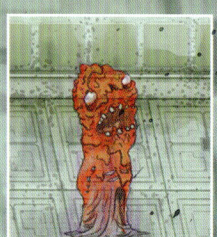
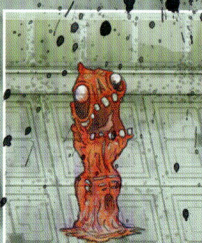
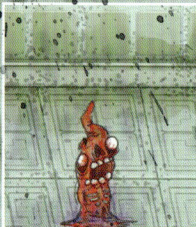
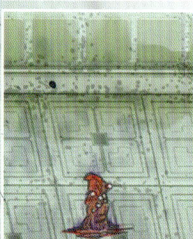
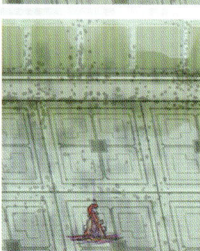
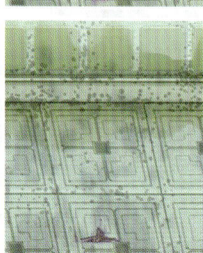

STACY HOLMES

Stacy was Megan's mother, wife to Luke Holmes, and mistress of Greg Montague. Stacy attempted to take down the cult, but was murdered by Luke.

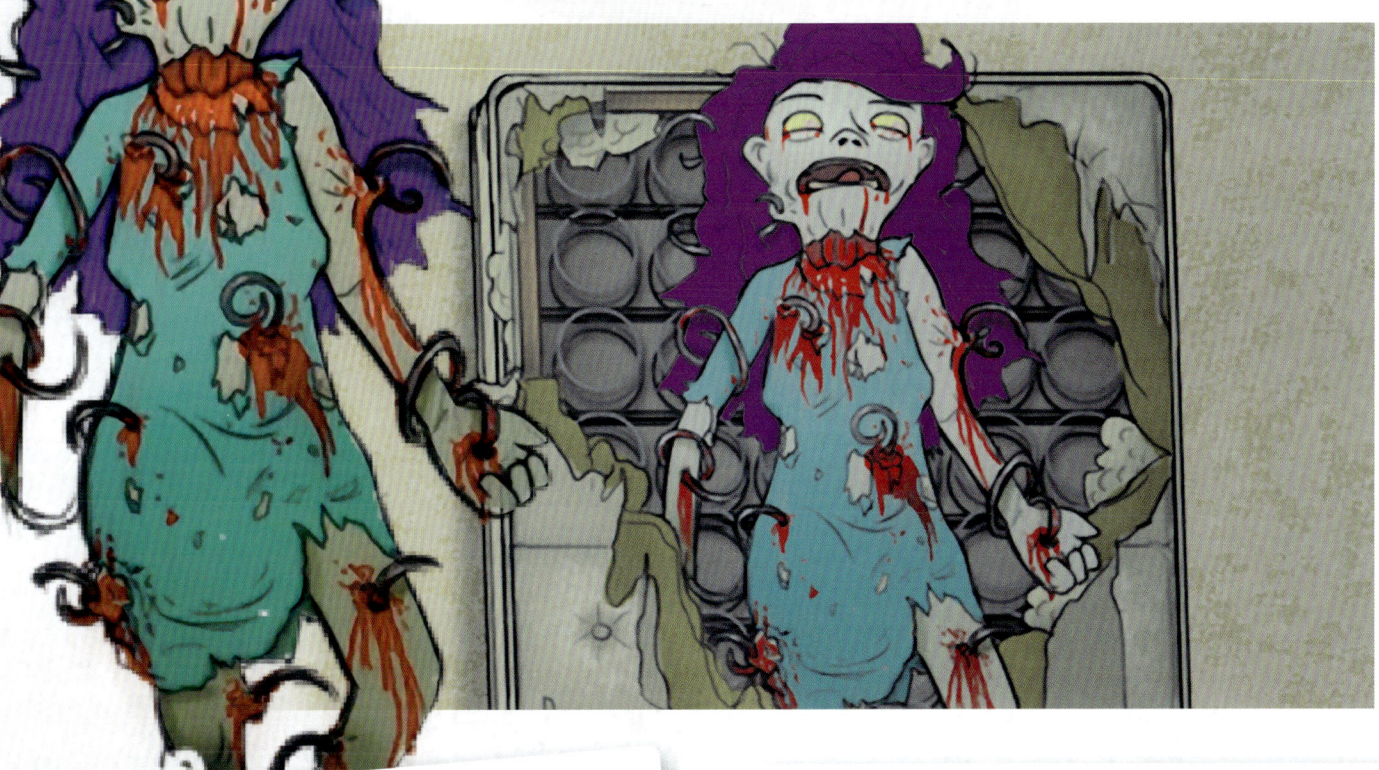

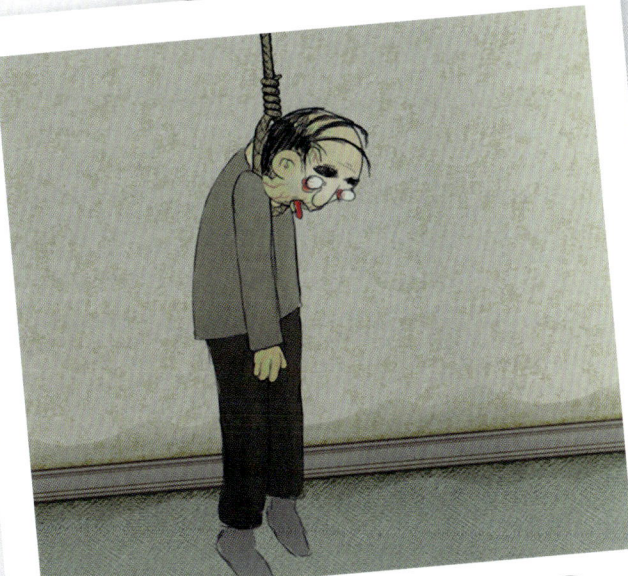

LUKE HOLMES

Luke Holmes was husband of Stacy, father to Megan, and a member of the Council of the Devourers of God. After murdering his family, Luke hanged himself.

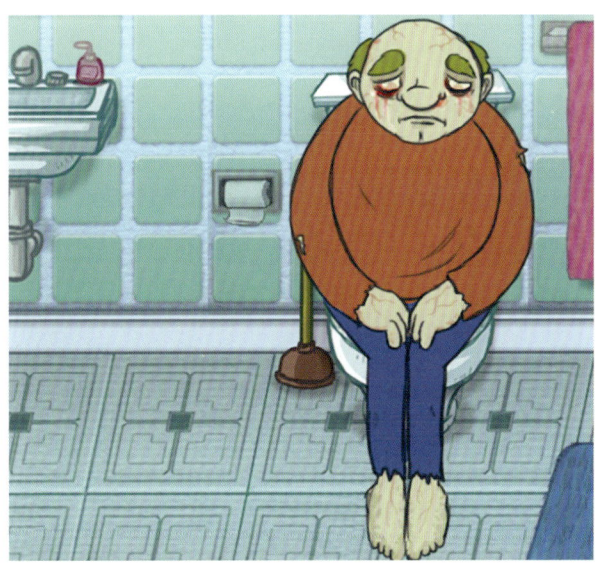

GREG MONTAGUE

Greg Montague was a simple working man who fell in love with a married woman. He blames himself for the deaths of Stacy, Megan, and Luke.

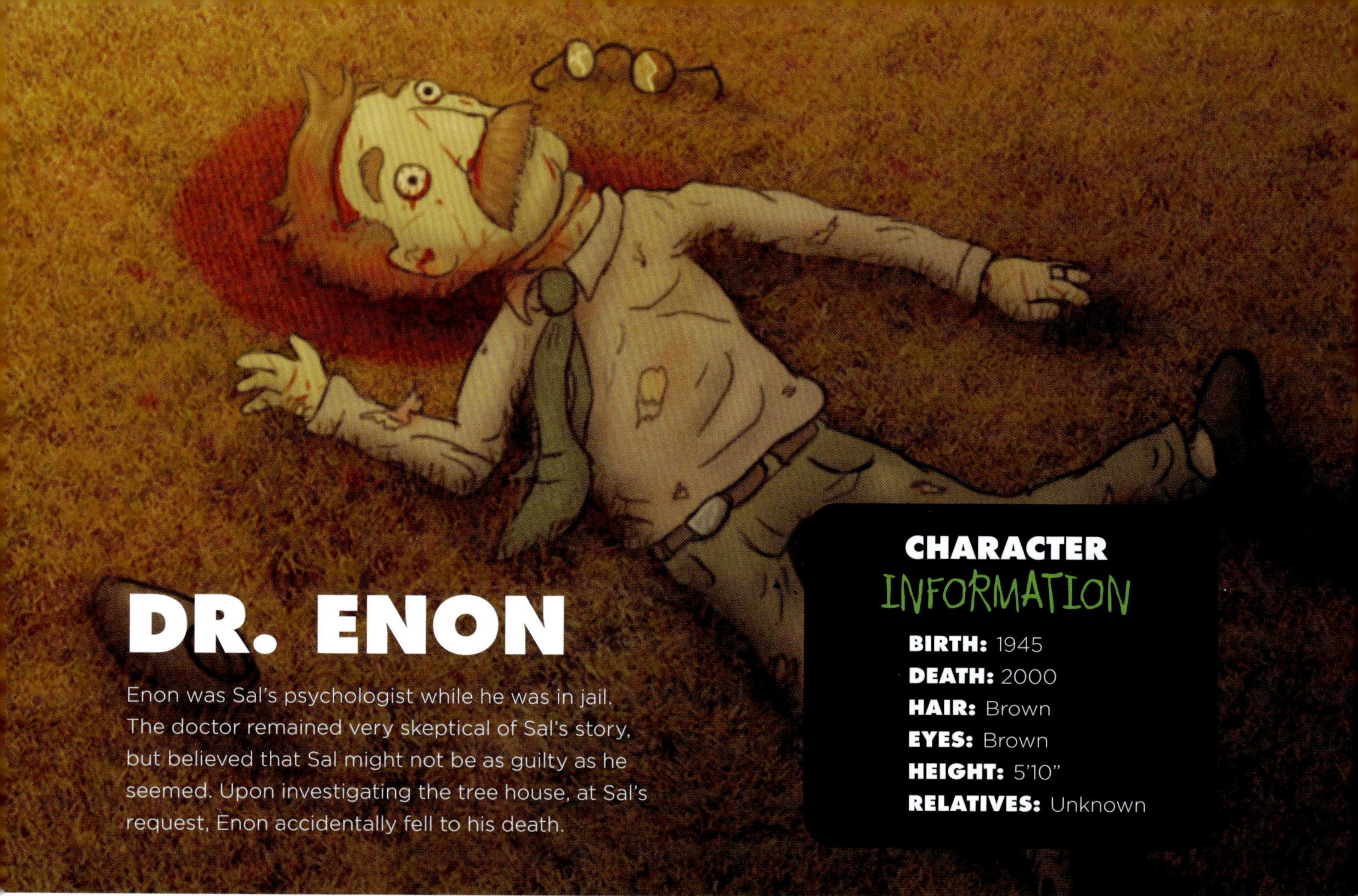

DR. ENON

Enon was Sal's psychologist while he was in jail. The doctor remained very skeptical of Sal's story, but believed that Sal might not be as guilty as he seemed. Upon investigating the tree house, at Sal's request, Enon accidentally fell to his death.

THE MYSTERIOUS MAN

The Mysterious Man appears on the top floor of the apartments with cryptic messages.

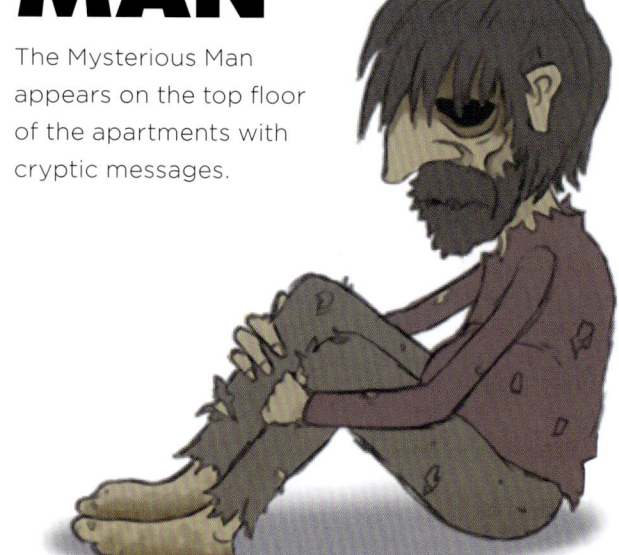

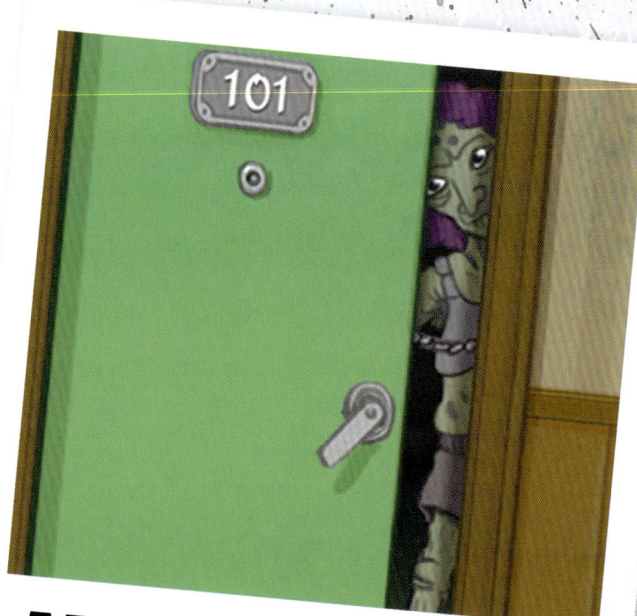

MRS. GIBSON

Mrs. Gibson is a cranky old woman that hates everyone and everything... even clothes.

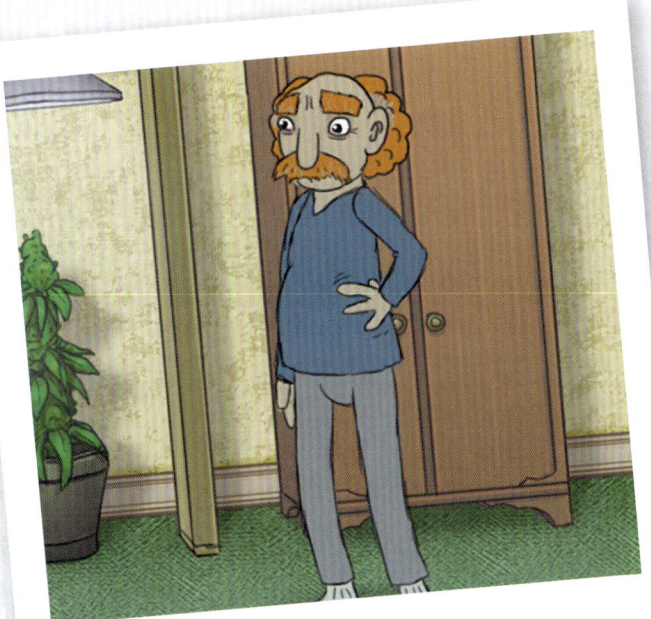

RAY MORRISON

Ray is Todd's father and a marijuana enthusiast.

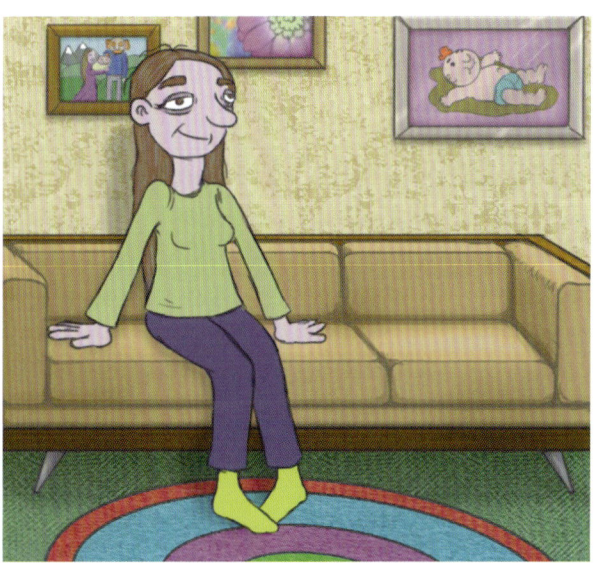

JANIS MORRISON

Janis is Todd's mother.
She's very kind, loving, and a bit spacey.

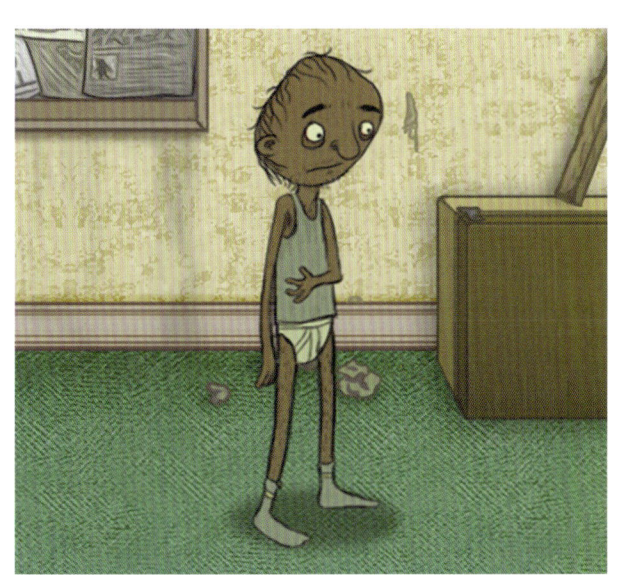

DAVID FINCH

David is a kind yinzer who is
married to a limbless mannequin.

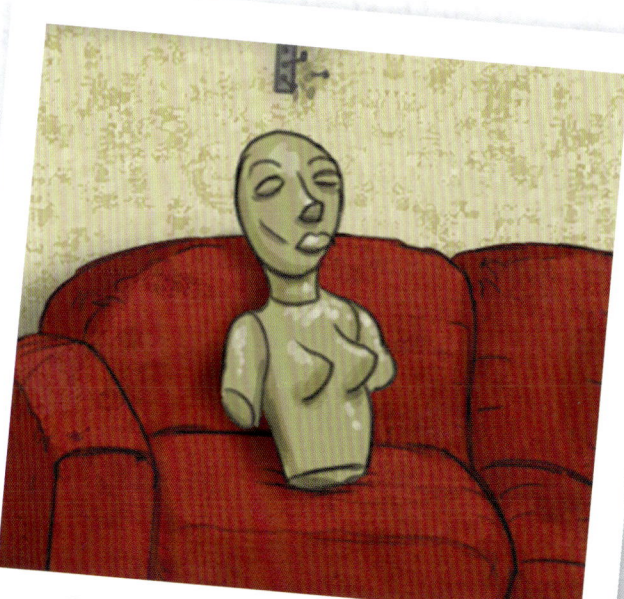

SARA FINCH

Sara is David's wife.
Weird, she kind of seems sad.

GIZMO

A therapy cat given to Sal during a very hard time; after he lost his mother. Gizmo and Sal bonded instantly. The cat grew to be pretty large and developed quite an eccentric personality for a feline. After Sal's death, Ashley took care of Gizmo.

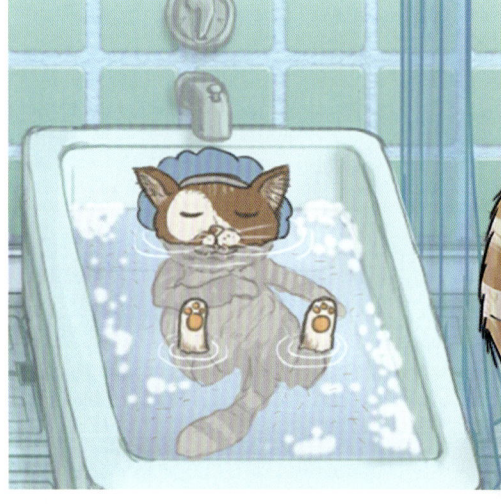

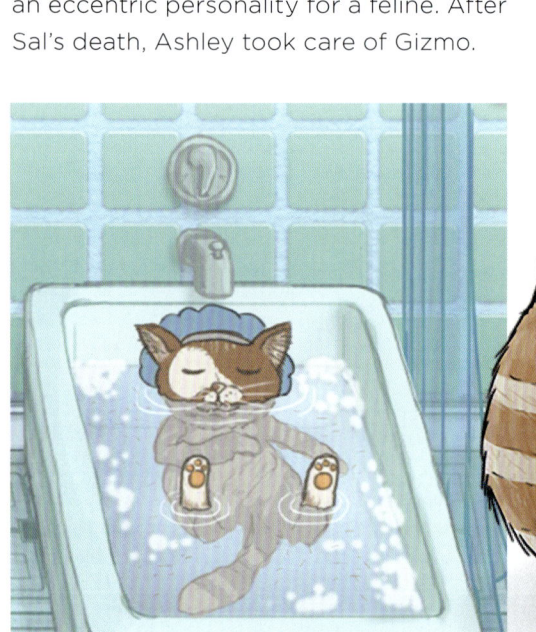

TALA GREY

Tala Grey is seen searching for her missing grandfather. She is a direct descendant of The Grey Tribe.

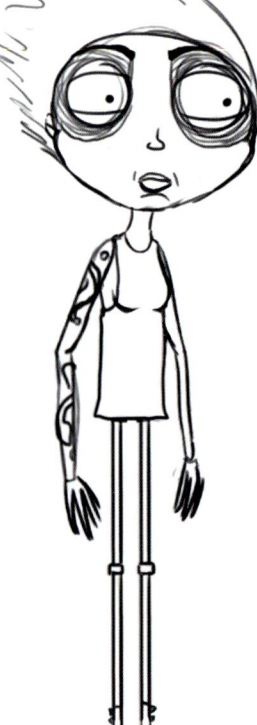

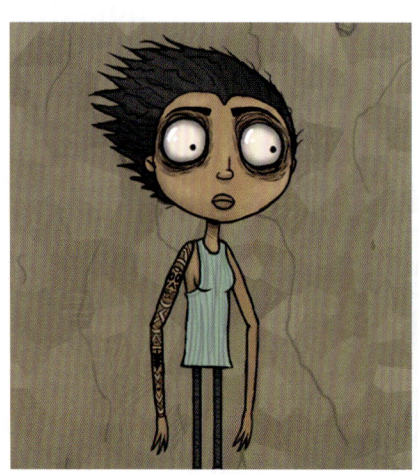

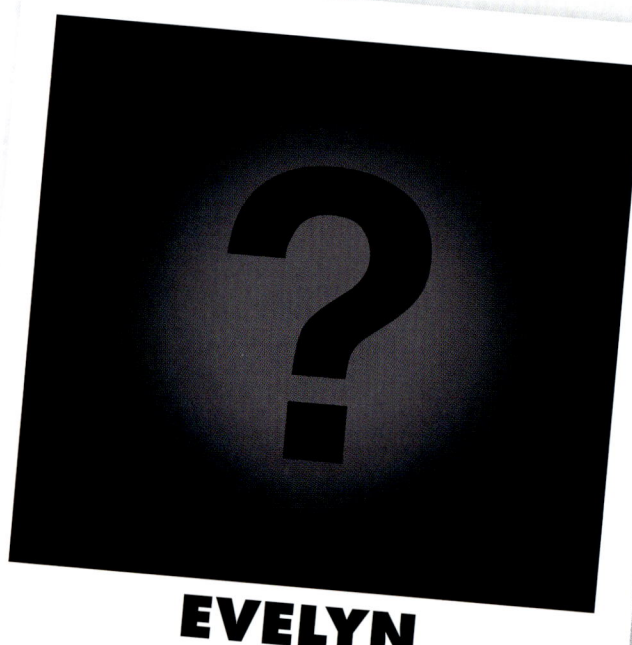

EVELYN

Evelyn was Jim Johnson's sister. When the two of them arrived on Earth, she went missing and Jim never saw her again.

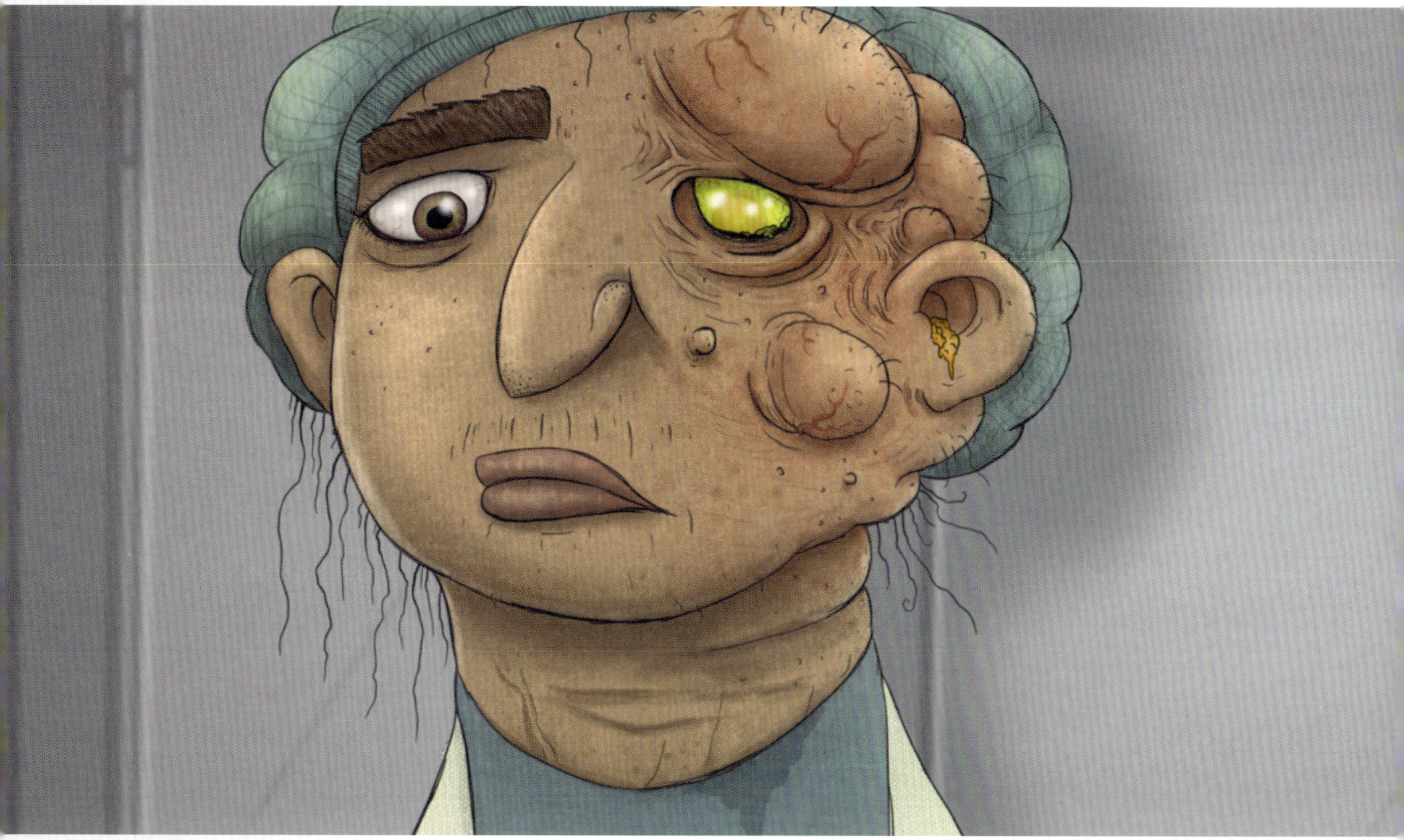

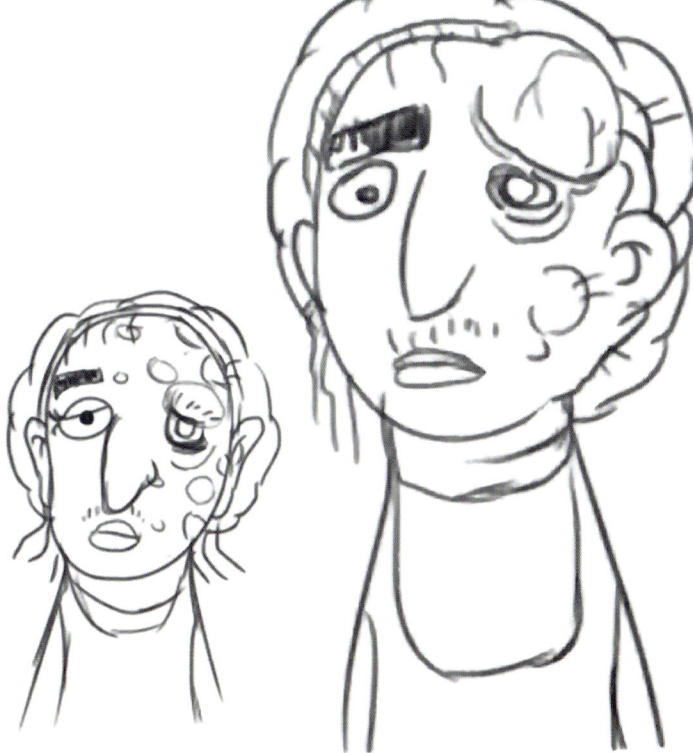

KIM
YAZZIE

Kim Yazzie is the lunch lady at Nockfell High
School. She has elephantiasis and a fondness
for nature photography.

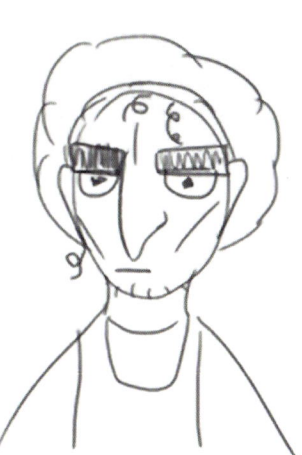

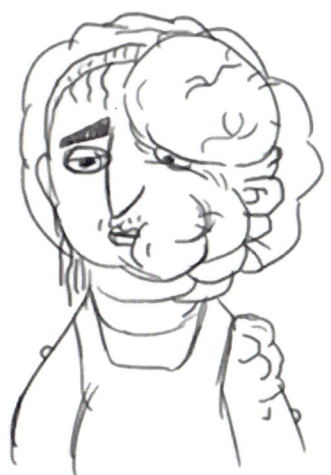

DETECTIVE

The detective who was investigating Mrs. Sanderson's murder is also suspected to be a cult member.

COP

This rude cop was seen guarding the crime scene in room 403 and is suspected to be a cult member.

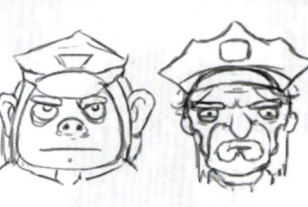 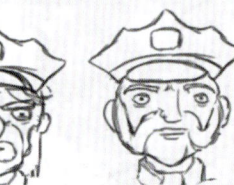 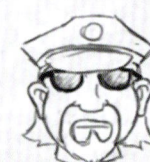
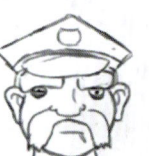 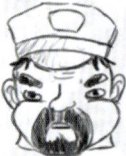 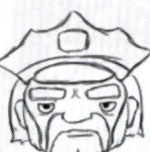 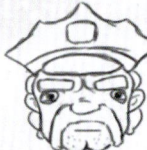
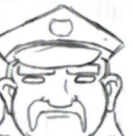 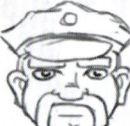 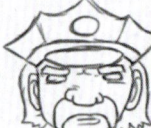 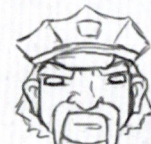

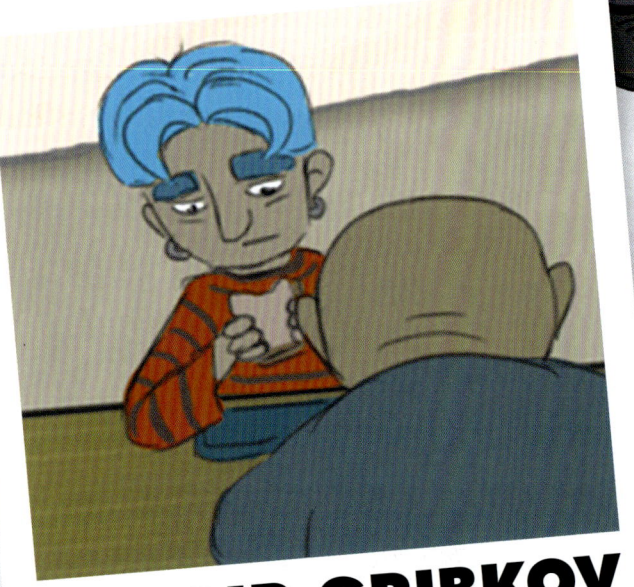

PHILLIP GRIBKOV

Phillip Gribkov is a classmate of the main crew and can be seen in the background of Episode Three.

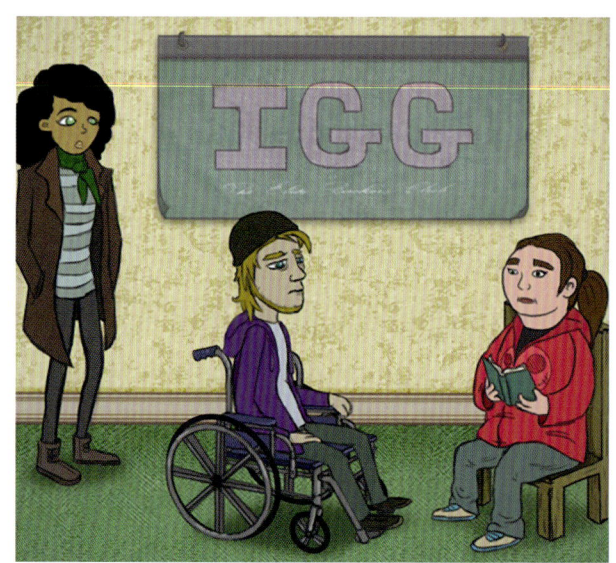

CJ, SIERRA, AND Z

CJ, Sierra, and Z are three college friends that often hang out in the Addison Apartments.

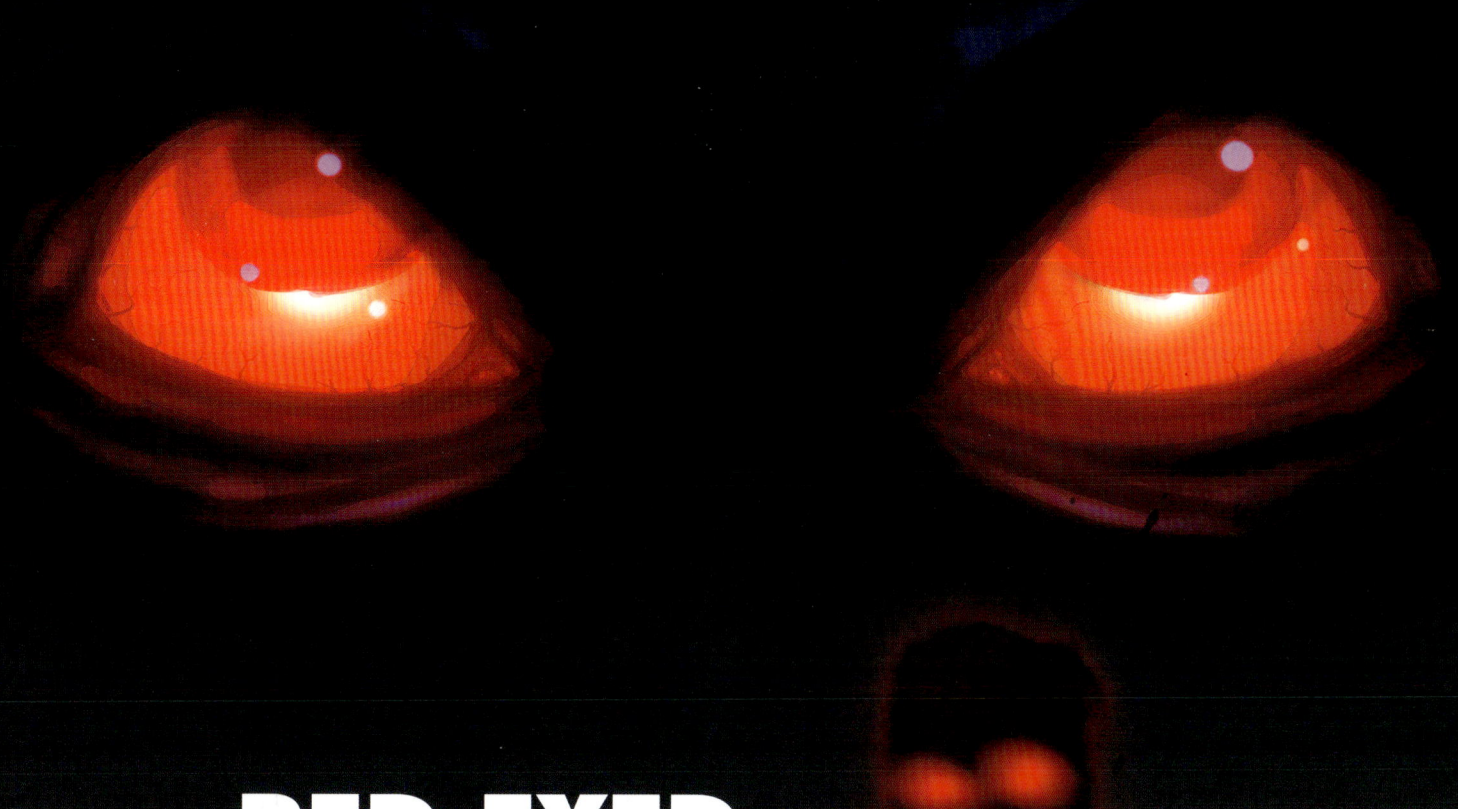

RED EYED DEMON

A mysterious cosmic being that belongs to the Plague of Shadows. It's able to take different forms and even possess humans to control their actions. The gang originally thinks there is only one but it turns out there are many.

CHARACTER INFORMATION

AGE: Unknown
HAIR: None
EYES: Red
HEIGHT: Any
RELATIVES:
The Plague of Shadows

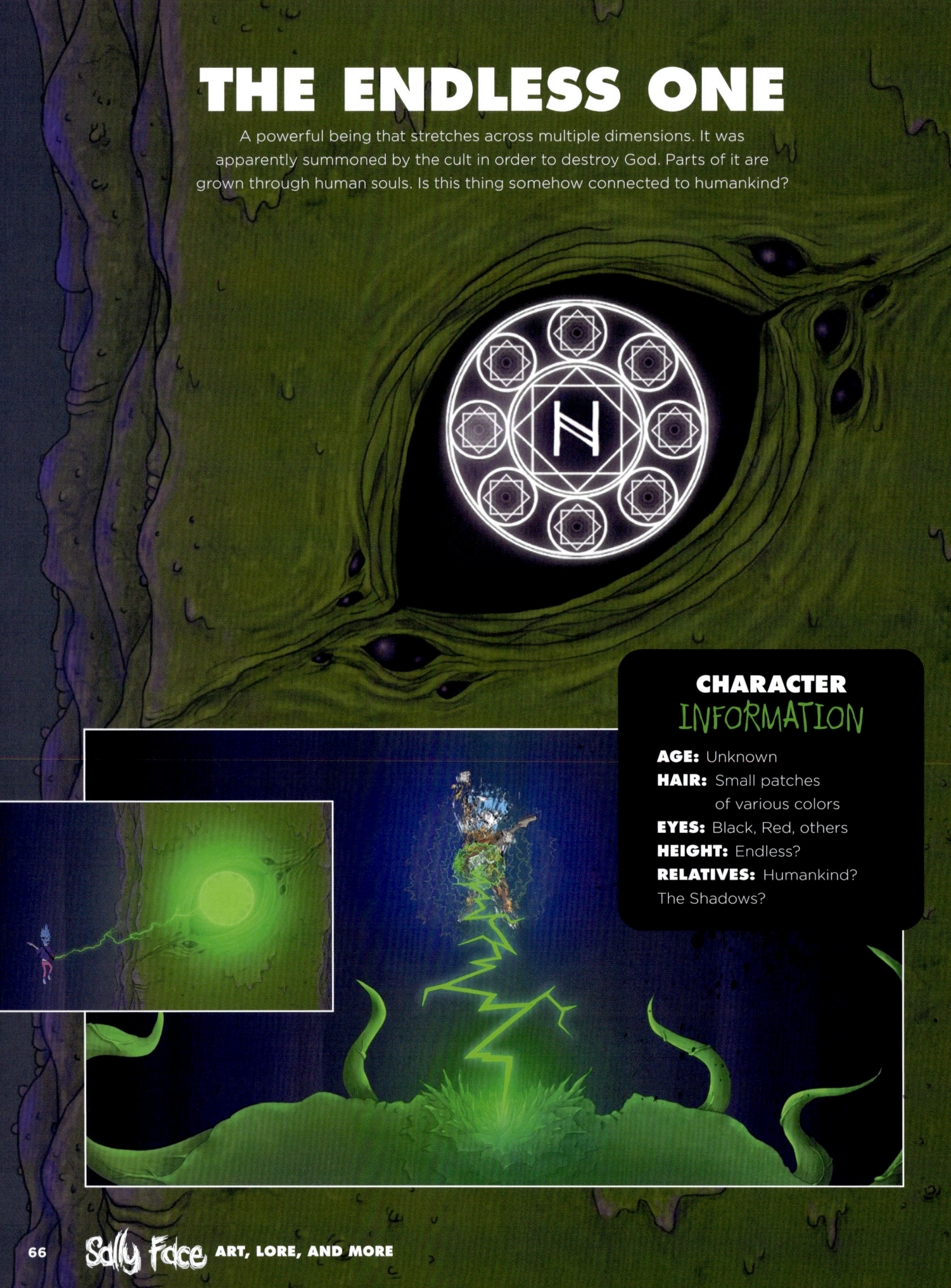

THE ENDLESS ONE

A powerful being that stretches across multiple dimensions. It was apparently summoned by the cult in order to destroy God. Parts of it are grown through human souls. Is this thing somehow connected to humankind?

CHARACTER
INFORMATION

AGE: Unknown
HAIR: Small patches of various colors
EYES: Black, Red, others
HEIGHT: Endless?
RELATIVES: Humankind? The Shadows?

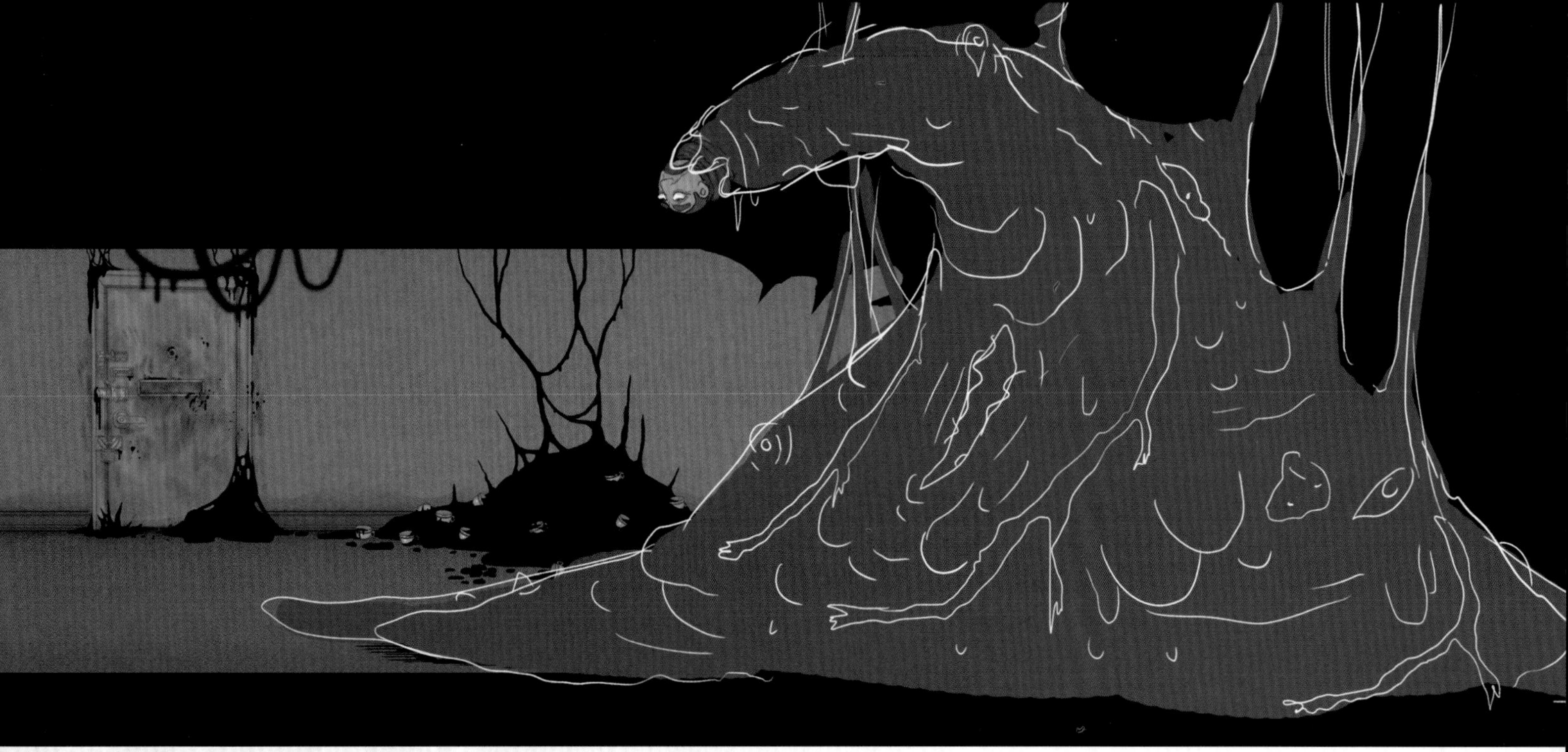

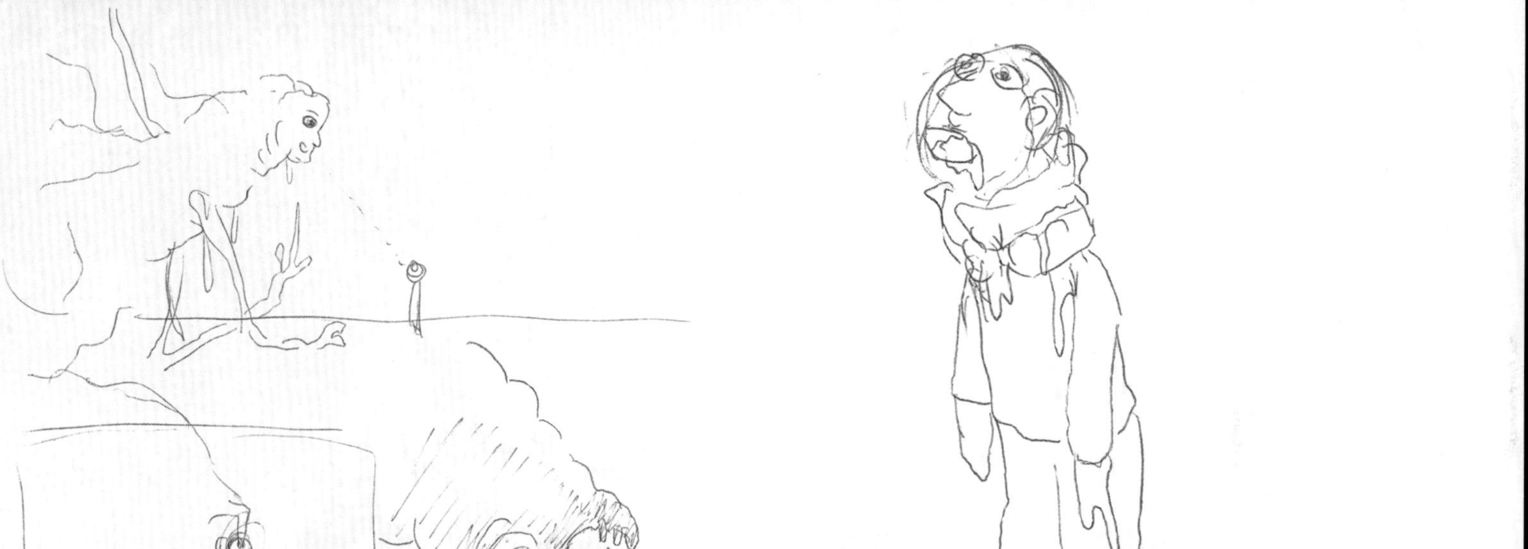

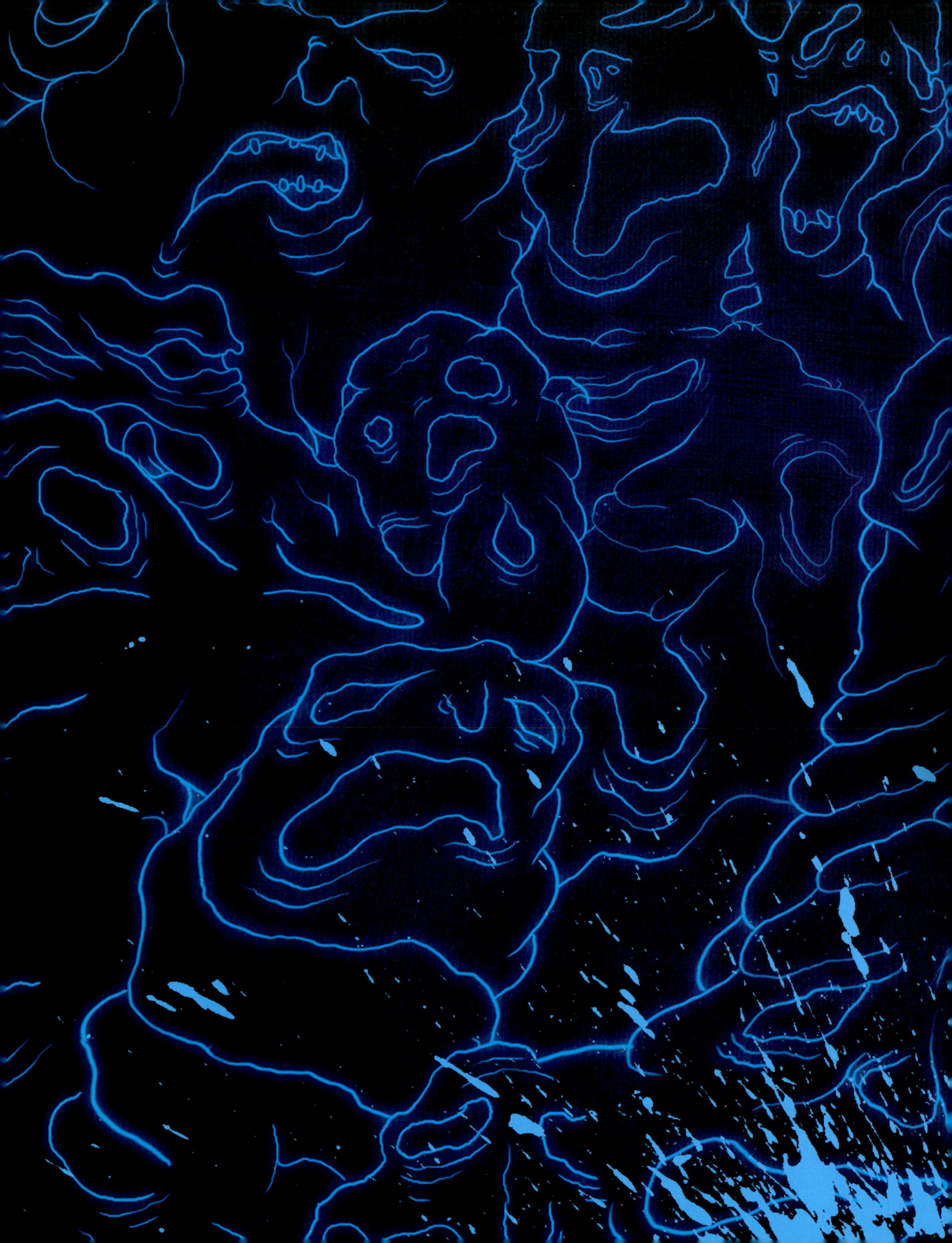

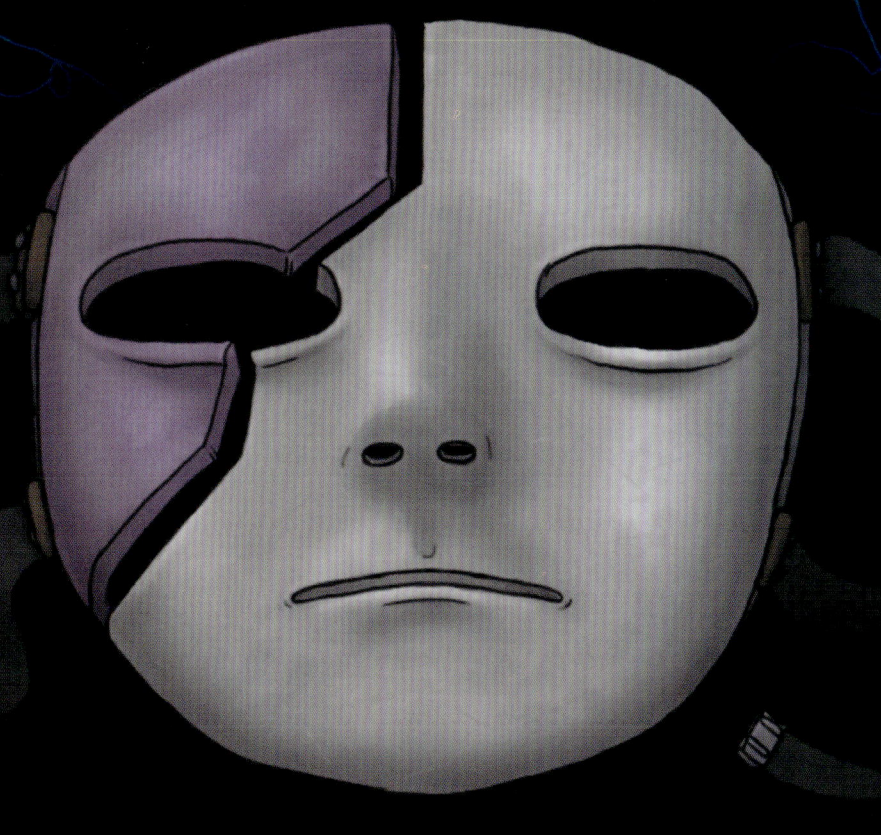

CHAPTER 2

Sally Face

LOCATIONS

NOCKFELL

Nockfell is a small rural town that is nestled in the woods, near a large lake. The town is centred around an old church from the 1700s that sits atop the rolling hills. A lumber factory employs most of the town.

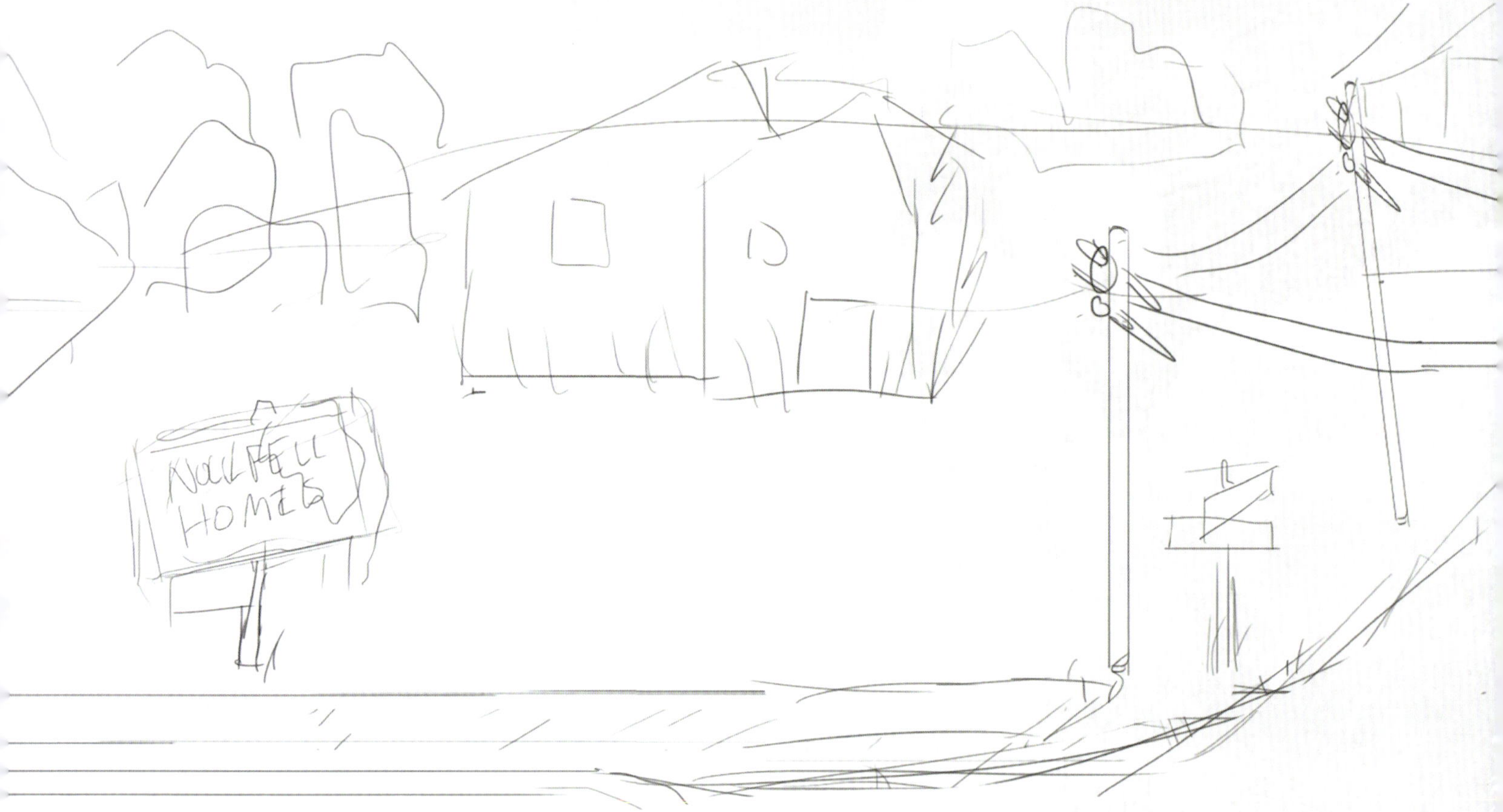

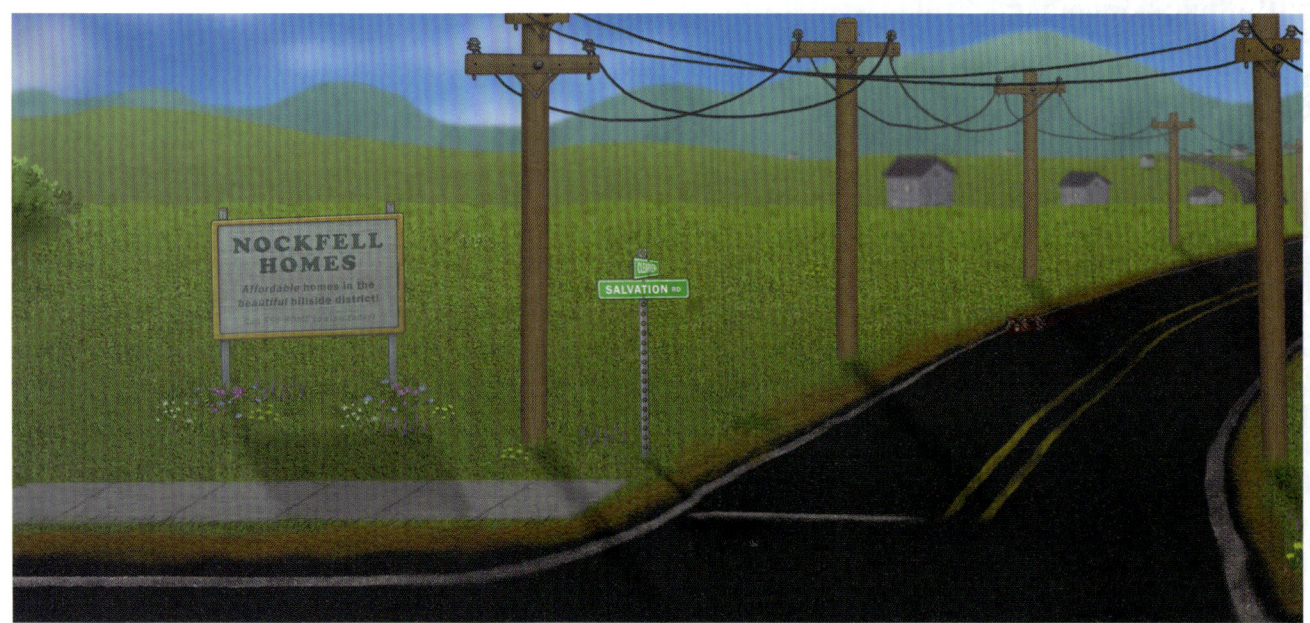

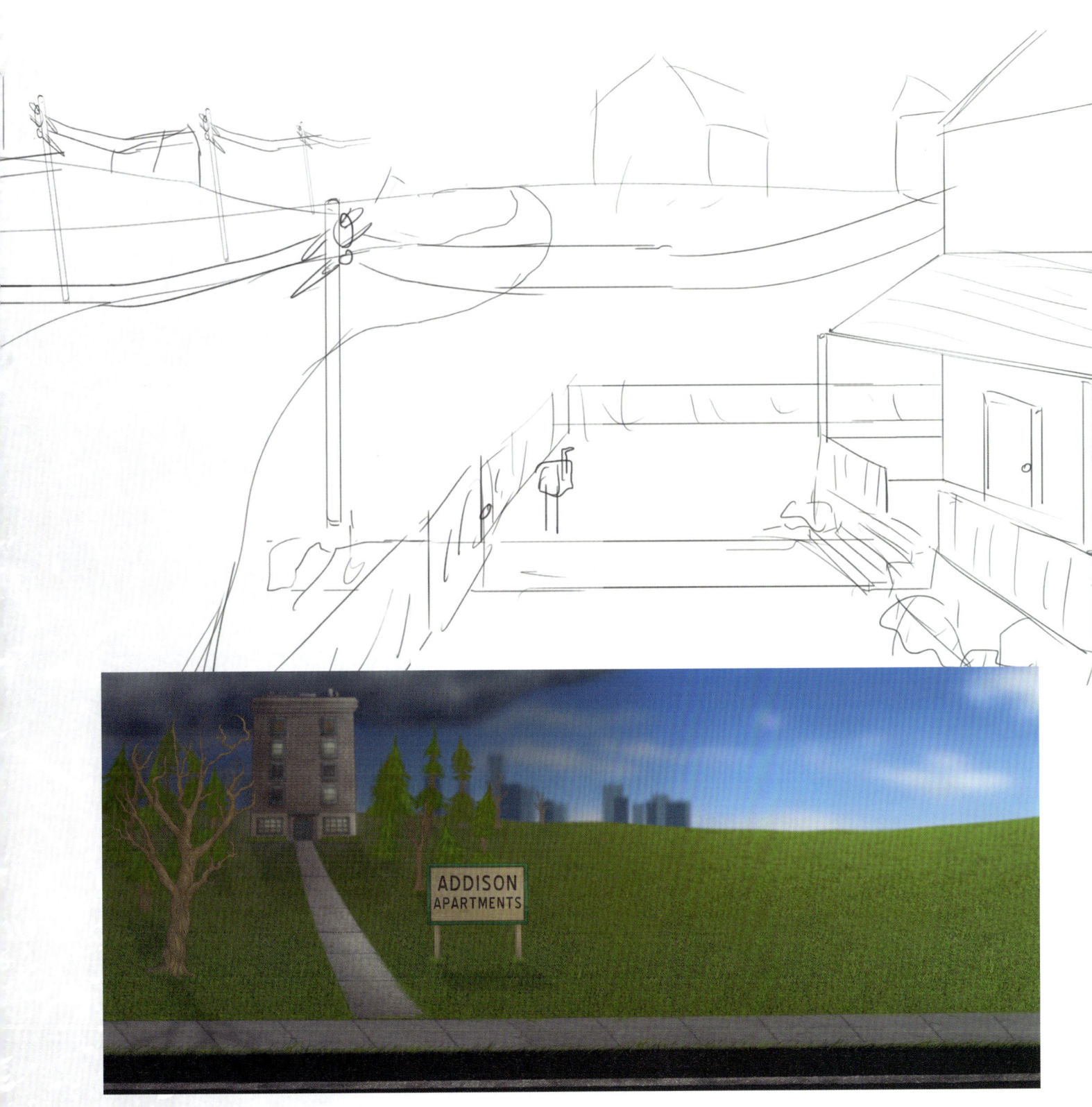

ADDISON APARTMENTS

A small brick apartment building, built by the Addison family in 1887.

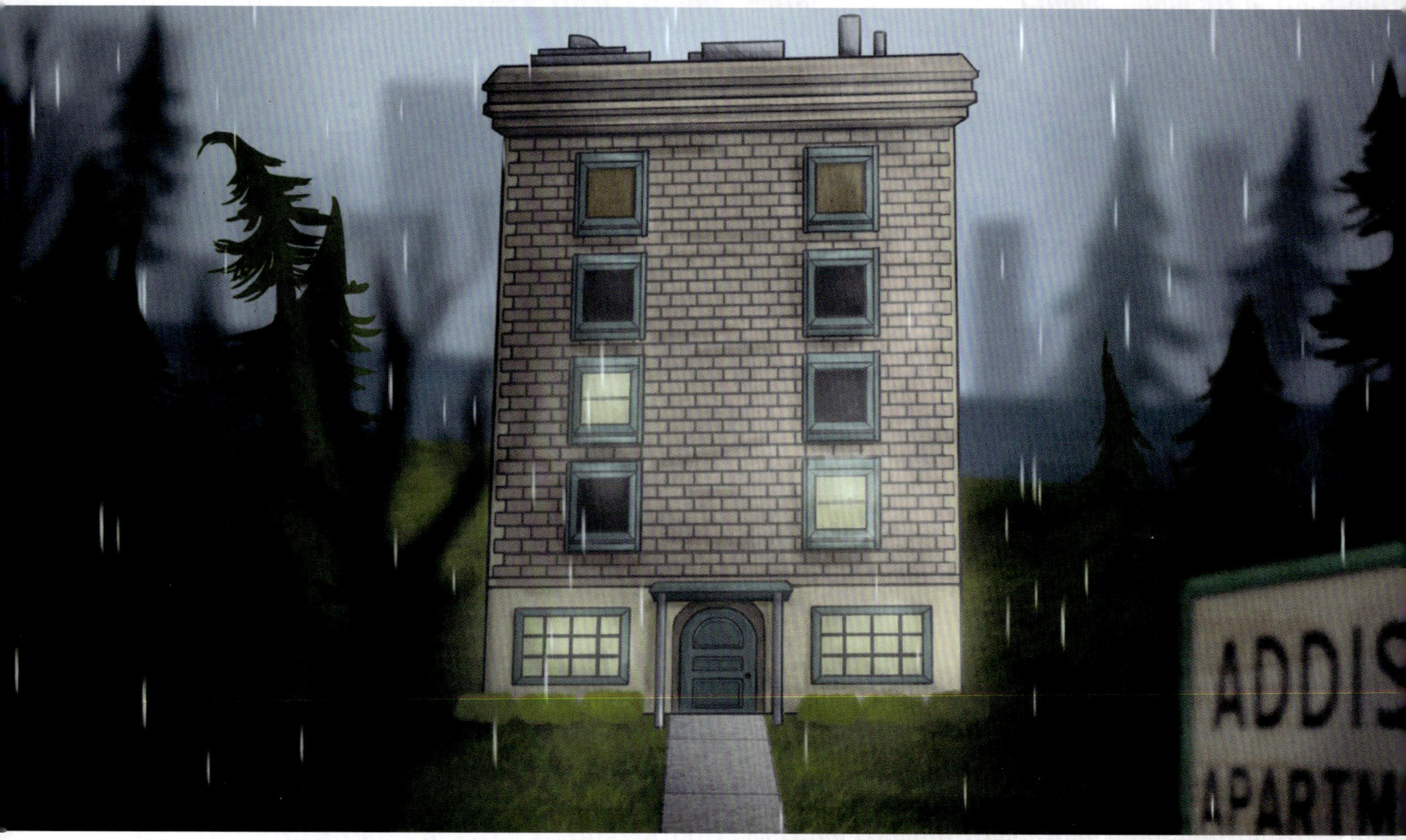

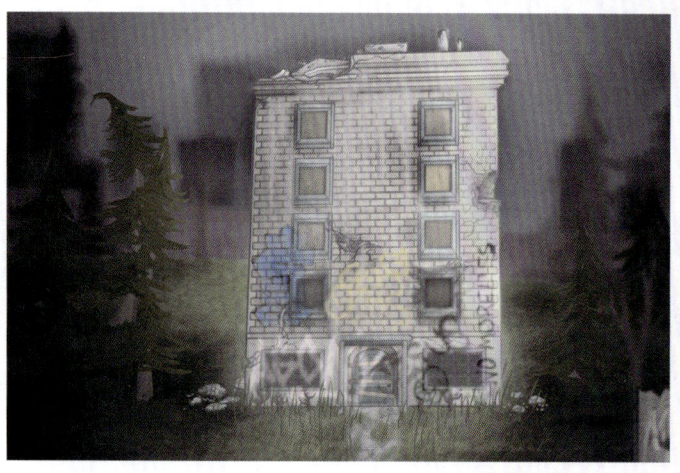

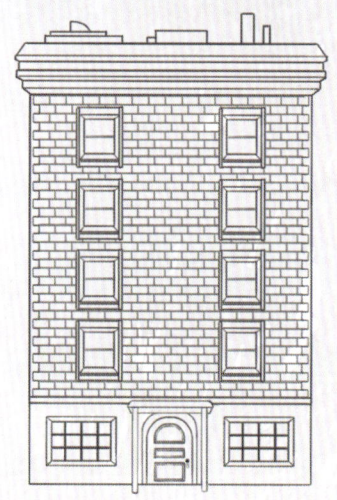

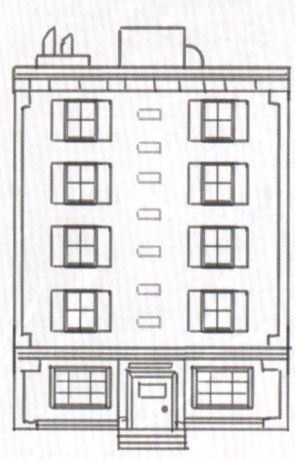

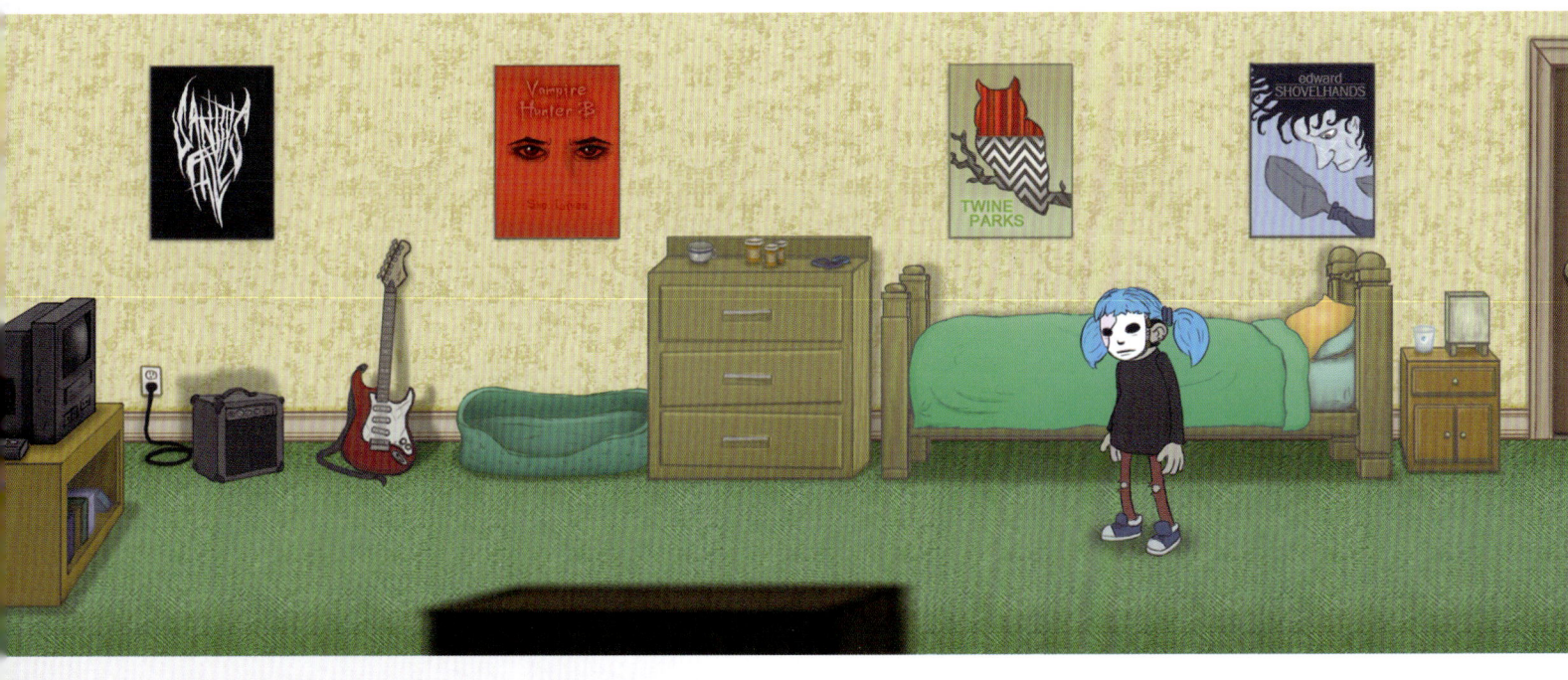

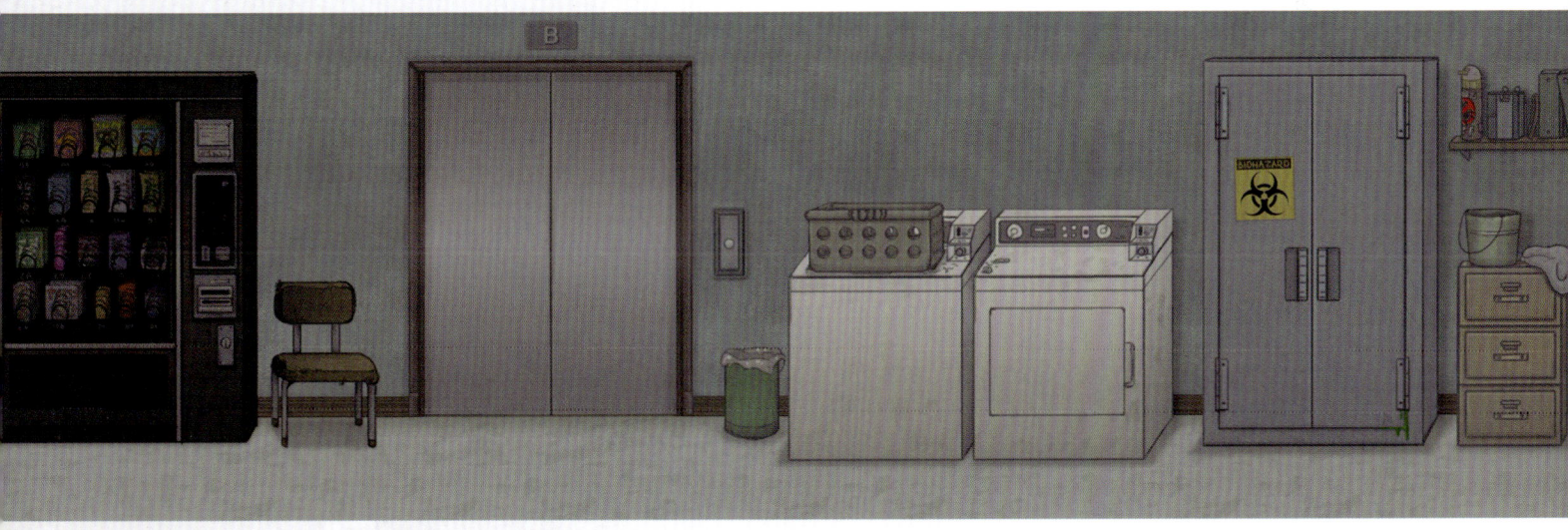

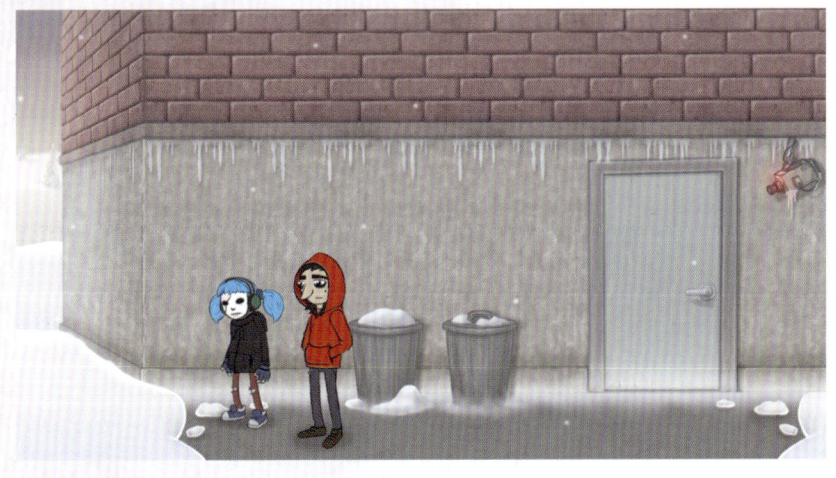

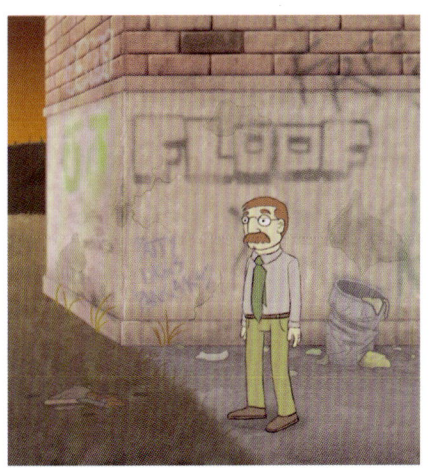

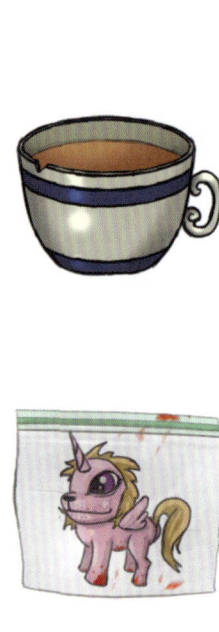
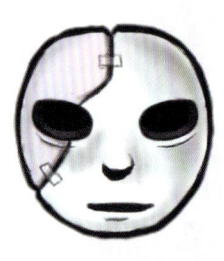
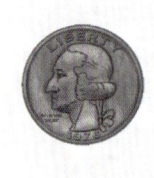

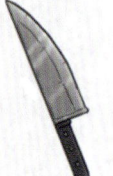

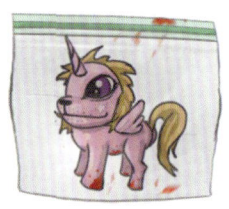
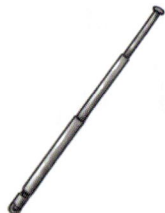
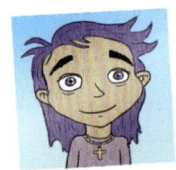
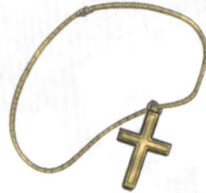
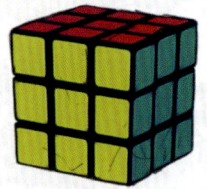

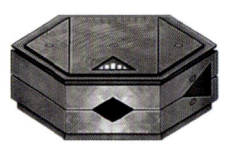
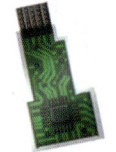
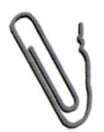
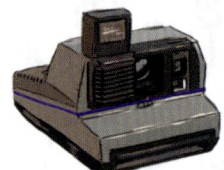
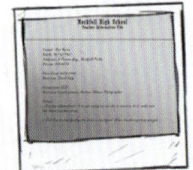

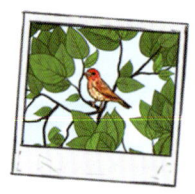
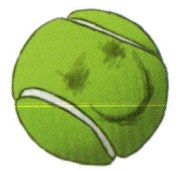

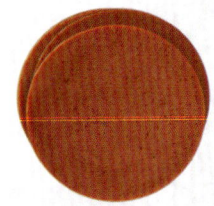
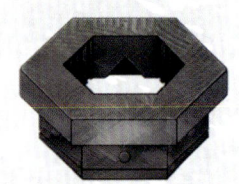

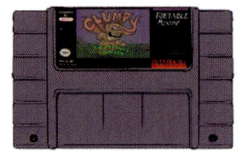
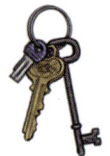
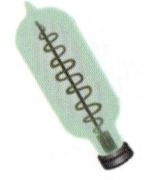
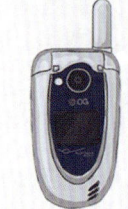

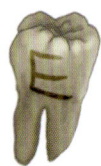
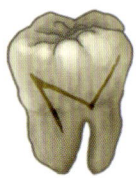
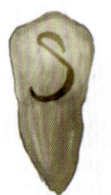
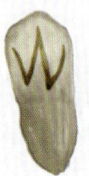
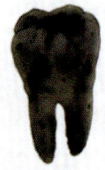

Sally Face ART, LORE, AND MORE

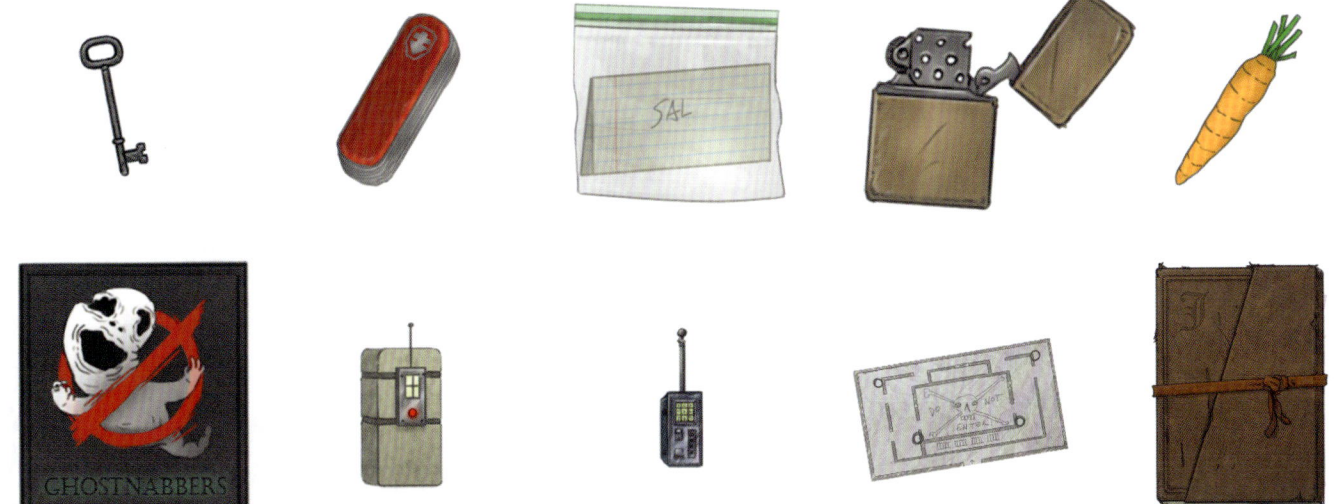

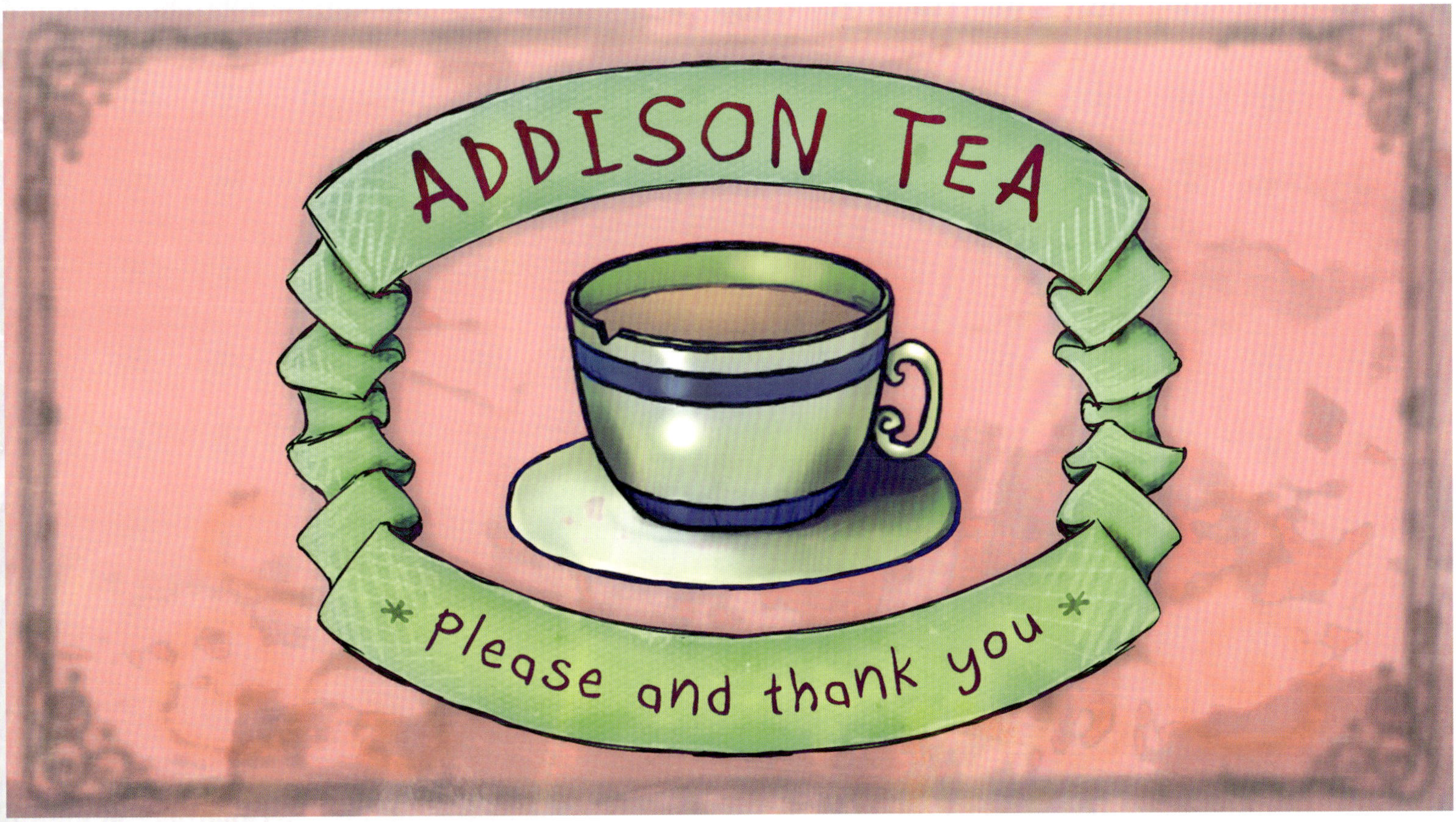

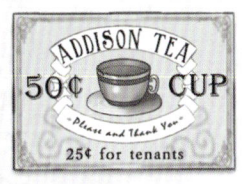

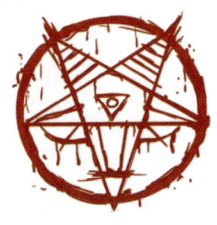

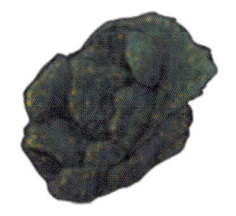

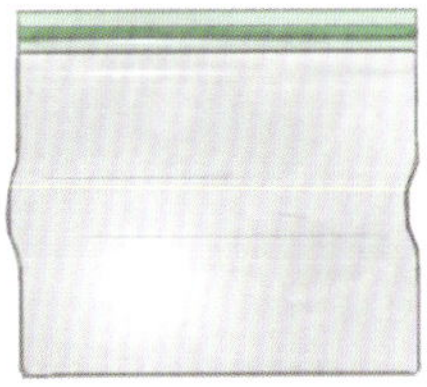

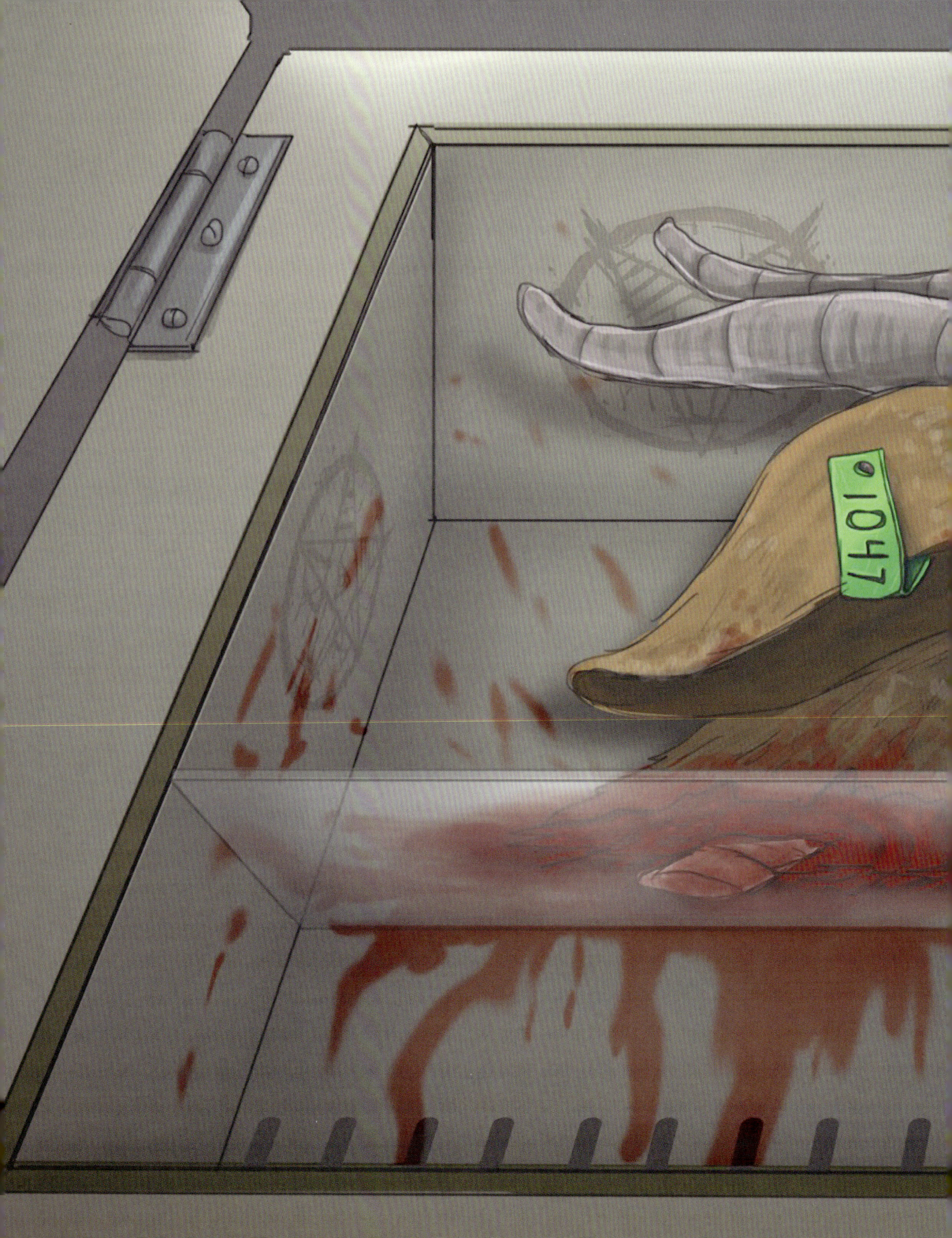

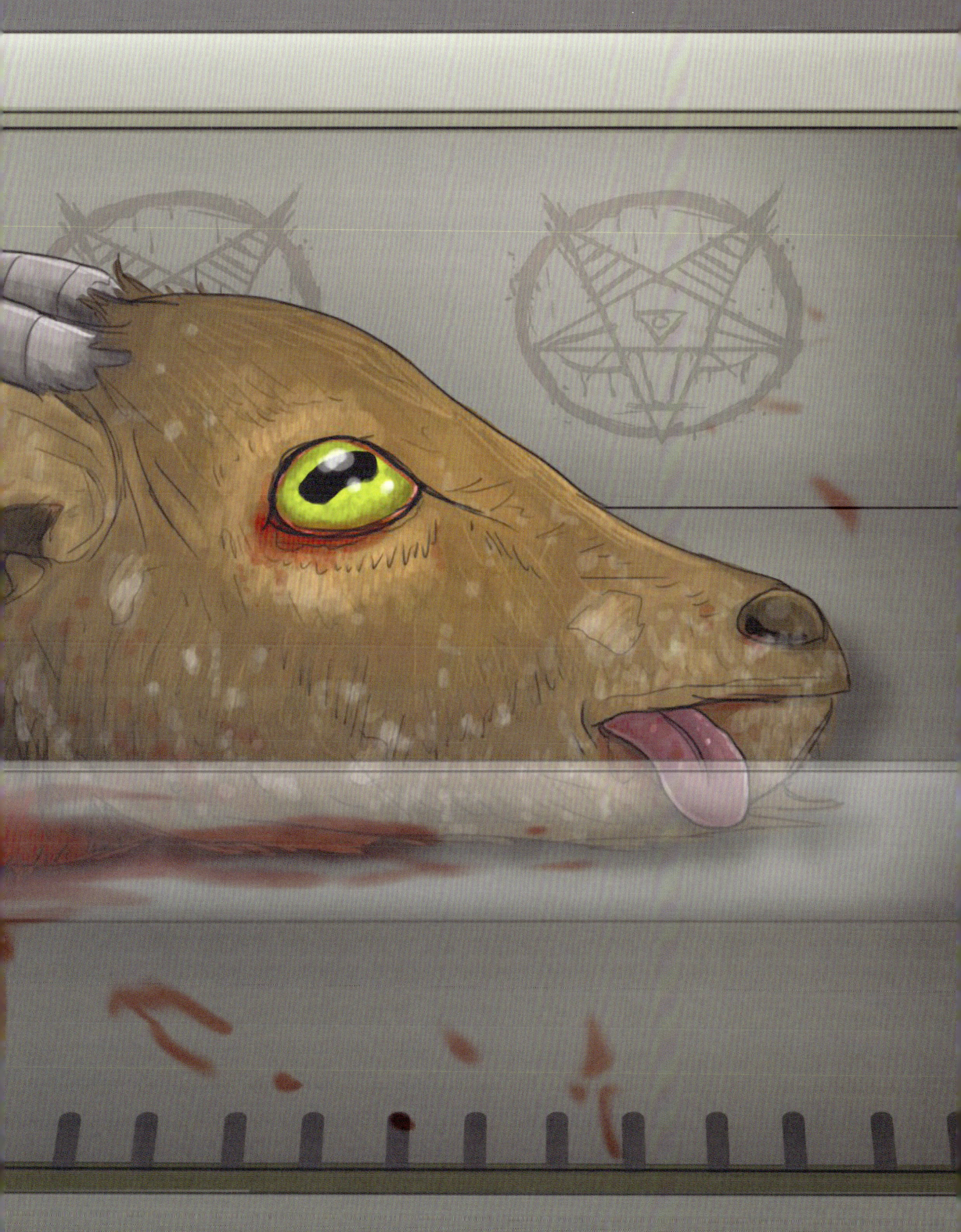

LARRY'S TREE HOUSE

Jim built this tree house for Larry, who lovingly refers to it as his "Fortress of Solitude". It's located behind the Addison Apartments.

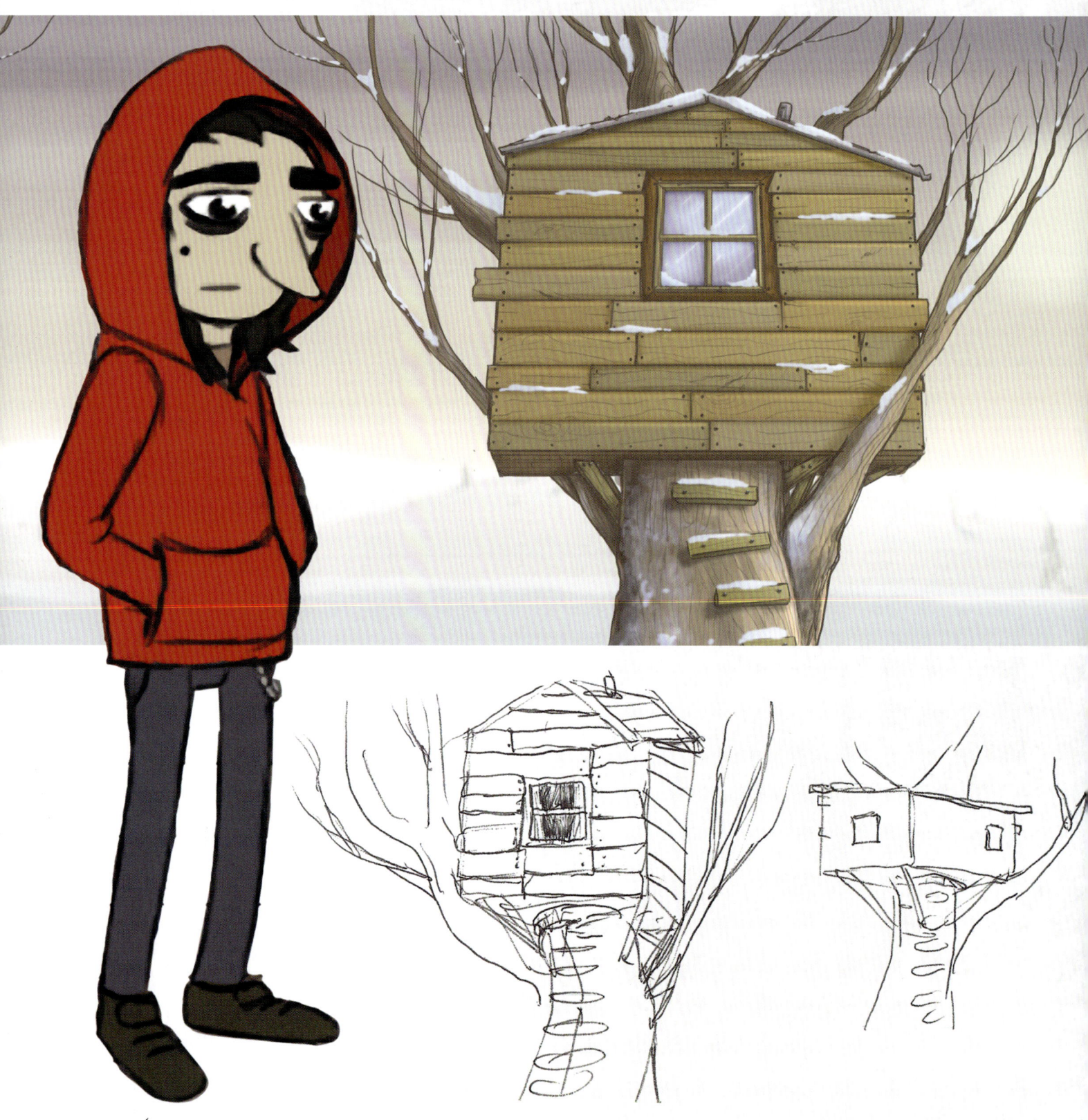

Sally Face ART, LORE, AND MORE

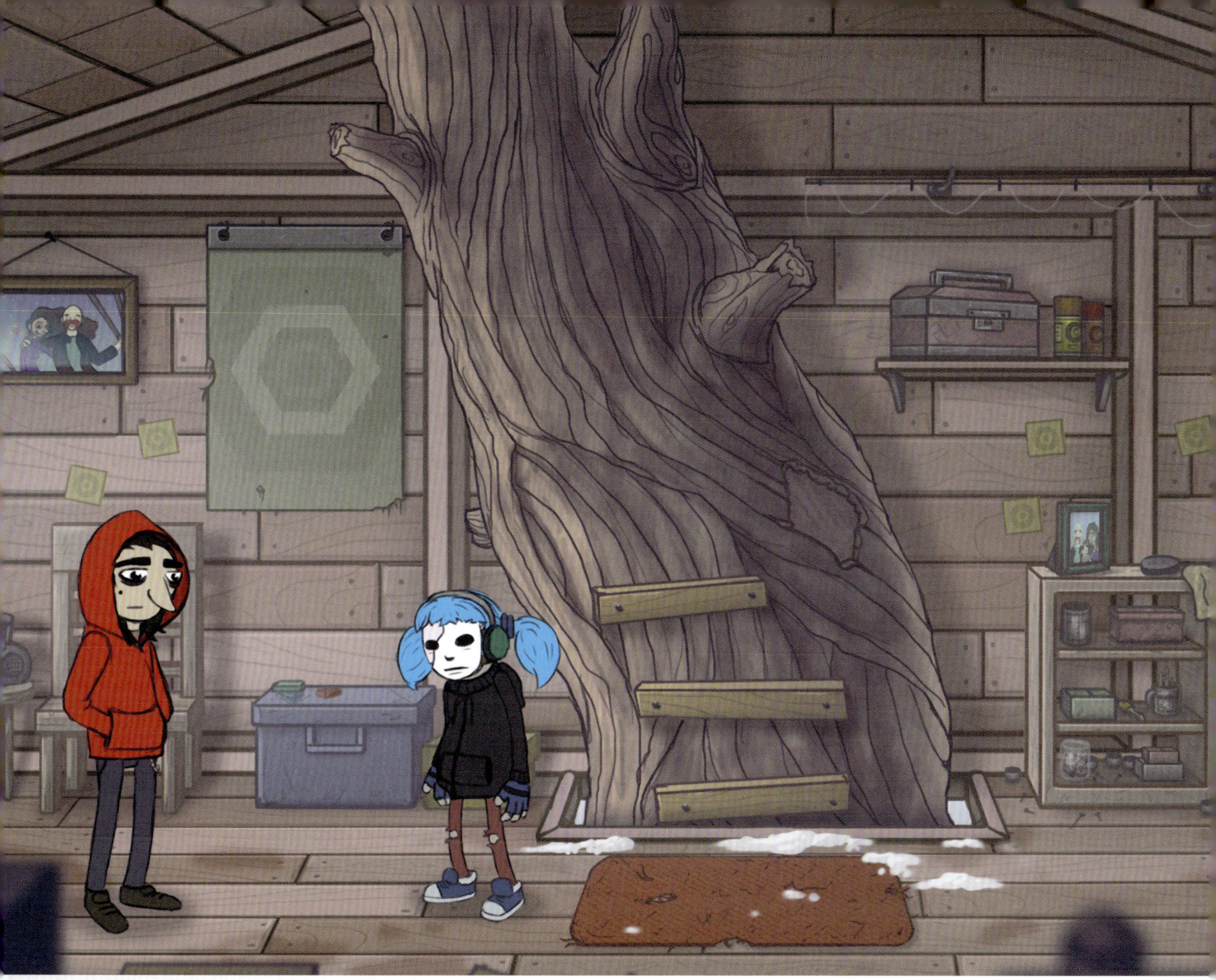

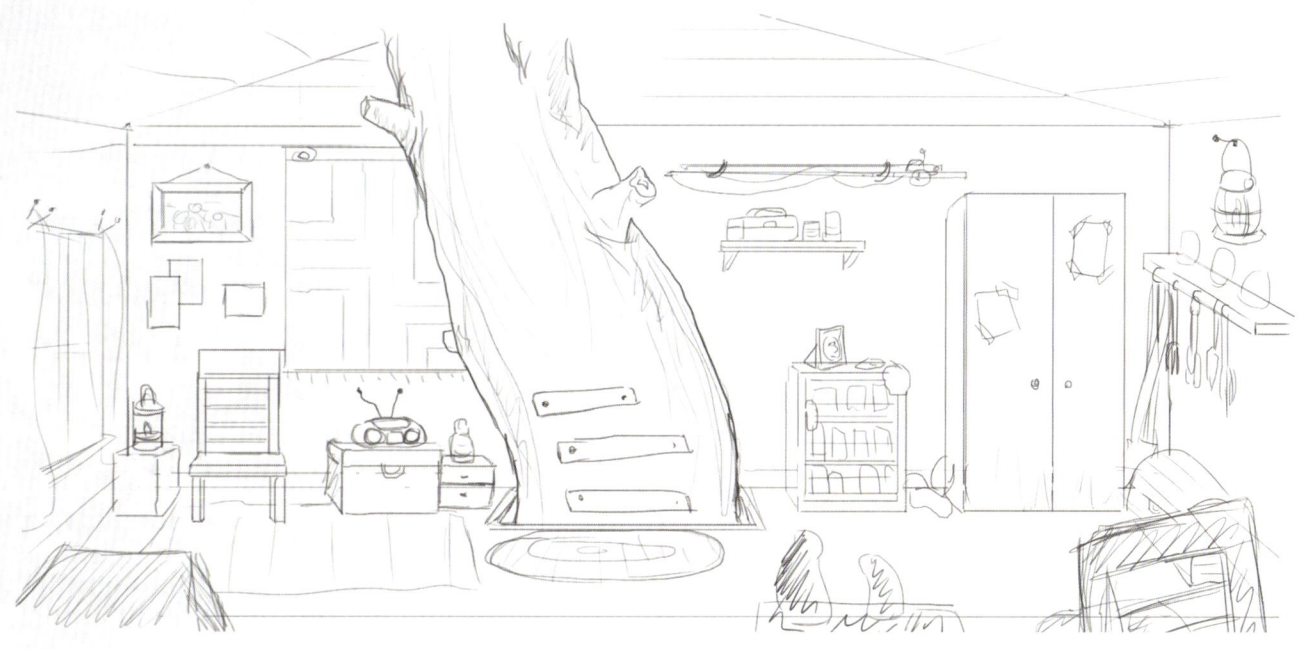

CHAPEL HILL

Chapel Hill is a hilly area of Nockfell that contains
Phelps Ministry (est. 1703) and Neveroak Cemetery.

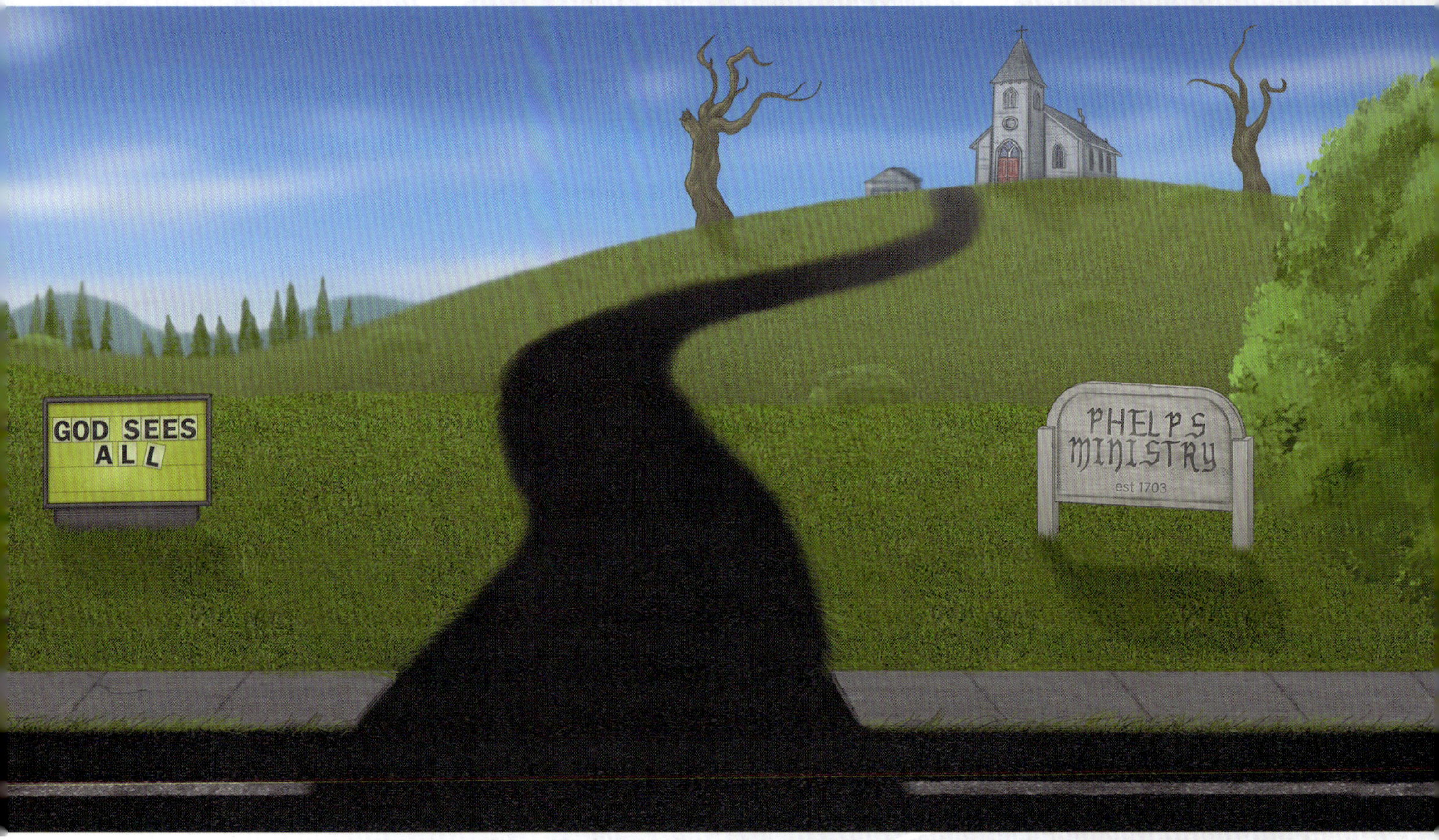

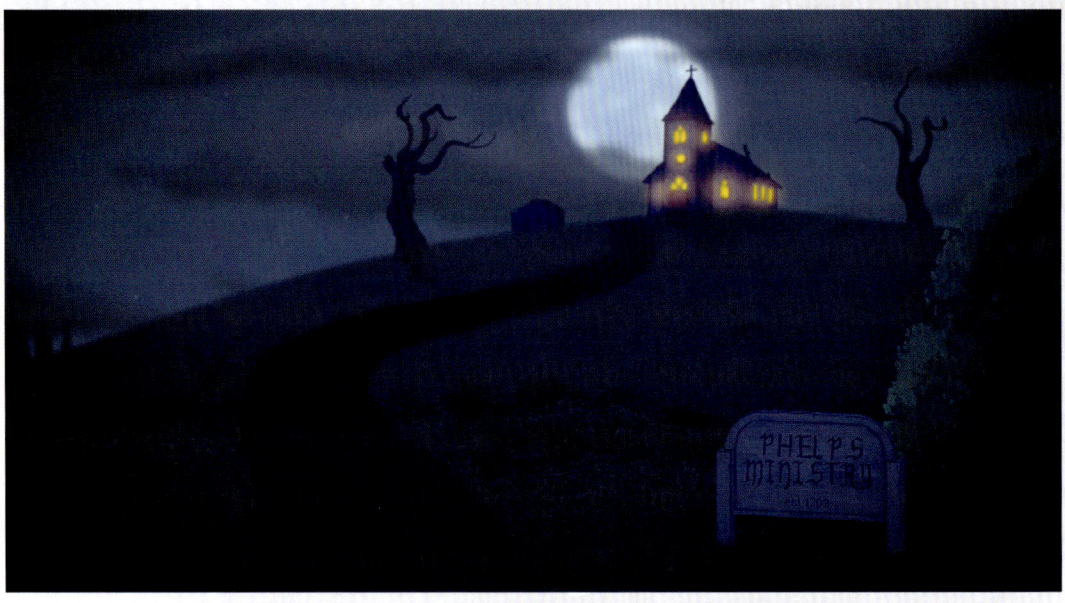

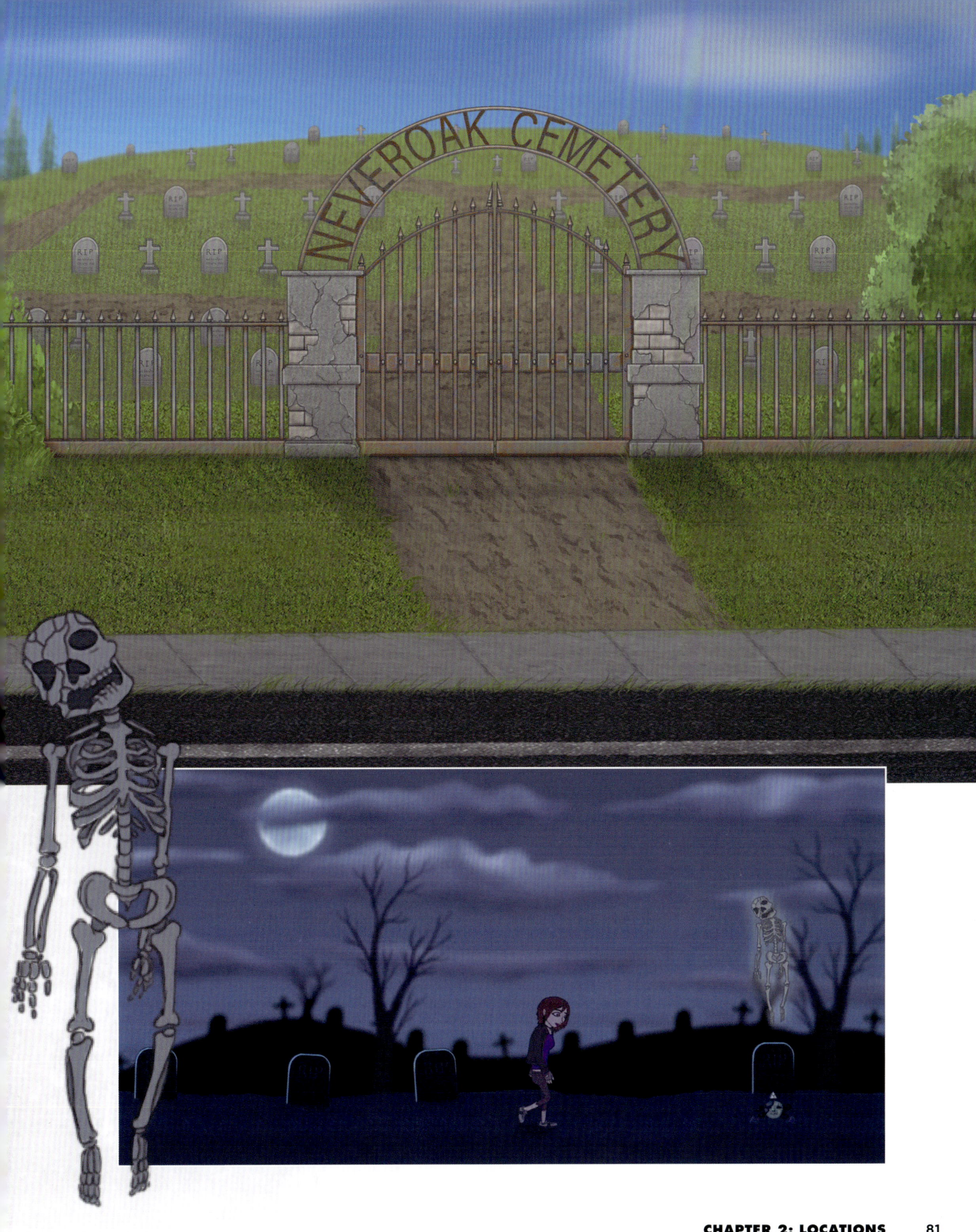

THE TEMPLE

An elaborate underground temple that was built
by the Devourers of God in the late 1600s.

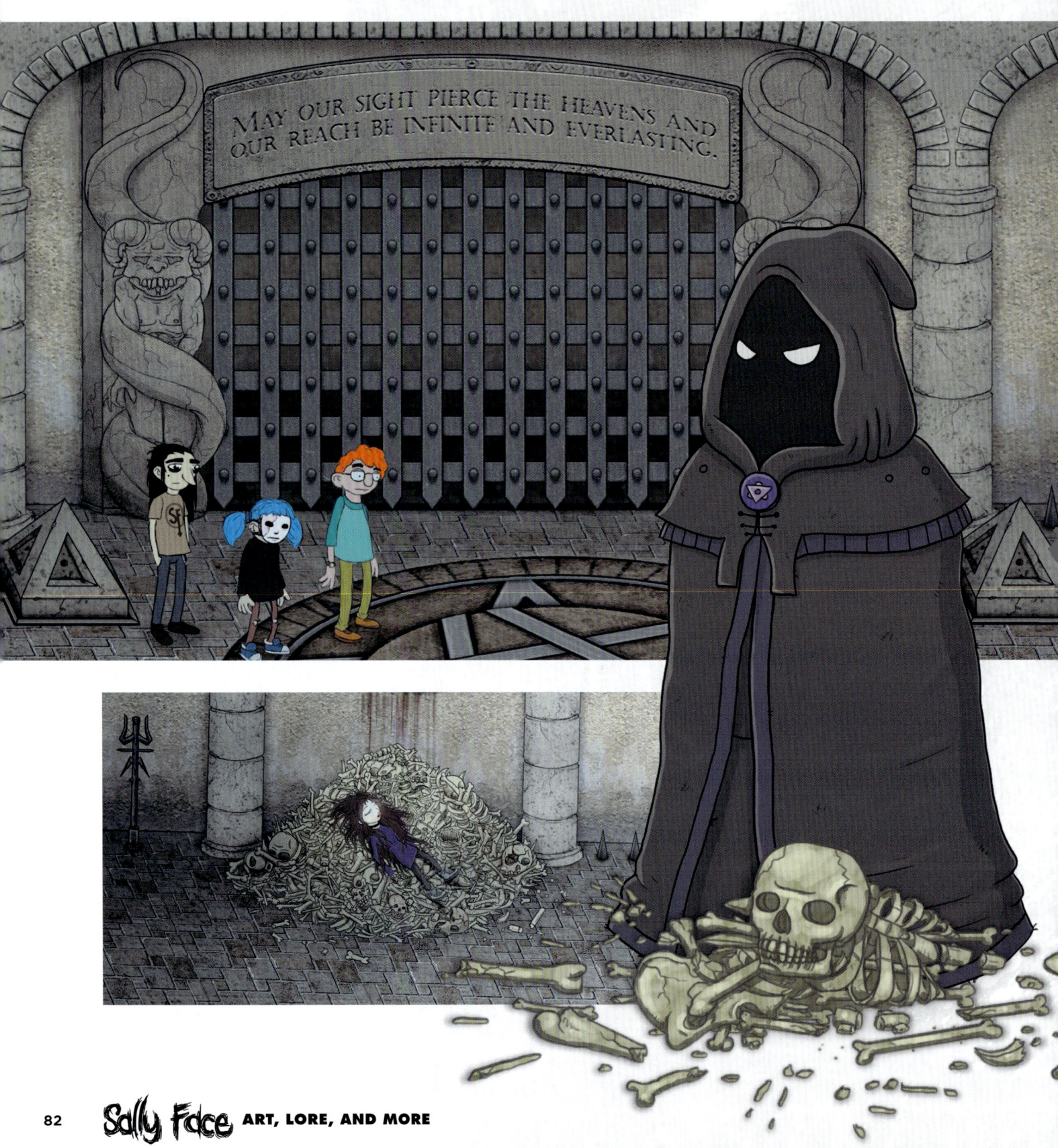

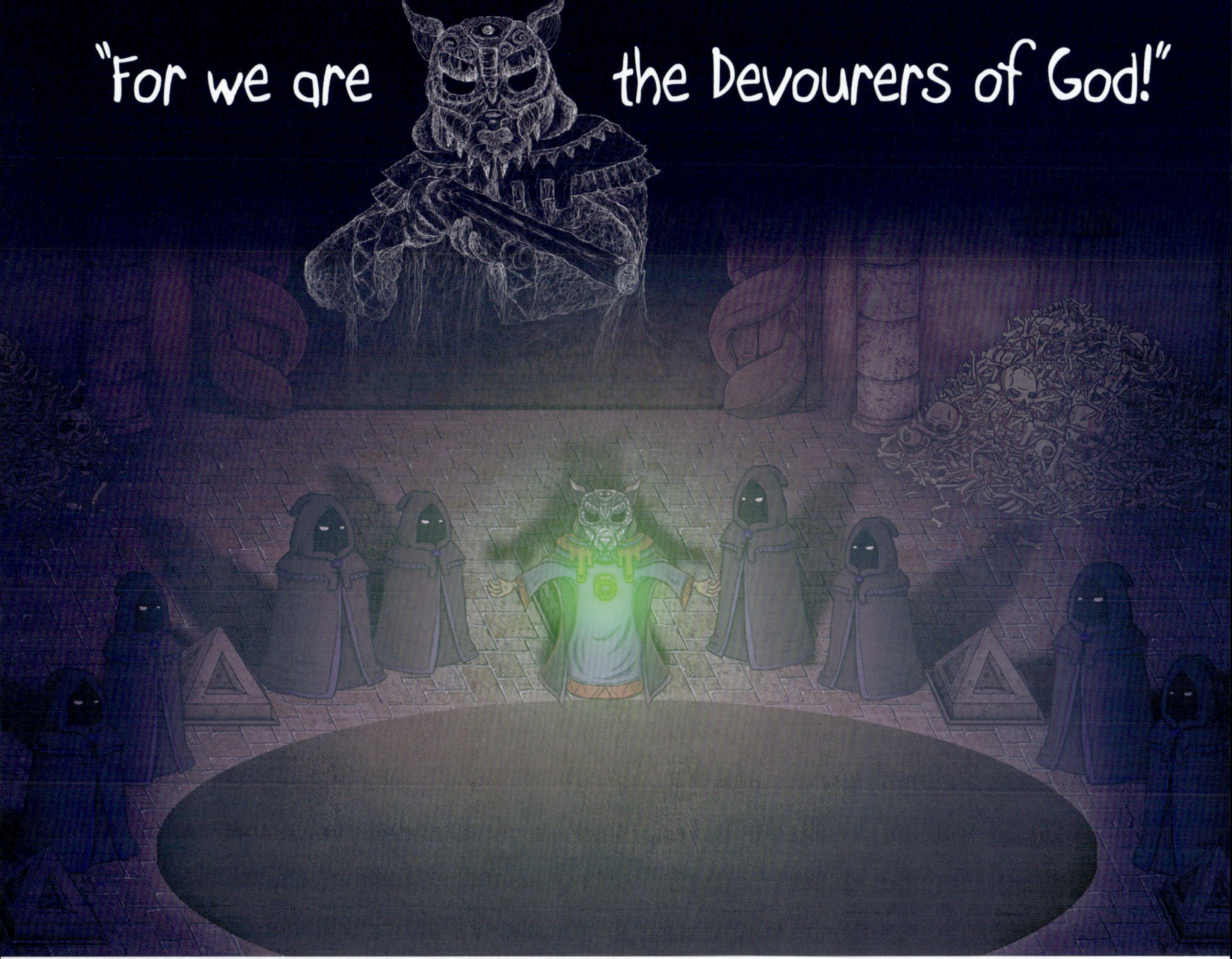

"For we are the Devourers of God!"

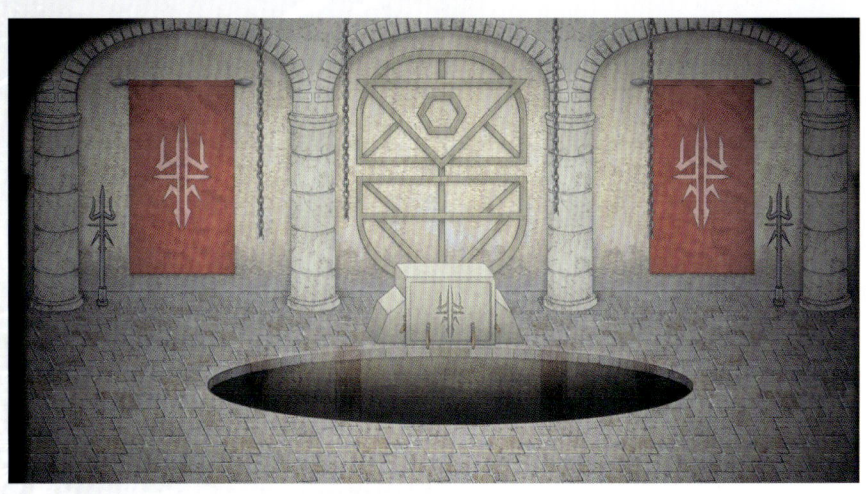

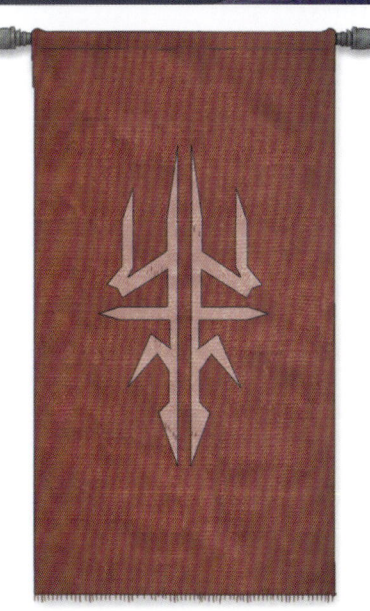

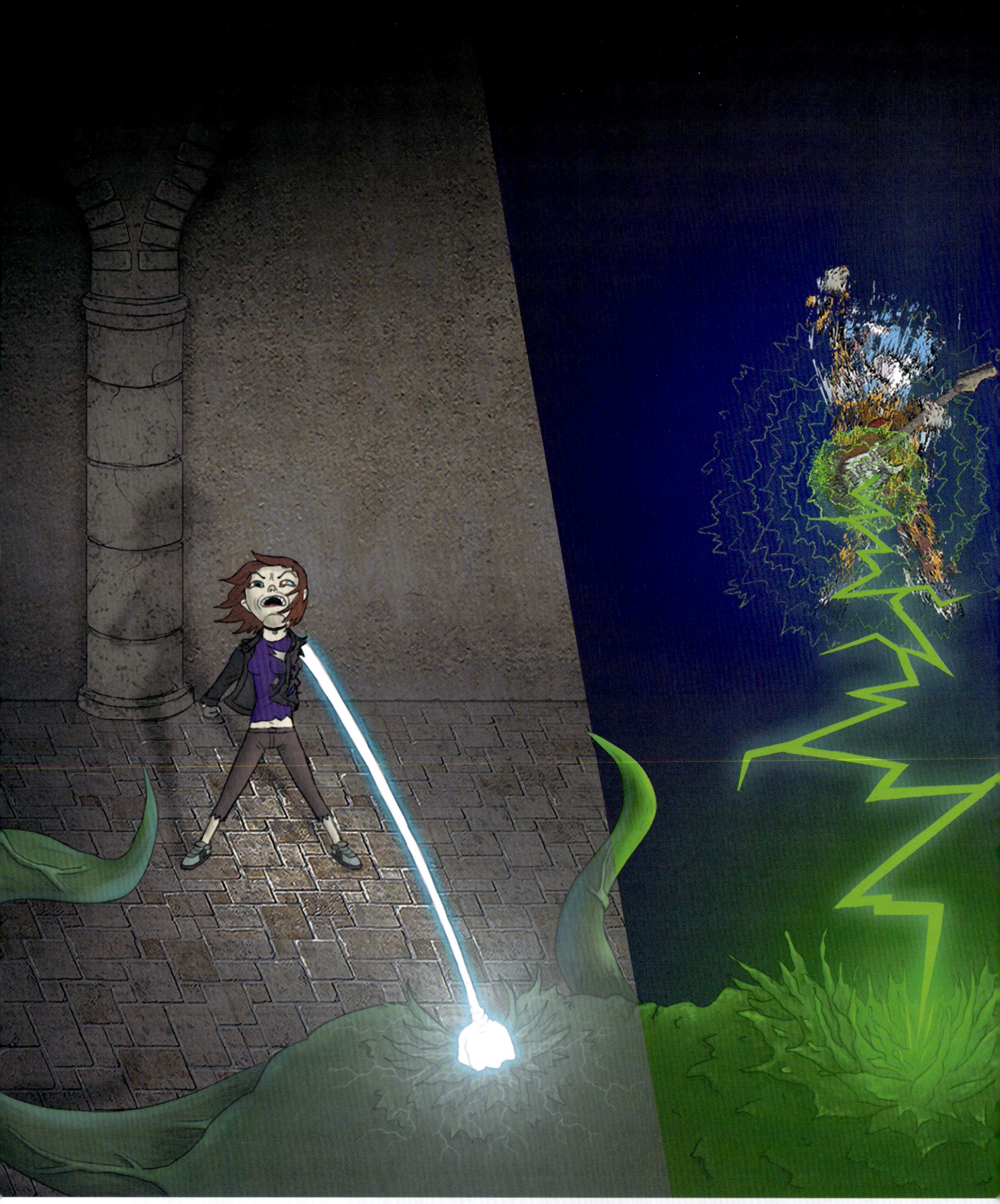

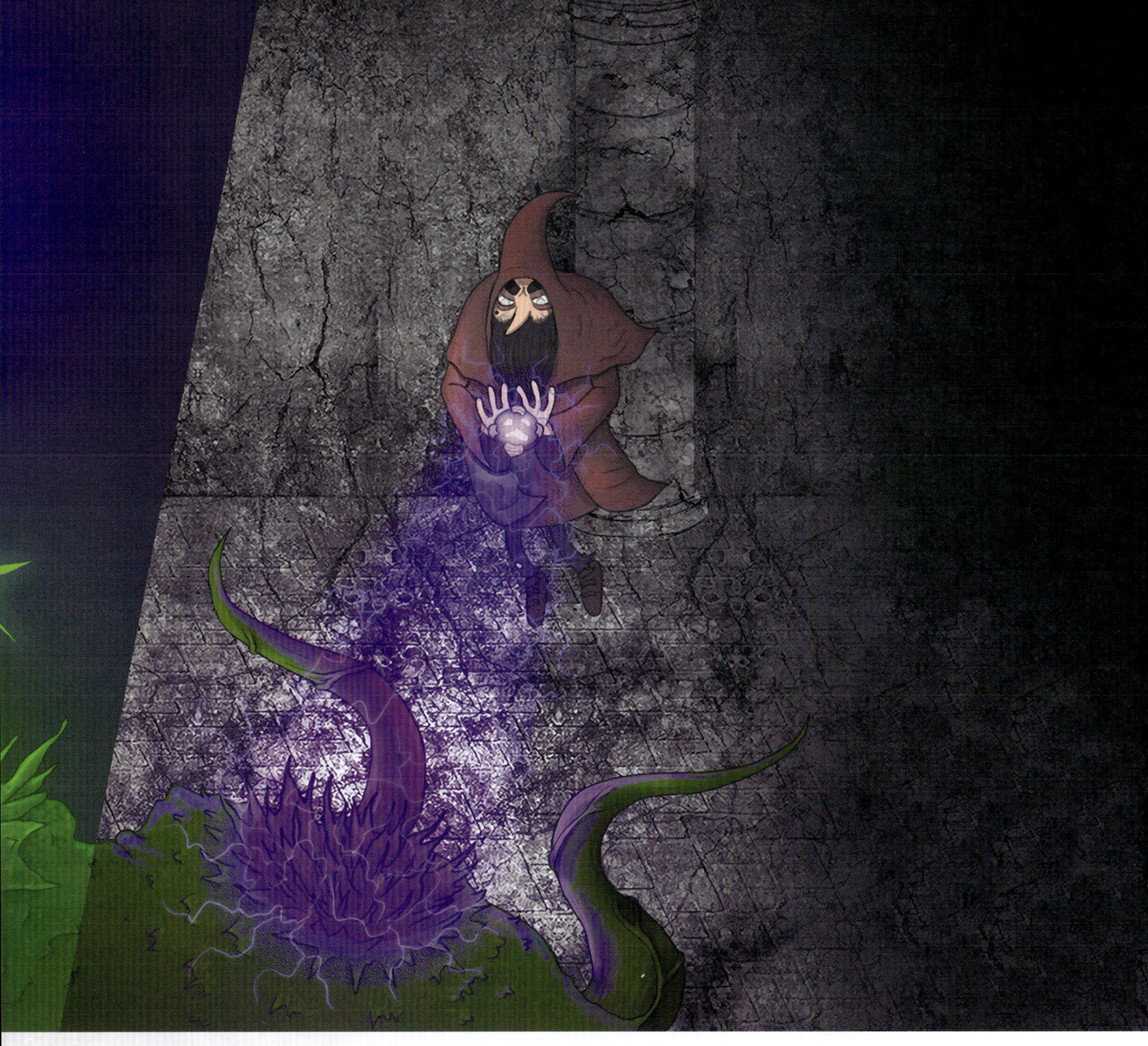

NOCKFELL HIGH SCHOOL

A modest school for the children of Nockfell and some surrounding towns.

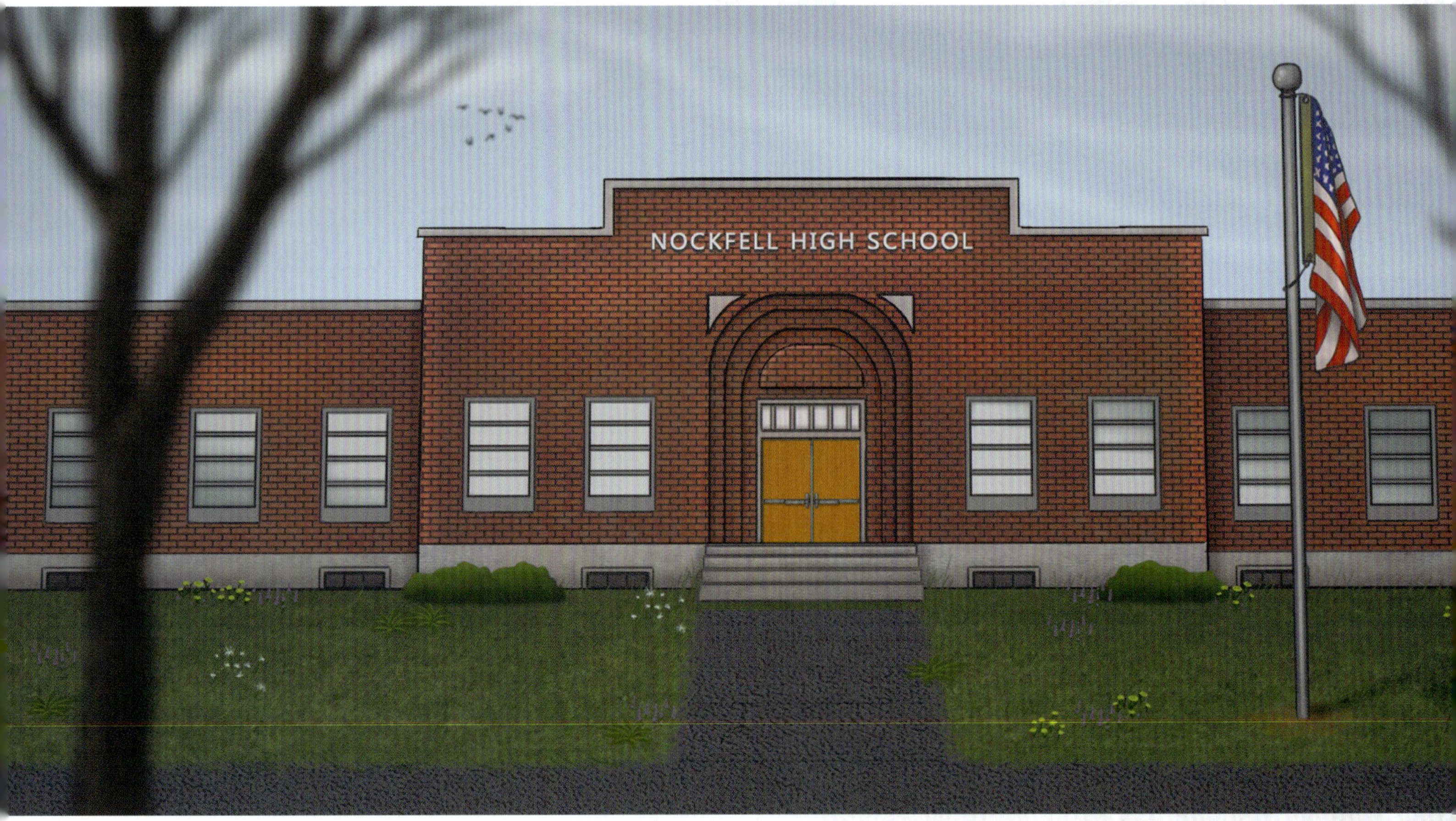

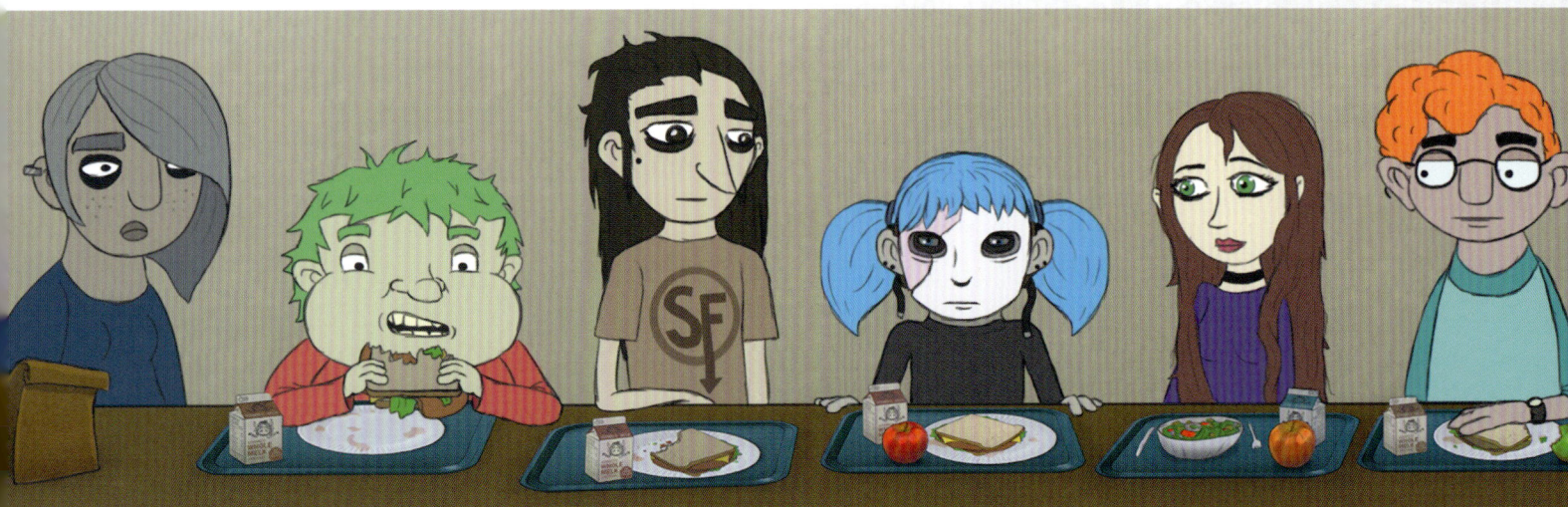

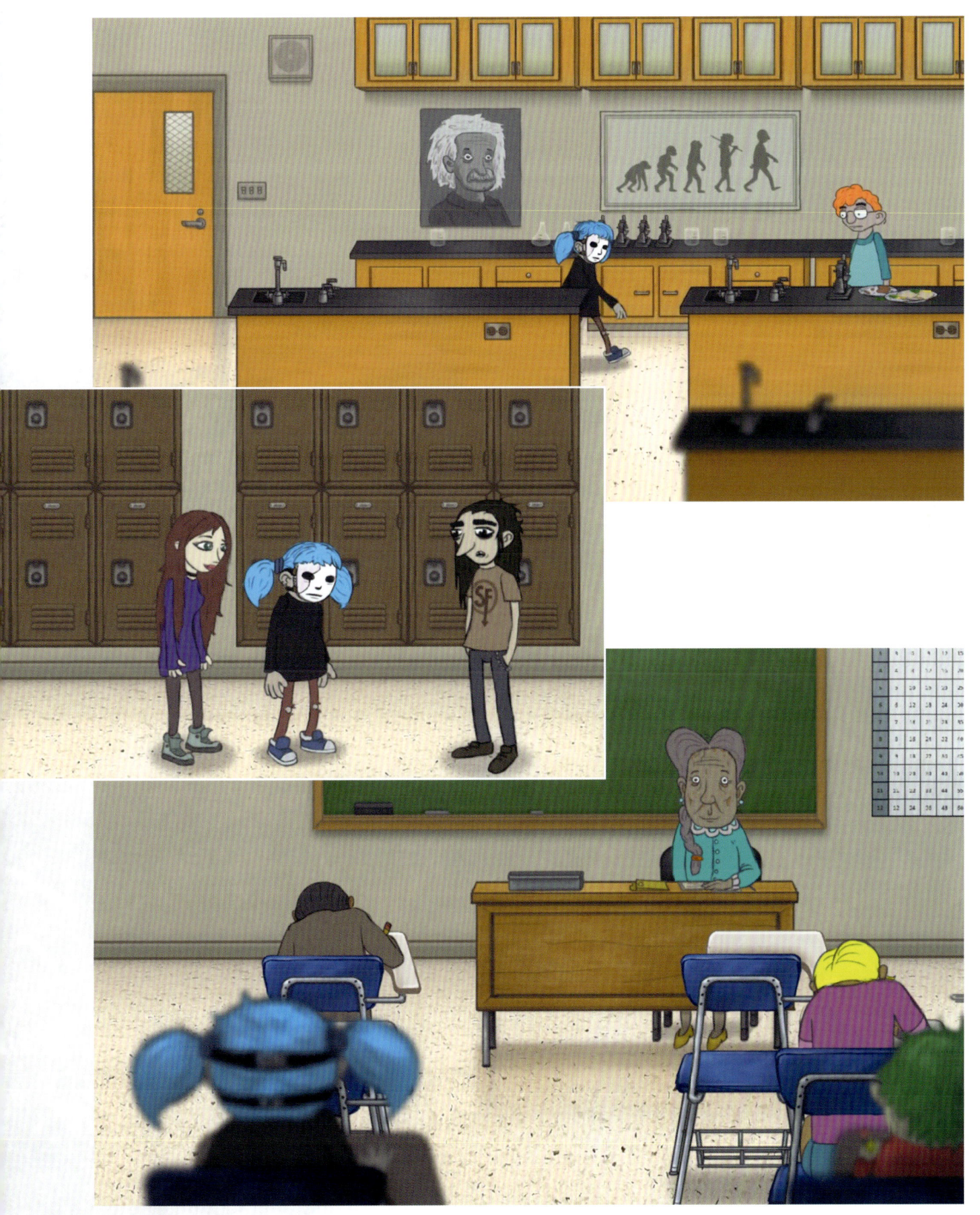

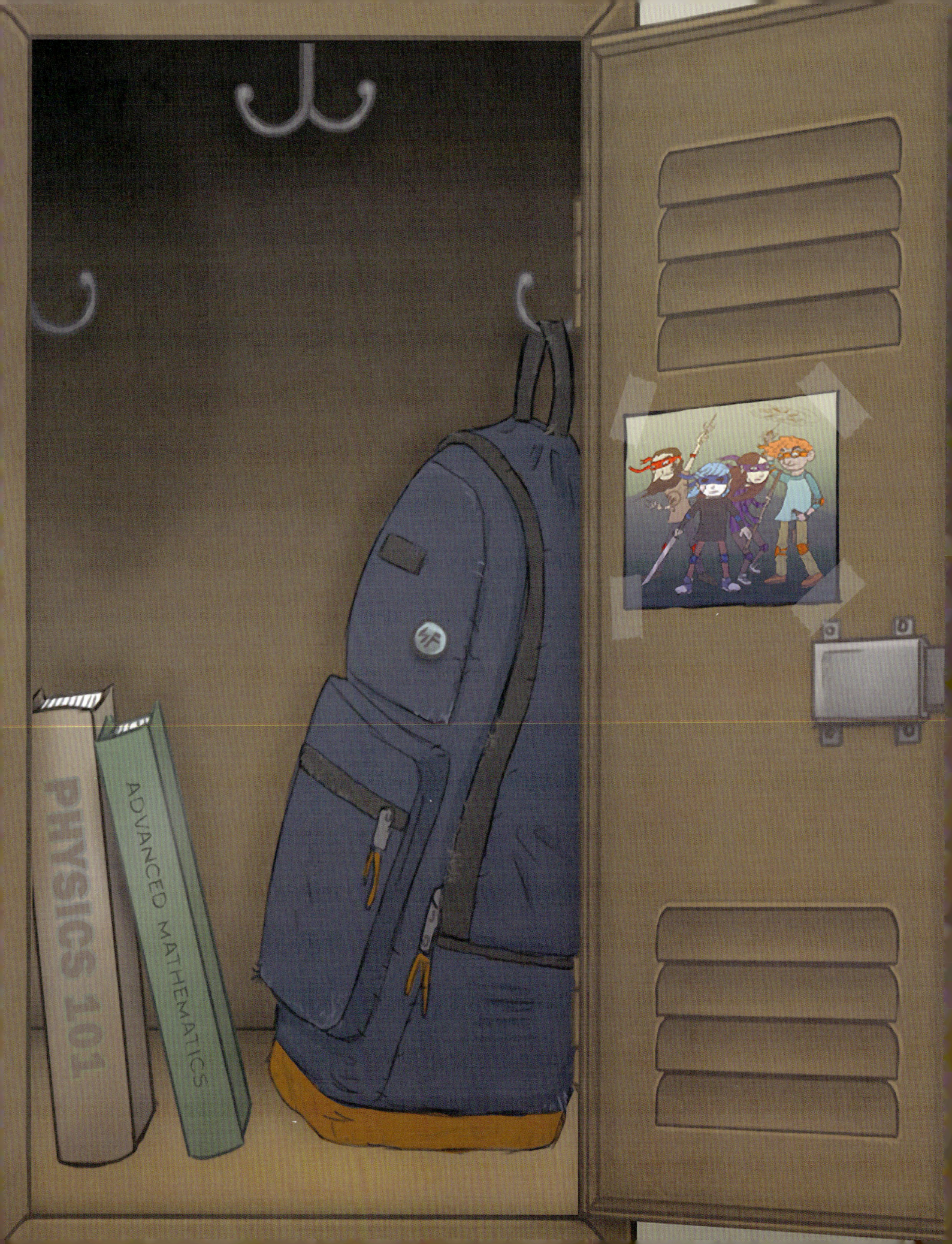

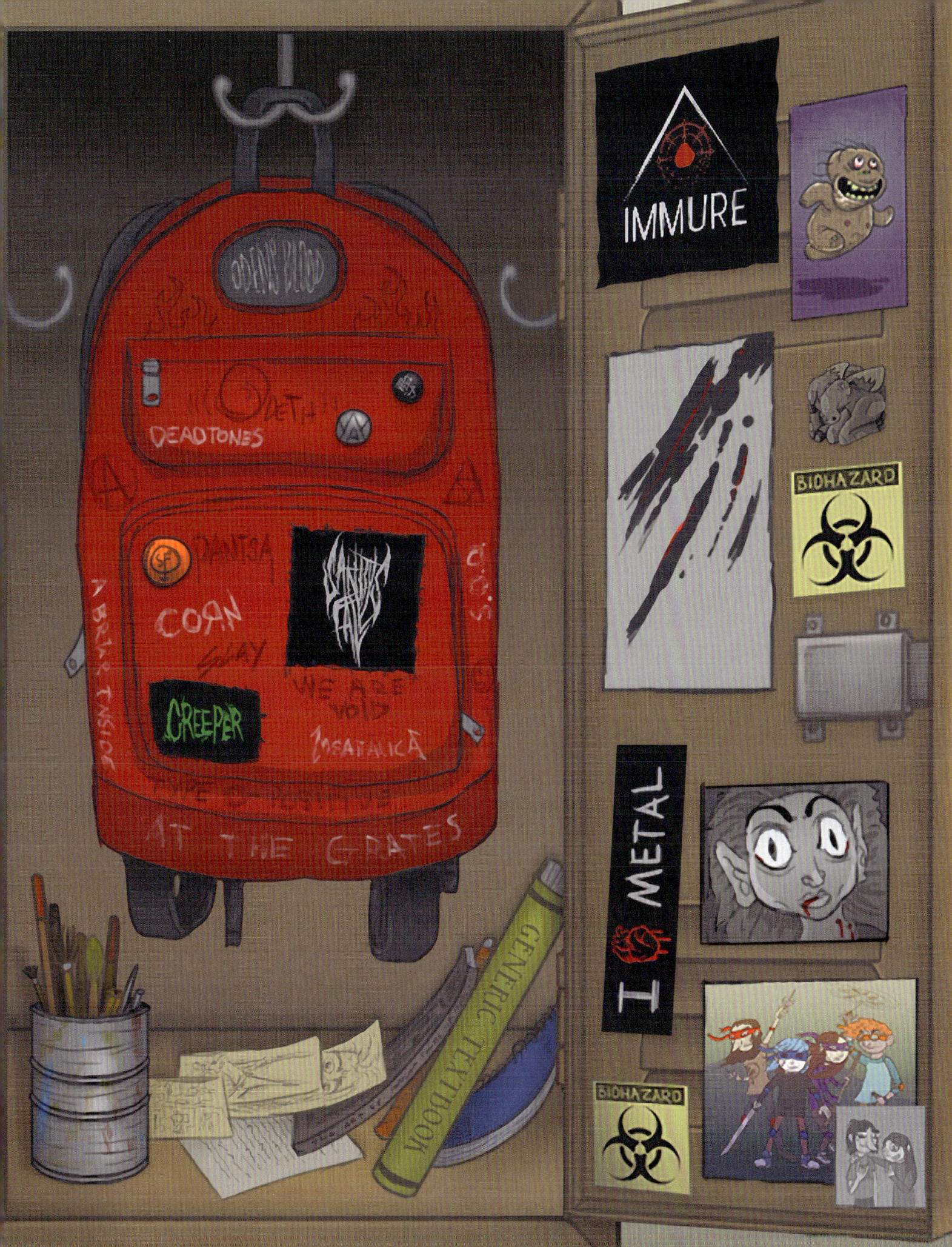

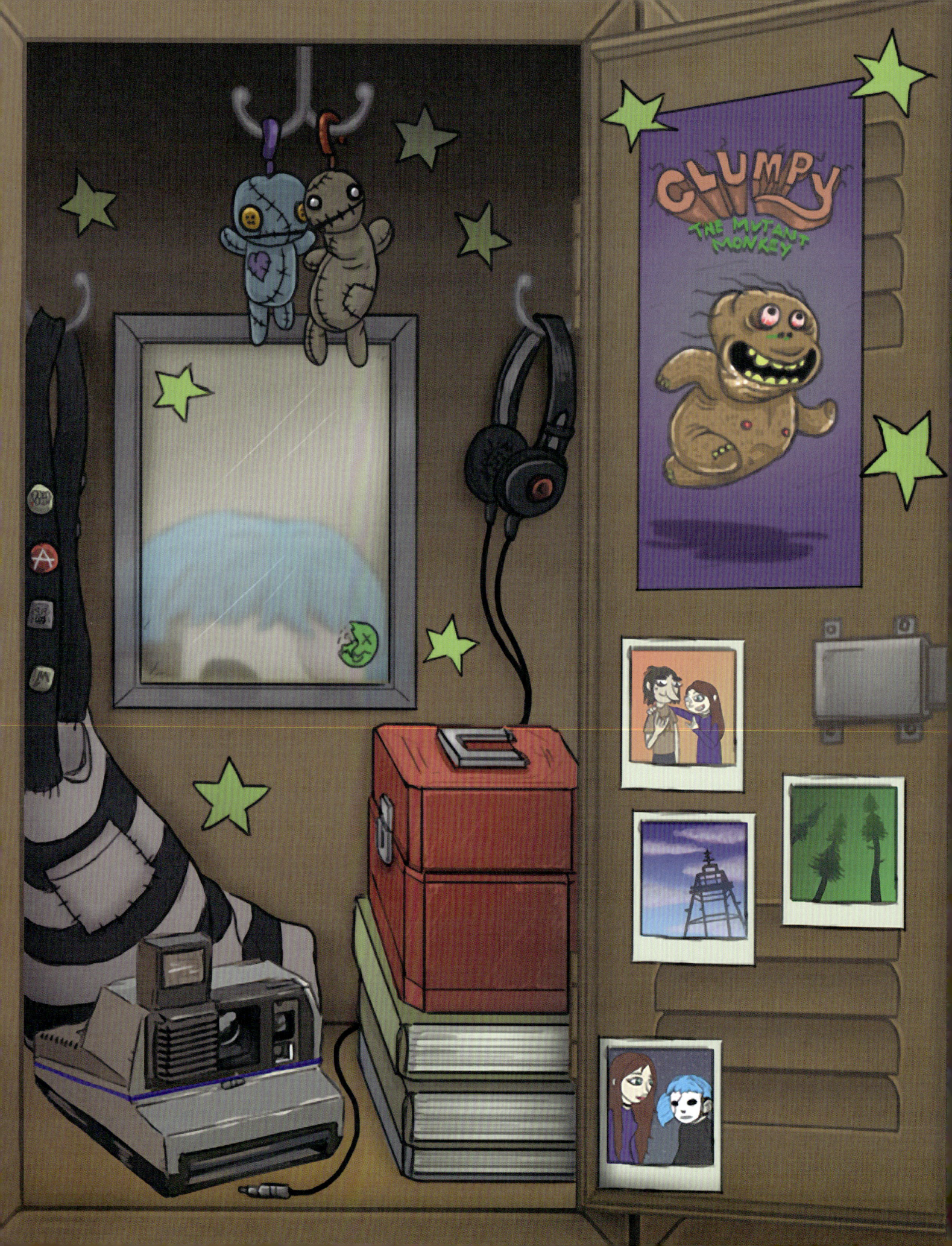

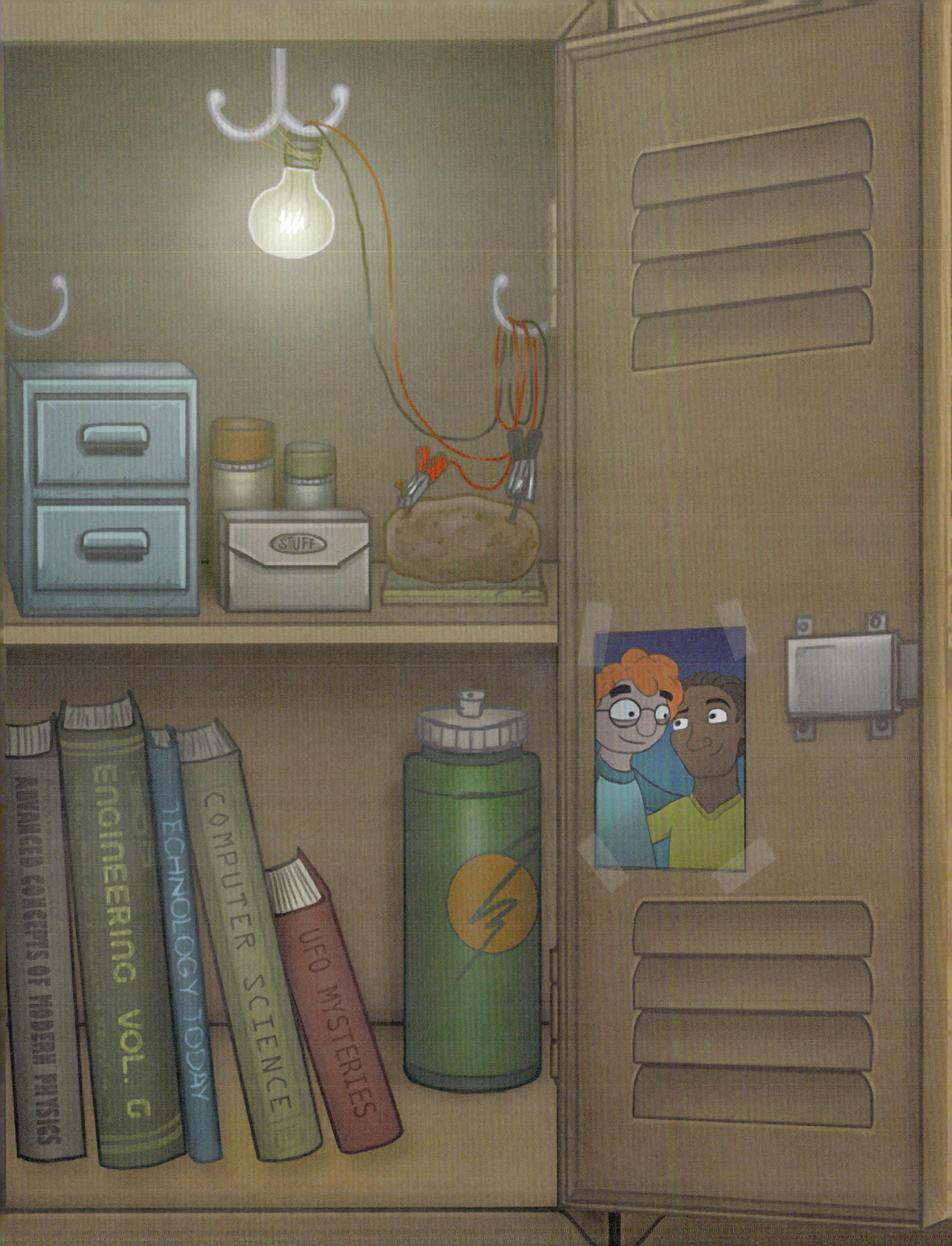

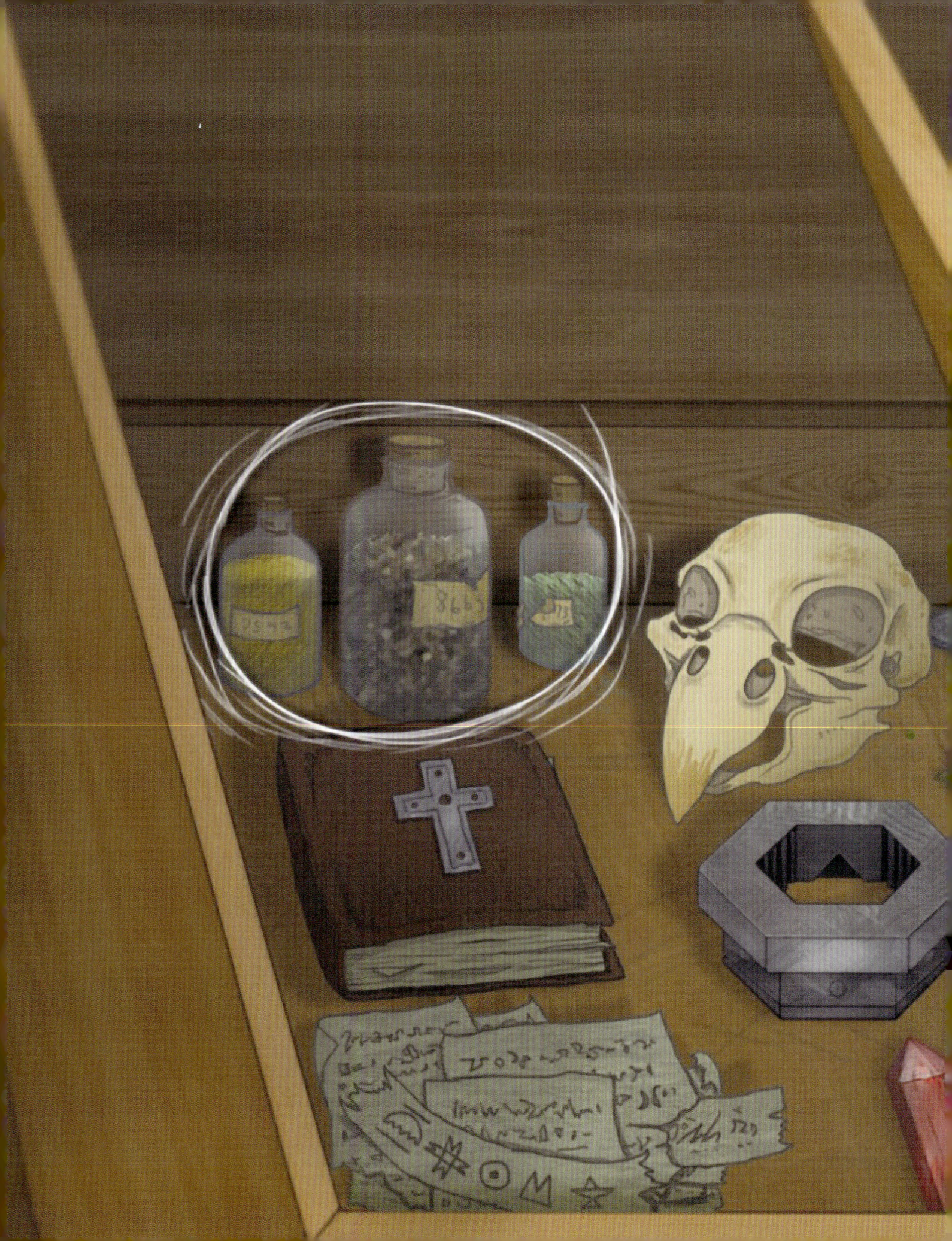

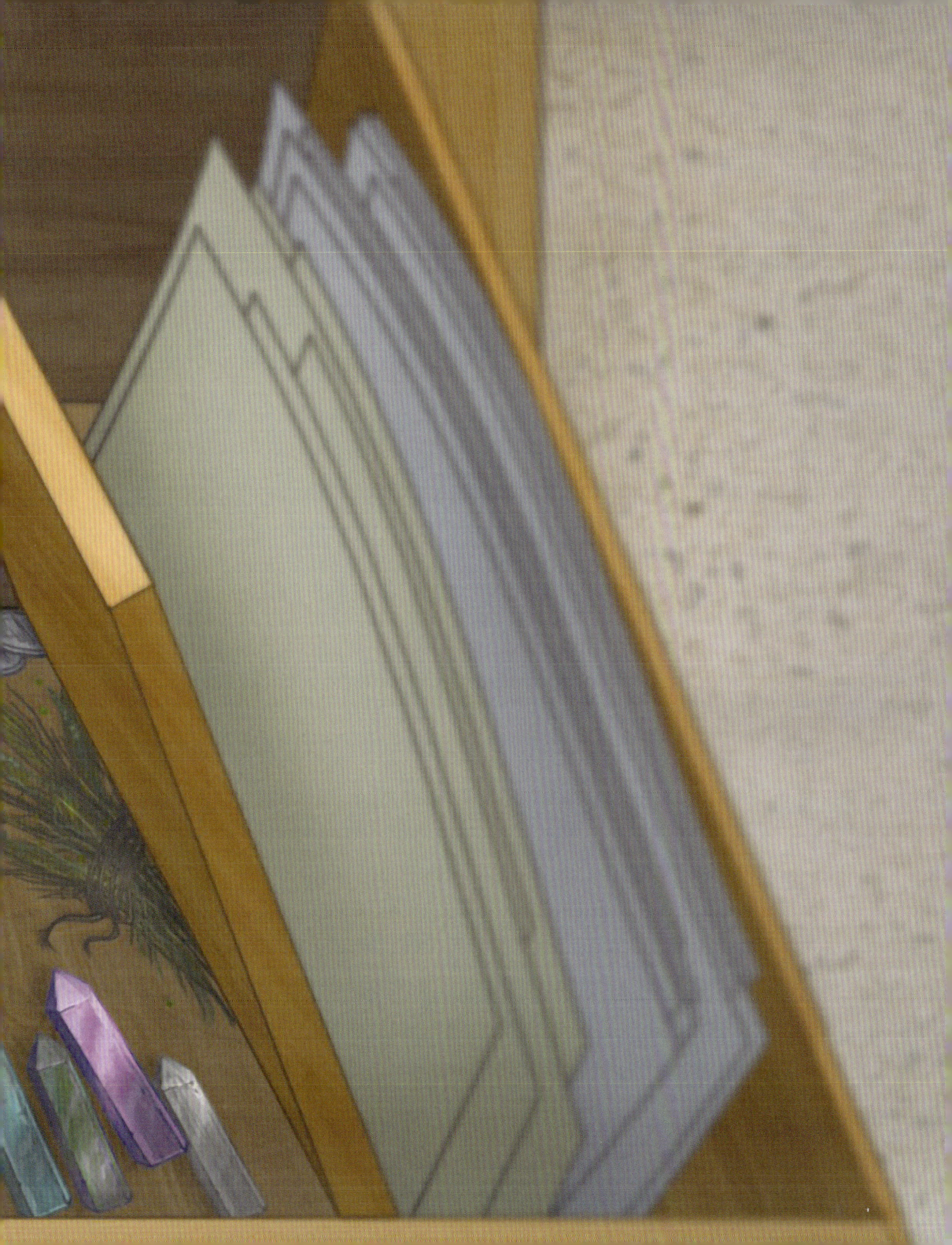

THE HOUSE

The house where Todd and Sal lived and conducted their paranormal research.

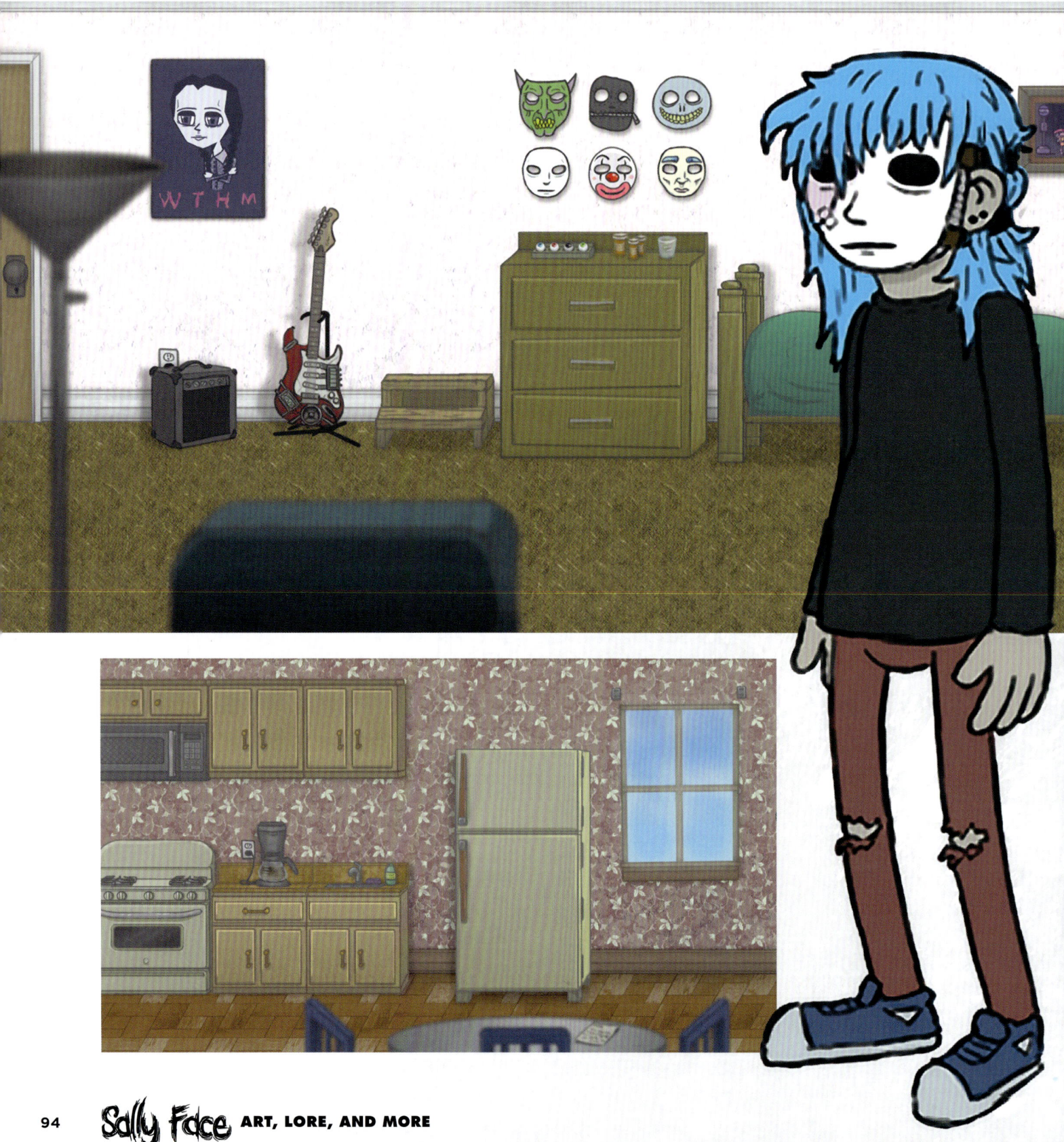

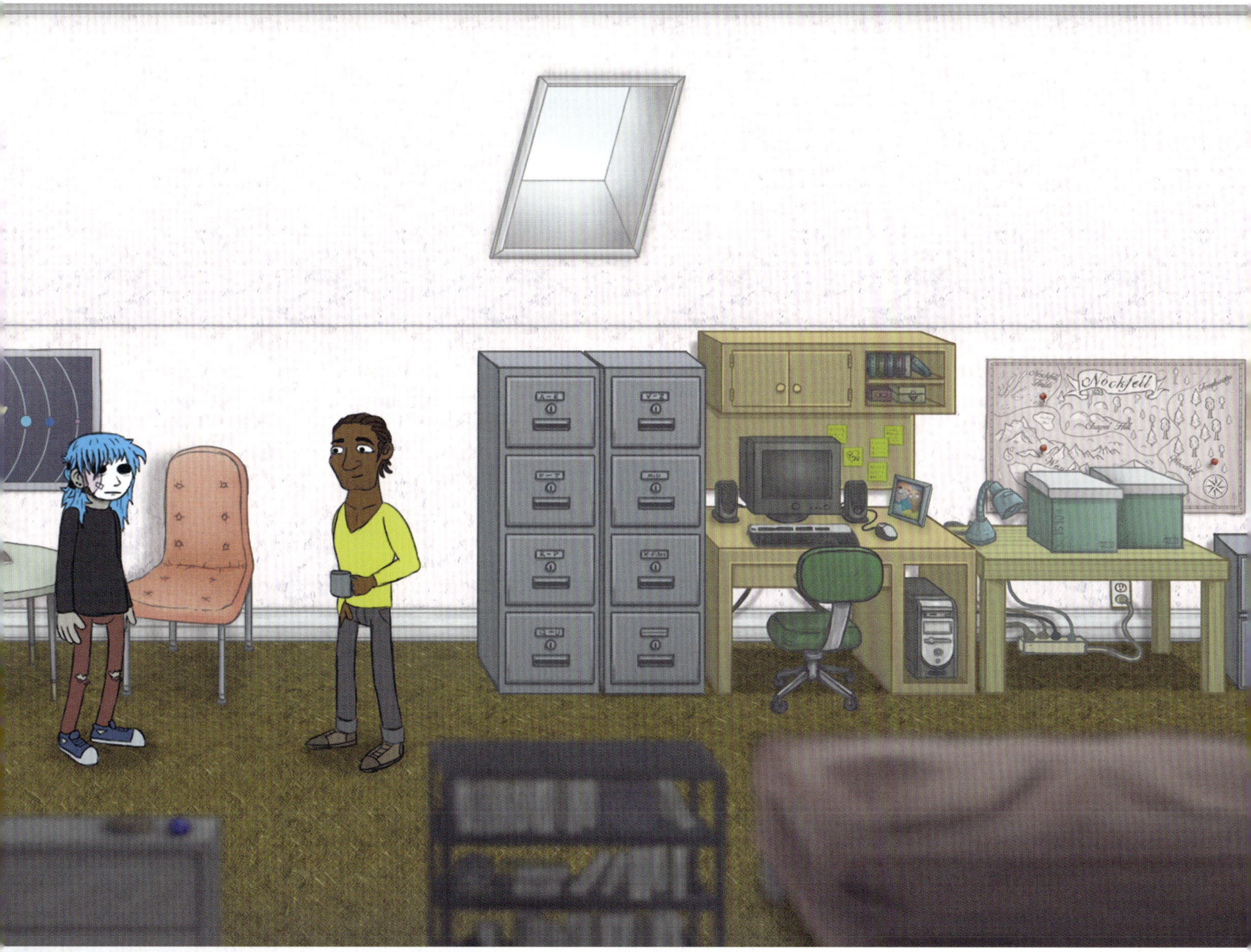

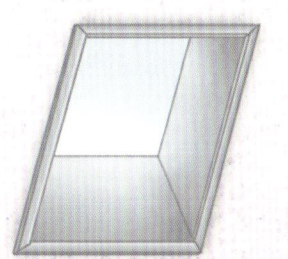

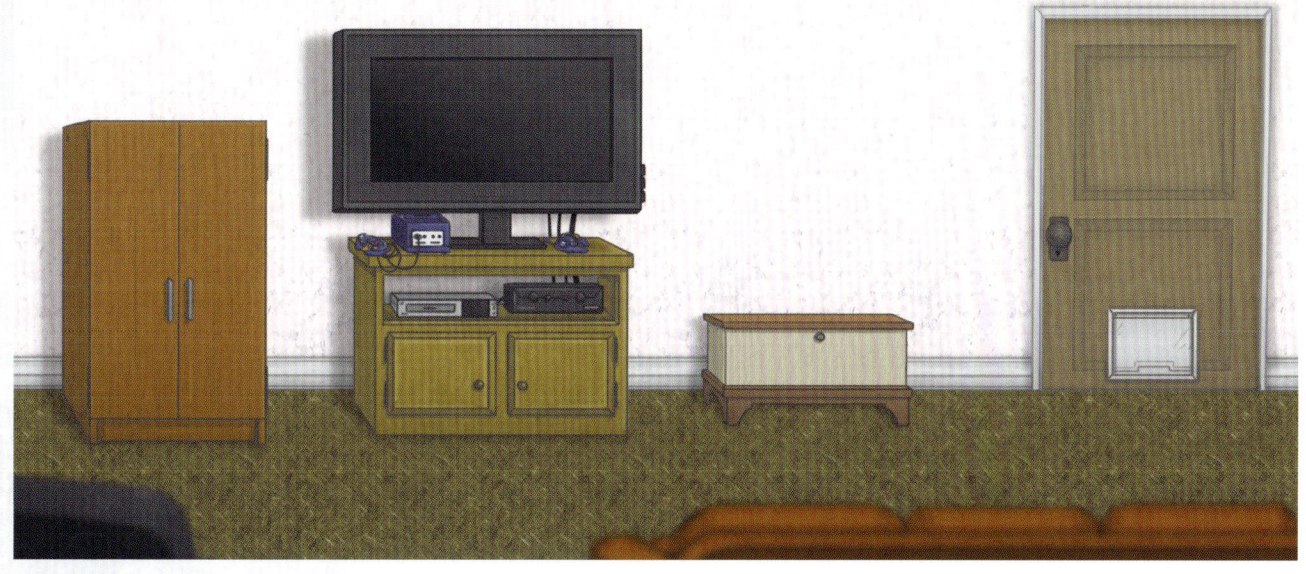

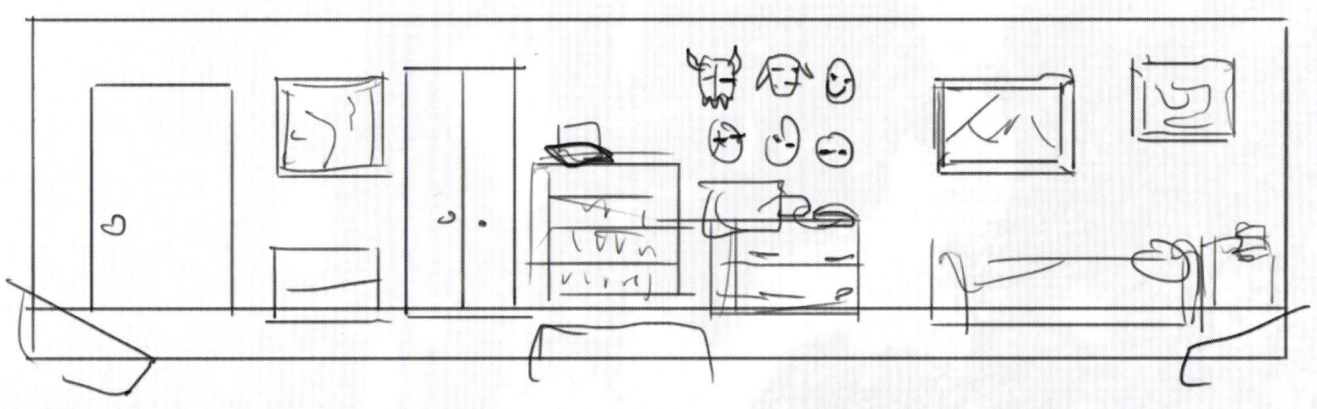

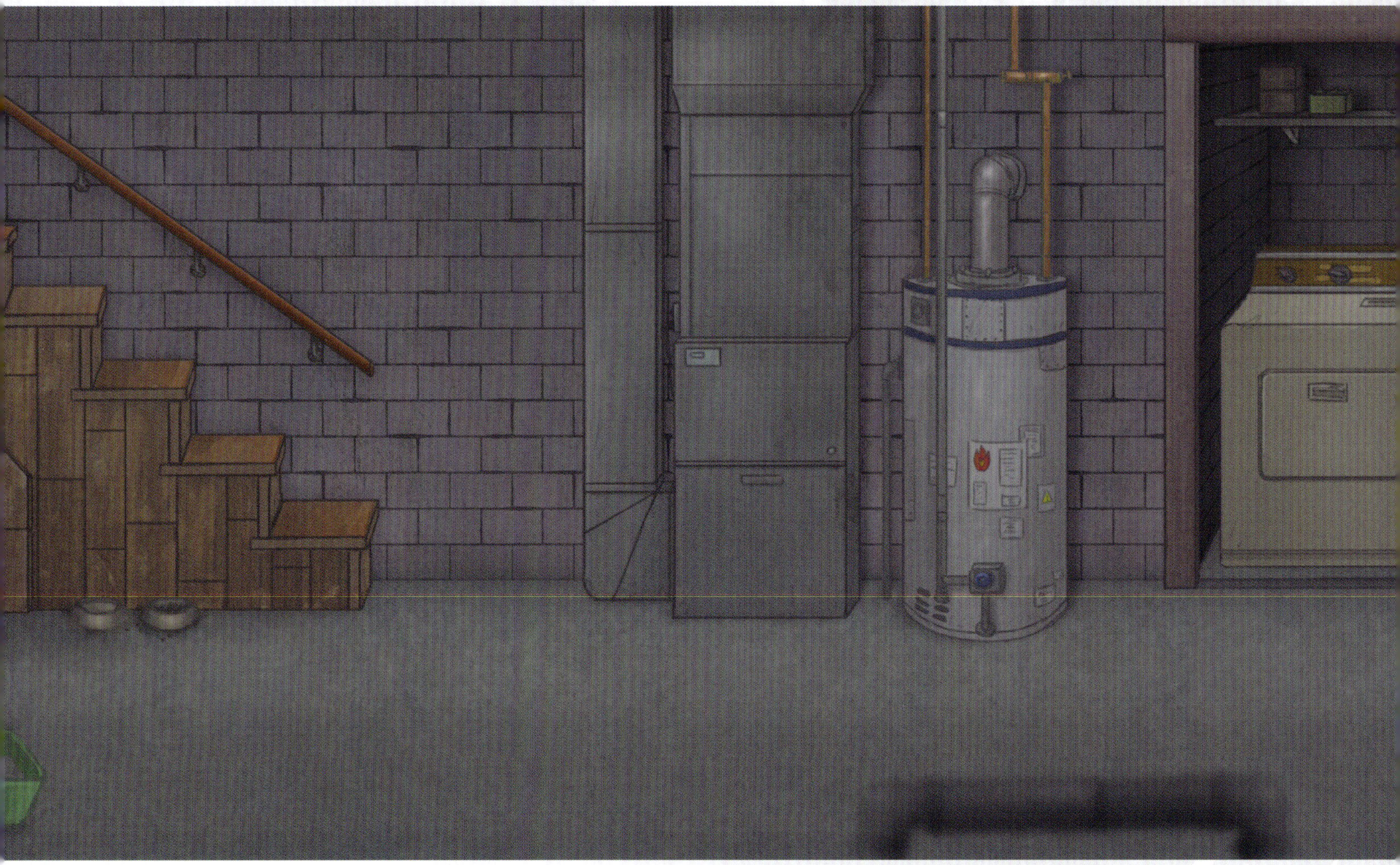

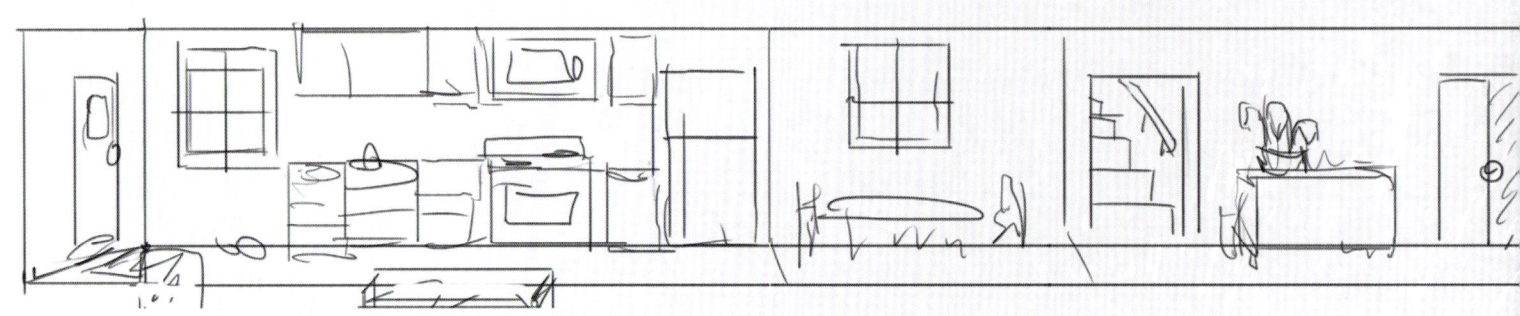

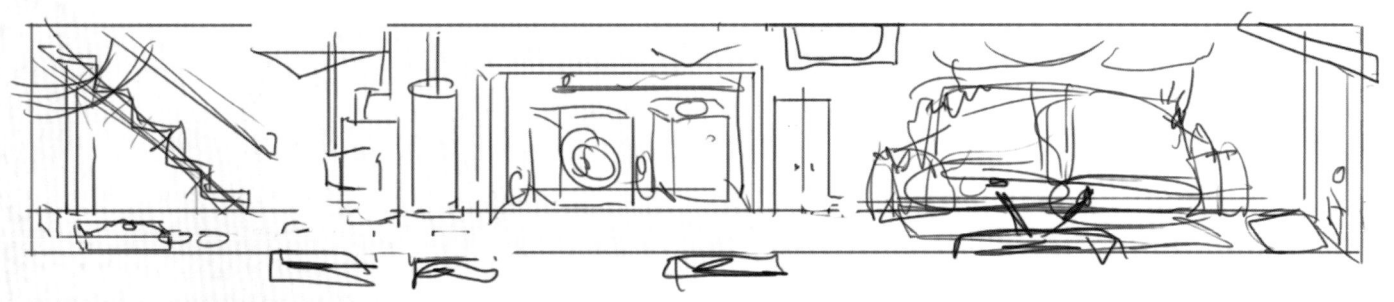

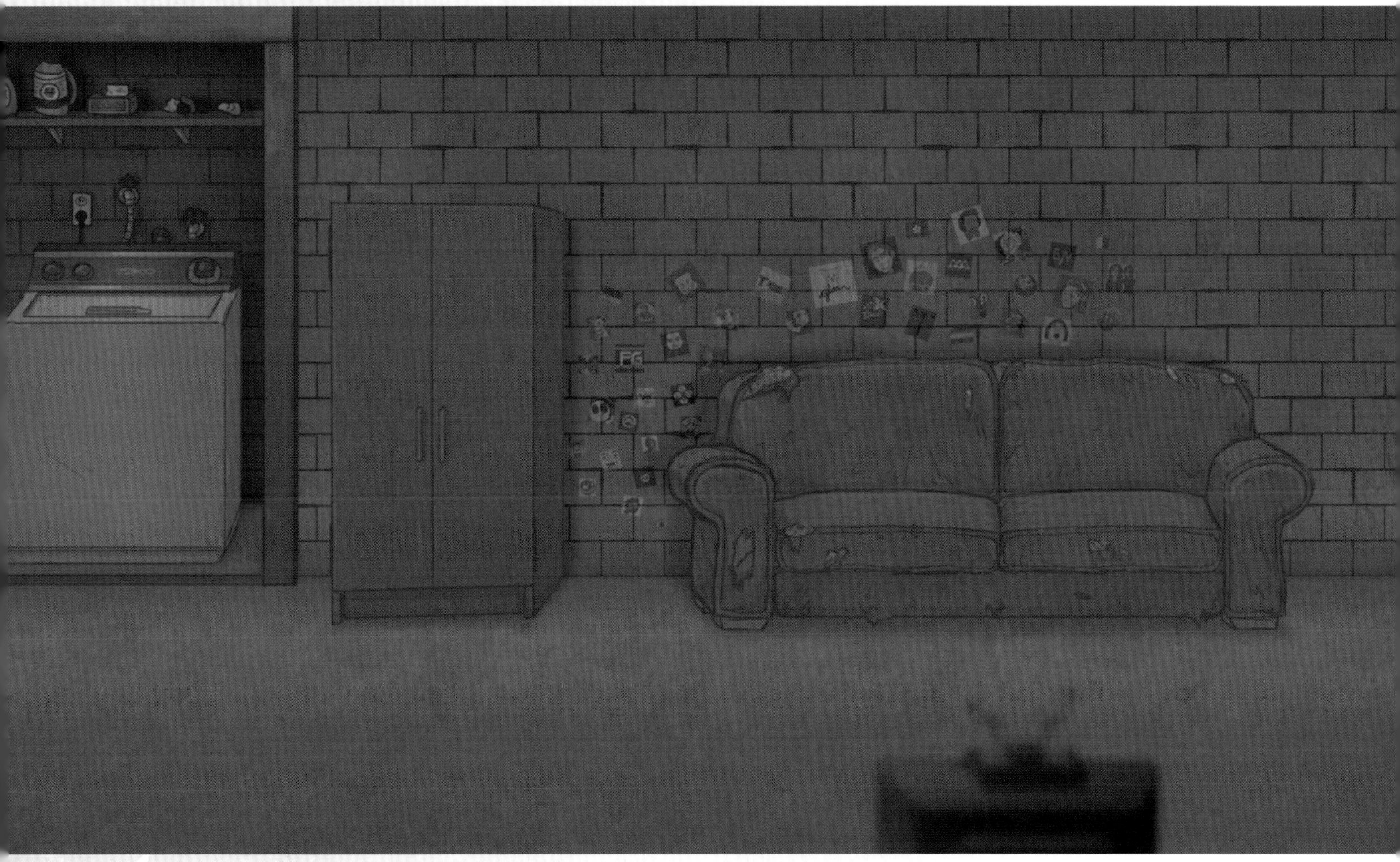

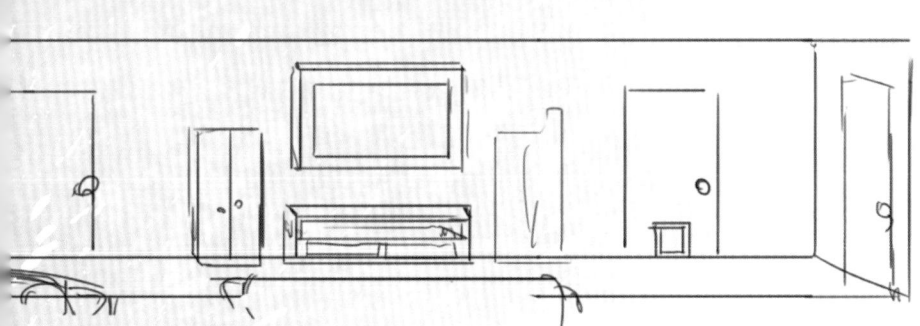

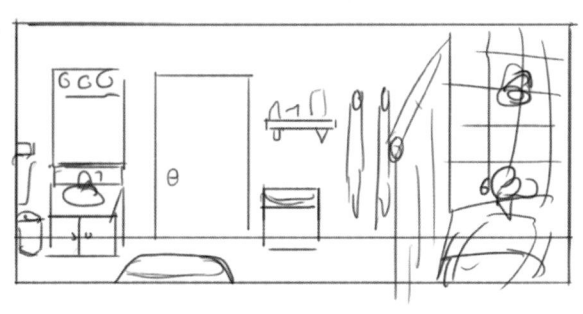

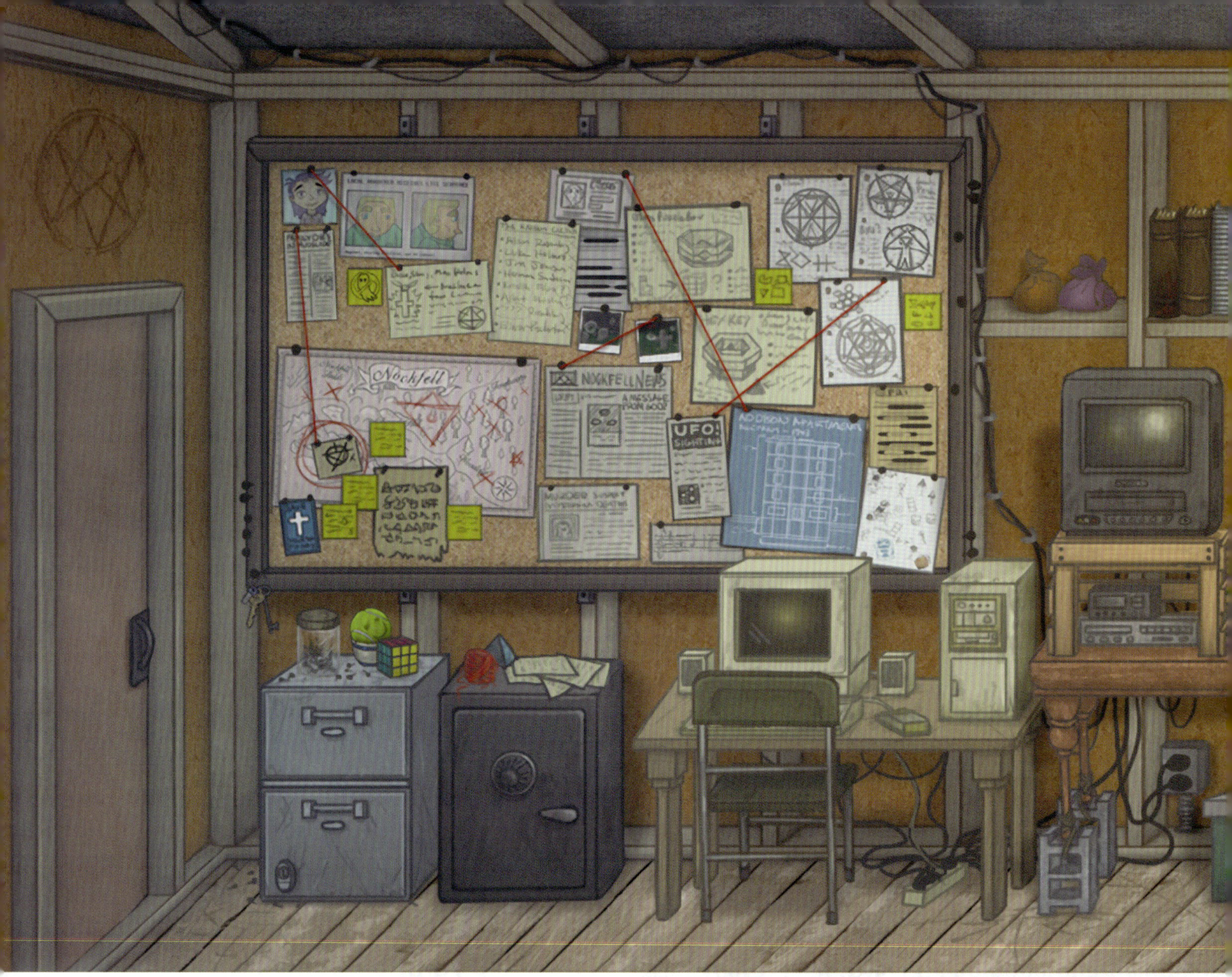

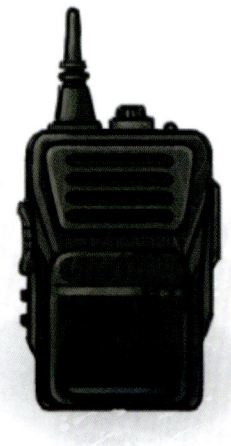

THE SHED

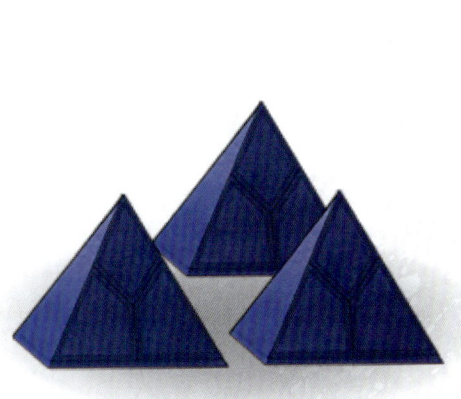

3 PYRAMIDS OF ASINTMAH

WALKIE TALKIE

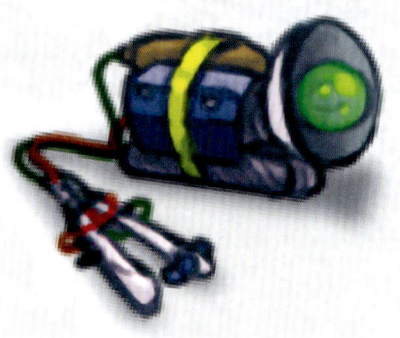

GHOST BLASTER

Sally Face ART, LORE, AND MORE

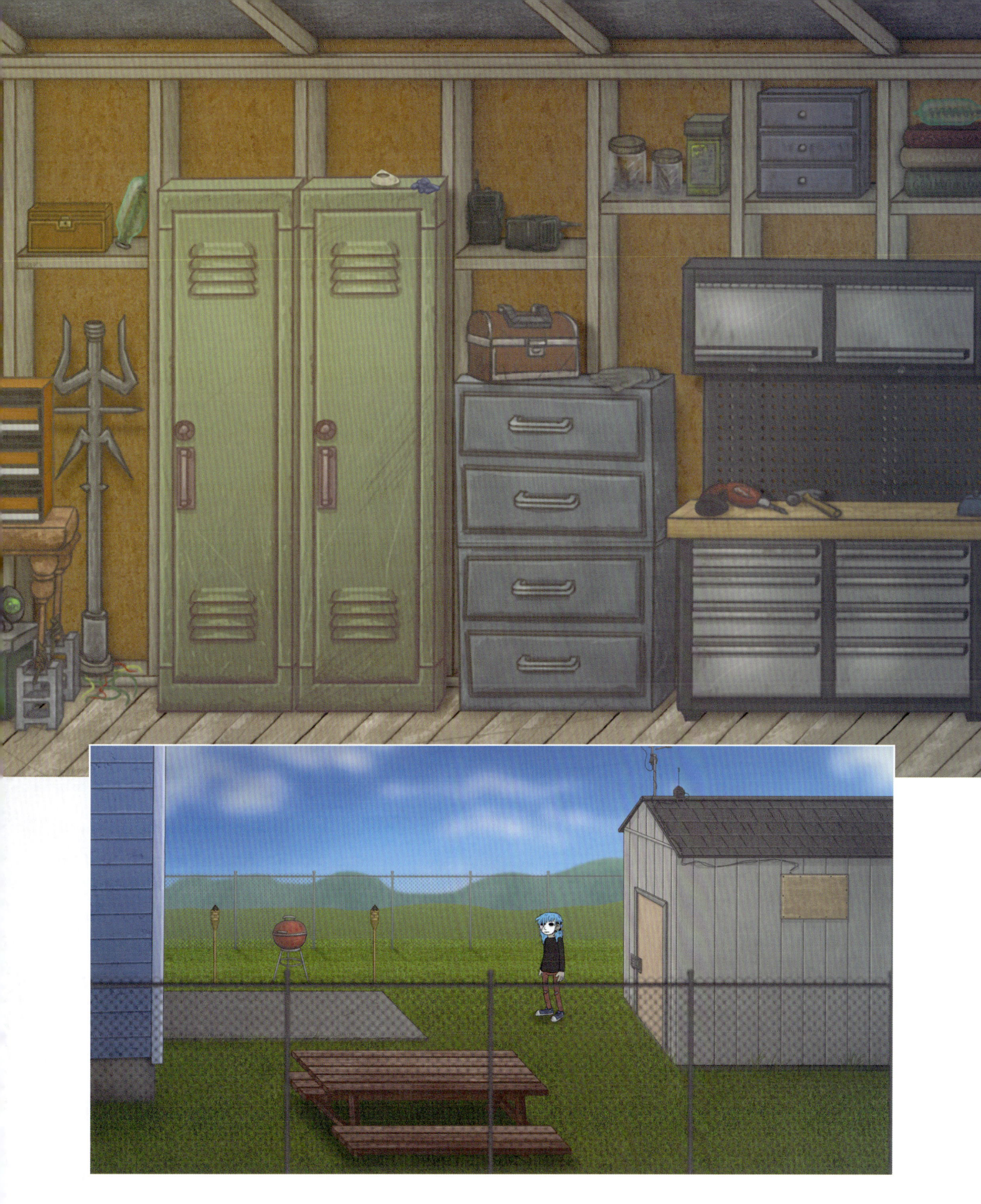

NOCKFELL COURTHOUSE

Across the road from the Nockfell Jail sits the local courthouse.

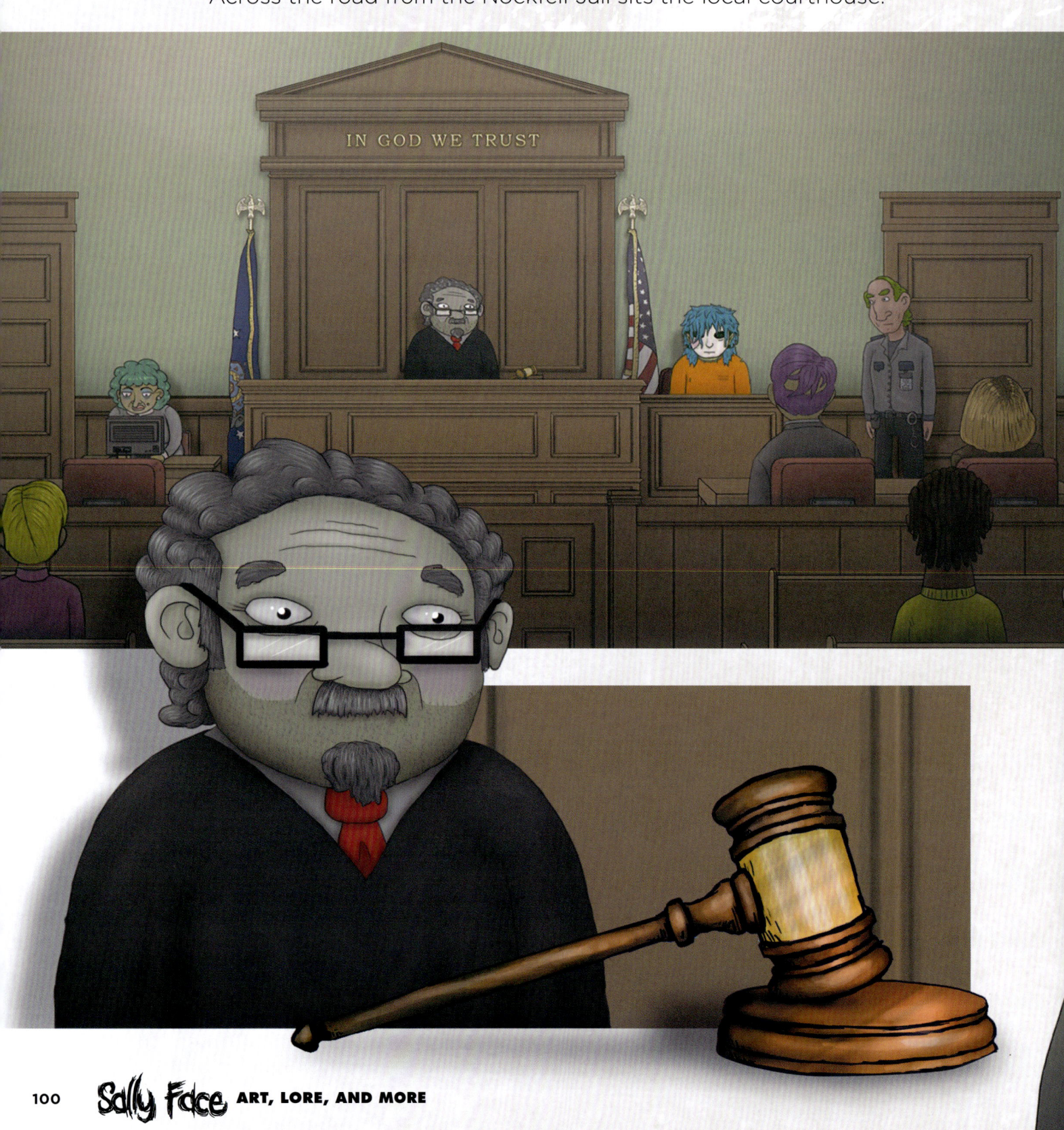

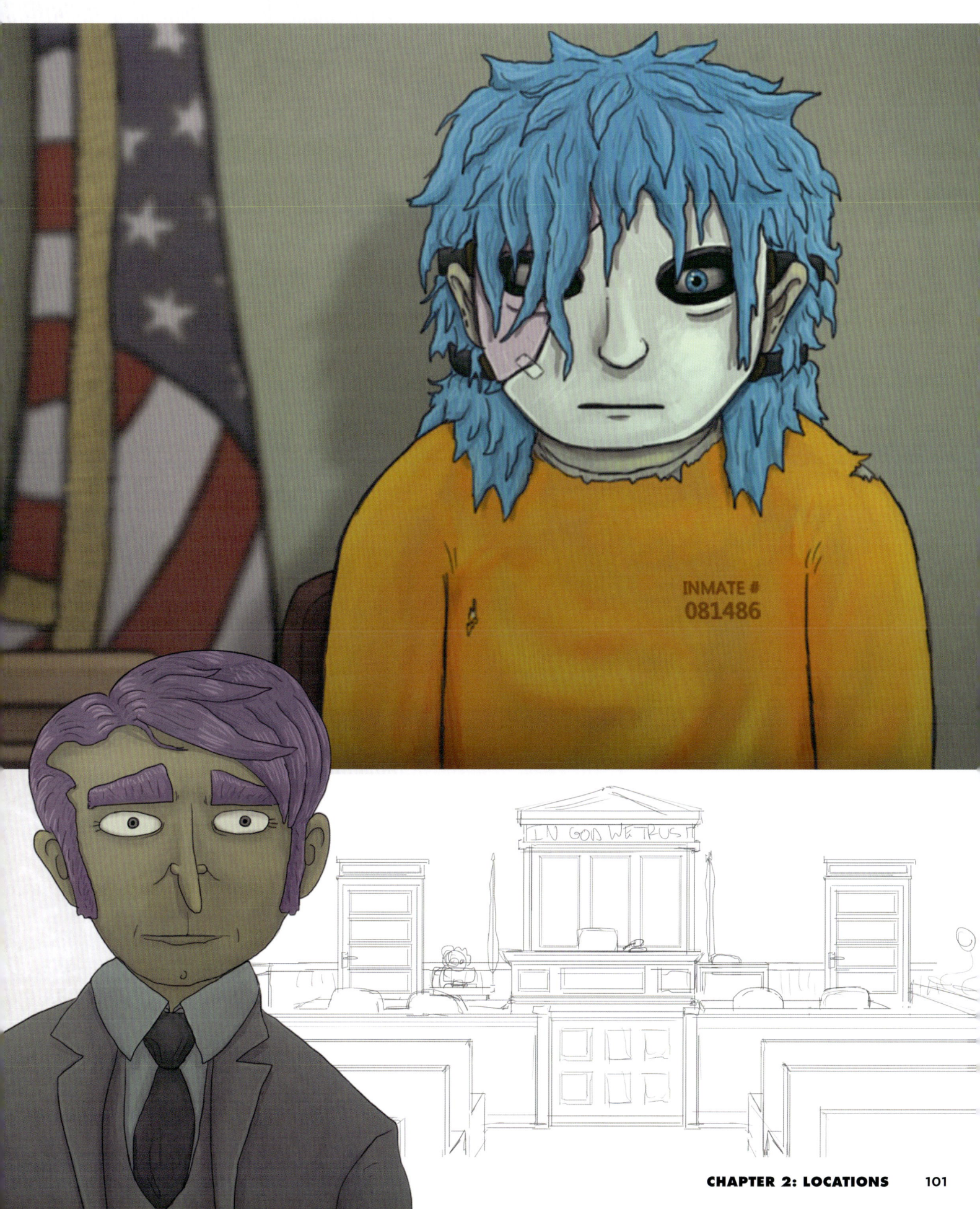

NOCKFELL JAIL

A small correctional facility on the outskirts of town.

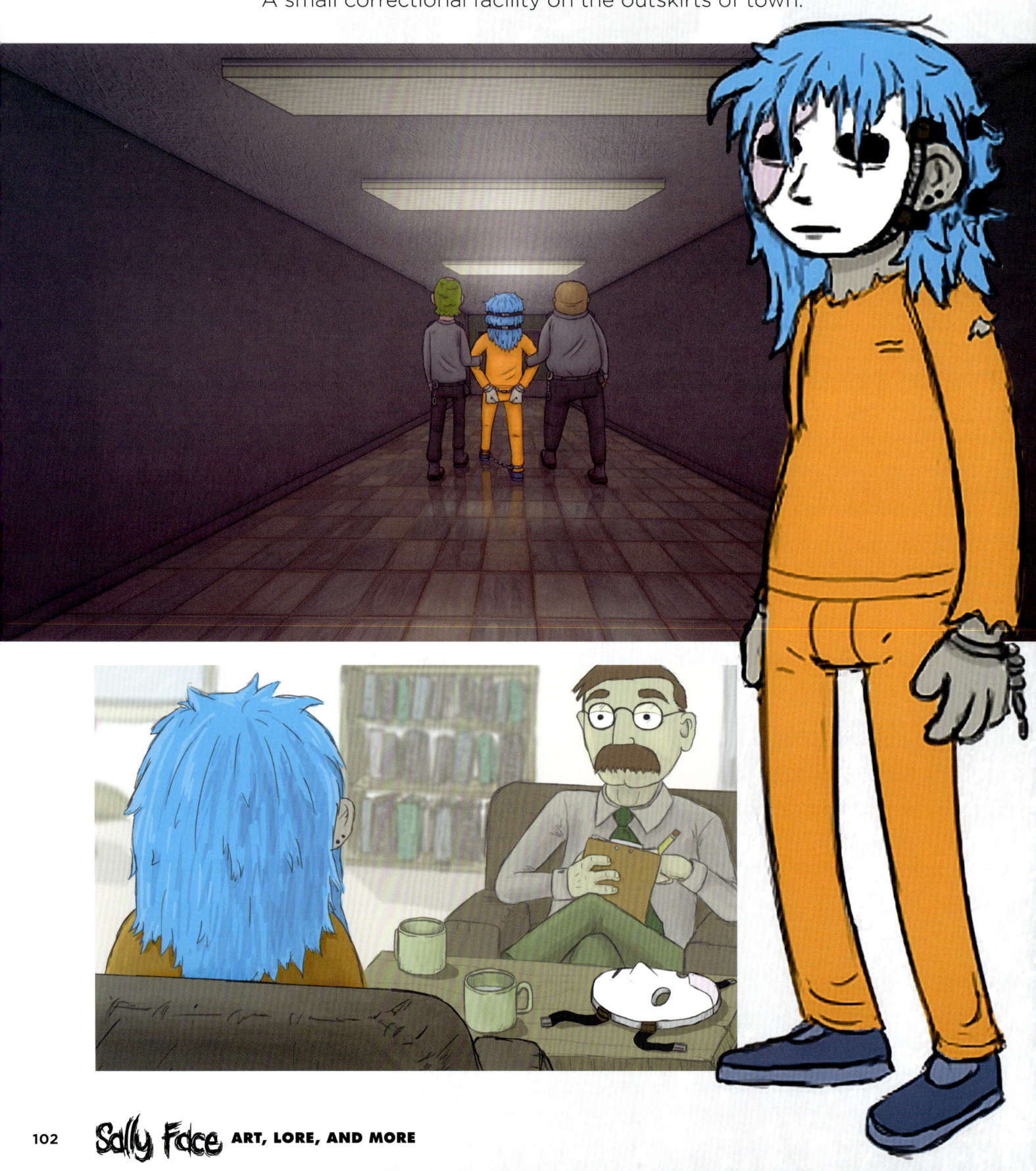

Sally Face ART, LORE, AND MORE

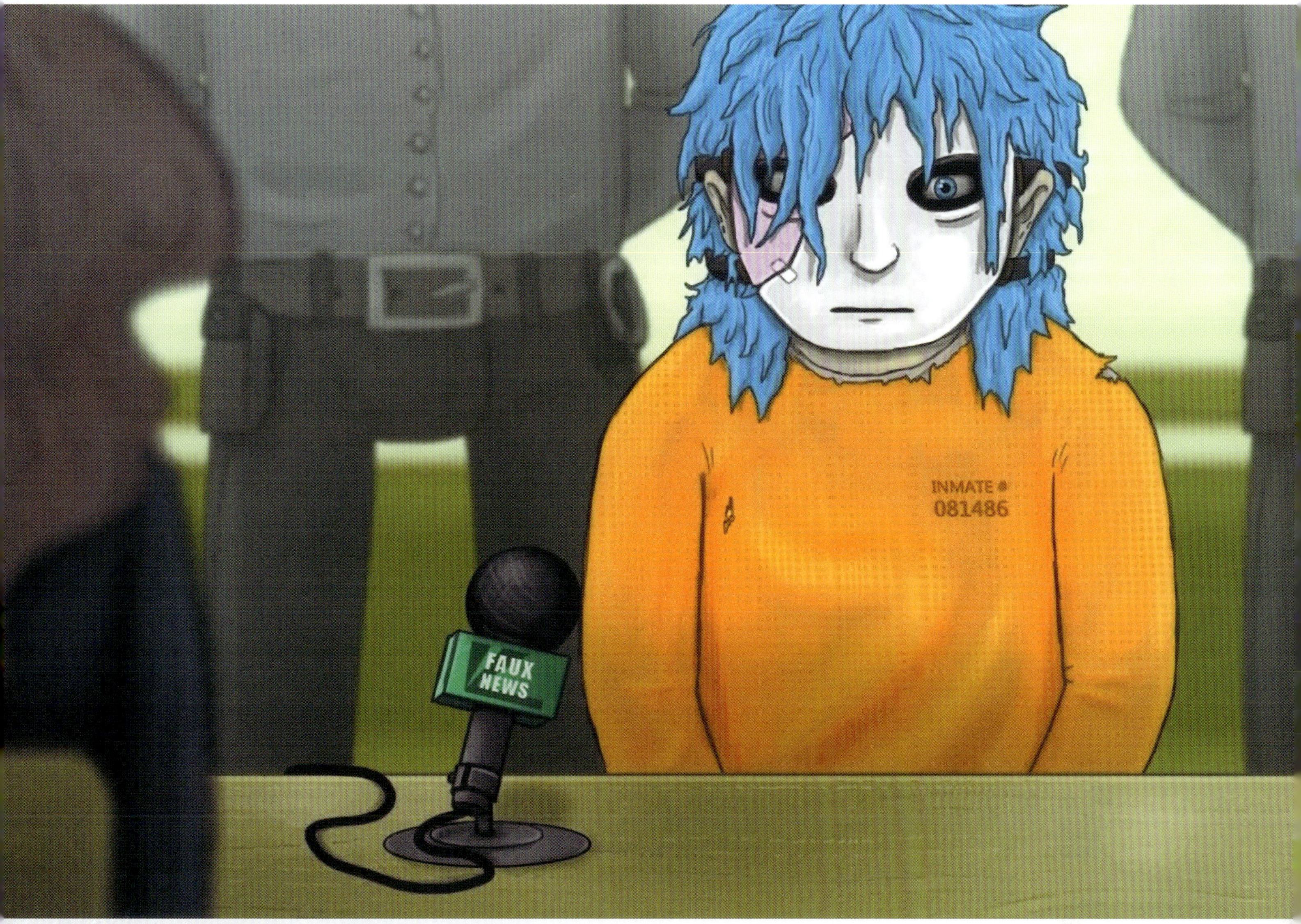

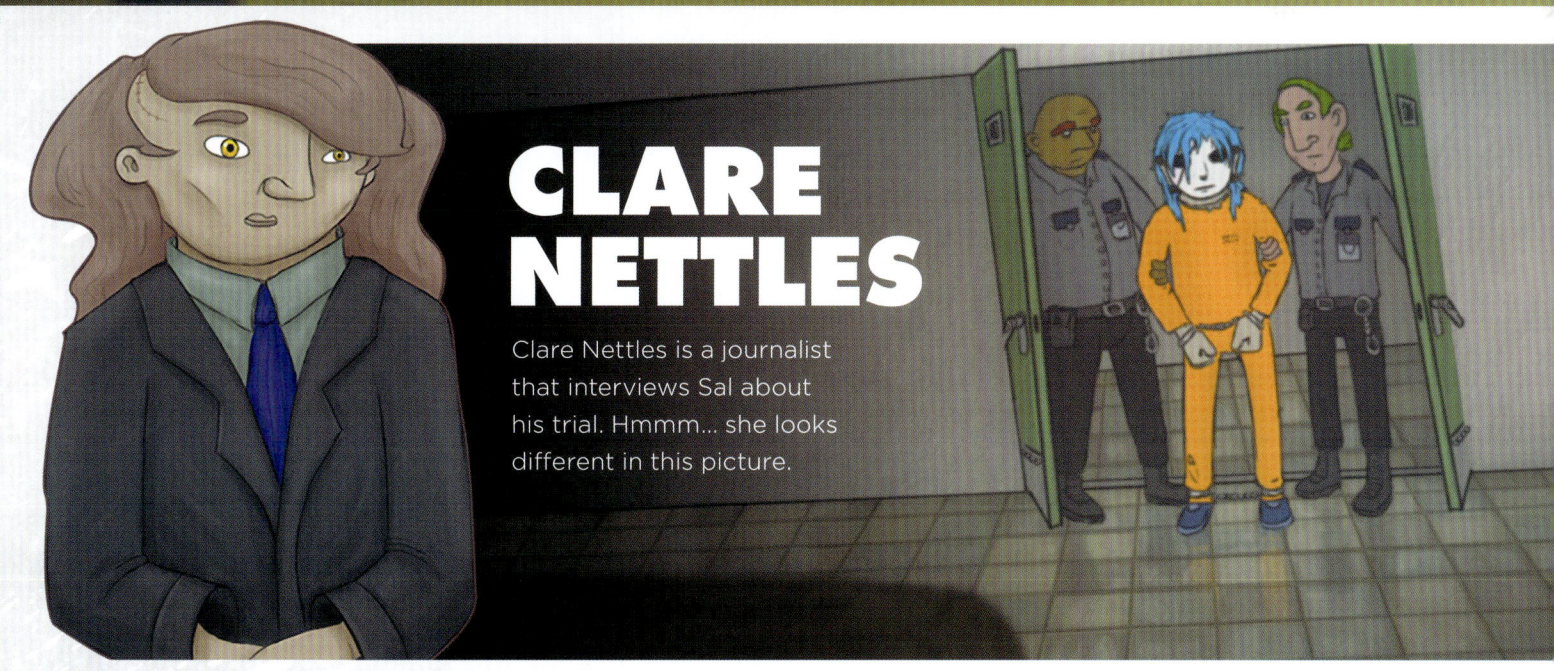

CLARE NETTLES

Clare Nettles is a journalist that interviews Sal about his trial. Hmmm... she looks different in this picture.

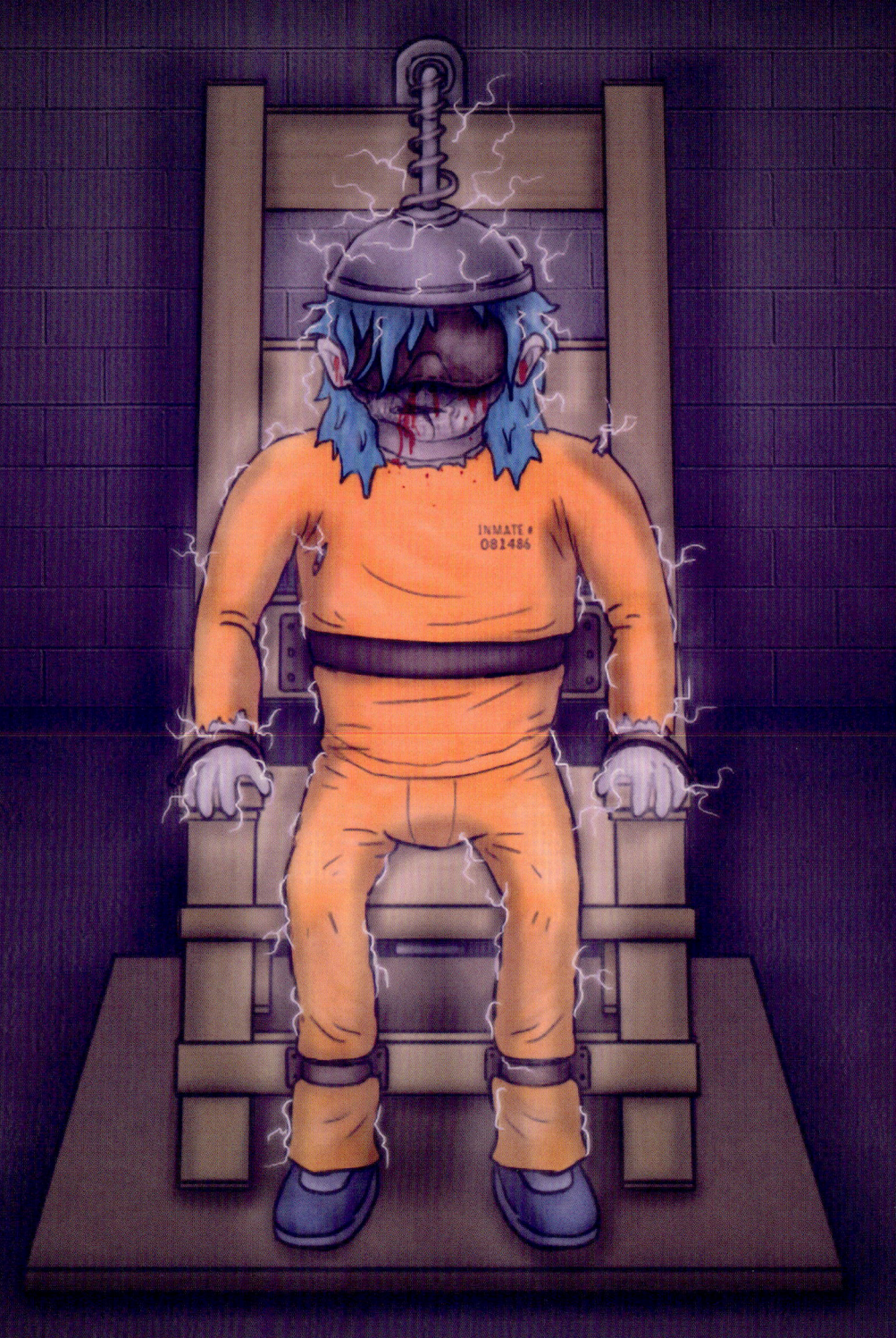

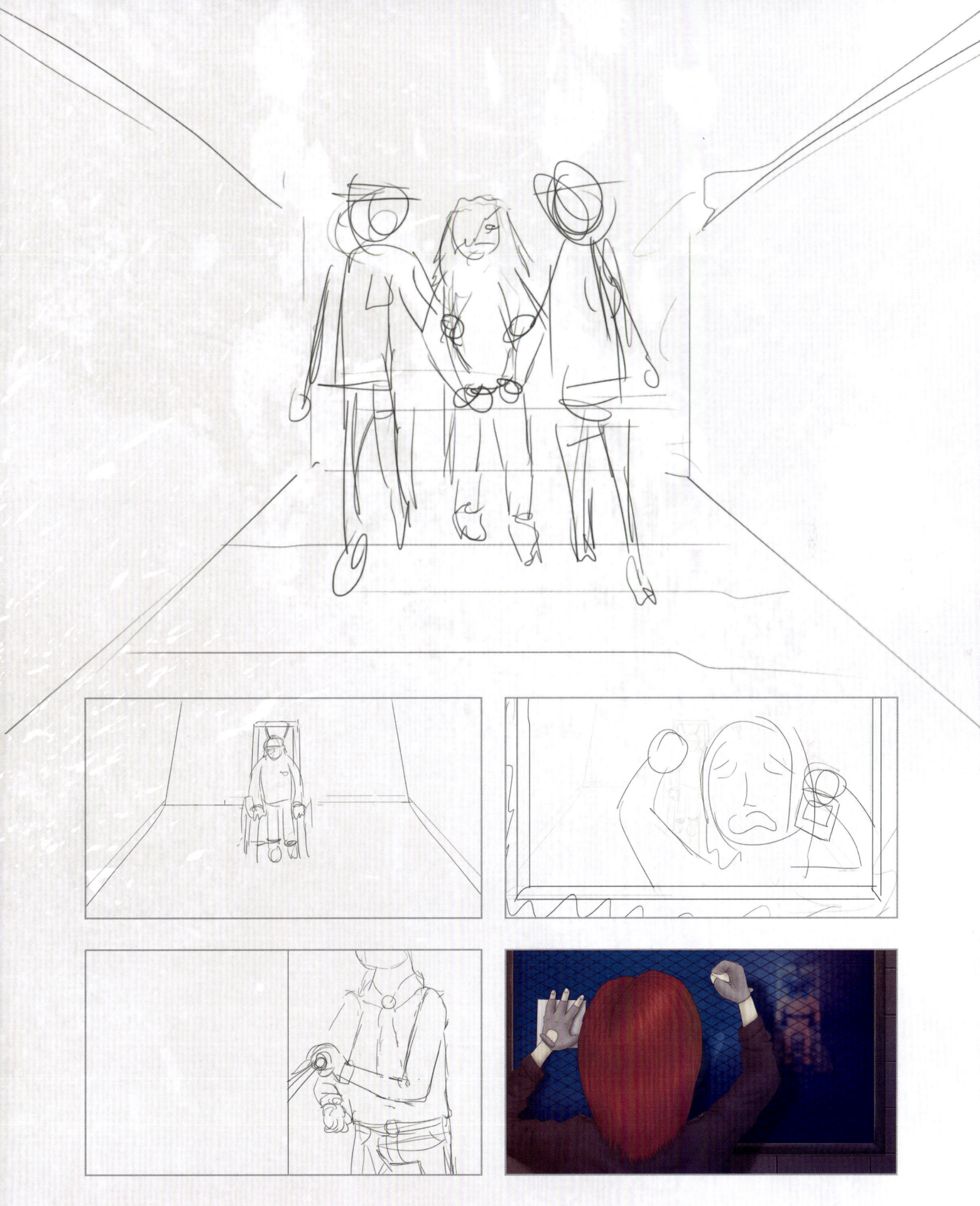

WENDIGO LAKE

A large lake in the southwestern part of town.

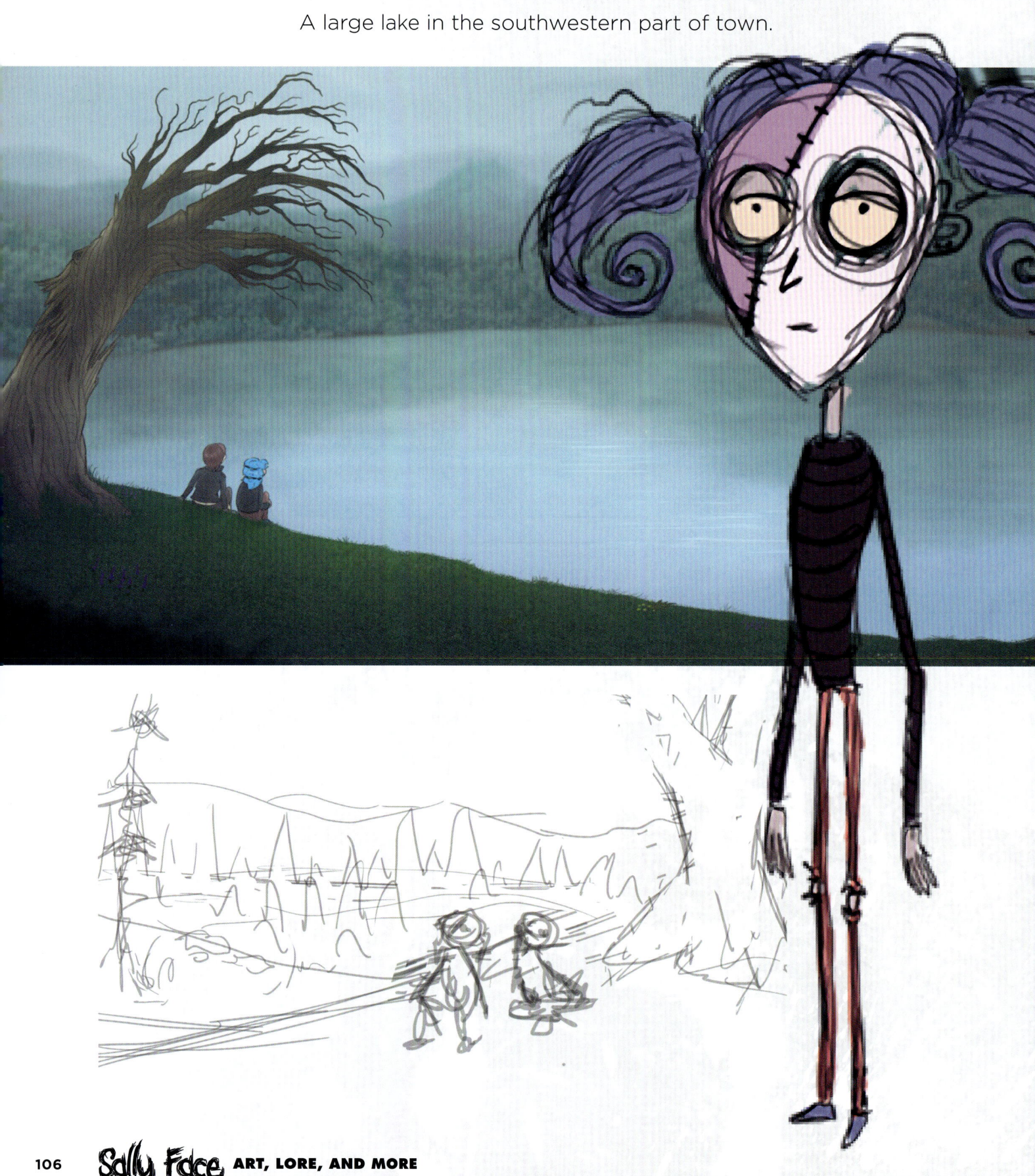

Sally Face ART, LORE, AND MORE

THE CAVES

Nockfell has a large natural cave system with openings around Wendigo Lake.

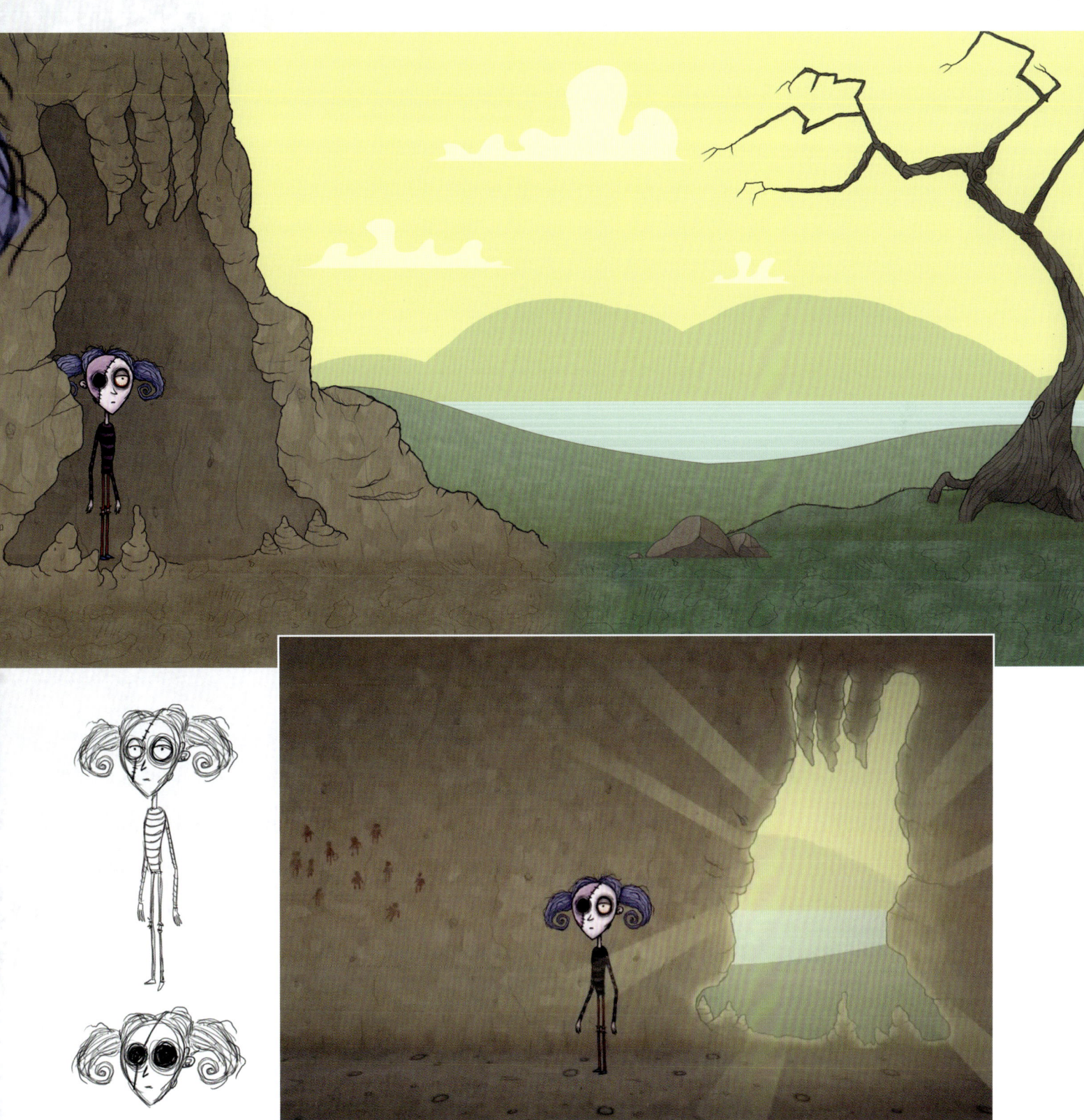

DREAMS

Sal suffers from frequent nightmares and disturbing dreams. Sometimes there seems to be something guiding him in those dreams or some meaning he is meant to find.

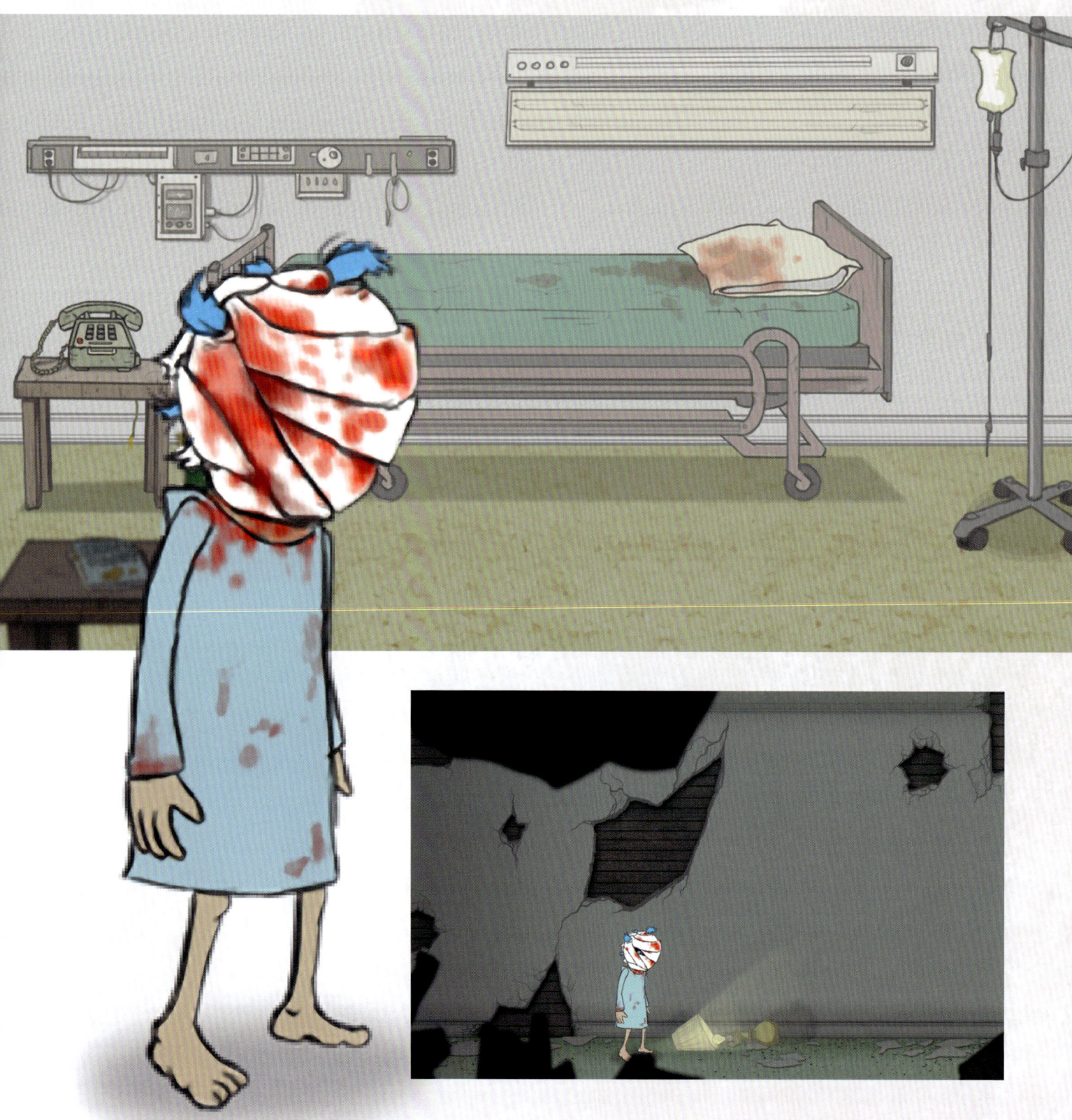

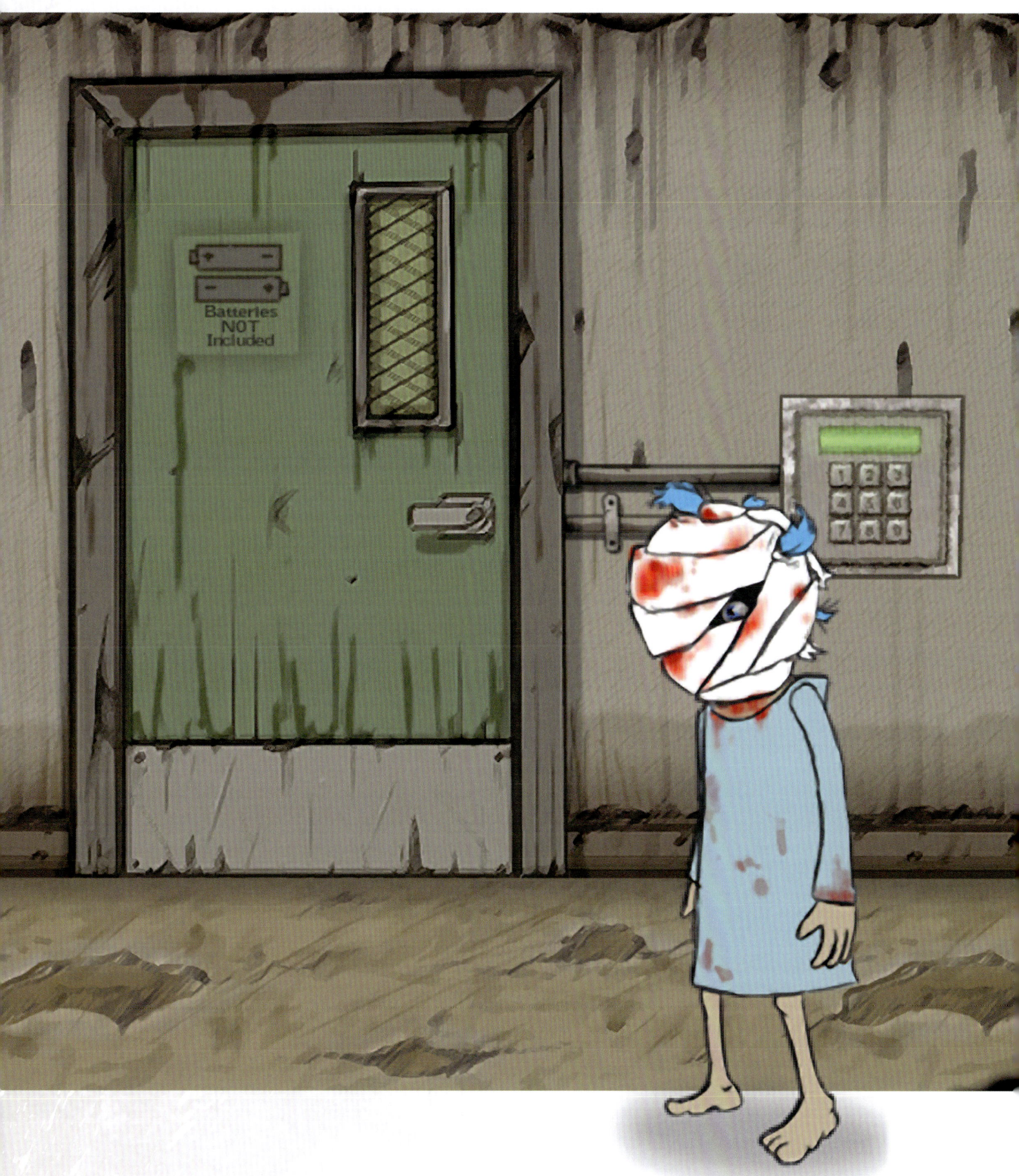

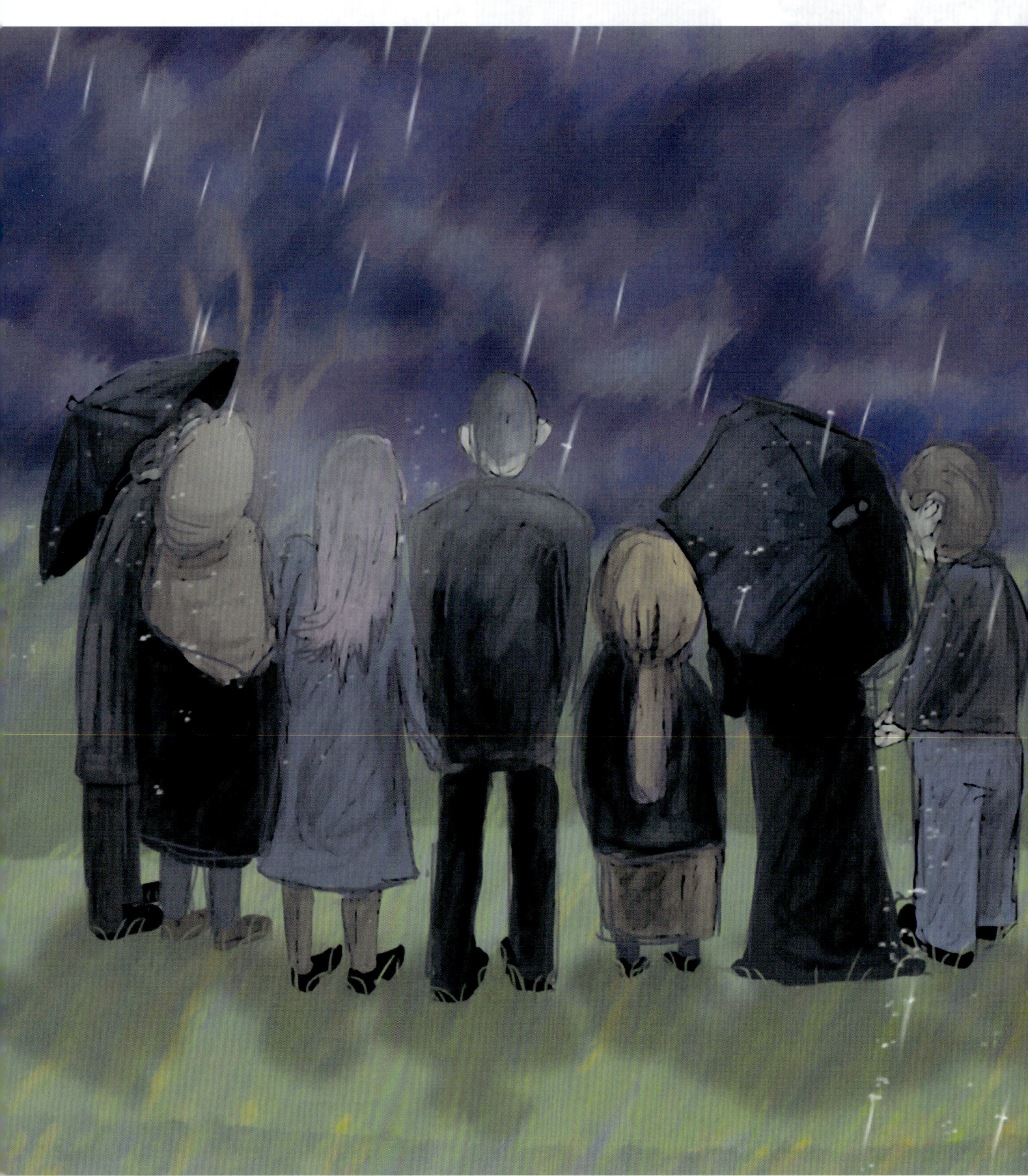

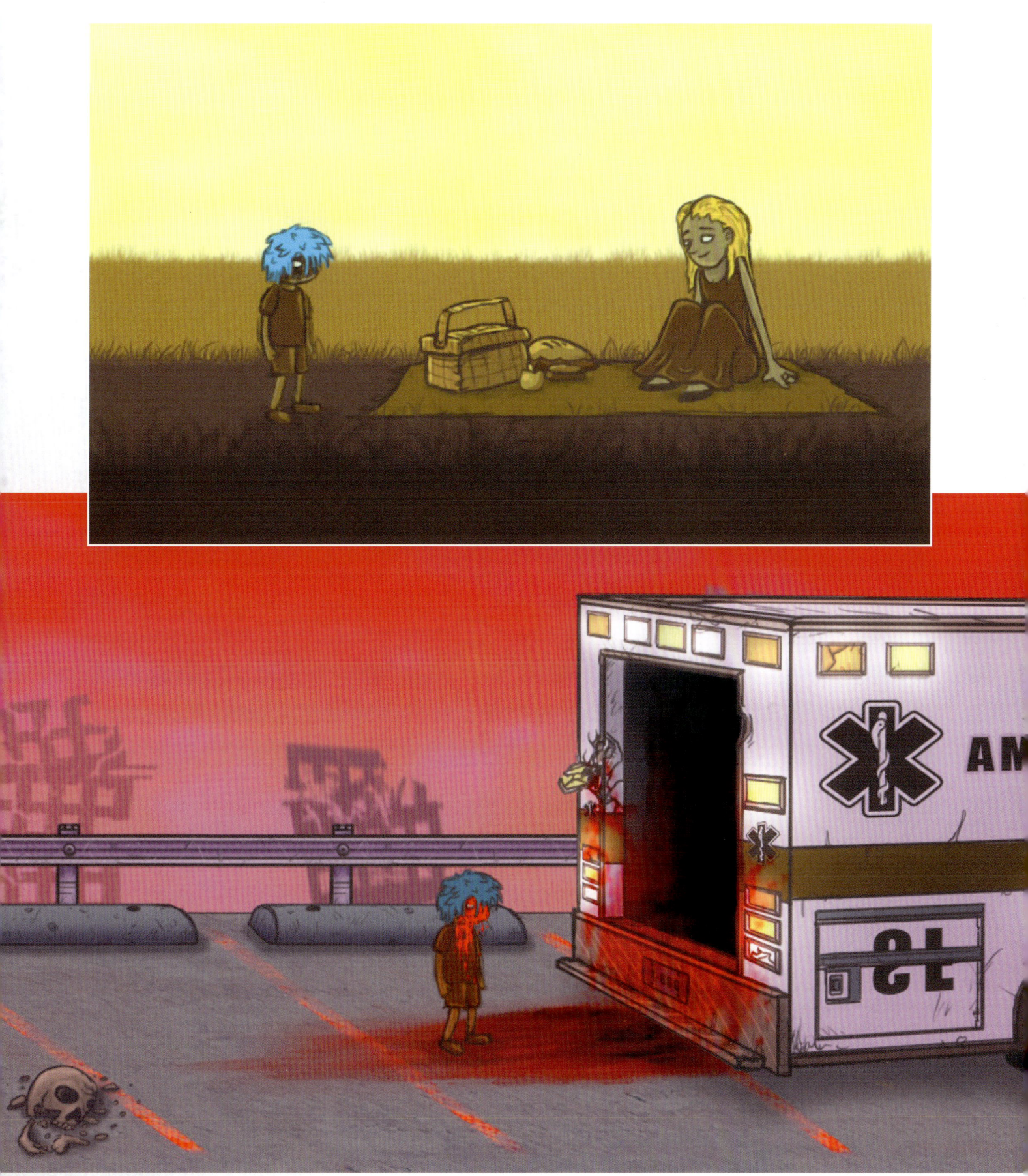

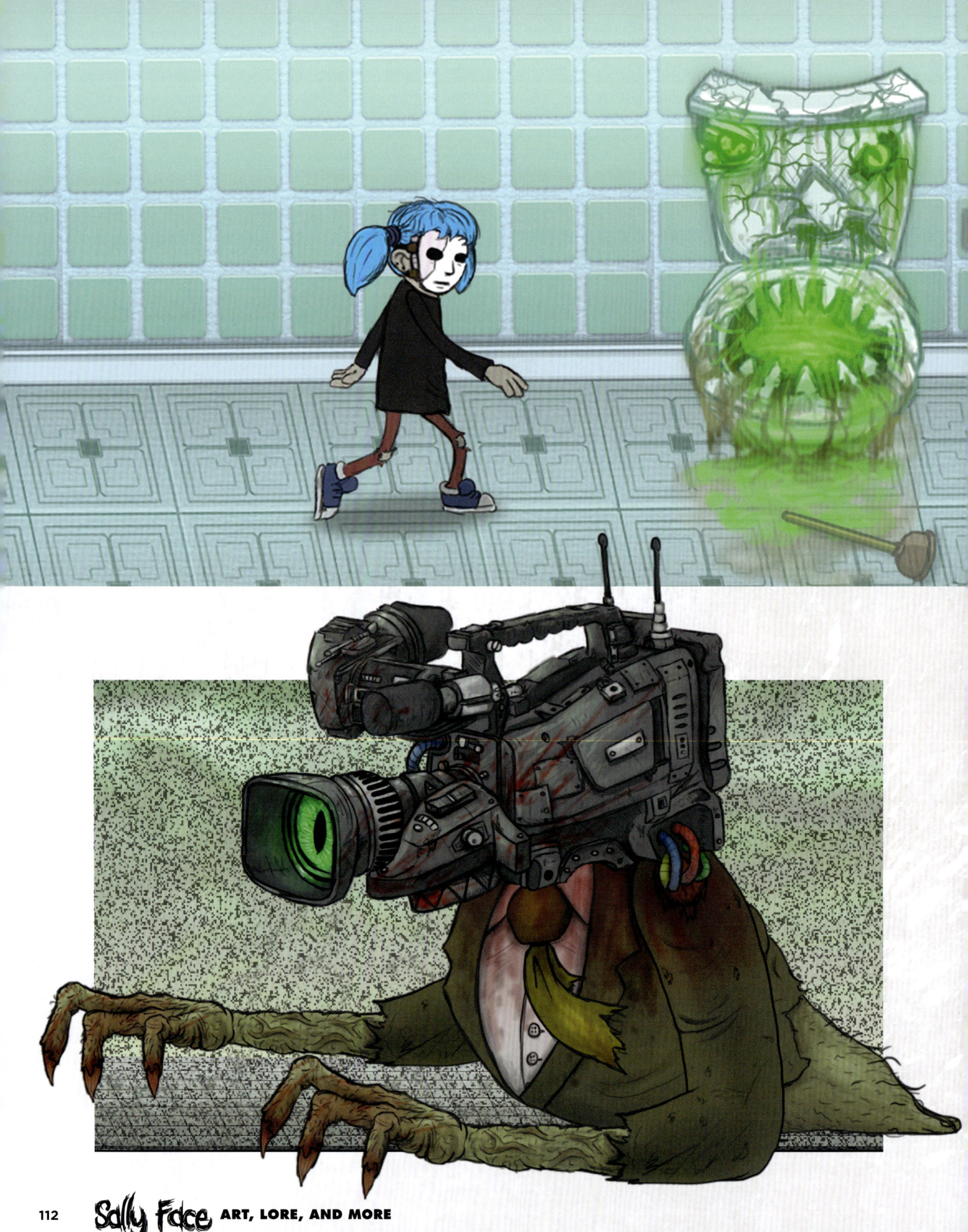

Sally Face ART, LORE, AND MORE

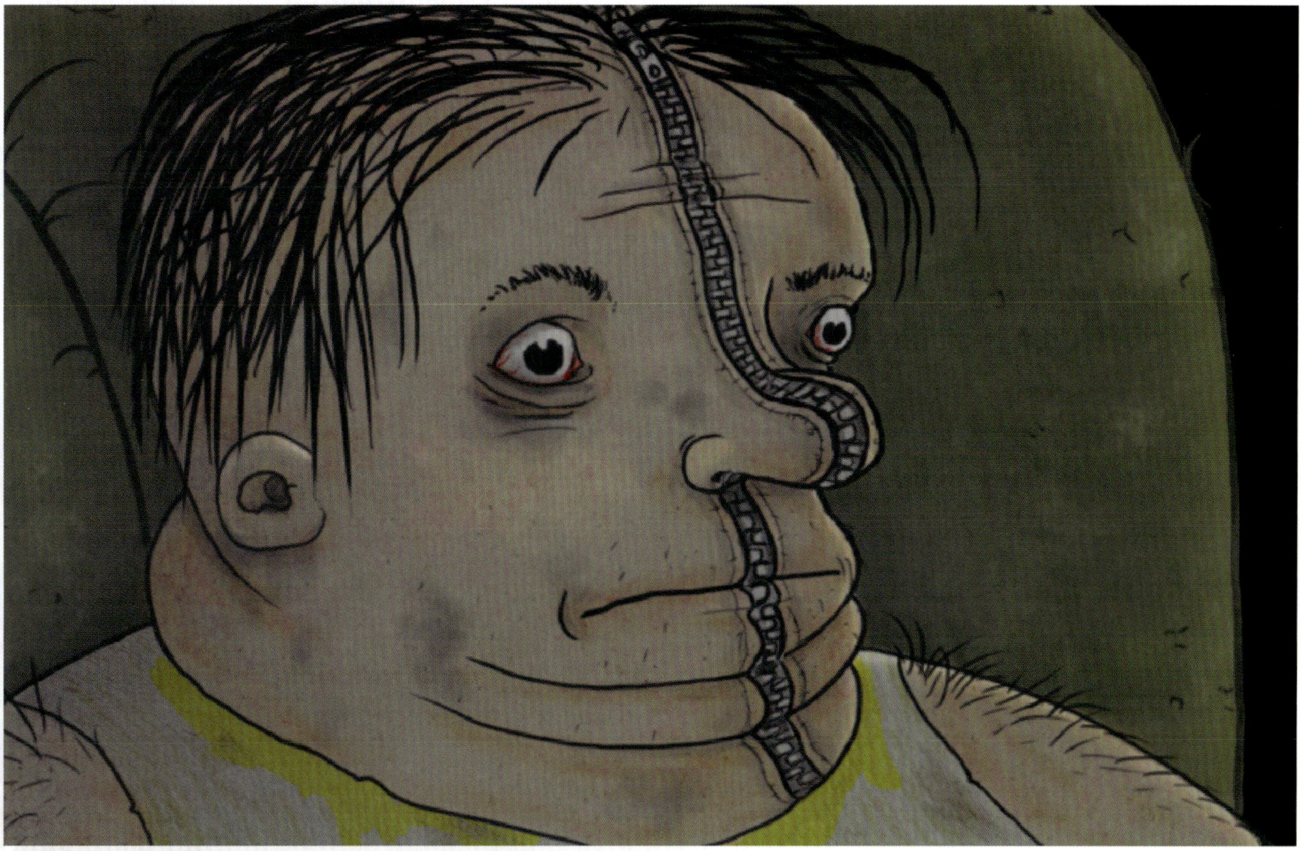

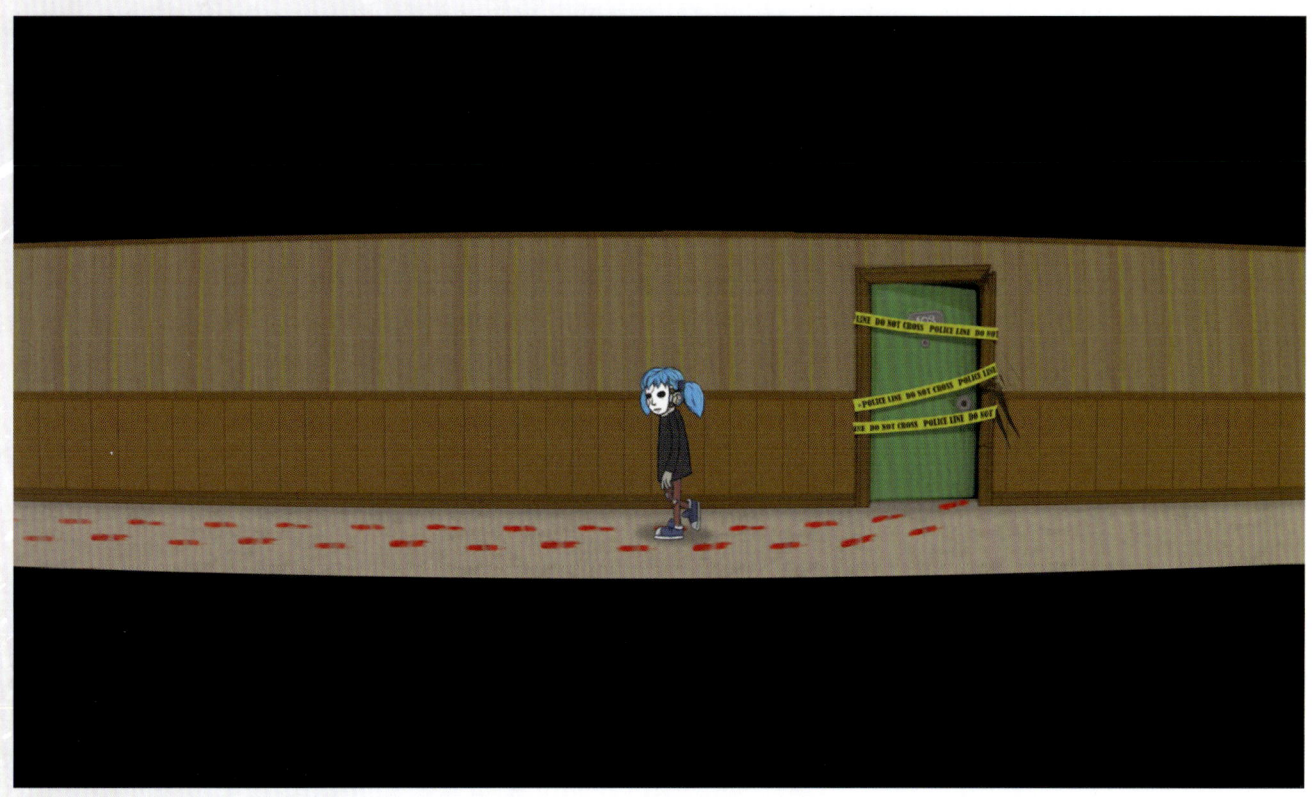

SOMEWHERE ELSE

Sal drifts between many places that other people are blissfully unaware of.
These include The Void, The Spirit Realm, The Black Room,
The White Room, alternate realities, and more.

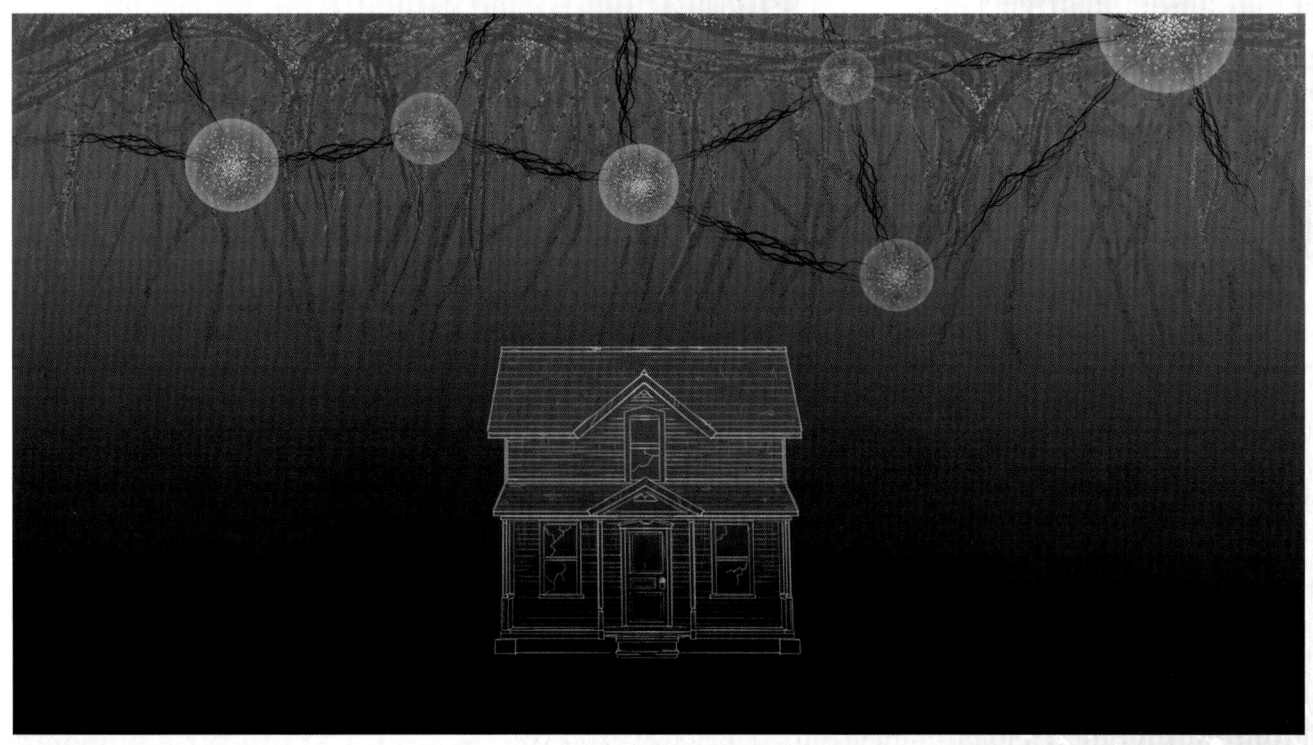

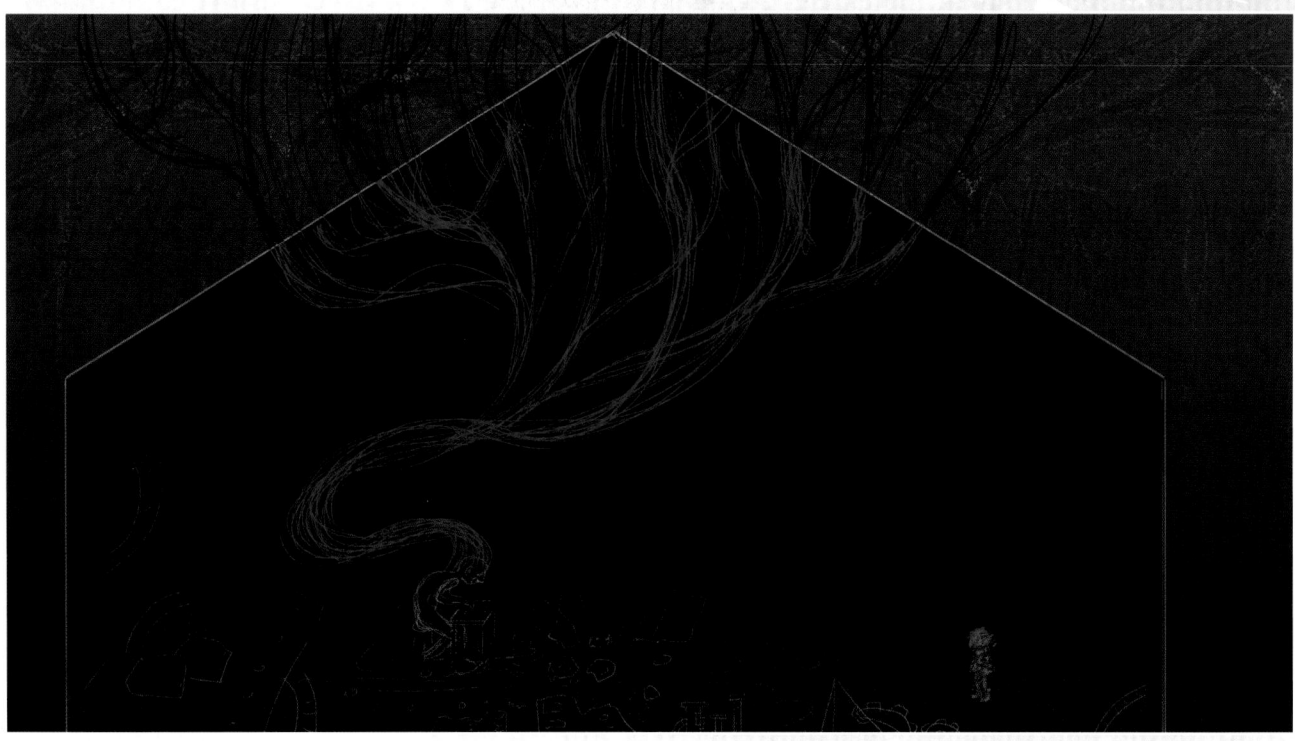

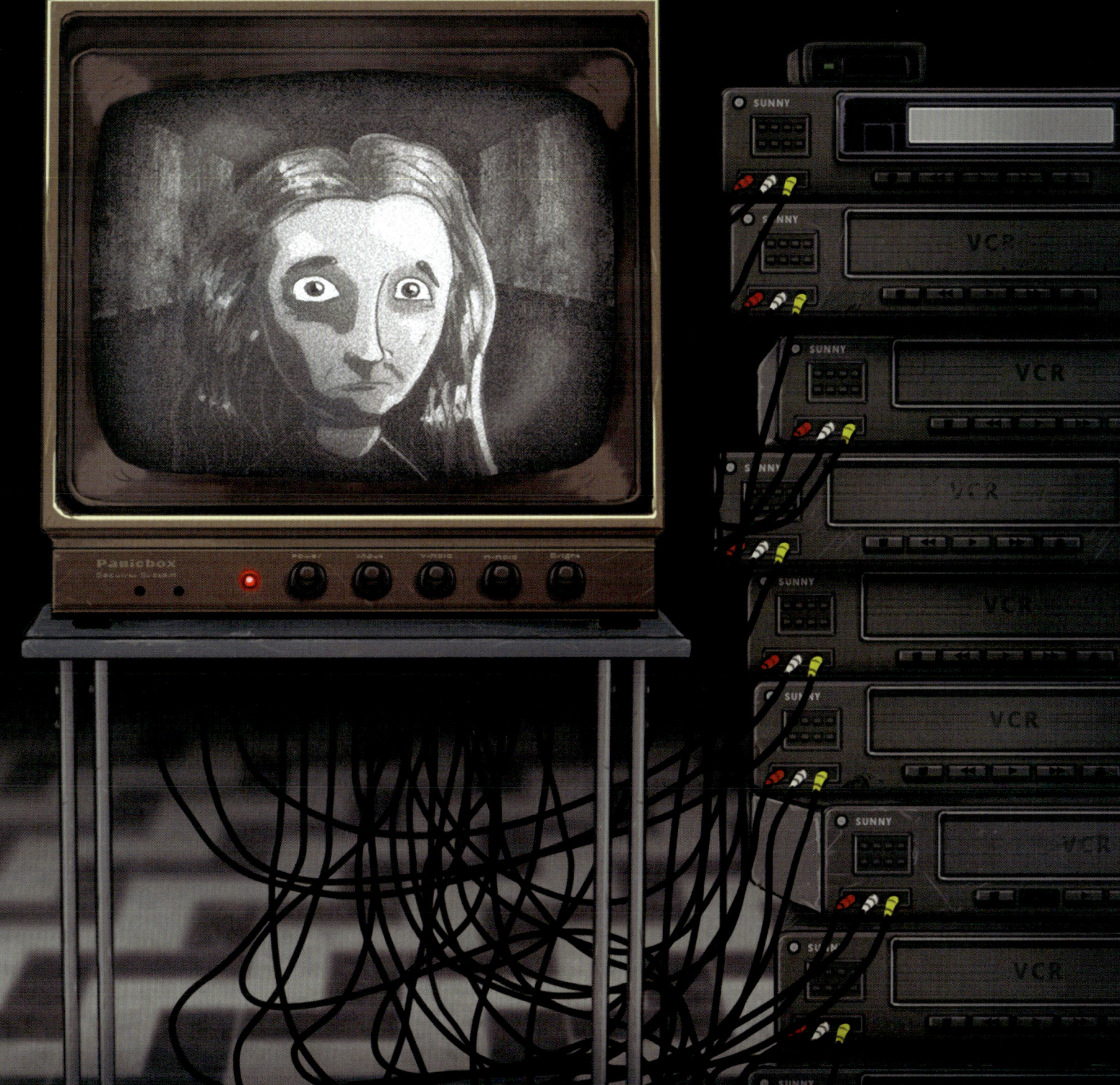

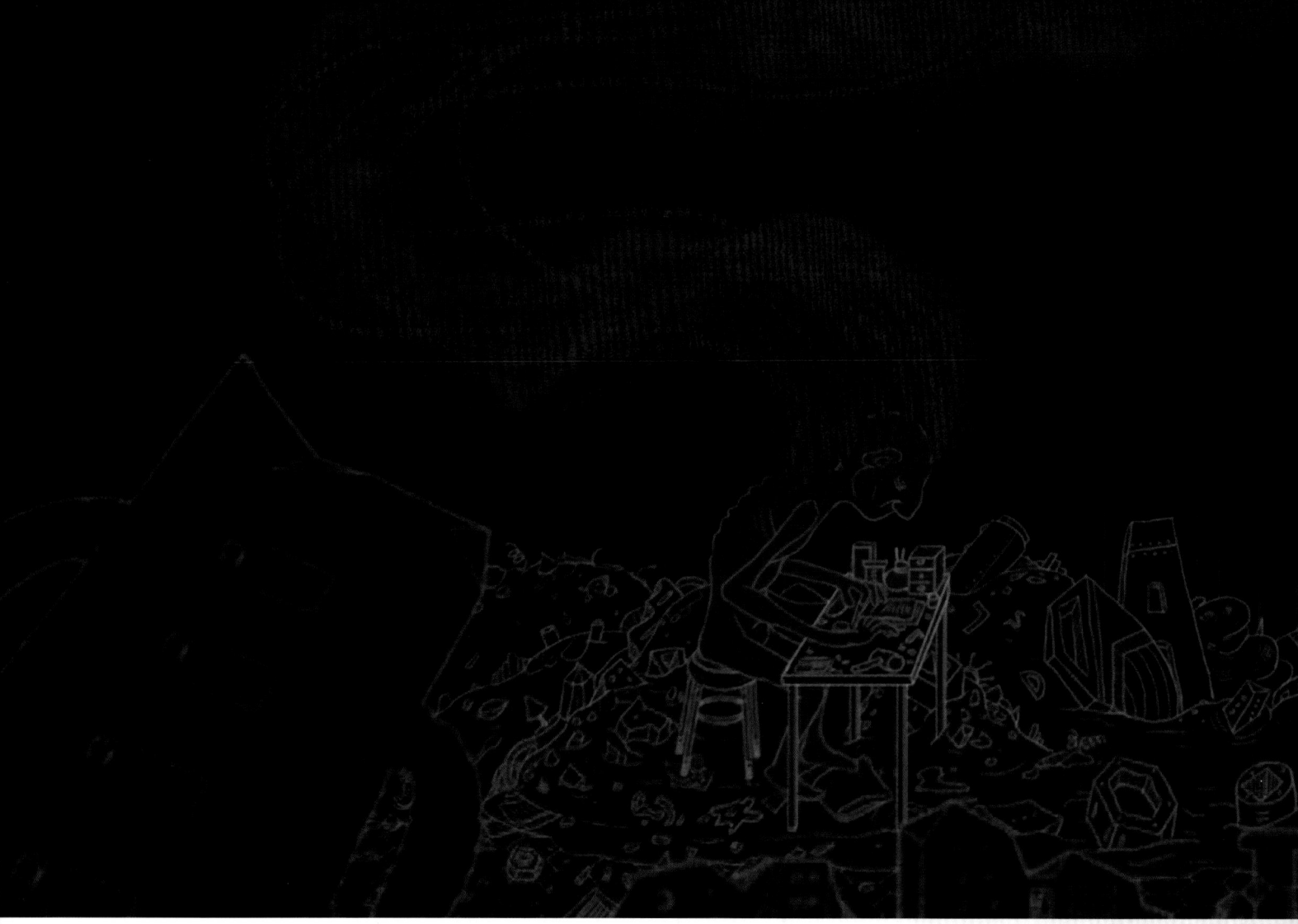

Sally Face ART, LORE, AND MORE

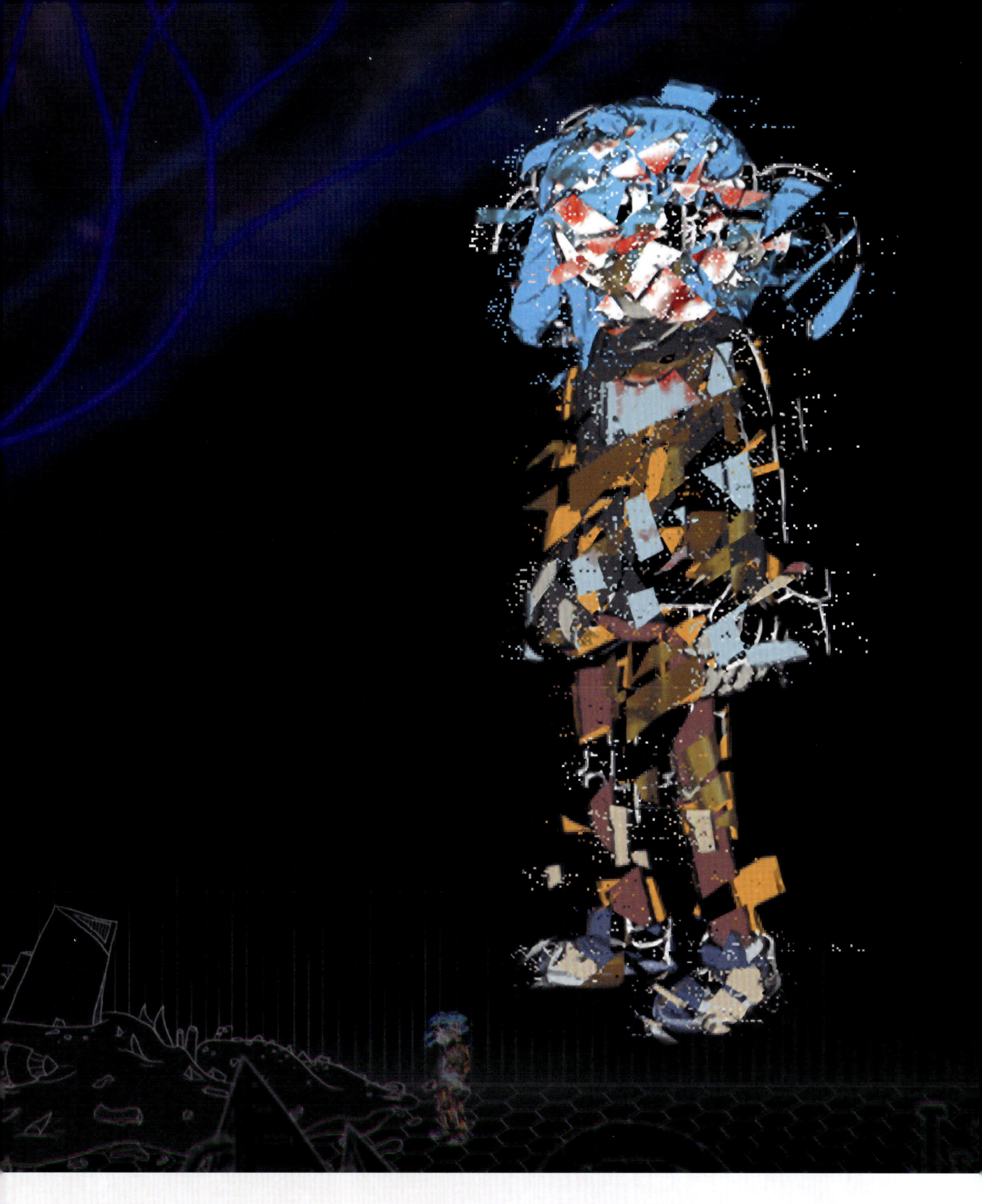

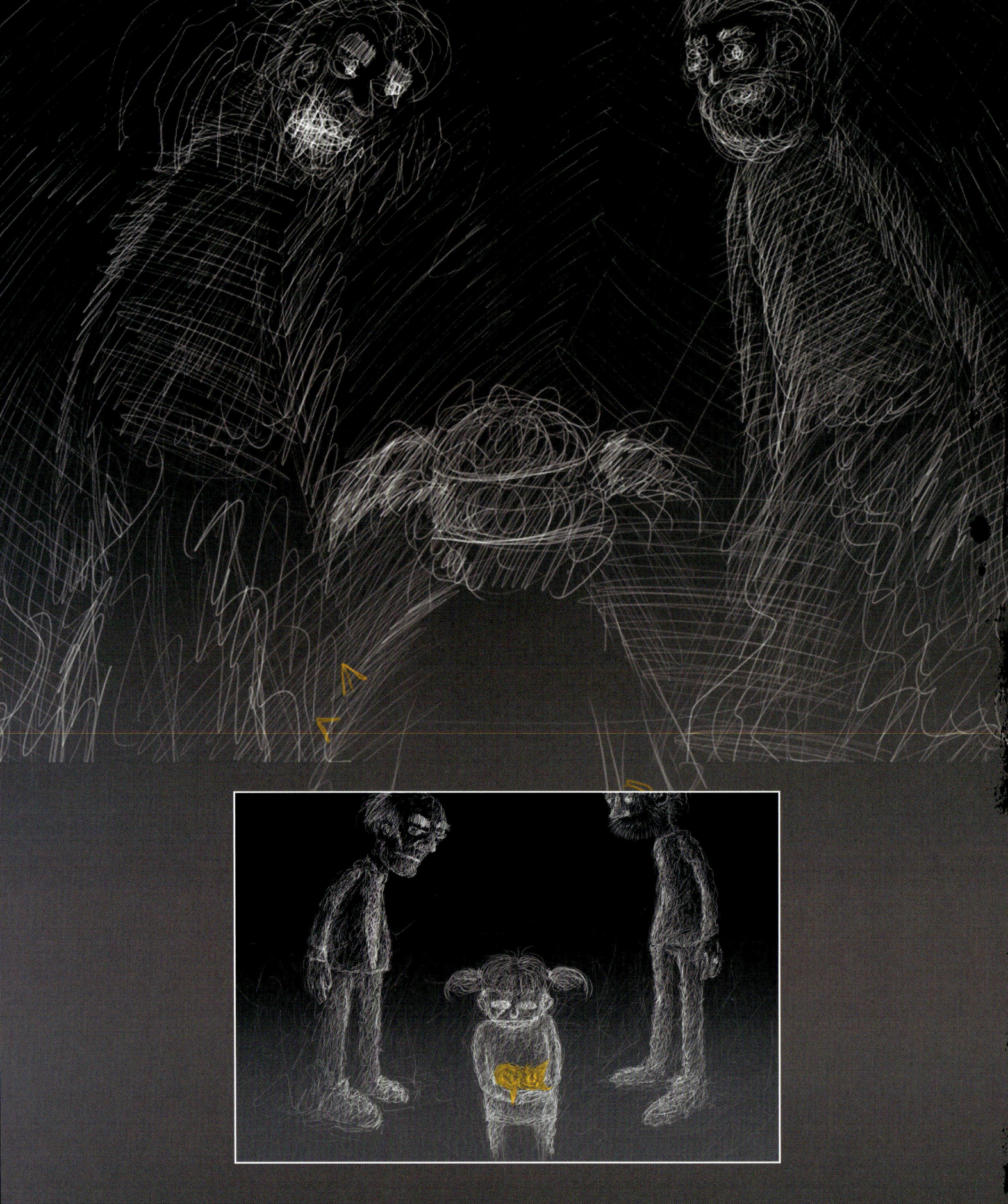

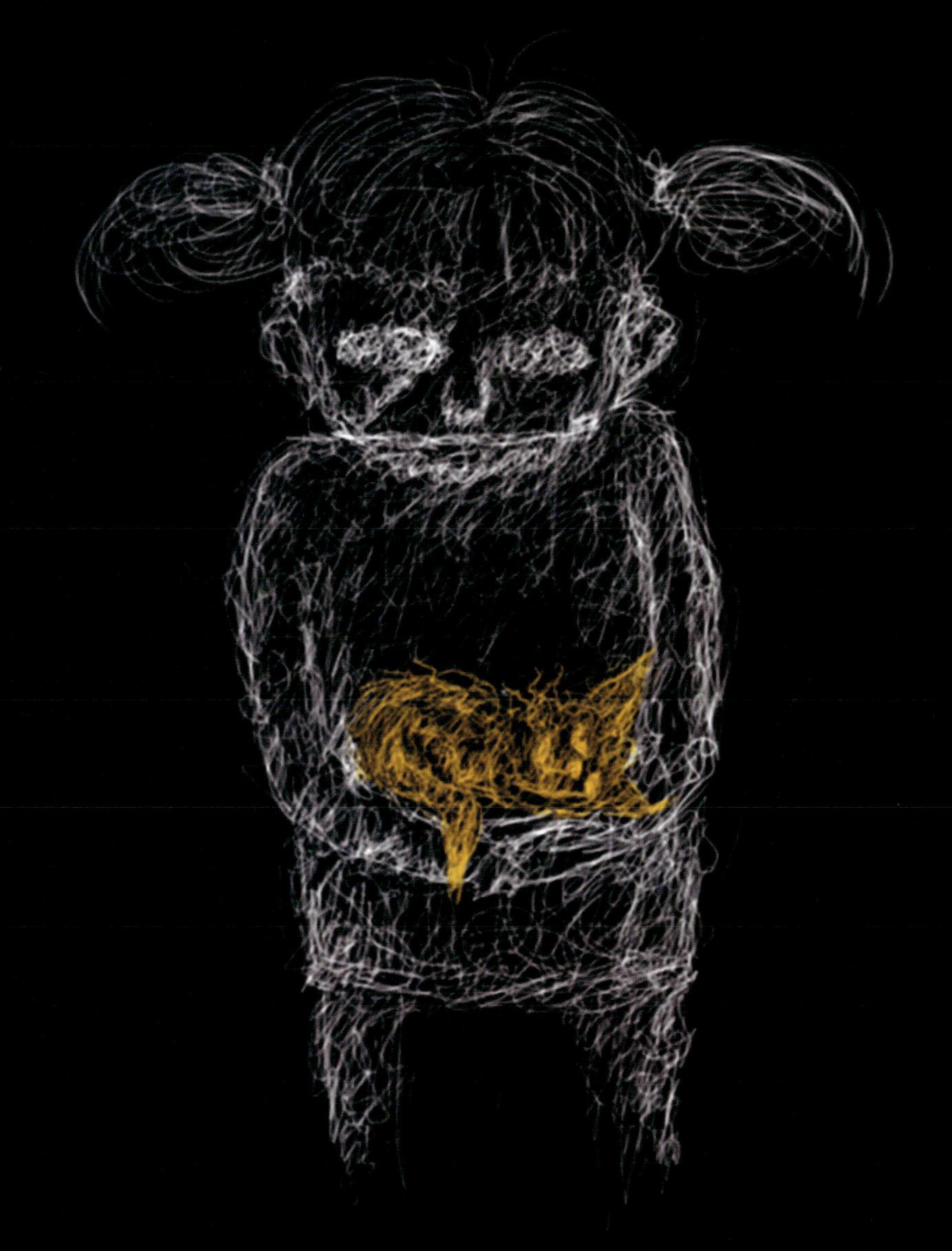

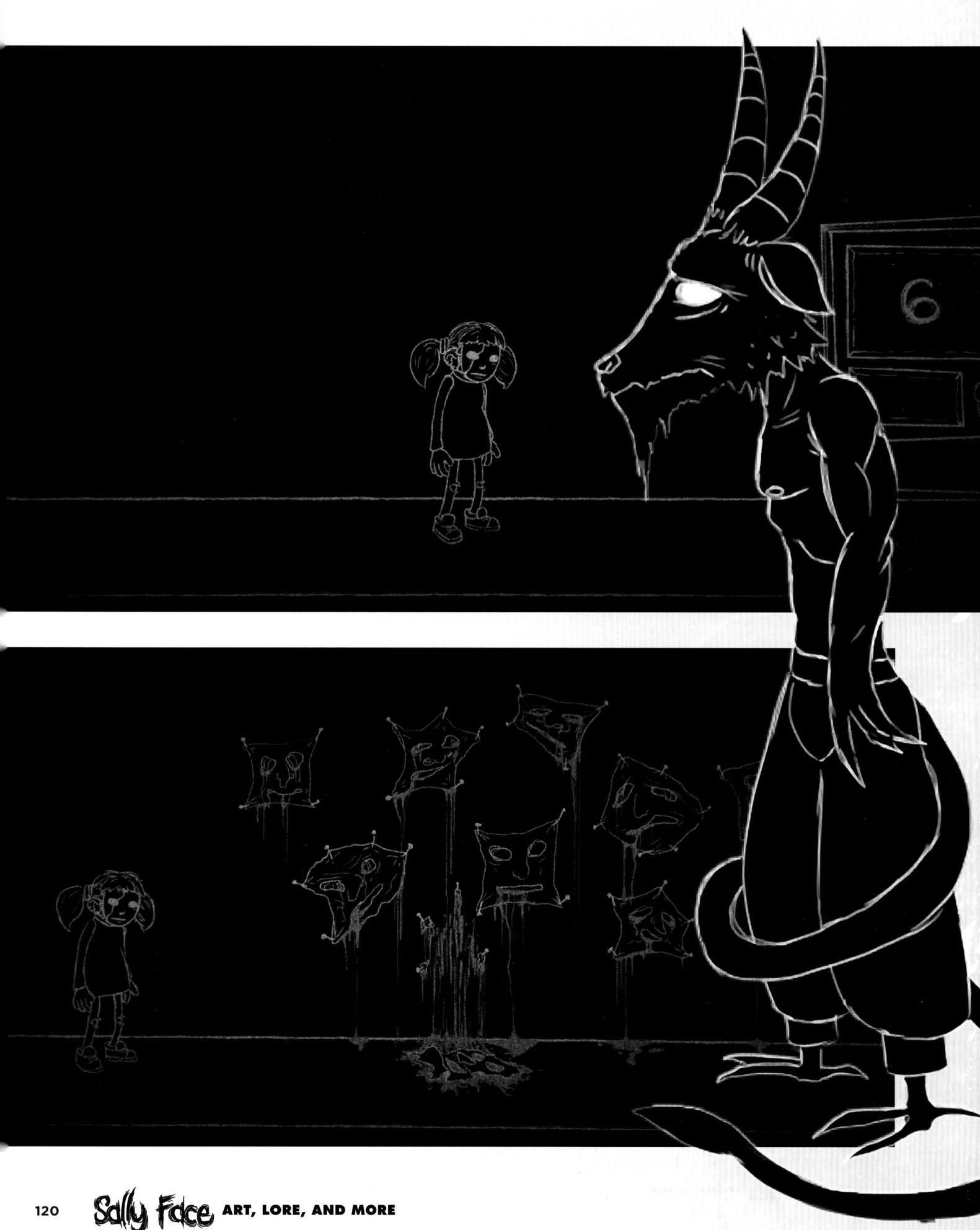

Sally Face ART, LORE, AND MORE

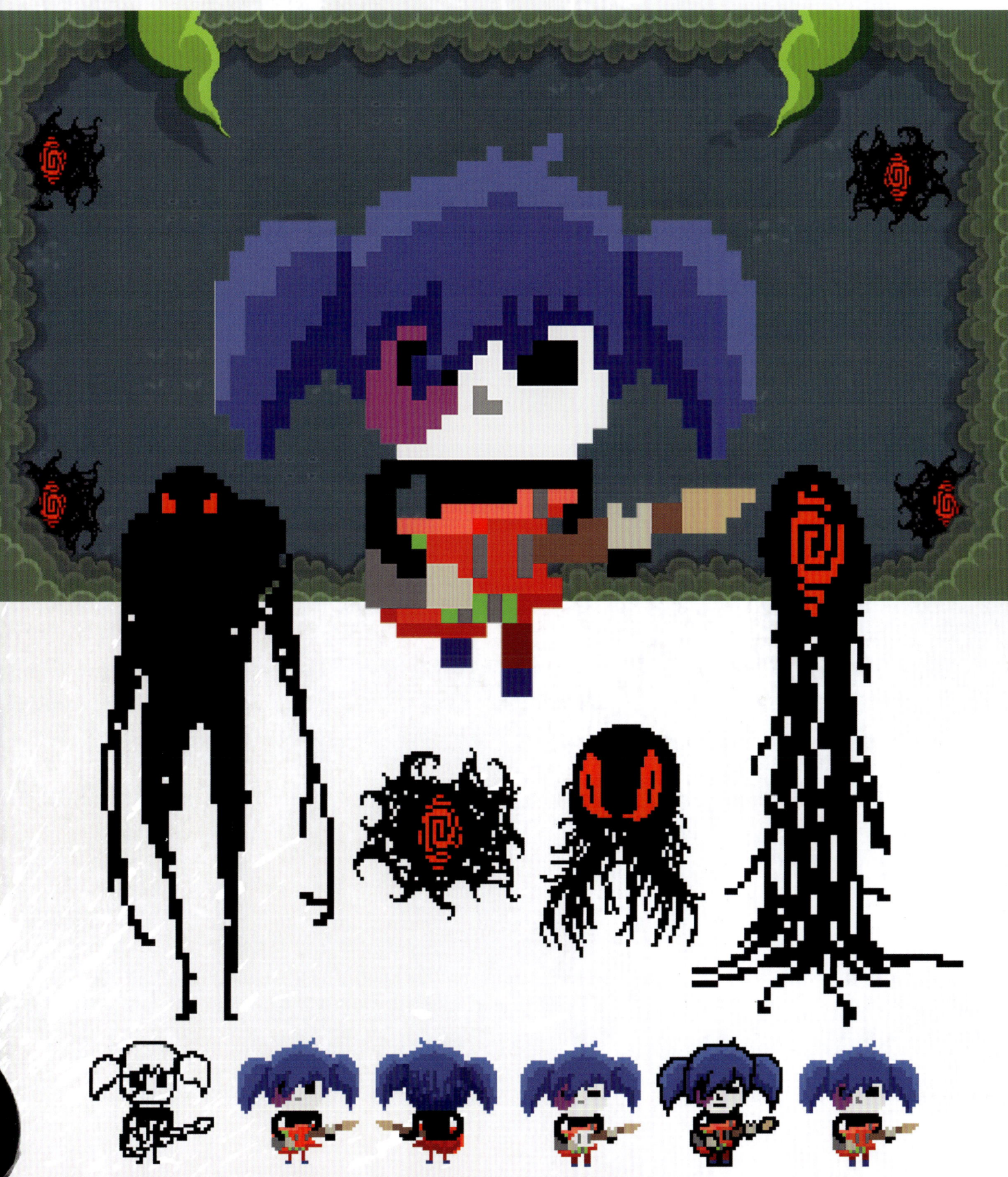

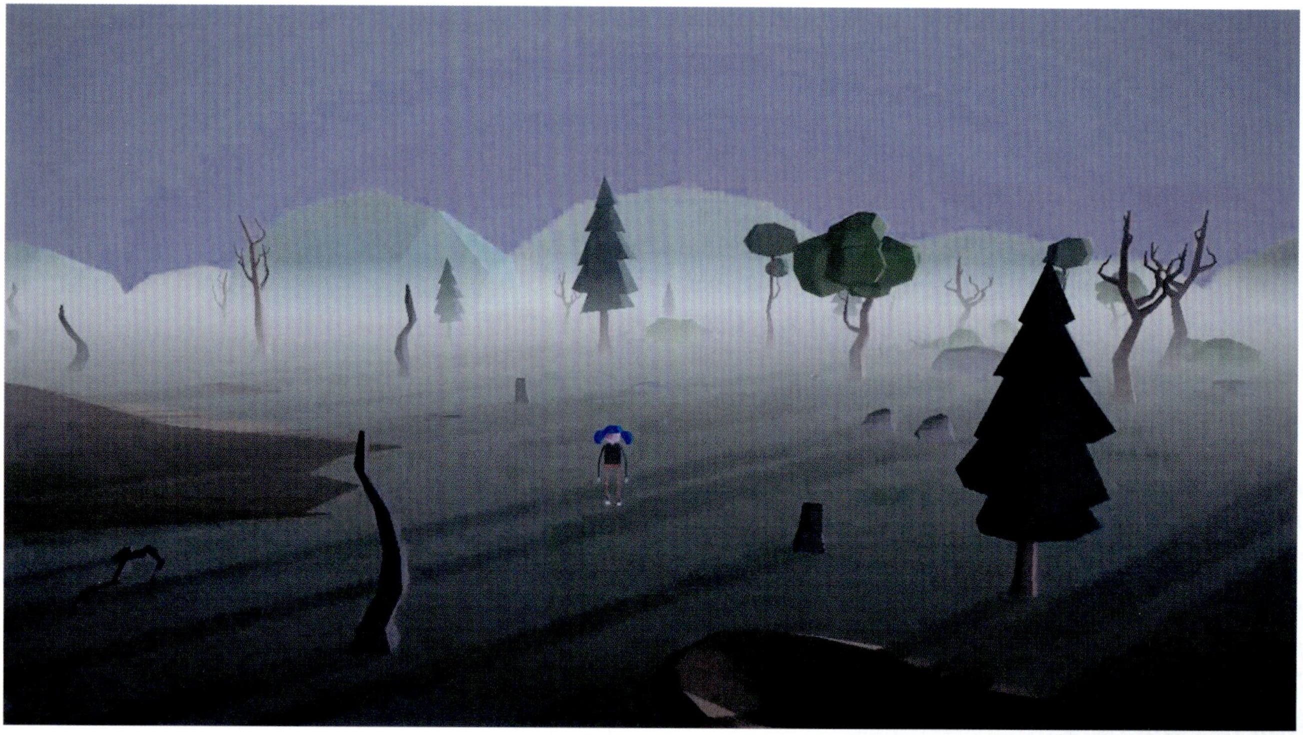

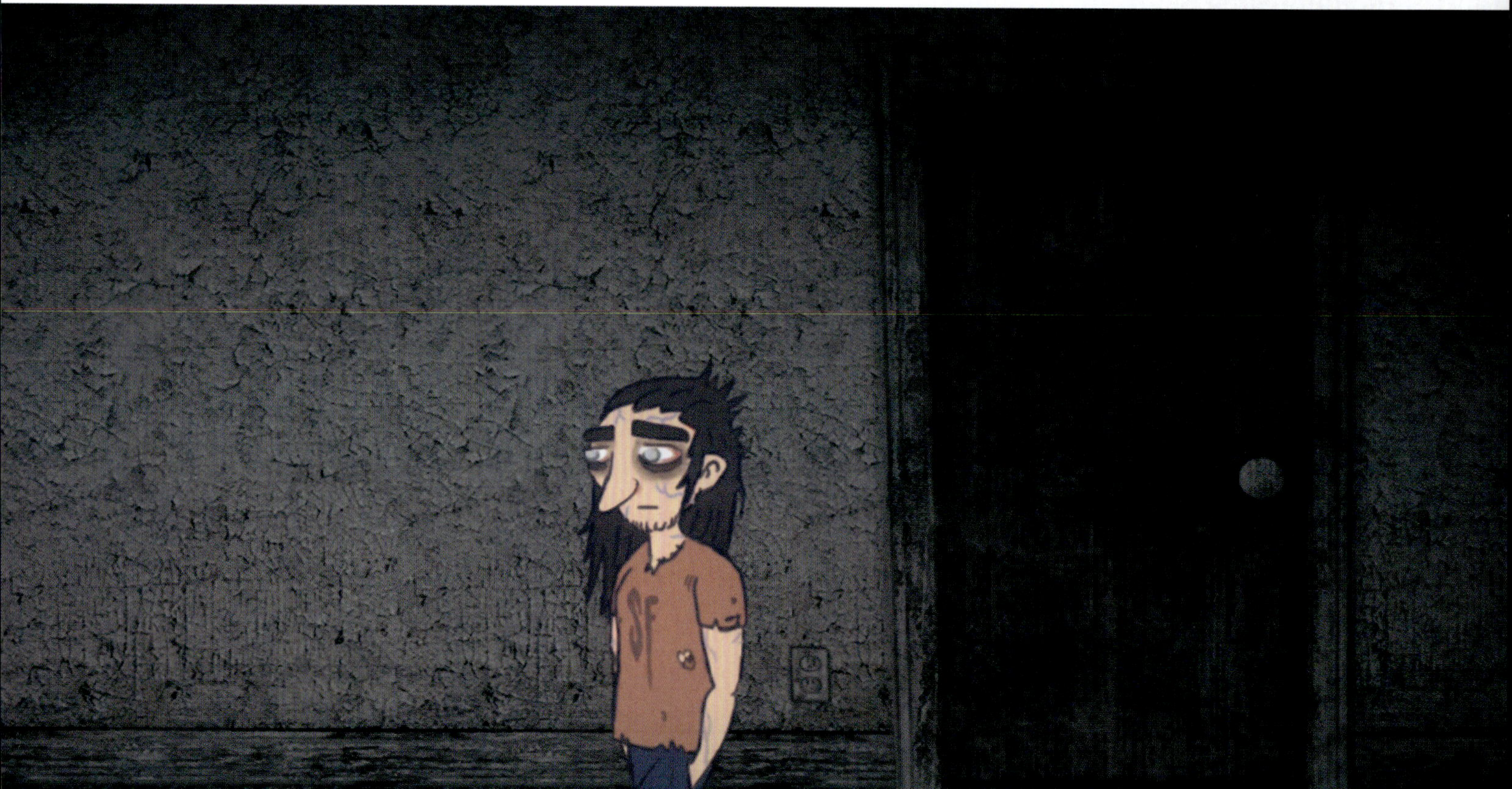
SF

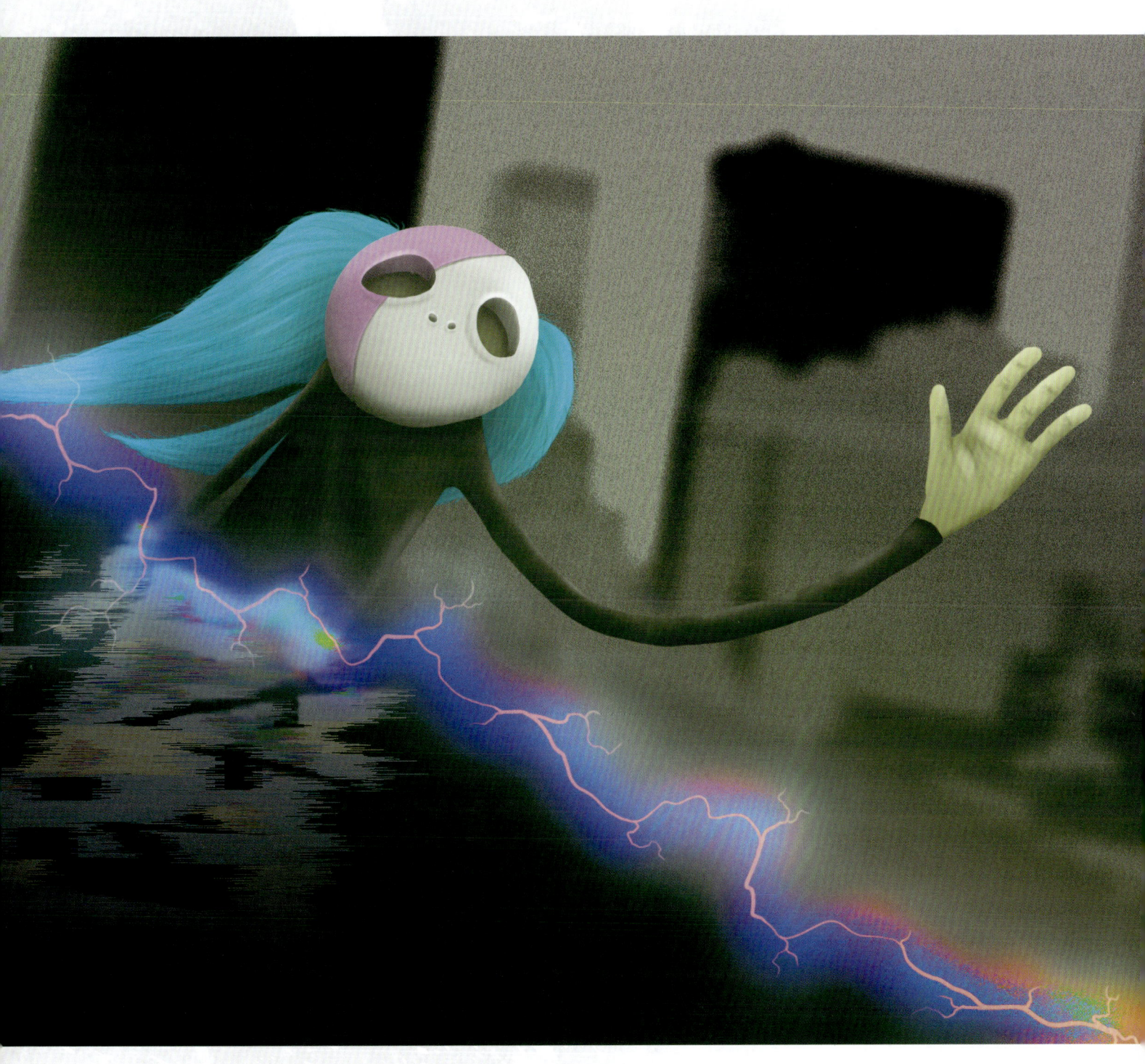

JIM'S LAB

A look behind the scenes of the stop motion world in Sal's journey.

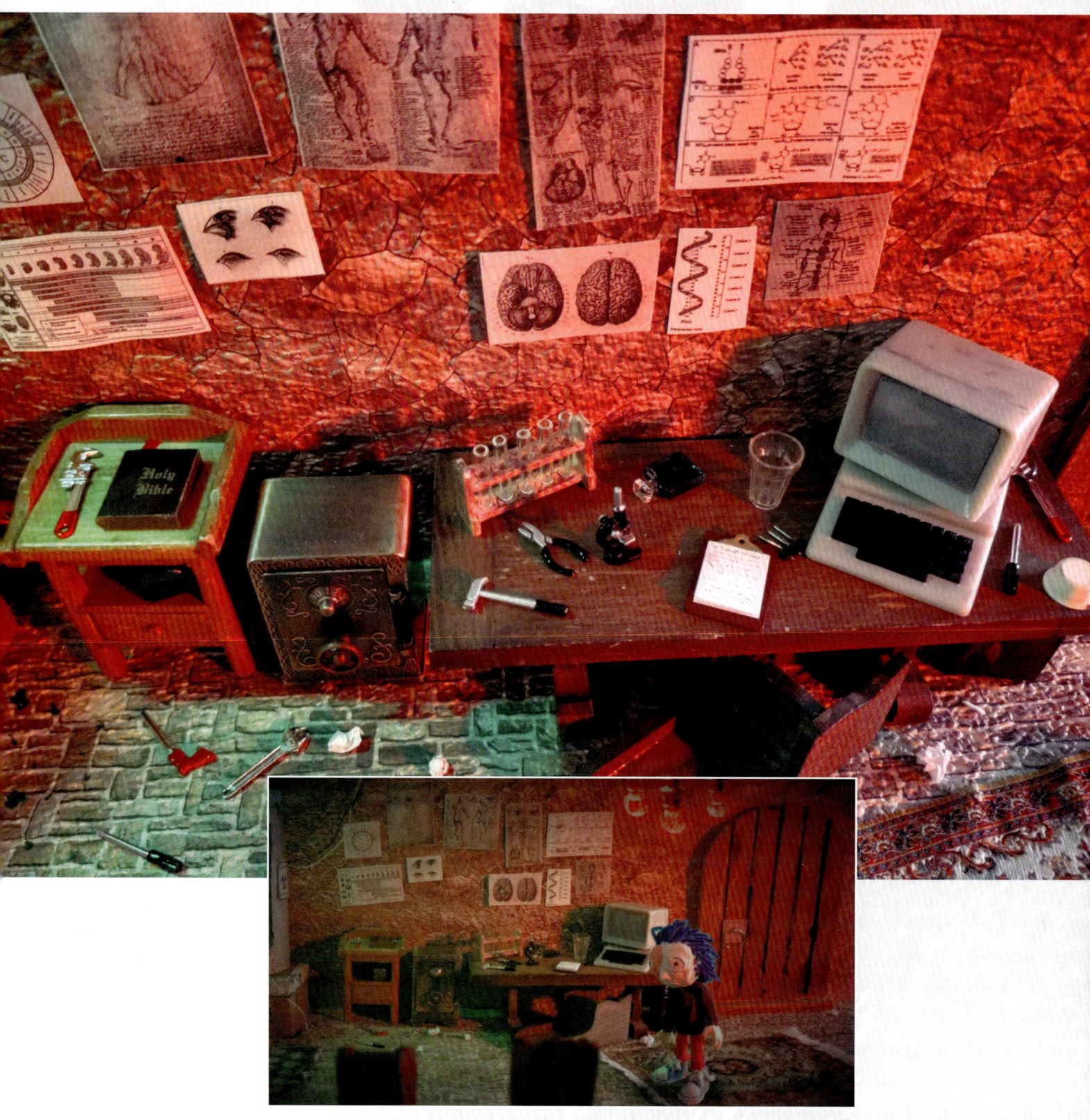

Sally Face ART, LORE, AND MORE

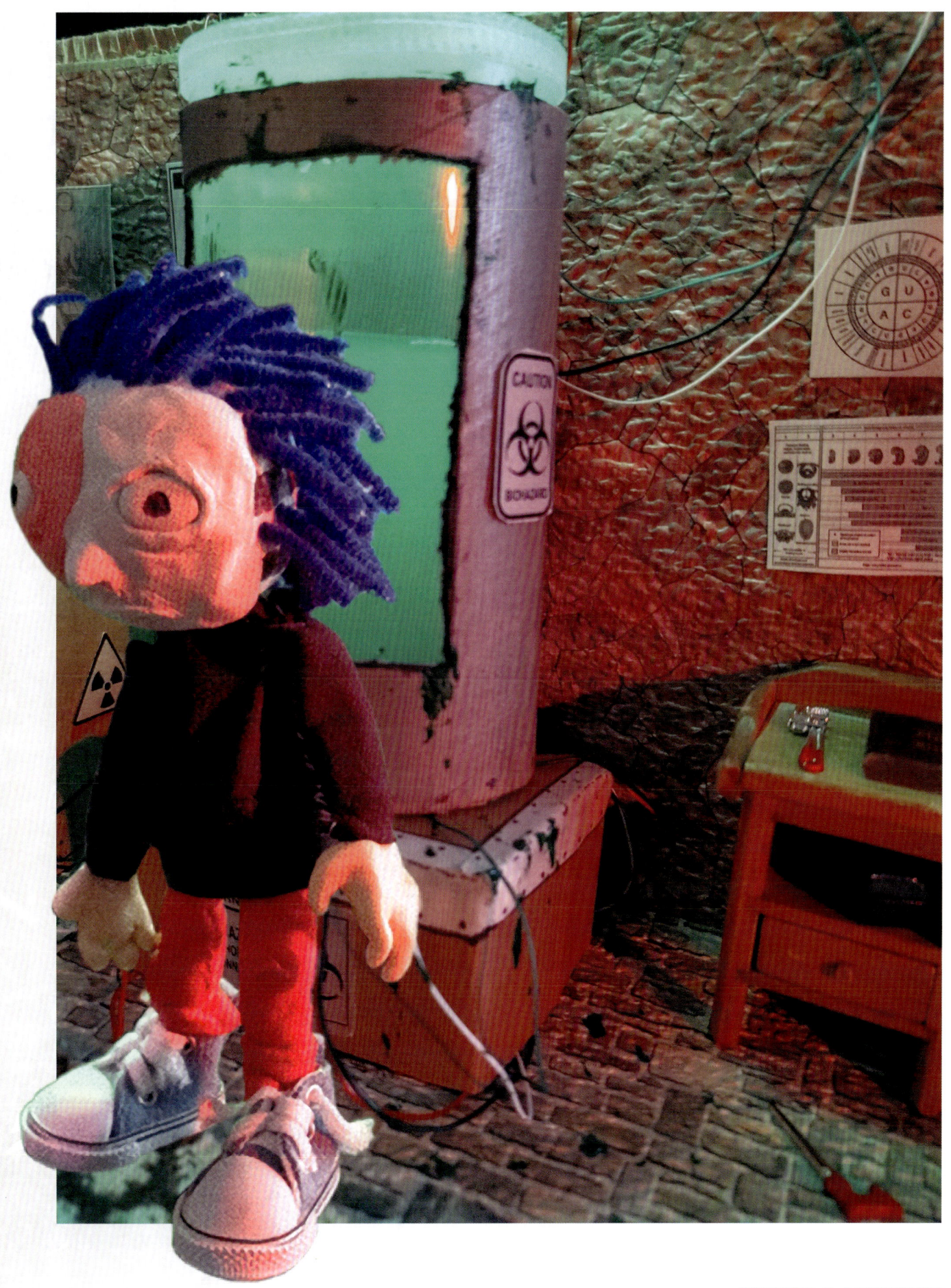

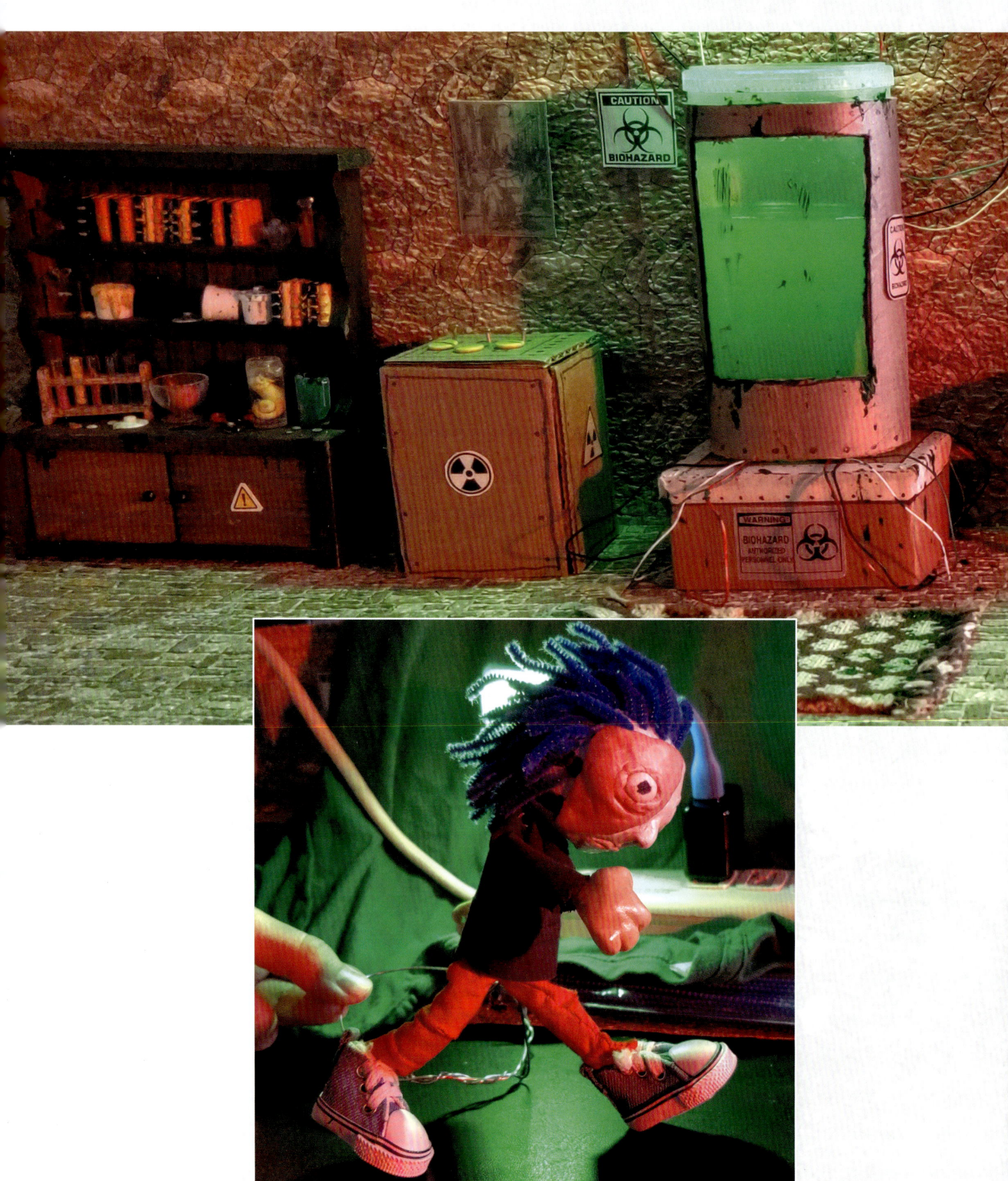

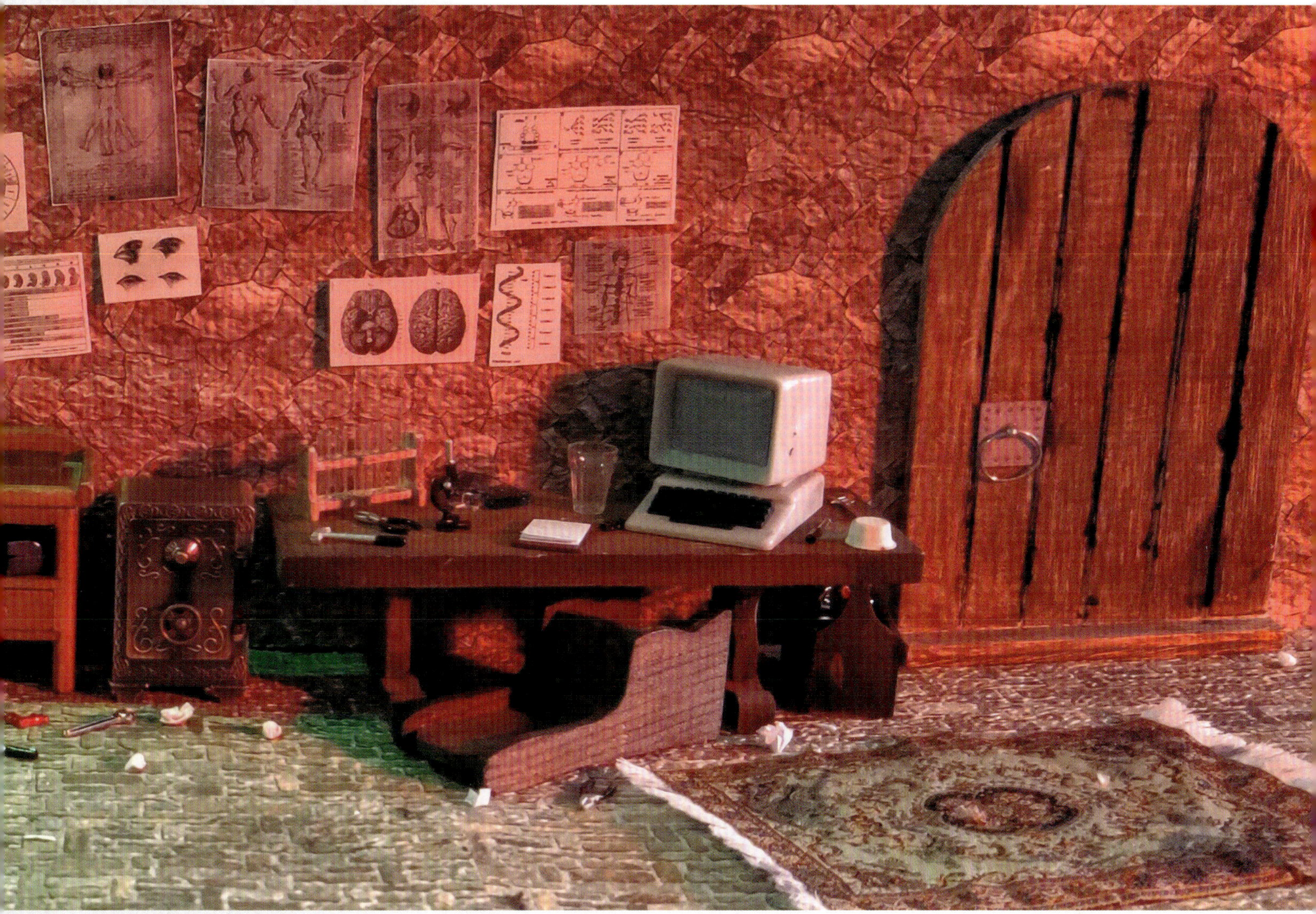

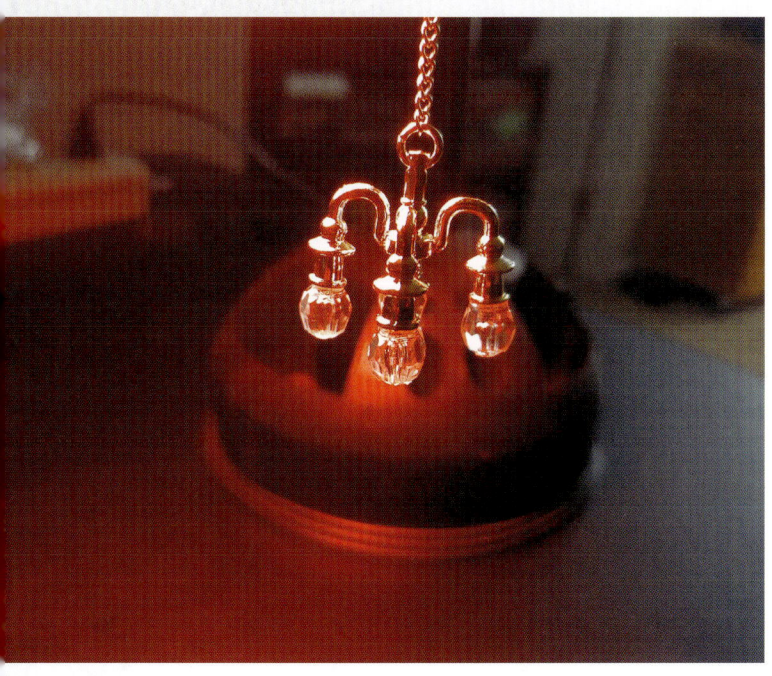

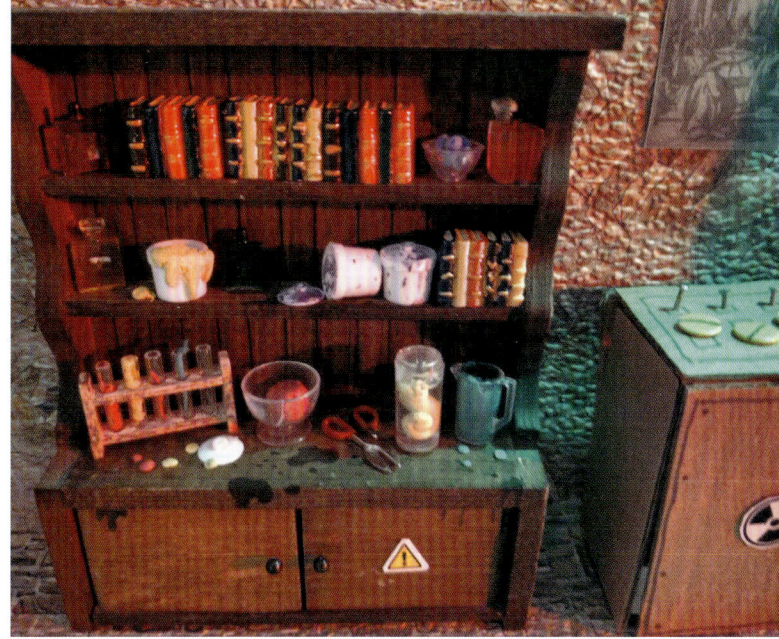

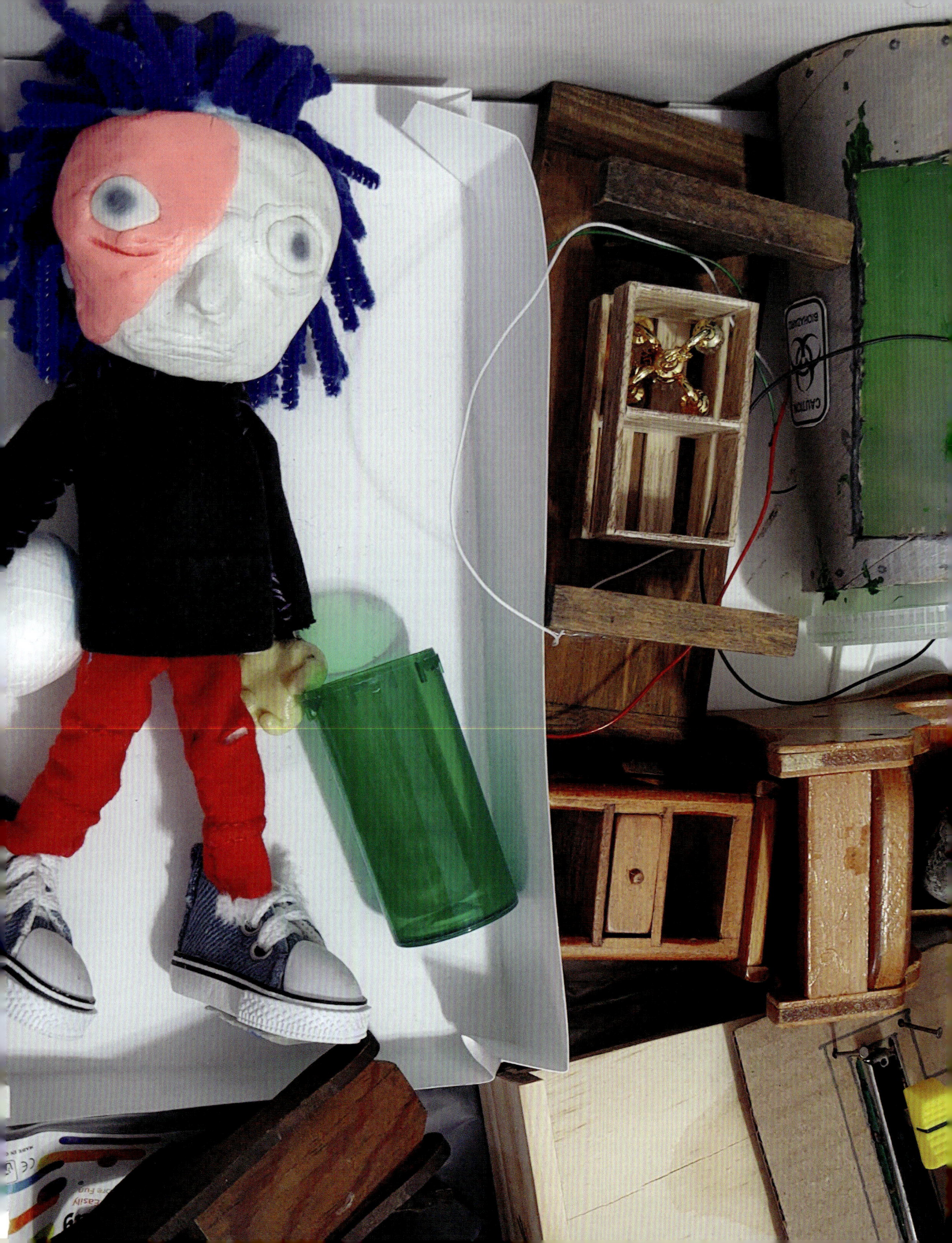

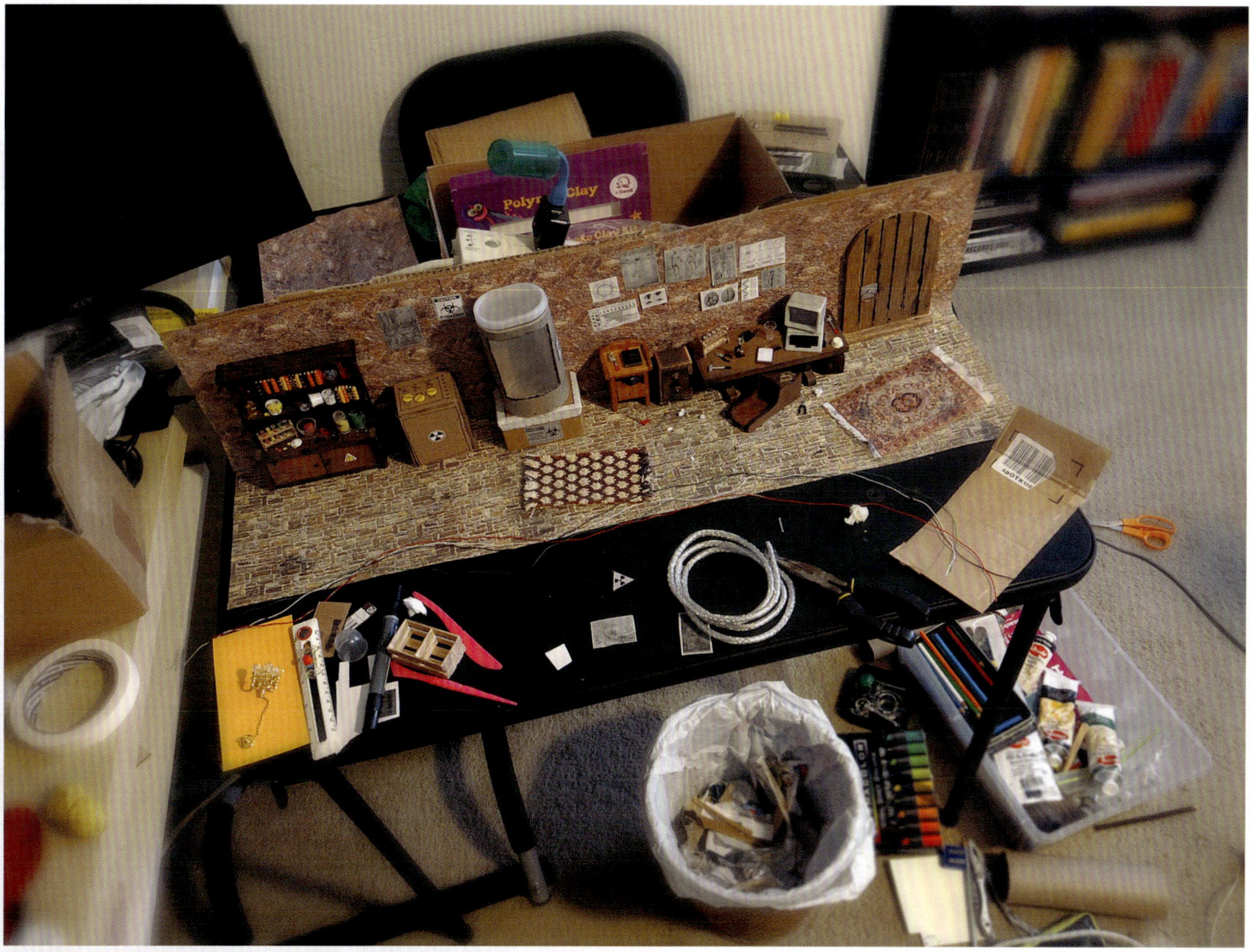

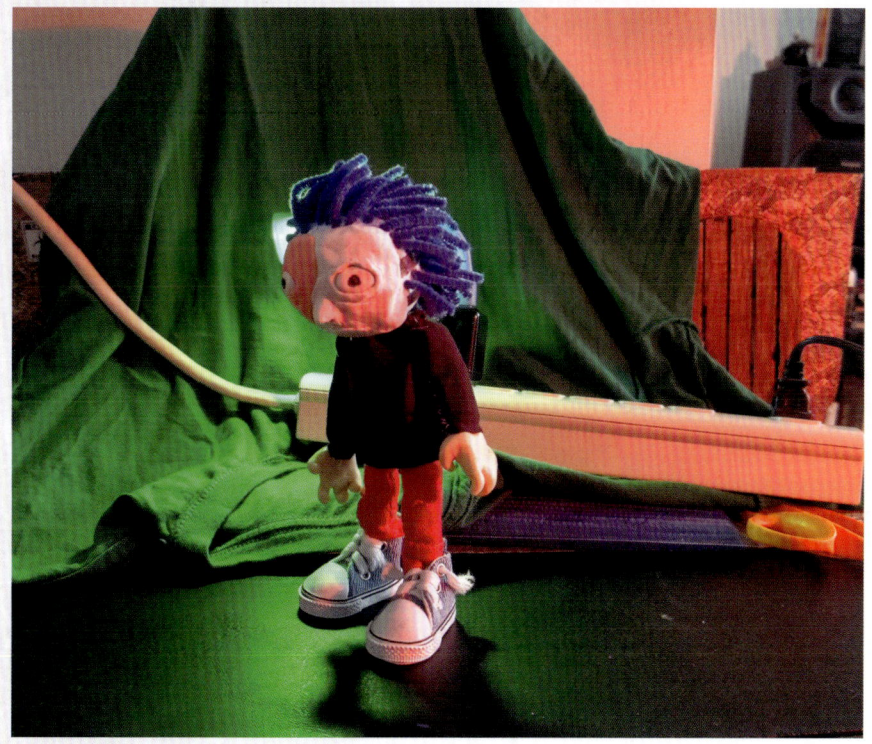

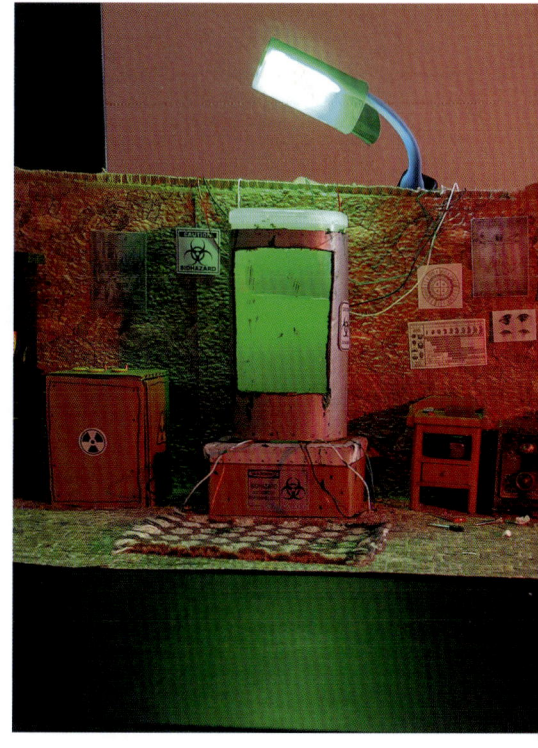

EPISODE 2
PUZZLE SKETCHES

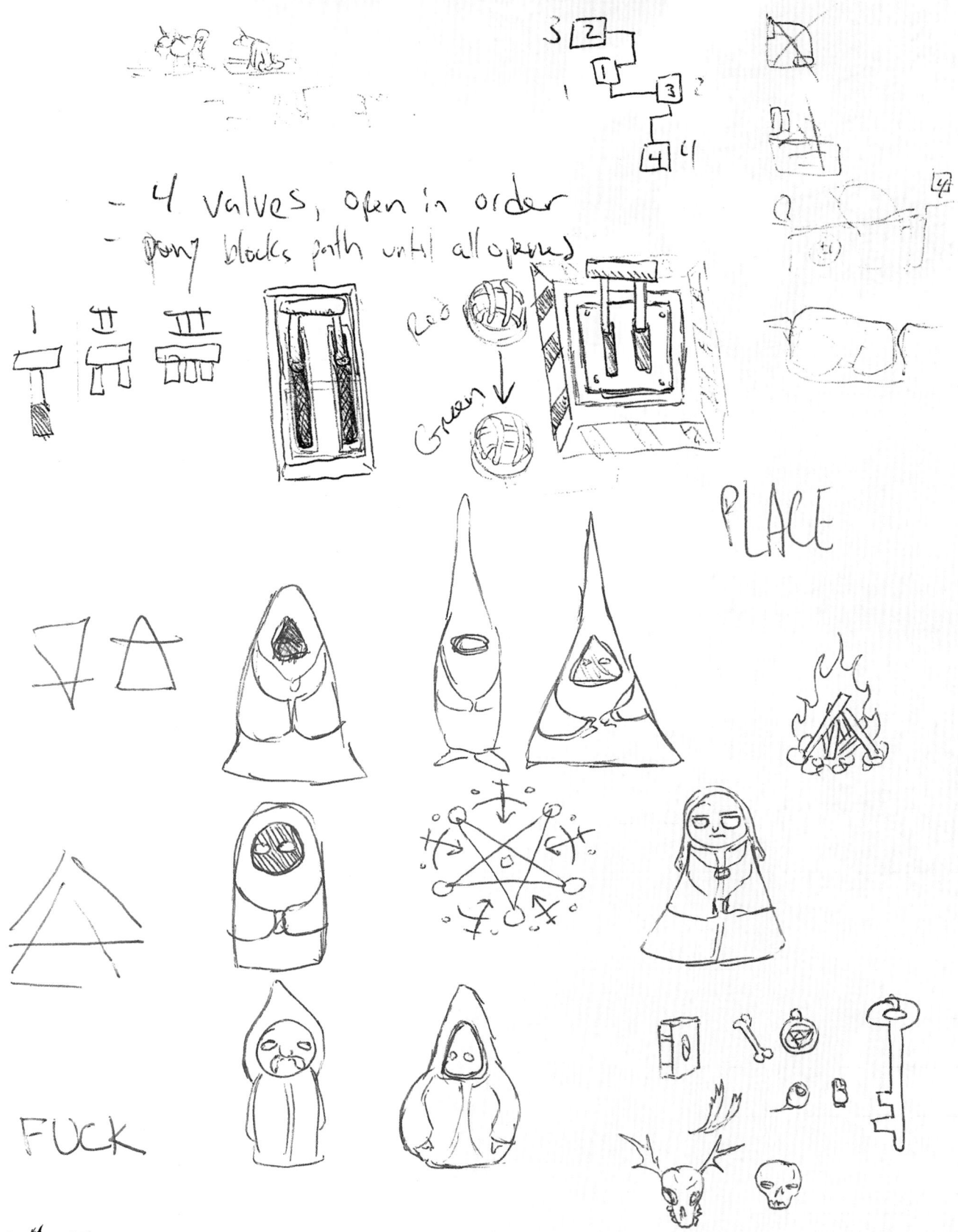

- 4 valves, open in order
- pony blocks path until all opened

Red

Green

PLACE

FUCK

WHAT'S IN THE BOX???

What is the Box? → A Key?

EPISODE 3
PUZZLE SKETCHES

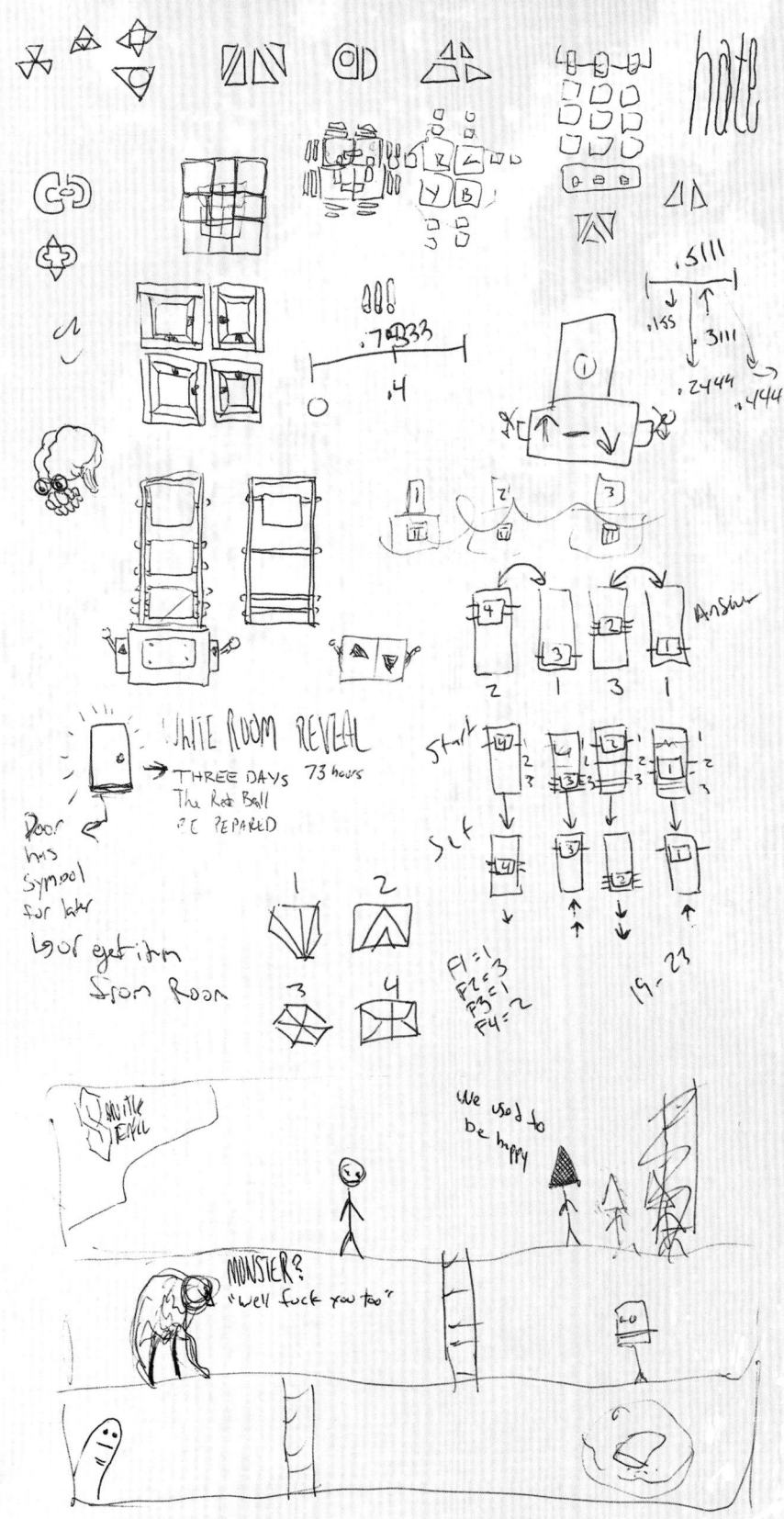

EPISODE 4
PUZZLE SKETCHES

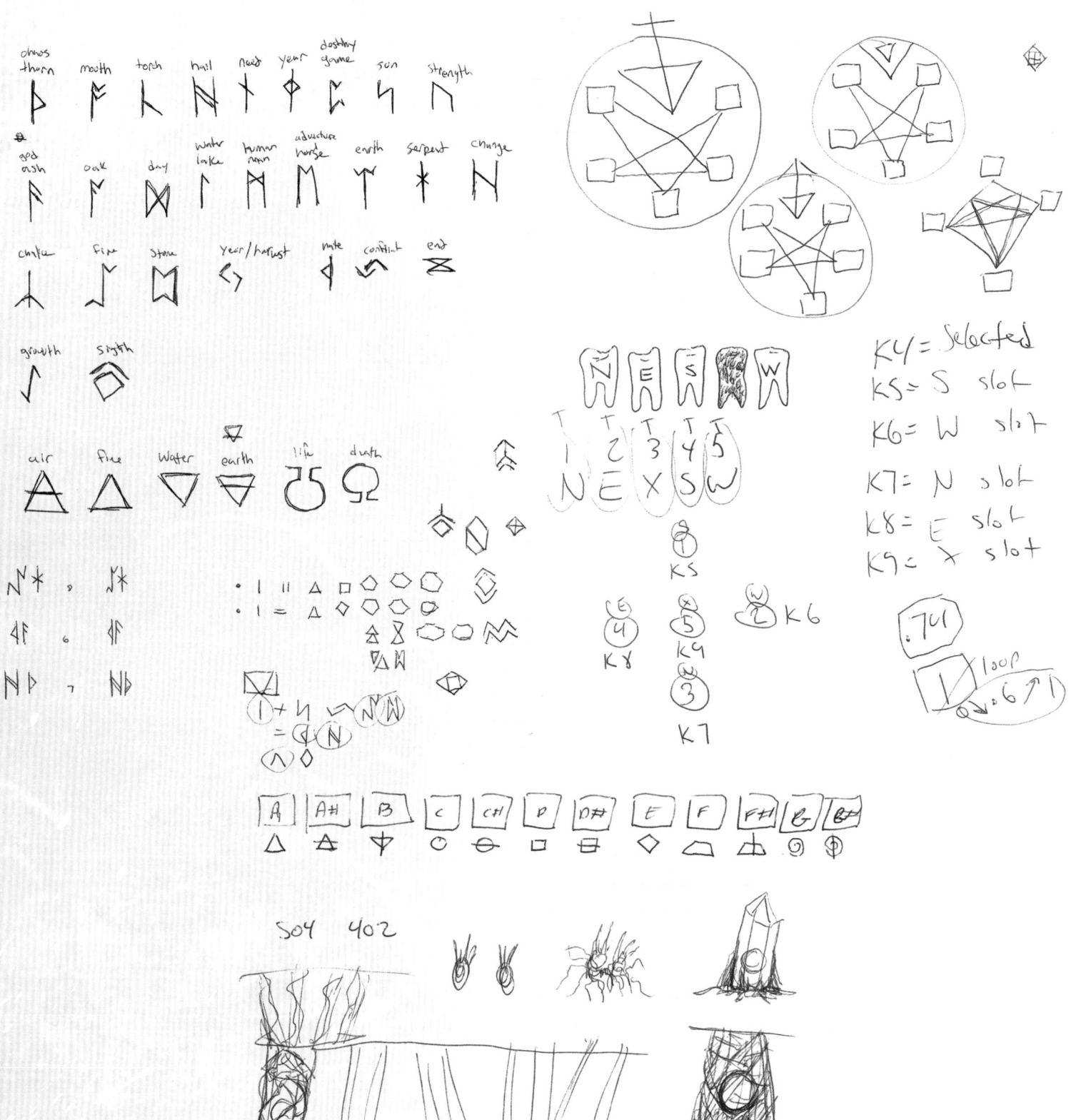

EPISODE 5
PUZZLE SKETCHES

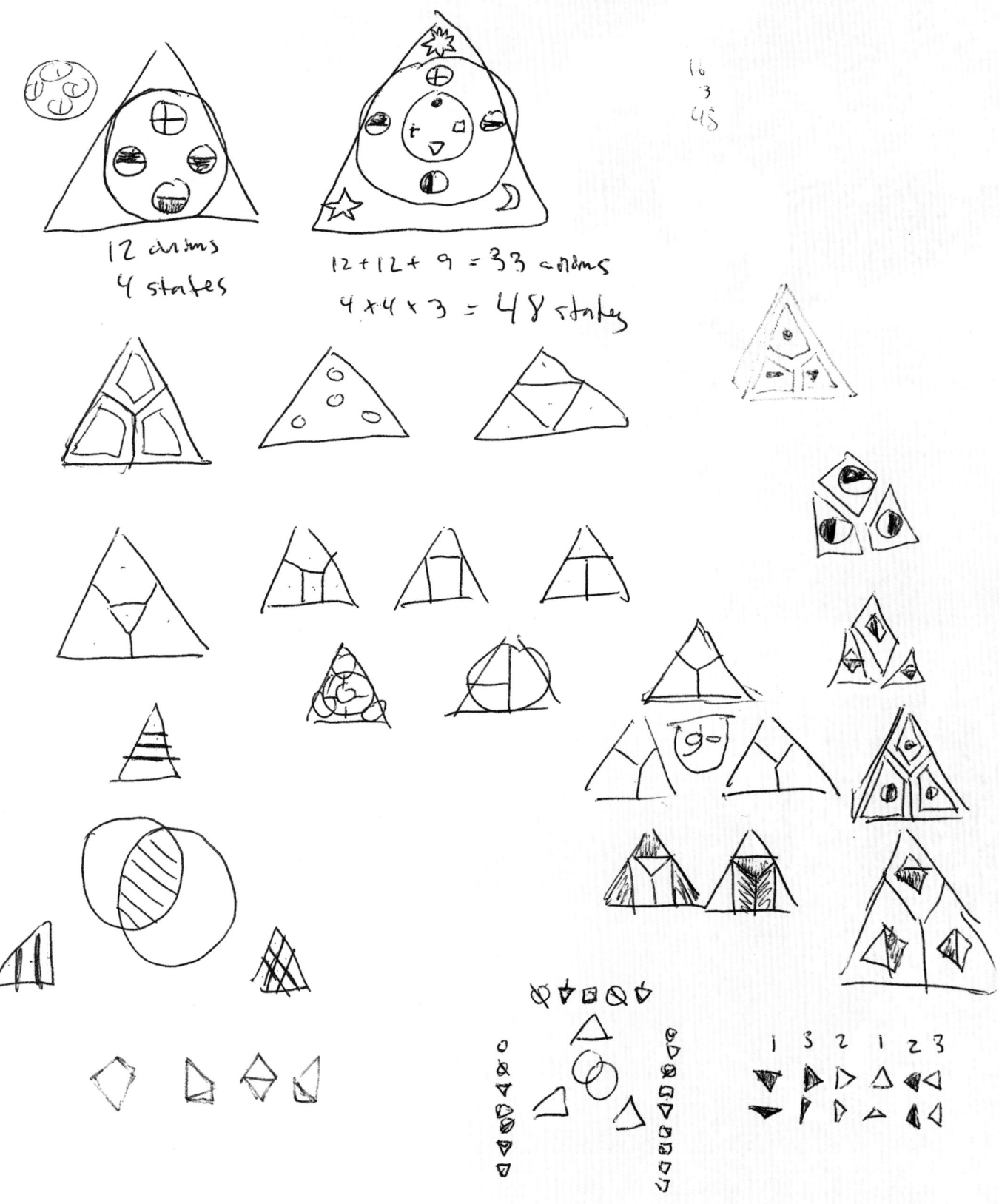

12 atoms
4 states

12 + 12 + 9 = 33 atoms

4 x 4 x 3 = 48 states

Sally Face ART, LORE, AND MORE

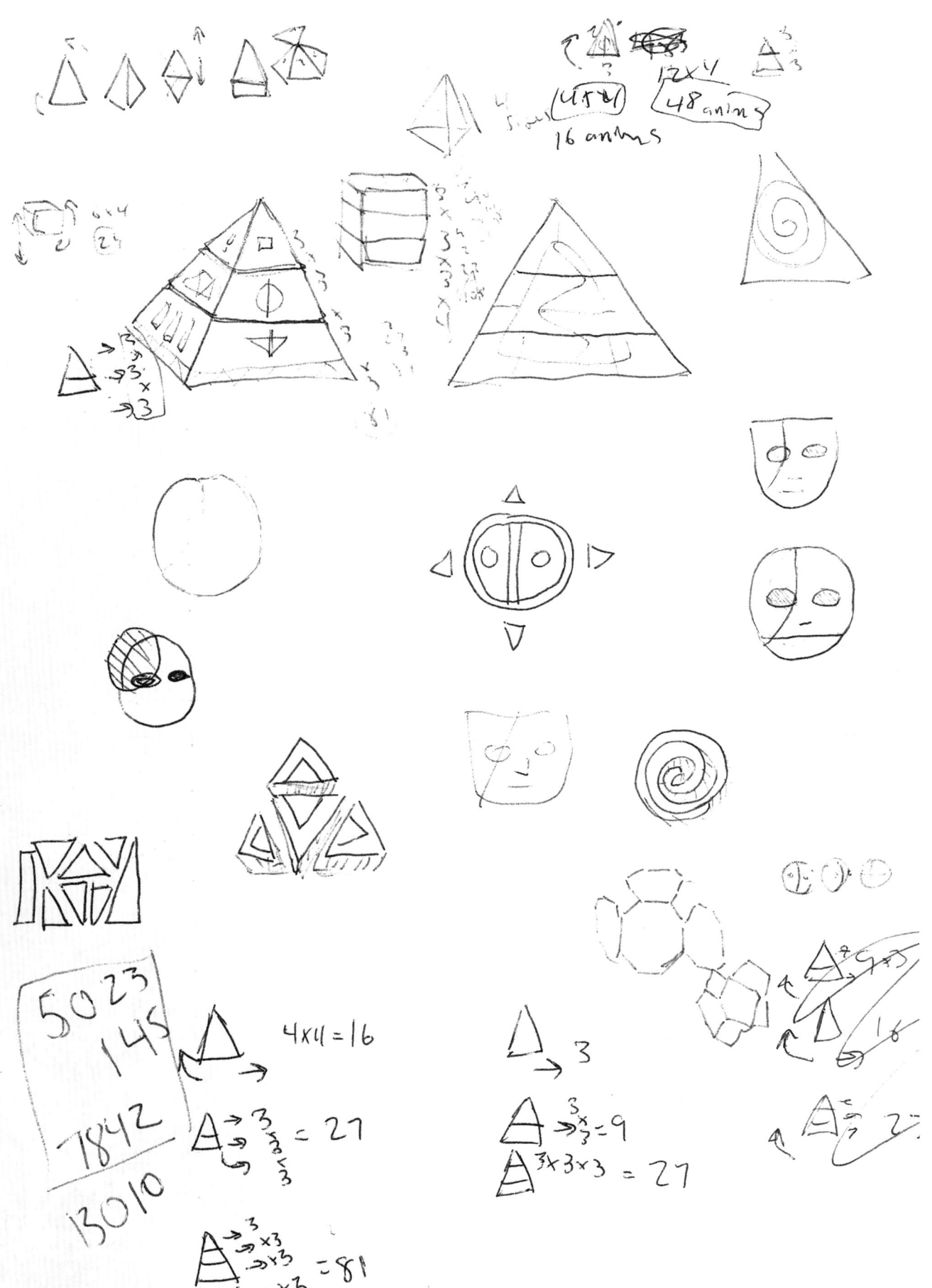

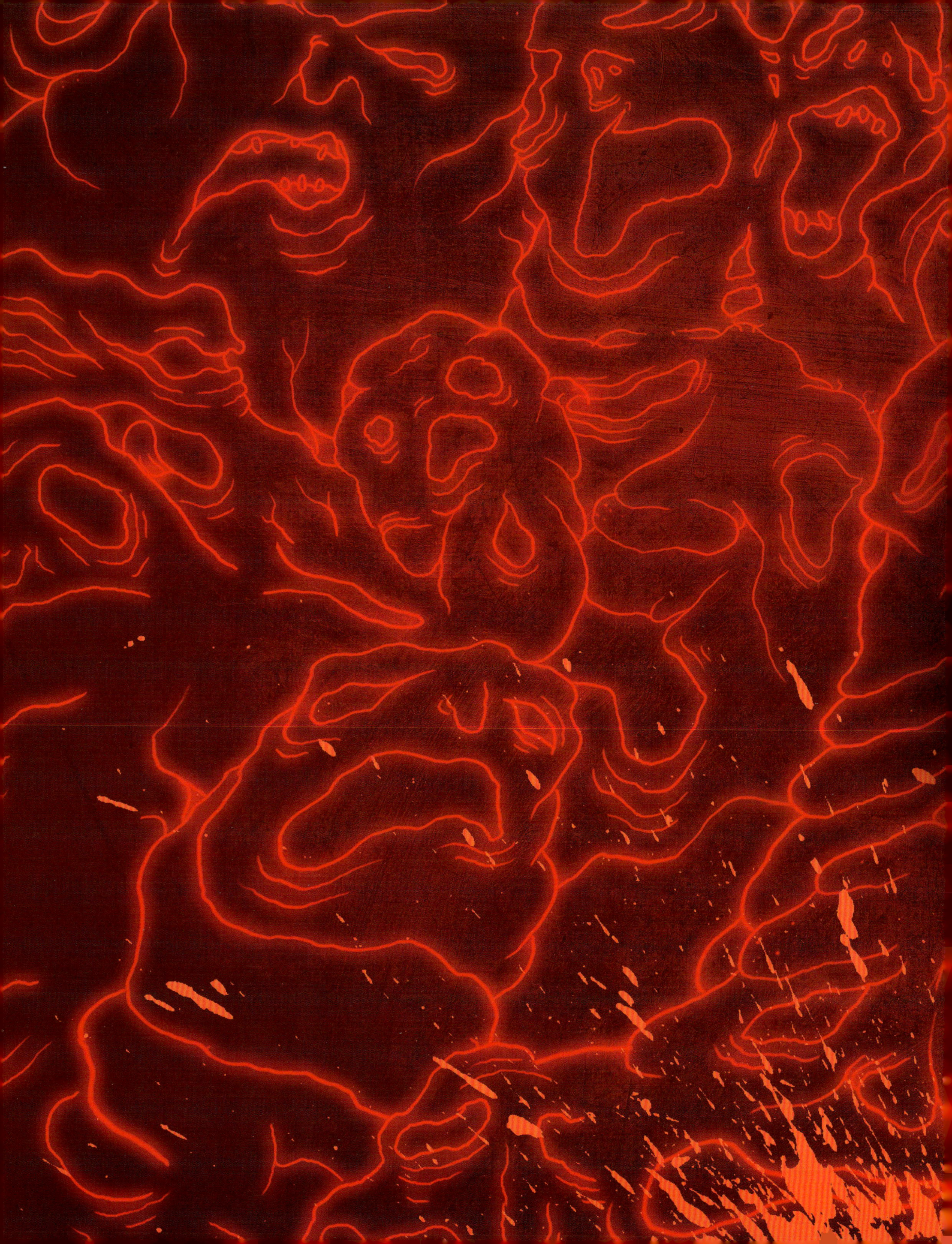

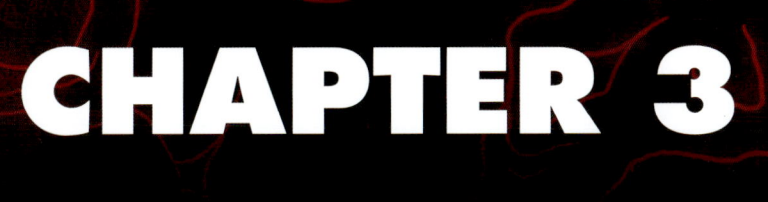

CHAPTER 3

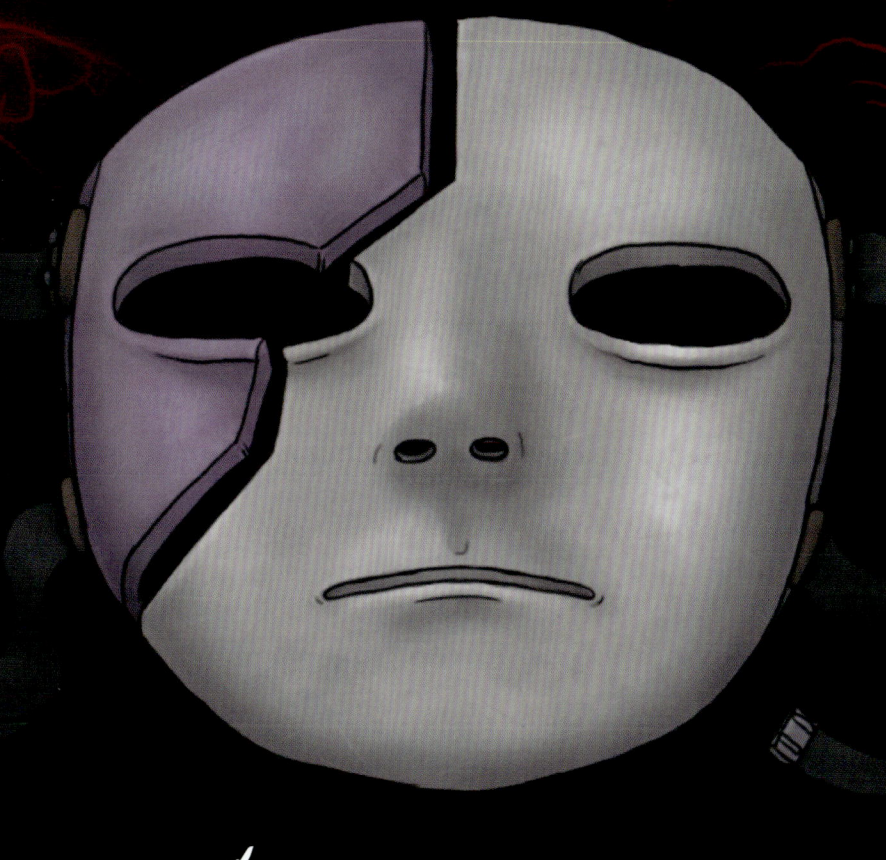

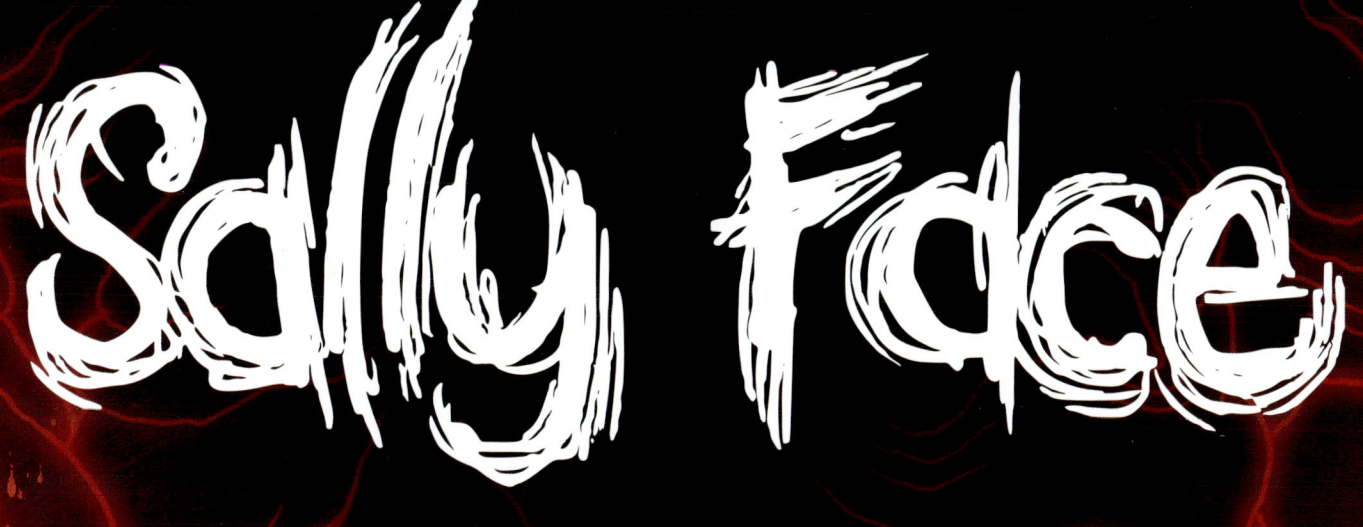

TIMELINE

TIMELINE

YEAR UNKNOWN: THE GREYS

The Grey family are a tribe of Native Americans, but there aren't many historical records of them. Even though there are relatives of the Greys living in Nockfell today, their ancestry appears to be more legend than fact. It is said that their family was formed when a great owl swooped down from the night sky and made love to a man who was lost in the woods. Weeks later, a beautiful young woman burst out from inside of the man. A nearby pack of wolves came to eat bits of the dead man's flesh. By doing this, the wolves became indebted to the young woman. Over time, the pack became human and, together with the young woman, they formed the first members of the Grey tribe. Descendants of the woman are said to have the ability to see the future.

1400s: THE ROSENBERGS

The Rosenberg family were originally from Germany, but by the 1400s they had spread out across Europe. There was a bloodline of witches in the family. As witch hunts became more prevalent, their numbers dwindled. Eventually, the last remaining witches traveled to America, the New World, in the hopes of escaping persecution.

1500s: NOCKFELL

The Grey tribe were traveling through the woods when they saw a large glowing light in the distance, so they sent their strongest hunter to check it out. Hours later, the light went out. The hunter soon returned, excited, after finding a beautiful lake. Over the next few months, the tribe migrated to live by this lake. However, people started disappearing in the middle of the night. They soon discovered that the hunter had been transforming into a beast and was eating people! They made a deal with the creature, so that they could continue to live on the land that had become home to the last of the Greys. Even though they were forced to make sacrifices to the beast, it was considered a balance between nature and man. This land came to be called Nockfell.

1663 — 1676:
THE DEVOURERS OF GOD

The first prophecy of Citlali Grey brought a small group of natives (a faction of the Grey Tribe) together. Colonists arrived in Nockfell, some of which were drawn in by the prophet. A marriage between Citlali Grey and Wesley Rosenberg (one of the colonists) united the two groups. This union ultimately led to the formation of the Devourers of God.

1677 — 1681
TEMPLE

The Grey/Rosenberg marriage gave the Rosenberg family rights to a lot of land in Nockfell. The newly-formed cult constructed a temple, hidden underground. The temple was built into existing chambers of worship within a natural cave system.

1703: PHELPS
MINISTRY

A church was built to hide the temple. It's used to indoctrinate followers and gain members. Another ceremonial marriage takes place between the Grey and the Phelps families.

MID 1700s: THE FINAL
PROPHECY OF CITLALI GREY

The prophecy about the "Child of The Abomination" was spoken and becomes a part of the Devourers' doctrine. Preparations for his execution began.

"The blue flame, not extinguished, still flickers in the night. He that sees between worlds, Child of The Abomination. Wielding light beyond man, pierces through the endless black. Betrayer of our kind, resurrected by Asintmah. His sword, blood of man, rises to protect the Great Atrocity and prevent the triumph of humankind."

A rough and incomplete translation.

1887: THE ADDISON FAMILY

Fredrick and Henrietta Addison moved to Nockfell to start a business. They quickly learned that the town is run by Phelps Ministry and the Addisons became involved with the cult in order to secure land. The Rosenberg family sold their land to the Addisons. The apartments were built over the recently expanded temple as a disguise and another access point for the quickly growing cult.

1905: TERRENCE ADDISON

Terrence Addison is born. His parents made a deal with the Council of the Devourers of God and so the boy was "blessed" from birth to be the entry point of The Endless One. The Council secretly fed him human flesh. This information was withheld from general members.

1906: A NEW PROPHECY

The new Oracles prophesize that they will alter the future by killing the Child of The Abomination. A man will fall from the sky and attempt to stop them, unless they persuade him to join the cult; then, he will help them greatly.

1917: THE ENDLESS

Fredrick and Henrietta Addison were murdered when they tried to push against the cult's wishes. Terrence was groomed to become the vessel for The Endless One and his soul was destroyed. From this point, the boy was tainted and controlled by the darkness and this had also slowed his aging.

1932: ROOM 103

Terrence's appearance began to change. The Council decided to lock him into room 103 to keep him hidden until he is at full power. They were able to draw power from the beast that he is transforming into.

1938: RED EYED DEMON

The first cosmic shadow was summoned by the cult: a relentless cosmic predator, older than time itself. Little was known about them besides for the fact that The Endless One demanded that the shadows be summoned. The ritual took a great toll on those who call forth these beings.

1972
Lisa Garcia moved to Addison Apartments and took the position of caretaker.

1973: JIM JOHNSON
Jim arrived in Nockfell / Earth. Evelyn was lost and possibly corrupted by the dark.

1975
Larry Johnson was born.

1974
Jim and Lisa got married.

1976
Sal Fisher was born. Ashley Campbell was born.

1977
Todd Morrison was born.

1982: PERSUASION
The cult reached out to enlist Jim, but he refused. Lisa gets pregnant, but the baby was stillborn. Jim suspected that the cult had something to do with the death of their child.

1983: INITIATION
In order to protect his family, Jim secretly joined the cult and made his way into the Council by earning their trust.

1987
Henry put their house on the market. Holmes family murder/suicide took place.

1984: SLAUGHTERED
Plans were enacted to stop the "Child of the Abomination". Despite not knowing the exact target, the cult had marked multiple potential children and had to act fast. 255 children and 32 adults were murdered across North America. Kenneth Phelps attempted to murder Sal and Diane. The cult thought that both were dead. Kenneth became an Archbishop. Jim betrayed the cult in an attempt to stop the slaughtering of the children and they killed him for it.

1988
Gizmo was born and adopted by Henry and Sal.

1990
Henry's house finally sold and he applied for a new job in Nockfell.

1991: STRANGE NEIGHBORS

Sal and Henry move to Addison Apartments in Nockfell. Mrs. Sanderson is murdered by Charley. Larry and Sal become friends. Sal finds a mysterious game cartridge in the basement.

1992: THE WRETCHED

Todd joins the gang with his paranormal expertise and gadget-making skills. The Super Gear Boy is made. Sal learns about an old cult in Nockfell. The boys work together to stop the Red Eyed Demon.

1993: THE BOLOGNA INCIDENT

Ashley, Todd, Larry, and Sal investigate the school lunch meat. They find out that Mrs. Packerton was killing people and using their flesh in the bologna, among other things. The gang finds an old cult temple below the apartments. They make a pact to fight the evil in Nockfell. Mrs. Packerton mysteriously dies in a car crash.

1994

The gang graduated from high school. Sal moved into the house with Todd.

1997

Ash leaves Nockfell. Neil moves in with Sal and Todd.

1999: THAT NIGHT

Larry commits suicide under strange circumstances. The cult imprisons the tenants of Addison Apartments as The Endless One infects their souls. Todd builds the Necro Guitar. Sal defeats The Endless One in battle and reluctantly kills the tenants to stop the spread of shadows. Todd is possessed by the Red Eyed Demon. Sal is arrested.

1998

Lisa and Henry get married.

2000

Sal is in prison and recounting his story to Dr. Enon. Todd is sent to a mental institution and thrown into a padded room. Enon falls to his death.

2001: THE TRIAL

Sal's on trial for mass murder. He decides to tell the truth, to warn people of what's out there. A heartbroken Ashley tries her hardest to help Sal, but he is found guilty and sentenced to death.

2004: EVERYTHING ENDS

Ashley continues to fight tooth and nail for Sal's release. Ashley meets the ghost of Larry. Sal is put to death via electric chair. Ashley and Neil, both devastated, continue to hunt the Devourers of God.

2005: MEMORIES AND DREAMS

Maple becomes infected by the dark. Larry's ghost disappears. Neil and Maple are taken by the cult. Sal finds The Vestige of Jim Johnson in the Void and learns to drift between worlds. Ash sacrifices herself for Sal and is resurrected with a new, powerful ability. Travis sacrifices himself in order to take down Kenneth. The Plague of Shadows is unleashed. An older Larry returns from the Void to give his final moments to help Sal and Ash destroy The Endless One. The Devourers of God and The Endless One are defeated. Larry's soul dies. The world is saved but something feels wrong.

AFTER

Even though the gang had stopped The Endless One from rising up, the Plague of Shadows destroyed 33% of the Earth's population.

It took Todd months to fully recover, yet remnants of shadow still remain within him. He's learning to keep it under control and perhaps, one day, will be able to wield its power.

Sal continues to acclimate to his new drifting abilities, and has been helping Ash and Todd clean up the devastation that the shadows left behind.

No contact with Larry has been made since his disappearance but the gang never gave up searching for him.

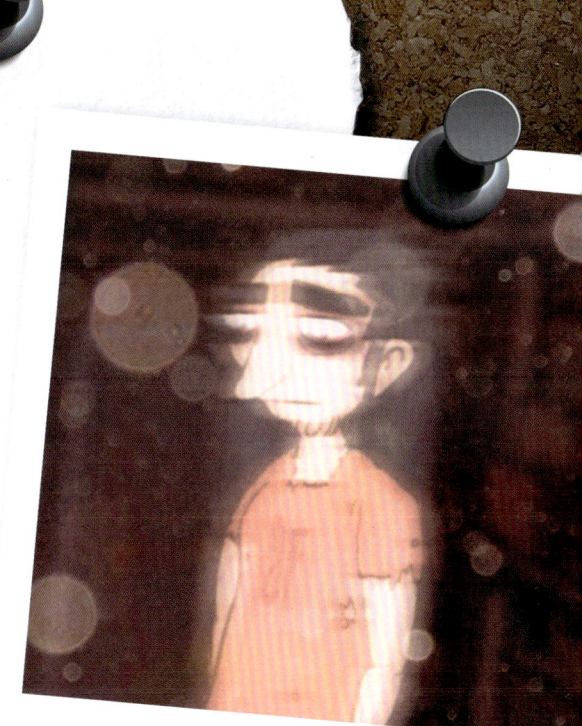

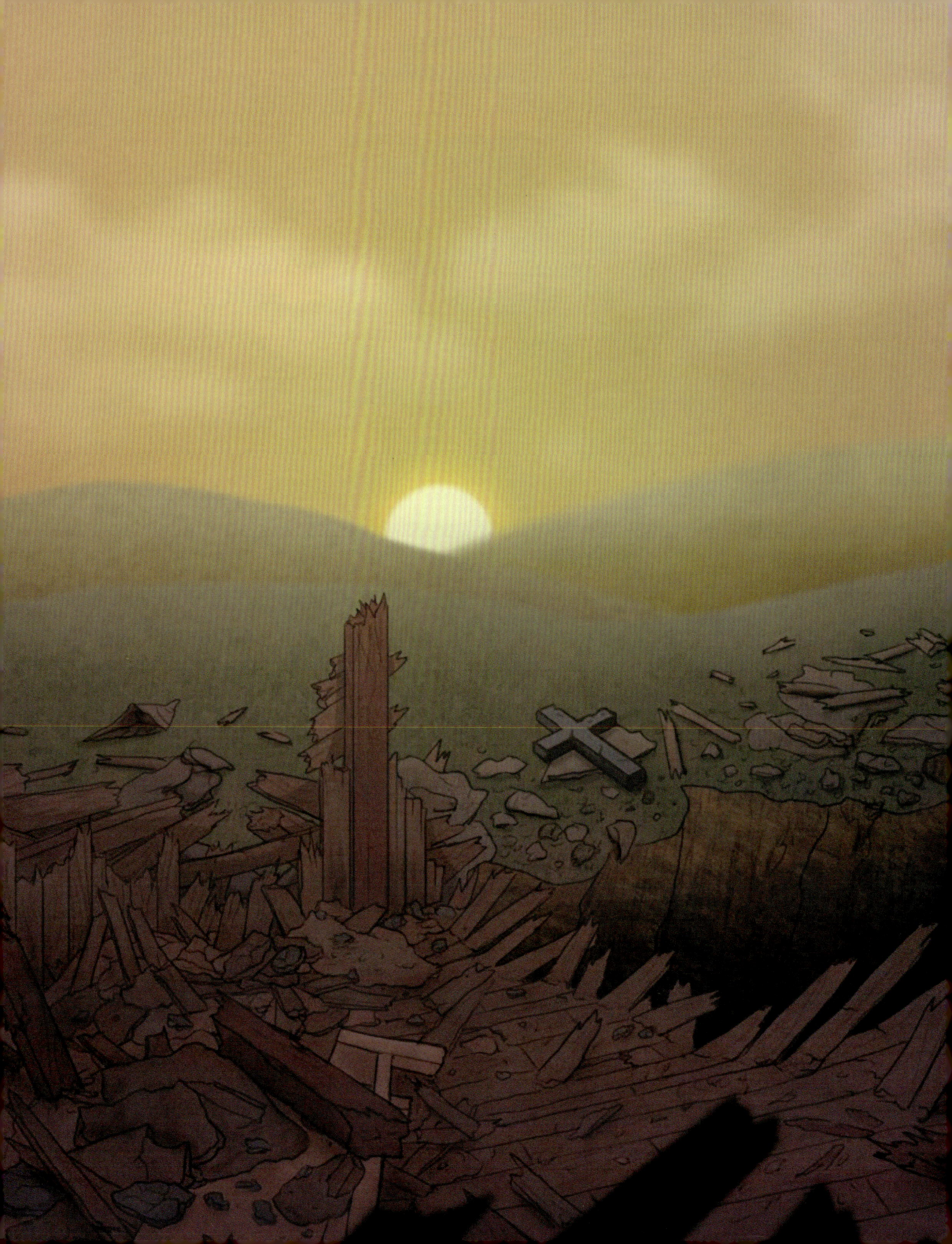

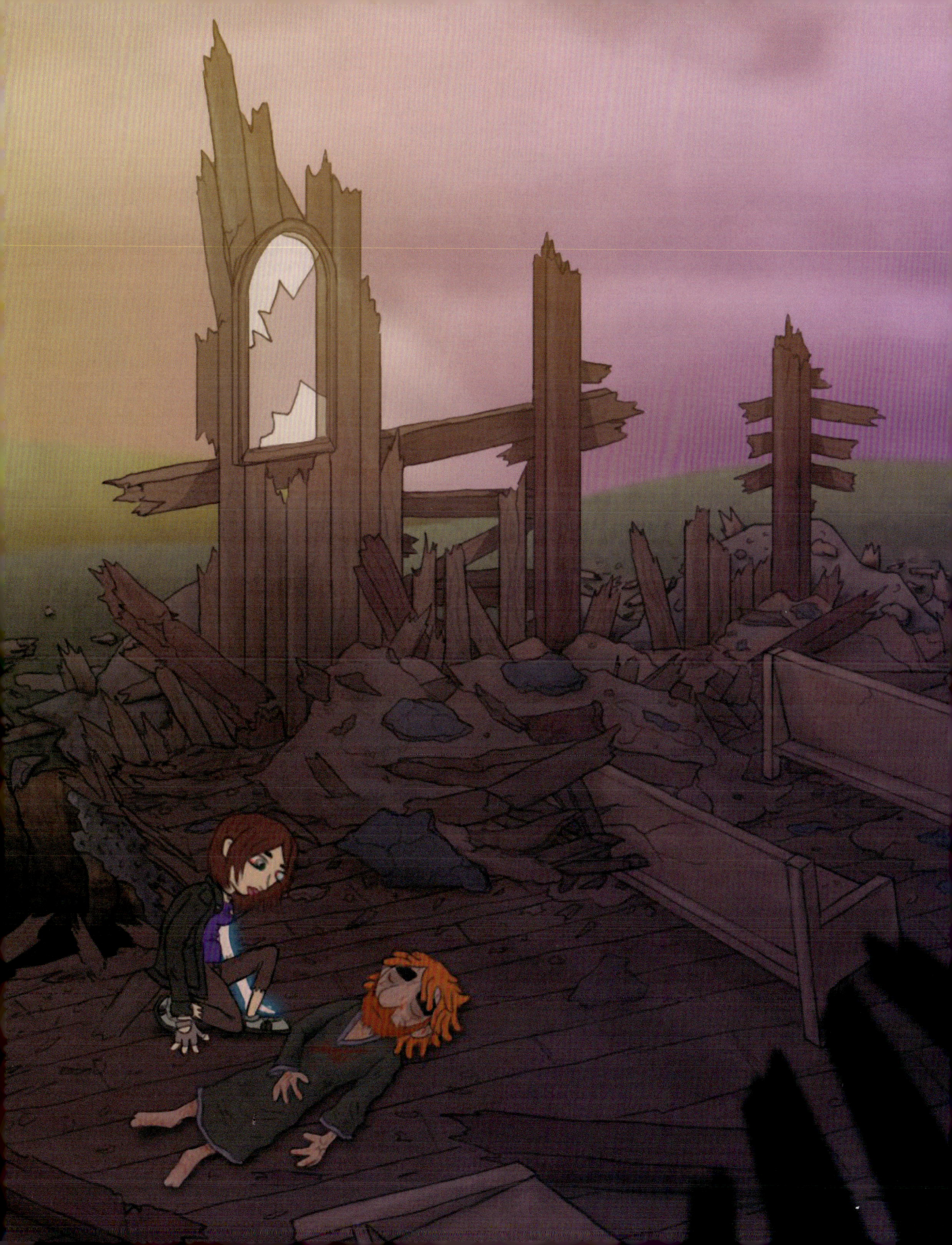

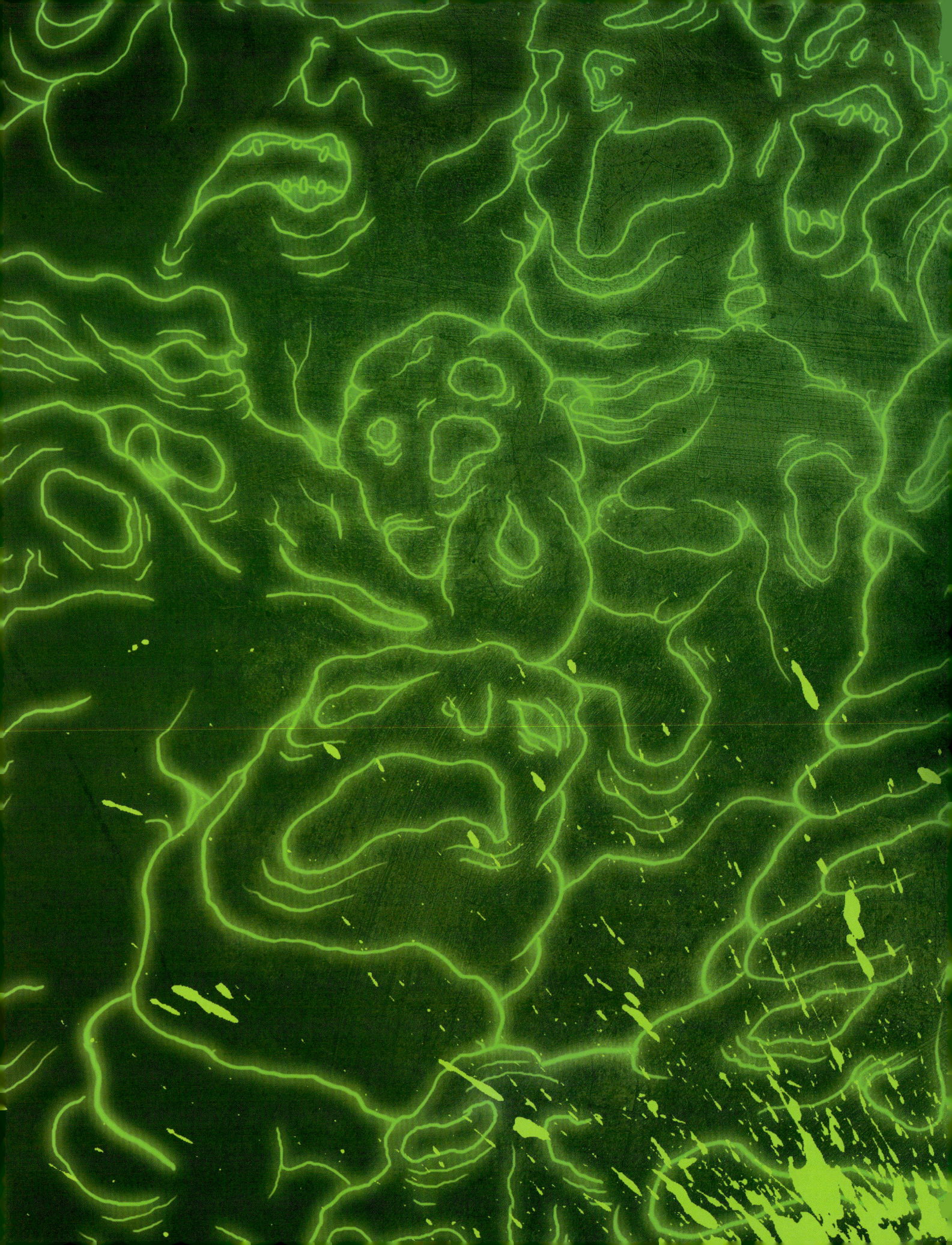

CHAPTER 4

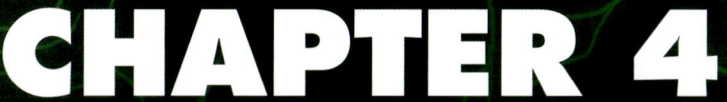

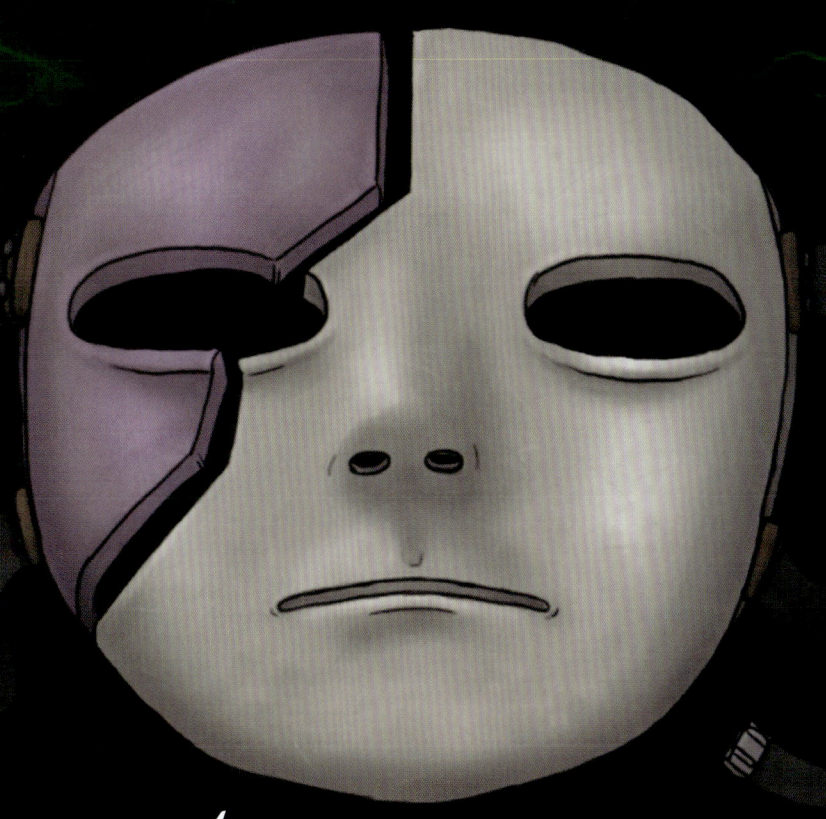

Sally Face

DEVELOPER BIOGRAPHY

A brief look at my life and the things that impacted me,
before the creation of Sally Face.

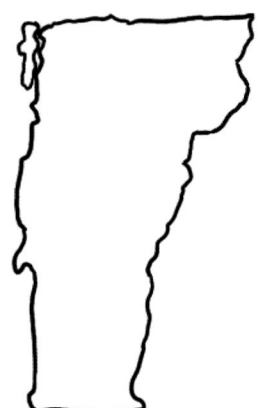 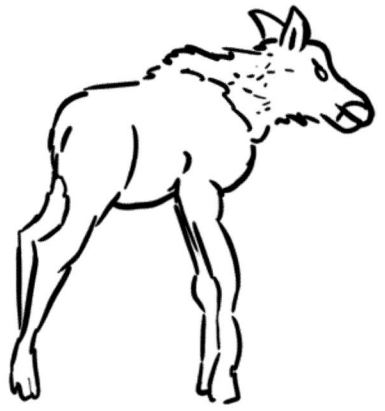 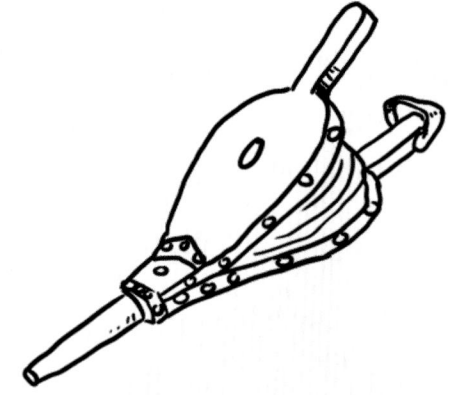

1986: A BABY MOOSE IS BORN

I WAS BORN in August of 1986, in Vermont. My stay here was brief, as my parents got divorced when I was only a few years old. My mom took care of me on her own while she was finishing college. Then, she met my stepfather when I was around five.

Some of my earliest memories are staying in his log cabin during winter and playing in the snow with his little dachshund. For some reason, I also distinctly remember having a lot of fun playing with the bellow (that thing you compress to blow air into the fireplace).

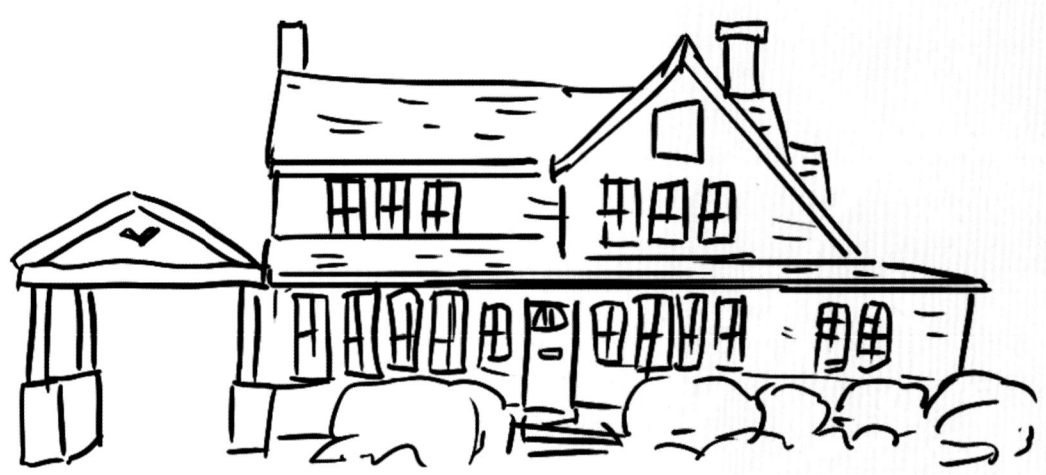

1991: A HAUNTING IN SOUTH JERSEY

WHEN I WAS ABOUT FIVE OR SIX, we moved down to southern New Jersey. The three of us lived in an apartment building before renting a house in Washington Township. The following two years significantly shaped the person I would become. Turns out, that house we were staying in was deeply haunted. Something that at first, as a child, I was blissfully unaware of. The house was one of the oldest homes in the area, built in 1835. It used to be a tavern and then a home for war widows. Later in life, I came to learn that my mother, some relatives, and even my

stepdad (who to this day is a hardcore skeptic) had a lot of unsettling experiences in that house. My mother told me that she didn't like to be in the house alone. I had a couple of unexplainable experiences there.

One in particular was the most paranormal thing I have ever witnessed. I was around eight or nine years old and this memory has stuck with me ever since. I was lying on the floor in my room, looking towards the hallway. The hall light was partially illuminating an otherwise dark bedroom. To my right, a small crate that was filled with toys sat nestled against the wall. Suddenly, without warning, the crate slid about five feet across the carpeted floor. This may seem relatively mundane compared to Hollywood visions of supernatural fiction but the difference is this was real. My little body was frozen in fear. It took me what felt like ten minutes but was probably closer to one or two minutes to jump to my feet and run downstairs, where my parents were.

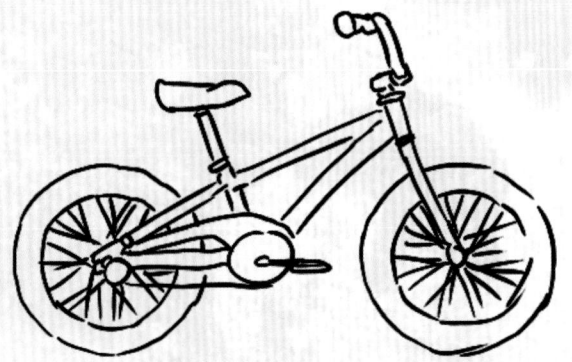

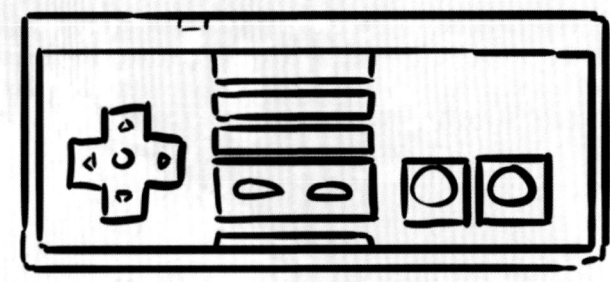

SHAPING MY INTERESTS

BESIDES THE SPOOKY HAPPENINGS, there were several other significant events in that house. My twin sisters were born and I was happy to be a big brother. When they got older, we didn't always get along but we always loved each other. Once we were adults, we became closer. The two of them mean the world to me.

There was a boombox in our garage with a bunch of my stepdad's cassette tapes. The two I gravitated towards were *Appetite for Destruction* by Guns N' Roses and a Beach Boys album. I listened to those albums a lot for a few years and they began to mold my music tastes towards rock and metal.

There were four things that I loved doing at this stage in my life: exploring outside, watching cartoons, drawing, and playing video games. I rode my bike all over the place, sometimes getting in trouble for cycling too far away. I loved collecting interesting stones and, one time, I even found a fossil while digging in my backyard. I received a Nintendo Entertainment System for my seventh birthday and spent many hours with Mario. I also highly enjoyed cartoons like Ninja Turtles, Ghostbusters, and the Simpsons. I think it was these cartoons that sparked my interest in drawing.

During my childhood, I was diagnosed with dyslexia. It's something I don't often talk about because I felt embarrassed by it for most of my life. It's something I still find myself resenting from time to time but I've come more to terms with it as I have grown older. After all, it's something I was born with and it can't be controlled or changed. While I don't have it as bad as others, it slows the speed at which I can read and has always made spelling difficult for me. Though, to be fair, English is not the most logical language.

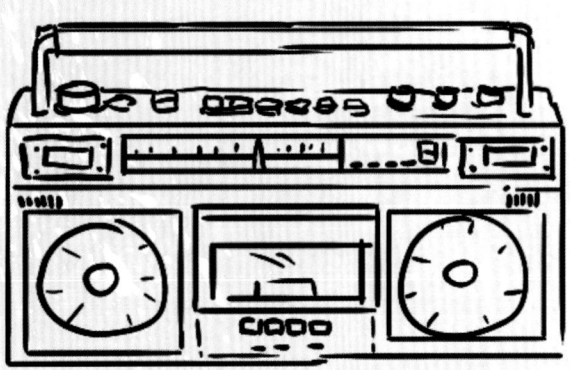

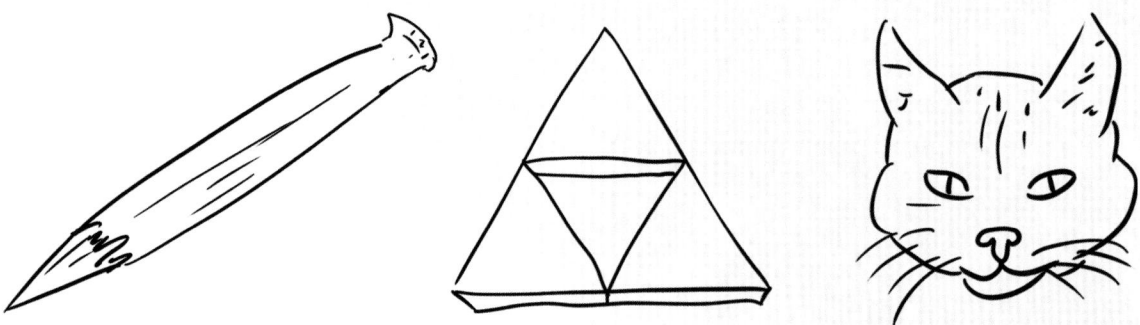

1994: MOVING TO NORTHERN NEW JERSEY

MY PARENTS eventually bought a house in northern New Jersey, in a rural town. This is where I spent most of my youth. I lived there for about eleven or twelve years. Here, I continued drawing, watching cartoons, playing video games, and riding my bike all over. I became obsessed with '90s Nicktoons, *Buffy the Vampire Slayer*, and *The Nightmare Before Christmas*. I grew fond of writing and crafting my own stories. A new interest sprouted in me and I began taking toys apart to see how they worked.

Over the years, our family had a couple of different cats. The first one was this big orange cat who would always sleep with me. He was part of the inspiration for Gizmo. Later, I was devastated to find him dead on the side of the road. We eventually got a German Shepherd mutt that I grew up with. I loved that guy so much.

There was a family next door with four kids, two of which were close to my age. I became very close

to them; the boys were like brothers to me and to this day I consider their family as part of my family. I used to be a very picky eater when I was a kid, so I do regret not trying more of their Arabic food (which everyone else loved).

On my thirteenth birthday, I got a Nintendo 64 with *Mario 64* and *The Legend of Zelda: Ocarina of Time*. I immediately fell in love with Zelda. Up until that point, I had played mostly platformers, beat-em-ups, shooters, fighting games, but nothing with this much depth. This was the game that completely changed my perspective of video games. It showed me that they can be great works of art, tell interesting stories, and have huge worlds you can explore. I spent that summer playing *Ocarina of Time* with my friends—this is a great memory that will always have a special place in my heart. *Zelda* and other video games were also one of the first big things I bonded with my sisters over. Later in life, the three of us even got Triforce tattoos together.

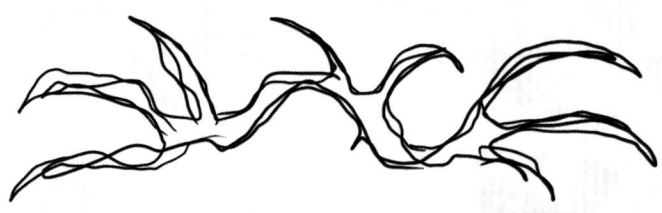

IT COMES AT NIGHT

DURING MY CHILDHOOD YEARS, I suffered from frequent Night Terrors. This meant a lot of extreme nightmares, sleep paralysis, sleepwalking, and waking up with intense fear. Sometimes I would have dreams within dreams within dreams. Waking up would feel hyper-real, but something was always wrong: a dead body in my bed, something in my room watching me, etc. When I actually woke up, it was always immediately apparent that it was just

a dream. Though, that realization somehow didn't make it any less scary to me.

One terror that stuck with me to this day is sort of hard to explain. I "woke up" in a dream and there was this indefinable mass floating over me. It was about the same size as me but made of shapeless bits of light. In that moment, I felt a cold emptiness like nothing I had ever felt before or since. I woke up with only one thought: that is what it feels like to die.

 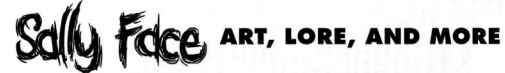

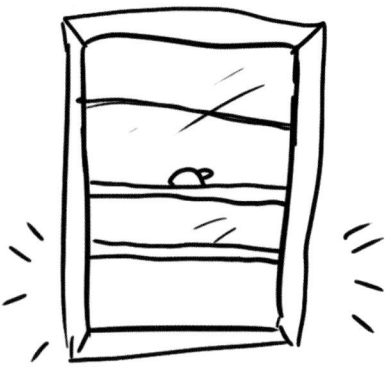

SOME MORE UNEXPLAINABLE STUFF

DESPITE HAVING MOVED out of the haunted Washington Township house, I continued to have a lot of unexplained experiences—many of which were corroborated by family members. Now, before I go on to describe these things, I need to say that I am very much a skeptical person. I use the term "haunted" lightly and I can't say that I definitely believe in ghosts or other supernatural things. I believe in the possibility of such things. Though, if they exist, they're probably not what we think they are. I do know for a fact that there are things beyond our current understanding of reality. I can say that with confidence because of my firsthand experiences.

Several times, in the middle of the night, we'd all be sleeping and then wake up to loud noises in the kitchen. It sounded like someone going through the cabinets. At times the dog would even bark at these noises. I can remember more than once my stepdad getting a bat and going downstairs to investigate, thinking someone was in our house. Of course, no one was ever there.

There are many stories that I and other members of my family have from this house but I want to share the two most significant to me.

I would often play in my room late into the night after everyone had gone to bed. Sometimes an eerie sound crept into my window from outside—a slow tapping sound, as if someone was rhythmically hammering on concrete right outside my window. It would scare me so much that I would run to my bed, get under the covers without turning the lights off, and just try to fall asleep as fast as I could. This was a frequent occurrence and to this day there is no logical explanation. I never really told anyone about it when I was a kid. But there are two things

that happened that make this a bit more substantial. 1) There was a concrete walkway in the front of the house (where my window faced). Over time, more and more circular chips appeared on the surface of the concrete. It got to the point where my stepdad got mad and was asking, "Who the hell is banging up the walkway?" 2) When I moved out for college, my sister took my room. Later on, I brought up the tapping sound and her face dropped. She said she had heard it too and it always freaked her out!

The second significant moment happened one night when our cousins were over. My sisters, my two cousins, and I were all hanging out in the living room. This was actually after I had moved out for college but I was home visiting. Someone was saying they kept seeing a weird light, though I never saw that myself. Everyone was getting a little spooked and the conversation came to a lull. Suddenly a voice emerged from downstairs! It was clear as day, a full sentence that sounded slightly electronic or inhuman in a way. When it finished speaking, we all stared at each other with wide open eyes. There was a beat of silence and then we all started whispering, "Did you hear that?" Everyone nodded to the question. Being older and a bit braver, and much more skeptical than I had been in the past, I jumped to my feet and quickly went downstairs. The rest cautiously followed. I turned on the lights and searched for signs of someone being there or maybe some kind of electronic toy or device that could have gone off. Nothing. There was nothing down there that could have made that sound. The worst part was this lingering thought in my mind: when it spoke it was so clear that I could hear every word, and yet somehow I have no idea what it said.

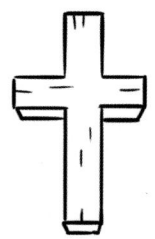

WITHOUT GOD

AS MUCH as I'd rather not talk about this part, I think it's an important piece of my journey. My parents are religious people. No, not the bigoted, gay-hating, woman-demeaning type. They're what I would call casual Christians. I grew up believing in God and going to church on Sundays. I repressed a lot of feelings because I thought they were "sinful" and that I wouldn't get a golden ticket into heaven if I did "bad" things. In hindsight, I would have had a much more enjoyable youth without that baggage. As I got older, I began to question the whole thing and I stopped going to church with them. It took a few years to fully shed myself of the religious thoughts and ideas but I'm glad I found my way out of it. I don't hold it against my parents, as I know they believed they were saving my soul.

I now firmly believe that no child should ever be indoctrinated into any religious belief. To me, that is morally wrong. I still remember the unraveling feeling of going from "It's okay, once I die, things will be cool" to "Damn, when I die, there will be nothing. How much of my life did I waste believing in this stuff?" It was a difficult transition, but it became so clear to me how nonsensical and hypocritical those religious belief systems are. However, when you grow up being told that "this is reality" then that's what you believe because you don't know any better.

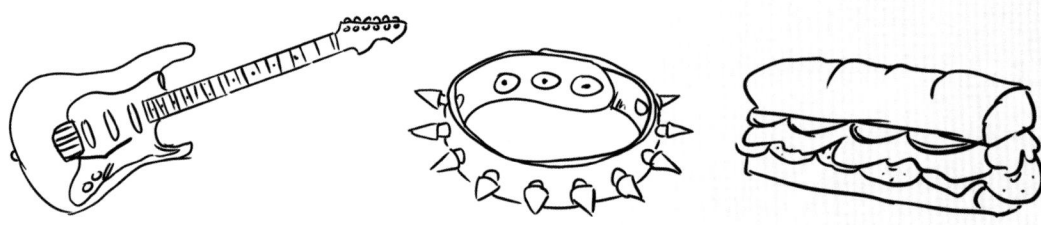

2001: HIGH SCHOOL

I WENT THROUGH A PRETTY BIG GOTH PHASE during high school. All black, bondage pants, spiked bracelets, the whole thing. This is also when I started teaching myself guitar. I mainly learned by playing different riffs from metal songs I liked. I was also in a few different bands throughout those four years. It was always a ton of fun playing on stage. It's a very special feeling. In another lifetime I may have pursued the band life. It was something I considered for a little while and something I do miss.

When I turned 16, I got my first job at a local sandwich shop. I was excited to earn my own money to buy a better guitar amp and other things for myself. Despite not liking the part where I had to deal with customers, I didn't mind the work and also made some good friends there.

Like many high schoolers, this was a time where I first discovered romantic love and loss. It's funny how when you're in school, everything feels so big and important. Not only relationships both romantic and platonic, but the whole experience. Then, later in life, you have a hard time even recalling details from that time.

Throughout my life, I would sometimes feel a sudden sadness and emptiness. This started happening more during my high school years. What I didn't realize at the time is that I was suffering from depression. My reaction was usually to go quiet, distance myself from others, and wait for it to pass. Since I didn't have a good way of describing it at the time, I was often left feeling alienated. Depression is something I still struggle with occasionally. I think that's partly why I seek out sad stories, artwork, and music; because they resonate with me.

 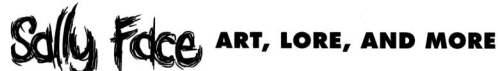

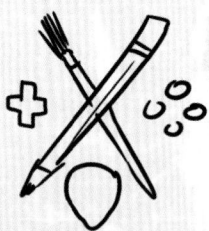

THE JOURNEY BEGINS

DESPITE HAVING come up with multiple ideas for video games, I never thought it was a thing I could actually do. I was getting close to finishing high school and I wasn't entirely sure of what I wanted to do next. I knew I'd probably go to college, since I was convinced I needed a degree to get a good job (spoiler: I didn't).

One day, my stepdad said he heard on the radio that there was a college teaching game design. That was the first time I realized that making video games was an option. I didn't know the first thing about what actually went into making games (this was a different time and there wasn't a lot of information online), though I knew that I loved the combination of art, storytelling, music, and interaction. So I decided that it was the perfect path for me.

There weren't many schools that offered game programs back then and none that were close to home. I applied to two schools, one in Pittsburgh and one in Chicago, and was accepted to both of them. Ultimately, I decided Pittsburgh was a better fit.

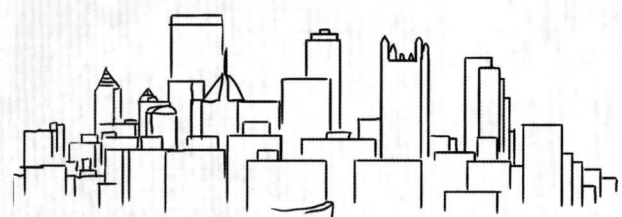

2005: OFF TO PITTSBURGH

MOVING TO PITTSBURGH started a new chapter of my life. I was far from home, my friends, my family, and everything I had become comfortable with. The change gave me room to figure myself out more and grow into myself in ways I may not have otherwise.

The class size of the Game Art and Design major was fairly small to begin with and more than half of them dropped out in the first year. Likely because they realized how much work it is to make games. In hindsight, I probably didn't need to go to college, but I don't regret the time I spent there; I learned a lot and met a lot of cool people. It was overall a positive experience. It's mainly that the debt accrued that may not have been worth it.

During college, I developed a strong passion for game design. I found myself overachieving on a lot of projects, simply because I really enjoyed the work. I remember staying up extra late many times and even working through the night on a few school projects. However, I was going to school full-time and also working full-time, so part of that was out of necessity. As you can imagine, I was consuming a lot of caffeine to keep my energy up.

Towards the end of my final quarter of school, I was hospitalized with a 5mm kidney stone that got lodged inside of me. Let me tell you, the pain was excruciating. I'm talking pain that put me on the ground, pouring sweat and throwing up. I missed a good bit of classwork and was failing some classes because of my absence. Luckily, I was able to reach out to my teachers to get extensions. I finished up the tail end of school on very strong painkillers that made me feel high and sick all at once. I was lucid enough to bring those grades from Fs to As and Bs. So I graduated by the skin of my teeth, at the end of 2009. From then on, I tried to improve on my diet, including quitting caffeine, which gave me a headache that lasted for two weeks. But the headache was nothing compared to the alternative, so it was worth it.

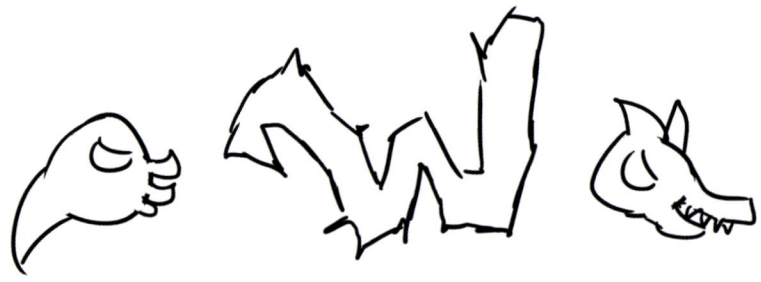

2010: WITHER STUDIOS

AFTER COLLEGE, I knew I wanted to start my own company instead of joining someone else's. I began by building some small prototype games and putting a team together. During the formation of Wither Studios and throughout the following years, I was in and out of side jobs, freelance work, and unemployment. All while trying to make the dream come true of working on our own games full-time.

The learning process of starting a development company was a lot of trial and error. We were developing an action-adventure game that we quickly realized was more than we could handle in our free time. So we switched gears to work on a platformer game based on a prototype I had made called Crowman & Wolfboy. We almost built the full game in an engine that our programmer was familiar with, but that programmer ended up leaving the team. At that point, we needed to change engines and start over. We ran a successful Kickstarter to get a little bit of money for software and other needs.

I traveled with the team to PAX East 2012, which was my first big game convention. In 2014, Crowman & Wolfboy was in the Indie Game Showcase at PAX East. It's always a good time meeting players and hanging out with other devs. In general, it was a ton of work to build games and start a company while maintaining full-time jobs. In order to do that, you have to sacrifice a lot of things in life. It takes a large amount of determination and maybe a bit of obsession for the work: two qualities I definitely have.

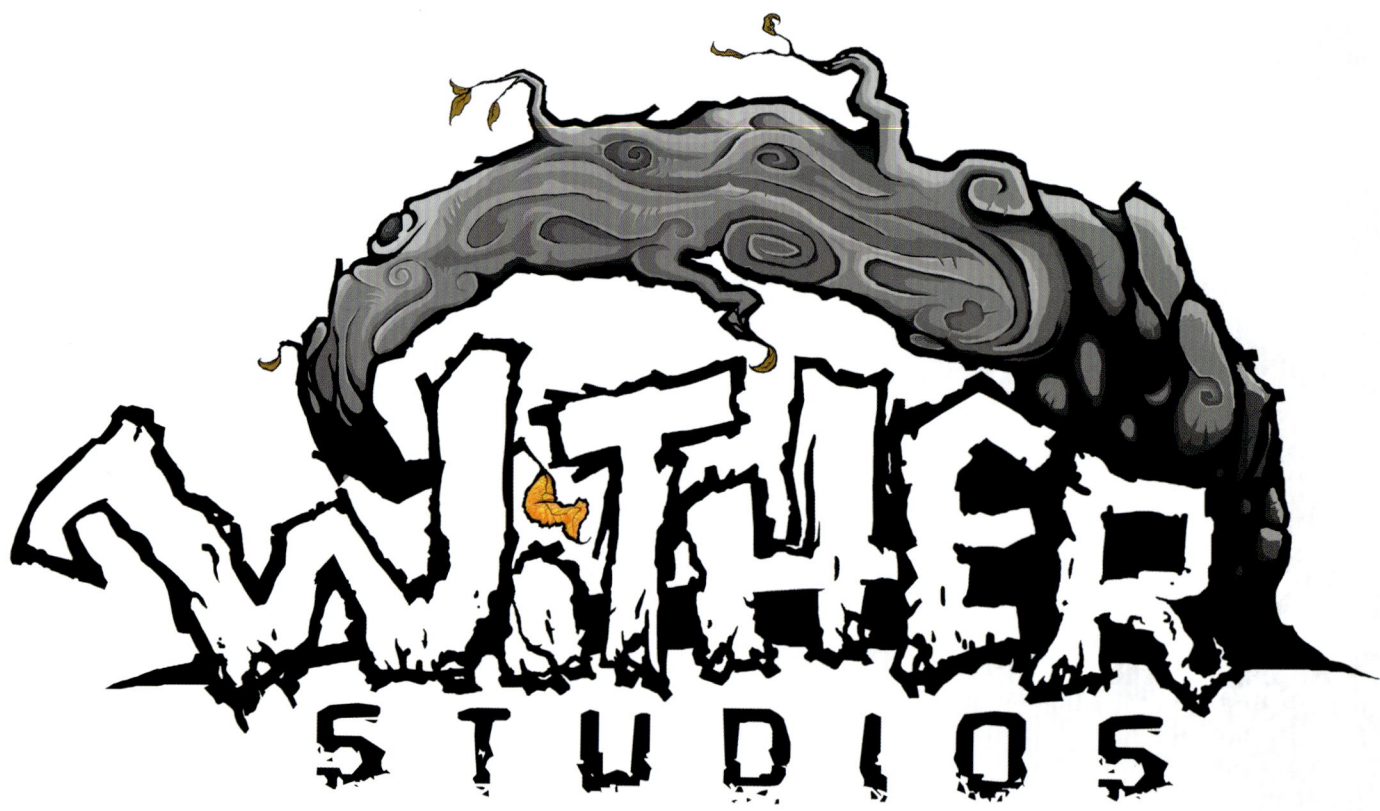

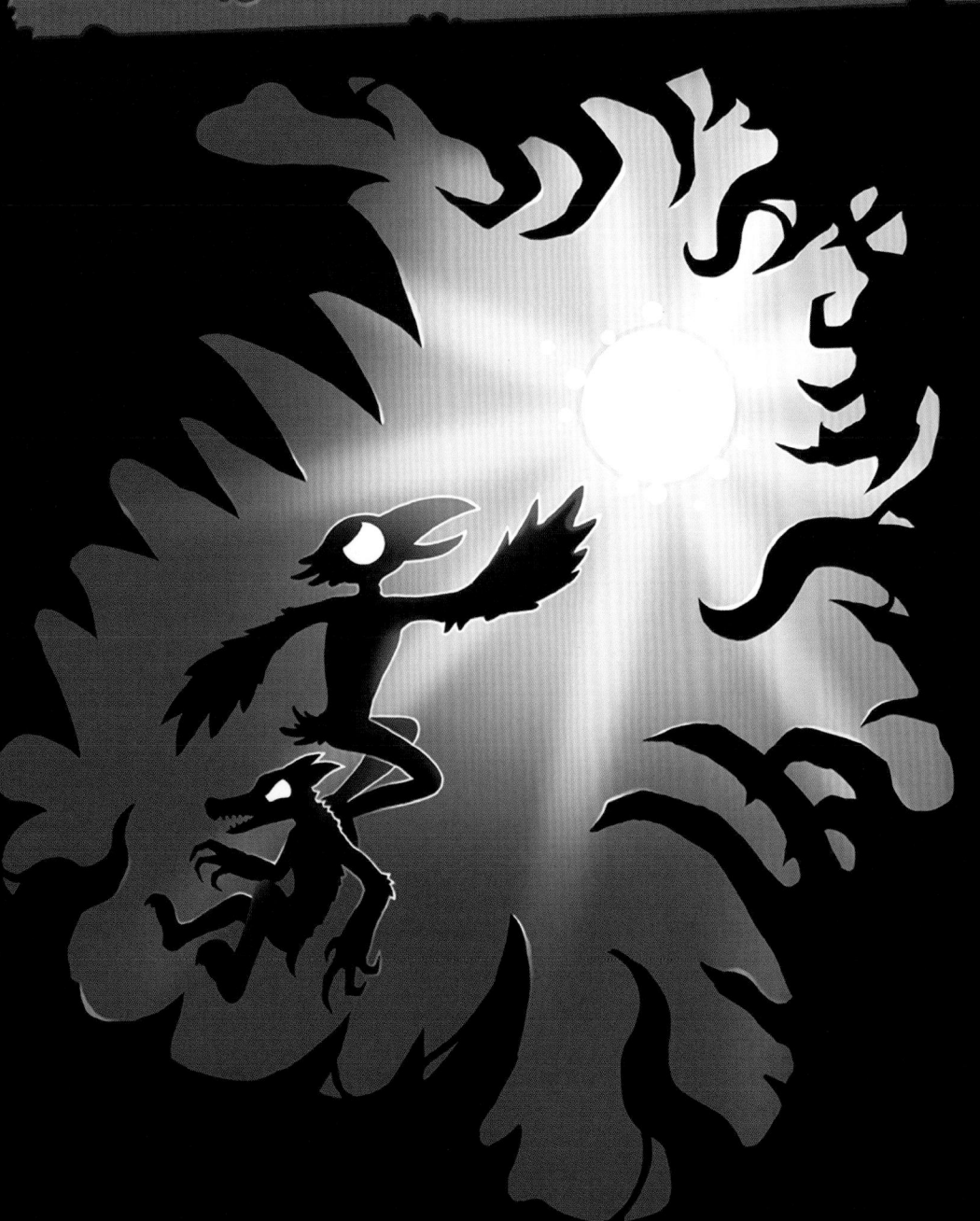

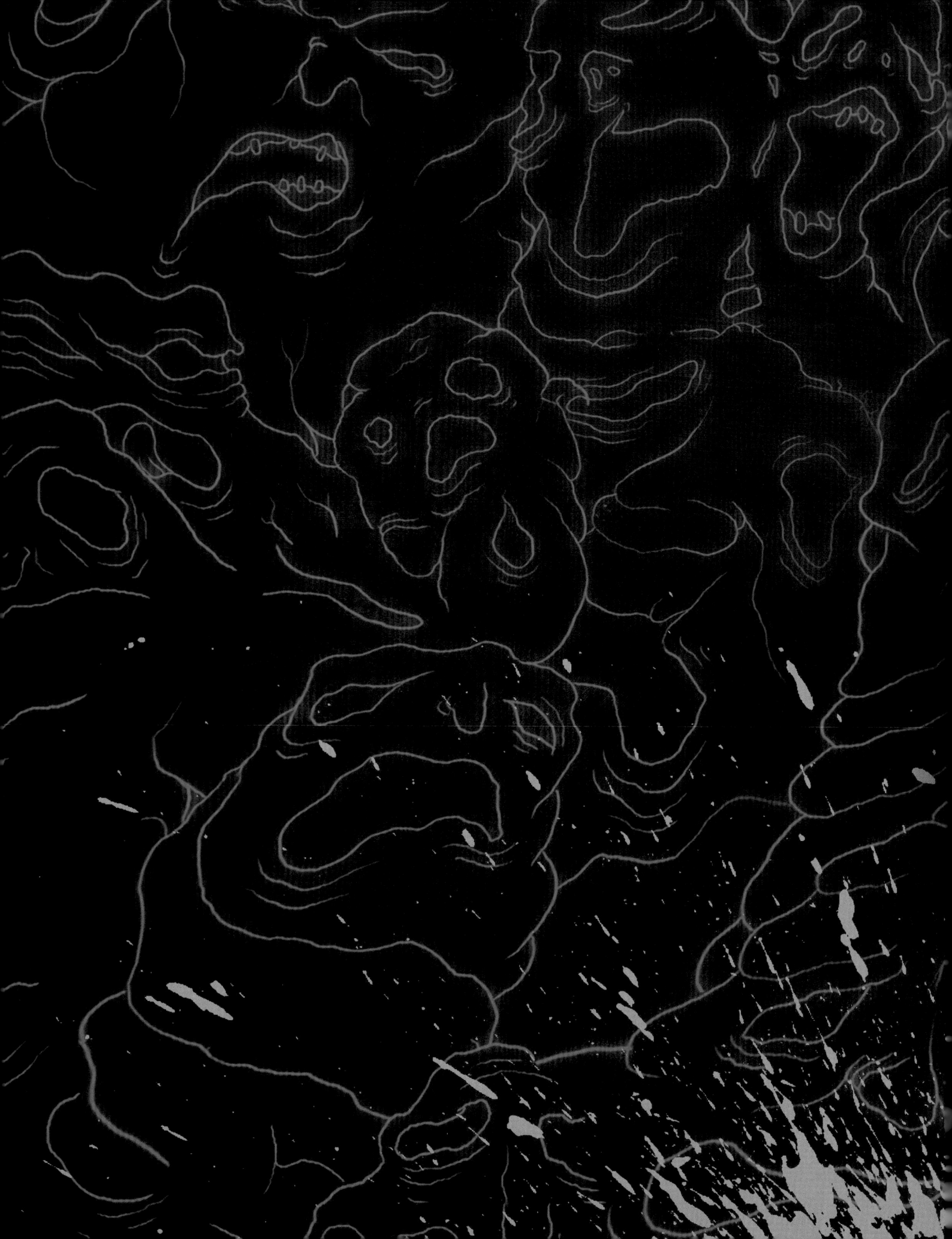

CHAPTER 5

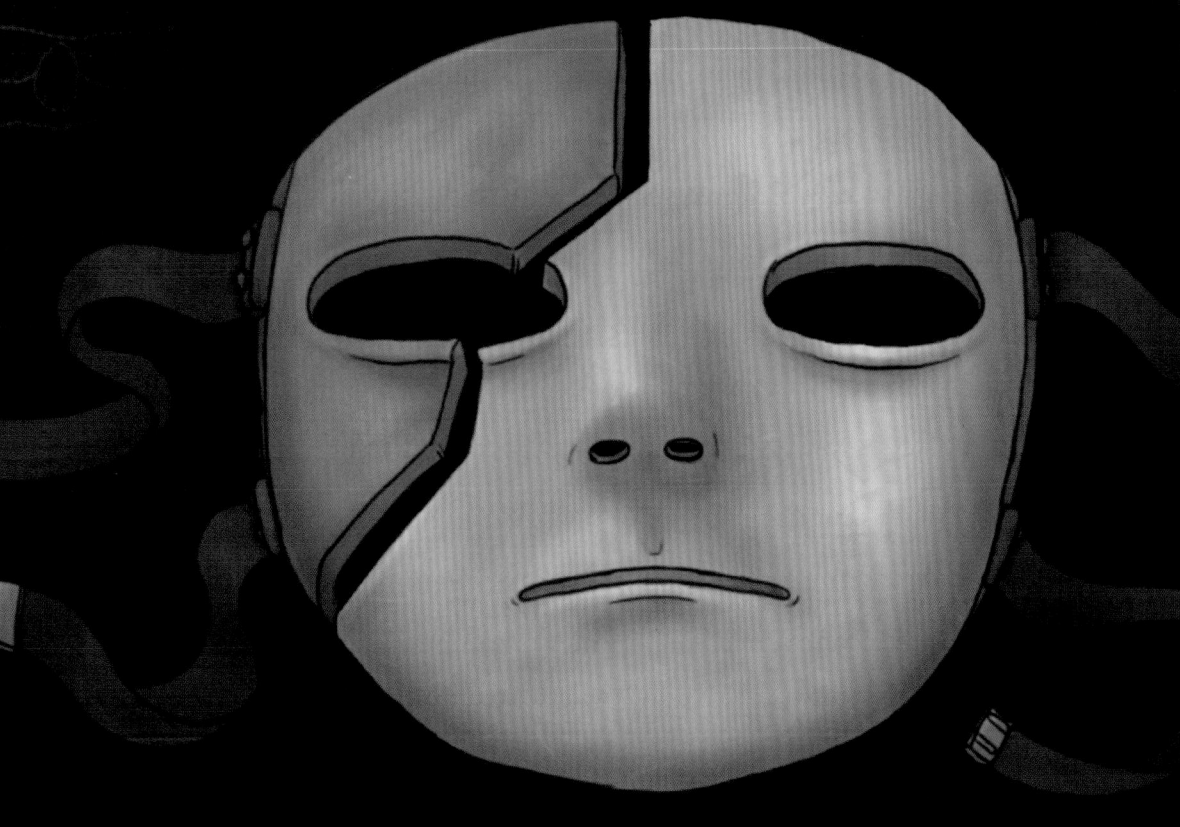

THE MAKING OF

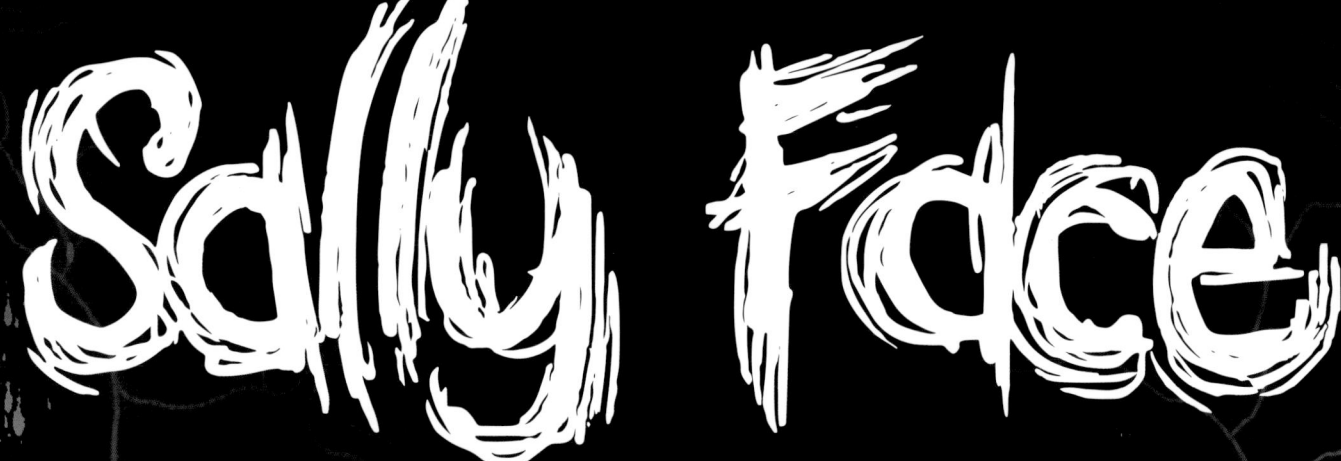

THE ORIGIN

How Sally Face came to be.

AROUND 2006/2007, I sketched a creepy character (as per usual) and the name "Sally Face" just popped into my head. Over the next few weeks, I began to imagine this character and what his life would be like. He was a boy with a girls face sewn on. I imagined him living in an apartment building filled with odd tenants. His best friend would be a lazy stoner who wore a cape and lived in the basement. This was the genesis of Sal and Larry. Here are the original sketches from that time.

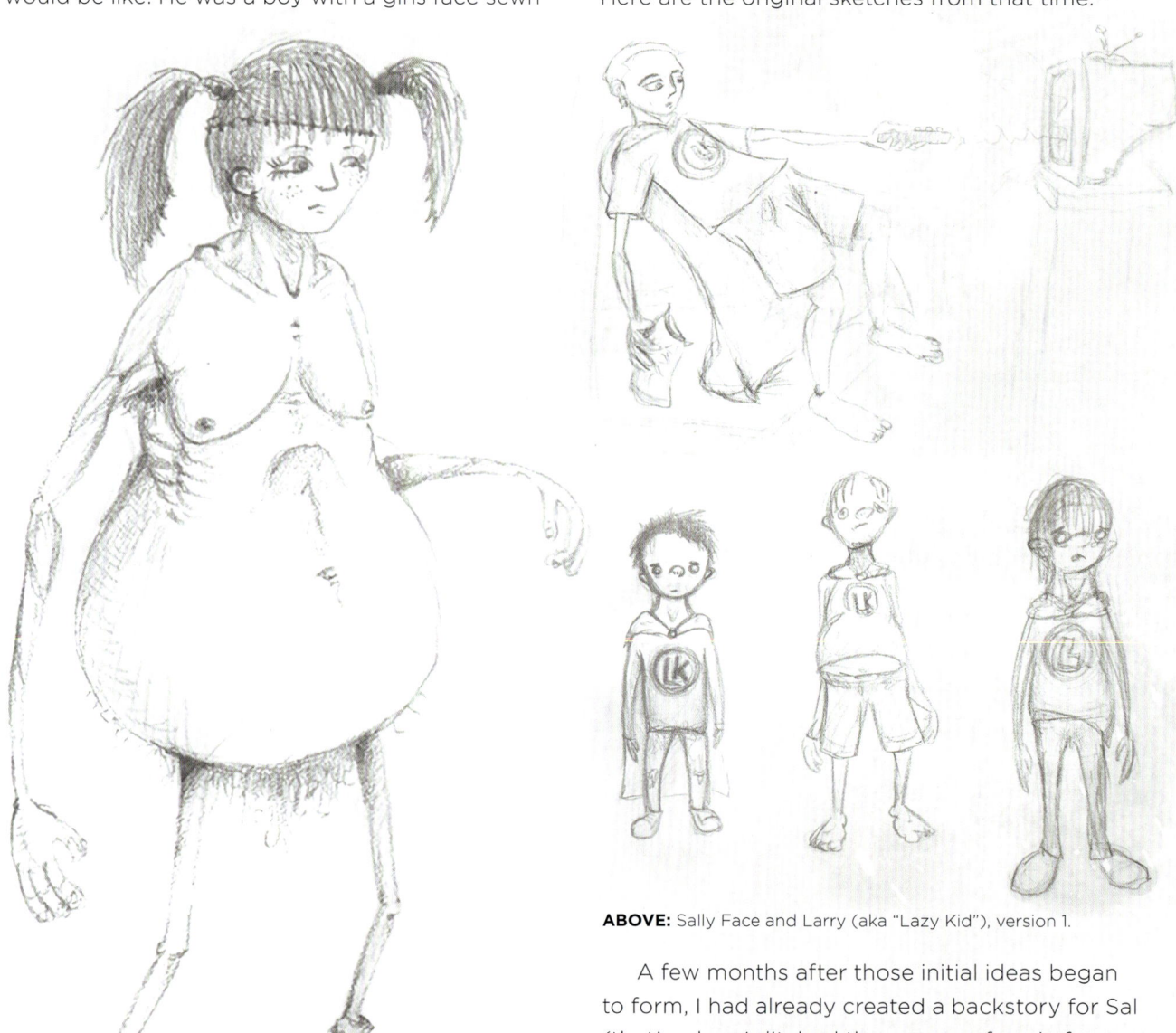

ABOVE: Sally Face and Larry (aka "Lazy Kid"), version 1.

A few months after those initial ideas began to form, I had already created a backstory for Sal (that's when I ditched the sewn on face in favor of the prosthetic mask), a world that he lives in, a cast of characters, and different stories I could tell within that universe. At the heart of everything, I wanted to create something that had the look and feel reminiscent of a '90s cartoon but with darker themes and more mature stories.

I knew from the start that Sal would be gender nonconforming. Part of that is because I've always been interested in breaking traditions (i.e. a boy with pigtails). Another part of it was inspired by my experience in high school. Back then, I felt like I didn't quite fit in. I was one of the "weird goth kids". In a small way, this was something that helped me to have more empathy for how tough it must be for LGBT+ people who struggle to fit in. There was this kid who transferred to my high school, who happened to be transgender. Even though I didn't have any classes with them, I did see them around a bit and they always seemed very quiet and nice. I had heard that this person was badly bullied and had to transfer schools a few times. That made my heart sink and I really dreaded what may happen in this rural high school, where I had been on the receiving end of bullying myself plenty of times. Sure enough, the bullies were very harsh to this kid and they ended up leaving after only a couple of weeks. The world can be cruel and unforgiving and I just hope that this person was able to find some peace in their life. So I really liked the idea of a nonconforming character who doesn't take shit from anyone.

Mental health was something that helped weave the story together as well. I have personally suffered from severe depression throughout my life and frequent night terrors when I was younger. I also have loved ones that struggle with various mental illnesses. I mostly wanted to use these elements as building blocks for the characters, without focusing too heavily on the subjects— though I did want to address them in the story and I tried to portray these aspects realistically. Some of the lines Sal says are direct feelings I've gone through (especially from the lake scene in Episode Four). The texts from Larry are inspired by real texts I received from someone I love deeply, who was attempting suicide. "I'll be gone soon" was the hardest thing I ever had to read. It tore me apart inside and to be honest it's still tough to read, years later.

During my college days, I got together with a few artist friends, and I attempted to assemble a team to make *Sally Face* into an internet cartoon series. Everyone got into the idea at first and we were all excited to start this project. However, between work and school schedules, no one could commit enough time and things quickly fell apart.

Sally Face sat in the back of my mind for seven years, as I moved on to other projects.

BELOW: Sally Face, version 2.

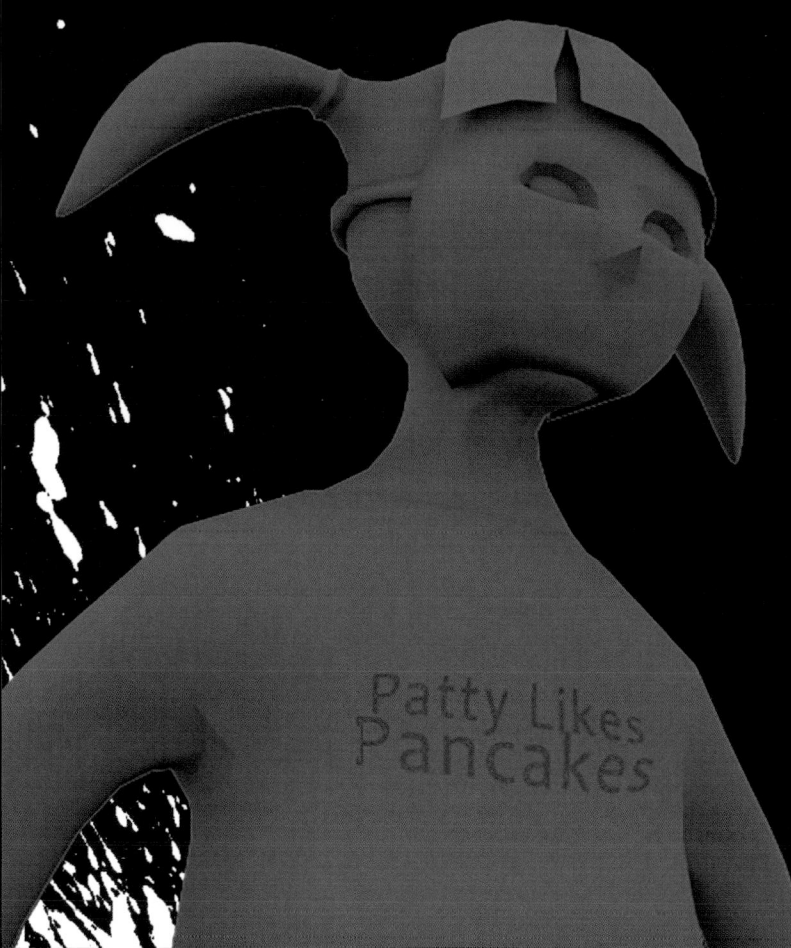

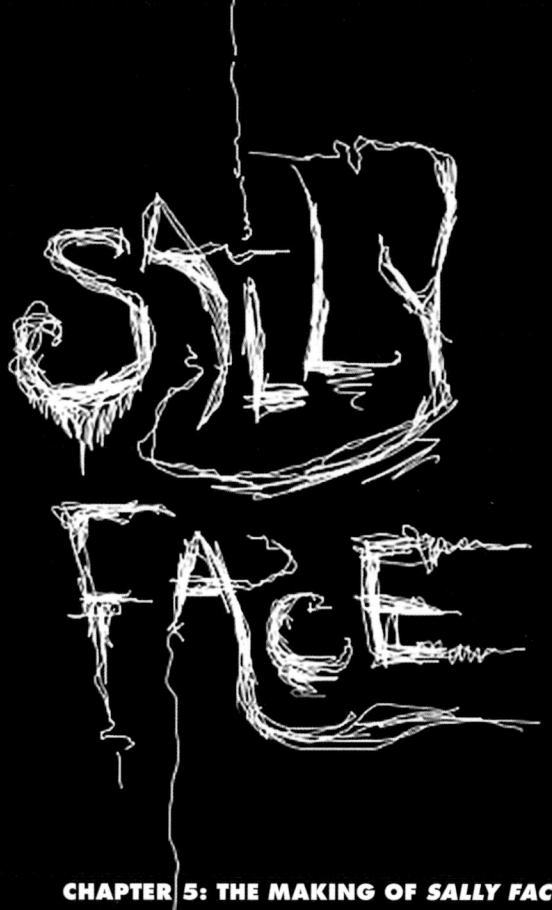

DEVELOPMENT HISTORY

My personal journey in creating Sally Face.

IN 2010, I started a small indie development team, Wither Studios, with some friends. We developed a mobile game called *Crowman & Wolfboy* that was released in 2013. The game got great reviews from media and users and was downloaded over 600,000 times. For our very first game, it was something to be proud of. Despite all of that, we still struggled to make money off of *Crowman & Wolfboy*. The team voted to abandon development on the planned expansions to the game. This had me pretty bummed because I had ideas for that game that I was excited to explore. A year later, our team was still struggling with what direction to take our second project. Eventually, at the end of 2014, we lost two of our team members over that conflict. It really sucked because not only were they good artists but good friends as well. A year's worth of work was thrown out.

The chaos that Wither had fallen into is what ignited my desire to work on my own project. I wasn't sure if the team would make it through that rough patch and I also needed a creative outlet of my own. There were a few concepts I was tinkering with when *Sally Face* came to mind. I thought it would be nice to finally do something with that idea and that it would transition pretty well into an adventure game, rather than a cartoon. So, in 2015, building from the original concepts, I re-wrote the story arc to fit a five episode narrative and began working on Episode One in my free time. It was a slow process, because I was working a full-time job and still working with Wither Studios.

My vision for the game was to make something that was filled with elements that interested me and to craft a non-conventional story. It would start off as a dark mystery and become more chaotic as things unfolded. I wanted it to have an underlying, tense feeling of being swept up in a dream.

In February 2016, I was unexpectedly laid off from my day job, during a company-wide downsizing. Finding a new job afterwards was turning out to be difficult. That's when I decided to focus on finishing Episode One of *Sally Face*. I had enough money saved, plus unemployment coming in, that I could be more casual about looking for other work for a while. My wife at the time fought me tooth and nail over this decision, which tore a giant hole in our relationship.

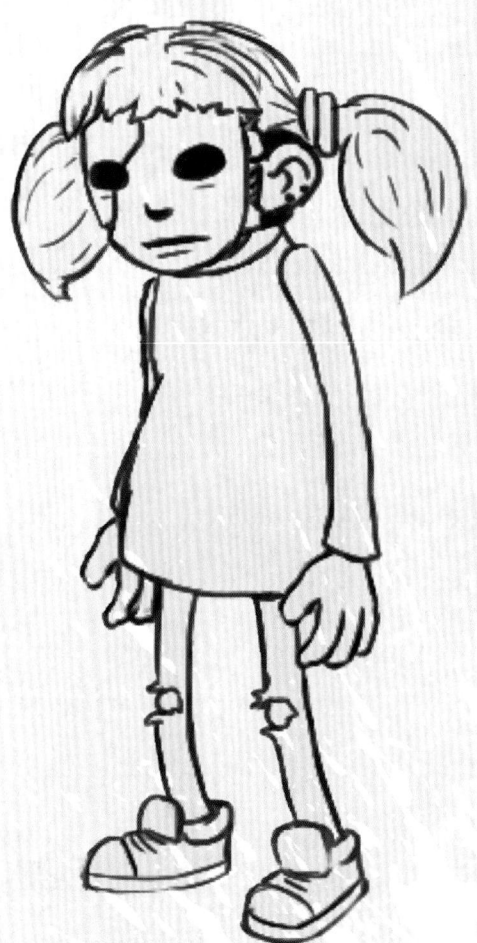

RIGHT: Redesigning Sally Face (third time's the charm?).

 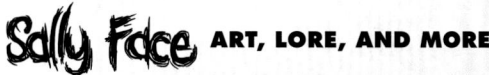

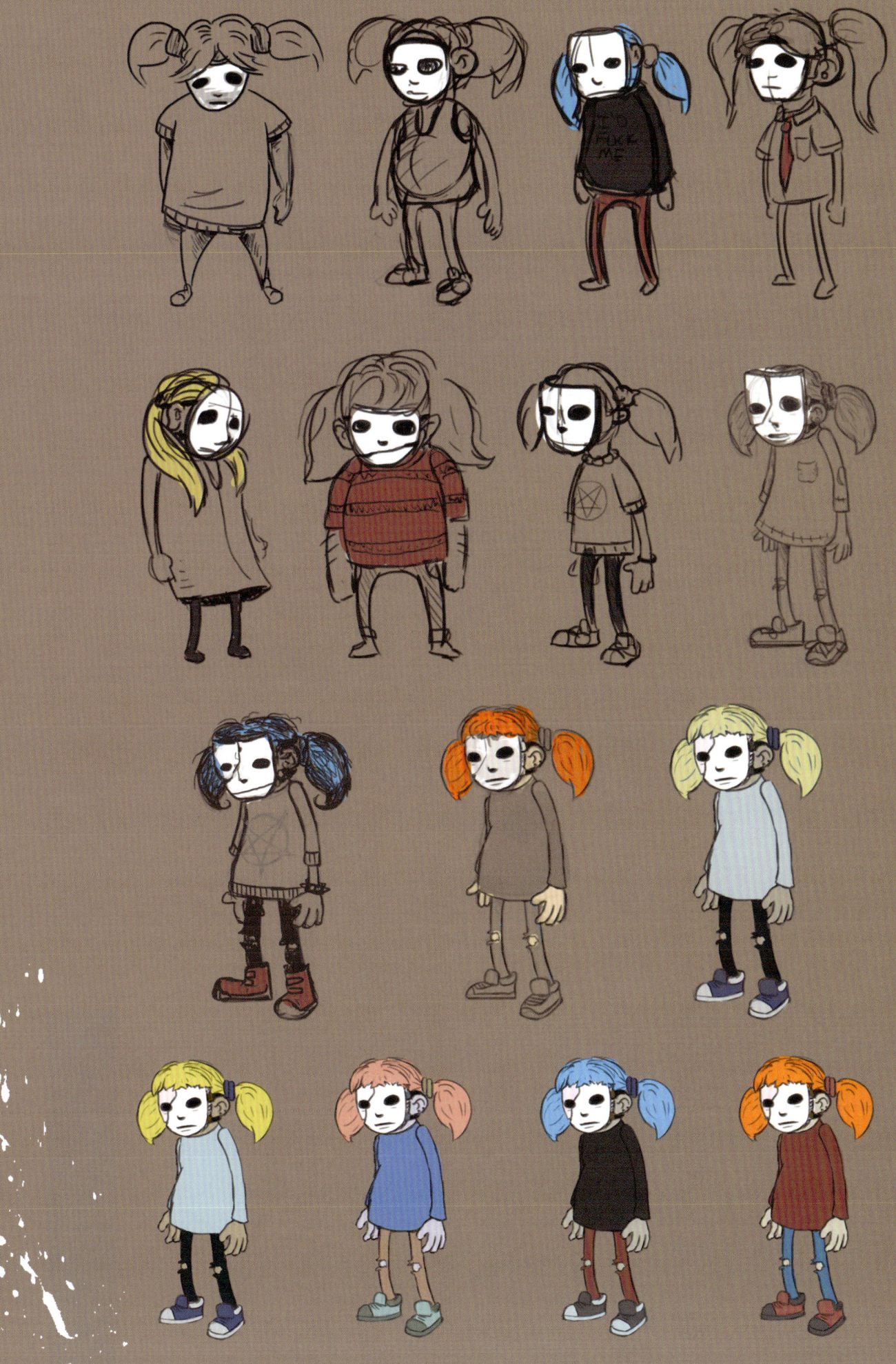

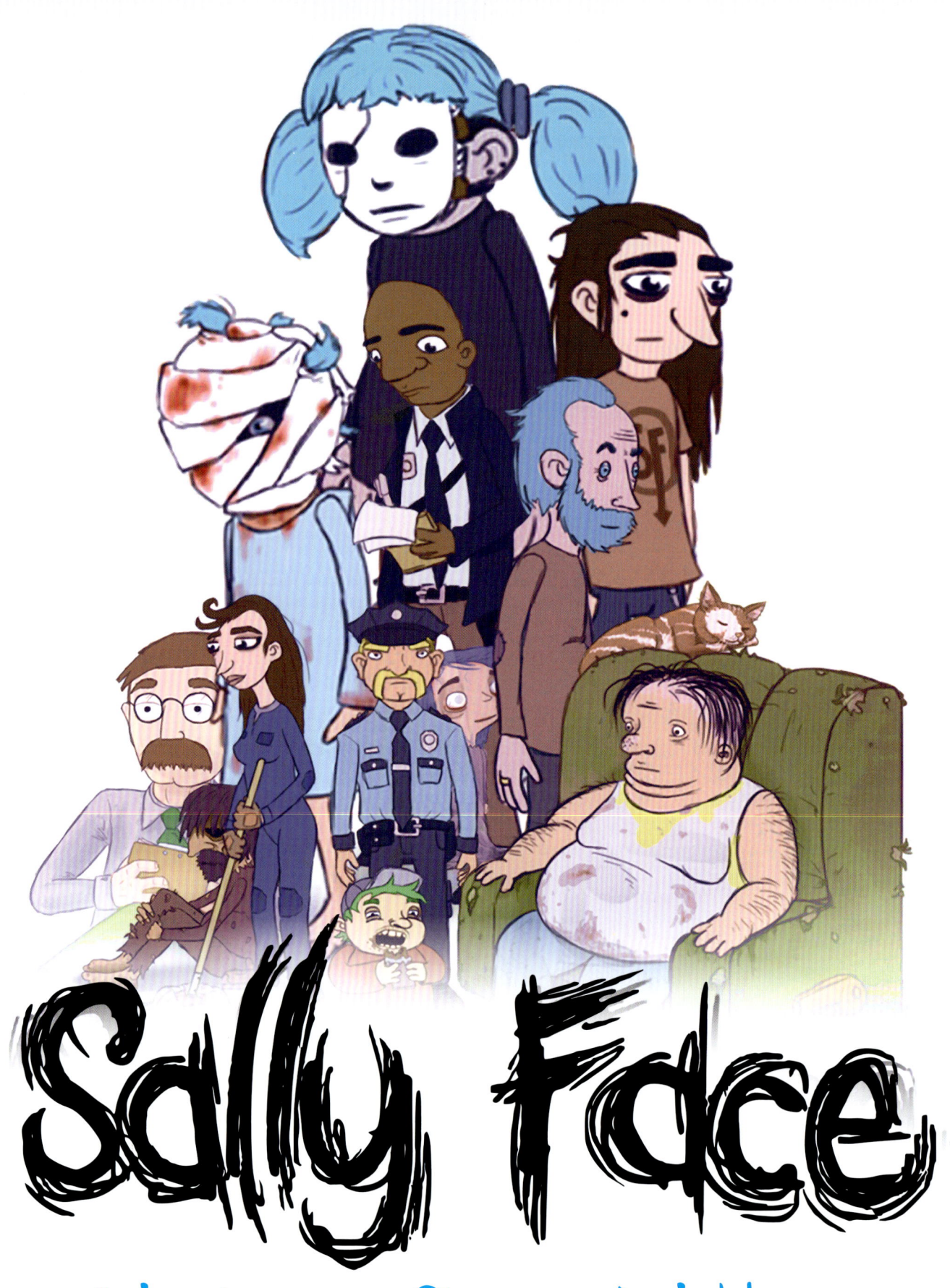

Sally Face

Episode One: Strange Neighbors

THAT SUMMER, I moved out and stayed with my parents while we figured out what we were going to do. During that time, I was able to finish up development on *Sally Face,* **Episode One: Strange Neighbors**. I released it on August 16th, on itch.io. Sales were dismal to say the least. I tried my best to promote it but I just couldn't gain enough attention. My funds were also starting to run low. So I decided to run a crowdfunding campaign, hoping to kill two birds with one stone (funding and attention).

That fall, I moved back to Pittsburgh with my wife. We began couples therapy to try to work through things. In November, I raised over $13,000 for *Sally Face* via crowdfunding. Luckily the game had started catching on with YouTubers and some of the bigger channels were starting to play Episode One. That was a huge help with getting more eyes on the game. On December 14th, I released *Sally Face* on Steam to great reception. I was finally able to focus my full time efforts into making a game, and not have to worry about finances. This was the dream I had been chasing for seven years prior.

Things were seeming to look up when tragedy reared its ugly head again. A very close family member of mine was reported missing (I don't want to name them out of respect for their privacy). There was a suicide note. I was seven hours away. The next few weeks were the darkest, saddest, and hardest times of my life. Thankfully, the police found the family member still alive. After days in recovery, a second attempt, and then more days in recovery, they started doing better. Obviously, this slowed production of Episode Two down quite a bit. Even after I had returned home, I was still dealing with an extreme sadness over what had happened.

Eventually, working on Episode Two actually became helpful for me to deal with what I was internally struggling with. As I was nearing the later half of production, in the spring of 2017, I went through a divorce. We had been together for eight years so this was a pretty big impact on me, especially with the emotional rollercoaster I had just been through. This all but halted production for a while, as I slipped into a deep depression.

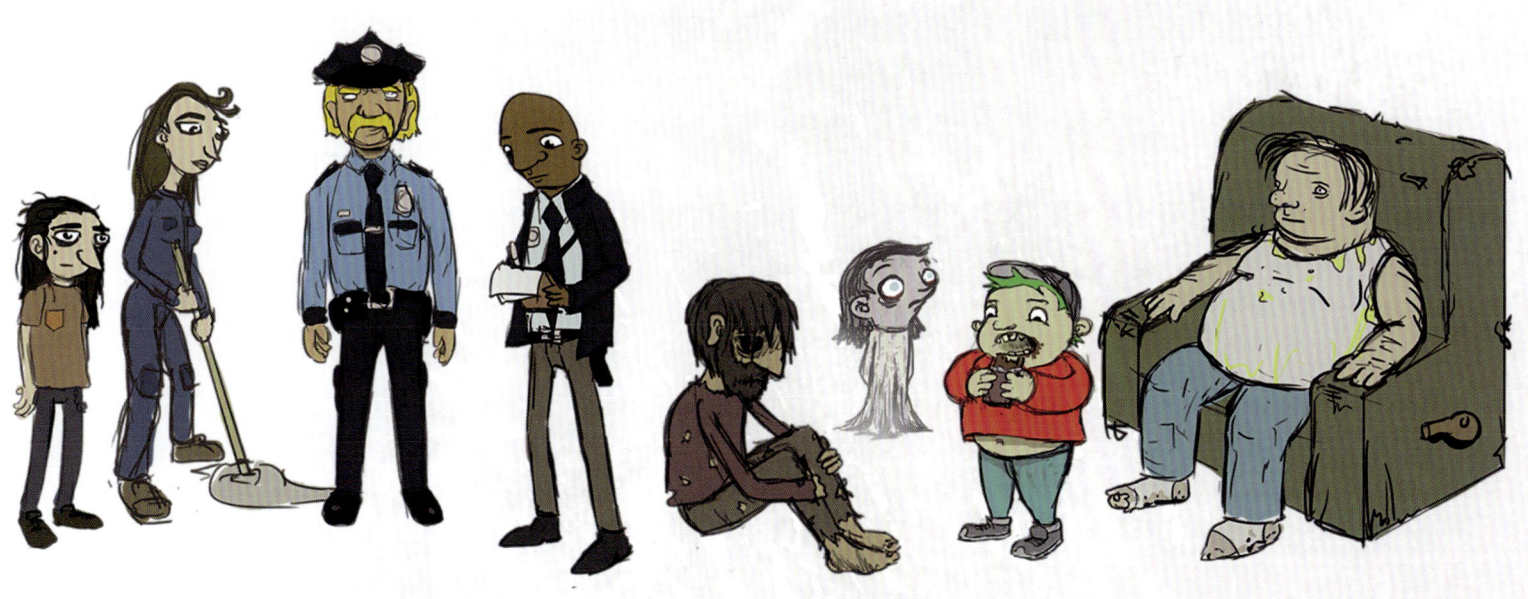

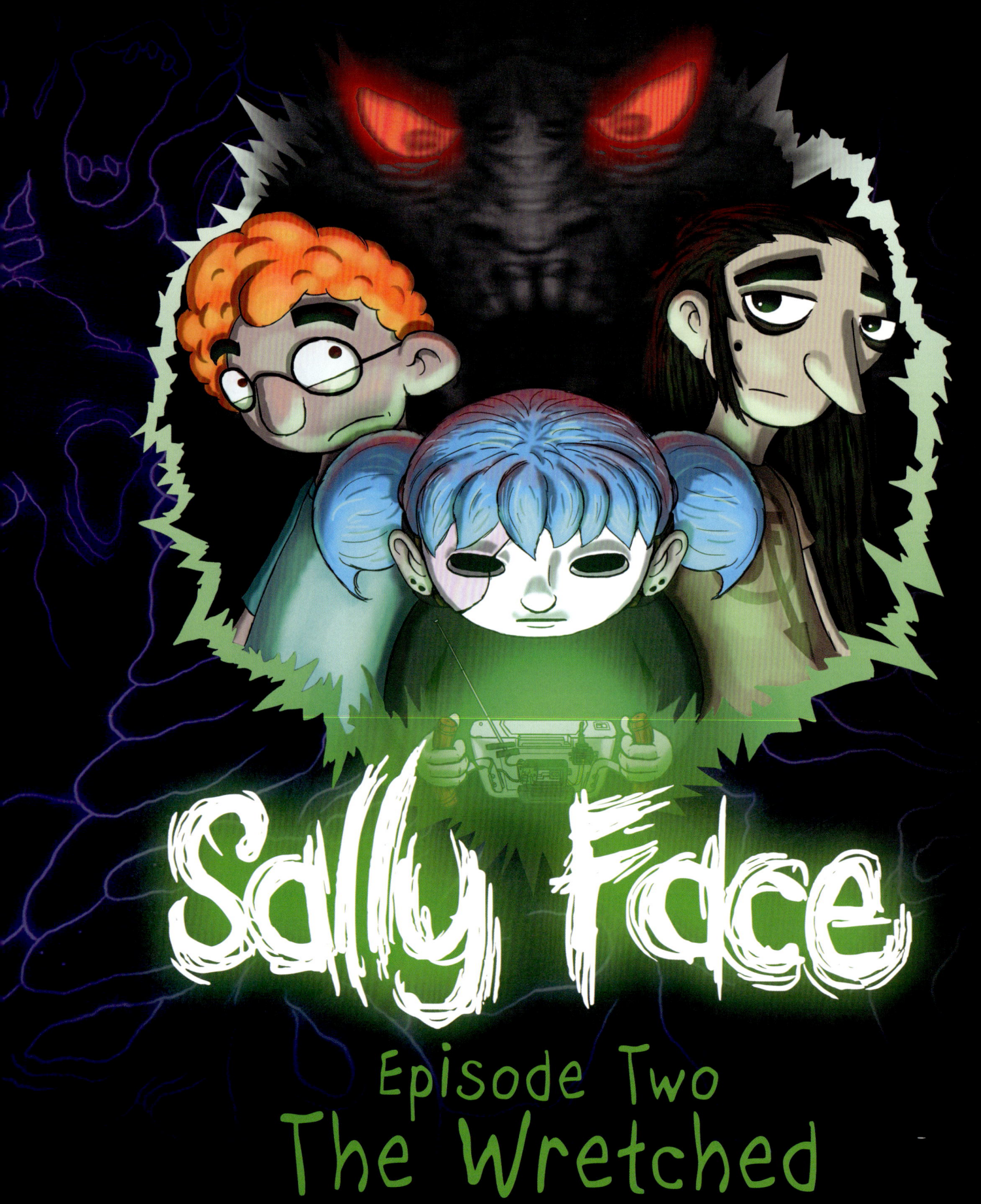

Sally Face

Episode Two
The Wretched

AFTER SOME TIME, I began getting back to development. Working on the game, again, became very helpful in getting me out of the dark hole I was isolating myself in. Seeing all of the excitement of the fans and how much the fandom was continuing to grow was also a big emotional gain when I needed it the most. I can't say how much I still appreciate seeing that excitement from fans every day.

Sally Face, **Episode Two: The Wretched** was released on July 7th, 2017 and was even bigger and better than Episode One.

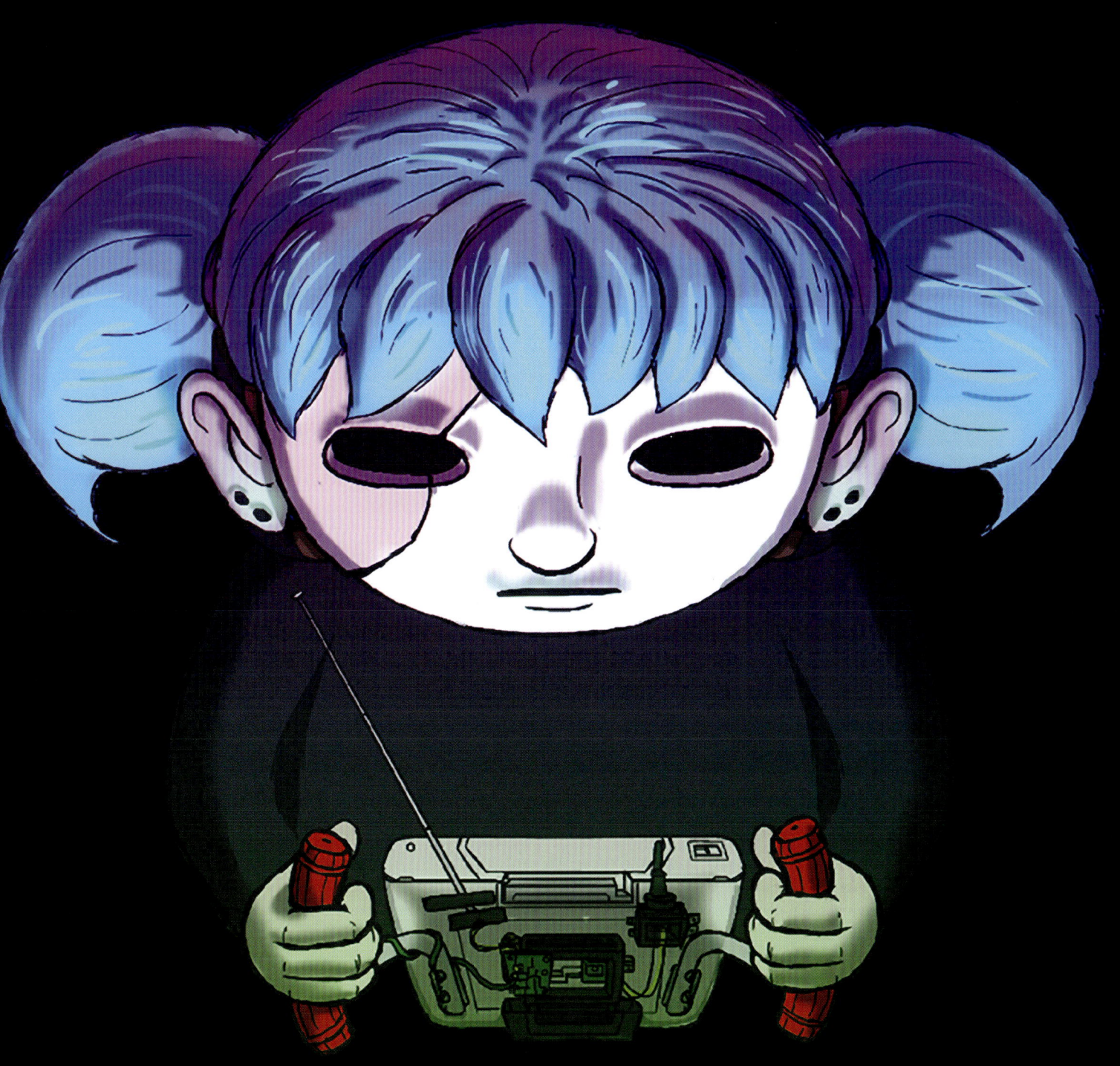

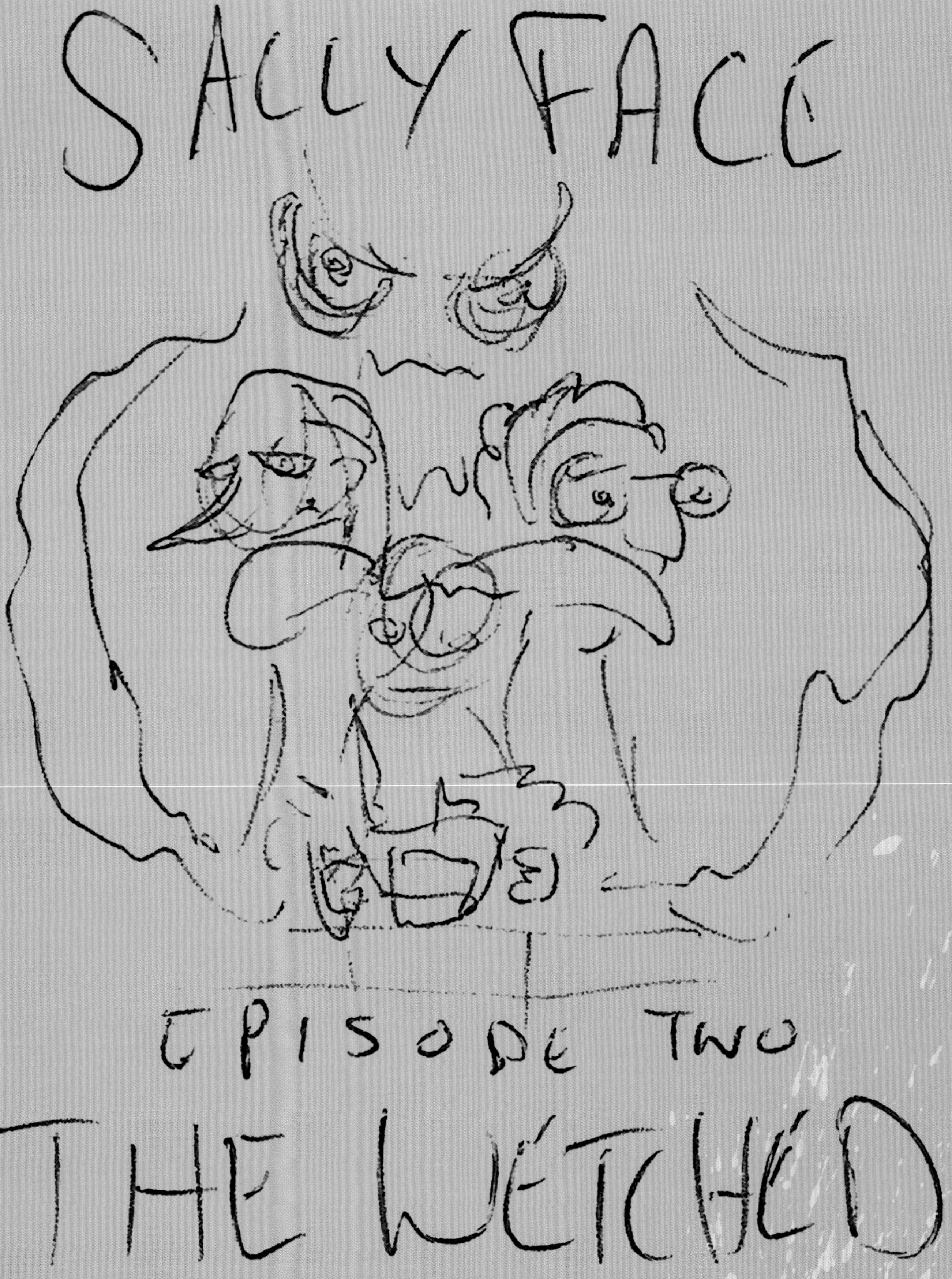

SALLY FACE

EPISODE TWO
THE WETCHED

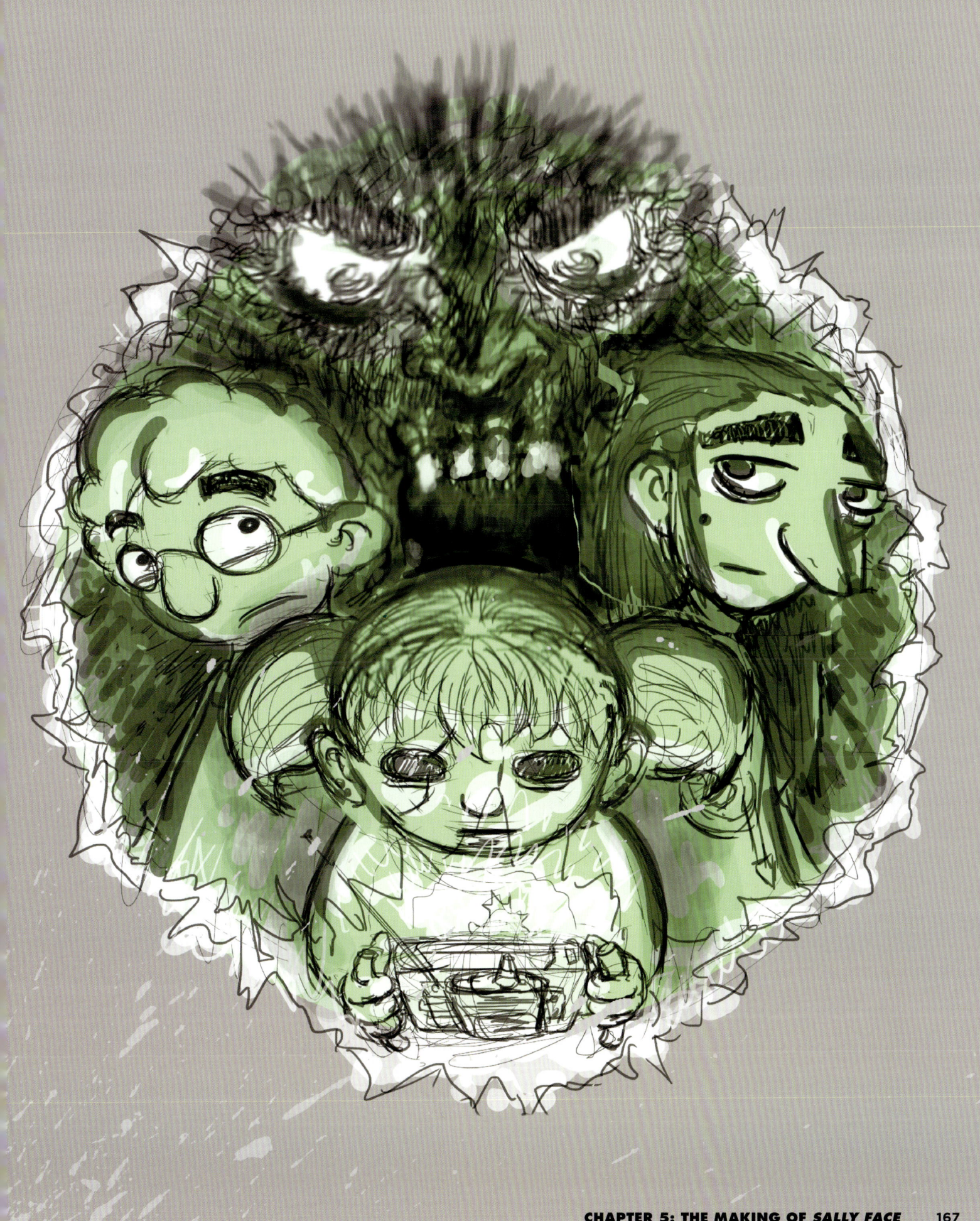

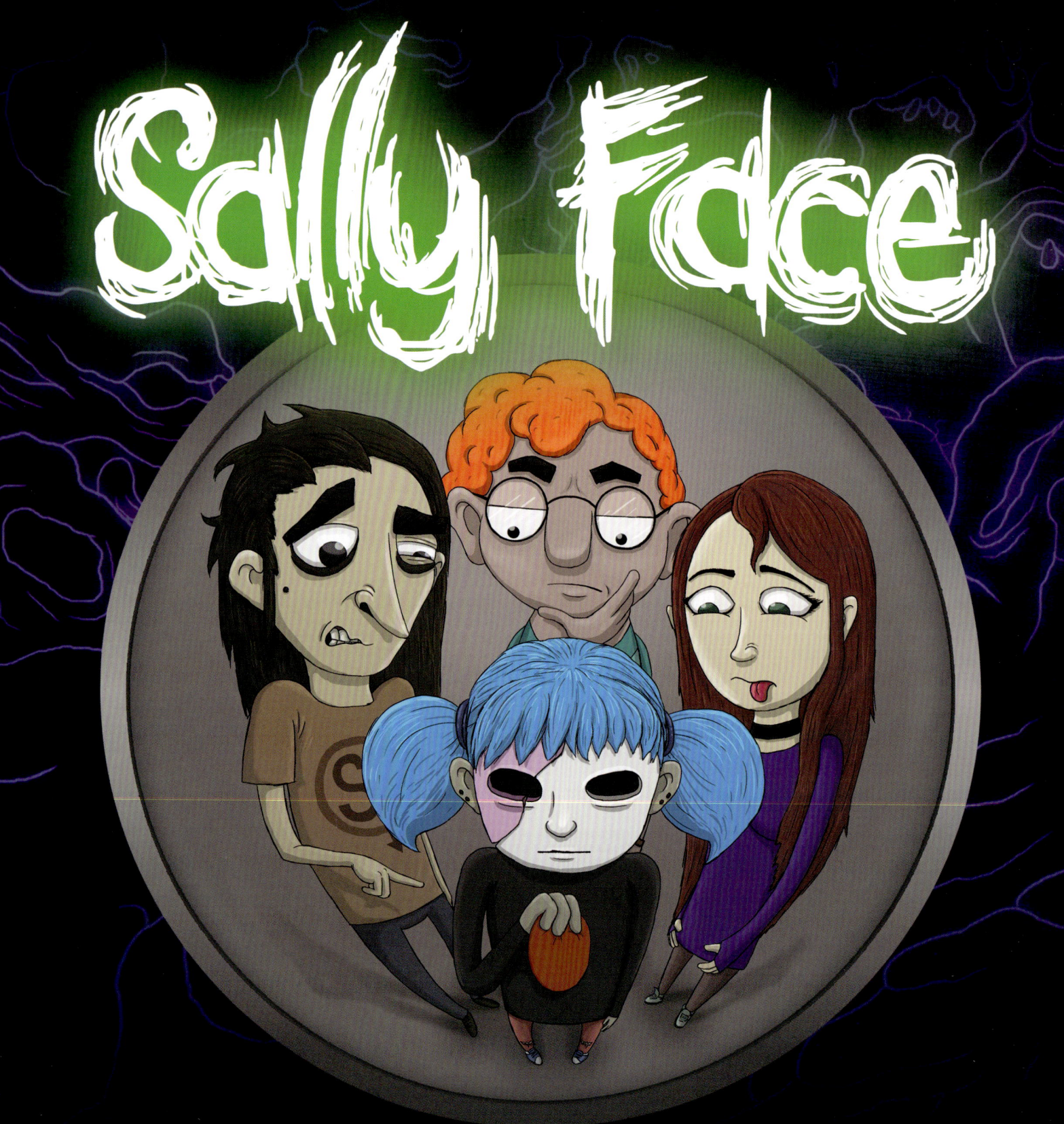

Sally Face

Episode Three
The Bologna Incident

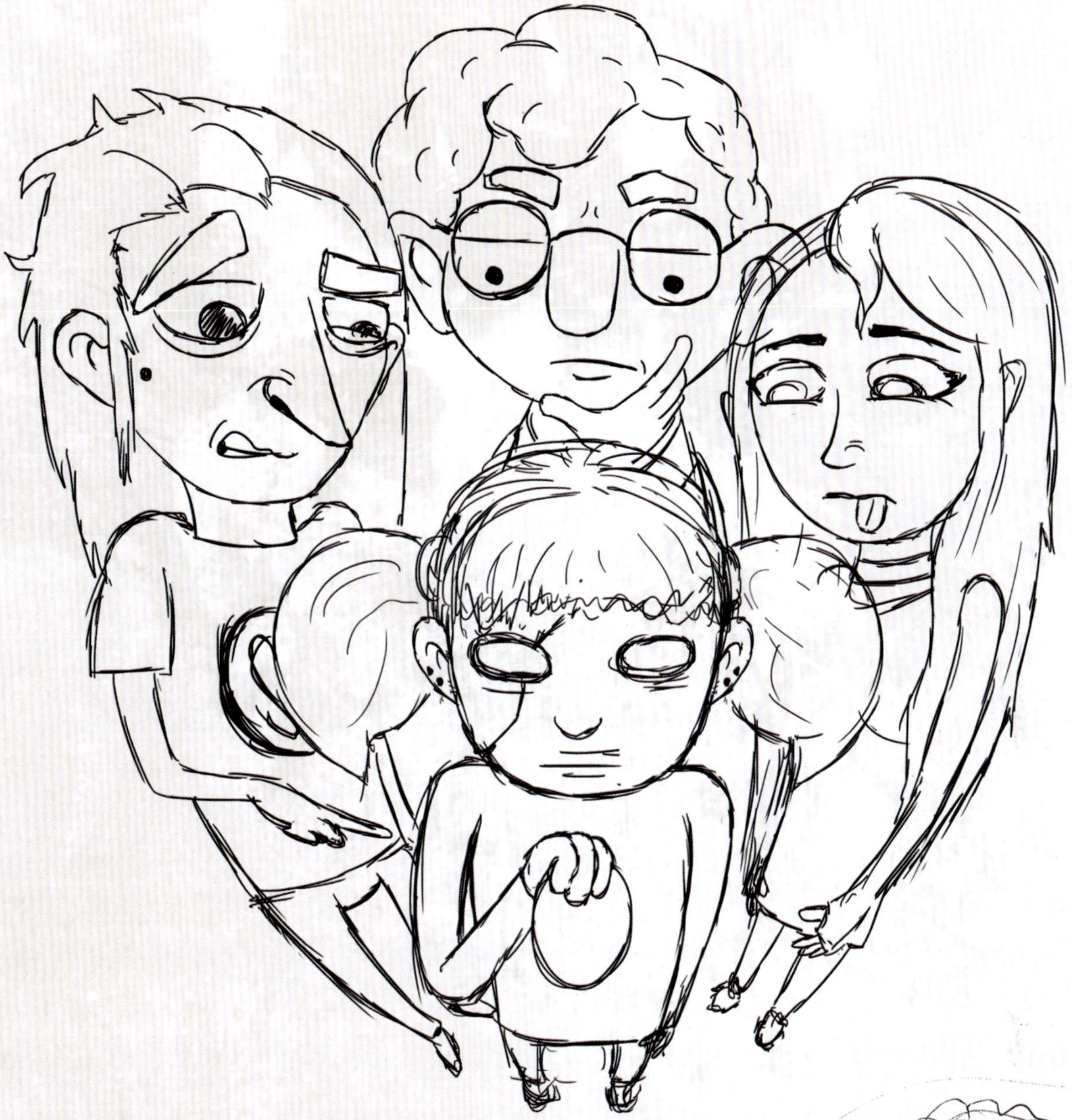

DURING WORKING ON EPISODE THREE, I was coming out of my depressive slump and leaned into development pretty hard. Maybe too hard. I didn't have a good balance of living my life and working. At first, it felt good and even helped me emotionally. However, the amount of hours I was working (over 80 hours a week) wasn't sustainable. I wasn't taking the best care of myself. I eventually started to feel the impact of that lifestyle, both physically and mentally, as it began to wear me out towards the end of production.

Sally Face, **Episode Three: The Bologna Incident** was released on February 10th, 2018 and quickly became a fan favorite.

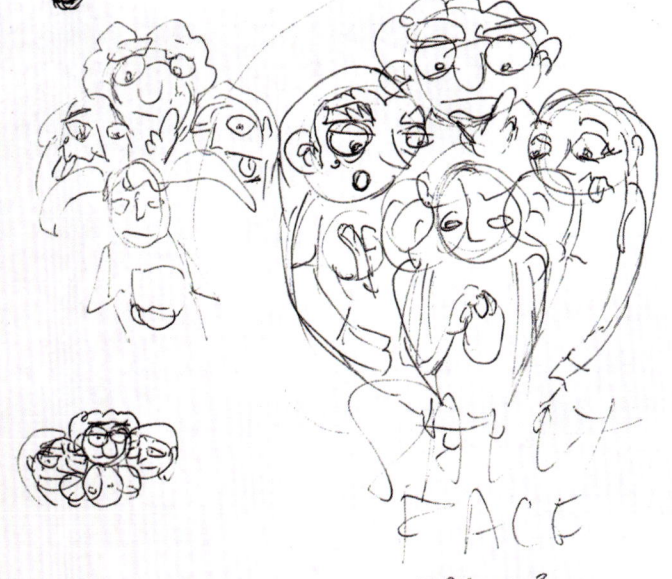

Sally Face

Episode Four
The Trial

SINCE THEN, I've made more of an effort not to overwork myself so much and to have a better work-life balance. Eating healthier, being more active, being more social, taking more breaks, etc. There's still a part of me that feels guilty, like, "oh, it's gonna take you longer to finish your work now!" But I know that this way is better for my health, my sanity and my work in the long-term.

Episode Four was much more involved and ambitious than the first three episodes. It was the biggest episode yet. In my original outline for *Sally Face*, Episode Four was split into two parts. However, I revised it early on to condense it into one episode.

Sally Face, Episode Four: The Trial was released on November 30th, 2018 and caused the fanbase to double in size within a couple of months.

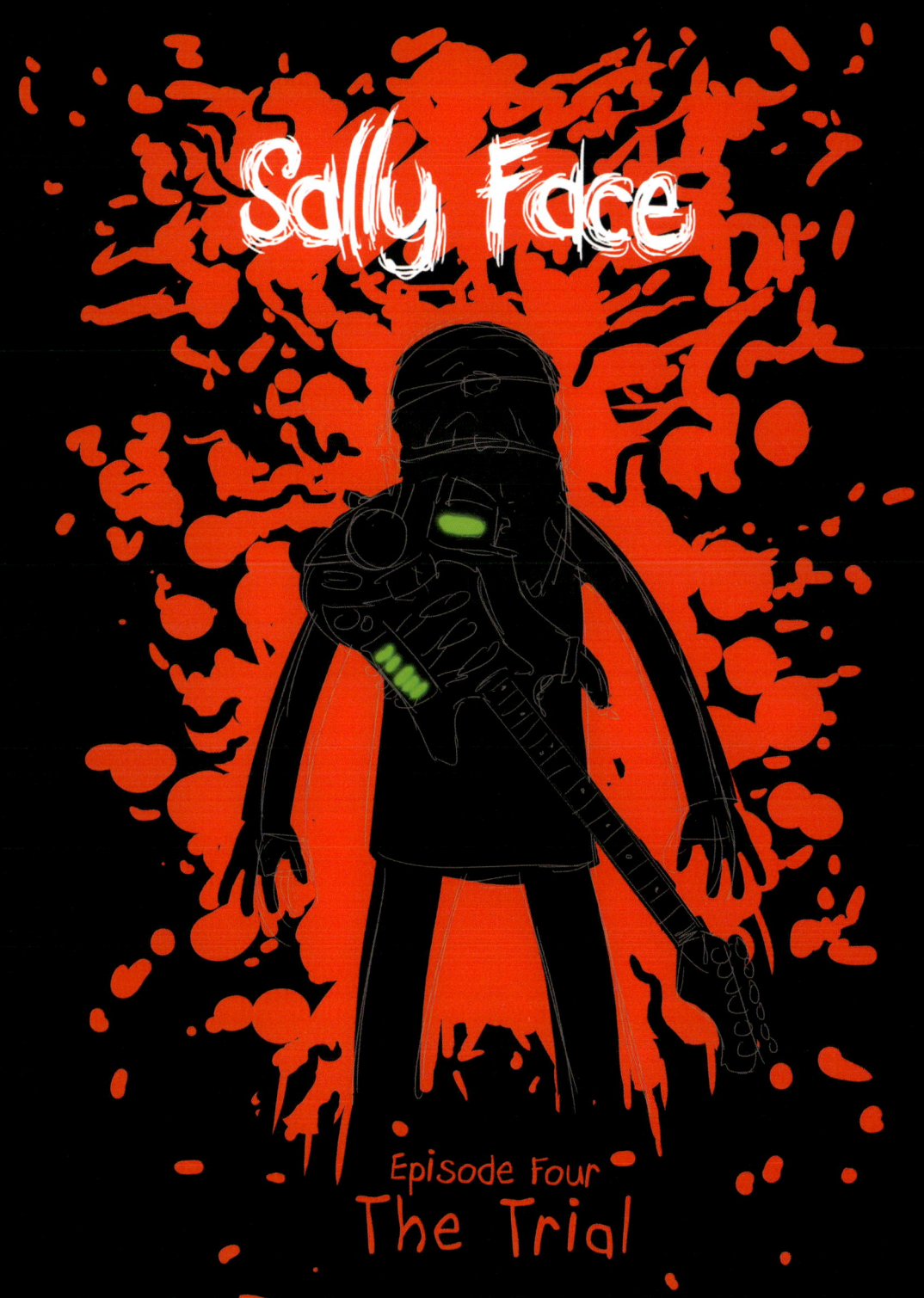

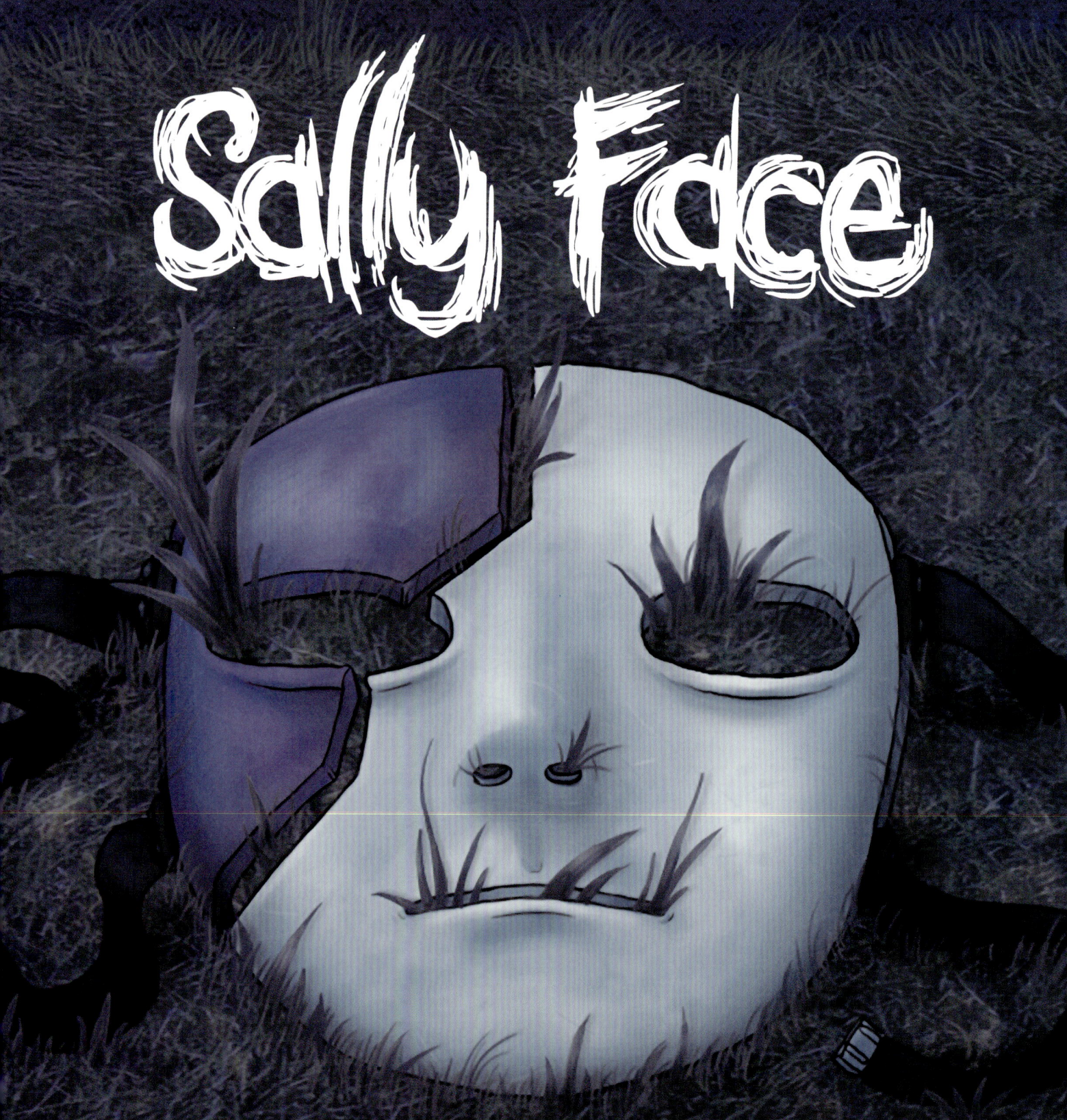

EPISODE FIVE took over a year to make. In the initial months, I had to modify the design to make it more realistic to accomplish. Originally, the size of Episode Five would have been close to all the other episodes combined. As such, some aspects and storylines had to be cut. It was a difficult process that I tried to take great care in doing. My hope is that I'll still be able to explore some of these elements in the future.

Being the final episode of the game, Memories and Dreams was meant to feel chaotic and semi-dream-like. It had to have a resolution to the story but also leave enough mystery open. It was a difficult tightrope to walk, especially since endings can be challenging. On top of that, I had to learn new programs and animation techniques. In the end, I am happy with how it turned out.

***Sally Face,* Episode Five: Memories and Dreams** was released on December 13th, 2019 and concluded the first game in the *Sally Face* series.

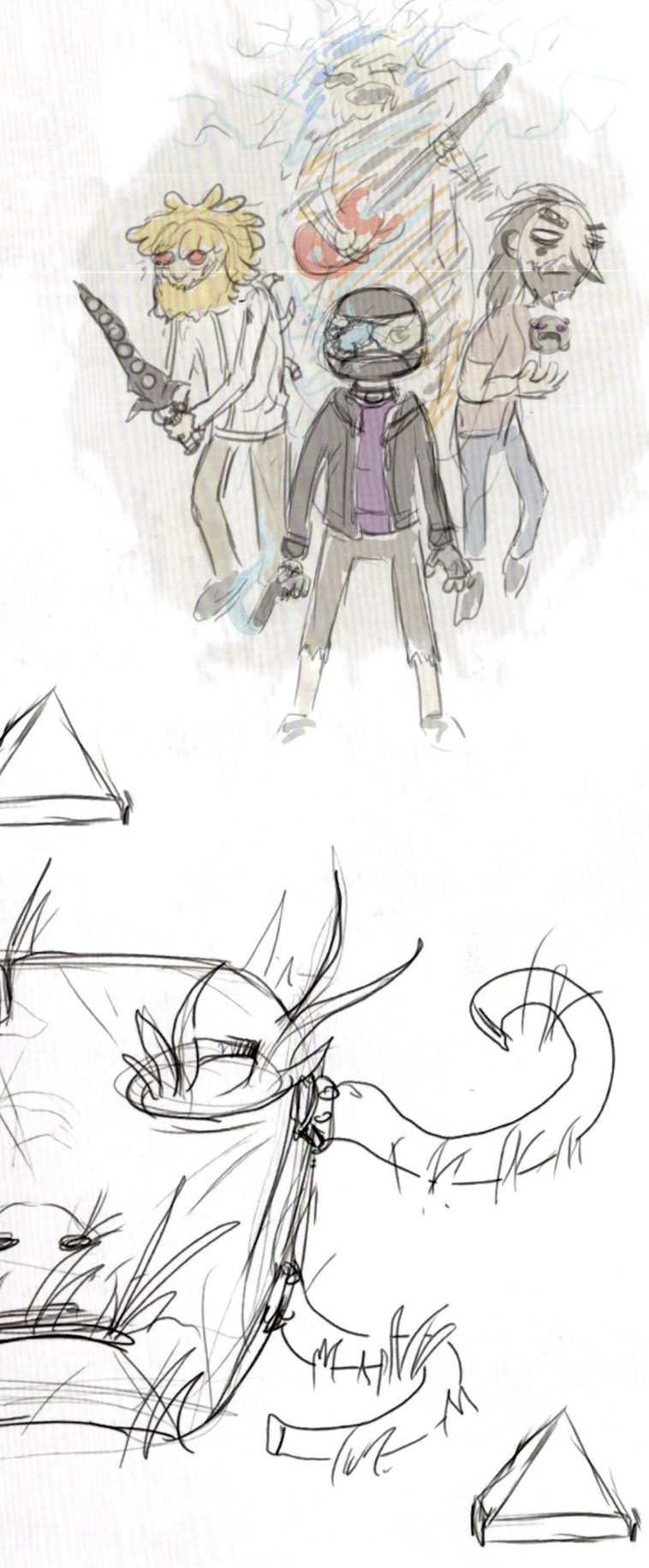

HOW THE SAUSAGE IS MADE

A look at how the game was developed and what went into it.

THE STORY started as an outline and a few pages of notes for the five episode arc. Then, at the start of each production cycle, I would flesh out each episode into a large detailed script. Based on that script, I'd design some rough ideas for puzzles that fit in with the story. Next, I would refine the script and flesh out most of the dialogue. As I built the game, some of the scripts were adjusted, added to, or cut. This was basically my process for each episode. All while making sure it fit within my overarching outline and notes.

STORY TOOLS USED: Pen and paper, writing software.

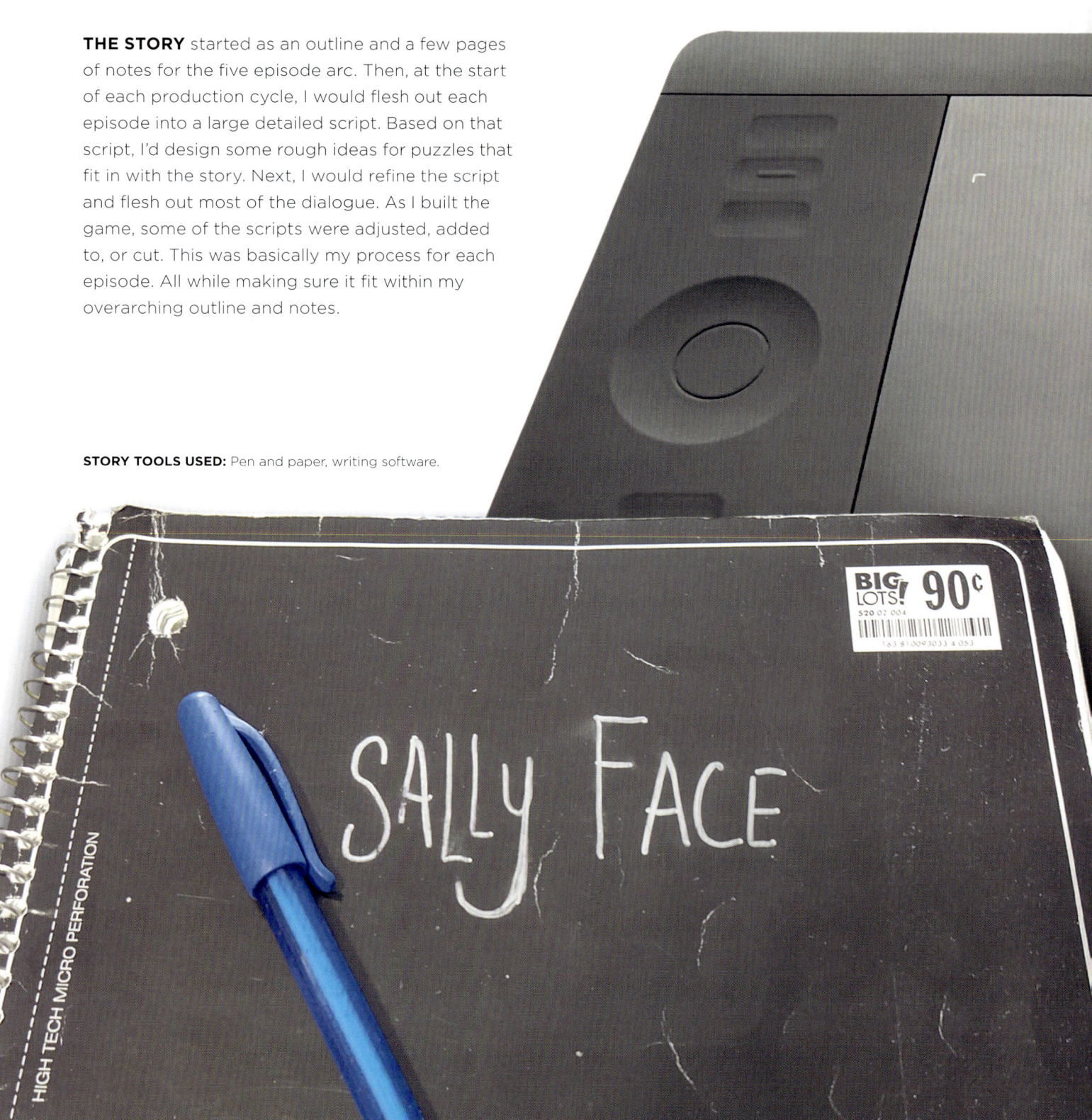

THE ARTWORK was to be reminiscent of '90s cartoons, but with a bit more of a creep factor. I also wanted it to have an unfinished, rough look. Thus, the sketchy linework. This was partly to add to the hand-drawn aesthetic and partly to save myself some work by not having to make everything super polished. Giving the characters odd features and shapes helped to add to the bizarre feeling of the game. Most of the animations are traditional frame by frame drawings (to fit with the cartoon look). Some characters and areas I would sketch out concepts for while deciding on how they should look. However, quite a lot of the art seen in game is the first iteration of what I drew.

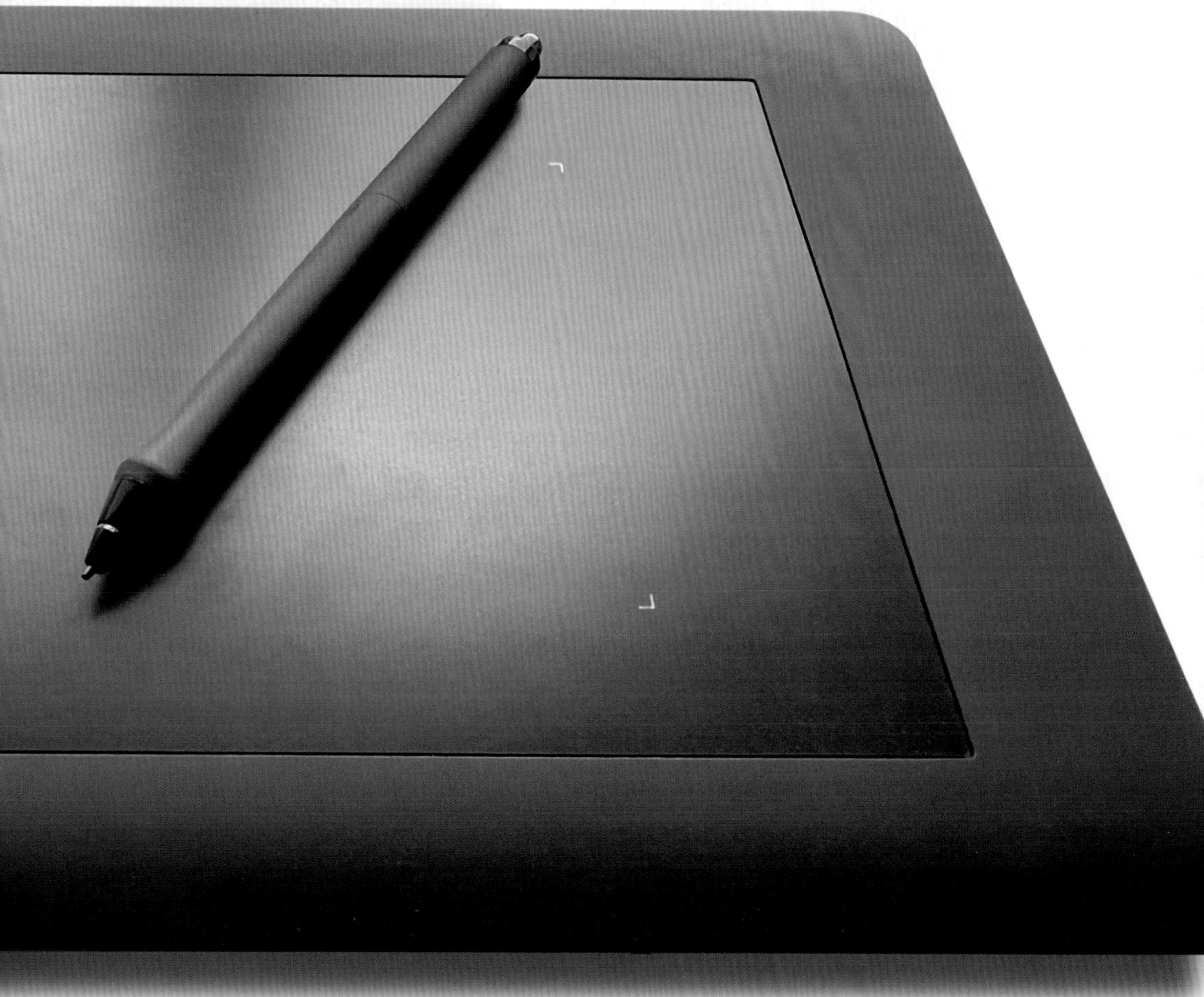

ART TOOLS USED: Pen and paper, Wacom Tablet, Photoshop, Unity, Blender.

THE MUSIC of *Sally Face* was fun to create. I had never really made music on this scale before. Most of my experience came from playing guitar in high school metal bands. Some of the melodies in the game are directly from or inspired by melodies I came up with back in high school. Like the artwork, I wanted the music to have an unrefined quality to lend to the game's unsettling atmosphere. As such, many of the songs are recordings of myself jamming on the guitar. My general strategy was to think about, and even sometimes look at, the area of the game that the music would go to. I would think about what that part of the game should feel like and then try to play that feeling. I never studied music theory or learned to read sheet music or any of that. So I never write any of my music down, it all just lives in my head. Additionally, Sanity's Fall is a fictional band I created for the game. I did all the guitars and screaming myself and then programmed the drums in.

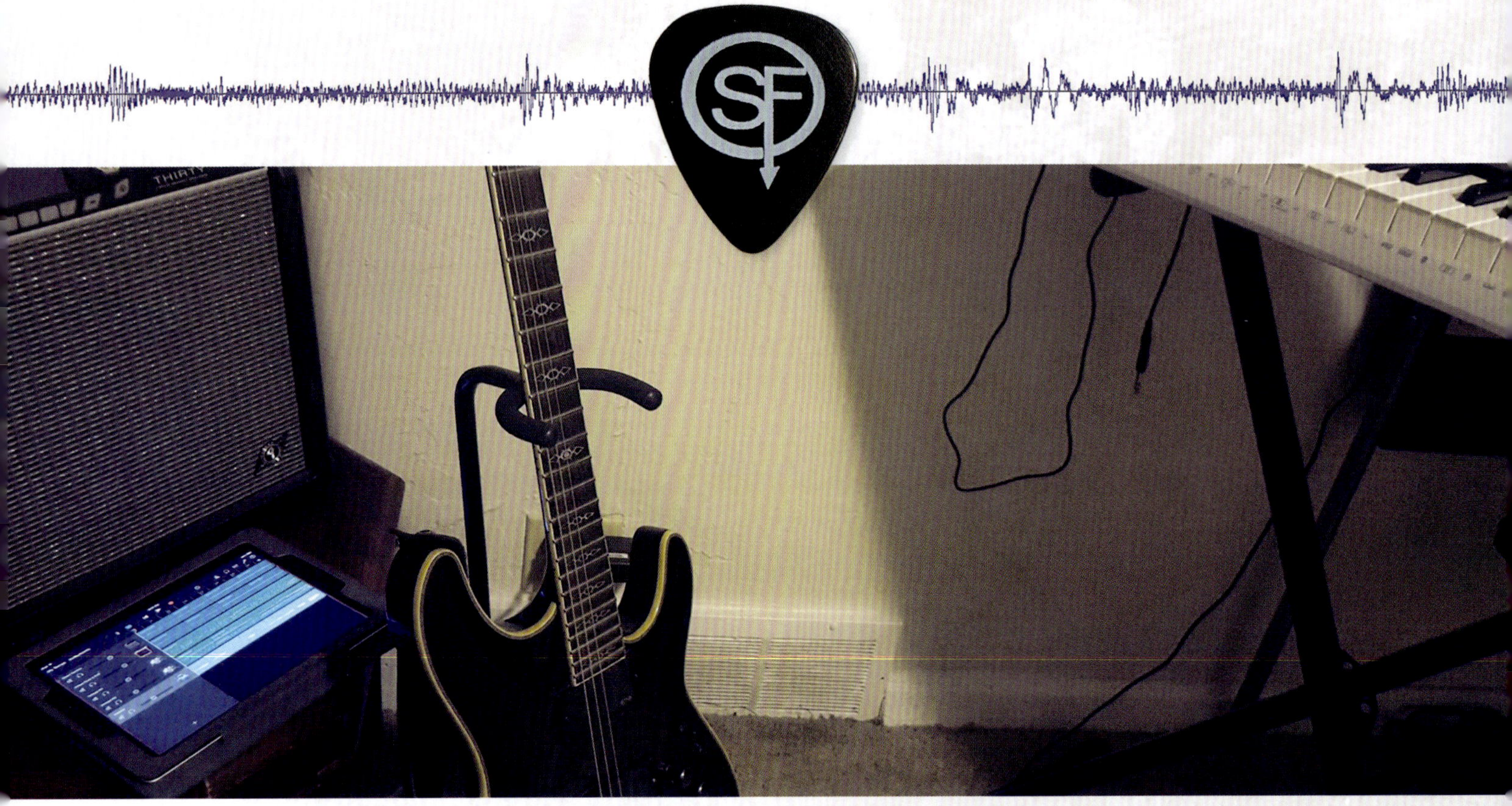

MUSIC TOOLS USED: Guitar, keyboard, iPad/GarageBand, Audacity.

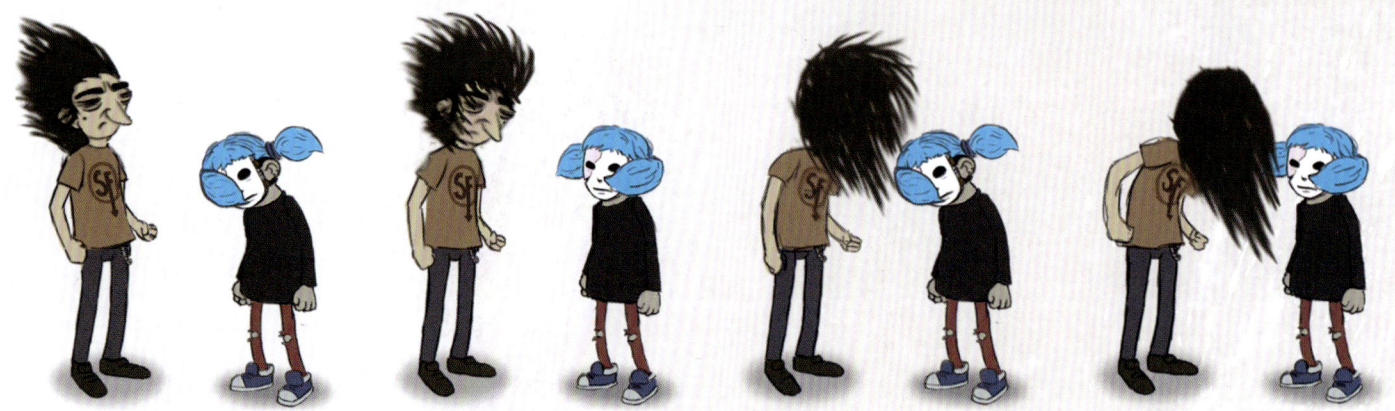

DESIGNING THE GAMEPLAY was important and always took its direction from the narrative. I wasn't particularly trying to break any molds with gameplay, though I did do some experimenting. I'm not a programmer, so that was a hurdle for me and did put some restrictions on what I could do with mechanics. I used a visual scripting tool within Unity in order to build the game logic. I designed the game to introduce new mechanics with each episode. This was to help keep the game feeling fresh, to add to the sense of uncertainty in the game, and to give myself something new to do/learn/improve on with each development cycle. I wanted to have at least one difficult "side quest" in each episode that filled in additional narrative for those that figured it out. While designing the puzzles and the gameplay in general, it was important to never make the player guess-and-check. So progression should feel clear and each puzzle should feel logical within that world.

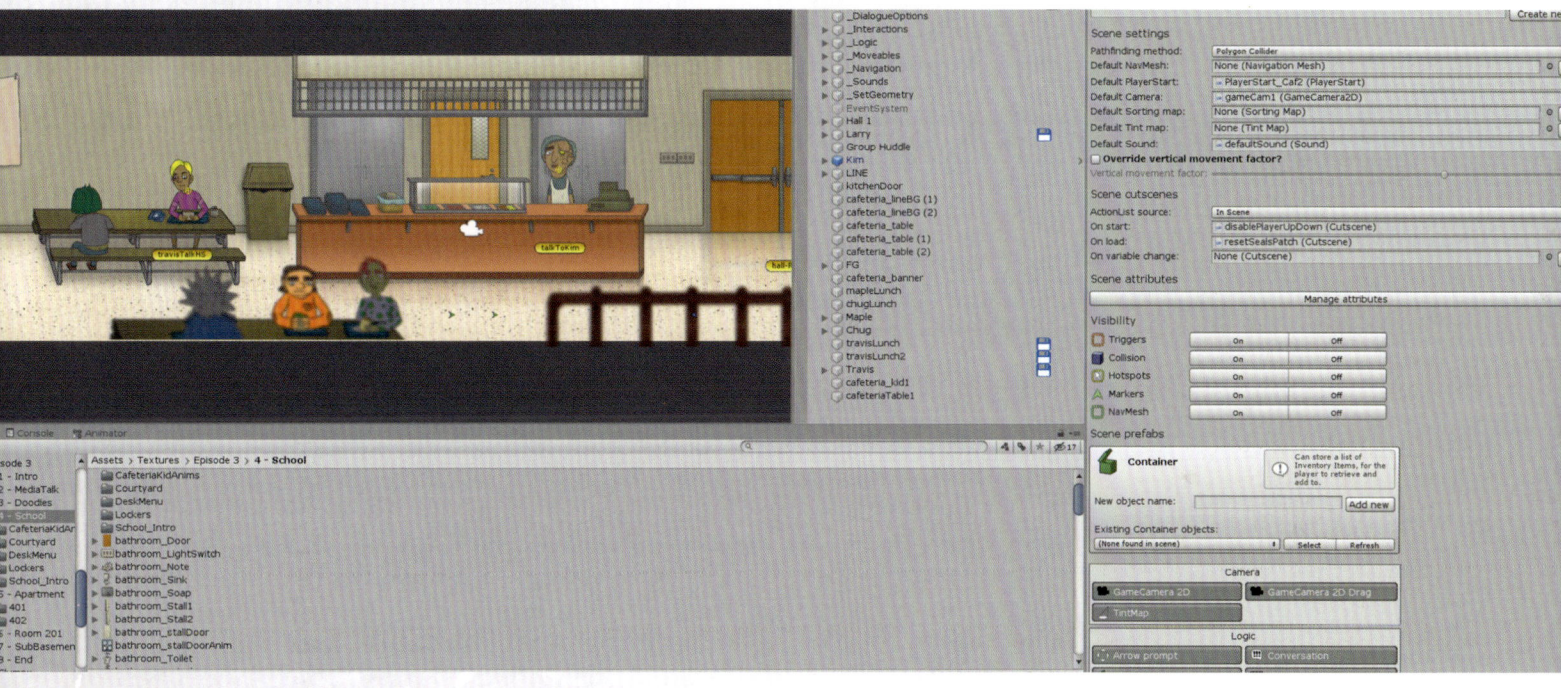

DESIGN TOOLS USED: Pen and paper, writing software, Unity, Adventure Creator.

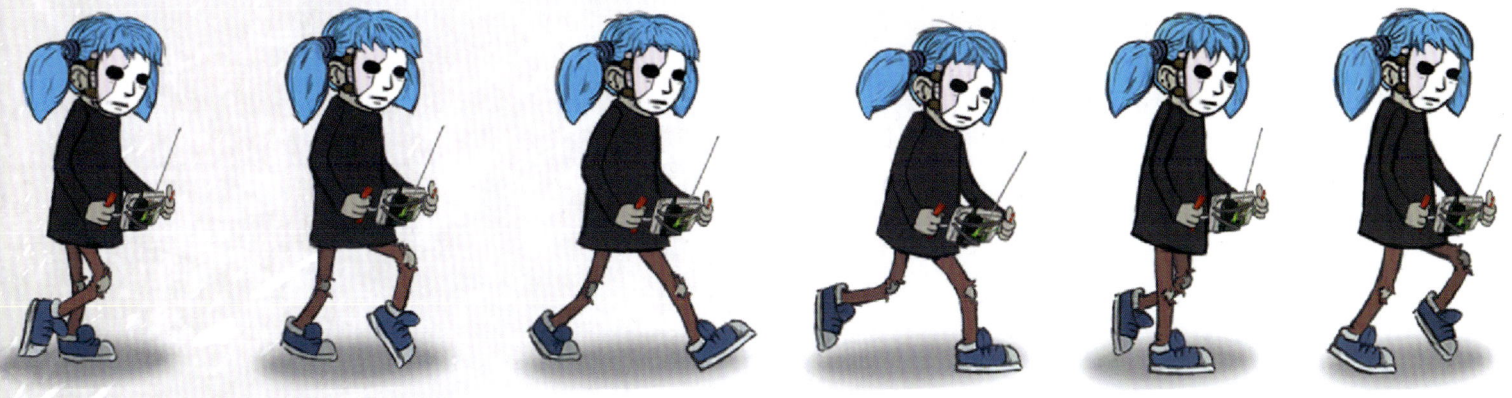

A RISE IN POPULARITY

IN THE EARLY DAYS of *Sally Face*, the game had gathered a small cult following. That following grew quite a lot over time and continues to grow. As a solo developer and solo business owner, it's been a huge change in my life. Even though this has been a dream come true, it's also been very overwhelming and very stressful at times.

THE FANS

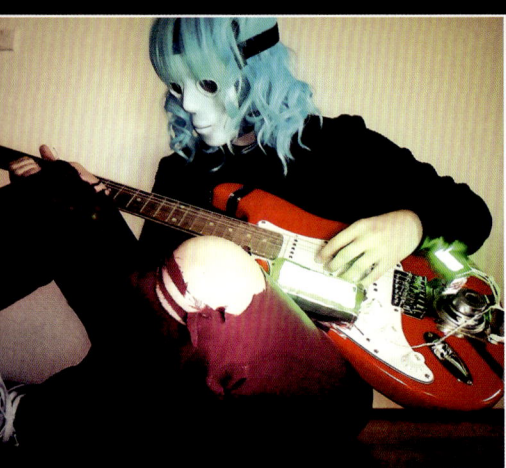

COSPLAY: Ruffneckcat (Jasmin Farr)

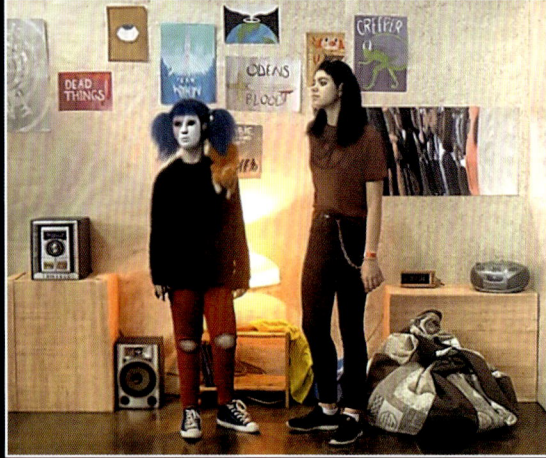

COSPLAY:
SAL: Dario Botvich
LARRY: Alyona Larchenko
PHOTOGRAPHER: Nadezhda Semionova

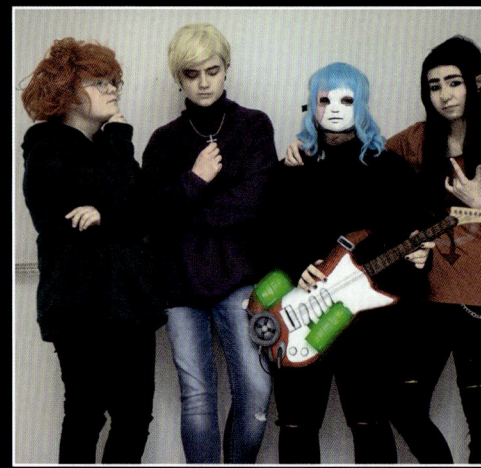

COSPLAY:
TODD: Annie Kuukkanen
TRAVIS: Pyry
LARRY: Iina
SAL: Janika
PHOTOGRAPHER: Riku

IN THE BEGINNING, I was able to connect with every fan and answer every question and every message. I really enjoyed that connection and seeing their excitement. Now, I get so many messages that I can't even read them all, let alone answer them all. When more started coming in, I tried to keep up with it at first. I really wanted to continue to talk with everyone and continue to interact with their posts of fan art and cosplays. But it began eating up hours a day. It took me a little while to stop putting so much time into that. I felt a sadness at not being able to answer everyone. Especially since I often get messages saying heartfelt things about how much *Sally Face* has changed someone's life, or saved them from depression, or saved them from suicide, or helped them in some way. In general, my fans mean a great deal to me and these kinds of letters really mean a lot. I think that strength to get through tough times is already inside of all of us but if my game can help bring that out in any way, that's something special.

For my own sanity and for the sake of productivity, I had to learn to cut back on fan interaction. I still like to engage when I can, though. I very much enjoy seeing the cool things *Sally Face* fans create and how much they get into the story and characters.

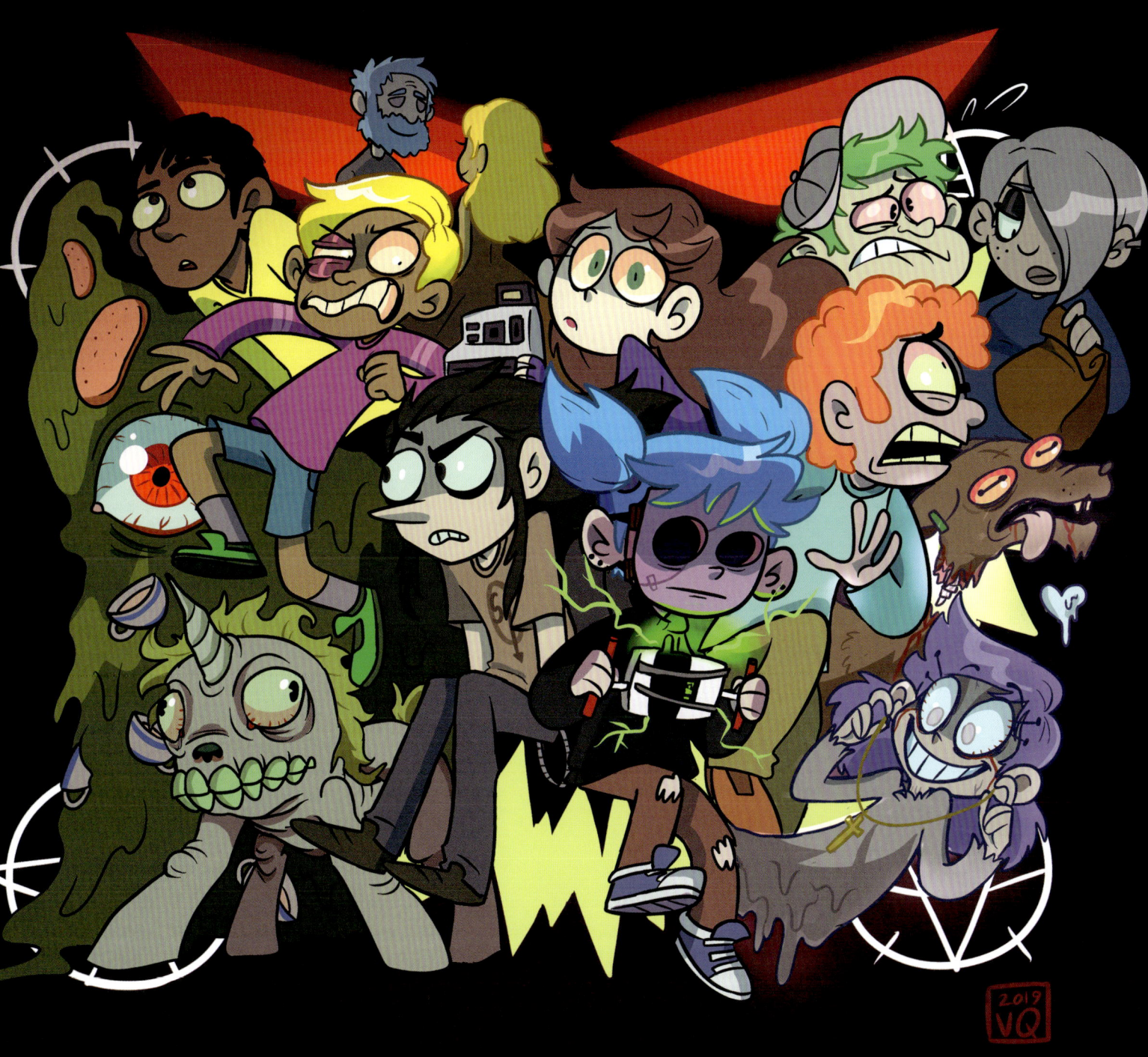

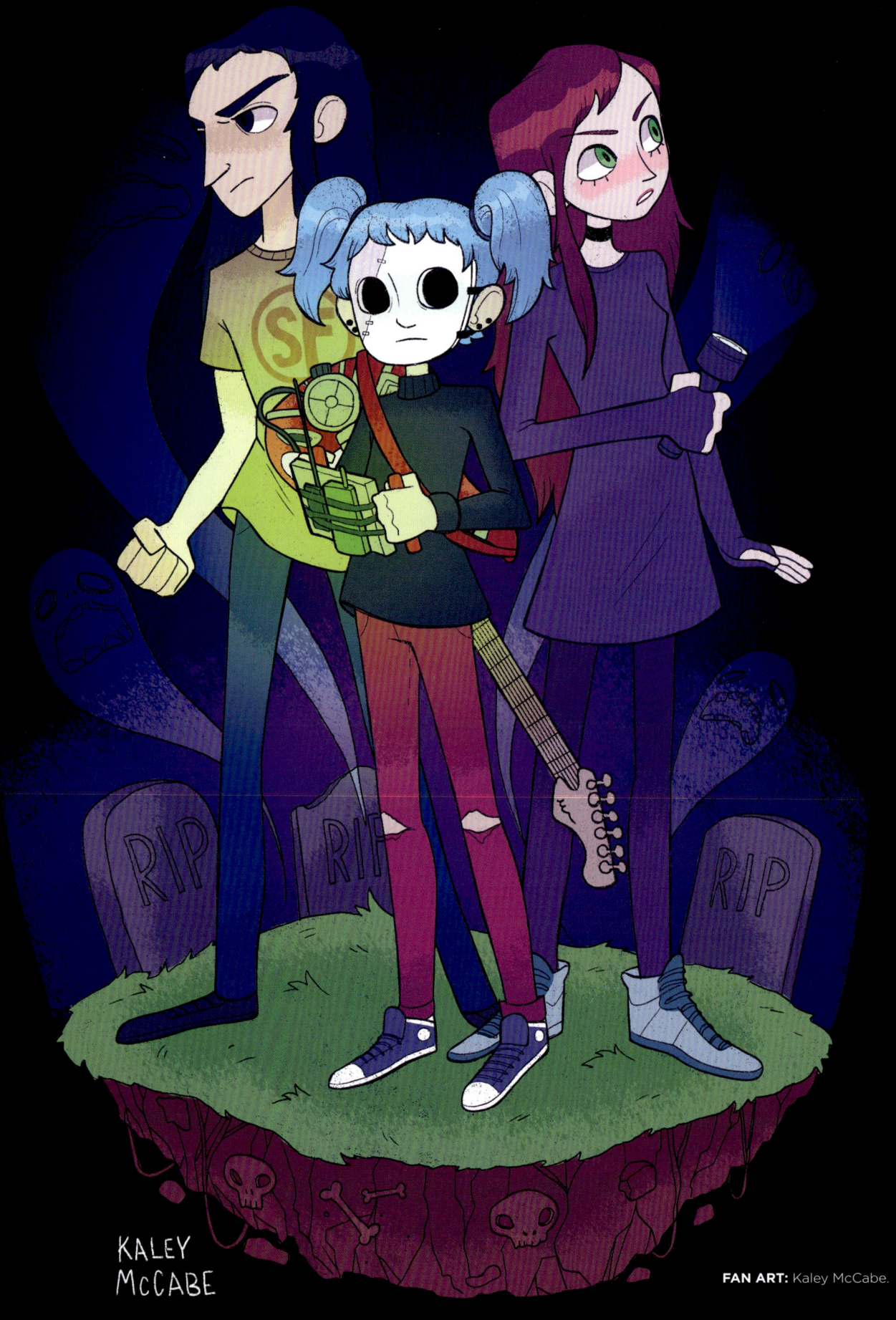

KALEY
McCABE

NEGATIVITY

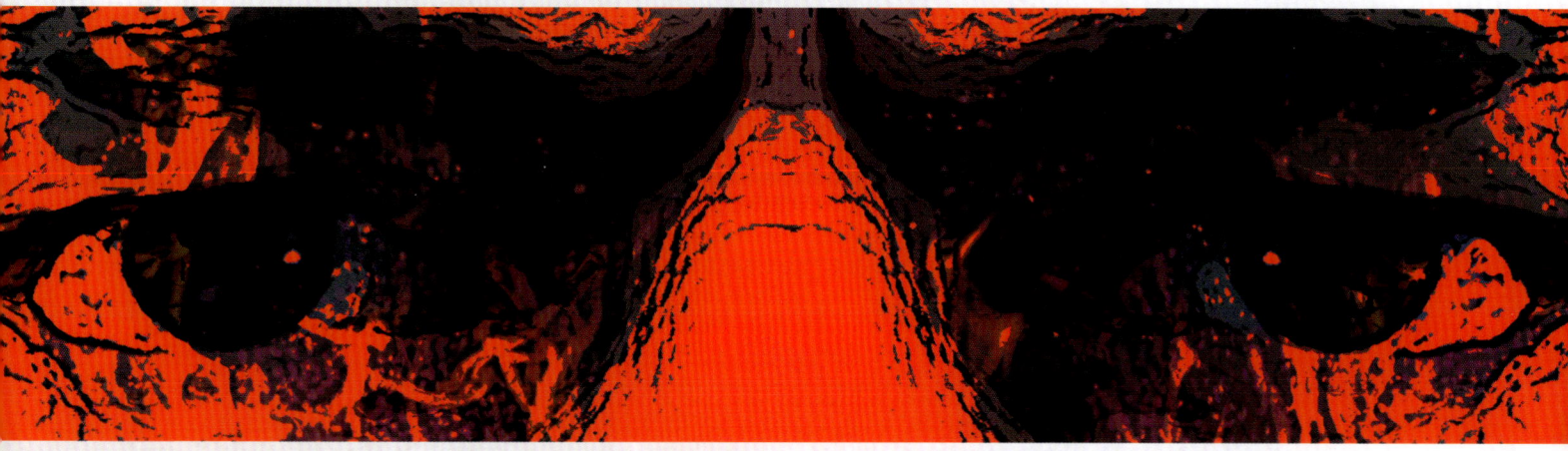

MY INTERACTIONS WITH FANS have been overwhelmingly positive overall. Though, with more attention and bigger numbers, some negativity and trolling comes my way as well.

There was a rumor started about Episode Five releasing in the summer of 2019, even though I had been saying "end of 2019" in all official channels. And when it didn't come out in the summer there were some people who were mad at me for "lying" or "delaying the game", even though neither were true. These people acted very aggressively towards me. A lot of the fans are patient and understand that it's a ton of work to make a game on your own. However, there are some that like to yell at me through the internet for "taking too long!" While I'm happy that they are anxiously waiting for my game, yelling at me doesn't help anything.

I've received negative reviews saying that having DLC makes me "greedy". This really shows me that those people don't understand game development. In fact, me charging only $15 for all of *Sally Face* is

pretty cheap. That's about five years of work for $15. I initially thought that the episodes would all be shorter but I wanted to make it the best I could, so more production value went into it. Despite that, I didn't want to raise the price (even though I probably should have) because I wanted to keep it fair and accessible to players. Not to mention, I only take home about 45% of the game revenue (after platform cuts and taxes). So when people call me "greedy" for "charging so much" it's unbelievable to me.

And then there are the small number of trolls that spew meaningless anger in my direction. I've found it best to not engage with these people and to just ignore them. If someone wants to start a genuine conversation, they don't do it by starting with insults. If they come at me particularly aggressively, I just block them. Interacting would achieve nothing, since they are just looking to fight. My thought is that they are most likely kids who are not happy with their lives. And I hope that they will someday find happiness.

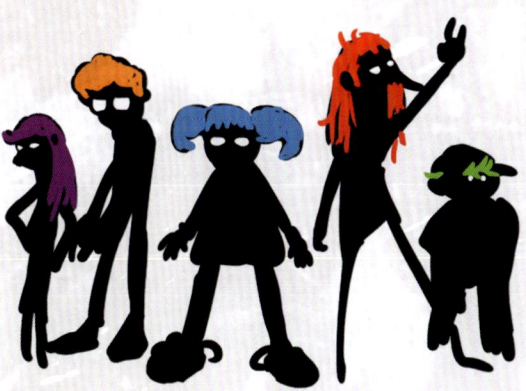

MERCHANDISING

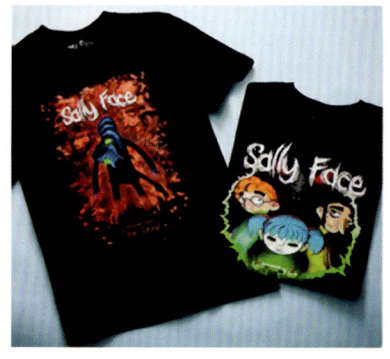
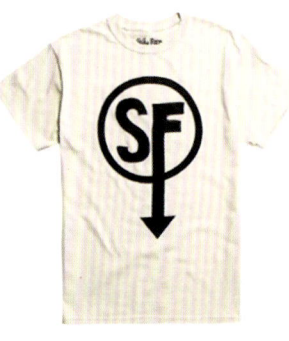
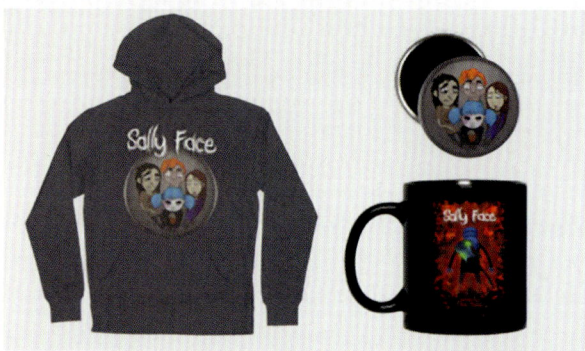

WITH THE RISING POPULARITY also comes new opportunities such as merchandising and other exciting things. I've partnered up with Brand Central, who handles *Sally Face* merch. Through them, I've signed deals with Hot Topic, Funko, BandMerch, Trick or Treat Studios, and more. All of these new opportunities are great, though they also take up extra time as well. Including flying out to LA for meetings, prepping documents, phone meetings, and so on.

Along with the merch, there comes other people (especially Chinese companies) selling counterfeit

Sally Face merchandise and stealing my work. It's a shame that people do this to anyone, let alone a solo artist such as myself. This has caused a lot of frustration, stress, and time wasted fighting these cases. Fans purchase these counterfeit items, without knowing they are fake, and that harms the future plans I hope to build upon. The money raised through merch sales goes into making the next game. When other companies steal my work, they are directly affecting my projects. To be clear, I don't blame fans for this, the issue here is 100% on these counterfeit companies.

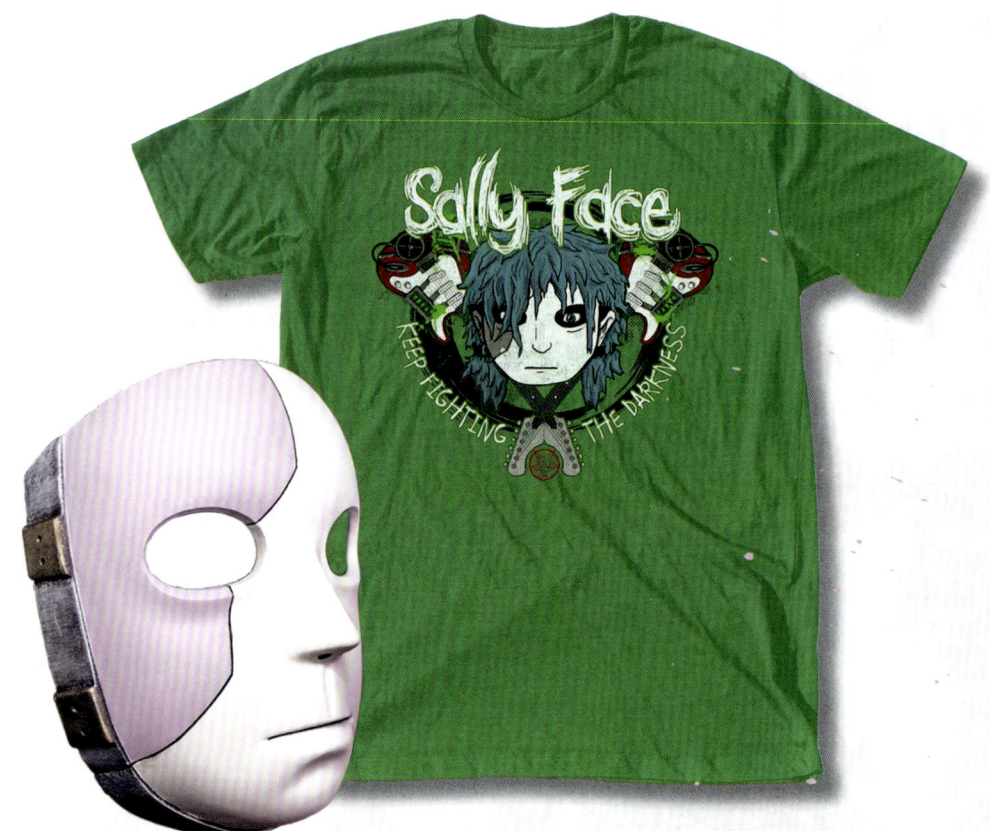

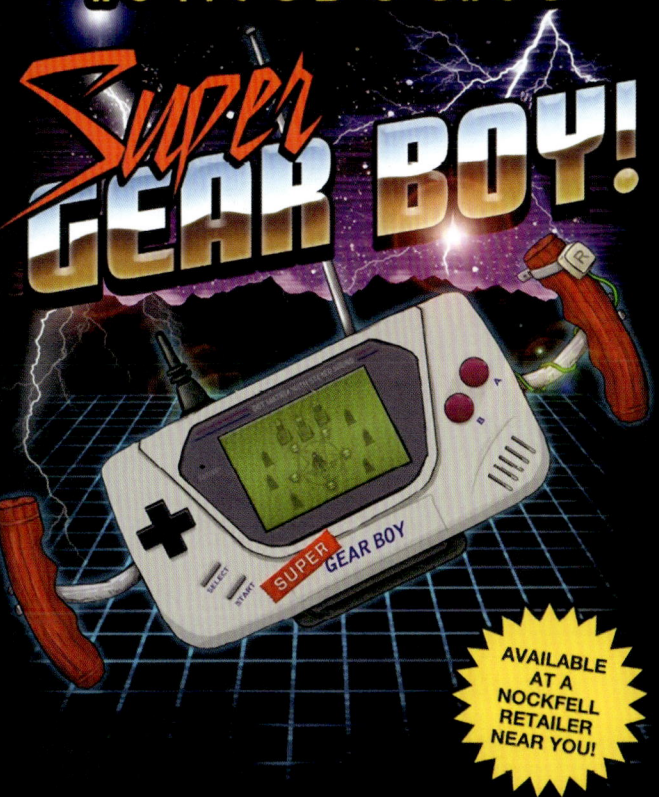

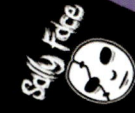

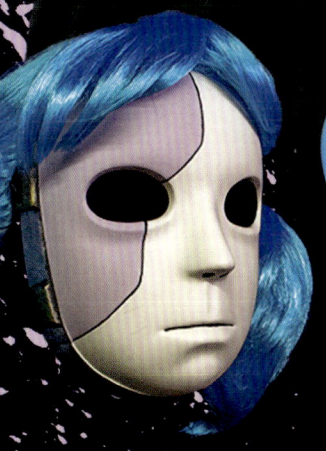

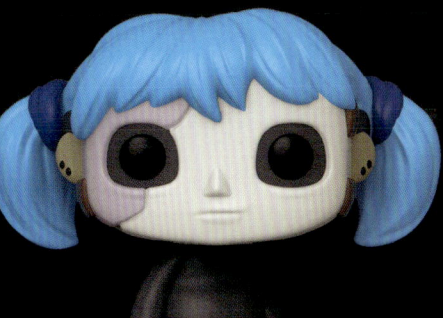

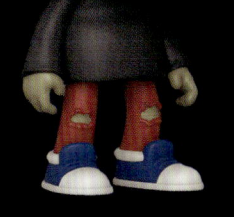

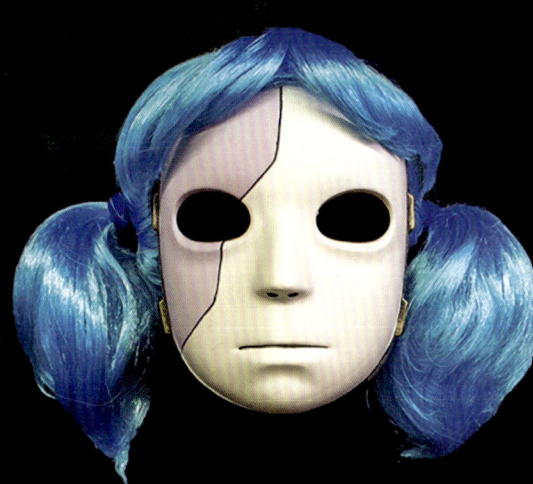

A TANGENT ABOUT YOUTUBERS

I'LL BE HONEST, before releasing *Sally Face*, I didn't know much about Let's Players, Streamers, "Content Creators", etc. I knew they existed and I knew a little about the controversies between them and game developers. They have definitely played a role in my journey with *Sally Face*.

I've spoken with and have met a lot of these people and it's always been a pleasure. Everyone has been super nice and it seems like a great community. In the early days, bigger YouTubers like JackSepticEye, Gloom Games, John Wolfe, and others really helped to spread awareness of the game. I even put little Easter Eggs in the game, to show my appreciation for them.

Some developers think that these Let's Plays and Streams are a big negative force for the game industry, essentially because more and more people are watching games instead of playing them. Which is stated to be a big reason why single player games are "dying". But I don't think it's that simple. I mean, this issue is undeniably a double-edge sword: on the one hand, the exposure can do great things for small indie developers, and on the other, it could hurt more linear, story-driven games by spoiling them. It's very important that players, who are able to, support the games they love by buying them. Otherwise, those developers won't be able to make more games. Of course, playthroughs can be great for those who don't have the means to play or want to see what a game is like before purchasing it.

As of the time of writing, my view is that these gameplay videos are a net positive for small indie developers, but that the process can use some improvements. At a minimum, YouTubers/Streamers should be sharing the official links to any games they play. I think a good amount of them do this already. And if they really enjoy the game, they should encourage their viewers to purchase it. Promoting the game is important if you want to see more work from that developer. I don't think that's asking for much and I believe most YouTubers/Streamers would understand that point. If we got some help with reminding their viewers of the importance of purchasing games they like, I think that's a good first step. I do recognize that some already do this, which is great, but it doesn't seem like the standard.

Similar to talking about piracy (which is another can of worms), this is a delicate subject matter. People tend to take sides and be very passionate about that. But I think it's important to look at both the pros and the cons of gameplay videos online and to continue to have a conversation about it. Whatever your opinion, for better or worse, this is definitely something that's changing the game industry in big ways.

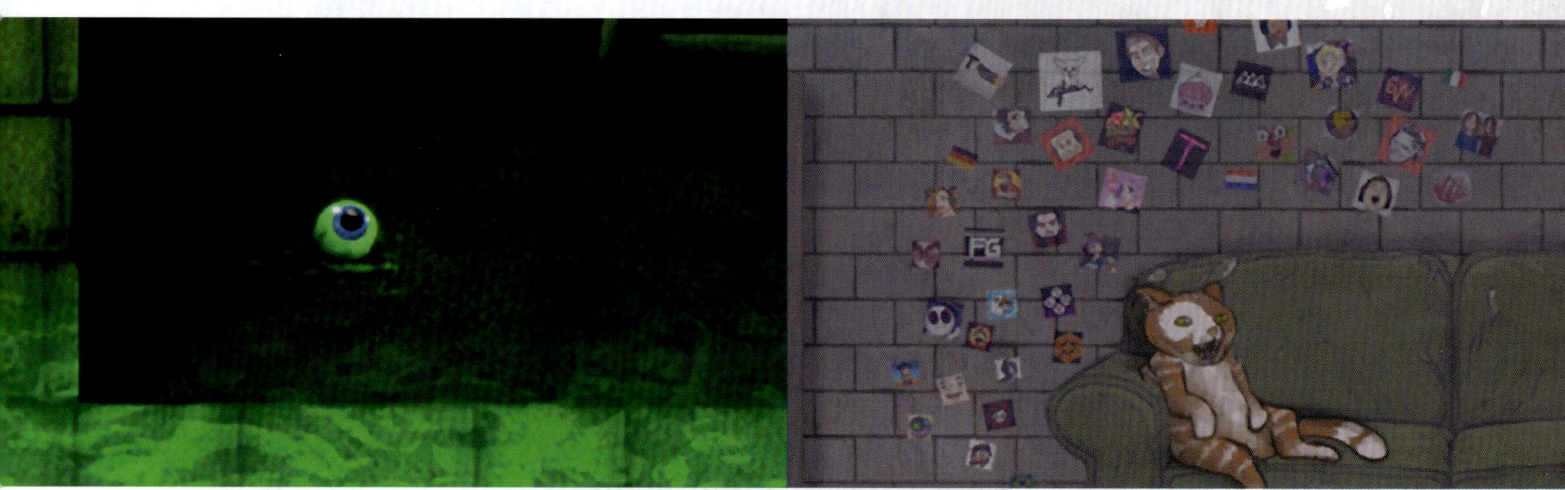

POST-MORTEM

A reflection on my first solo game creation.

I'VE BEEN WORKING on *Sally Face* for the last five years of my life. In that time, I've created over 80 characters, 54 environments, recorded 56 songs, wrote thousands of lines of dialogue, designed 70 puzzles/challenges and mixed over 500 sound effects—all within the span of five episodes. The final project has over 4,000 art assets and over 1,000 animations.

My blood, sweat, and tears went into this project. I've poured so much of myself into making this game, at times giving too much and then learning to find a better balance. For many people, it's tough to understand how much work goes into developing a game. I hope that the above stats can shed just a little bit of light on the sheer amount of work involved. Though honestly, t hat's only the tip of the iceberg. To me, this work is very rewarding and I wouldn't trade it for anything.

The side project I started eventually became my dream job of working on my games full-time. It literally changed my life.

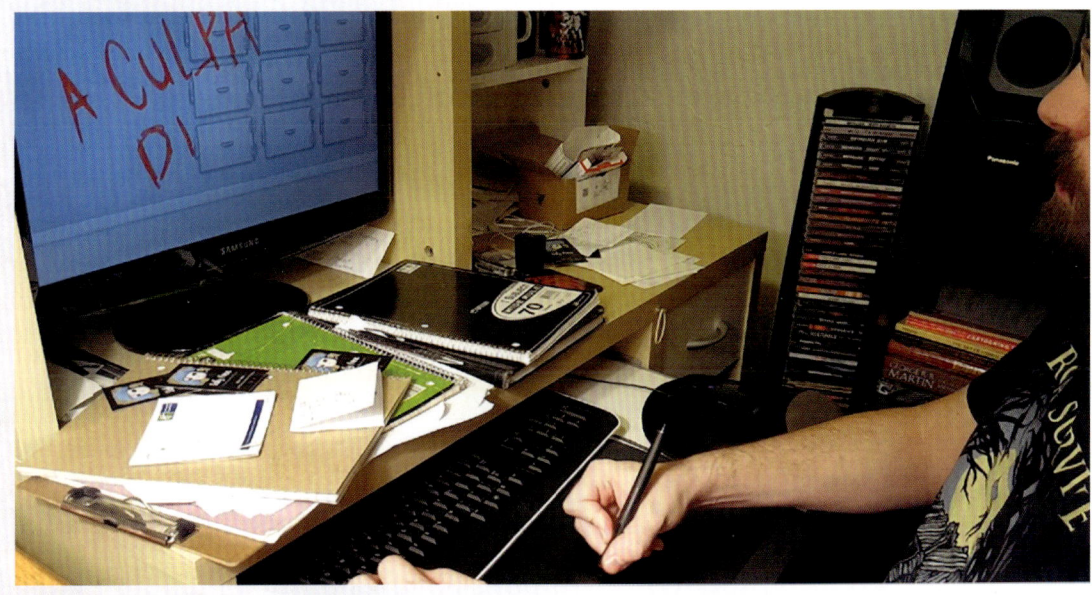

THIS PAGE: Old work space (top) vs new work space (bottom).

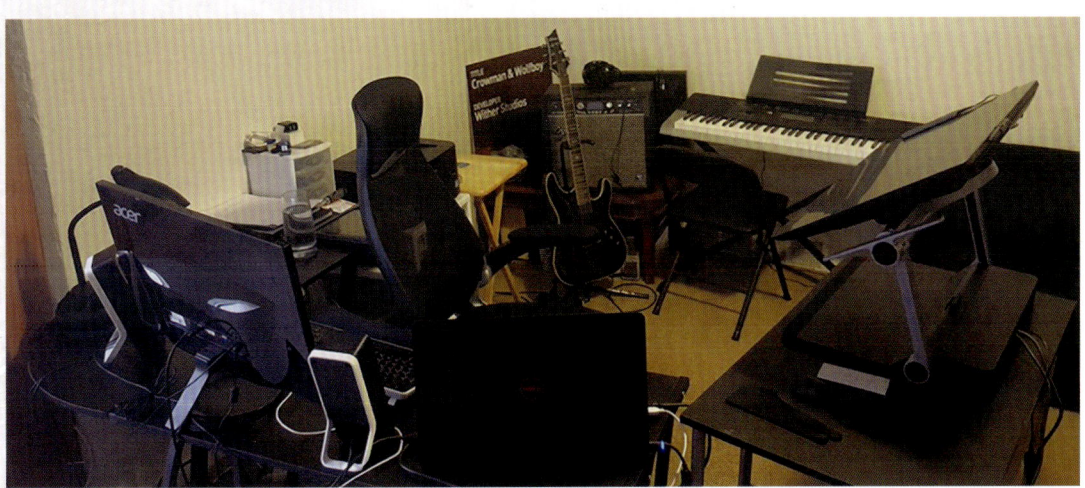

WORKING ON MY OWN

THIS PROJECT has been a solo endeavor for me, creating everything in the game myself: art, music, writing, design, sound, animation, and so on. Not only that, I also do every other aspect from marketing to PR to support. That means answering emails, fixing bugs, cutting trailers, making marketing materials, writing press releases, traveling to conventions, doing bookkeeping, managing social media sites, etc.

I began working on my own out of necessity (I didn't have any budget) but also out of passion. I have a strong drive for this work and find it to be very satisfying when it all comes together. So even when the game started making some money, I still wanted to see it through on my own. Partly because of my love for the work and partly as a personal goal/challenge to create a full game by myself.

Most of the time, I do enjoy working alone. I can make my own hours, work on what I want when I want to, and have full creative control over the project. That means I can really let my vision shine through without having to make compromises. That said, I do sometimes miss the group environment and there's also a lot to be gained with working as a group.

I also want to do a shout out to the group of awesome volunteers that helped translate *Sally Face* into other languages. They helped to bring the game to players around the world, which was huge!

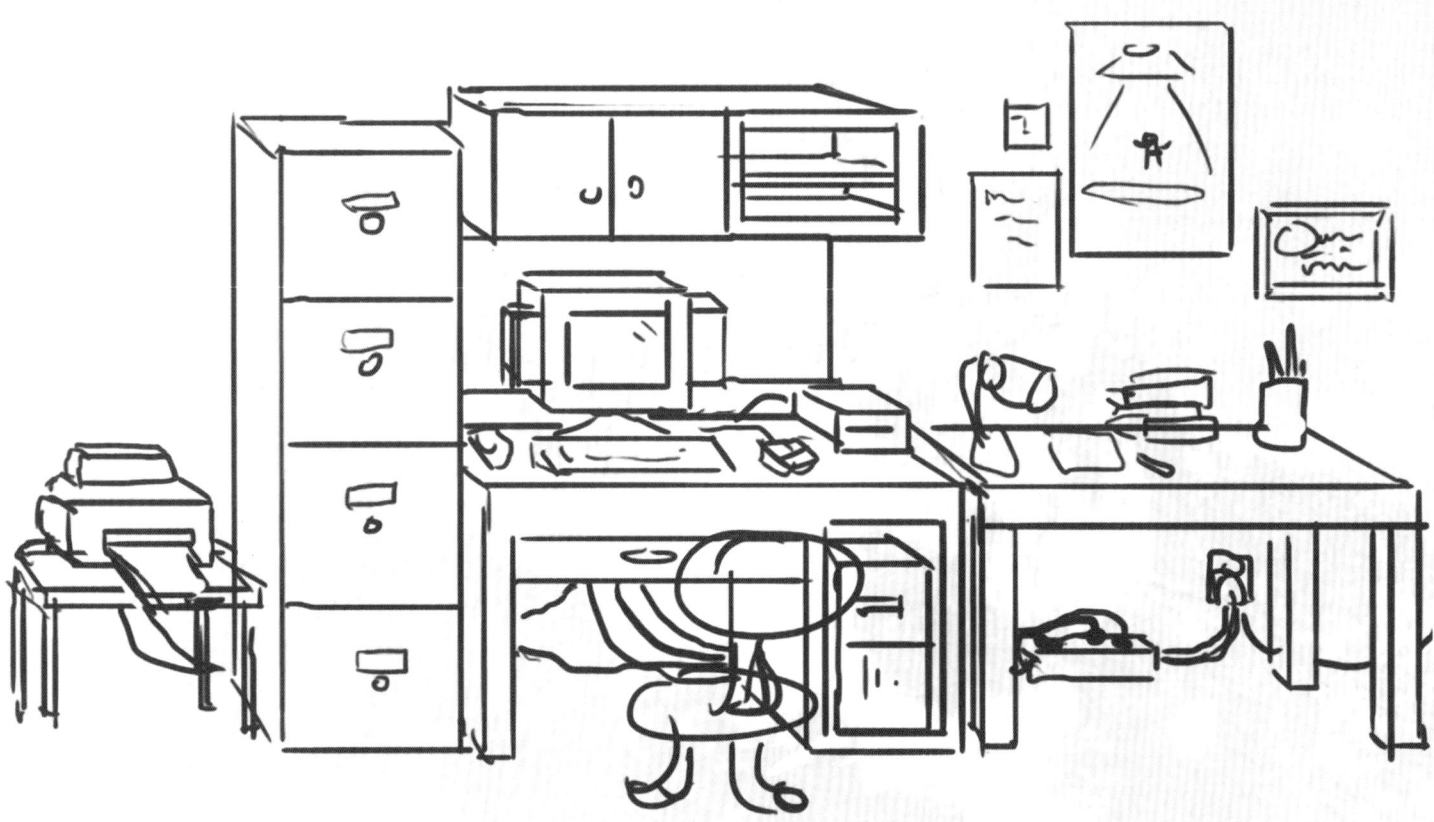

SOME OF THE THINGS I'VE LEARNED

1 Keeping the project short and taking breaks in-between really helped to prevent burnout. So the episodic format was great in that regard. From the beginning, I also planned to evolve the game as I went, so that I was always looking forward to making the next episode and pushing myself as a developer. That turned out to be a helpful component in keeping my motivation going.

2 The episodic format has become a technical nightmare to manage over time. Whenever I have to do an update or a patch, I currently have to make 14 builds and upload them to four different sites (these numbers will increase with new platforms). It's very tedious and time consuming. Additionally, when there are big gaps in releases (with new episodes) plus software updates (Unity and plugins) it can sometimes create issues when users update their older files. In the future, I might rethink how I'll be distributing a game, in order to simplify that process.

3 Working 80+ hours a week is not sustainable. I used to work like this for long stretches of time without breaks. But it's not healthy and I want to continue making games without burning myself out. Occasionally, I'll still slip into that overworking mode for short spurts but I've learned to keep a better balance overall.

4 I will never do a midnight launch again. Every time I plan this, I try to get everything set up early and every time I think that I'm not going to be up too late, I always end up staying up super late anyway. For Episode Five I stayed up past 4am and it was just too much. From now on, I'm going to plan on doing launches in the mornings. This will give me the full day to work with a clear head and not running on zombie brain.

5 Avoiding crunch is hard, though I've been getting better at it. I think the key is to get the project in a near finished state before even talking about a release date. I've seen a lot of people online saying things like "drop the new episode already" but I don't think they really understand what they're asking for. These things take a lot of time and even when they are "finished" they still require a lot of work before launch. You have to get the bugs out, do testing, work on translations, ready platform-specific implementations, work on marketing materials, etc. Asking for a rushed game is like asking for a shittier version of a thing you like. No one wants that. Especially not the person working hard on the project so that players will enjoy it.

6 No matter how hard you work and no matter how much testing you do, there will always be bugs. Always. Once thousands of players are playing the game on all different devices and interacting in different ways, issues will pop up. It's inevitable. It used to really stress me out. And I'd be lying if I said that stress was totally gone but I've come more to terms with that. Just knowing and expecting to have to fix some things after launching has helped.

THE RESPONSE TO THE ENDING

THE RESPONSES to Episode Five were positive overall. Most players really like it, which is great. Though the thing with endings in general is that they don't always please everyone. *Sally Face* is not an exception, as a good amount of fans didn't like the ending. Even though it doesn't seem to be the majority opinion, I still feel a bit disappointed in that. This is a project I've poured my heart into and a community that I love and care about very much. So I do care what they think and it does affect me.

It seems that most of those who were disappointed were so because they wanted more. And at least that's something good. This was one of the feelings I wanted people to have at the end. I wanted them to want more, I wanted them to wonder, "what happens next?", I wanted there to still be mystery remaining for people to talk about. I wanted to keep it open so that I could revisit the world of *Sally Face*. I have too many ideas to let it die and too many things I want to explore.

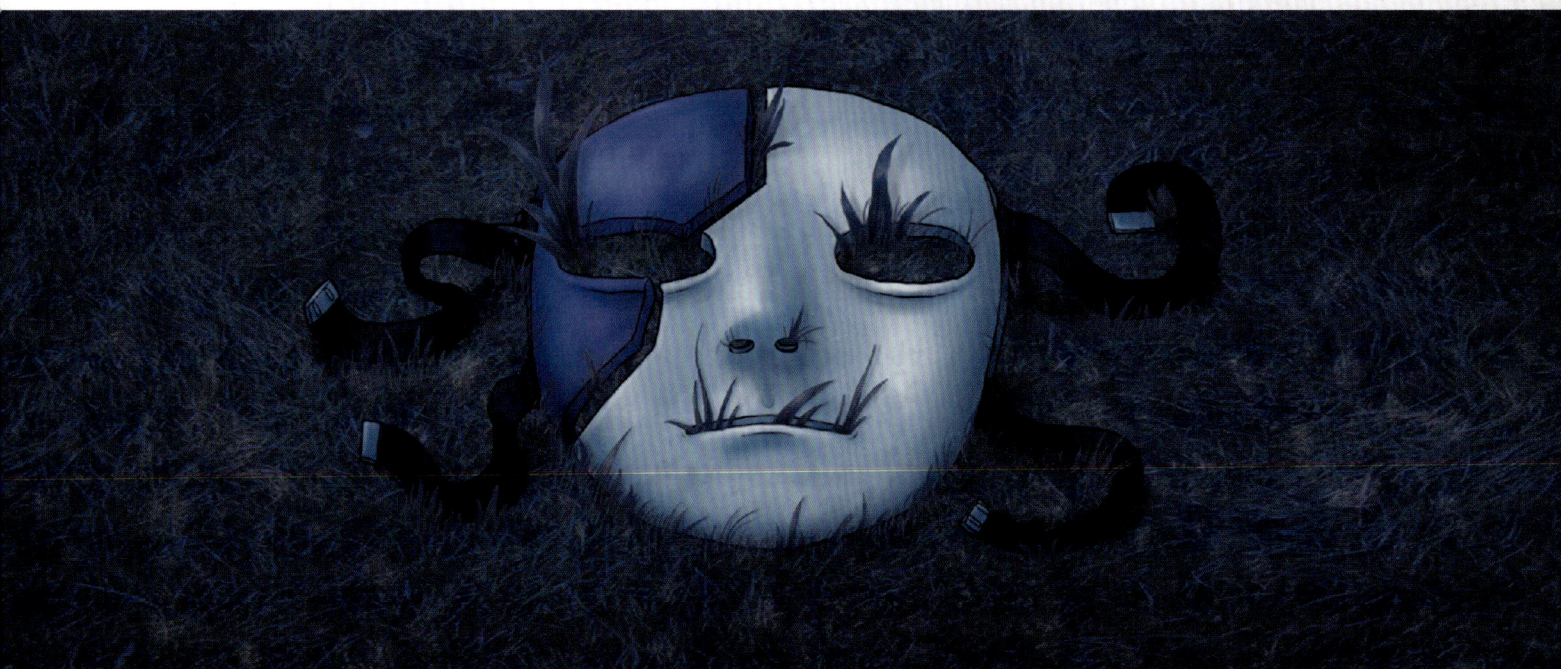

WHAT'S NEXT?

SO WILL THERE BE another *Sally Face* game in the future? Yes! I have several ideas for *Sally Face* that I am excited about. However, I also have other game ideas that I'd like to explore too. Life is short and games take a long time to develop, so I have to choose what I do carefully.

In general, I want to work on games that mean something to me. That's why I'm an indie developer; to have the freedom to make things

that I care about. And I hope that whatever my next project is, that *Sally Face* fans will also enjoy it.

In addition to my solo work as Portable Moose, I still work with Wither Studios. The team lineup has changed a little since we started, back in 2010, but the company survived that rough patch. We continue to pursue our passion of making games we love, to share with the world.

 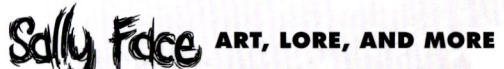

GAME DEV ADVICE

I get asked quite often by hopeful developers for advice.
So I wanted to include some of the tips I usually give them.

1 Do some research to find the best path for YOU. There are a lot of ways in, so think about what you want and what your short term and long term goals are. Keep in mind, what worked for someone else, may not work for you.

2 There are a lot of free programs/tools out there. Apply what you figure out from the first tip, to figure out which programs would be best for you to start learning. And start learning it today, there's no good reason to wait.

3 Start VERY SMALL. Seriously. Make little prototypes and release them online, share them with your friends, etc. Don't worry about making a full game yet. You will need to build your skills up first.

4 You will fail a lot. It's a ton of work, sometimes very frustrating and it's an extremely competitive field to get into. Don't quit your day job and make sure you have a back up plan. Game development is not for everyone.

5 Learn from your mistakes and failures. This is the best way to hone your skills. You will learn and grow so much more from actual hands-on work, than from reading or taking classes.

6 DON'T become an indie dev to get rich. If you're in it for the money, maybe think about a different field to get into. DO become an indie dev because you're passionate about the work, love the creative process and get excited about the connection you're creating.

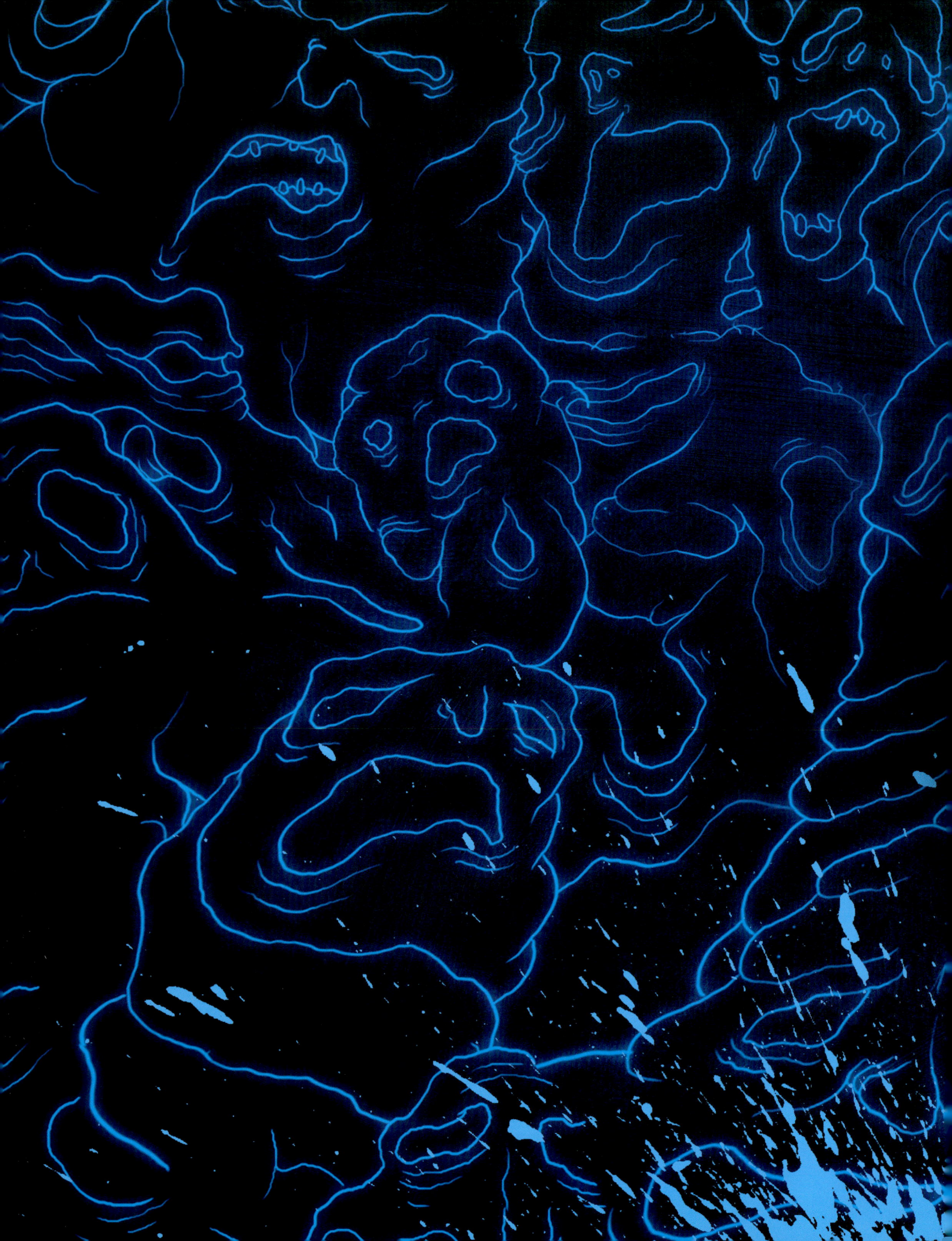

CHAPTER 6

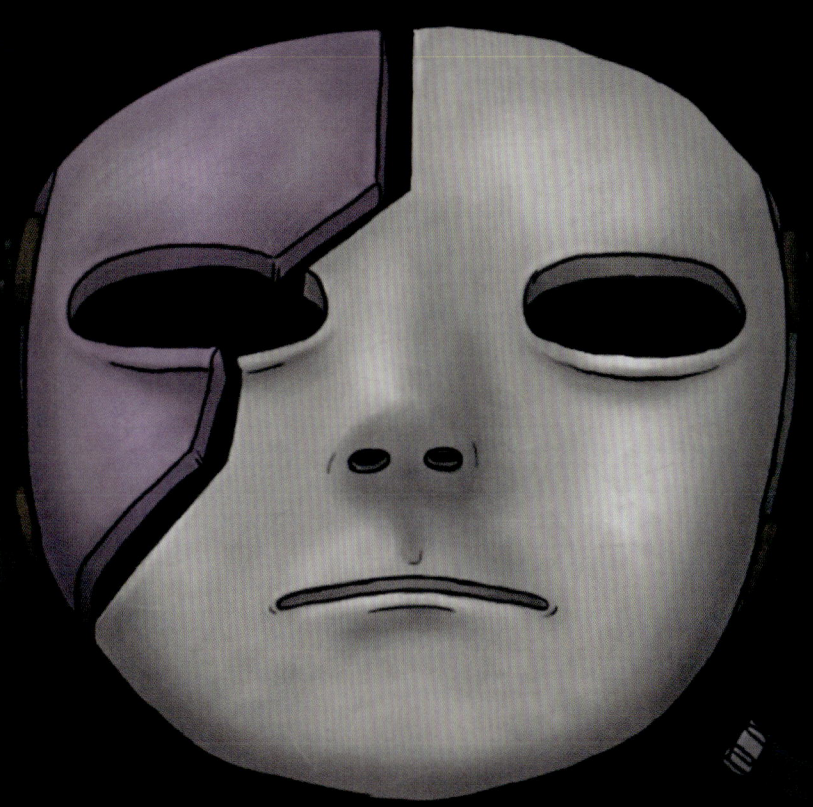

Sally Face

GAME SECRETS GUIDE

GEAR BOY

1) In the intro dream, you'll find four numbers hidden throughout.
Enter those numbers in order, 5364, into the locked door inside Diane's grave.

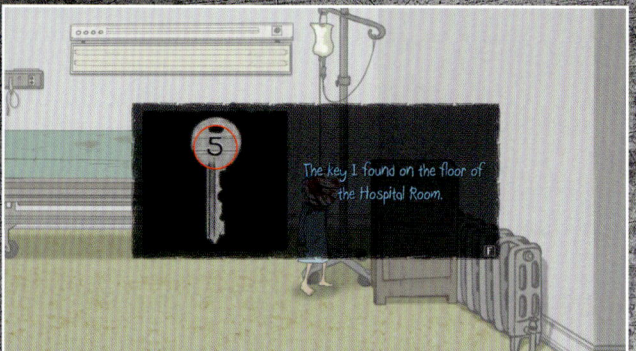

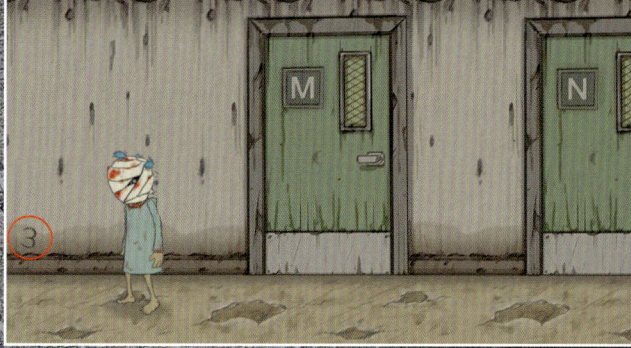

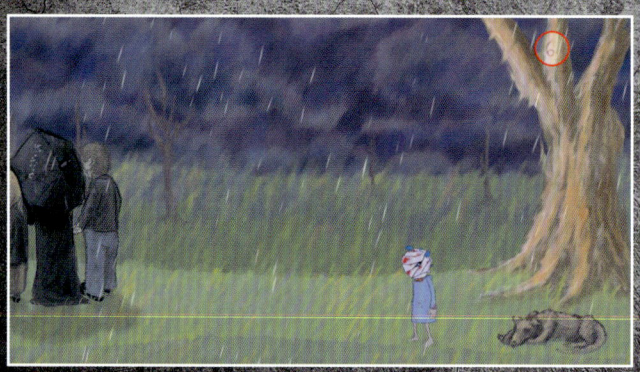

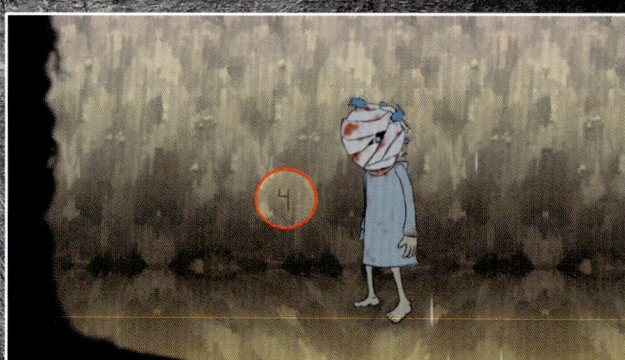

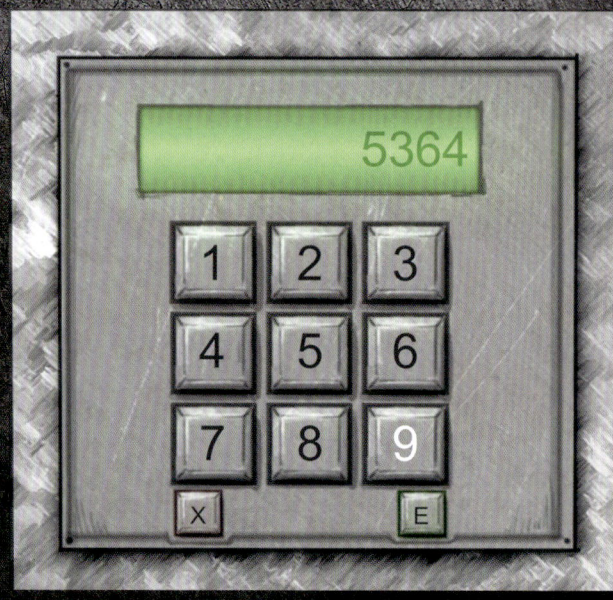

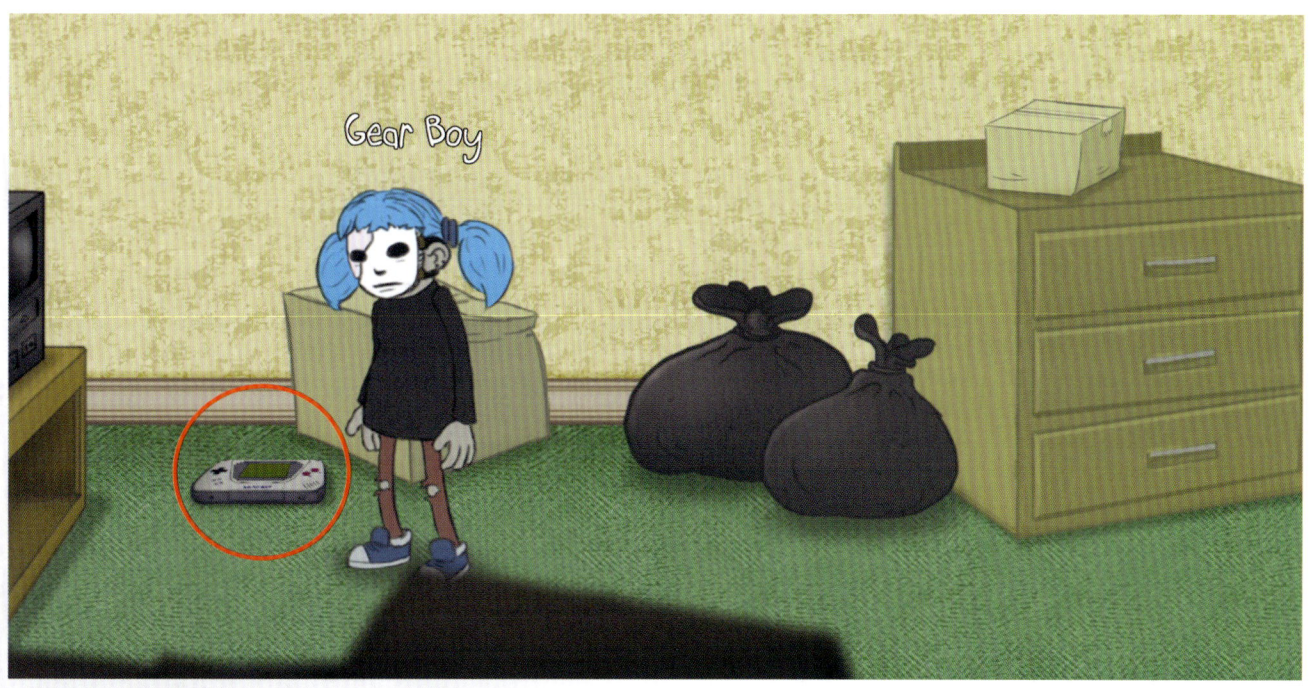

2) Find the Gear Boy in Sal's room, behind the TV.

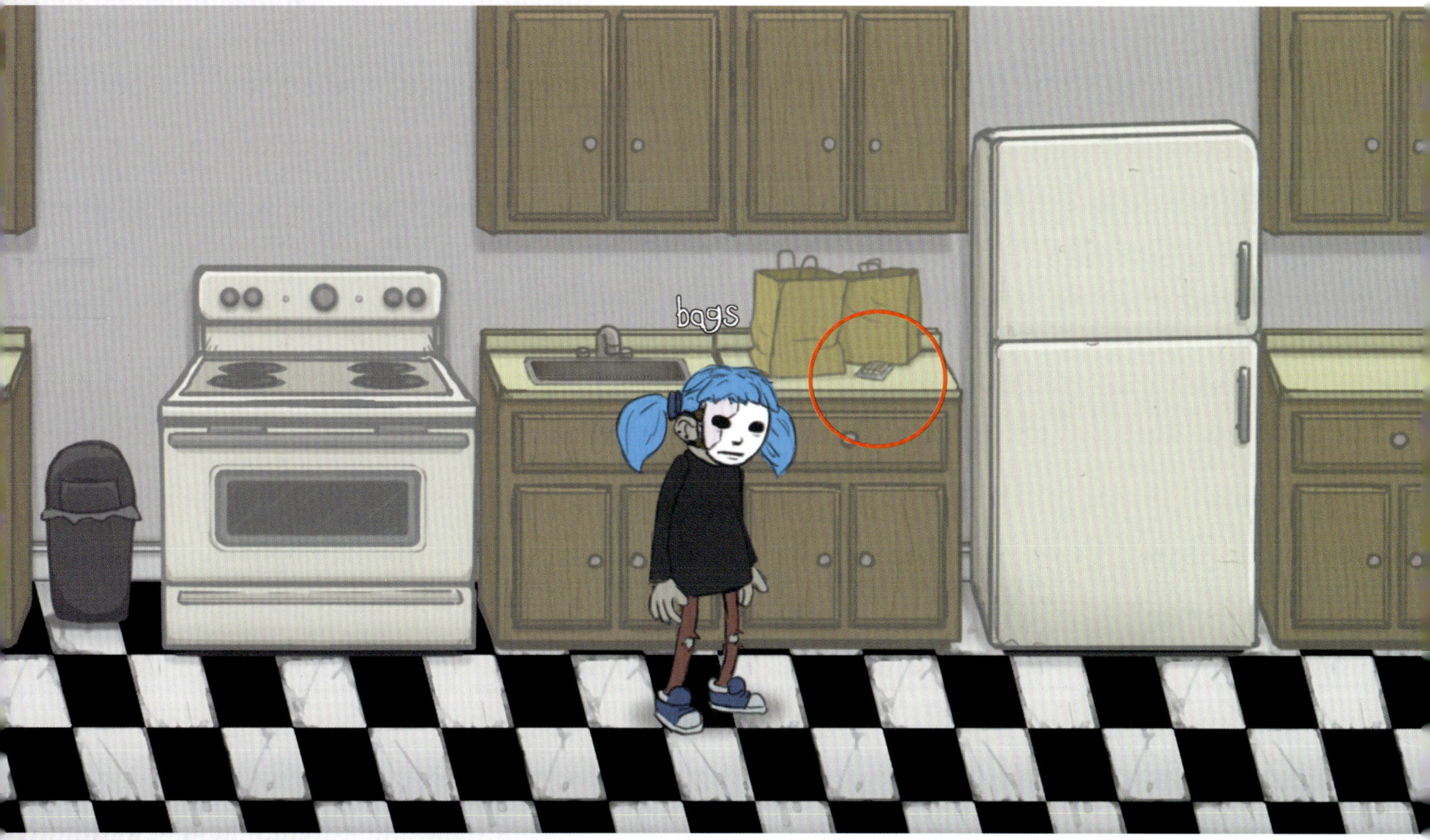

3) Grab the batteries from the grocery bags in his kitchen.

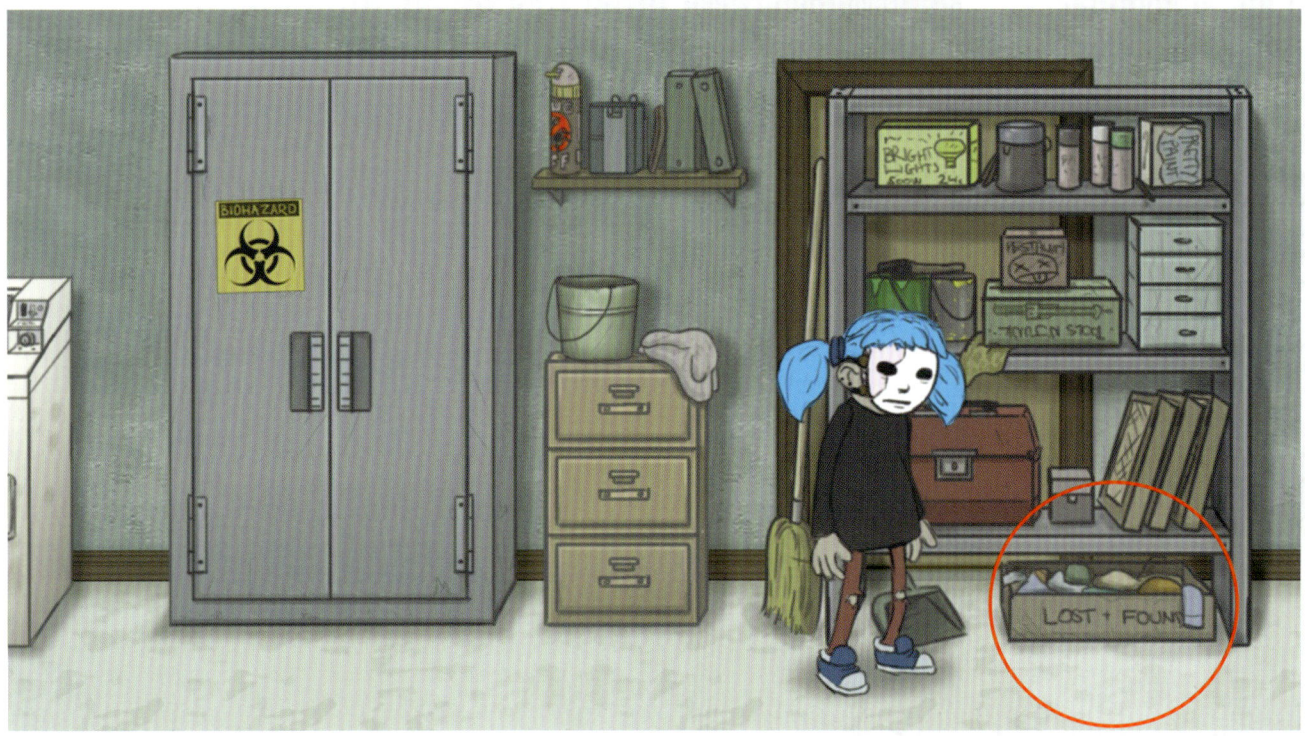

4) Find the old game cartridge in the basement, in the "Lost + Found" box.

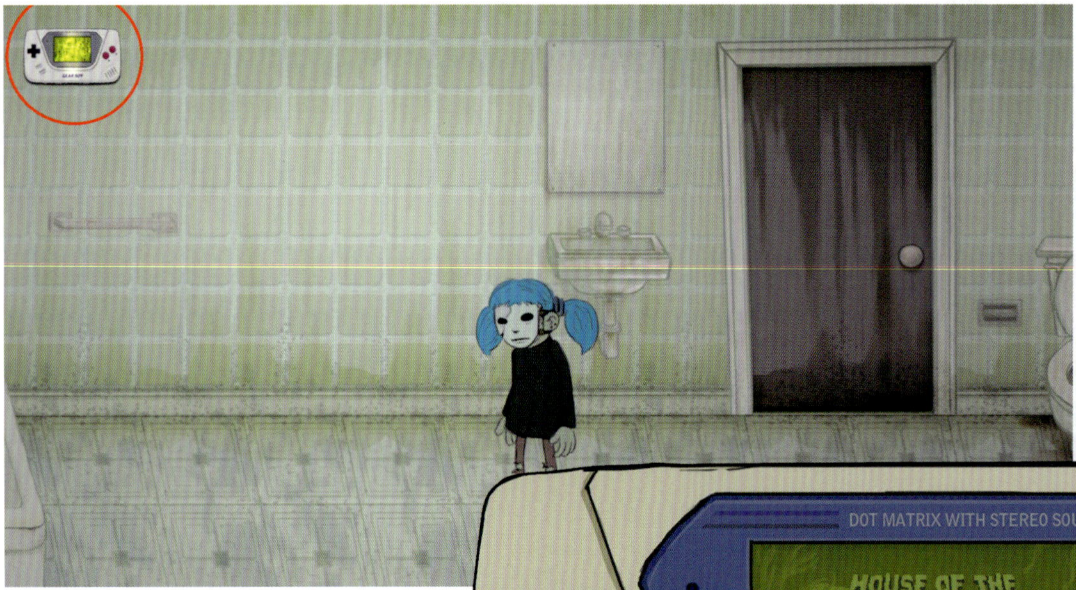

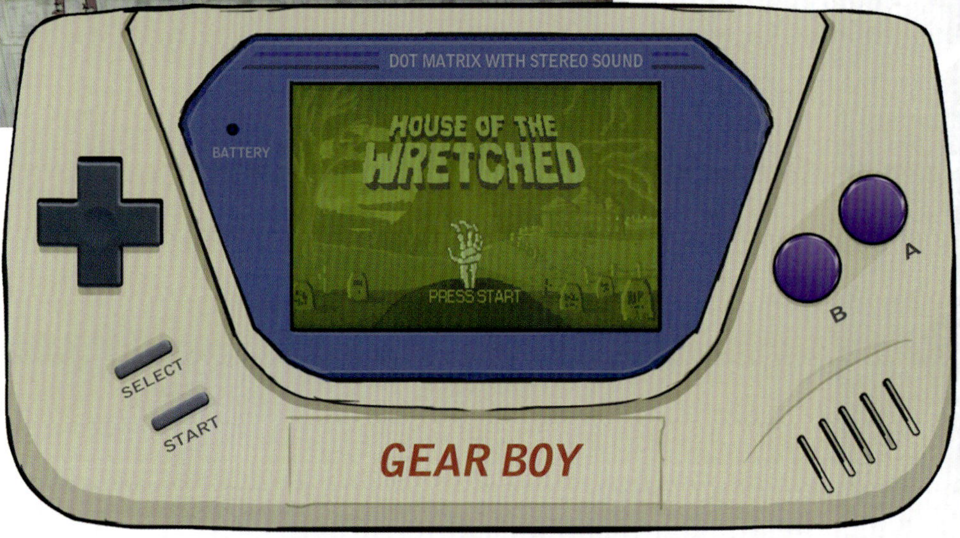

5) Finally, go into the bathroom of 504 to access the game (requires Ghost of Megan, see next guide). After talking to Megan, leave and then come back to the room. Once you see the Gear Boy icon light up, you can now access the game from your inventory menu.

DOT MATRIX WITH STEREO SOUND

HOUSE OF THE WRETCHED

PRESS START

BATTERY

SELECT

START

GEAR BOY

A

B

GHOST OF MEGAN

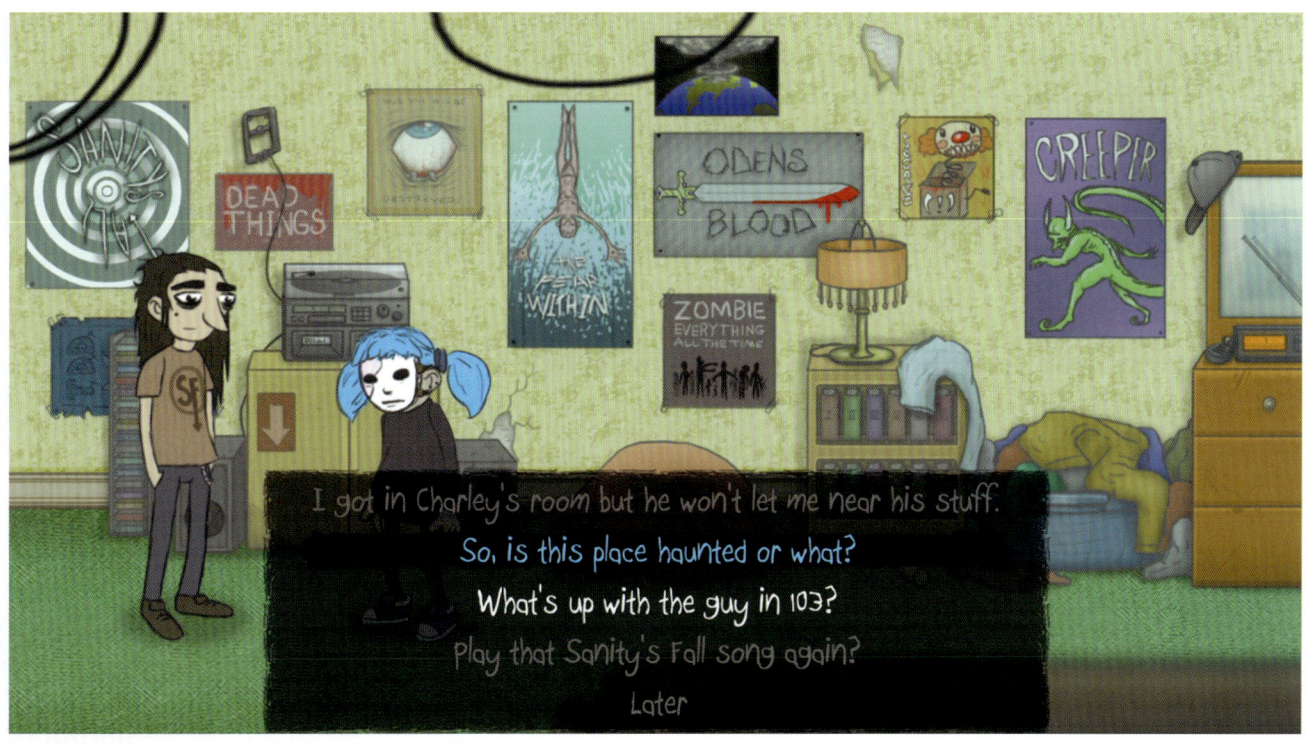

1) After sneaking into room 403, ask Larry if the building is haunted.

2) Grab the quarter in 402 from Henry's room.

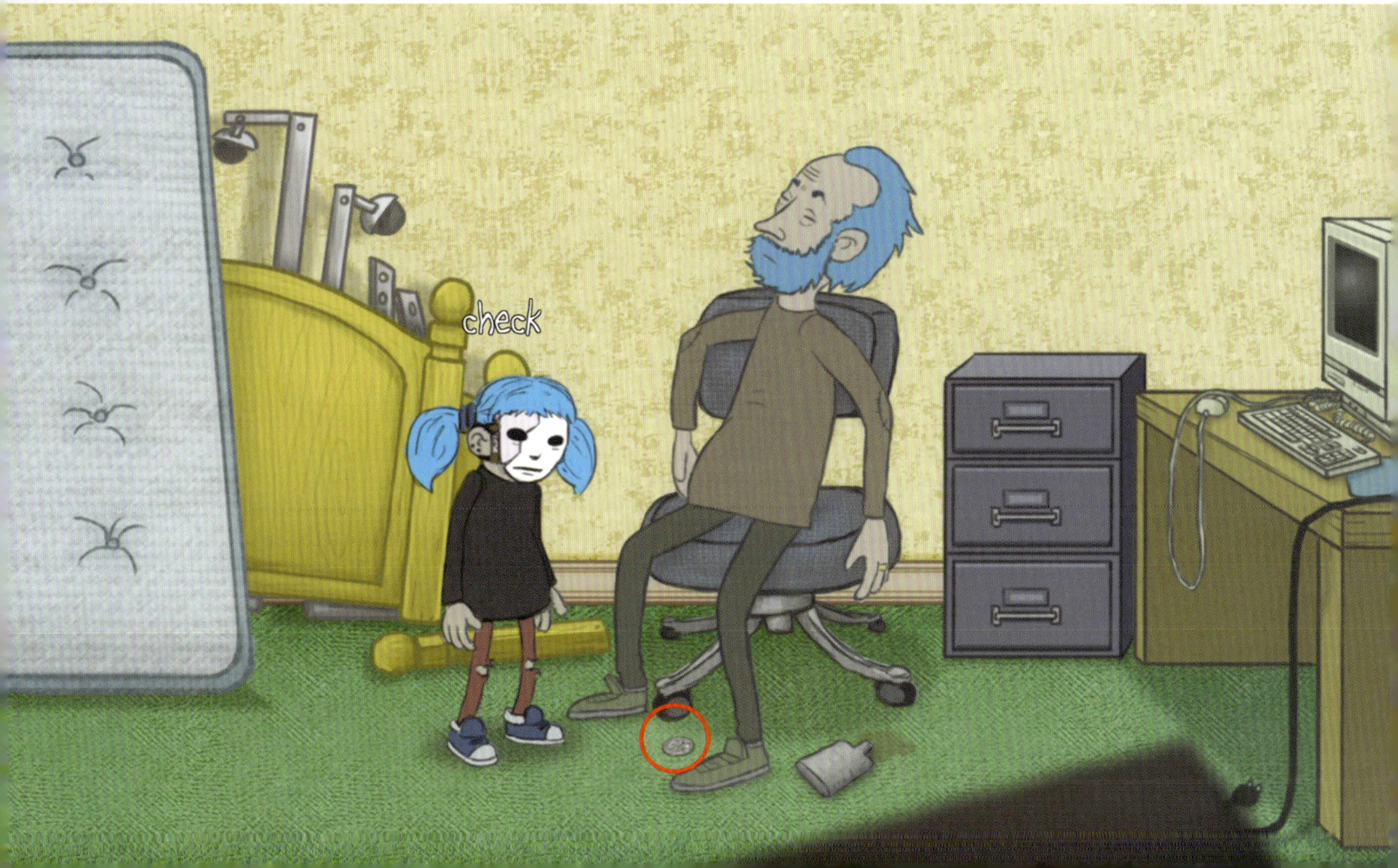

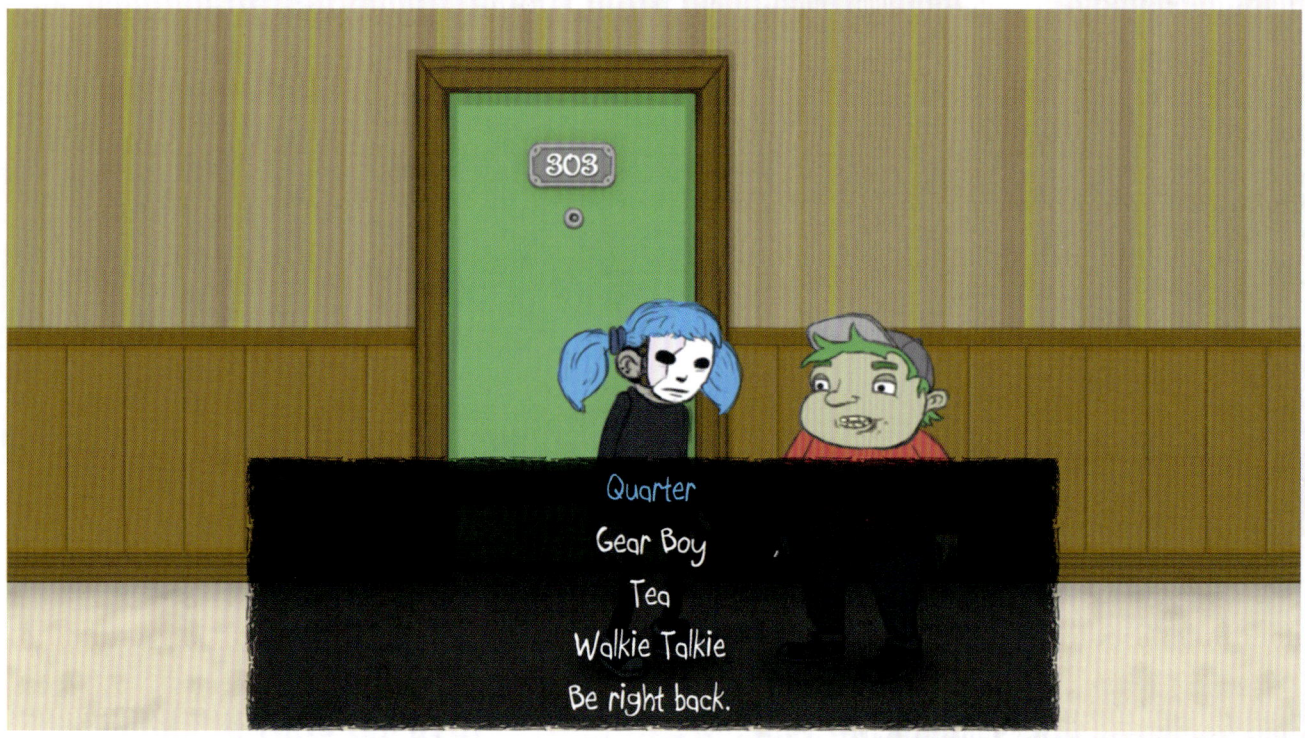

3) Next, visit Chug on floor 3 and trade him the quarter for the key to 504.

4) Go into the bathroom of 504 to speak with Megan.

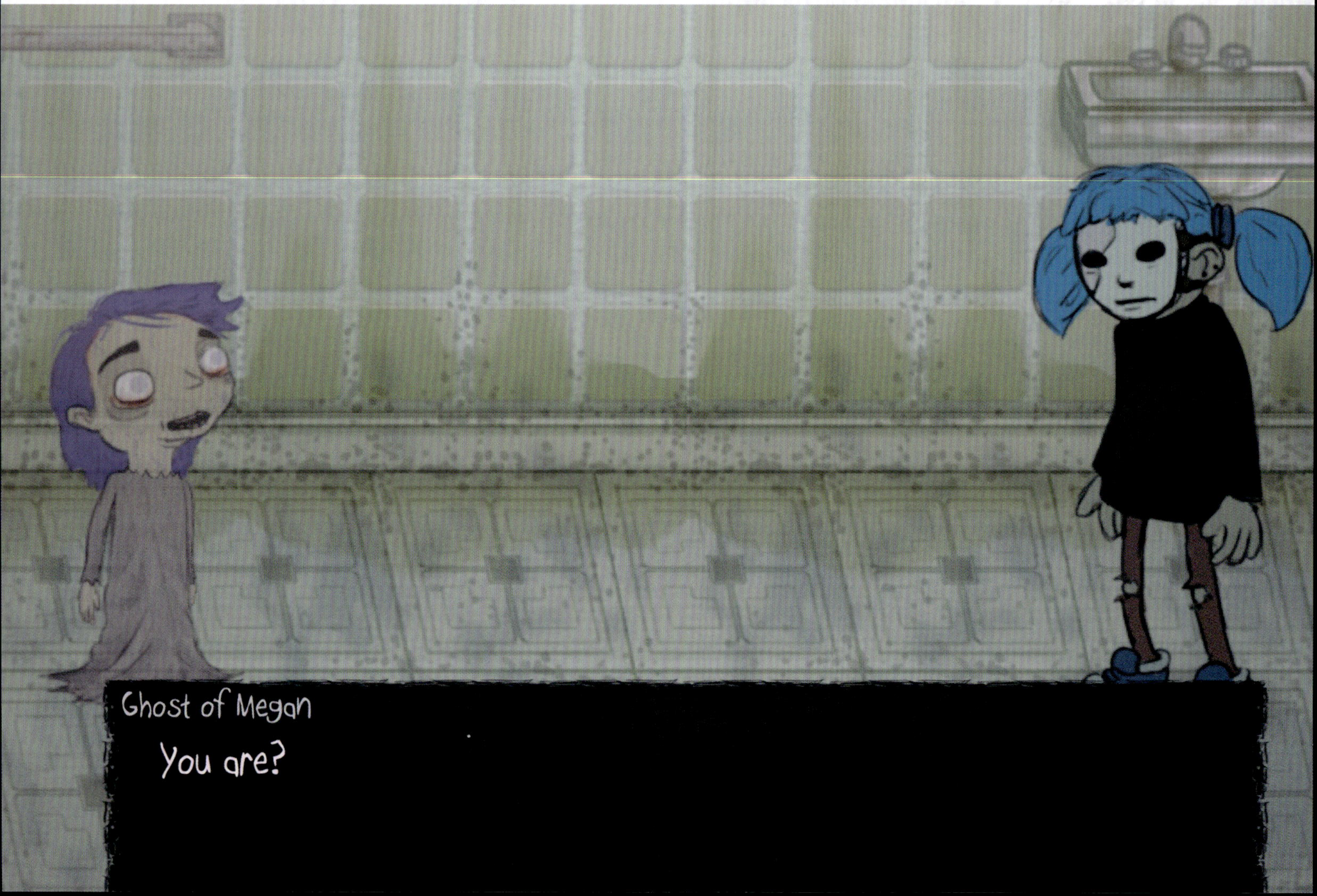

Ghost of Megan
You are?

HIDDEN THINGS

COLD FEET

Open the morgue drawer in Sal's dream to see a hidden body. Who's in there?

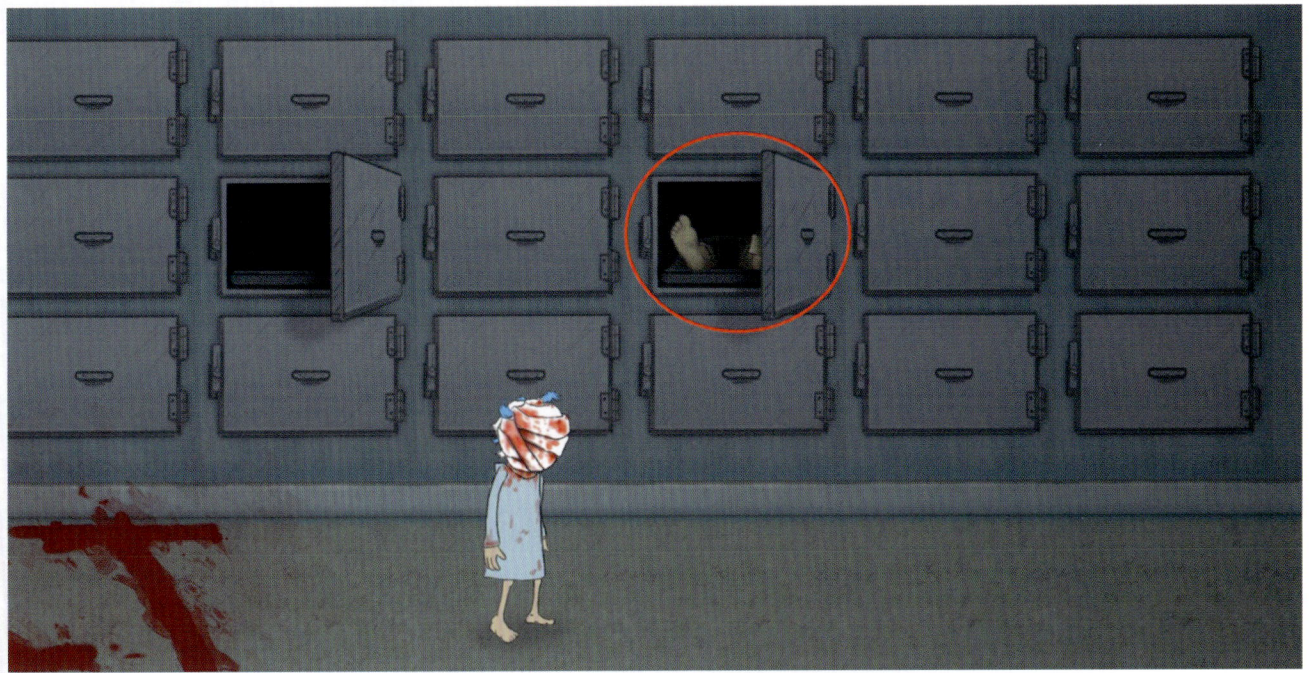

LAXATIVE

Visit Megan without using the Sleep Aid on Charley. Instead, you'll find a laxative on the bathroom floor of 504. Sal will mix this into the tea. This can be used as an alternative to the Sleep Aid.

THE EYE

On floor 5, go all the way to the left of the hallway. You'll see a small hole in the wall. Interact with it.

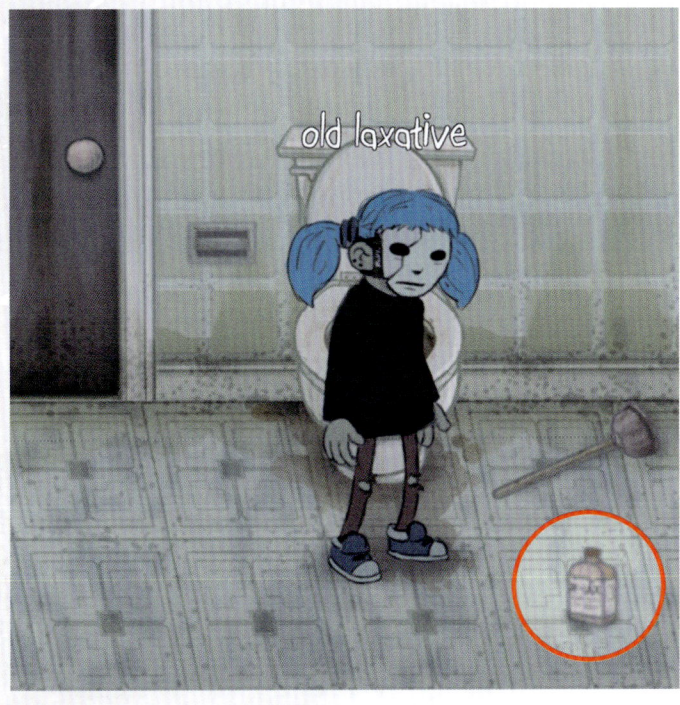

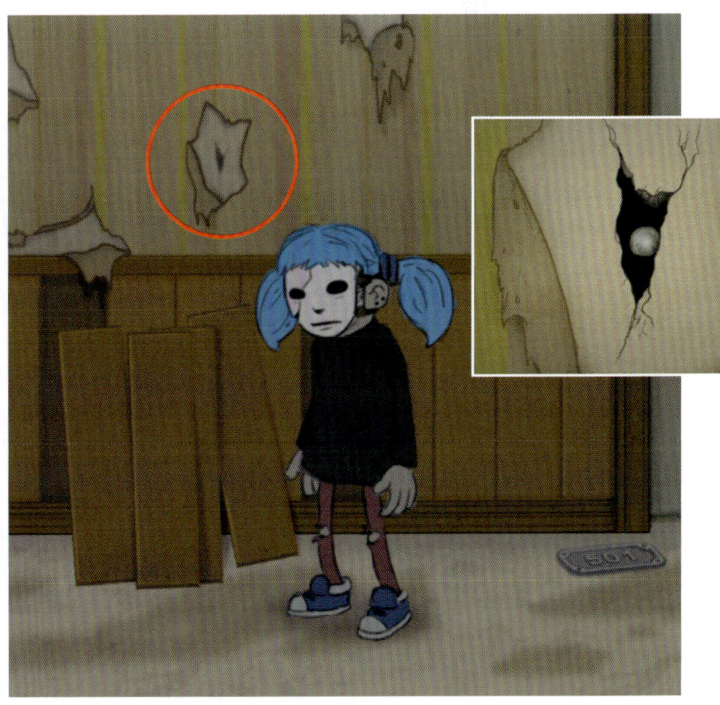

EPISODE TWO
The Wretched

JIM'S PUZZLE BOX

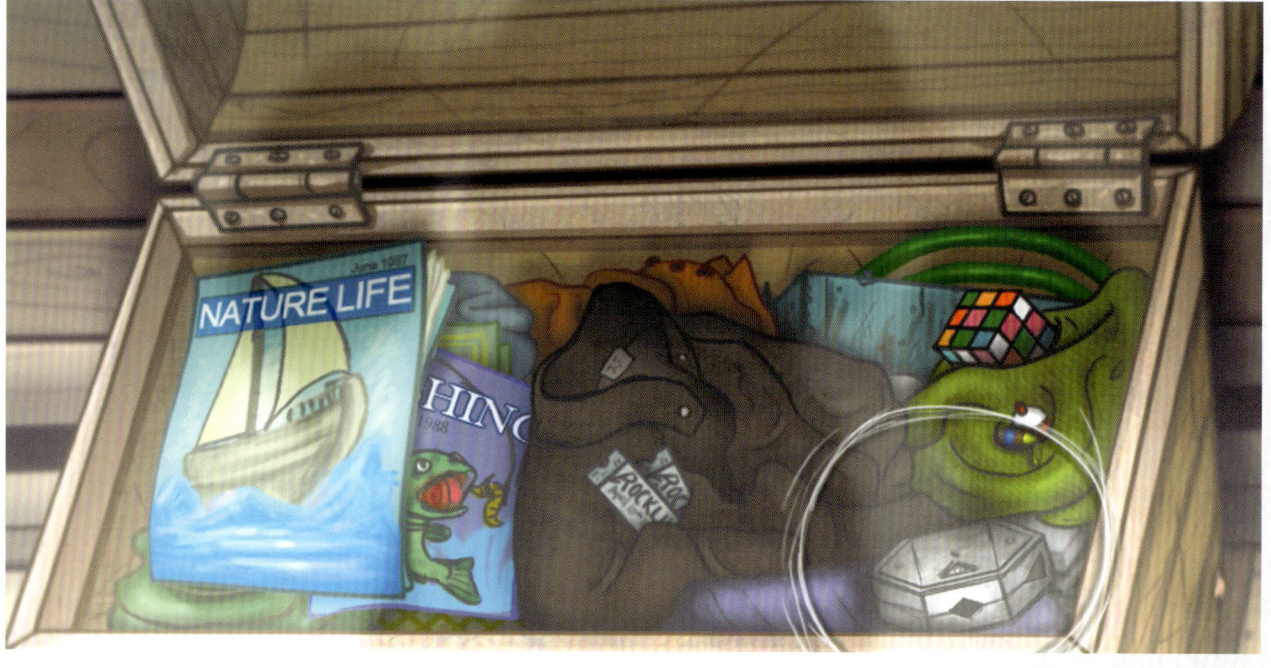

1) Get the puzzle box from Tree House Chest in beginning of game.

2) Unlock Chapter 2 in the Gear Boy game by speaking with the Phantom in the Tree House (after Gear Boy upgrade).

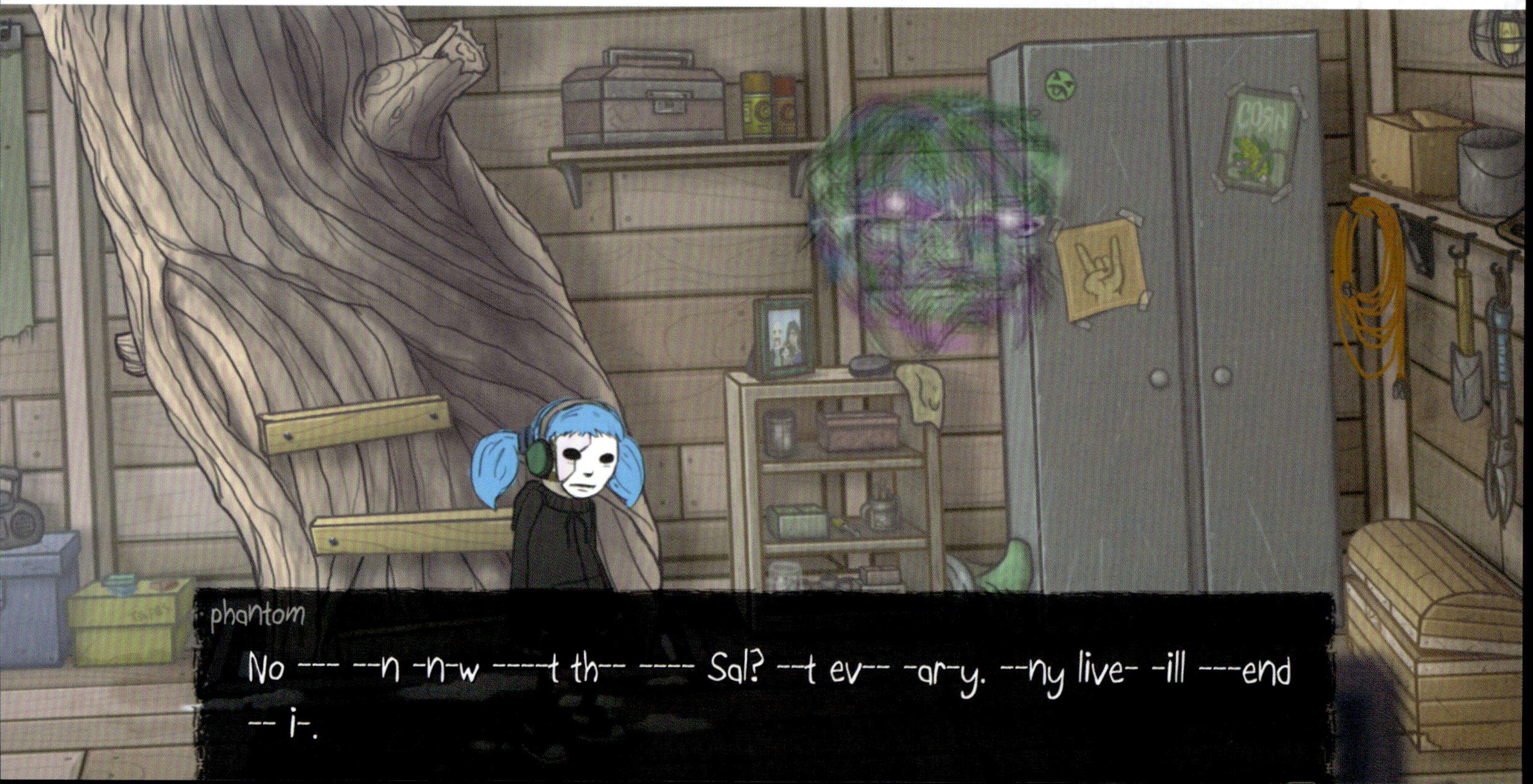

phantom

No --- --n -n-w ----t th-- ---- Sal? --t ev-- -ary. --ny live- -ill ---end
-- i-.

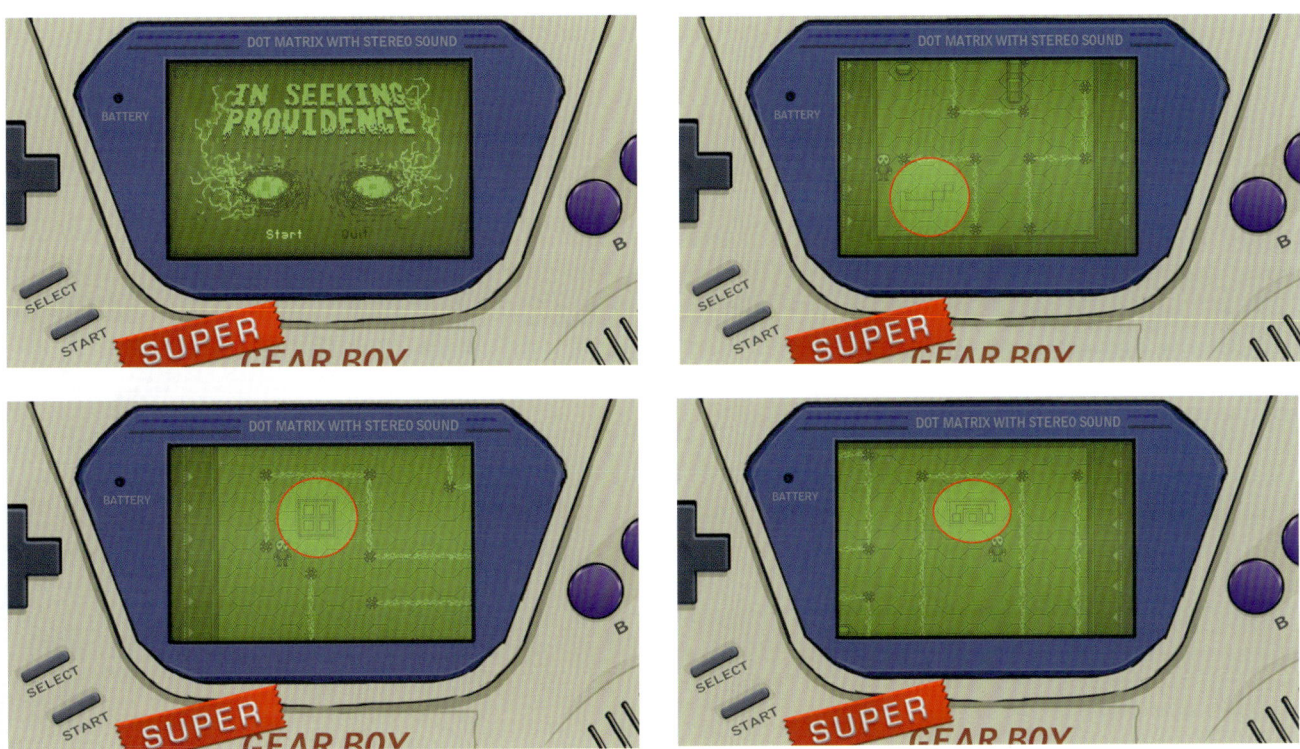

3) Play through In Seeking Providence – Chapter 2 and take note of the symbols on the floors in Level 1, Level 2, and Level 3.

4) After you've gotten the Crowbar from David, talk to him again to go into his room.

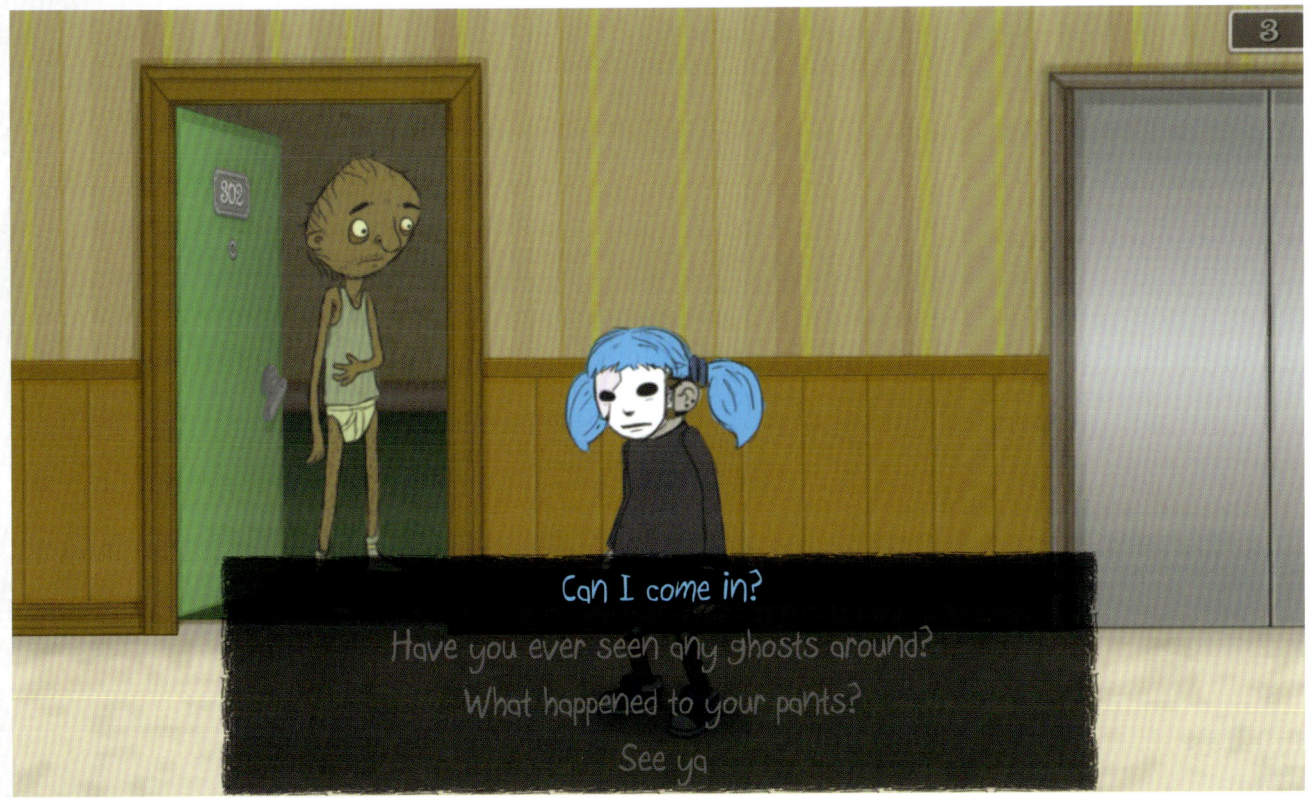

Can I come in?

Have you ever seen any ghosts around?

What happened to your pants?

See ya

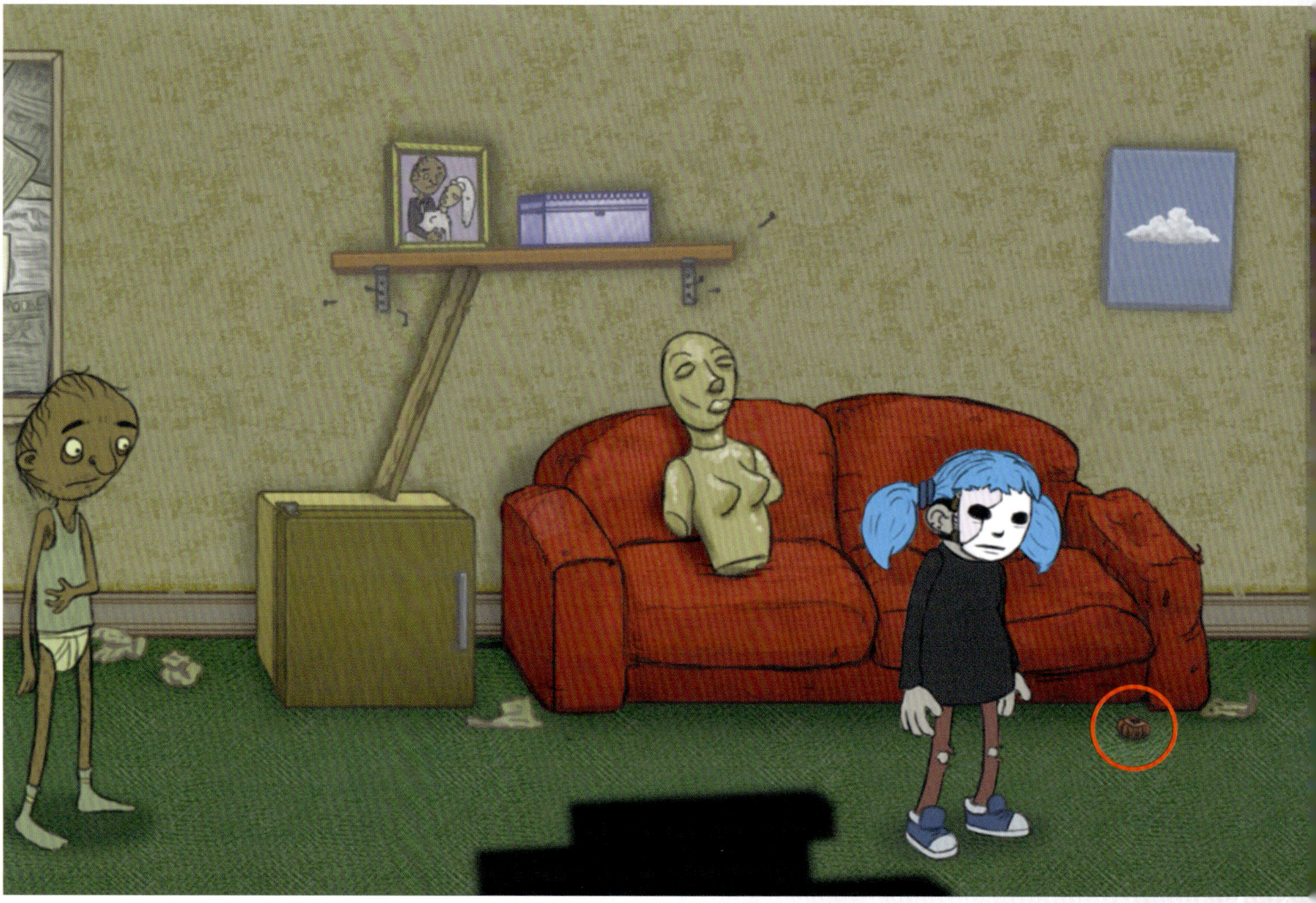

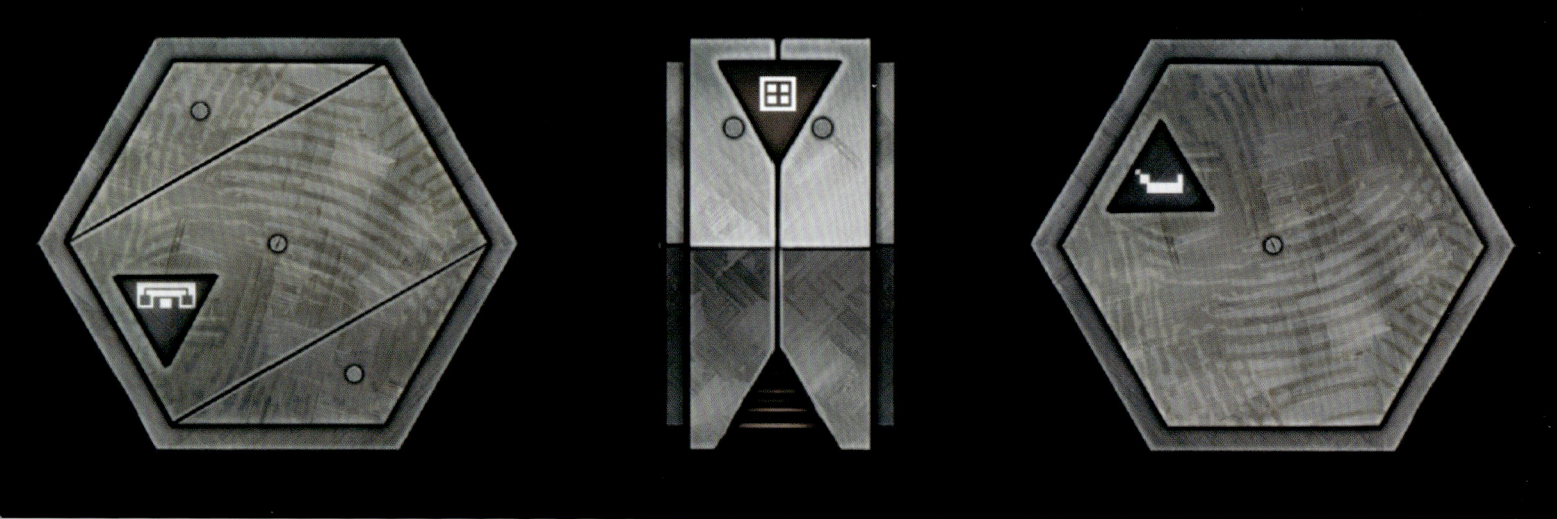

5) In David's room: there is a small dial on the floor, on the right side of the couch. Pick it up.

6) Now you can interact with the box from the inventory. Notice that each side has a different number of screws: 3, 2 and 1. Select the symbols from In Seeking Providence – Chapter 2 where the number of screws corresponds to the level the symbol is found. Solution below:

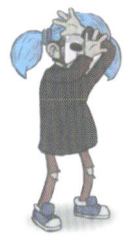

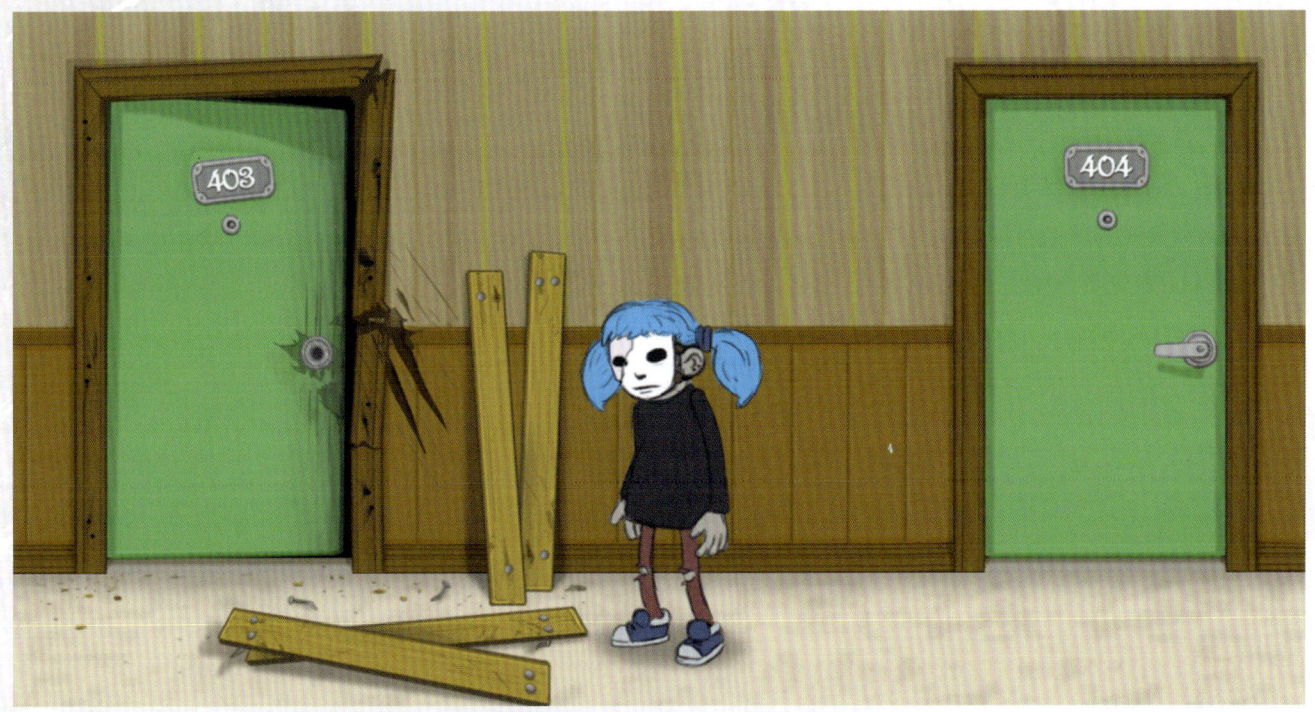

?????

yek noitingoc eht dnuof evah uoy

7) Bring the key to Todd and show it to him. This will trigger a cutscene that brings Sal to the White Room for the first time.

IN SEEKING PROVIDENCE – CHAPTER 8

After you get the crowbar and before going into the hole in 504, use the crowbar on 403.
Once inside, use the Super Gear Boy to summon Mrs. Sanderson.

EPISODE THREE
The Bologna Incident

COMPLETING THE FULL INTRO

1) In the first section, the answer is given when the Phantom is speaking, but it's jumbled up. In order to decode it, pay attention to the number of notches on the sides of the mechanisms.

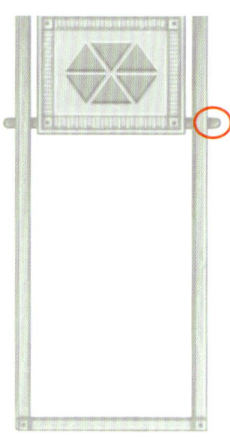 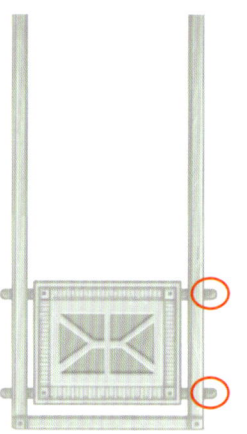 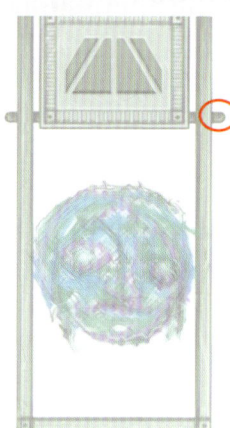 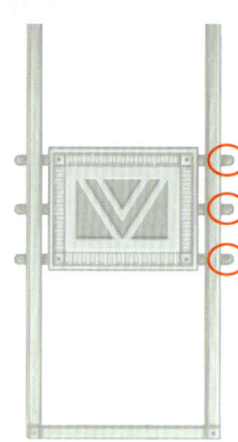

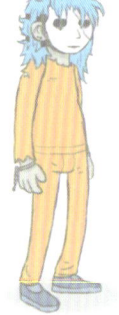

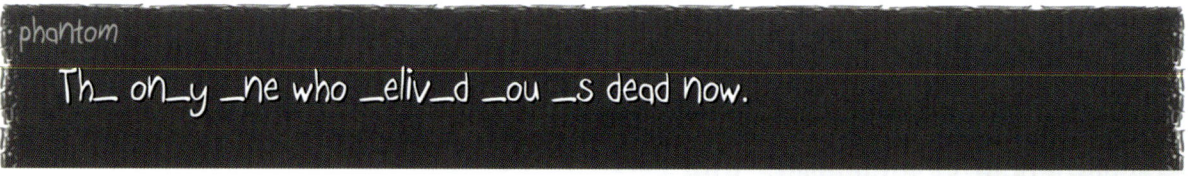

phantom

Th_ on_y _ne who _eliv_d _ou _s dead now.

2) Pull the levers of each mechanism in this order: 1) Up 2) Down, Down 3) Up, Up 4) Down.

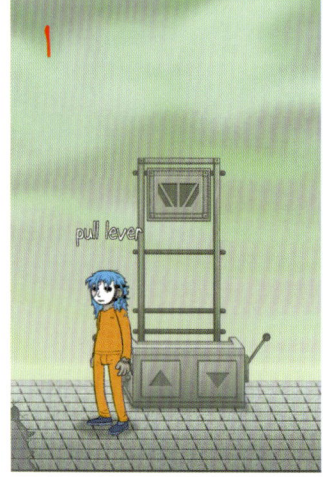 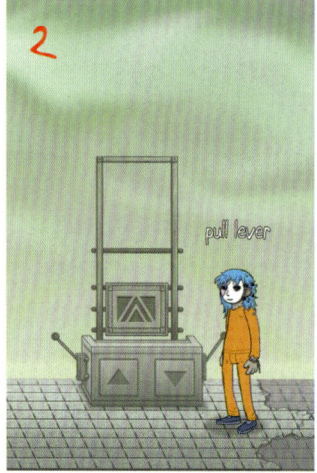 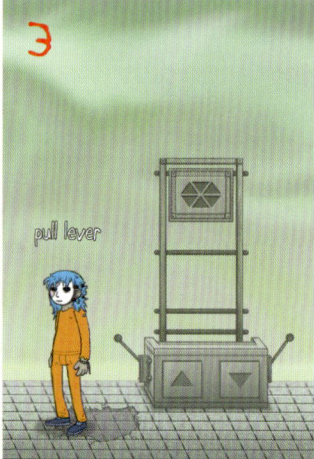 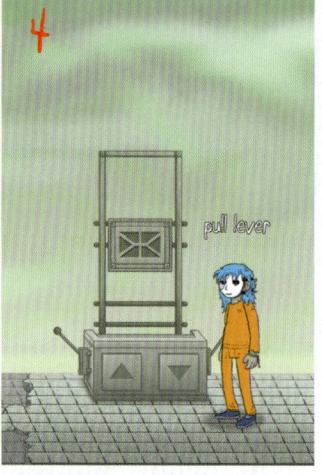

Sally Face ART, LORE, AND MORE

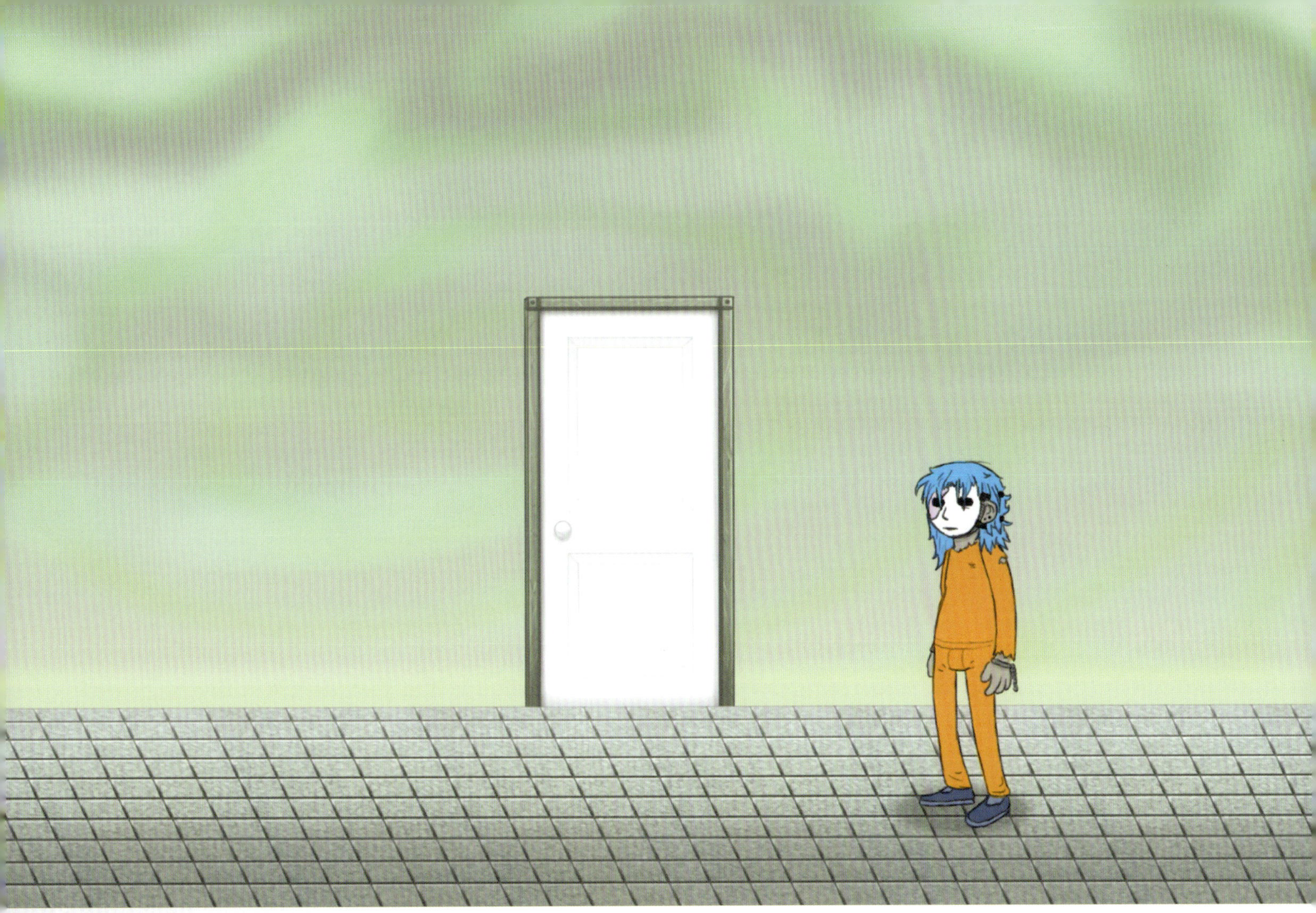

3) If you do the first code correctly, a door will appear that leads to the second area.

4) In the second part, you'll need to type in the number that the phantom gives you.
When he gives you the number, it's glitched into two parts. Combine the parts to get the full number.

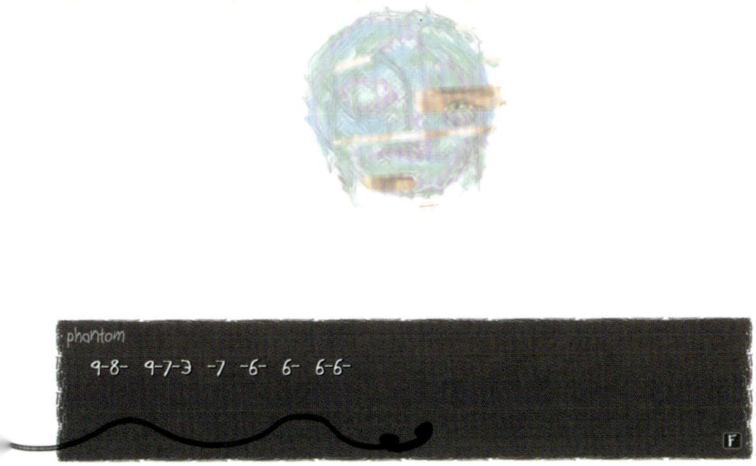

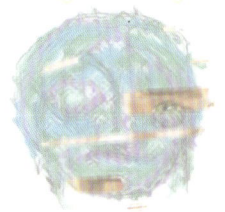

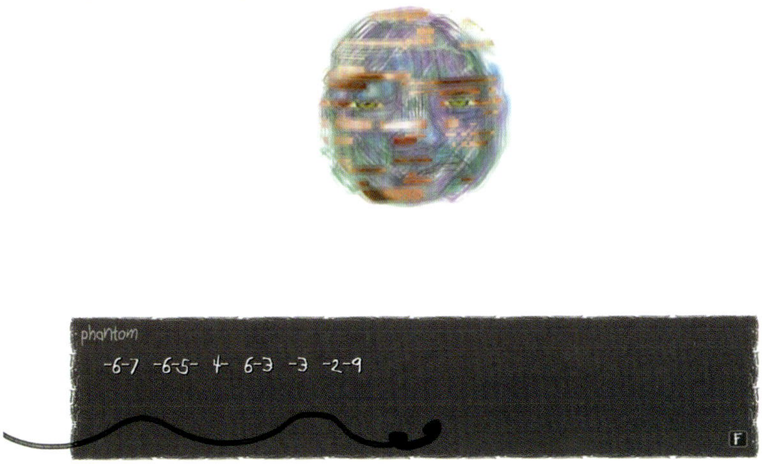

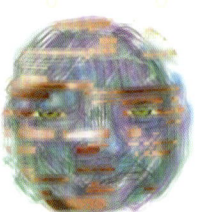

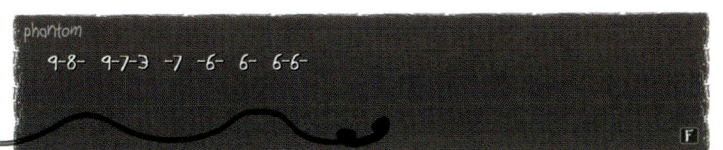

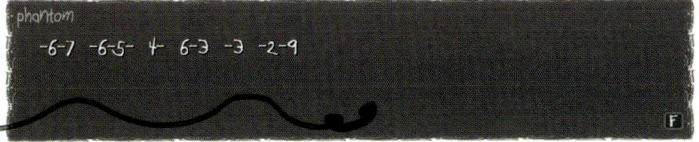

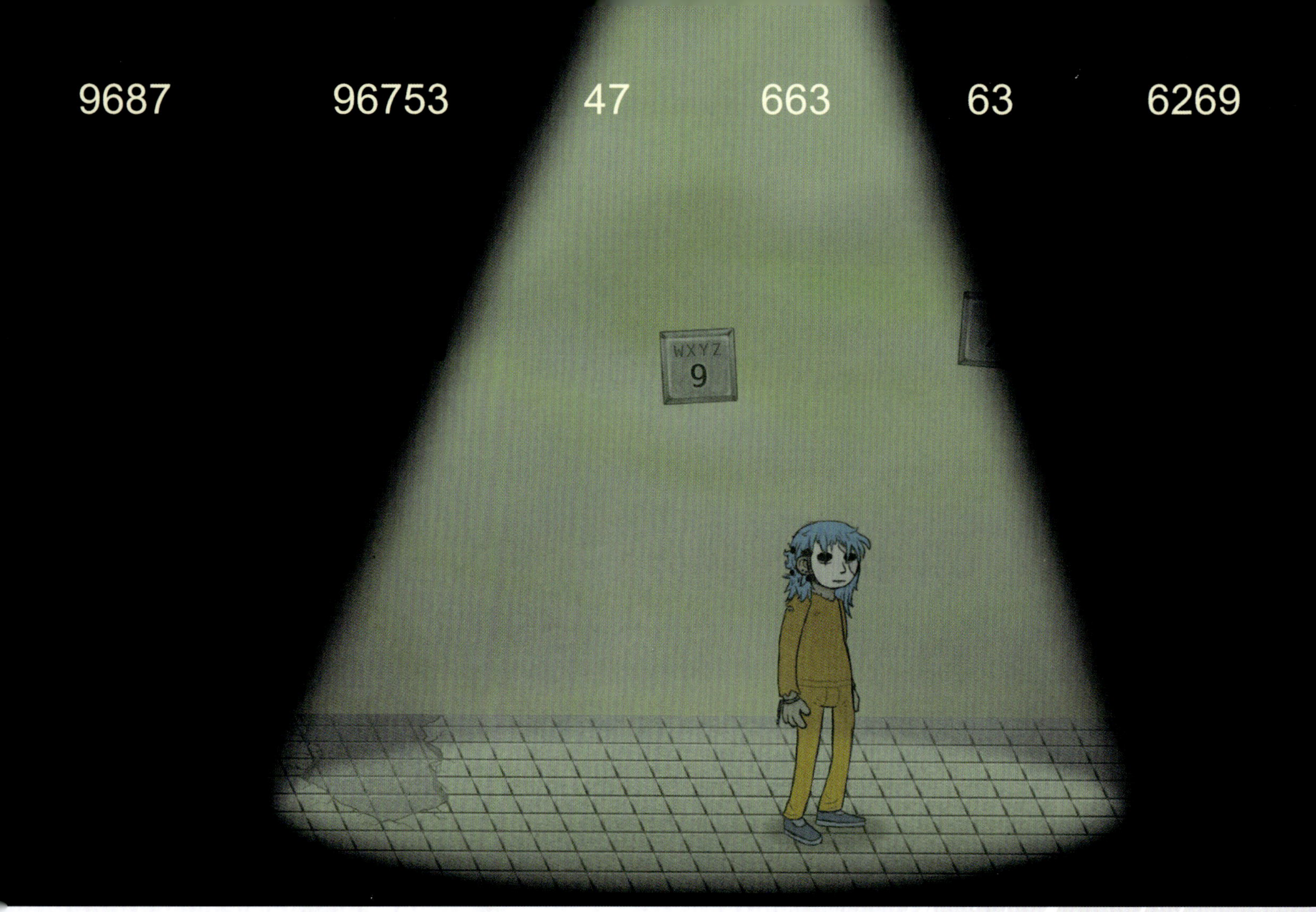

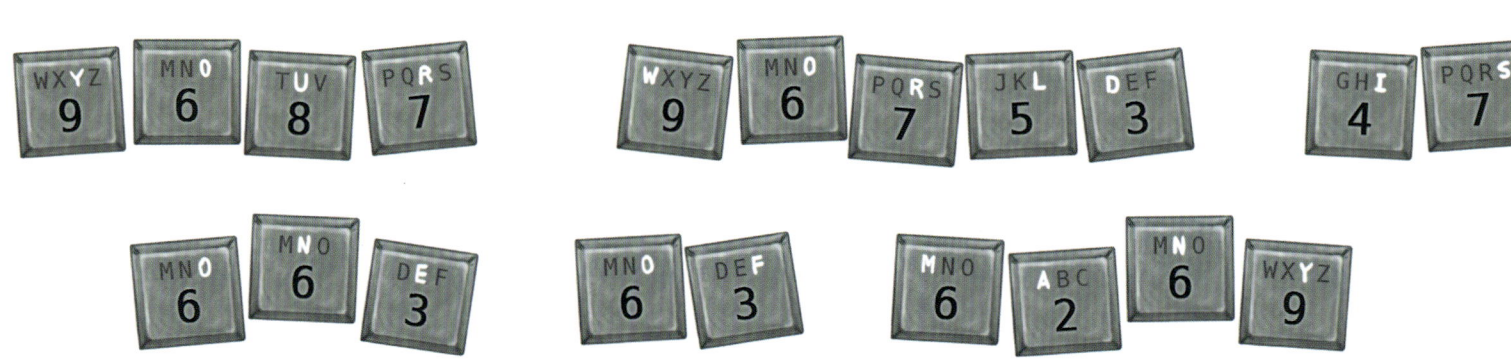

9687 96753 47 663 63 6269

5) This area is timed and there's a "hidden" section immediately to the right, when you first start. Here is the full sequence: **9687 96753 47 663 63 6269**.

If you decode this number (using the alpha-numeric phone buttons) it reads as follows:

"Your world is one of many."

JOURNAL PAGES

1) You'll get the journal by completing the intro sequence (previous guide). It is not possible to get any pages if you do not do this step first. NOTE: If you want to get Clumpy! (page 214), those steps will overlap with this.

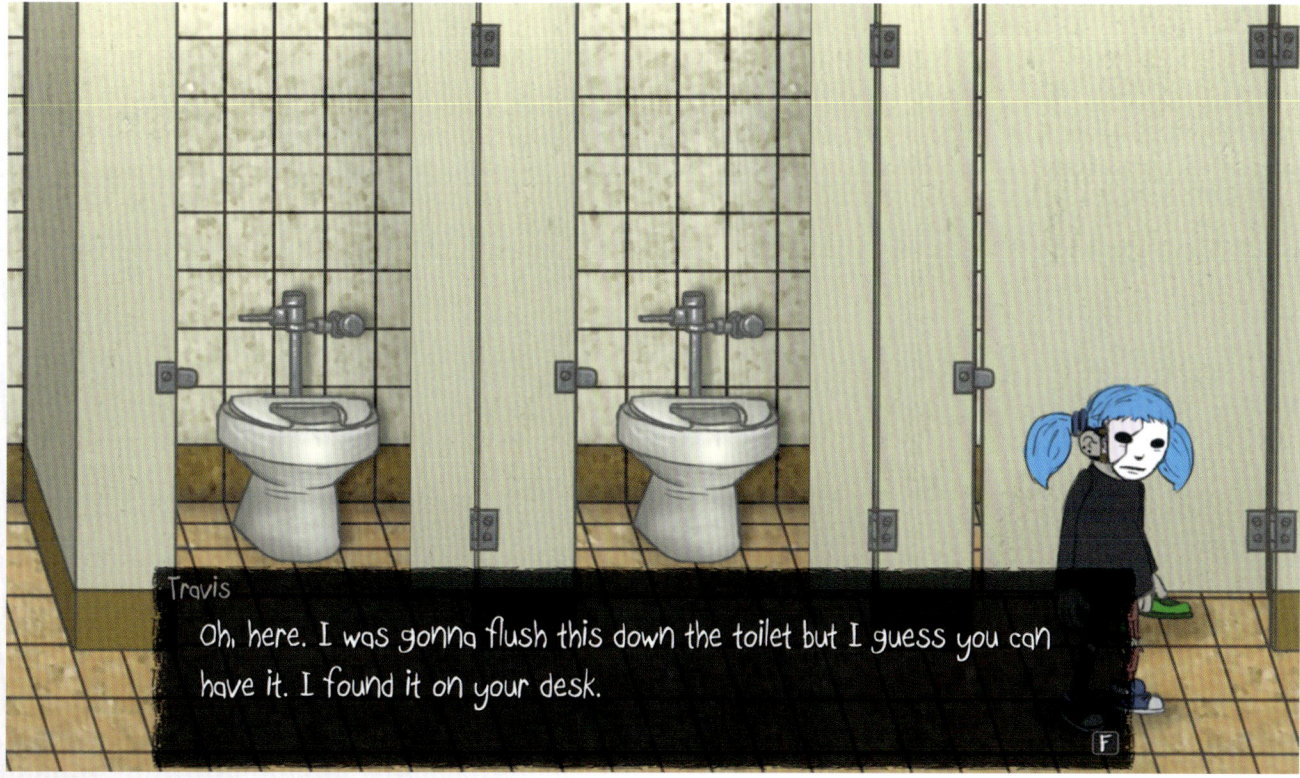

Travis

Oh, here. I was gonna flush this down the toilet but I guess you can have it. I found it on your desk.

2) After getting the Bologna from Kim, you may notice that Travis isn't in the cafeteria. If you go into the bathroom, he's in the last stall. Talk to him and choose the right options to get to the end of their conversation (3rd, 2nd, 3rd, 2nd).

3) Talk to Rosenberg, in 102, then use the Super Gear Boy on her (get the Super Gear Boy from Sal's room).

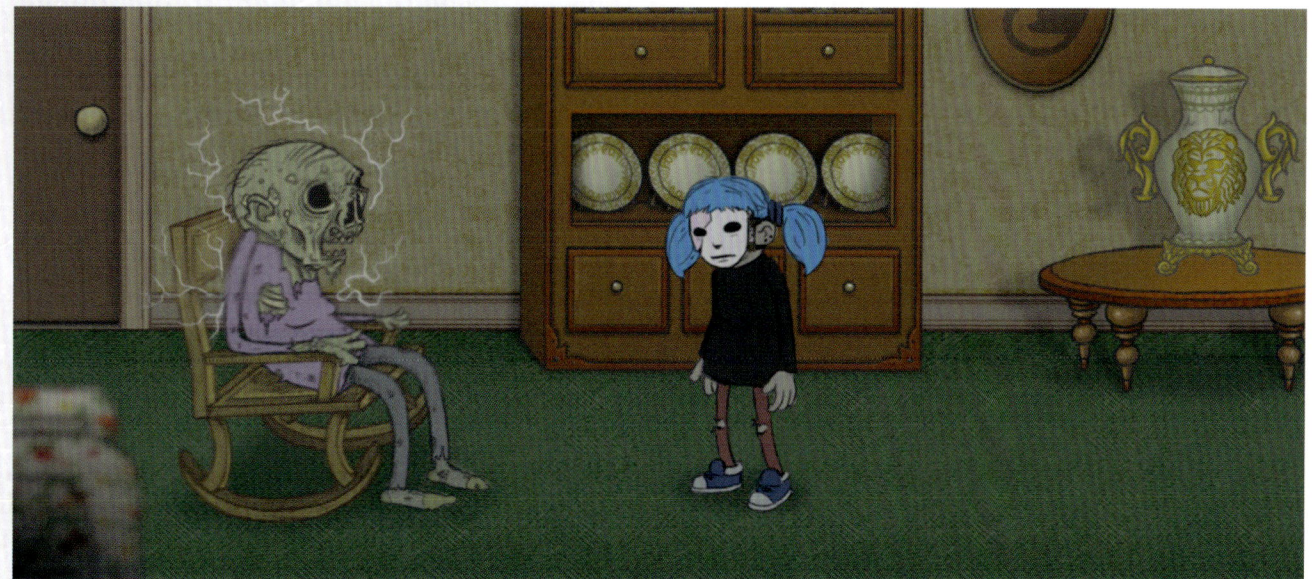

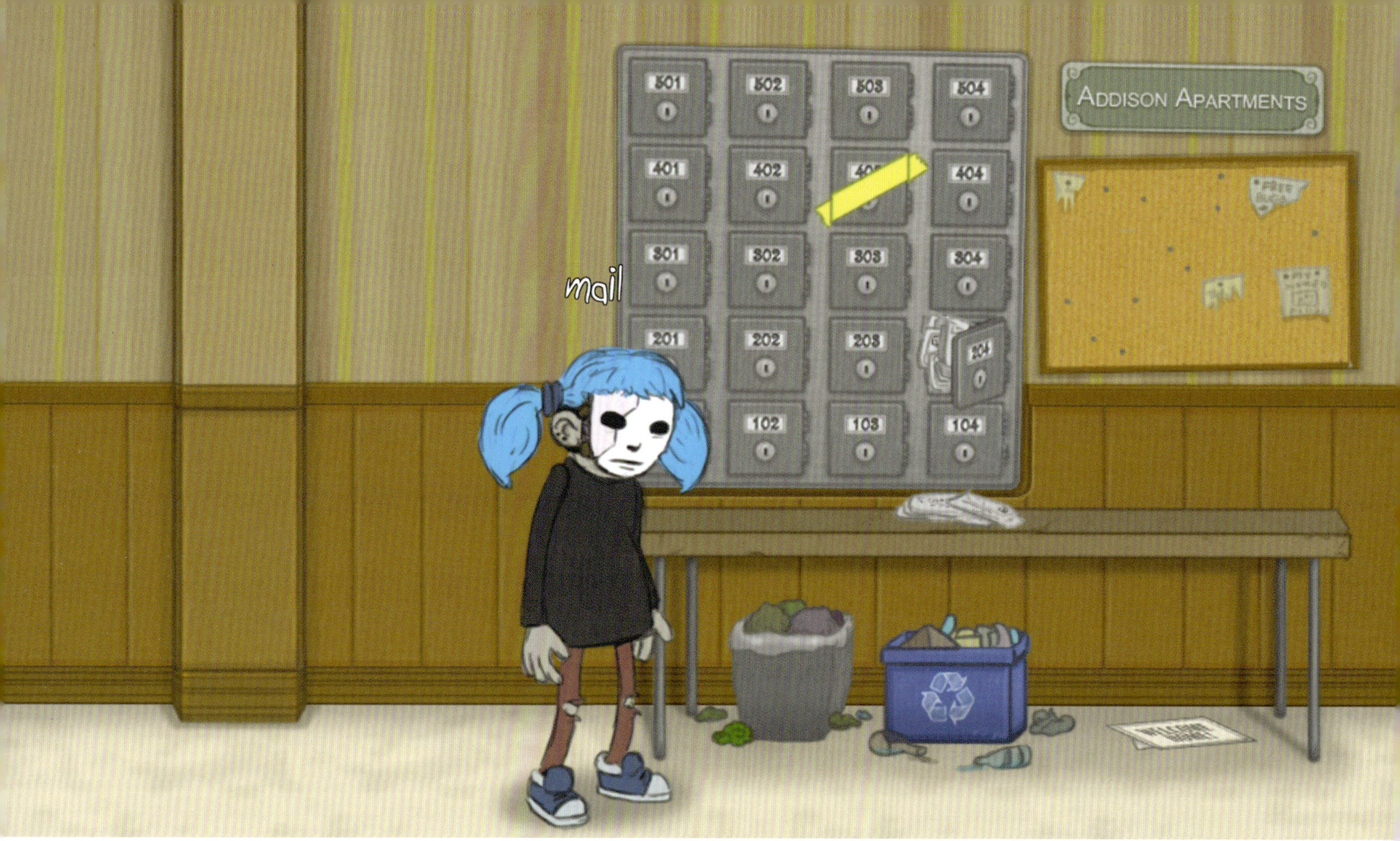

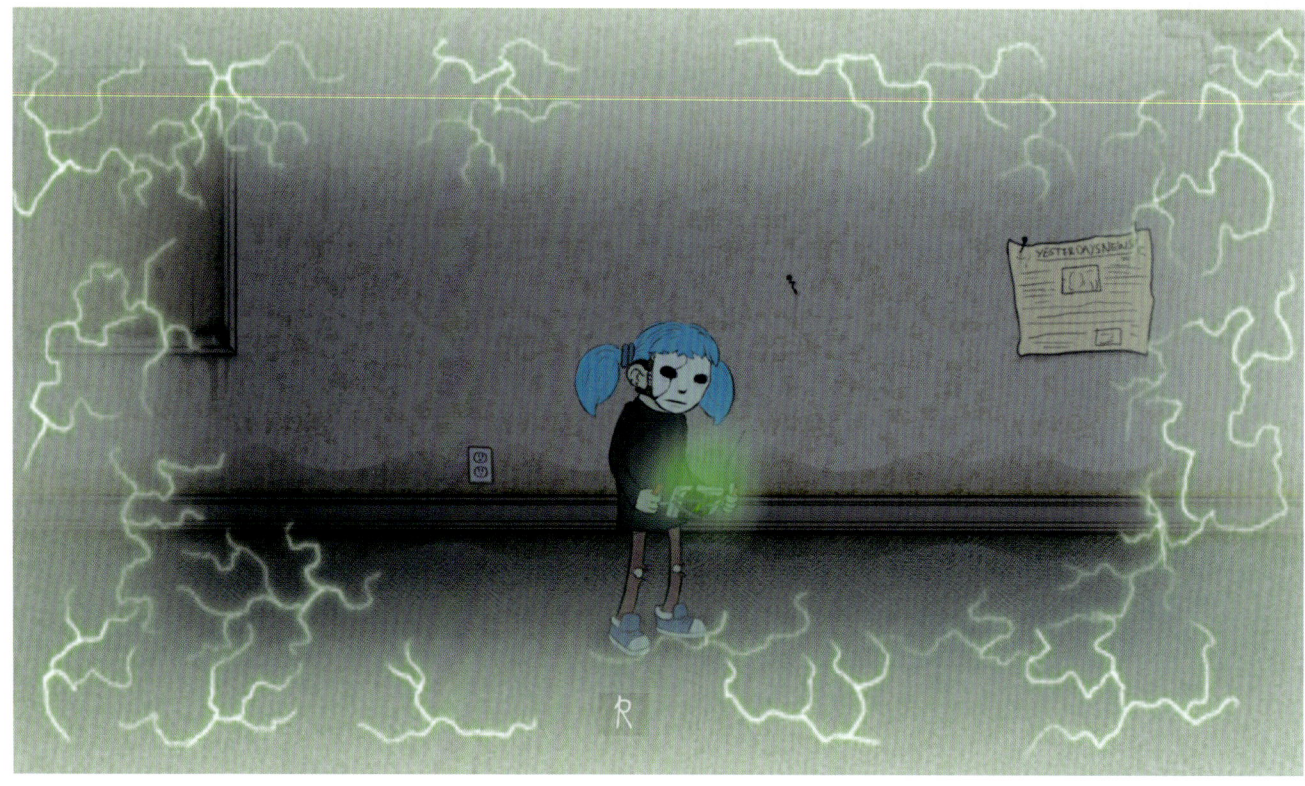

4) On the first floor of the apartment building, check the mailboxes.

5) In room 501, use the SGB on the nail with no paper on it.

Sally Face ART, LORE, AND MORE

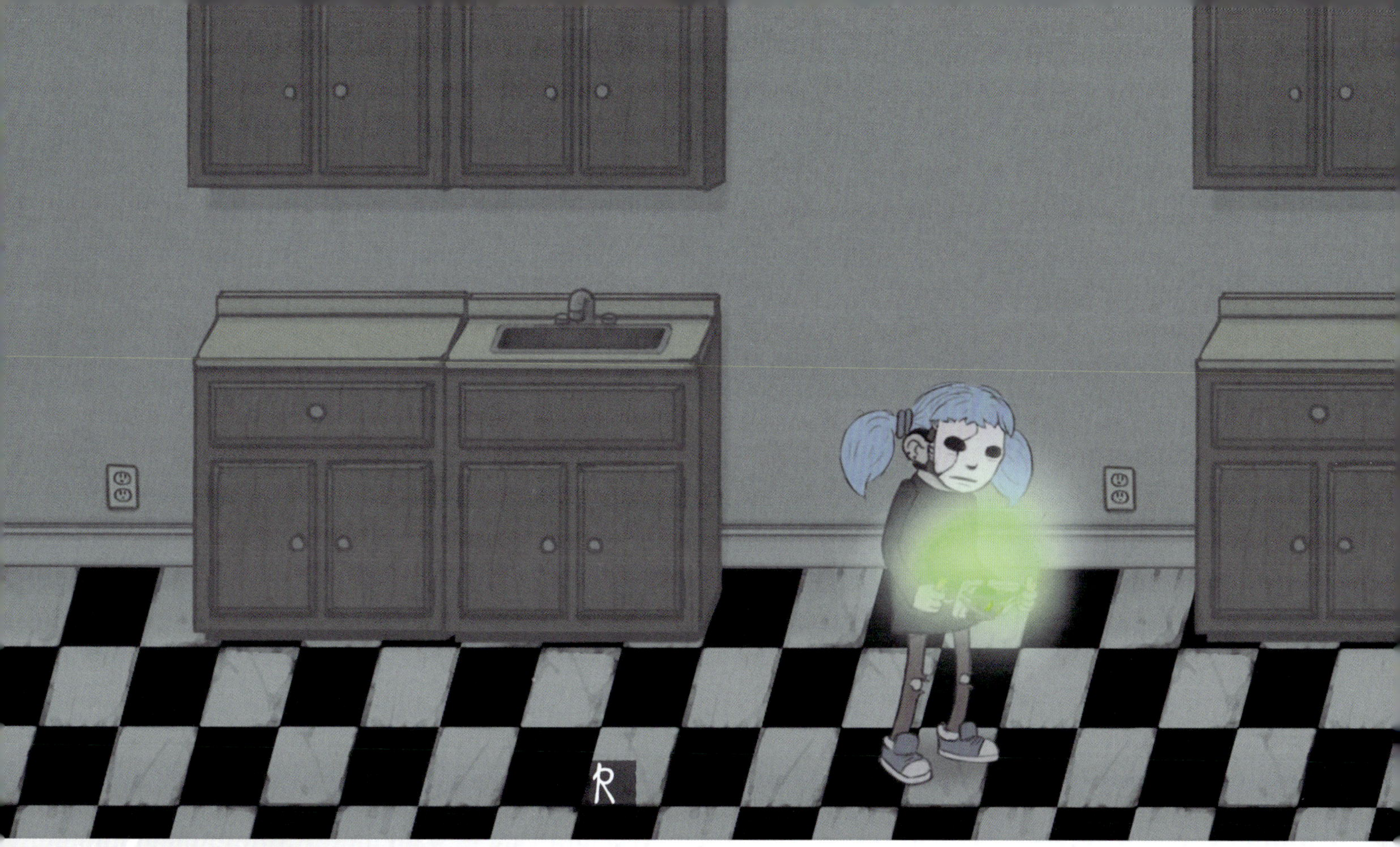

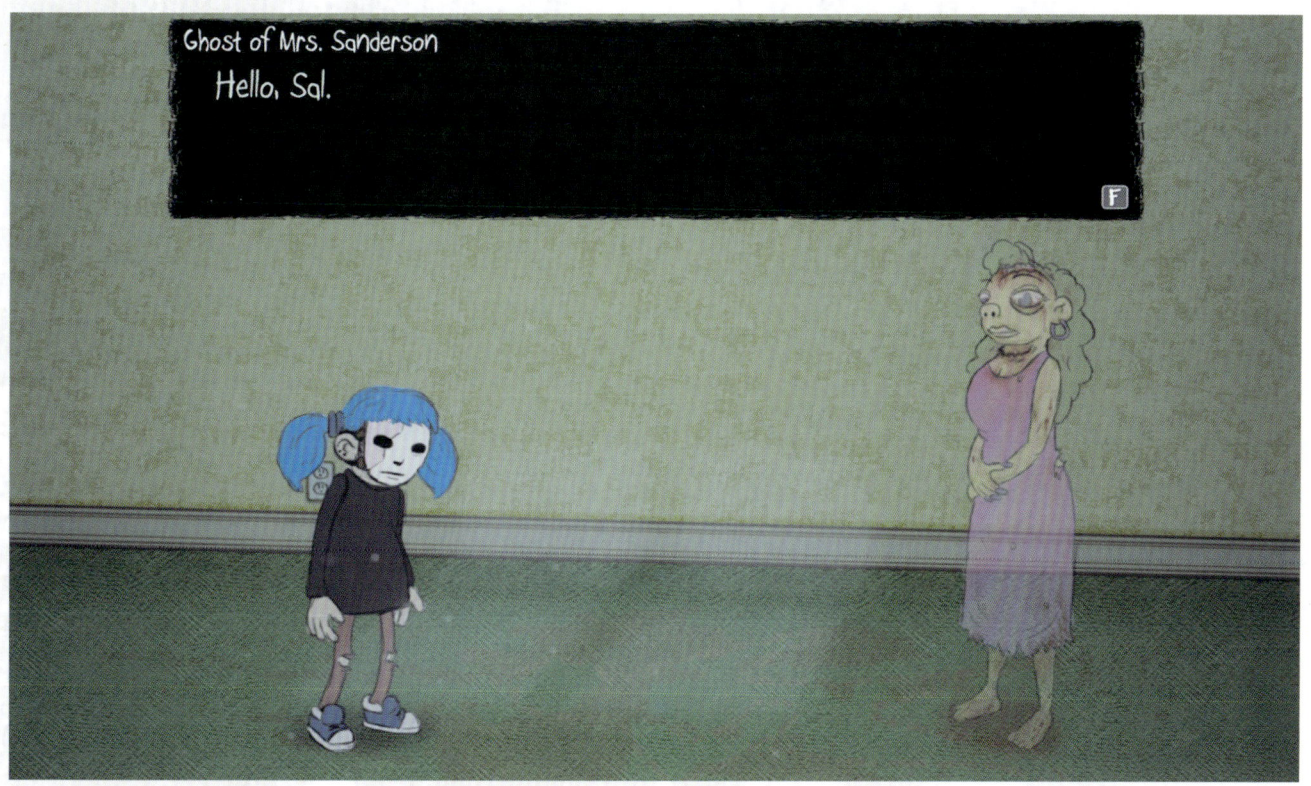

6) In room 304, use the Super Gear Boy in the kitchen.

7) In room 403, use the Super Gear Boy to talk with Mrs. Sanderson.

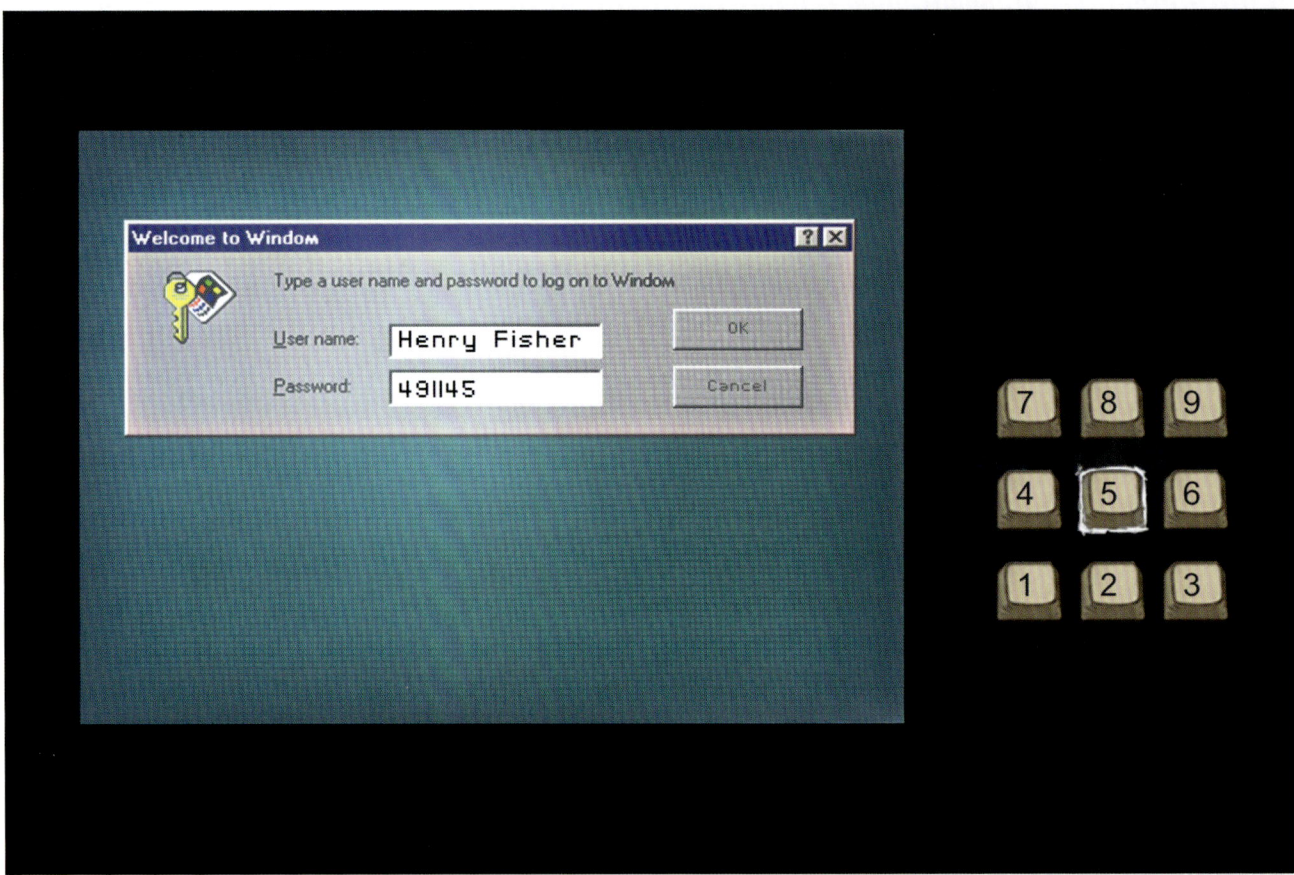

8) In 402, enter the correct password for dad's computer.
It's "Diane" converted to numbers, D=4, I=9, A=1, N=14, E=5: 491145.

9) In the Main Temple Hall (first room of the cult area), go all the way to the right edge of the screen and keep walking. You'll find a secret room with a chest. Open that baby up!

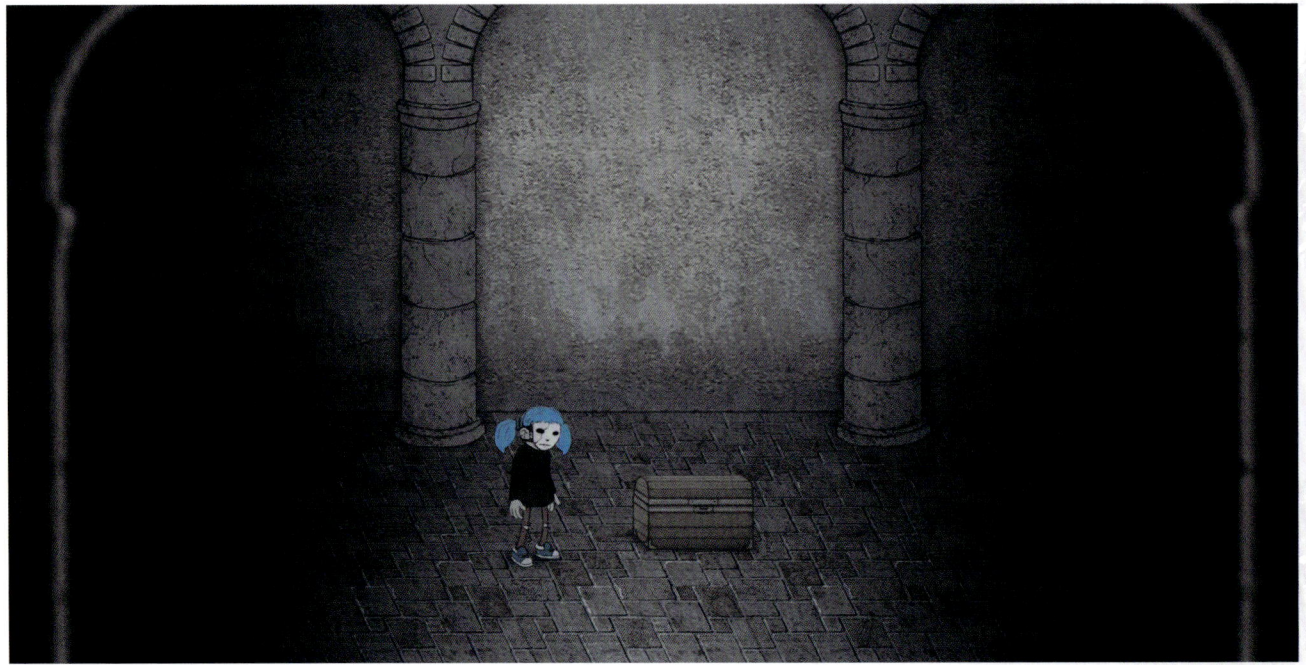

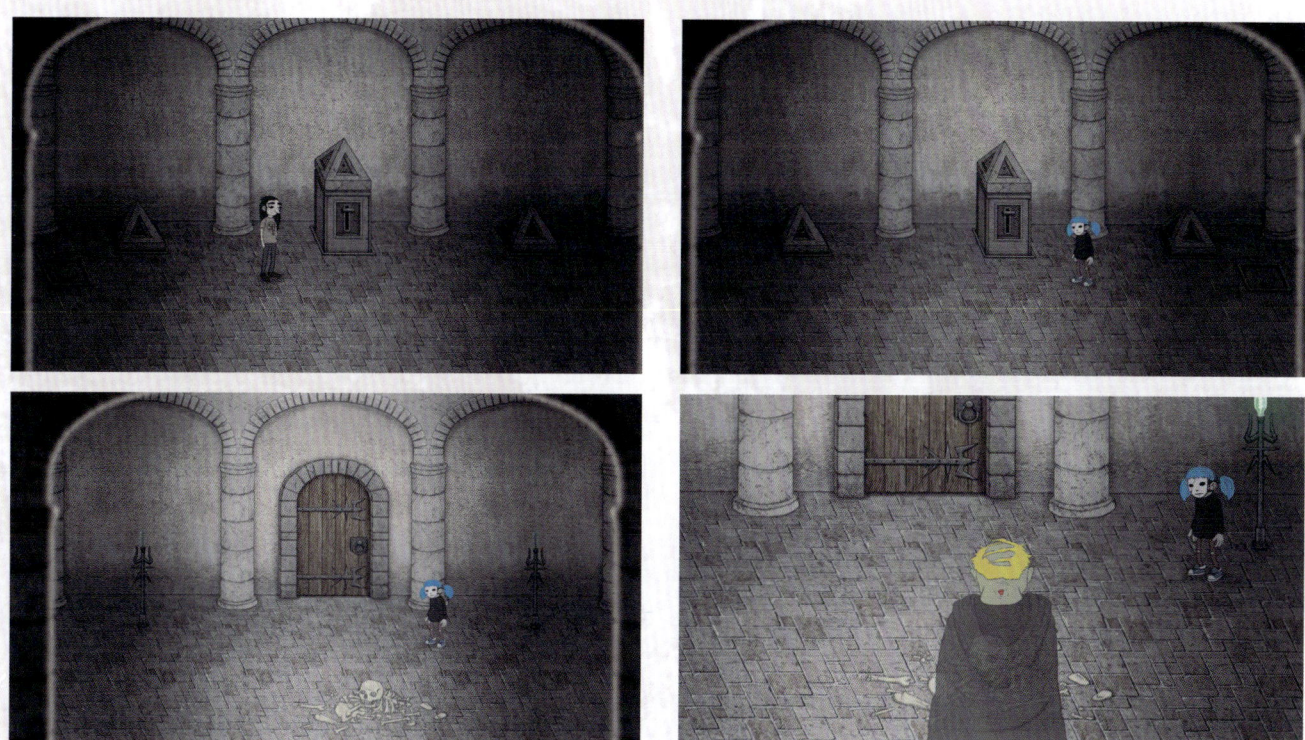

10) In the two Temple mazes, there are secret rooms in the last halls of each maze. The best way to tell the last halls is by knowing that the last three rooms (of both Larry's and Sal's maze) are empty besides for having three doors each (no spikes, spires, or foreground pillars). In the last room of Larry's, go all the way to the left, past the edge of the screen, step on the switch, and then finally pull the lever. In the last room of Sal's, it's to the right. Now in the next room, the second door will be unlocked. Go there and use the Super Gear Boy on both lights to summon the Ghost of Cultist.

11) In the center of the Temple (the final room), go to the right before finding Ash. You'll see a pedestal with the last letter/page. NOTE: This page will only appear if you've gotten all of the other pages first.

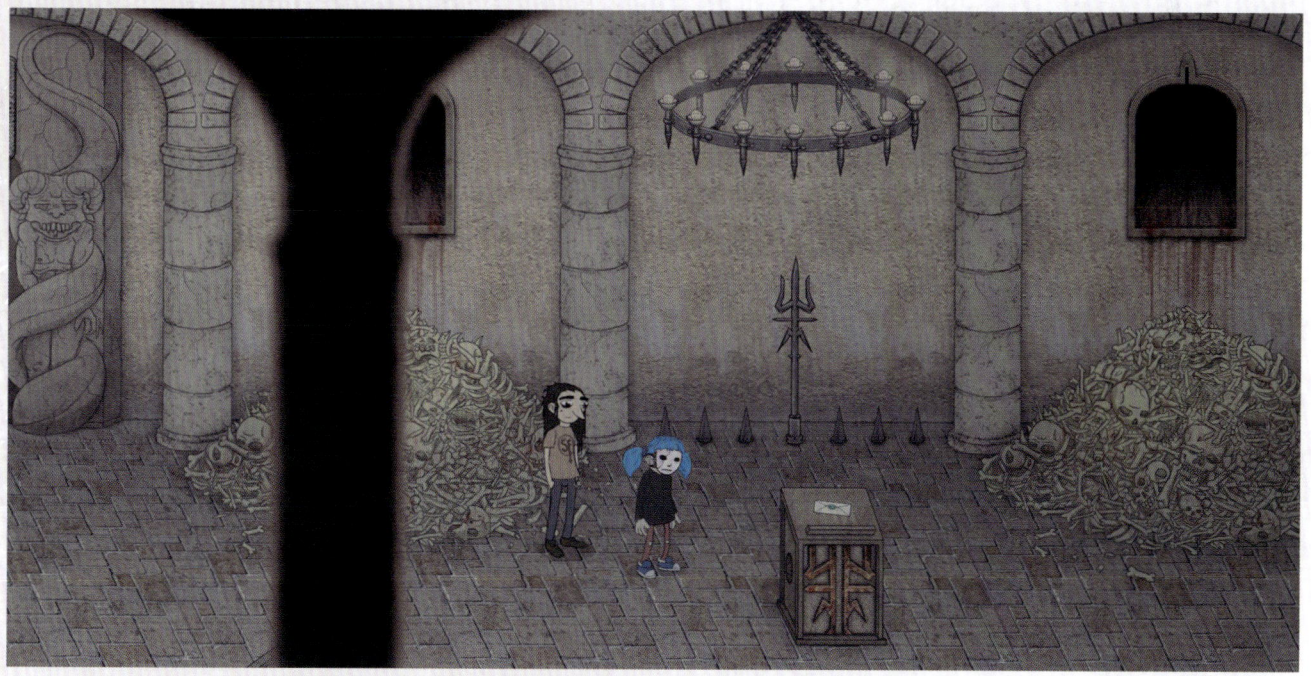

CLUMPY!

1) Grab the sticky tack from the science lab (to the left), but after grabbing the tack do NOT talk to Ashley while she's in the hall.

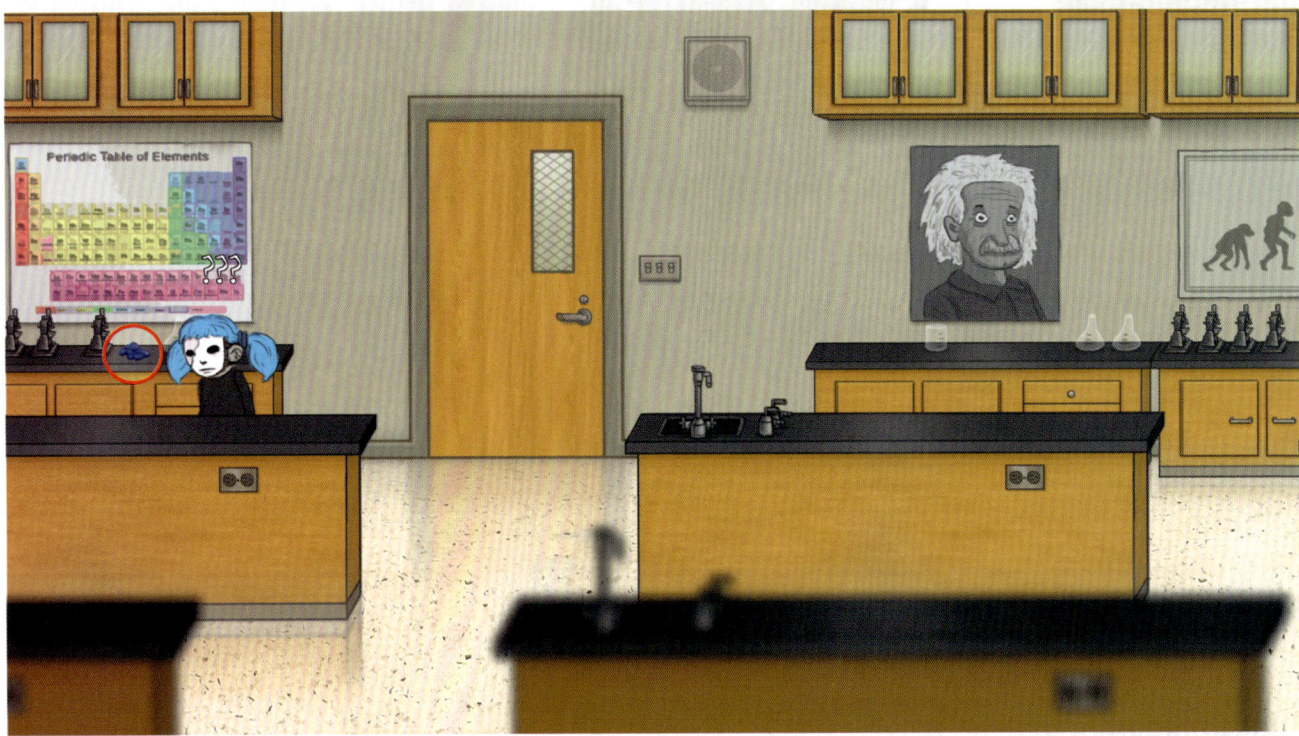

2) Once at the apartment, go up to room 401 (Rob's room). Interact with the poster that's falling down. Rob will give you a quarter.

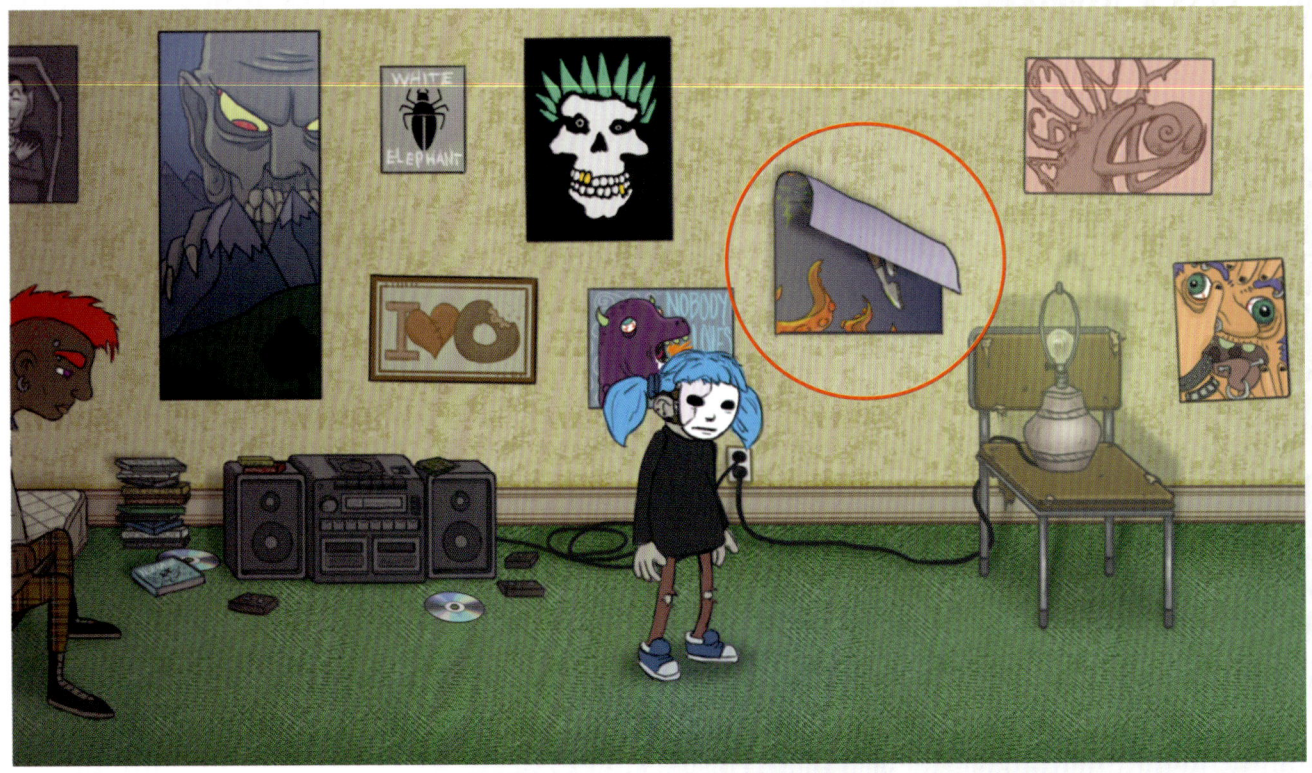

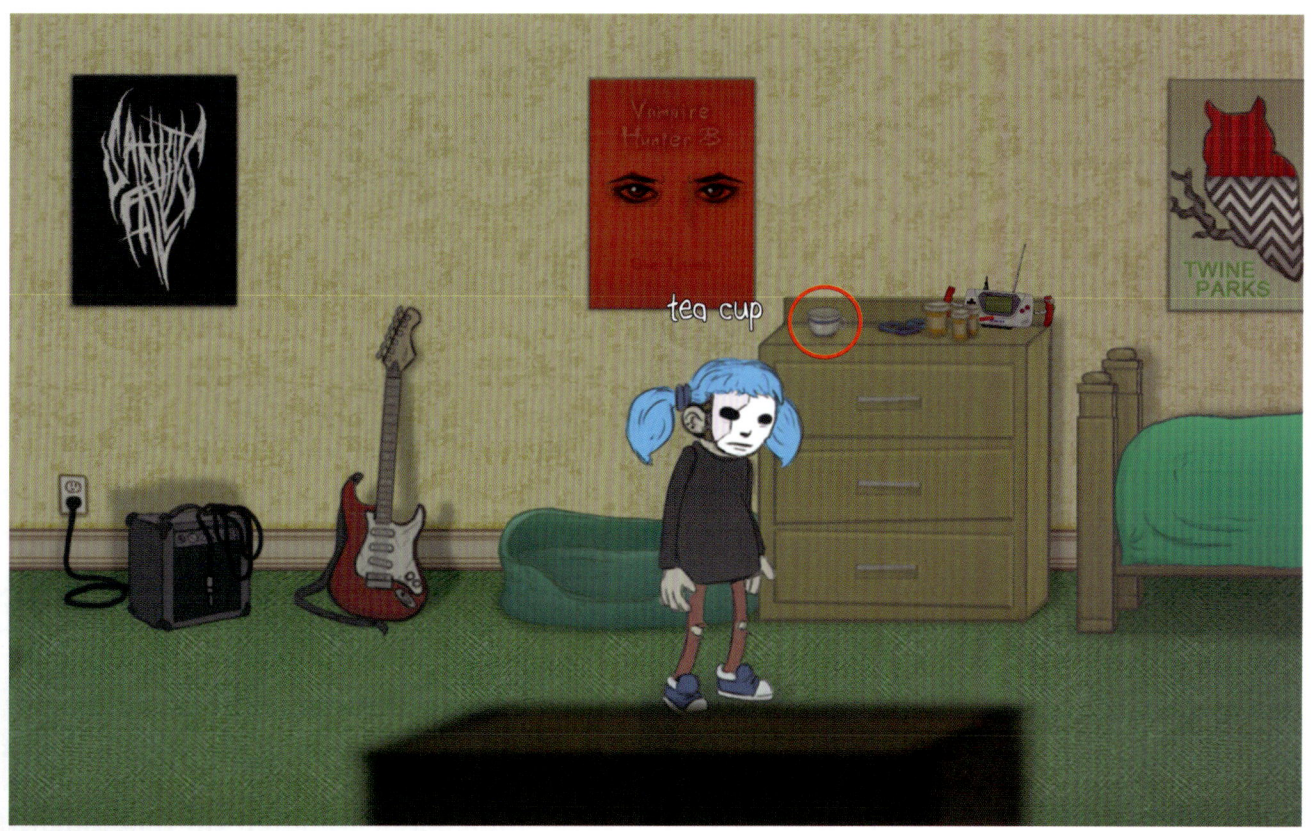

3) Get the tea cup from Sal's bedroom, in 402.

4) Give Addison the quarter to make you a cup of tea.

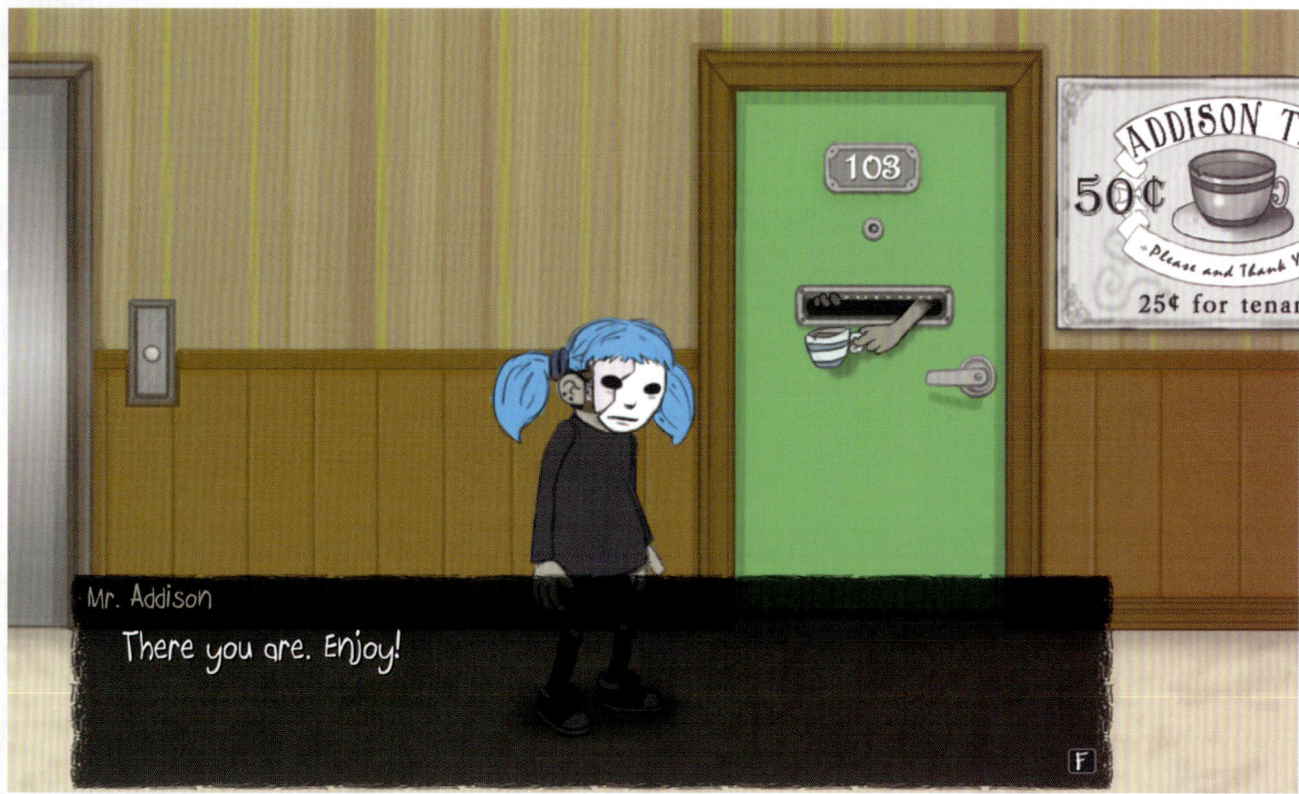

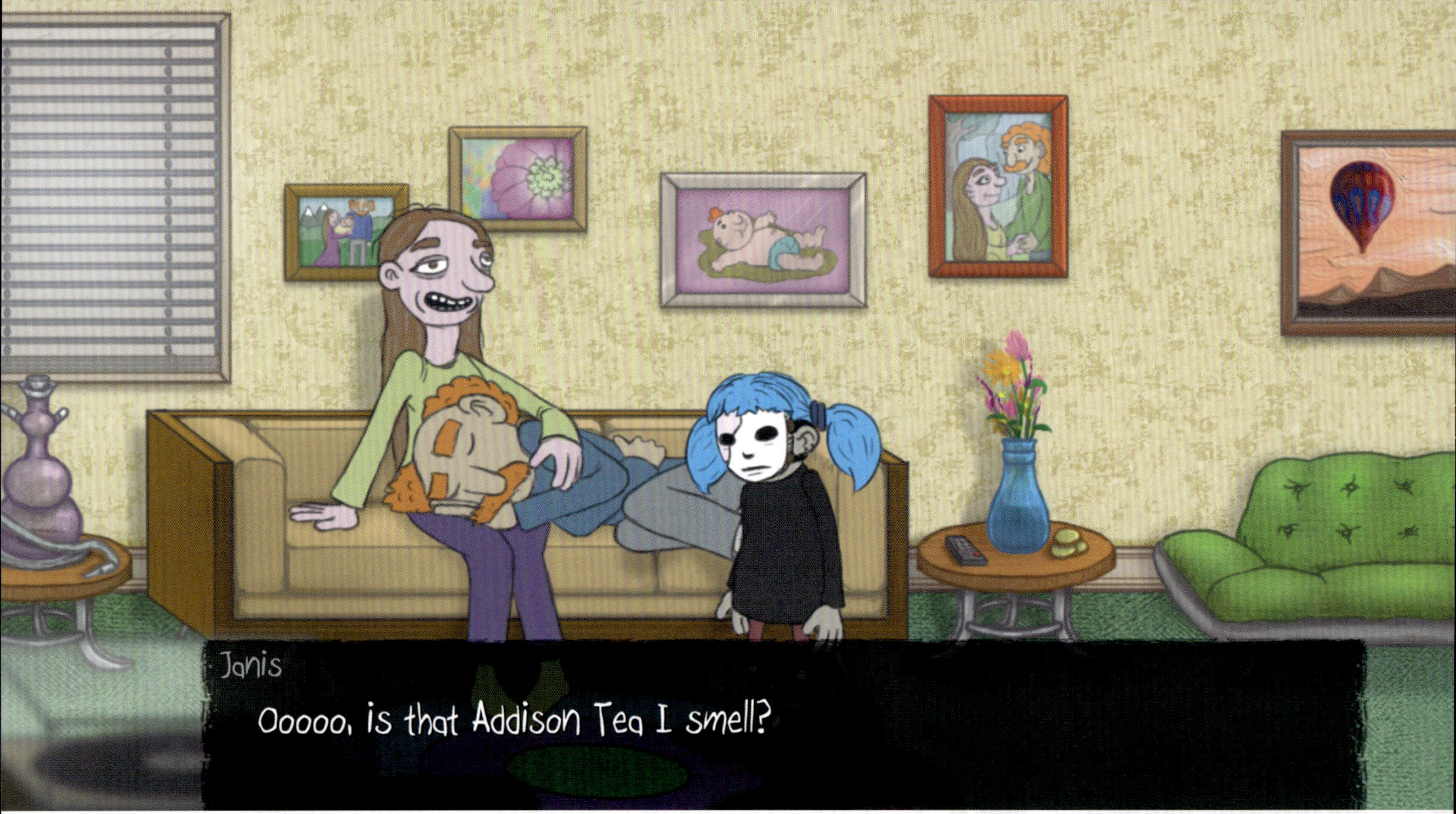

Janis

Ooooo, is that Addison Tea I smell?

5) Go to room 202 and give the tea to Todd's mom, Janis. She'll give you a chocolate bar.

6) Give the chocolate to Chug on floor 3. He's standing by room 303 and you'll need to talk to him a bit before he'll ask for the chocolate. Then he'll give you the game, Clumpy!

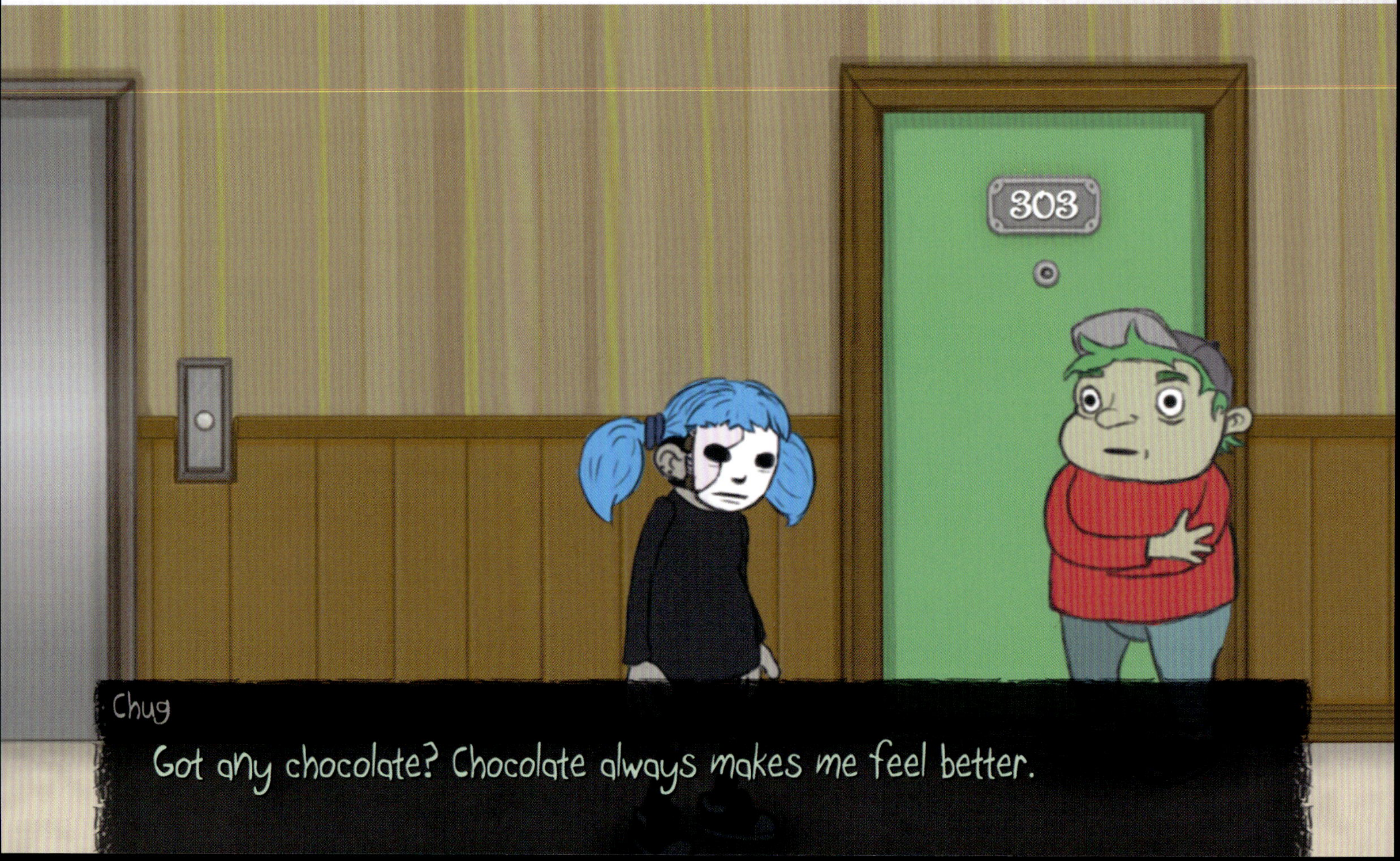

Chug

Got any chocolate? Chocolate always makes me feel better.

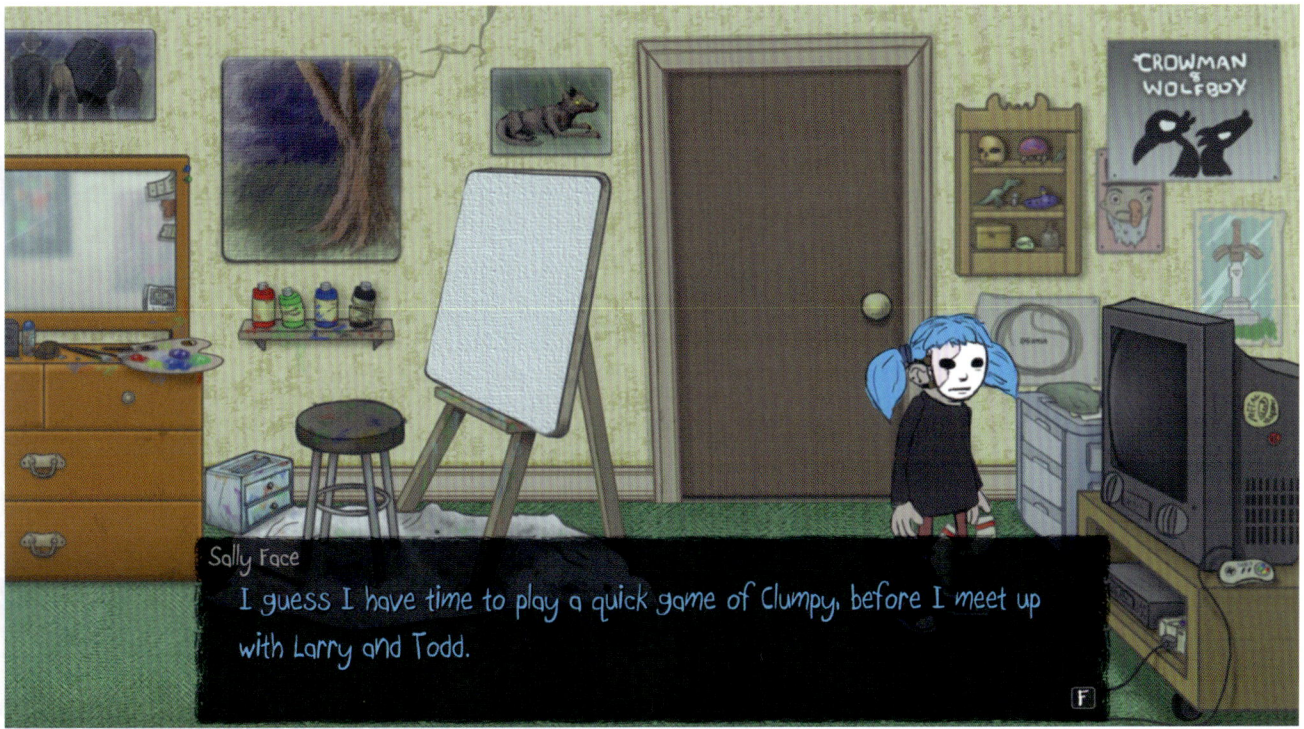

7) Head to Larry's room, in the basement, and interact with his TV.
Sal will play the bonus level of the Clumpy! game.

8) If you beat the level of Clumpy!, you'll get an achievement.

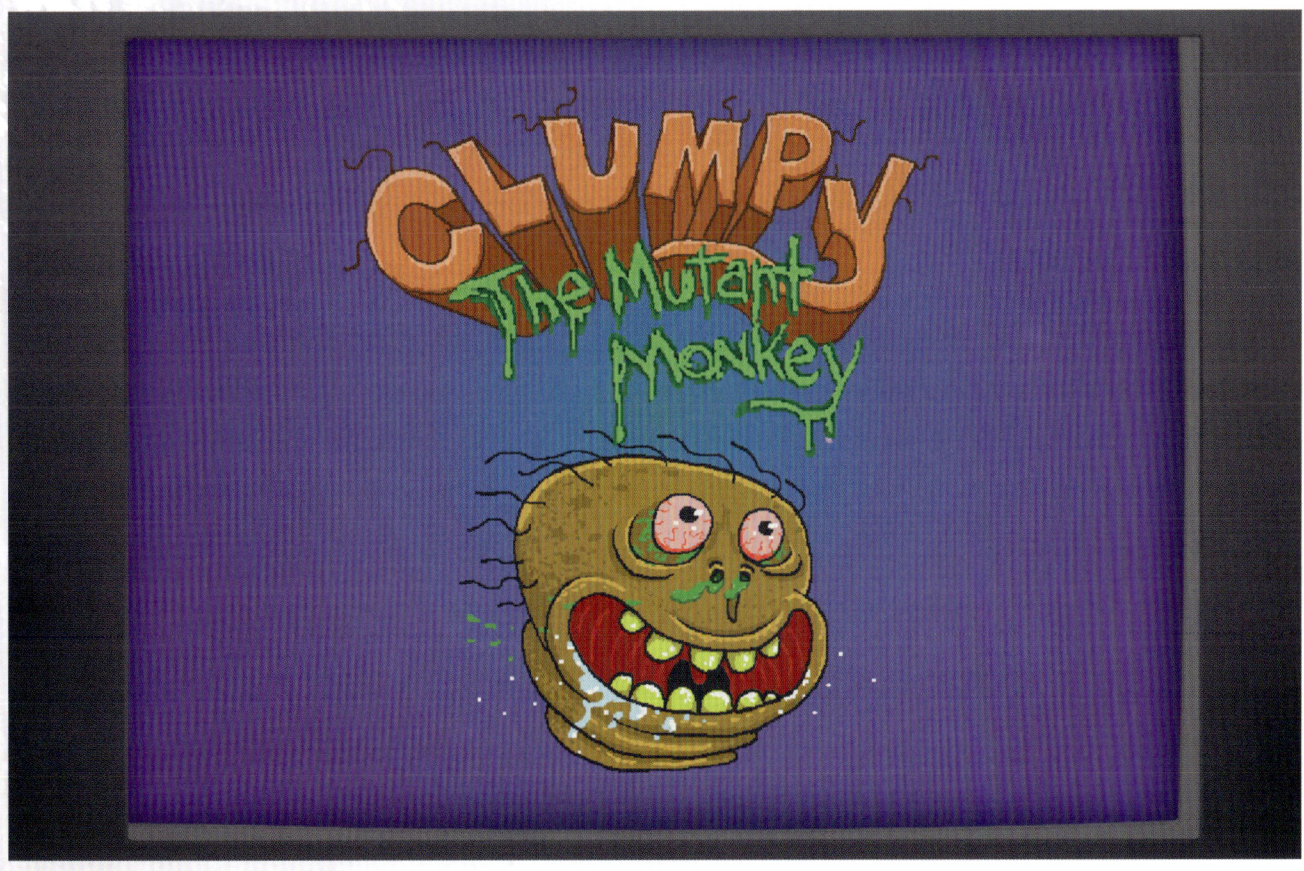

EPISODE FOUR
The Trial

THE DARK PLACE

1) In order to figure out the code for the fourth door, you'll need to examine the symbols in the first three rooms. Count the number of lines in each symbol to get three numbers: 8, 6, 7.

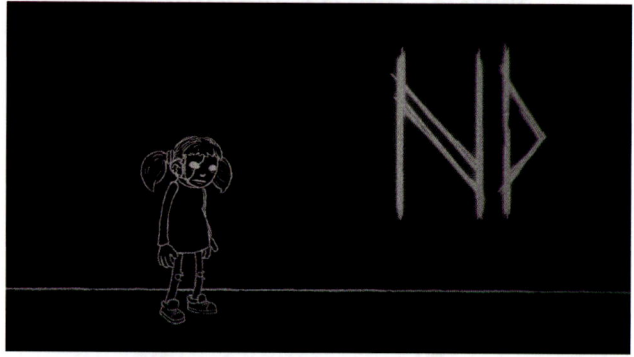

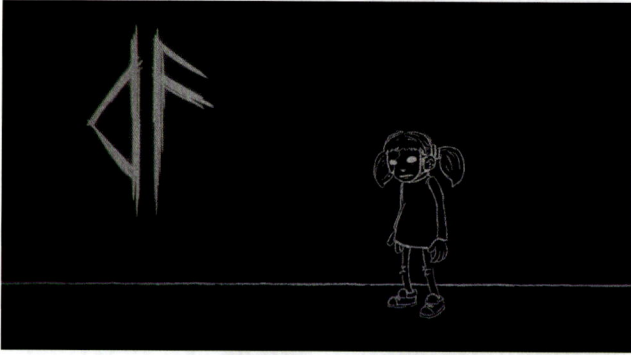

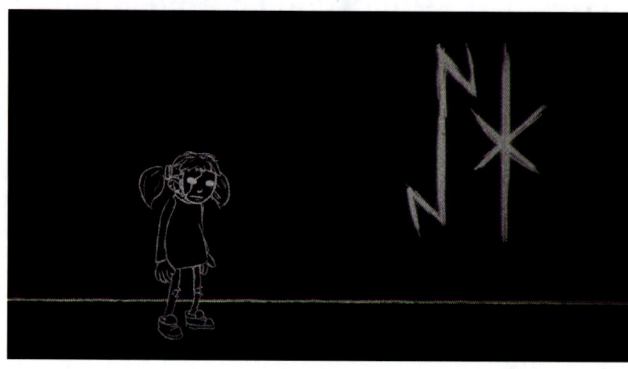

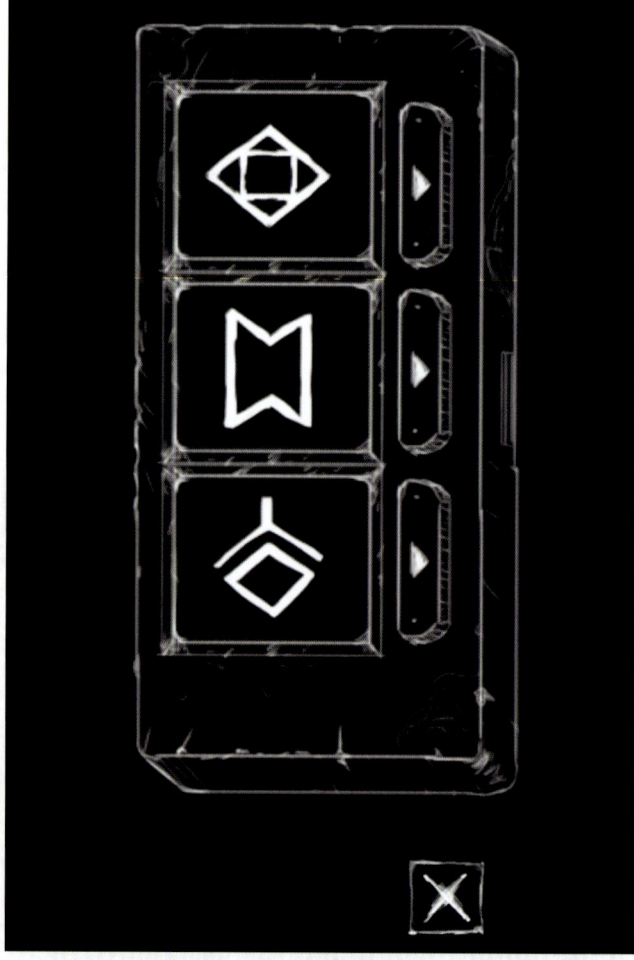

2) On the Door 4 lock, select the symbols that have the same number of lines as the numbers you found.

Sally Face ART, LORE, AND MORE

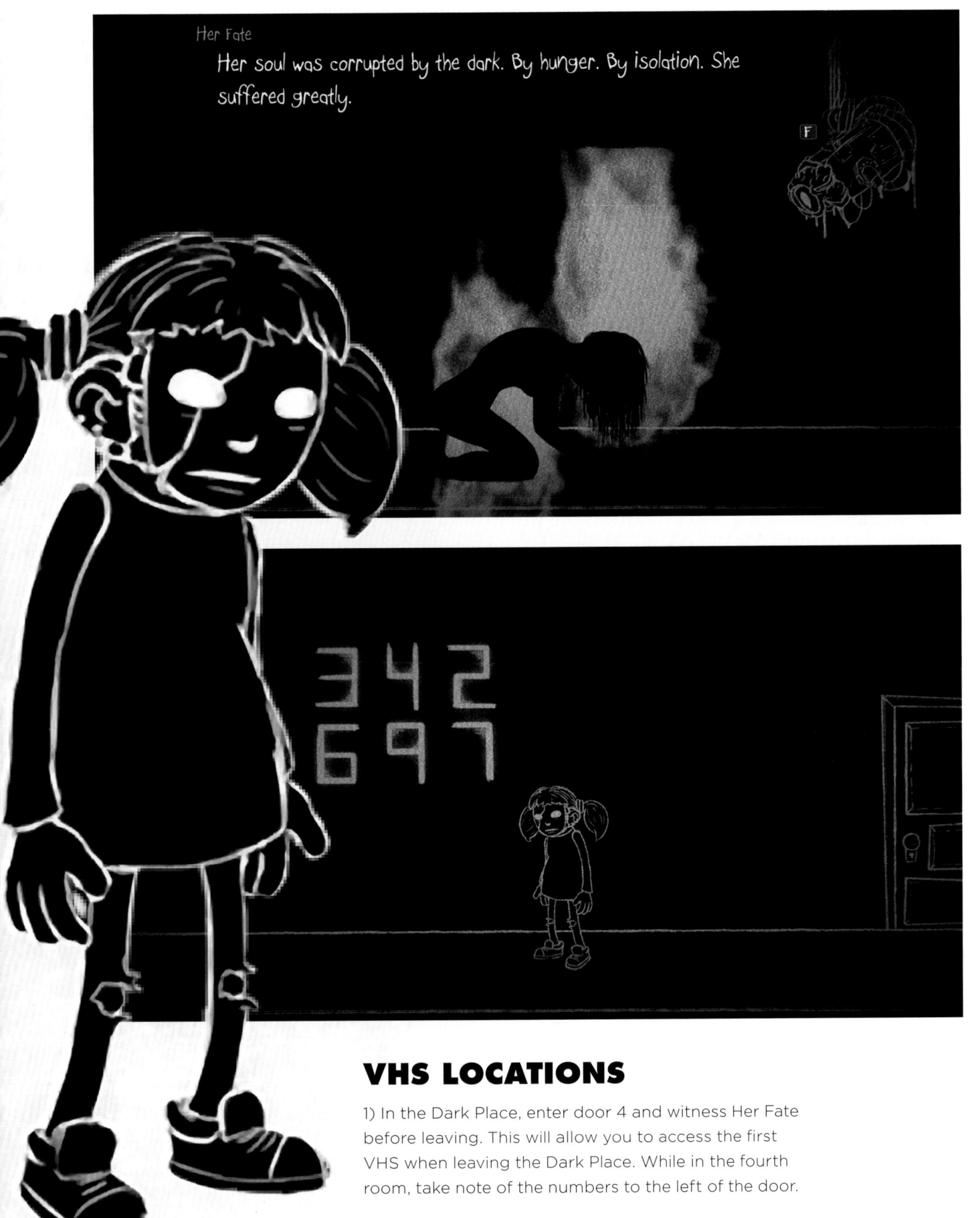

Her Fate

Her soul was corrupted by the dark. By hunger. By isolation. She suffered greatly.

VHS LOCATIONS

1) In the Dark Place, enter door 4 and witness Her Fate before leaving. This will allow you to access the first VHS when leaving the Dark Place. While in the fourth room, take note of the numbers to the left of the door.

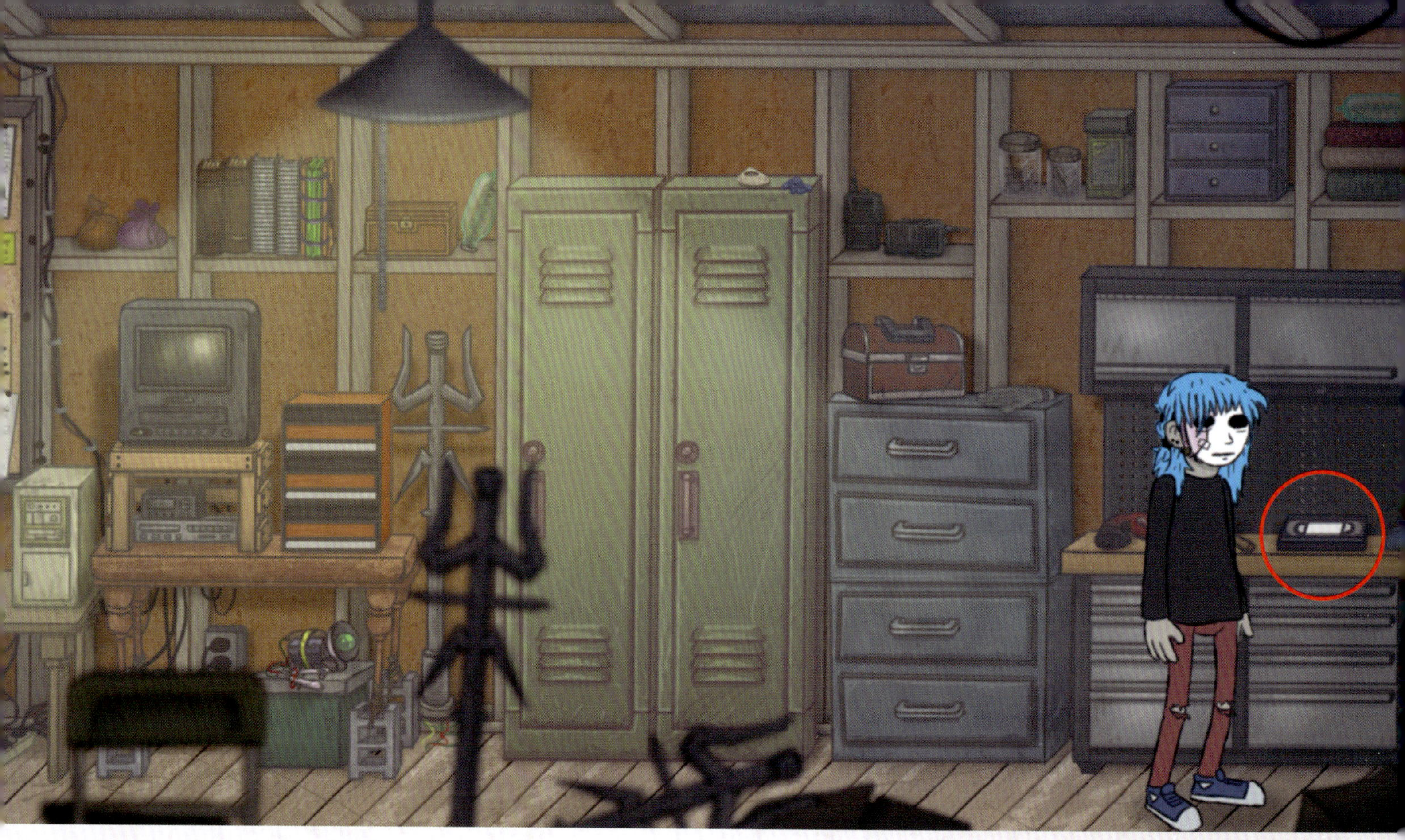

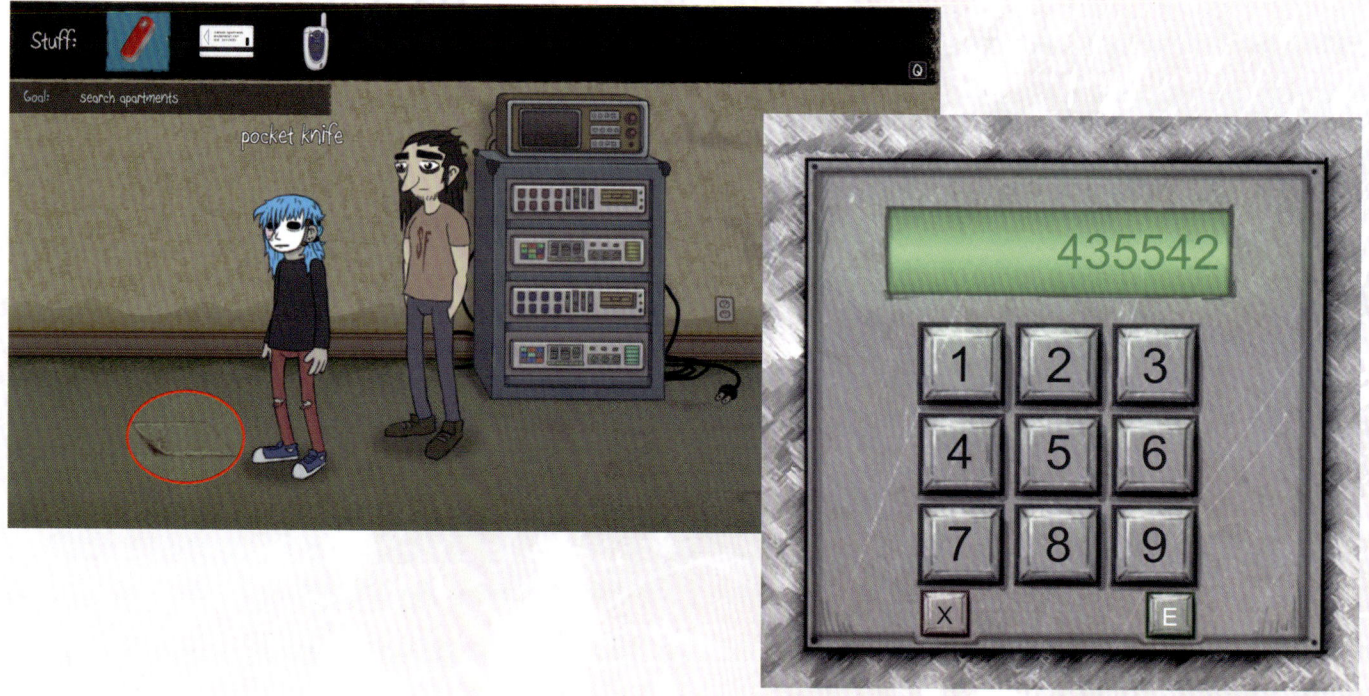

2) In the shed, on the far right. You can find the code on the note in Todd's room: **4035364**.

3) In room 201, specifically in bedroom 1 during your first visit, use the pocketknife on the torn carpet. Then enter the following code: **435542** (This number is decoded from the number found in the fourth room in the Dark Place. They are decoded by counting the lines of the numbers).

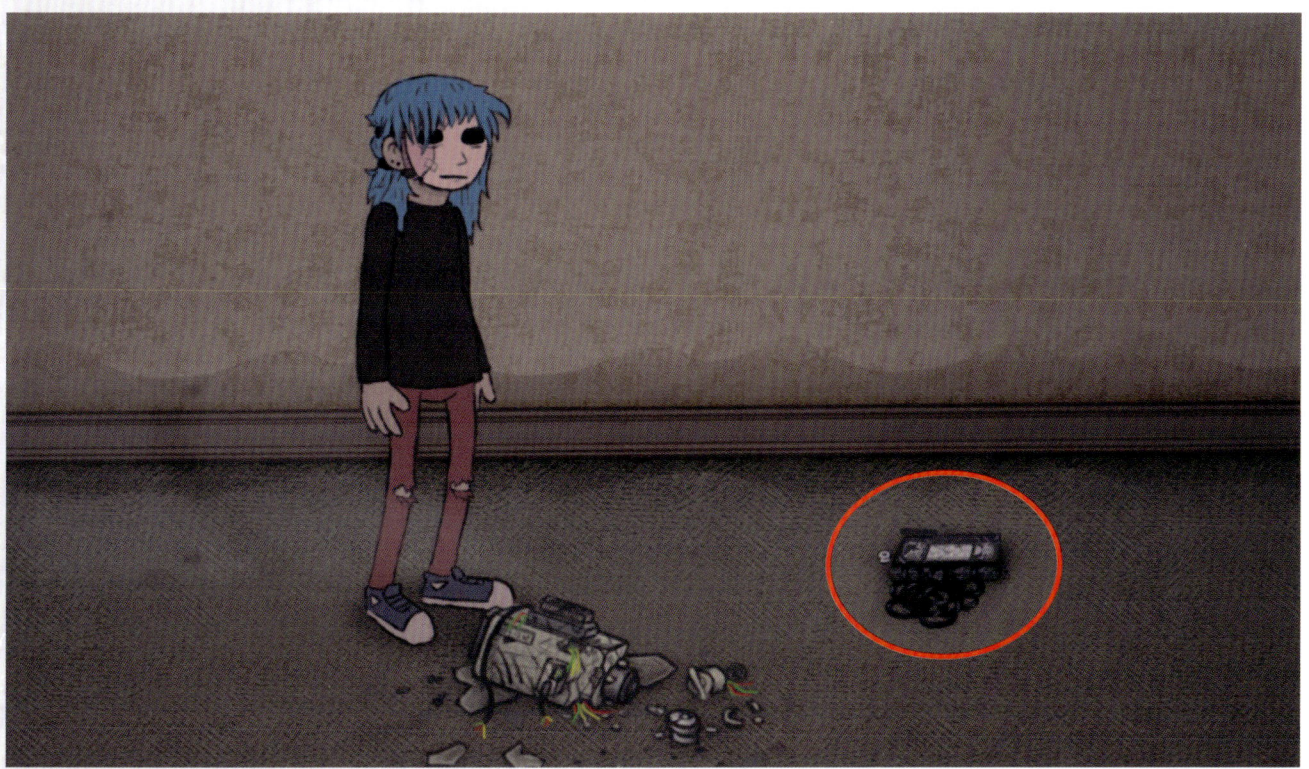

4) In room 404, during your first visit, use the pocketknife on the broken tape.

5) In room 503, during first visit, find the hole in the wall and interact with it until it breaks.

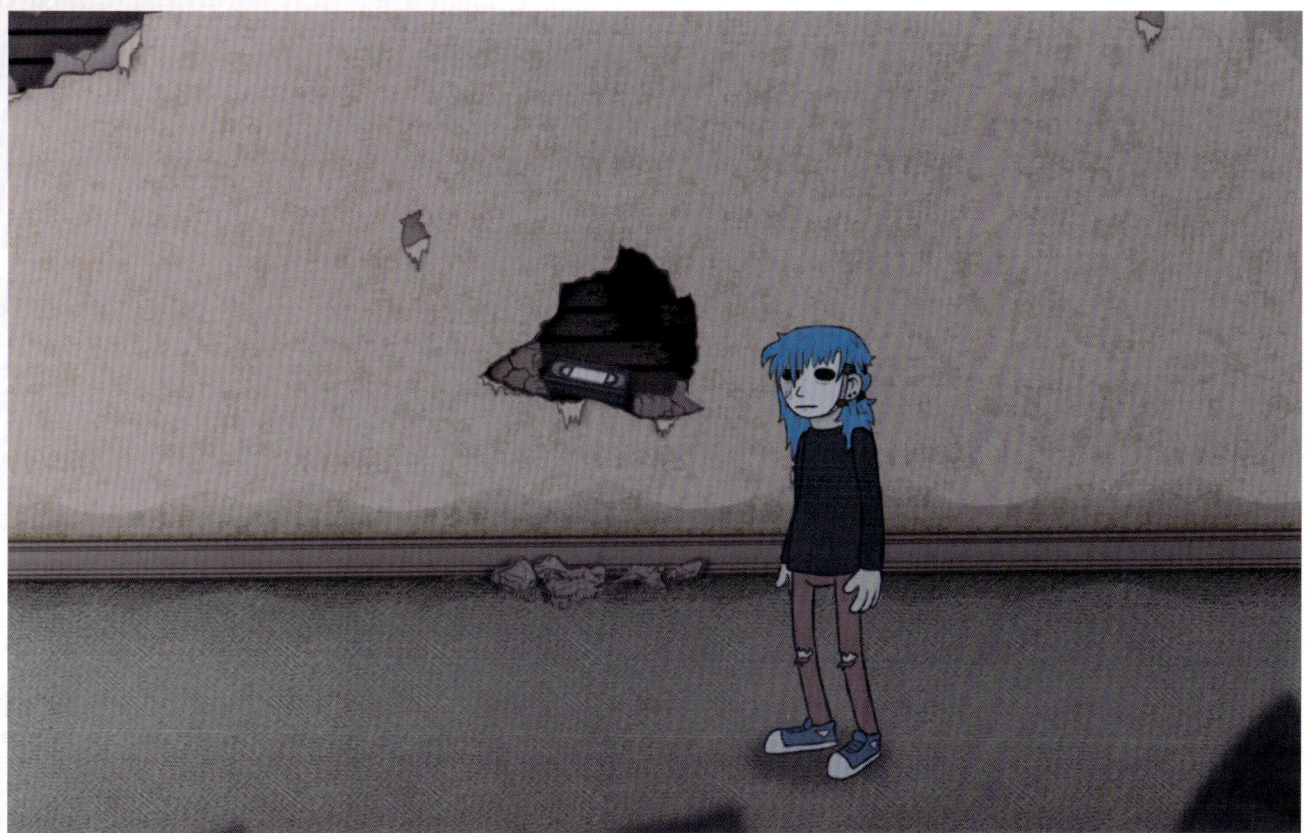

6) Room 504, second visit, in the bedroom. Blast it with Larry, then grab with Sal.

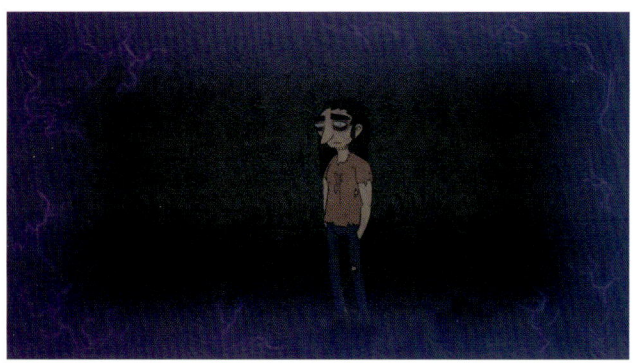 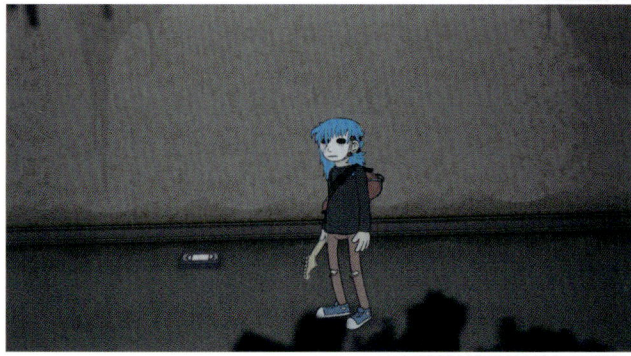

7) Room 404, second visit. Blast it with Larry, then grab with Sal.

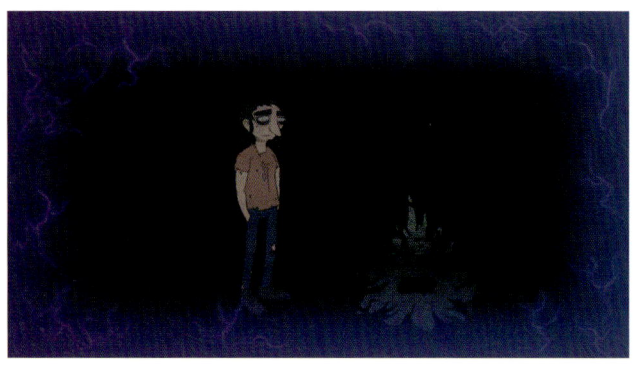 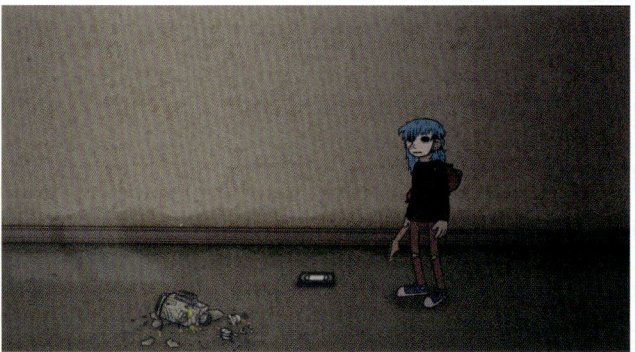

8) Second visit. Get the Dark Pony from the Other Side in 303. Place the pony on the symbol in 204. Switch to Sal and get the tape from 204.

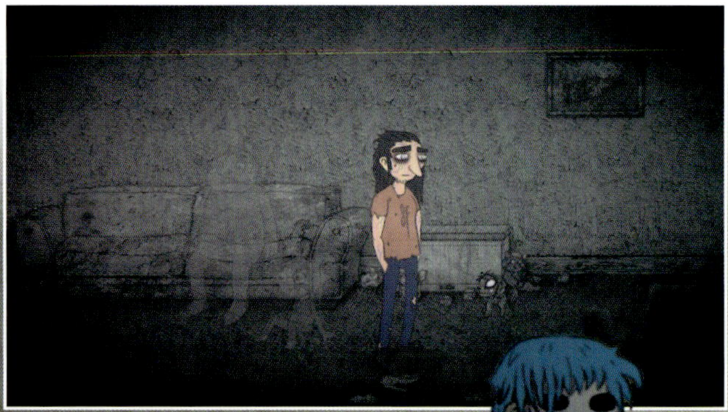

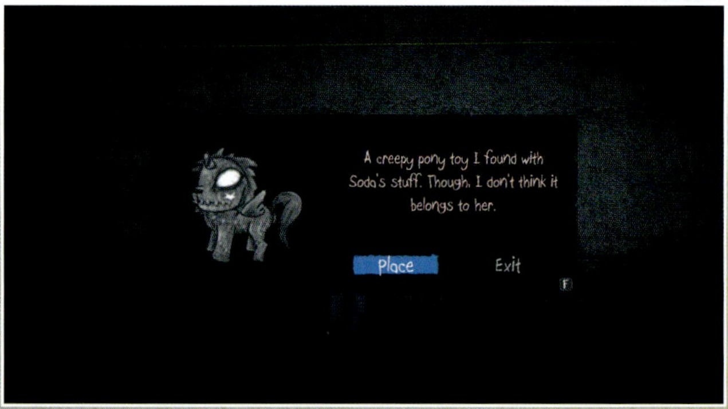

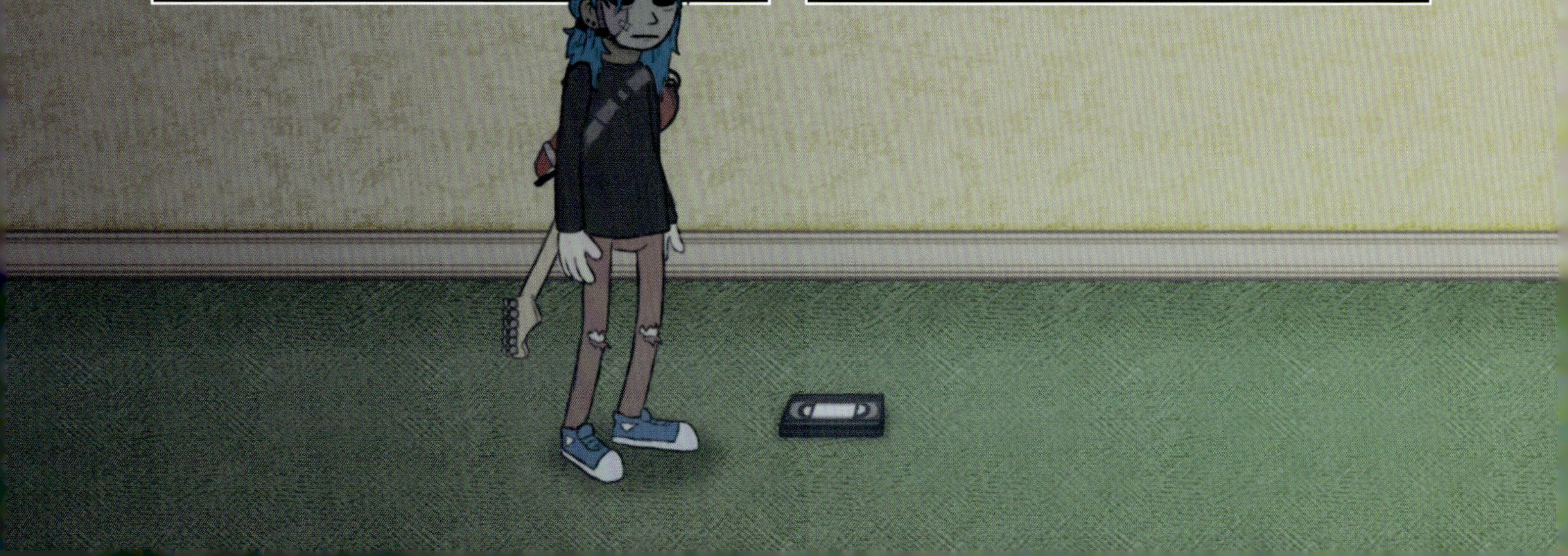

9) Floor 1, second visit. Open Mrs. Gibson's door as Sal, get the carrot from room 104, place the carrot by Gibson's door.

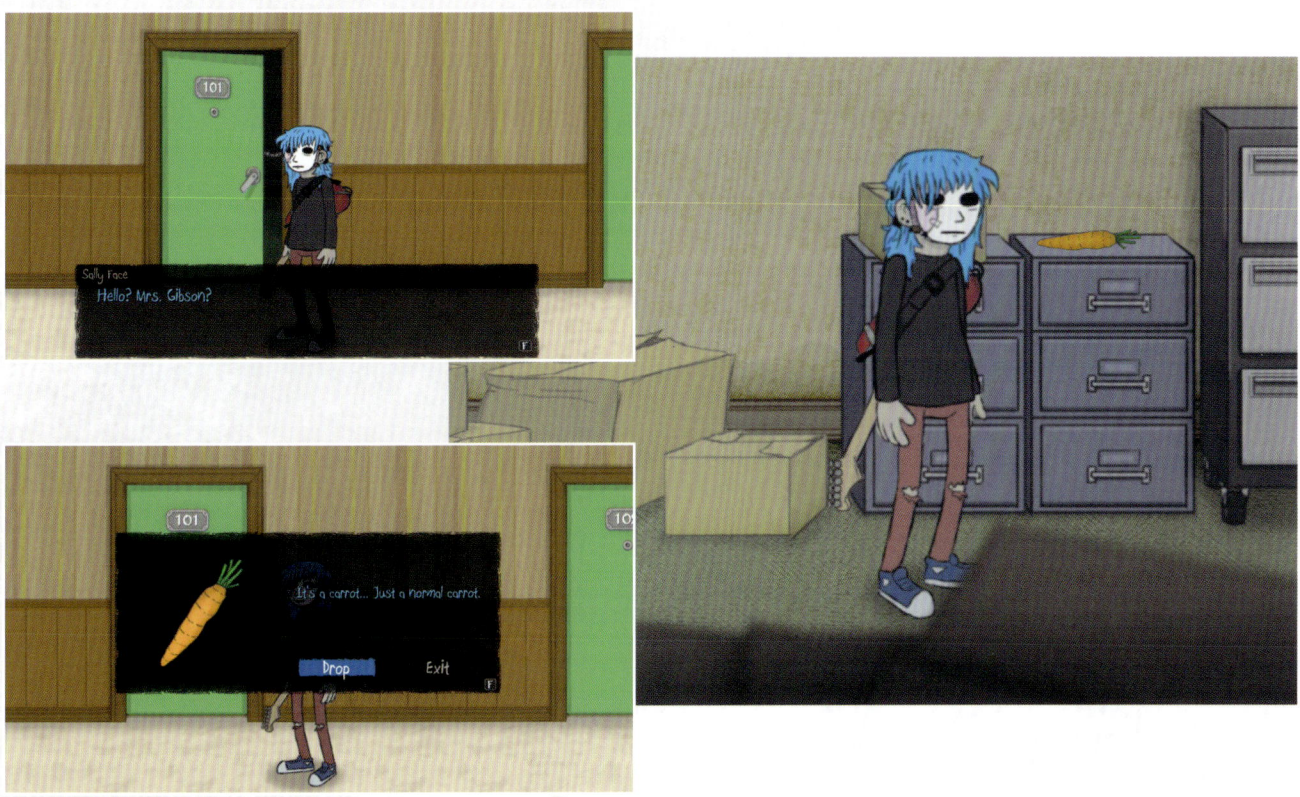

Switch to Larry, grab the lighter from far right of the hall, interact with rabbit, switch to Sal to get tape. If you remember, this is a reference to the story Larry tells in Episode Two about accidentally killing Gibson's rabbit.

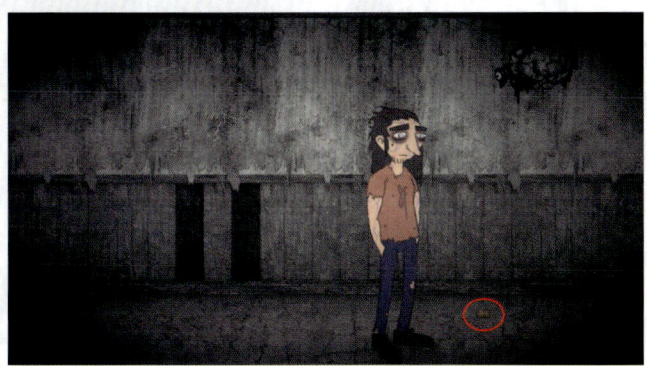
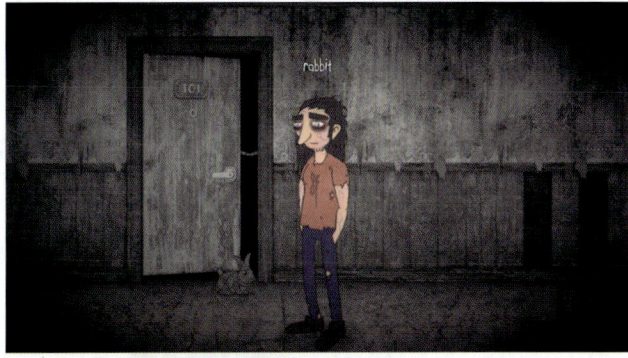

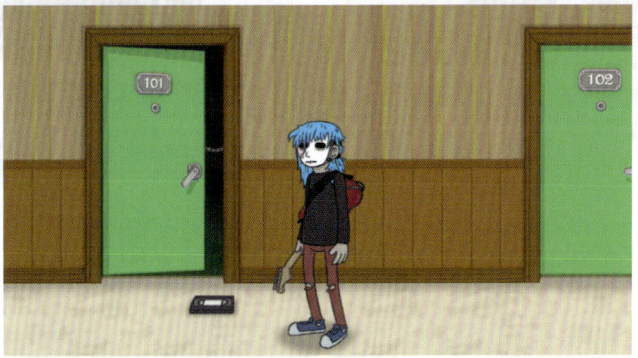

EPISODE FIVE
Memories and Dreams

SHED CODE

The code is the same from episode four: **4035364**.

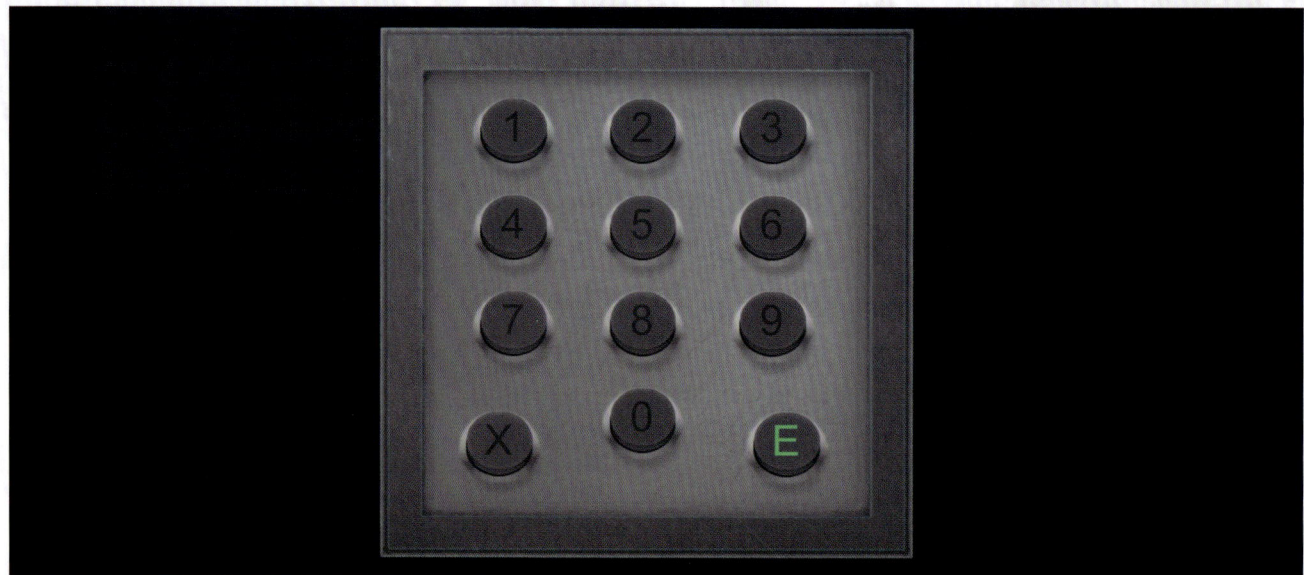

JIM'S SAFE, A LETTER TO LISA

The combo is the "initiation" date from Jim's notes: **1983**.

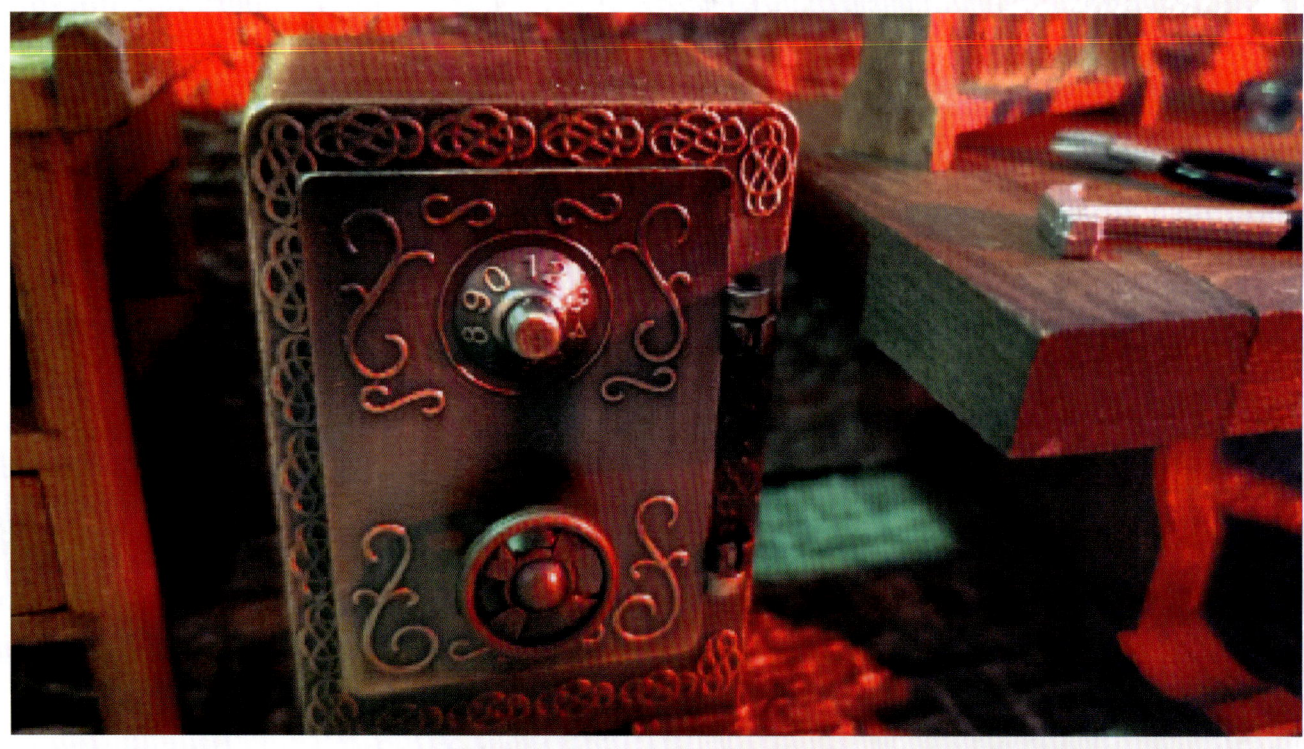

DOOR 5, THE FINAL MEMORY

1) First, you must find all six hexagons throughout the episode (and take note of the colored dots on each one). NOTE: You must interact with each of them in order to progress.

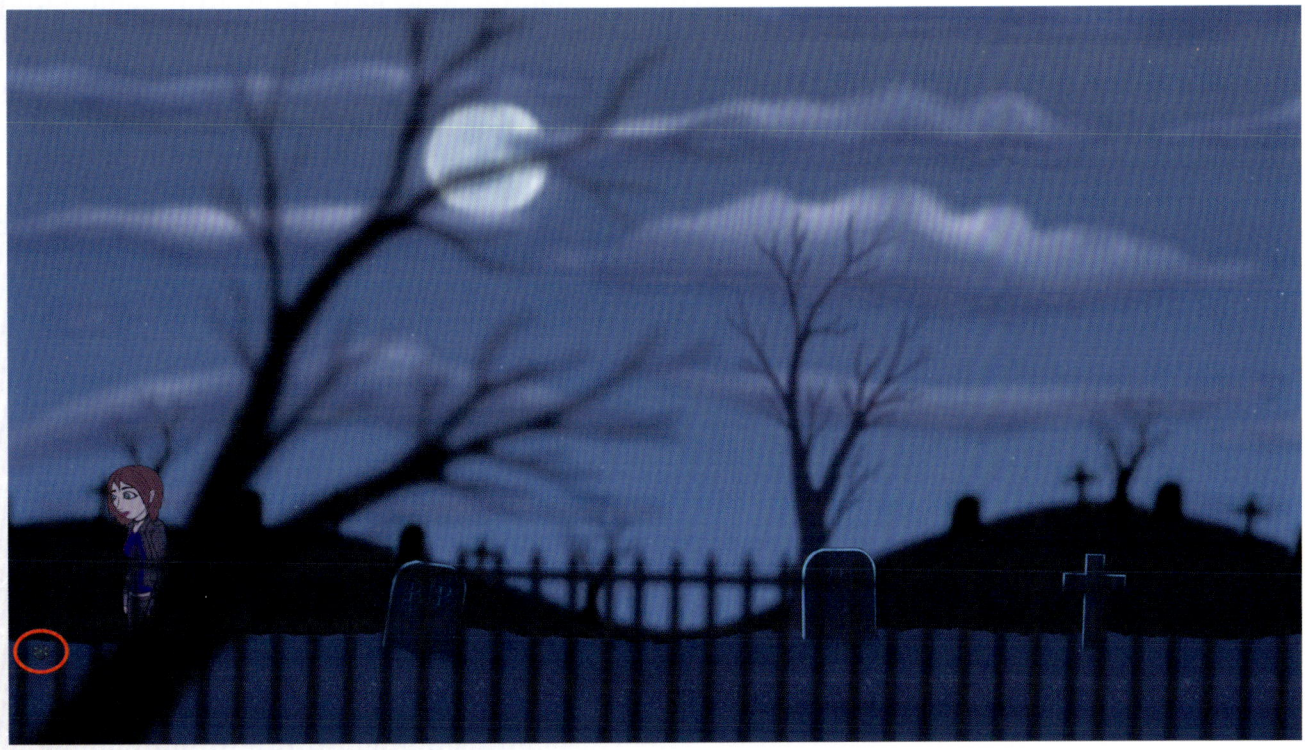

1.1) At the far left edge of the cemetery.

1.2) Neil's house, bathroom, left of sink.

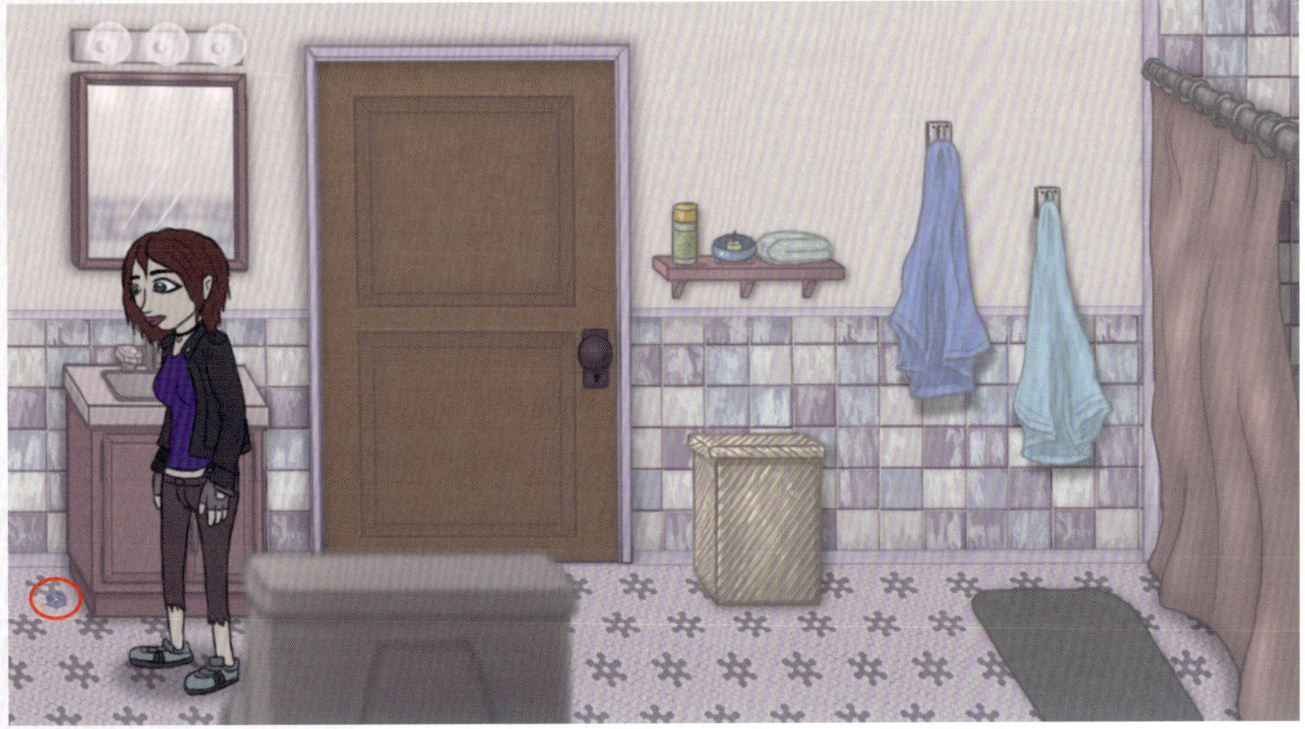

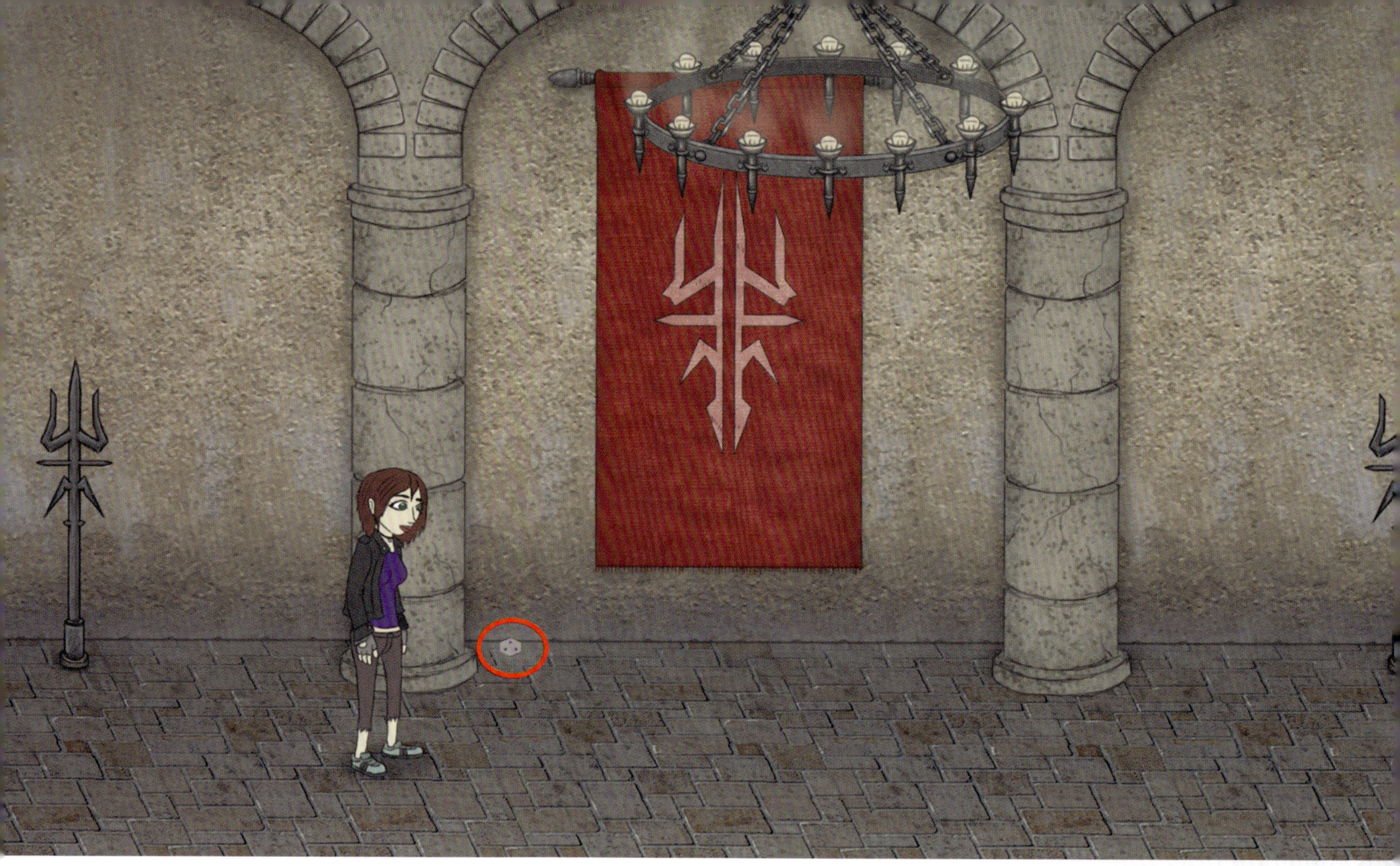

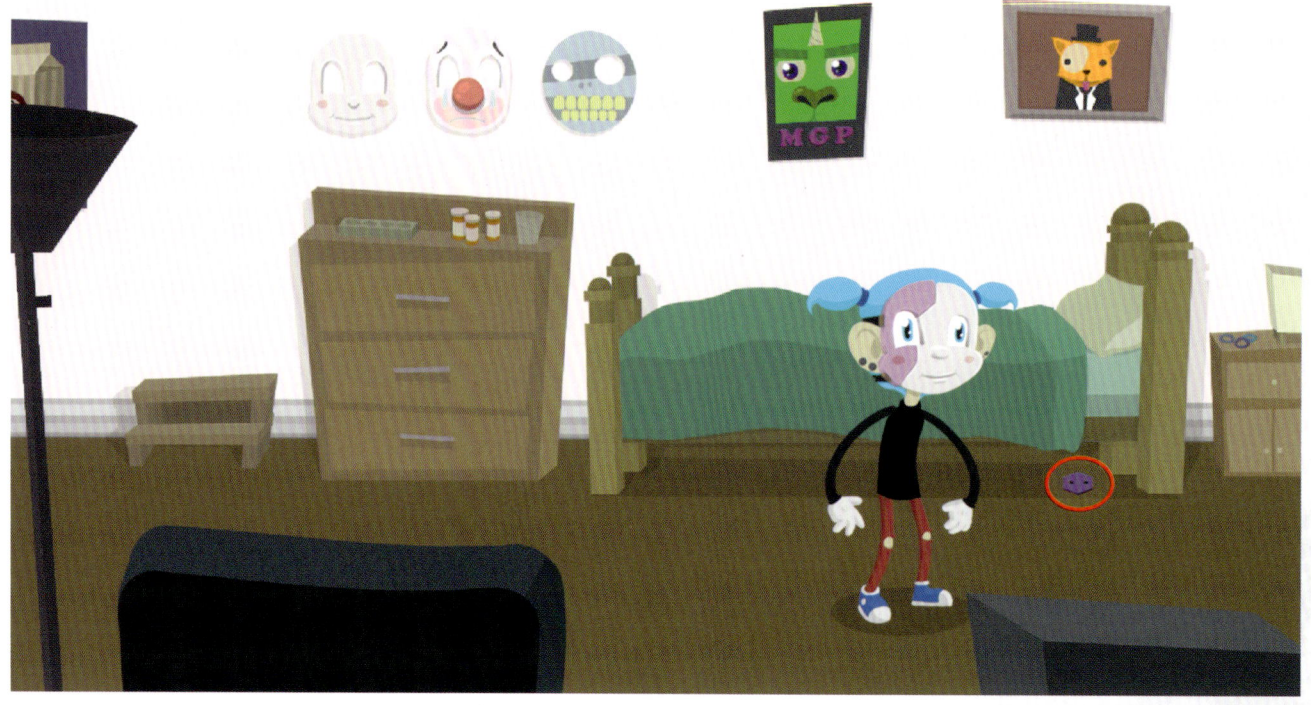

1.3) Temple, East Hall.

1.4) Cartoon House, Sal's room, under bed.

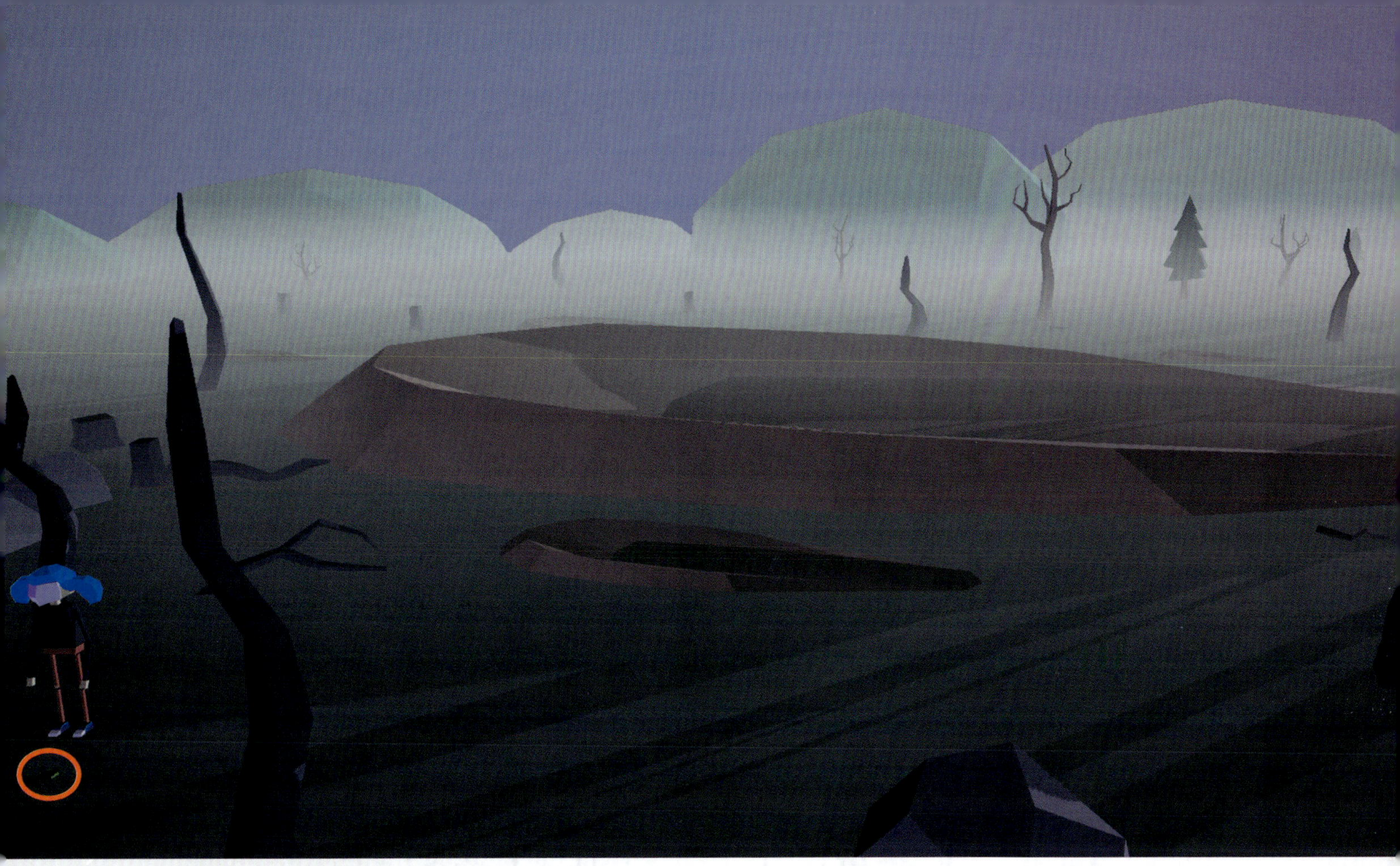

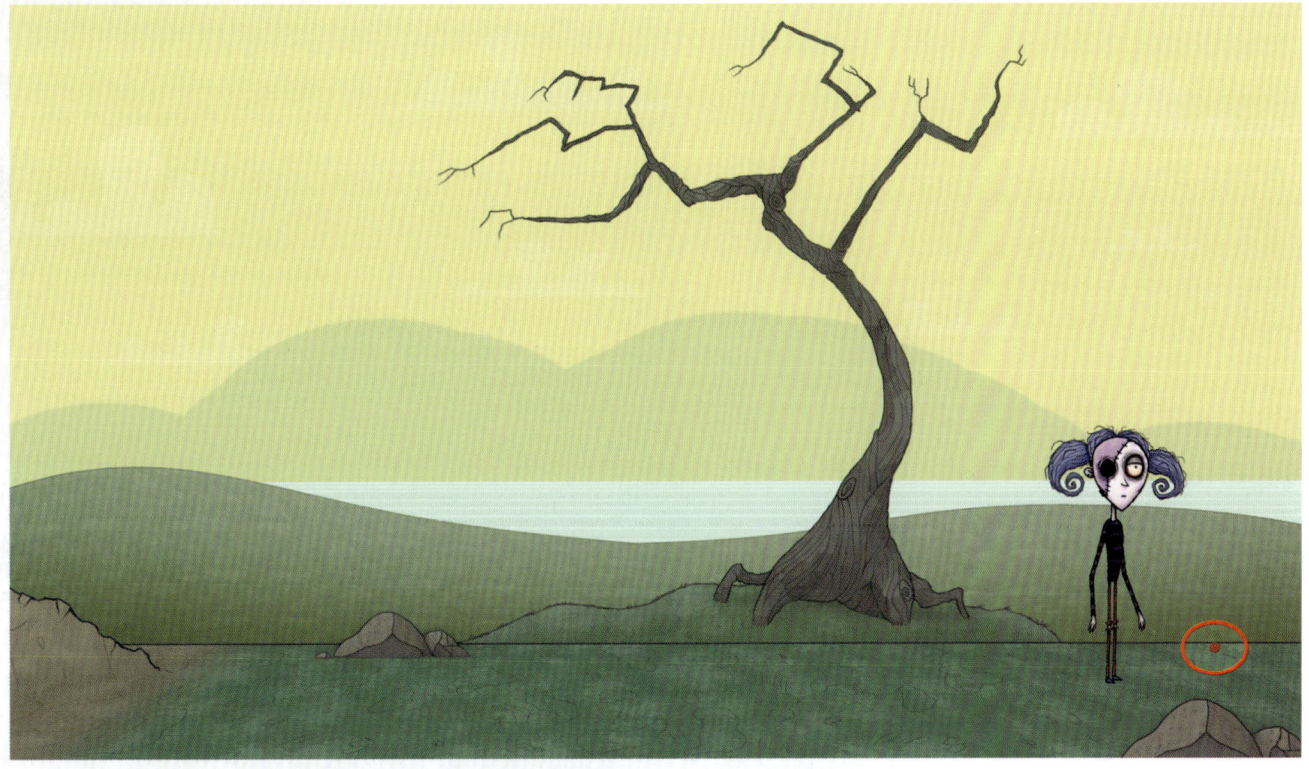

1.5) The crash site, bottom left of area.

1.6) The cave entrance, outside to the right.

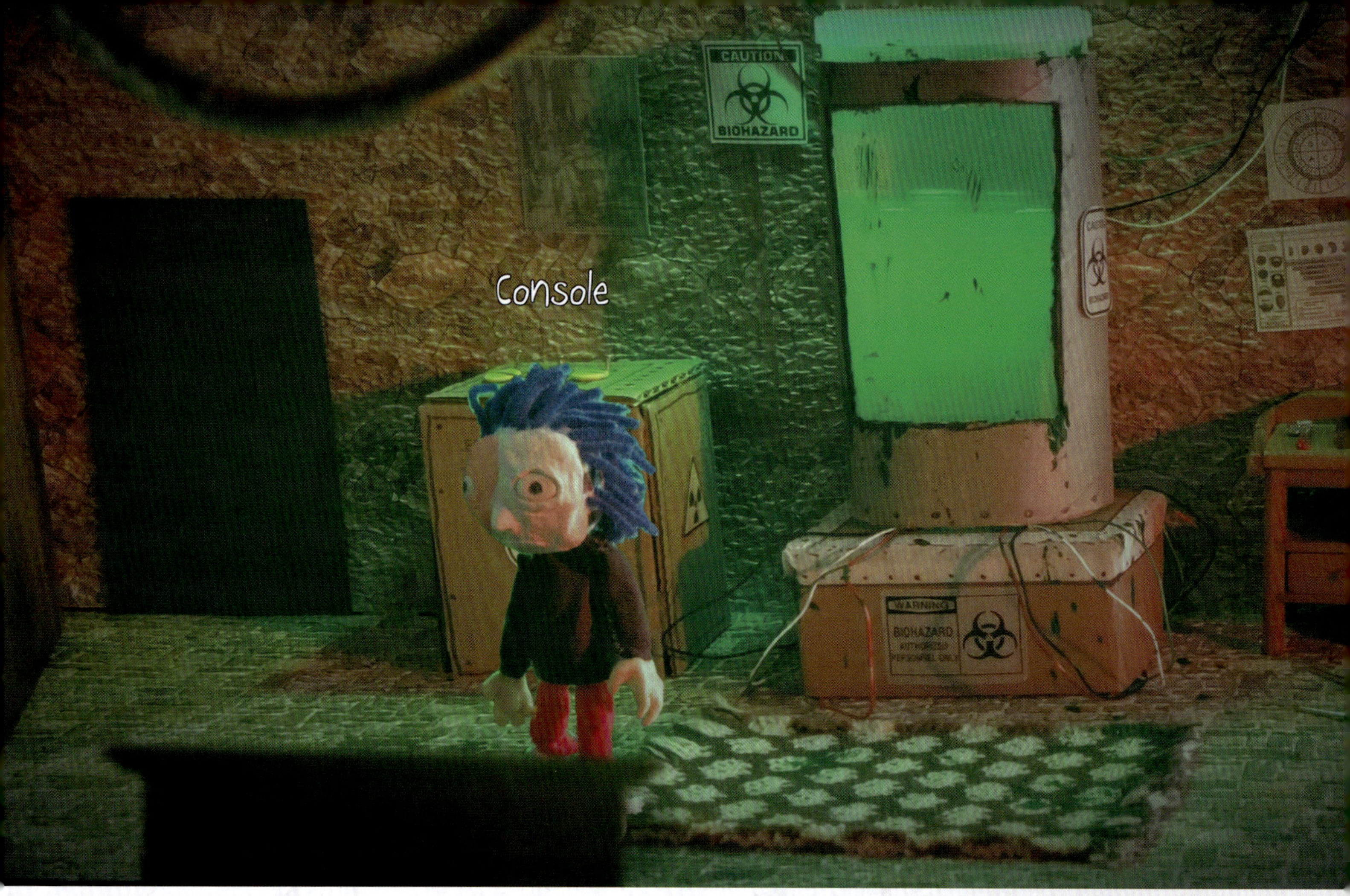

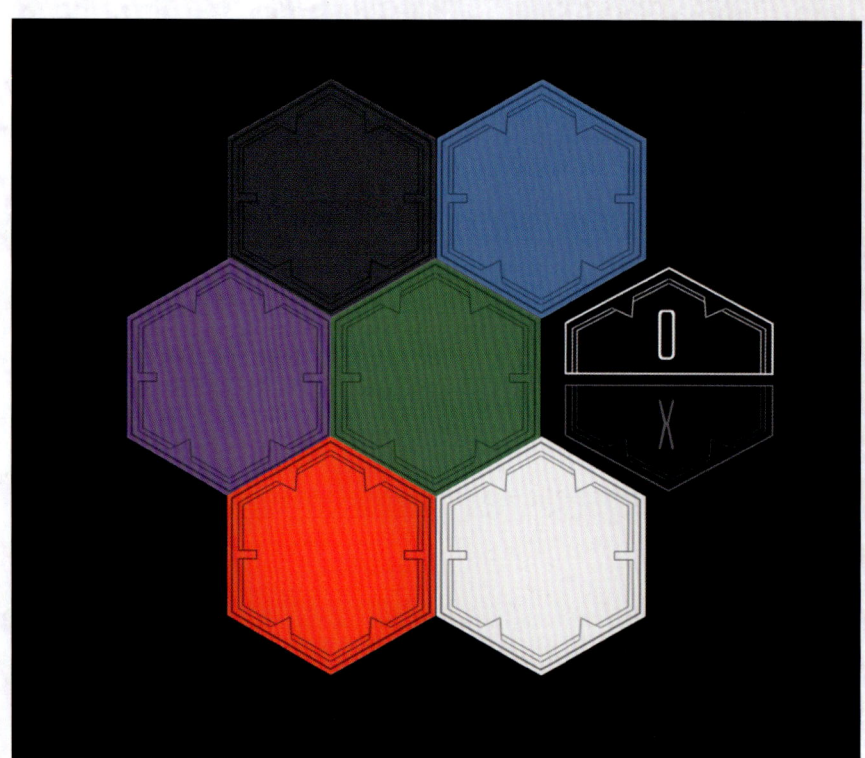

Console

2) In Jim's Lab, interact with the large shelf on the far left. This will reveal a black doorway.

3) You need to press the hexagon buttons in order. The order is determined by the colored dots: **White, Black, Blue, Red, Green, Purple**. Then press the "O" button.

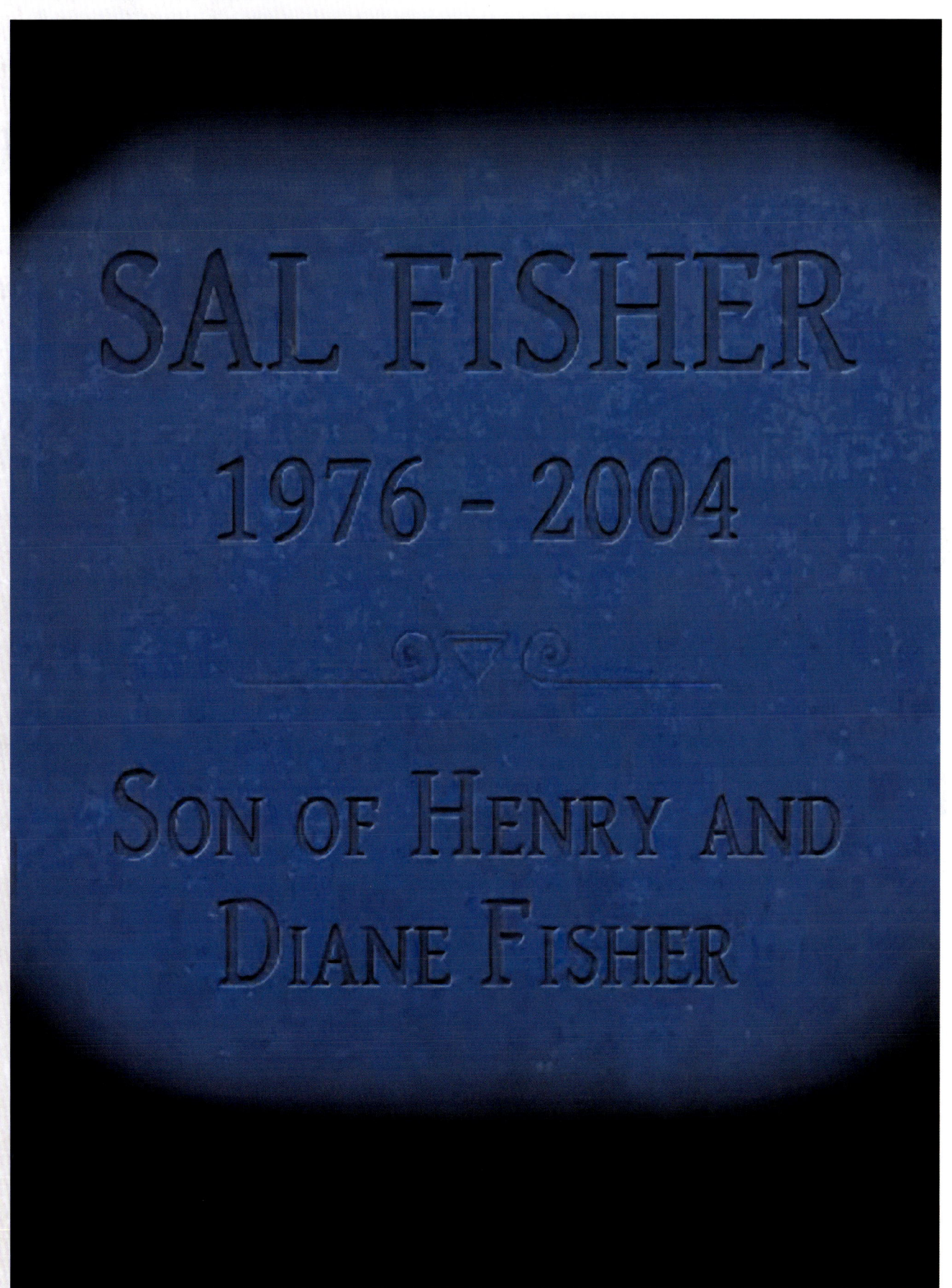

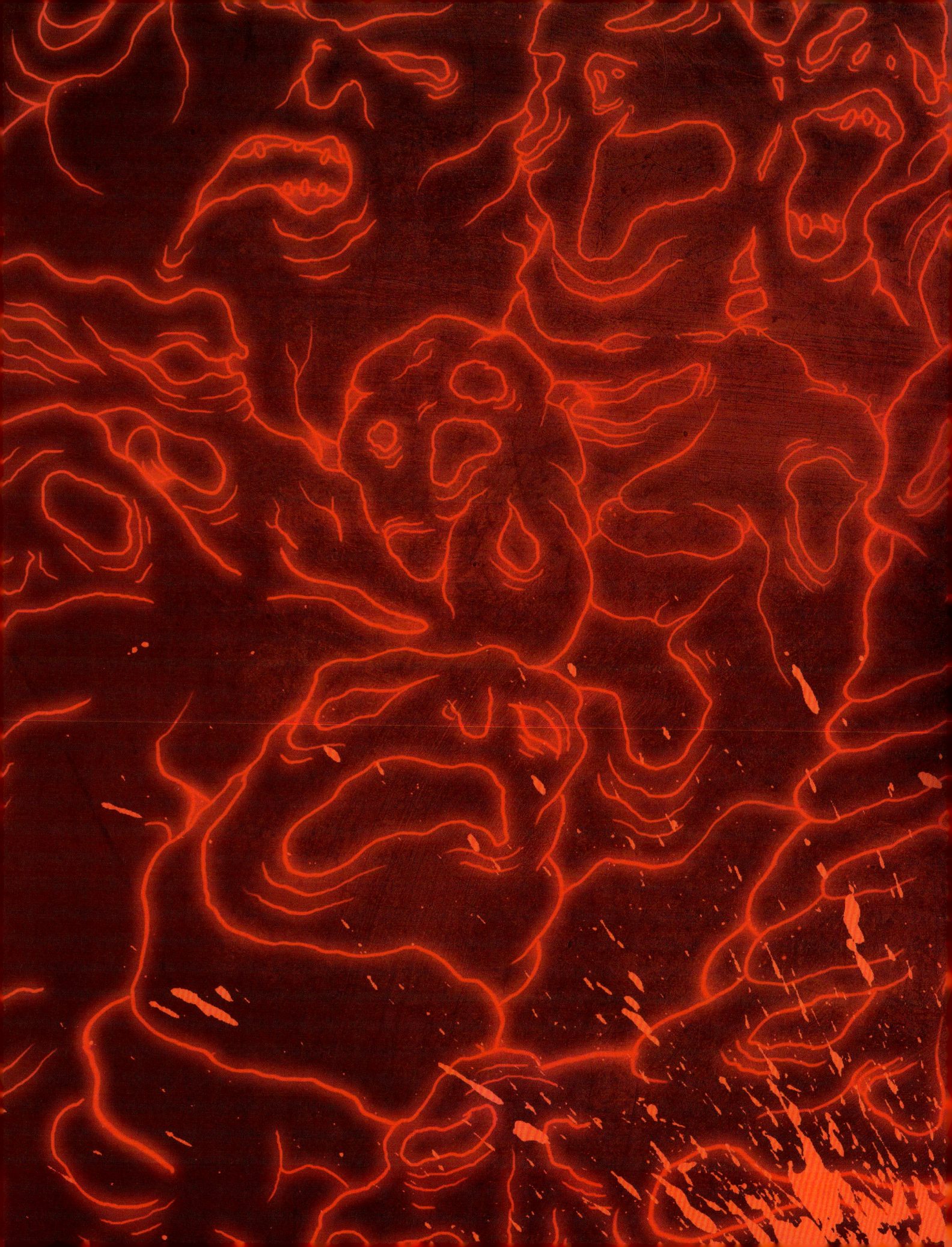

CHAPTER 7

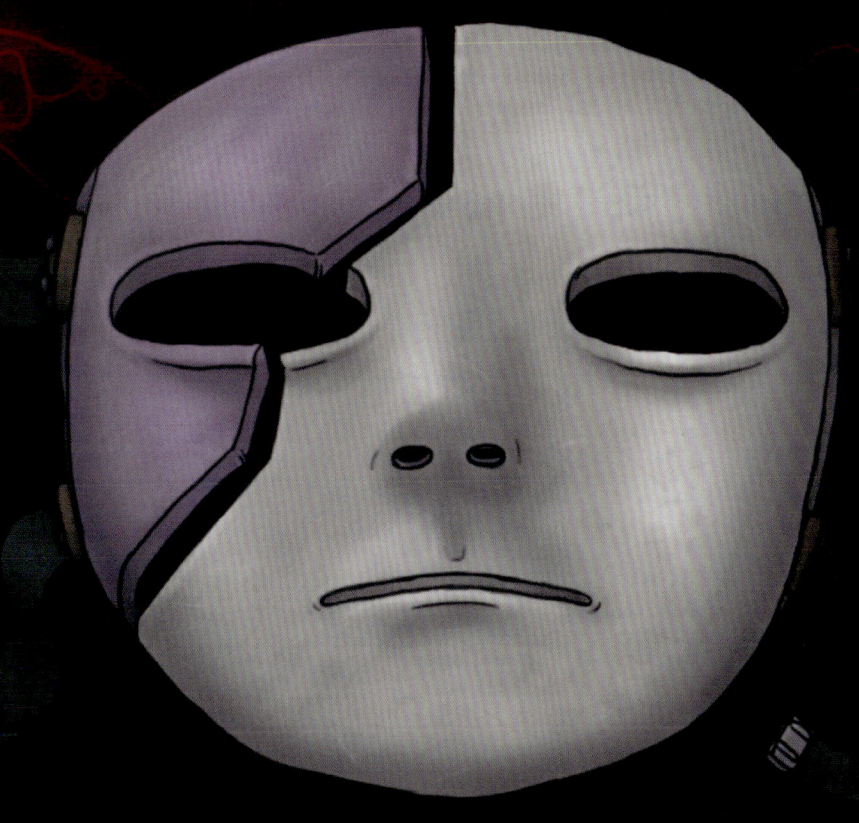

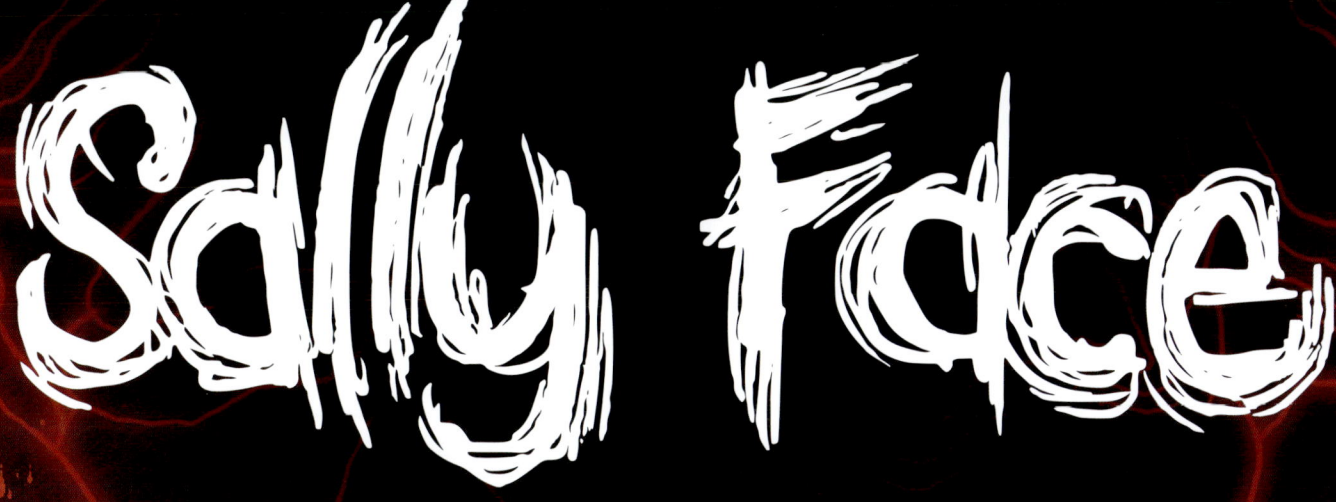

FAN ART GALLERY

A DEDICATION TO SALLY FACE FANS

THE FANS have been a huge part of this journey. I've been lucky enough to have a wonderful community of people from around the world who love and support *Sally Face*. I want to dedicate this section of the book to all of those fans. The following pages contain a small sample of the vast talent of the *Sally Face* fandom. Whether you're a skilled artist or not, I appreciate every person who has played *Sally Face*, purchased this book, bought merch, told their friends about *Sally Face*, or supported me in any way.

Thank you!

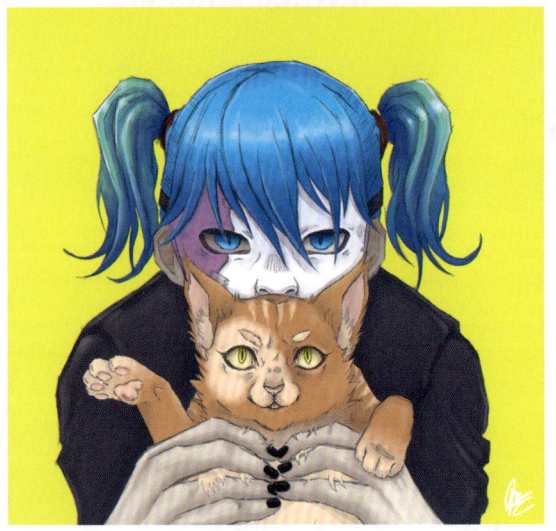

FAN ART: Jane McIlvaine.

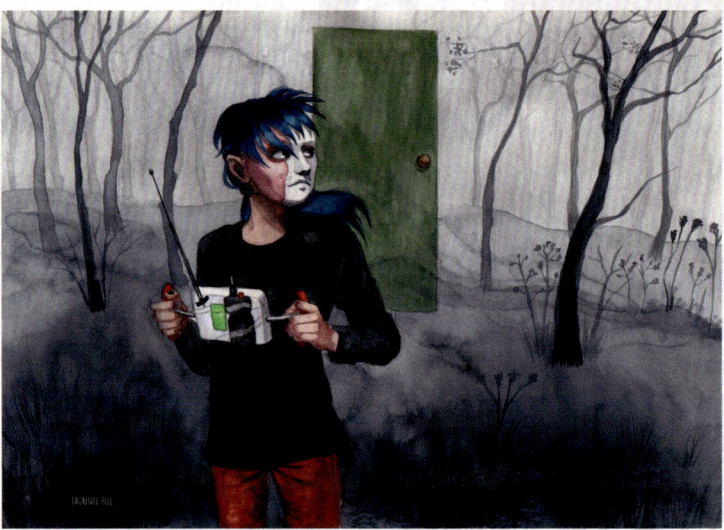

FAN ART: Laurence Hill.

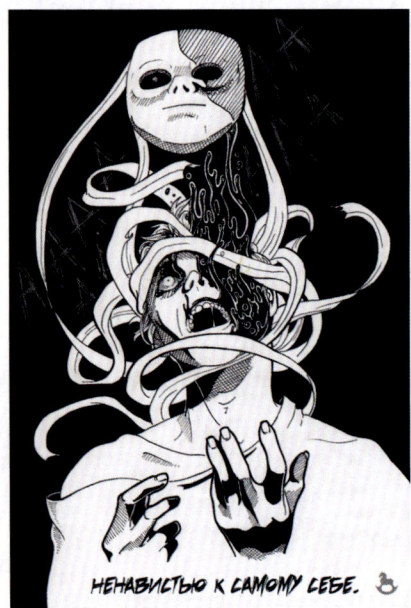

FAN ART: Rocking Horse.

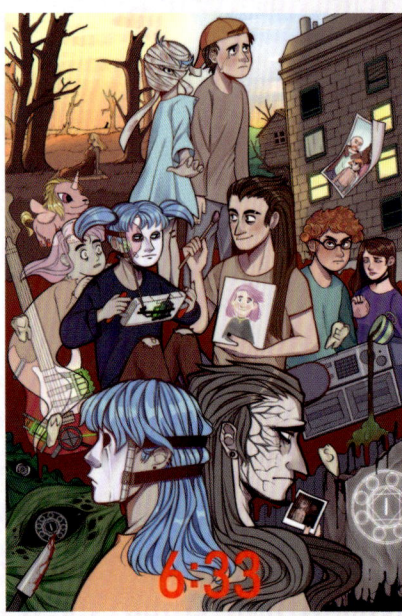

FAN ART: Giuls.

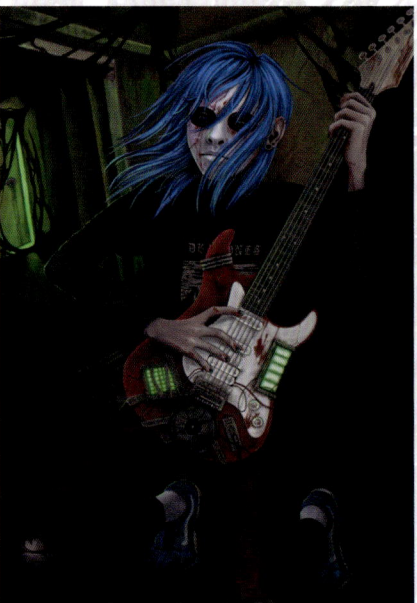

FAN ART: Lena Tõsjatova.

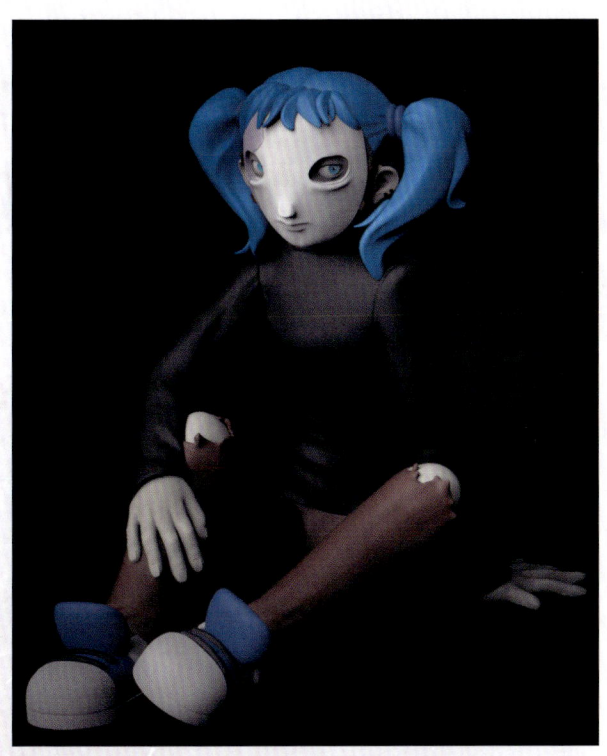

FAN ART: Anastasia Gorbacheva.

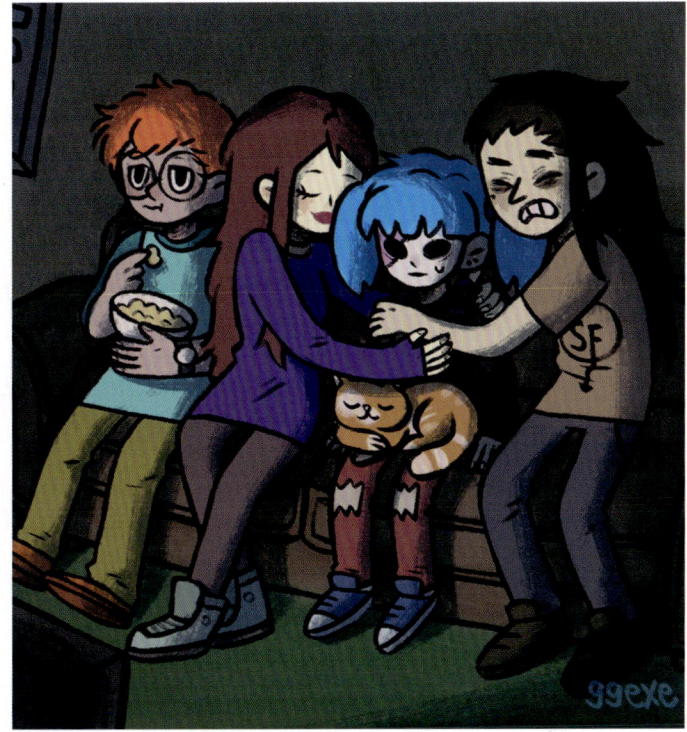

FAN ART: 99exe.

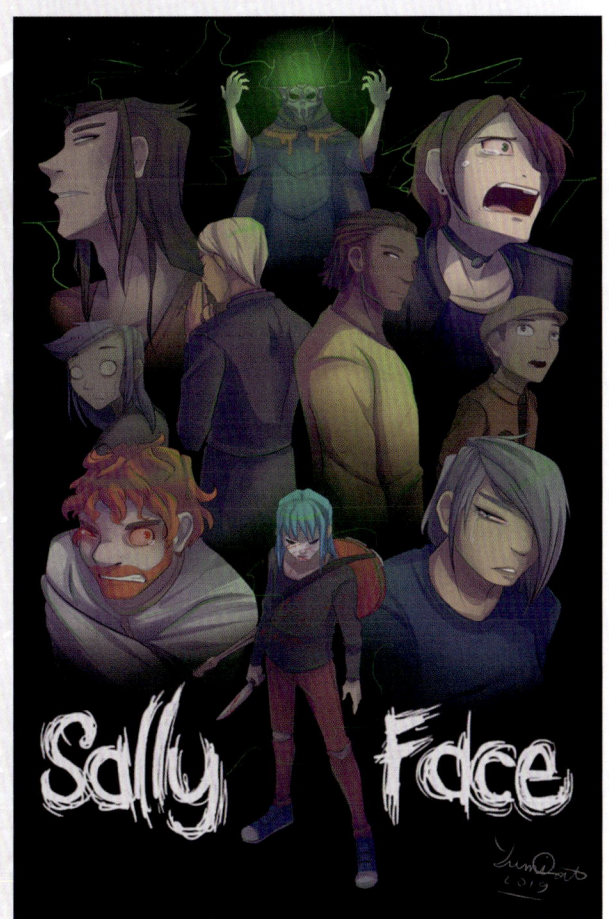

FAN ART: Yumi the Cat.

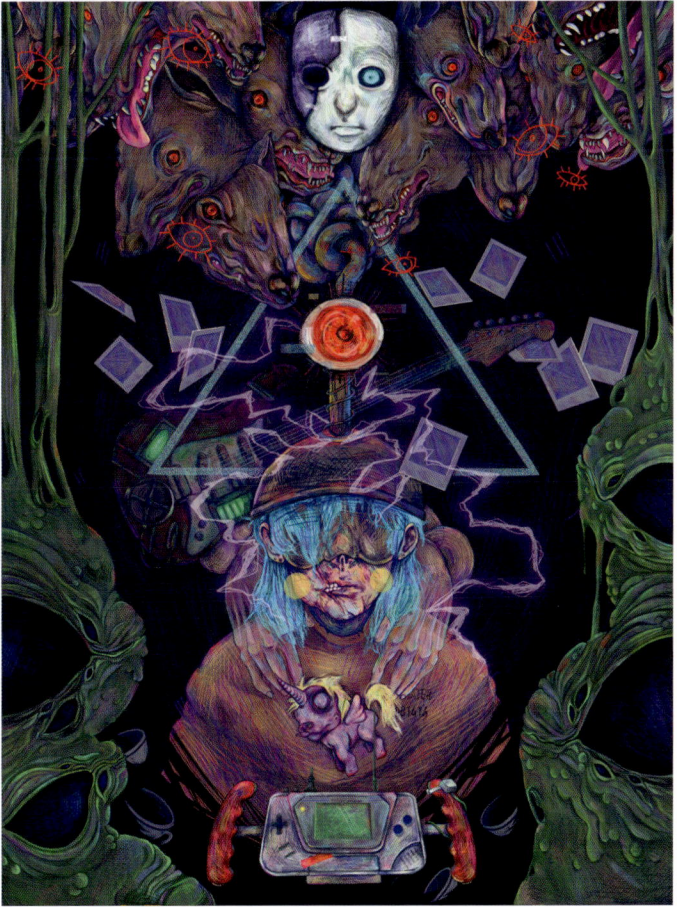

FAN ART: Sophia Moog.

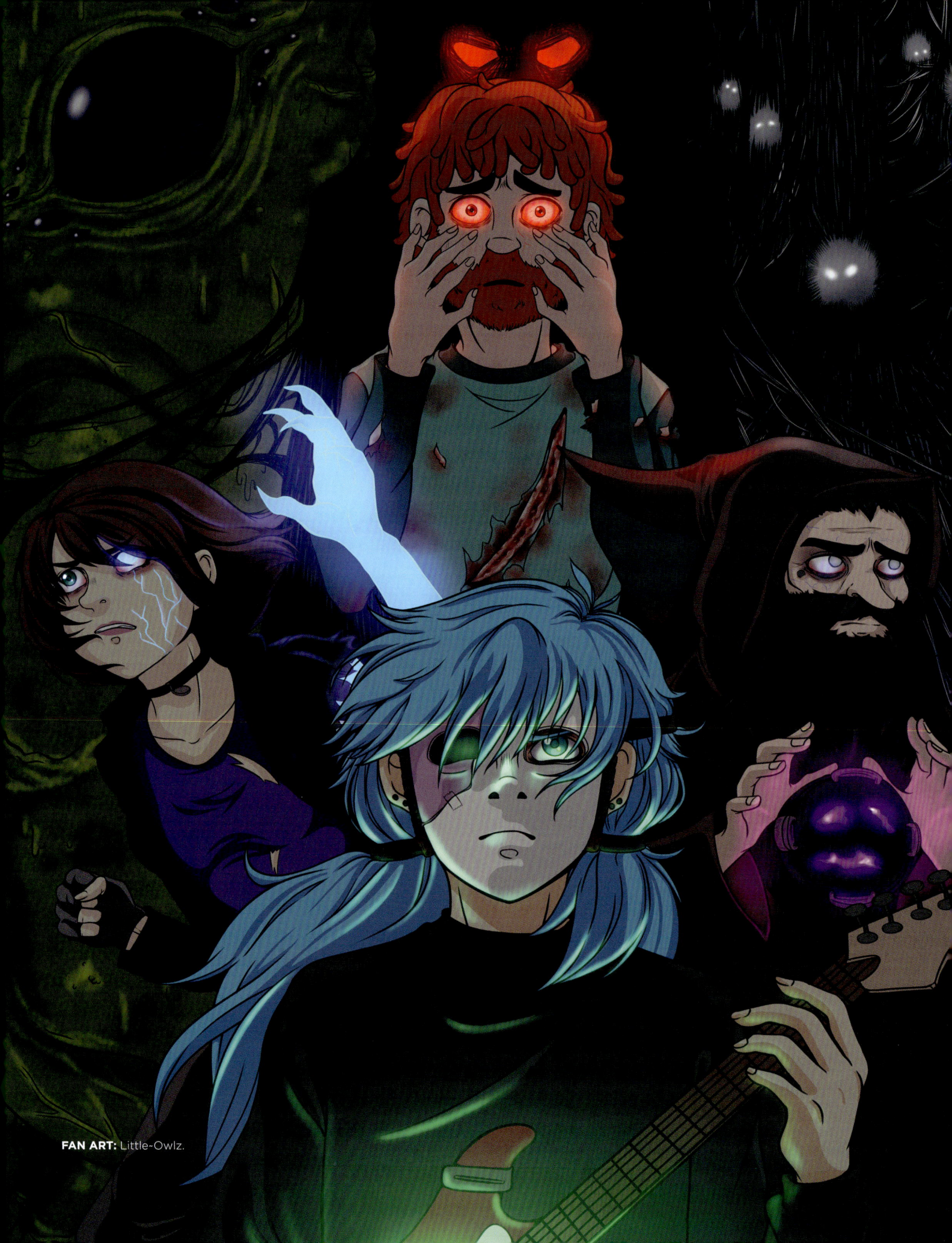

FAN ART: Little-Owlz.

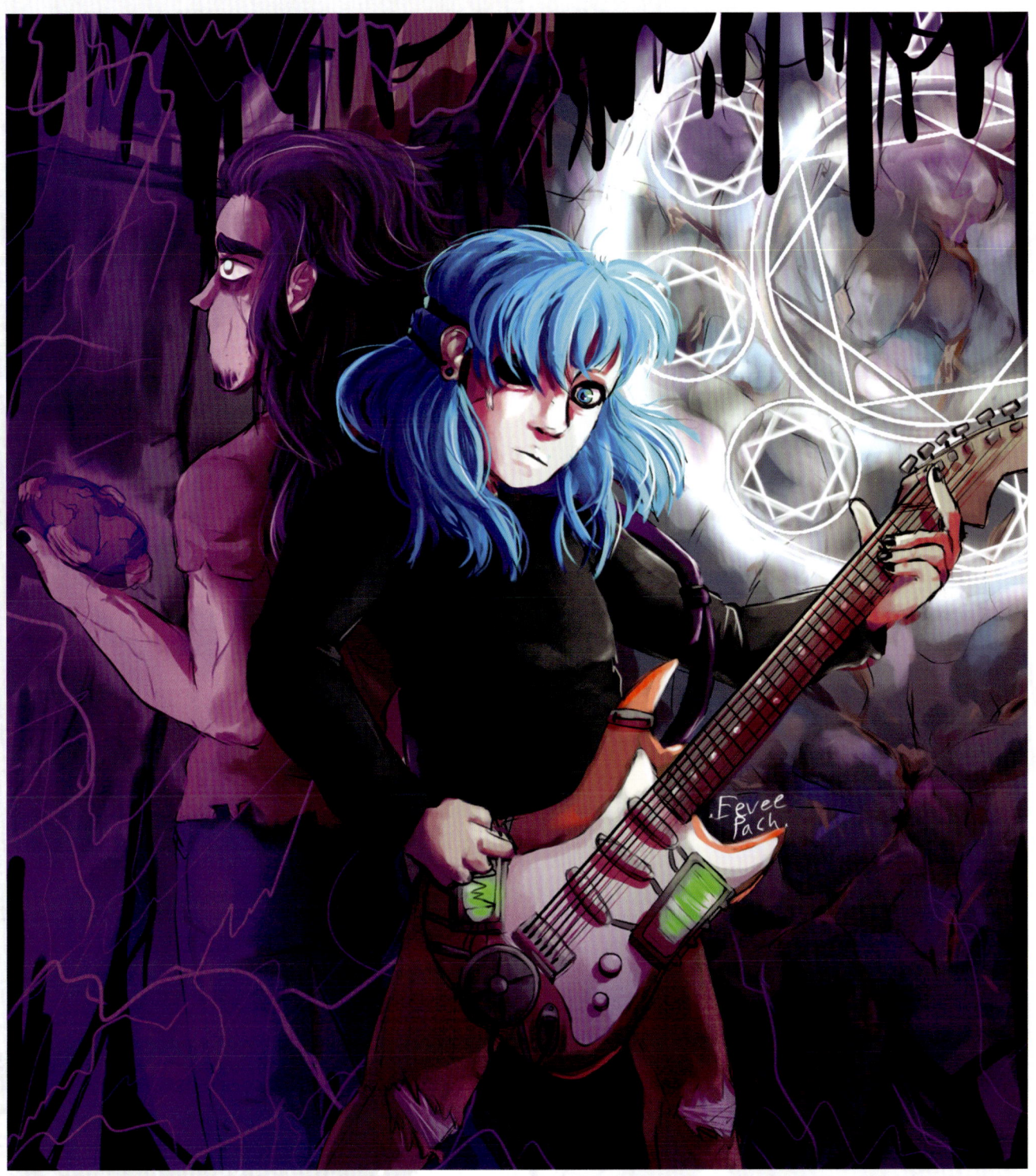

FAN ART: EeveePach.

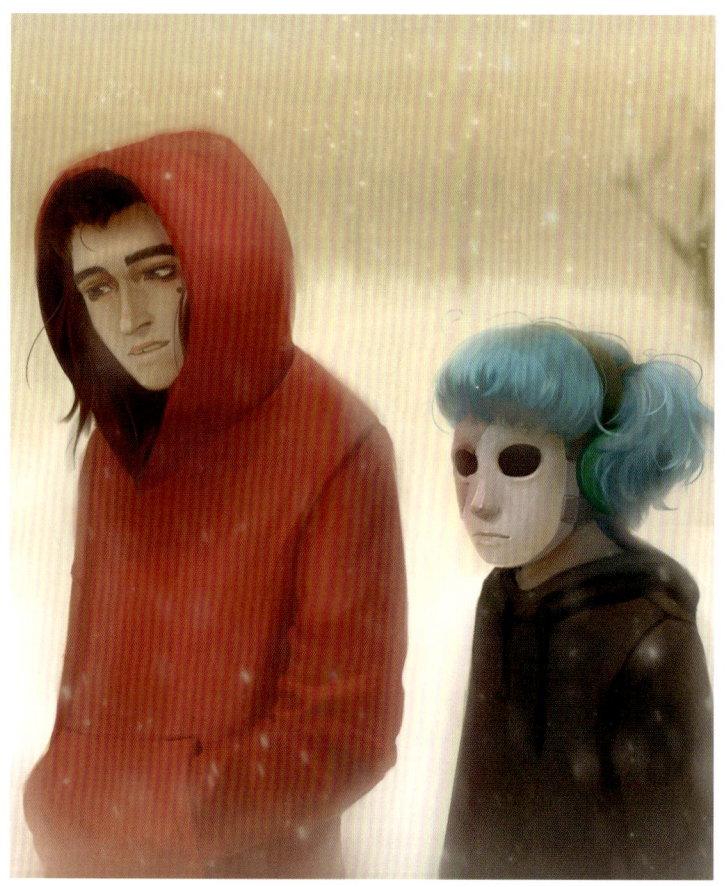

FAN ART: JeyKuto.

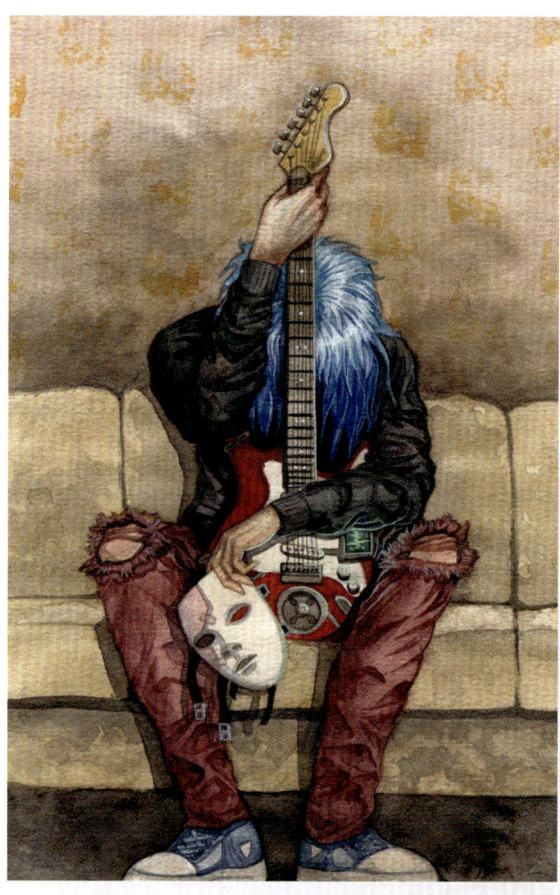

FAN ART: Greyn Periwinkle.

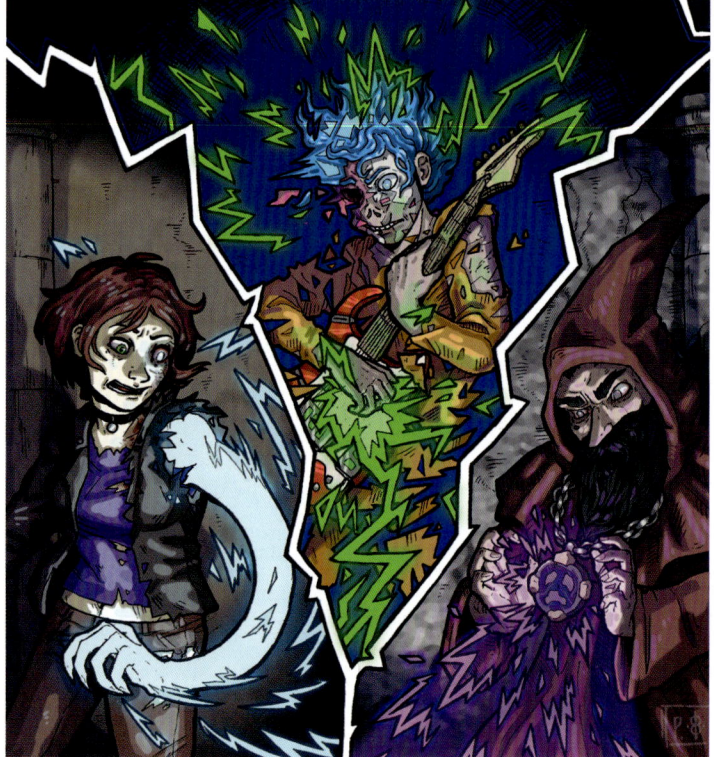

FAN ART: PolinaEnotArt.

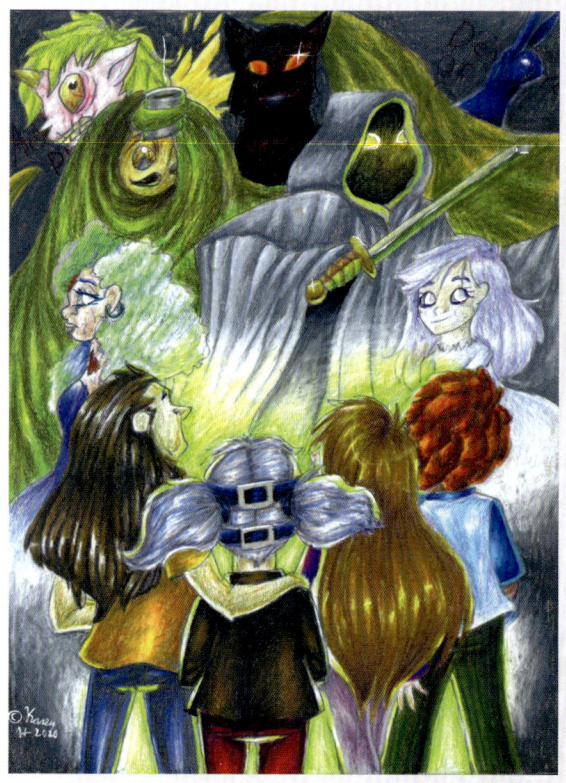

FAN ART: SpaceKase.

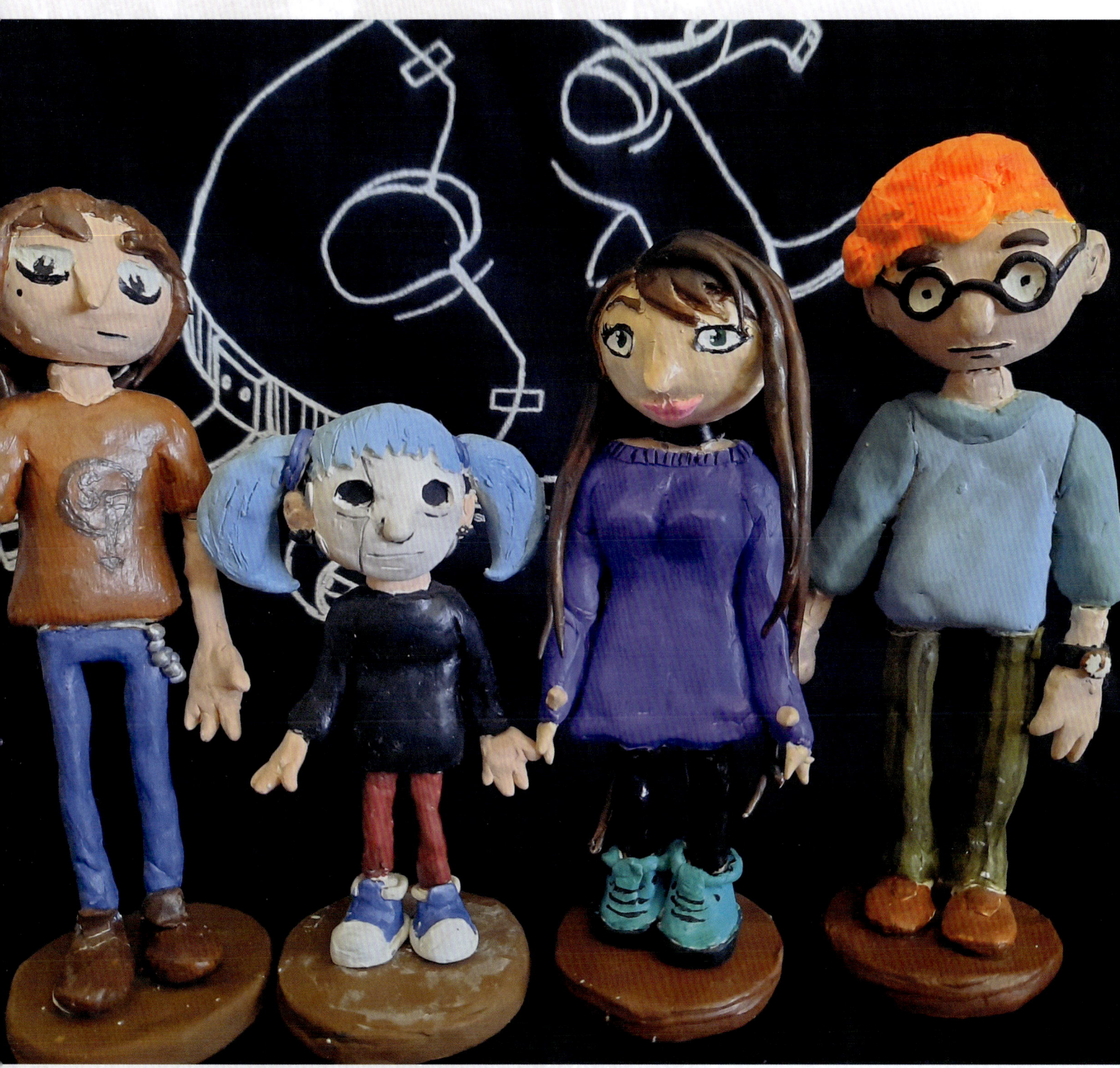

FAN ART: Hiza @lunaisaluna.

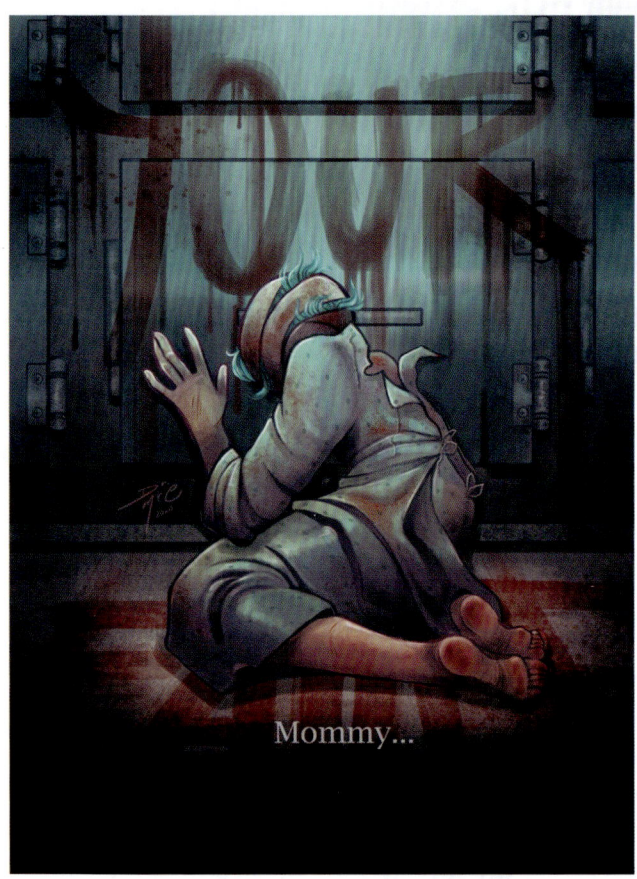

FAN ART: Dr. Mel the Creator.

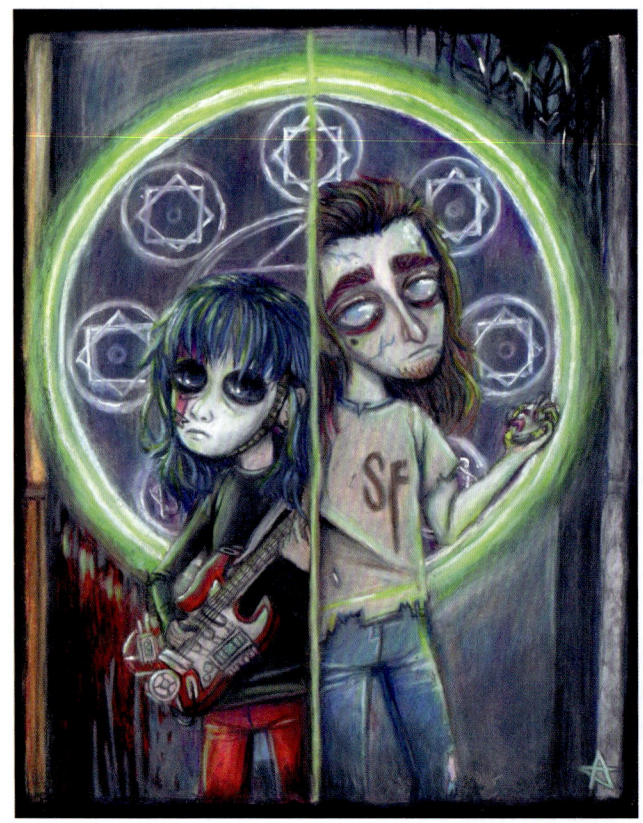

FAN ART: Alexis Irene Fucci.

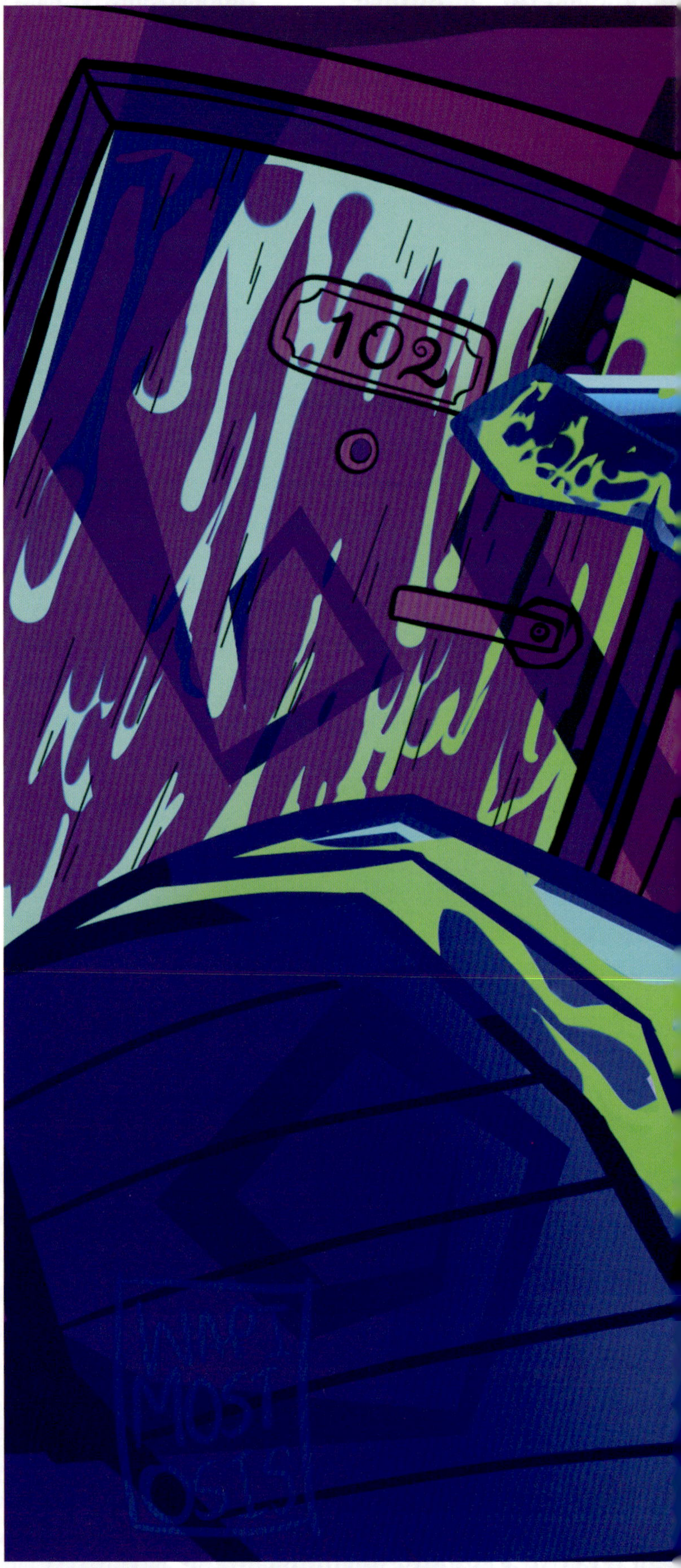

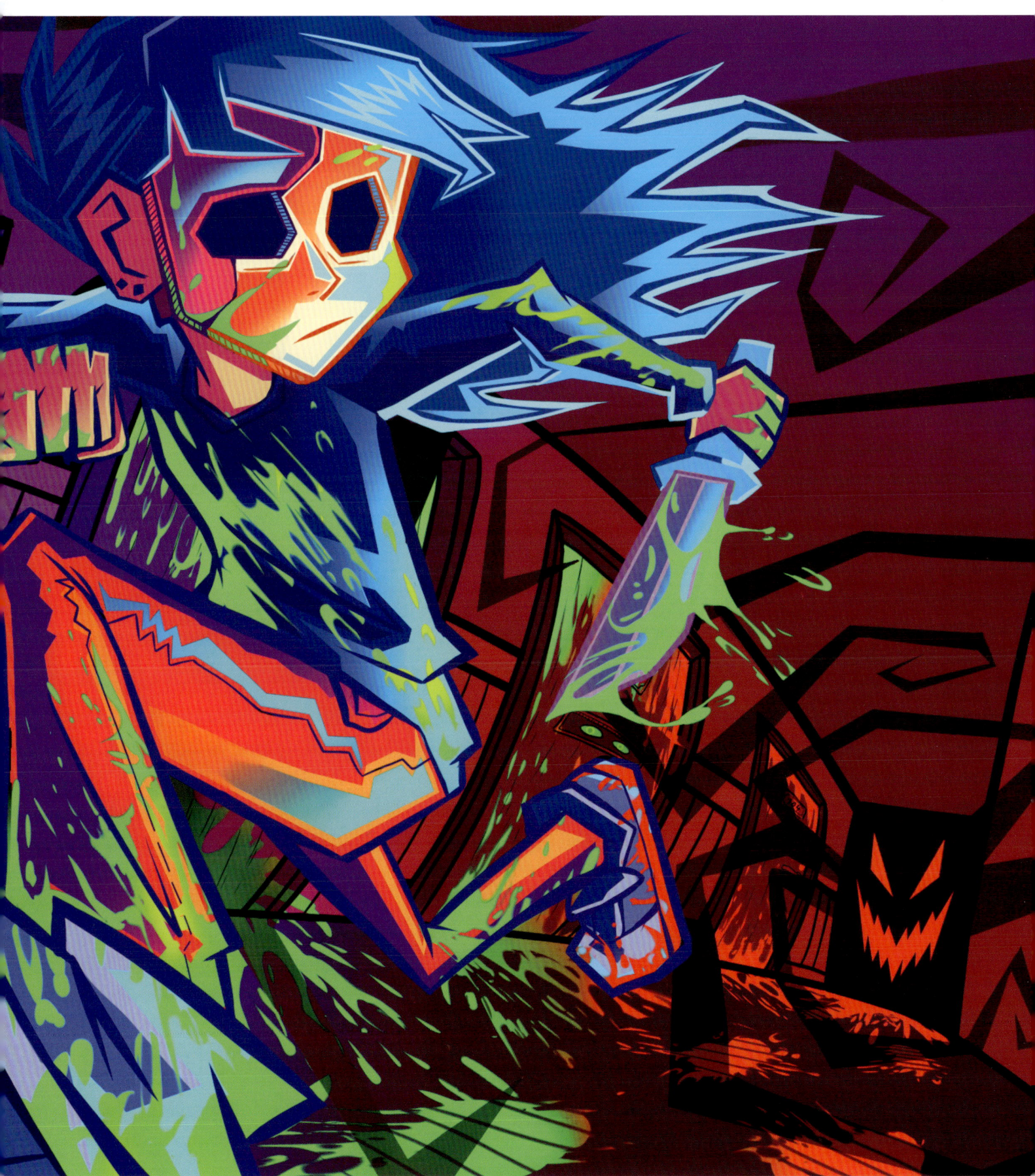

FAN ART: Azby Whitecalf.

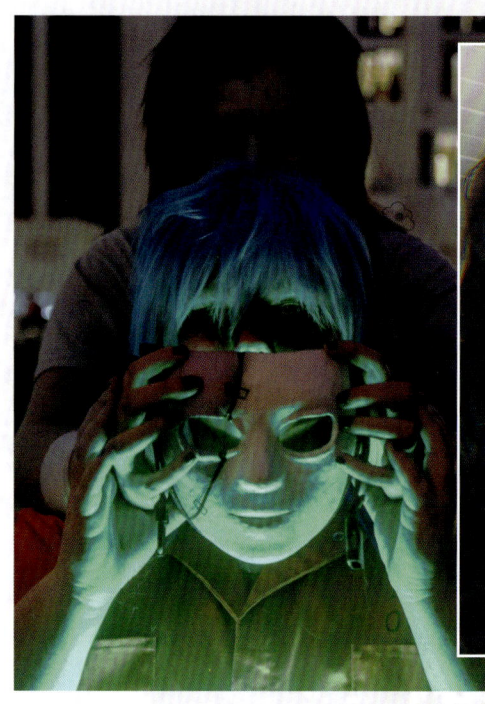

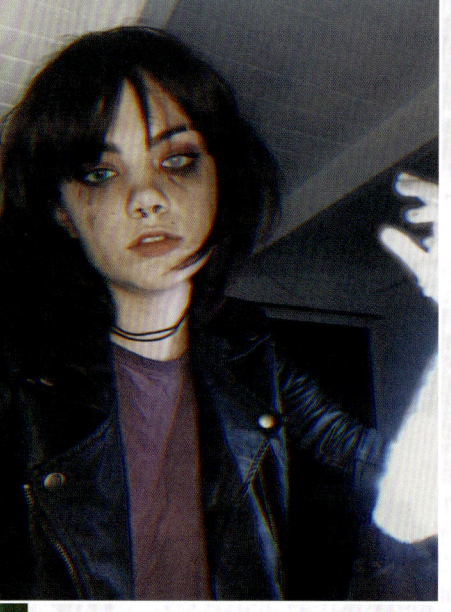

COSPLAY: Gigisoftboi.

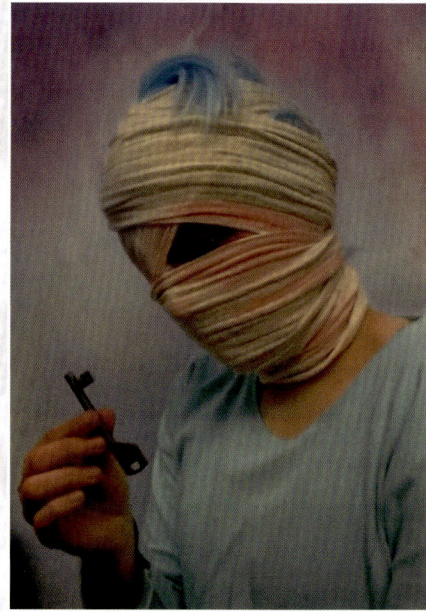

COSPLAY: _lamq.

COSPLAY:
SAL: Dallas Ingram (PikaCosplay).
LARRY: Isa Love.
PHOTOGRAPHER: Skylar Smith/
Skyleinphotography.
LIGHTING: Karamel.

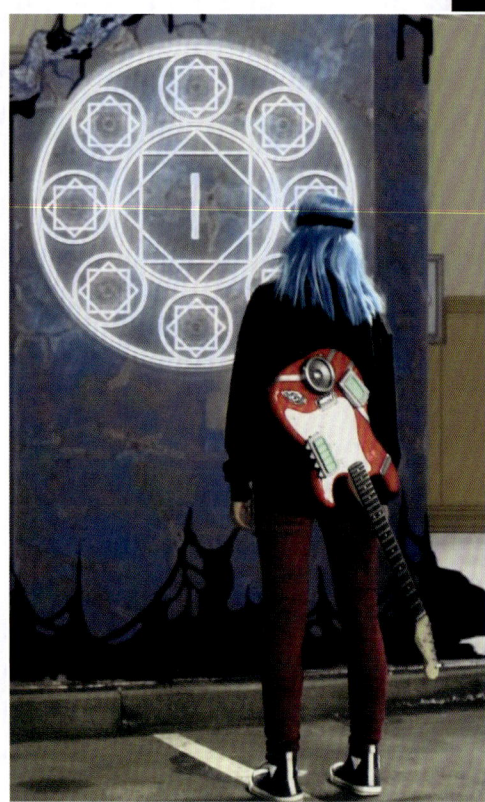

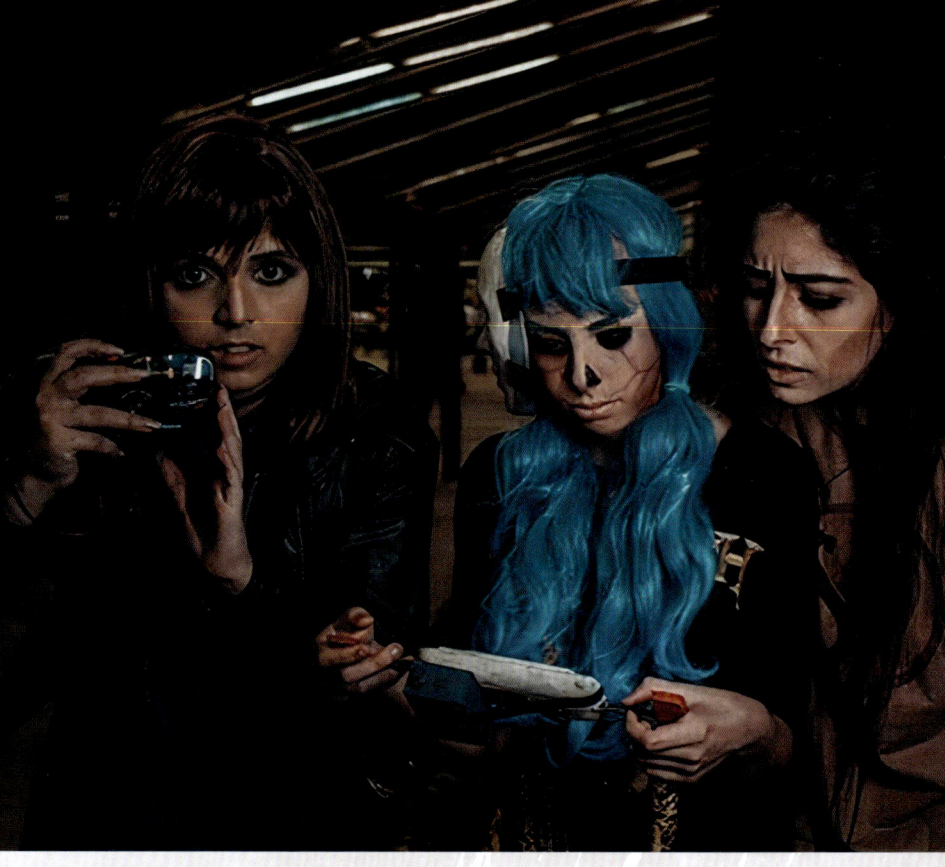

COSPLAY:
SAL: Demonanser.
PHOTOGRAPHER: Tea N.R.

COSPLAY:
SAL: Loli_Pops.
LARRY: Deadly Vu.
ASH: uchi riri.
PHOTOGRAPHER: Kenji Teoi.

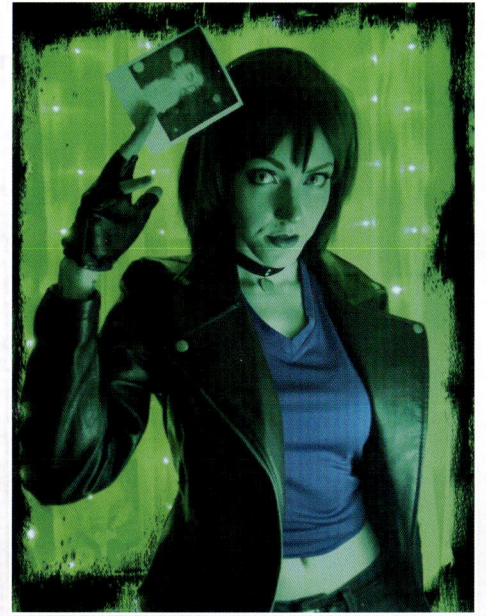

COSPLAY: Miss Mellowy.

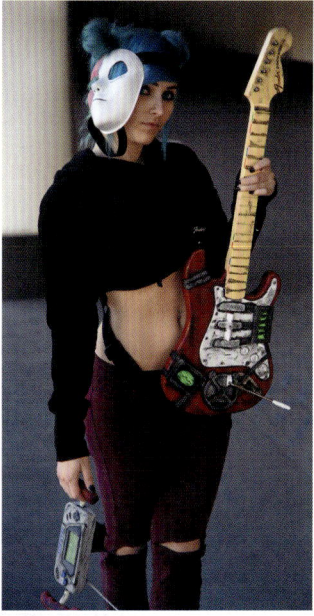

COSPLAY: @suteroozu.

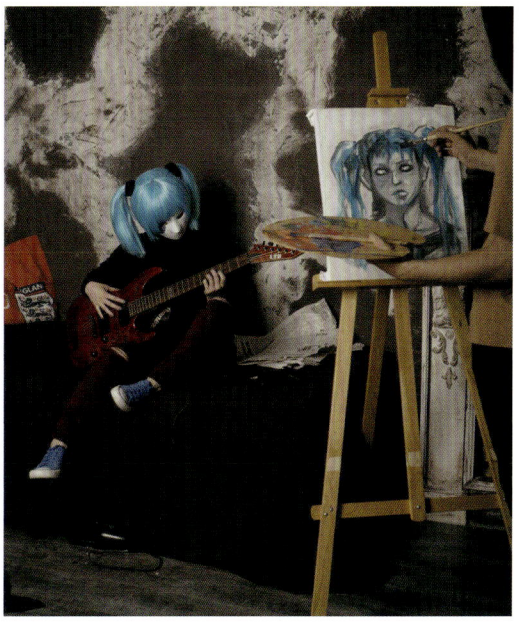

COSPLAY:
SAL: AppleAnarchy.
LARRY: Ritsko.
PHOTOGRAPHER: Serg.lyubetsky.
ARTIST: Milka Shtayger.

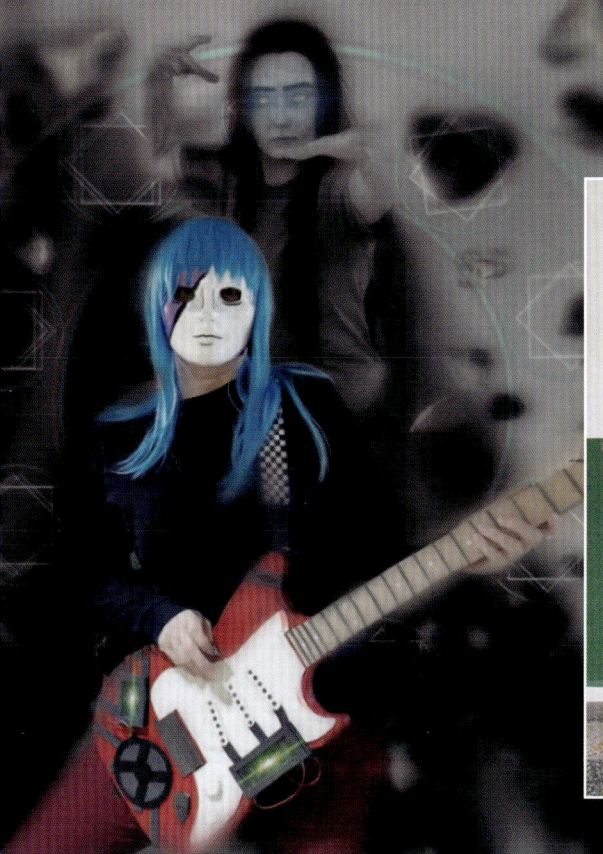

COSPLAY:
SAL: Galactic Prince.
LARRY: Sweaty Sensei.
PHOTOGRAPHER: Darth Hufflepuff Cosplay.

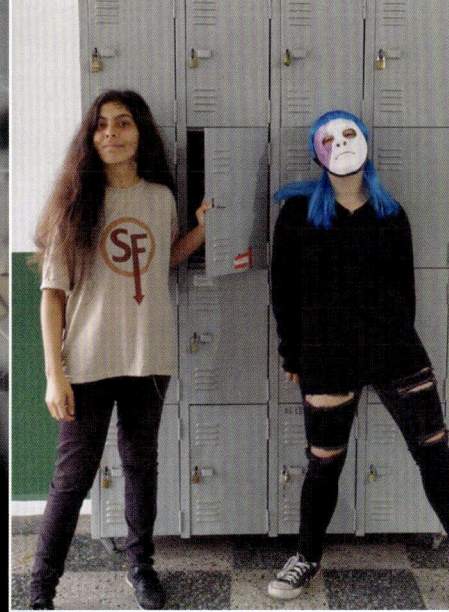

COSPLAY:
SAL: Bianca Madonna.
LARRY: Alanis Limas Caldas.
PHOTOGRAPHER:
Luciano Padilha Martins.

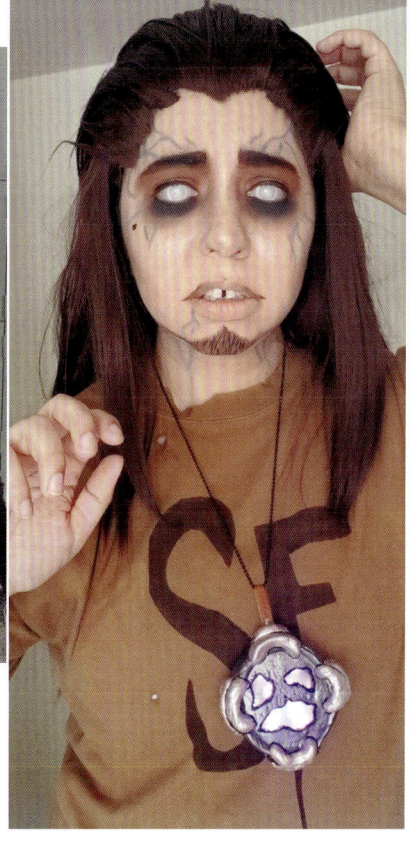

COSPLAY: S. Scott.

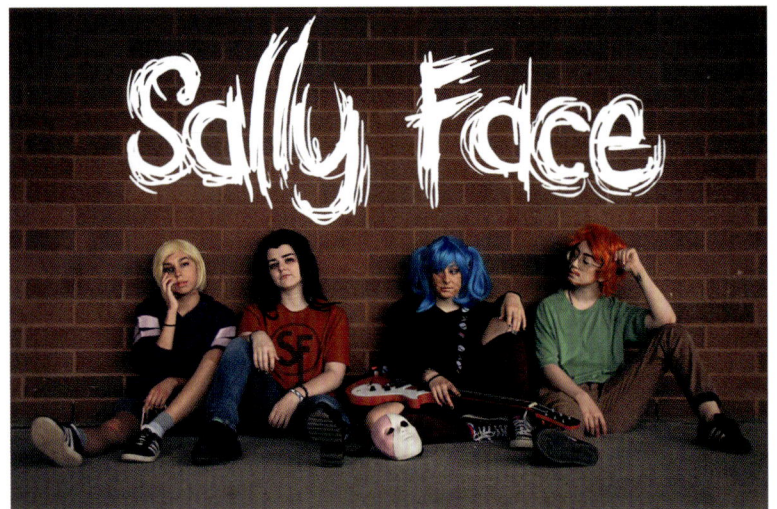

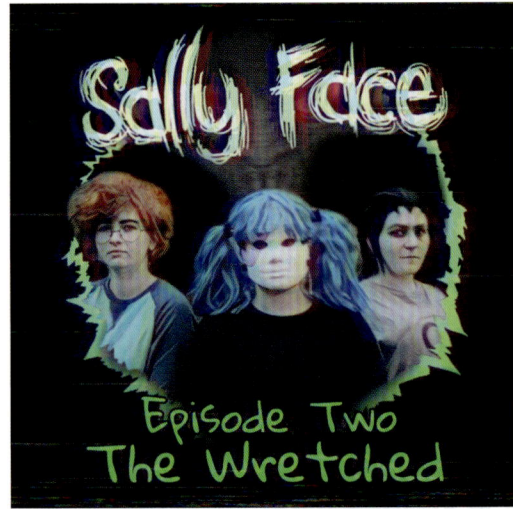

COSPLAY:
SAL: Kiki (@Kikiscosplayservice).
TRAVIS: Taylor (@Itsnotdoneyet).
LARRY: Nate (@Anxiouscrows).
TODD: Caitlyn (@CKsilverleaf).
PHOTOGRAPHER:
Haley Anna (@Haleyanna.h).

COSPLAY:
TODD: Jay N. Trylor.
SAL: Mochiliciious.
LARRY: Sir.Tedward.
PHOTOGRAPHER:
Jayngling.

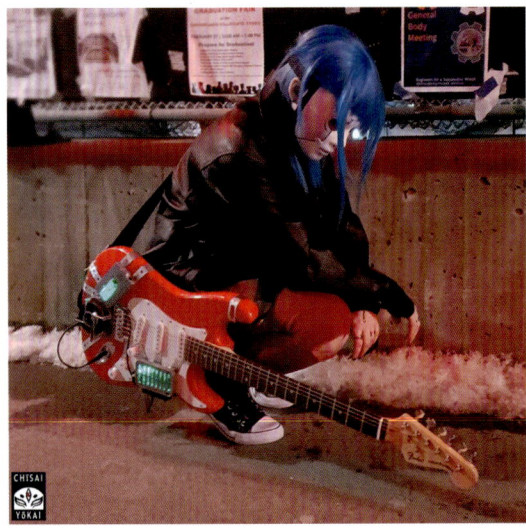

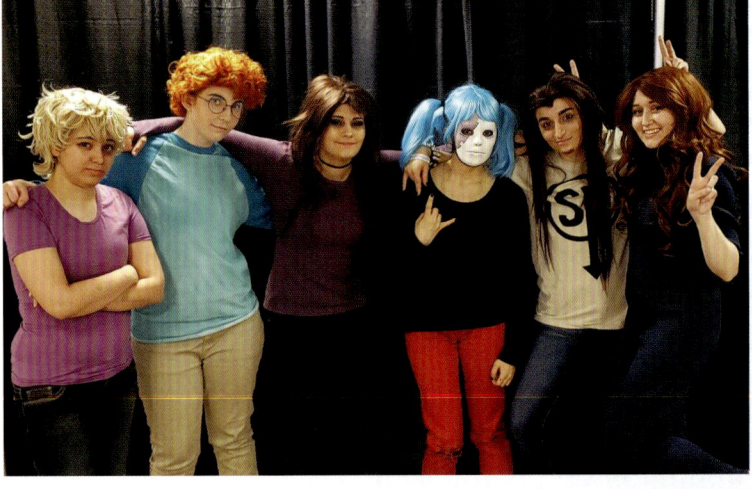

COSPLAY:
SAL: Chisai-Yokai (Alana Slattery).
PHOTOGRAPHER: Makina.

COSPLAY:
TRAVIS: Remy (softdirks).
TODD: Emily (ECNicktoons13).
ASH: Kristina (Creepy_Anime_Freak).
SAL: Ana (OnyxGlow).
LARRY: Victoria (Noravalkyrie).
LISA: Ellie (FreckledStardust).
PHOTOGRAPHY: AJ (Vorpal_Nova).

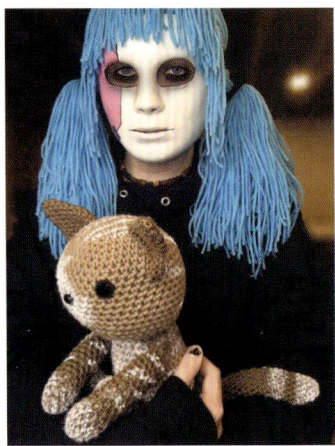

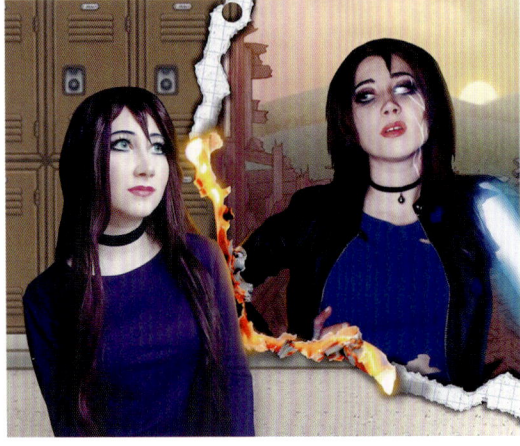

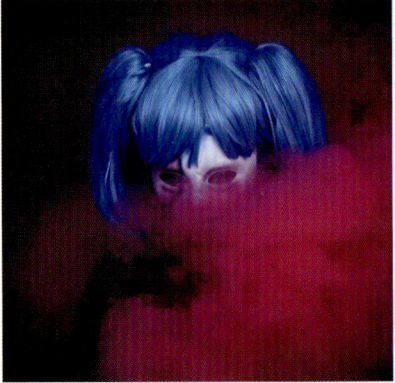

COSPLAY: shinju THE cosplayer.

COSPLAY: Dina Bay.

COSPLAY:
SAL: Haley Havok.
PHOTOGRAPHER: Jamie Webb.

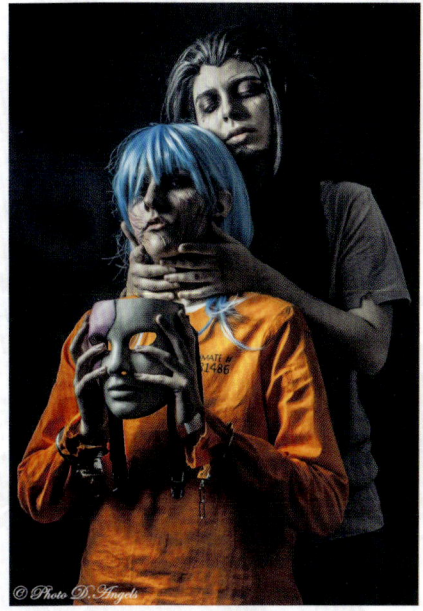

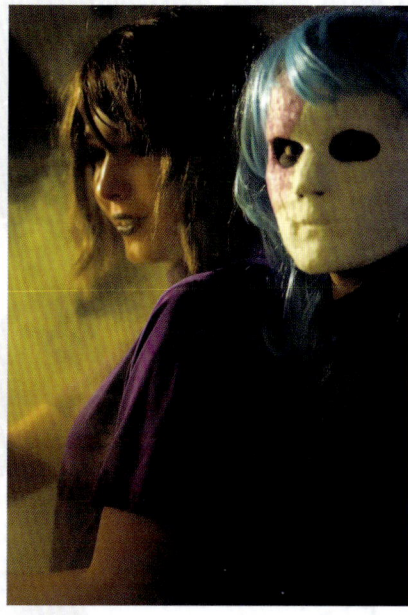

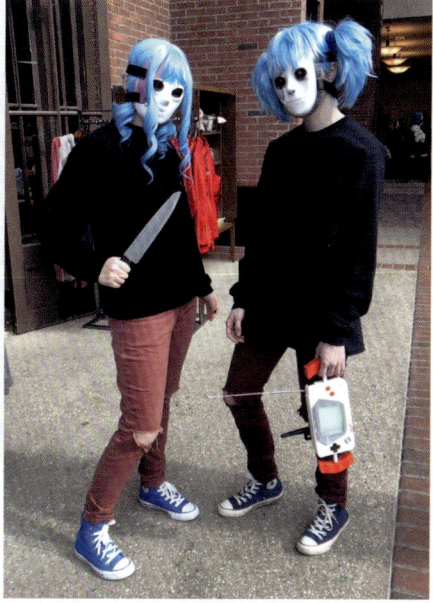

COSPLAY:
SAL: Lee Whiro Cosplay.
LARRY: Illy Cosplay.
PHOTOGRAPHER:
Photo D. Angels.

COSPLAY:
ASH: Elisabeth @a_pea.ch.
SALLY: Iris @theissmo03.
PHOTOGRAPHER:
Maya Åstrup @memyselfaneye_com.

COSPLAY:
SAL: Aster @asterisk_cos.
SAL: @chainedartist.

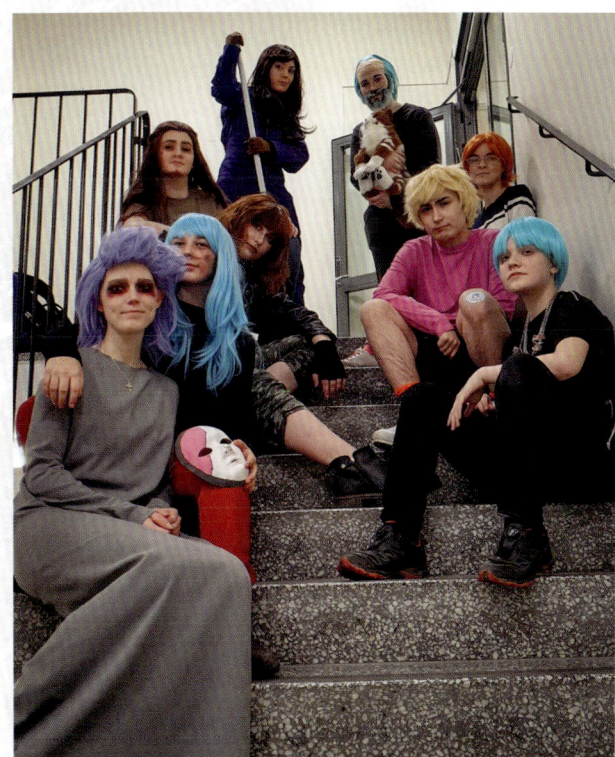

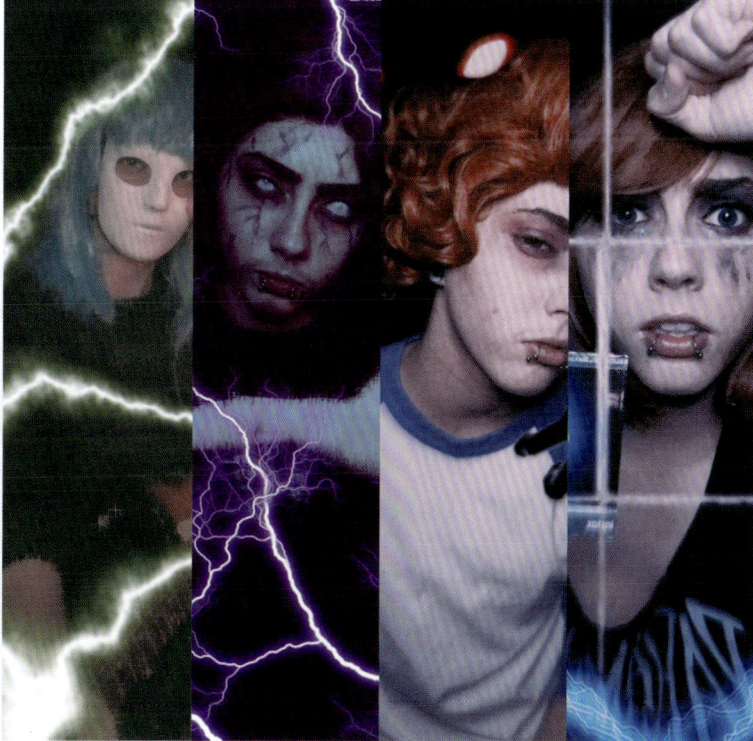

COSPLAY:
MEGAN: Sara Hiding.
SAL: Celine Forsman.
HENRY: Lovina Thorelli Bodin.
ASHLEY: Izabell Granat.
LISA: Poppy Palm.
TRAVIS: Elliot Celis Andersson.

PHILIP: Percy Rung.
TODD: Amanda Bogren.
LARRY: Linnéa Wallgren
(Nottitaniccal).
PHOTOGRAPHER:
Lisa Jansson.

COSPLAY: Jasper Jayy.

ACKNOWLEDGMENTS

I CREATED the first draft of this book in 2020 and over the following few years Brand Central searched for the right publisher. I appreciate all of the legwork that Ross Misher and Lexi De Forest have done in not only securing a publisher for this book but also in expanding the Sally Face brand by connecting me to great merchandising partners.

I was thrilled that we landed with Titan Books and thankful for their wonderful team. Richard Jackson (acquisitions editor) ensured a smooth onboarding process. Francesco Piscitelli (project editor) was a pleasure to work with and handled the project with great care. James King (layout designer) really did a fantastic job at taking my rough draft to new heights. And Charlotte Kelly (publicist) made sure that this book found its audience.

A special thanks to Liz Peters for always supporting me and proofreading my work. To my friends and family for their love and support. And to all the Sally Face fans who make it possible for me to pursue my dream.

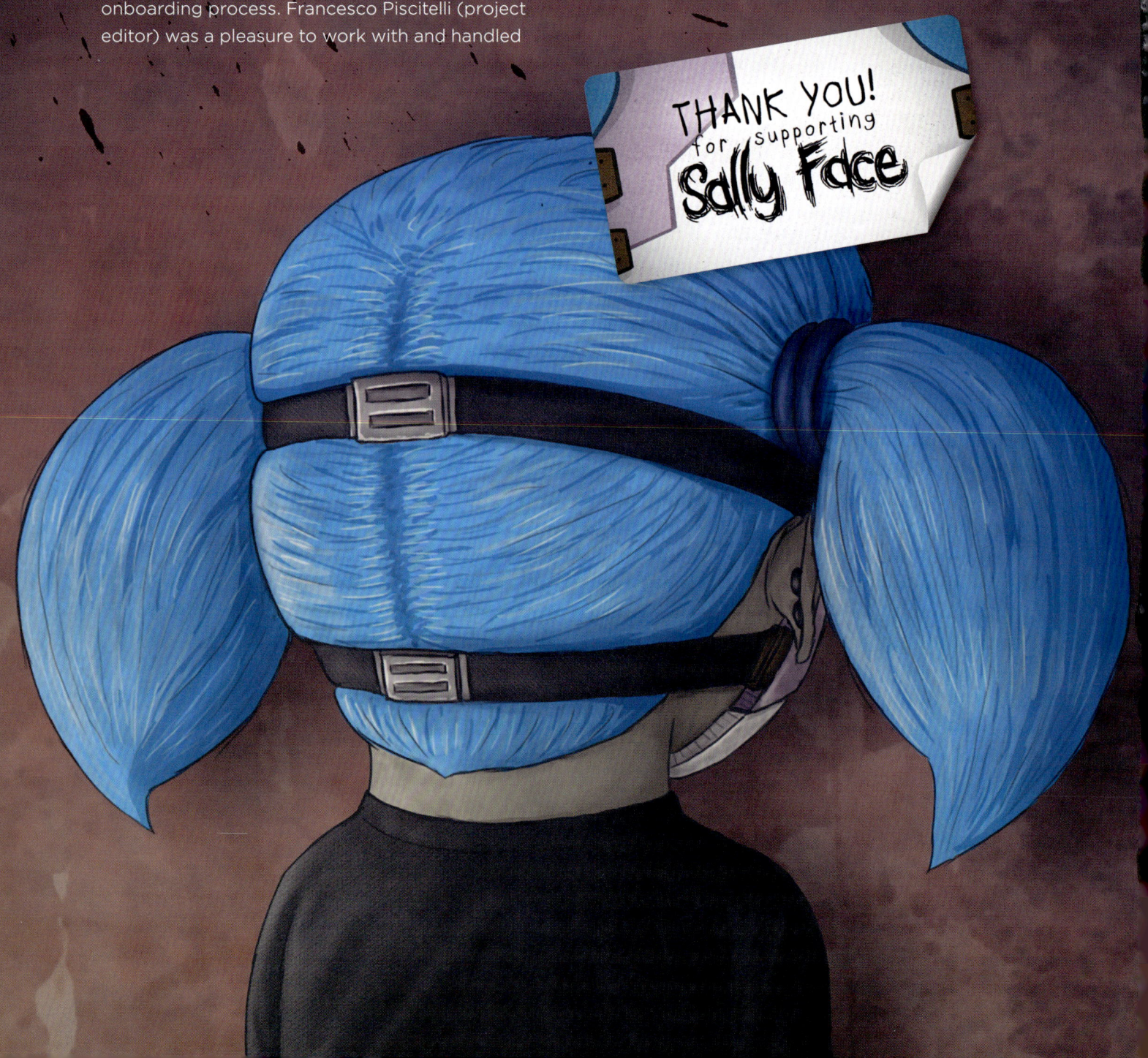

THANK YOU! for supporting Sally Face

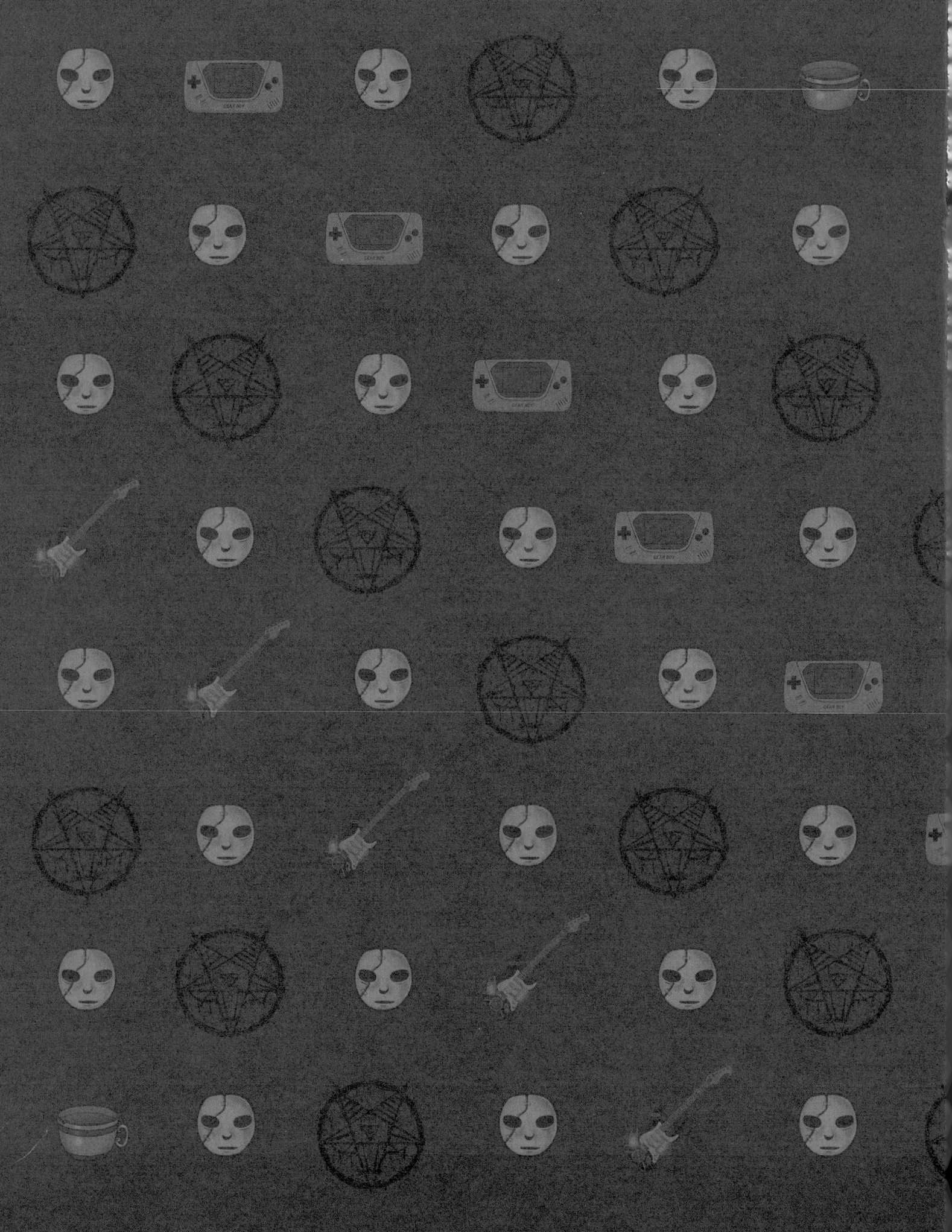